WOMEN'S STUDIES
ENCYCLOPEDIA

WOMEN'S STUDIES ENCYCLOPEDIA

Revised and Expanded Edition

G–P

Edited by

Helen Tierney

Greenwood Press
Westport, Connecticut

Library of Congress Cataloging-in-Publication Data

Women's studies encyclopedia / edited by Helen Tierney.—Rev. and
expanded ed.
   p. cm.
  Includes bibliographical references and index.
  ISBN 0–313–29620–0 (alk. paper)
   1. Women—United States—Encyclopedias. 2. Women—Encyclopedias.
3. Feminism—Encyclopedias. I. Tierney, Helen.
HQ1115.W645 1999
305.4'03—dc21   98–14236

British Library Cataloguing in Publication Data is available.

A CD-ROM version of *Women's Studies Encyclopedia:
Revised and Expanded Edition* is available from Greenwood
Press, an imprint of Greenwood Publishing Group, Inc.
(ISBN 0-313-31074-2).

Library of Congress Catalog Card Number: 98–14236
ISBN: 0–313–29620–0 (set)
ISBN: 0–313–31071–8 (A–F)
ISBN: 0–313–31072–6 (G–P)
ISBN: 0–313–31073–4 (Q–Z)

First published in 1999

Greenwood Press, 88 Post Road West, Westport, CT 06881
An imprint of Greenwood Publishing Group, Inc.
www.greenwood.com

Printed in the United States of America

The paper used in this book complies with the
Permanent Paper Standard issued by the National
Information Standards Organization (Z39.48–1984).

10 9 8 7 6 5 4 3 2 1

Contents

Acknowledgments

Our sister, Helen Tierney, the editor of this *Women's Studies Encyclopedia*, died on October 31, 1997, when the encyclopedia was almost complete, but before she had acknowledged the myriad of individuals who made this book possible. Helen worked on this edition, almost to the exclusion of everything else, for the better part of two and a half years because she considered the availability of information about women of the utmost importance—their contributions to literature, art, science, learning, philosophy, religion, and their place in history. Her family has taken the few remaining steps necessary to see this project to completion.

The encyclopedia is a collaborative effort of many women and men who have given generously of their time, experience, and expertise. Acknowledgment and special thanks are due to all those who contributed articles and to the consultants whose advice and counsel were essential in choosing topics, in recommending the professionals who wrote the articles, and in reviewing articles. Acknowledgment and thanks are due to Helen's colleagues in the Women's Studies Program and the History Department of the University of Wisconsin for their assistance and support, particularly Gloria Stephenson for her help with articles Helen was working on at the time of her death. We do not know all the names of the many individuals who provided their generous assistance along the way, but we would like to express our deepest appreciation to them on Helen's behalf.

The Family of Helen Tierney

Introduction

The *Women's Studies Encyclopedia* contains information about women from all fields and disciplines of study, written in nonspecialist language and in a style accessible to all readers. The idea for the encyclopedia grew out of the discovery, when I first began to organize a course in women's history, that to teach about women, information from beyond the confines of my own area of expertise was essential. Conversations with colleagues interested in offering introductory women's courses or courses in their own disciplines showed that we all shared the same problem: a need for knowledge outside our own fields of interest but with neither the time nor the training to find and understand the results of current research in disciplines other than our own.

Students discovering the then brand-new world of women's studies, male colleagues interested either in broadening their own courses to include something about the other half of humanity or at least in finding out "what the fuss was all about," and women in the "real world" of business and homemaking also evinced interest in a reference that would offer basic information with the latest research and reflection about women from a feminist perspective. The encyclopedia tries to meet these needs.

Since the publication of the first edition of the *Women's Studies Encyclopedia*, research on women has proceeded rapidly; feminist thought has grown and branched out; conditions for women have changed markedly in some areas of life, for good and for ill, and little in others; material conditions in various areas of the world have offered new opportunities or set back advances. Less than ten years after its publication, many articles in the *Encyclopedia* had become out-of-date. In fact, the rapid changes taking place in Eastern Europe a decade ago were making some articles obsolete even before the third volume was published.

Since the early 1980s there has been an increase in women's studies and feminist reference materials, but the need for a multidisciplinary reference tool that touches on all facets and aspects of the female condition is still needed. To better meet that need, the new edition of the *Encyclopedia* has been somewhat enlarged, but, of course, three volumes cannot do more than scratch the surface. There are new articles; some articles have been completely rewritten; many others have been revised or updated. Some omissions have been corrected, and the number of articles in some areas has increased. There is more complete coverage of violence against women, as well as additional materials on women in public life. There are also more articles on contemporary conditions for women in specific countries or regions, but it was impossible to cover every country and every region of the world.

The entries in the *Encyclopedia* are meant to convey information to an educated audience without expertise in the subject under discussion. The bibliographic apparatus is, therefore, limited. The references included at the end of many of the articles are meant primarily to direct readers to works from which they may obtain a fuller explanation, more detailed information, or different perspectives on a subject.

The focus, as in the first edition, is on the American experience. Although a wide array of articles deal with women in other areas of the world and other cultures or on women in general, unless otherwise specified articles deal with women in the United States.

The articles are not written from a single feminist perspective. One aim in inviting contributions was to incorporate as wide a variety of feminist approaches as possible, so that all shades of opinion, from those so conservative that some will deny they are feminist, to the most radical, are represented. They do not, therefore, necessarily represent or agree with my own perspective.

As in the first edition, uniformity of organization and structure for articles of such widely varying subjects was not feasible, but one feature, the omission of the word "women" from entry titles, is fairly consistent, since every article is about women.

This edition is arranged more simply than the last, in alphabetical order. In cases where it was thought that the grouping of entries would make locating them more convenient, individual entries will share a common heading (e.g., articles related to French women's history, such as the Code Napoleon, are listed under "France"; articles about dowry in Western Europe and in India are listed under "dowry").

Cross-references have been reduced to a minimum. When a word or phrase used as the heading of an entry appears as a noun in another entry, the cross-reference is indicated by an asterisk. When a major topic might be listed under several different headings, cross-references to the heading are given.

The names of the authors of entries follow the entries and are also listed under Consultants and Contributors. Those articles that are not signed were written by the editor.

Helen Tierney
October 1997

G

GATHERING/HUNTING SOCIETIES include all cultural groups, past and present, that subsist exclusively on noncultivated foodstuffs. They do not raise animals or practice agriculture but depend on collecting wild plants, fishing, hunting, and a variety of intermediate food-procuring activities. Because the terms "hunting" and "gathering" do not fully describe the variety of food-collecting activities that these groups engage in, and because of the cultural bias that associates hunting with males and gathering with females, some anthropologists have suggested the term "forager" as a more accurate label for this type of society.

Both prehistoric and modern foraging bands have several characteristics in common, although there are exceptions to these generalizations. Most are small, with a maximum of 50 individuals. They are generally nomadic and move within a prescribed territory in order to exploit the area's resources. They are considered to be egalitarian, meaning that there is no ranking of individuals within the band, and no band member, male or female, can dominate another. This last feature is a behavior observed in several modern foraging societies; therefore, we cannot be sure that prehistoric peoples were also egalitarian.

The assumption in most traditional studies of foraging bands has been that women are inferior to men. Males were seen as the major protagonists in humanity's past, with women having a secondary or incidental role. This bias led anthropologists and archaeologists alike to focus on the hunting activities of band societies as exclusively a male activity, while underestimating the importance of gathering, which is generally assumed to be a female activity. Women were thought to have little power within the group, based on their low status as gatherers and mothers.

Feminist anthropologists saw the danger of the man-the-hunter myth in its underlying support of the "natural" inferiority of women. Their studies and a move toward a more objective viewpoint in ethnographic studies led to a shift away from the male orientation to a more balanced view of gender roles. A new picture of band societies that is beginning to emerge includes a realization of the importance of plant collection in the subsistence strategies of many past and present societies. However, it is also important to understand the enormous variation in gender roles* that is possible among foraging peoples. Many cultures may not assign hunting and gathering tasks based on gender, and these tasks need not be an indication of status.

Prehistoric Gatherer-Hunters. For most of human history, people have practiced a foraging way of life. Our earliest ancestors, who lived 2 million years ago, during the Lower Paleolithic (Old Stone Age), collected wild plants, insects, and small animals. They left no evidence of large-scale hunting activity and probably scavenged meat from the remains of larger carnivores' meals. Because there is so little evidence of variation in tools and in food-procuring techniques, it seems reasonable to assume that hunting and gathering were not specialized activities until later in human evolution. Females and males probably took part in all these activities, with little regard to gender-assigned roles.

With the emergence of the first member of the human species, the Neanderthal, 125,000 years ago, there is growing evidence that human society was becoming more complex. Neanderthals made more sophisticated tools and buried their dead. There is still no evidence that anyone had higher status within the group, however, or that men dominated women.

The beginning of the Upper Paleolithic, about 35,000 years ago, marks the appearance of modern humans: Homo sapiens. This period coincided with the drier, colder climatic conditions of the late Pleistocene. Vast areas of Europe were covered with grasslands, upon which roamed reindeer, mammoth, bison, horse, and woolly rhino. Archaeological research reveals that the number of sites increased dramatically at this time, as did the complexity of society. There were more specialized tools for working wood and bone and for making clothing.

Spectacular cave paintings and carvings appear during this period, including the first representations of the human figure, often called the "Venus" figurines. It was traditionally assumed that these figures were fertility or sexual symbols and were made by men, but it is equally possible that they were made by women. Interestingly, they appear when, for the first time in human history, there was a rapid rise in population. Women were having more children and may have encouraged fecundity by weaning their children at an increasingly earlier age.

The late Paleolithic people of Eurasia were dependent to a great degree on hunting, but this is no reason to assume that women did not enjoy equal status. The usual technique for hunting the grazing herds was to organize animal drives, in which animals were driven into ravines or into artificial enclosures to be killed. These drives required the entire community's co-operation, and ethnographic studies indicate that women and men could have had similar roles in this operation.

Archaeologists have held firmly to their conception that all prehistoric people were hunters. This must be seen as an intrinsic problem in the nature of the archaeological record. Animal food leaves a greater amount of waste in the form of bone, which is well preserved in most soils. Plant foods leave less waste and are poorly preserved. Stone tools may be interpreted as hunting and butchering implements, although they may actually have been used for plant harvesting and preparation. Also, many tools may have been made of wood or other perishable substances and, hence, not survive as well as stone, which would also skew the bias toward hunting. There is even speculation that the most indispensable tool of a foraging culture would have been the carrying pouch, used to carry foodstuffs and children. These, too, being made of skins or plant fibers, would have perished long ago.

The hunters of the Eurasian plains were only one type of society during the Late Paleolithic, albeit the most intensively studied. Other groups, in Africa, Asia, and the Middle East, were practicing more intensive food-collecting techniques that would eventually lead to the emergence of plant and animal domestication and the growth of stratified society.

Modern Gathering and Hunting Societies. There is no culture group living today that has not been deeply affected by modern Western society. However, there are small bands of people who still practice a "Stone Age" economy, getting most of their food by foraging. These groups have been investigated in an effort to understand our human ancestors. Modern foragers, however, have had as long a history as any present-day society and therefore cannot be considered to behave like prehistoric people.

Women's status in these societies is extremely variable, and anthropologists have had a difficult time interpreting gender roles objectively. Most anthropologists have been male and have tended to bias their studies toward male activities, interviewing only the men of the band. Anthropological research is now focusing on the entire experience of the community of women, men, children, and the elderly. The outcome of such research shows that women's status in these groups often cannot be described in our culture's terms and that our ideas of power and aggression may be inadequate to understand the experiences of people in other societies.

The !Kung of the Kalihari Desert in Botswana are often used as an example of a typical hunting and gathering community. The men traditionally hunt with poisoned arrows, while the women collect nuts, roots, and fruits. Eighty percent of the !Kung diet is provided by the women. Females and males enjoy equivalent status within the group structure. Their economy is based on sharing and cooperation, and anthropologists have postulated that prehistoric humans were similar to the !Kung. Although this is a simplistic approach to understanding prehistoric behavior, the !Kung do offer an alternative to Western society's biased attitude toward male/female roles.

The Agta Negritos of the Philippines, a present-day tribal people, are an example of a culture whose women and men share all subsistence activities. Most interestingly, the women of a number of Agta tribes hunt large game with bows, arrows, and hunting dogs. The women are prevented from hunting only during late pregnancy and the first few months after giving birth. Teenagers and women with older children are the most frequent hunters. The women space their children to allow for maximum mobility. They maintain that they keep their birthrate down through the use of herbal contraceptives.

By studying these ethnographic examples and by questioning the assumptions that have been made about female and male roles in prehistory, it becomes possible to understand that Western society's traditionally low view of women's status is by no means universal. If the study of human culture has one thing to teach us, it is that human behavior and culture allow for adaptation and that gender roles are not determined by biological laws but can be changed.

References. Frances Dahlberg (ed.), *Woman the Gatherer* (New Haven, Conn., 1981); Margaret Ehrenberg, *Women in Prehistory*, vol. 4 (Norman, Okla., 1989); Joan M. Gero and Margaret W. Conkey (eds.), *Engendering Archaeology* (Oxford, 1991).

WENDY R. EISNER

GATHERING/HUNTING THEORIES OF EVOLUTION. Anthropologists have put forward several theories of human evolution based on the assumption that females gathered and males hunted. These theories seek to understand how our early ancestors developed into modern humans. Although physical evolution is often confused with cultural evolution, it is important to keep the two concepts distinct. Physical evolution is the actual morphological changes that led to the development of modern Homo sapiens. Humans have gone through virtually no physical changes in the past 40,000 years. Cultural evolution, however, which follows the development of human society, is in a constant state of flux and is also much more difficult to analyze than physical evolution is.

Early anthropologists had little information on the physical development of humans and concentrated instead on the evolution of human society. One of the first comprehensive evolutionary theories was that of Lewis Henry Morgan, who introduced the idea that early societies were "matrilineal"; that is, they traced descent through the mother's, rather than the father's, line. He speculated that women would have higher status in such a society, but he never seriously considered that women would wield any real power. Later work by Friedrich Engels and archaeologists like V. Gordon Childe echoed these ideas, which assumed an early, male-dominated culture of hunters. This gave way to a more egalitarian and peaceful era of plant gathering and incipient horticulture. All these evolutionary theories take for granted that the later phases of civilization are not only the most highly evolved but those in which the males dominate.

Most recent theories of evolution seem unable to escape from the early assumptions that differentiate between peaceful female gatherers and violent male hunters. When anthropologists began to unearth real evidence of physical evolution, a debate began on the question of innate human aggression, a debate that continues today. Findings of hominid (prehuman) bones with large numbers of animal fossils were supposed to indicate that those hominids killed large numbers of animals and even their own kind for food, giving rise to a man-the-killer theory. The subsequent discovery that the entire assemblage of bones, the hominid bones included, were the remains of hyena meals has not erased the popular notion that we became human through violent behavior and that the female's only duty was to raise the children and prepare the meat brought home by the successful hunter.

In response, a number of experts have been reconsidering the evolution of human society. Nancy Tanner is among those who have constructed an alternative to the man-the-hunter evolutionary model. The early human female, says Tanner, having the greater investment in reproduction and child care,* would have more influence in mating procedures. Therefore, the male would have to be more attractive in terms of sociability and willingness to share food and time with the children, rather than resorting to aggression and coercion.

Toolmaking is the first archaeological indication we have of early human culture, and this may well have emerged out of a gathering, rather than hunting, tradition. A container for gathered foods or a baby carrier would have been an early necessity, as would digging sticks for gathering root vegetables. This does not mean that there was an early division of labor between the sexes, however. Big-game hunting was a late evolutionary development that did not necessarily exclude females from participation. Additionally, human physical evolution shows a trend away from sexual dimorphism.* The most probable evolutionary model for early hominids was nonspecialized hunting, gathering, and collecting activities that stressed flexibility in food choices and cooperation among all band members. This emphasis on flexibility and cooperation, rather than on dominance, may have led to the survival and success of Homo sapiens as a species.

References. Frances Dahlberg (ed.), *Woman the Gatherer* (New Haven, Conn., 1981); Friedrich Engels, *The Origin of the Family, Private Property, and the State* (Chicago, 1902; New York, 1972); L. M. Fedigan, "The Changing Role of Women in Models of Human Evolution, *Annual Review of Anthropology* 15 (1986): 22–

66; Lewis Henry Morgan, *Ancient Societies* (New York, 1877); Nancy M. Tanner, *On Becoming Human* (Cambridge, U.K., 1981).

WENDY R. EISNER

GAY AND LESBIAN MOVEMENT consists of a set of grassroots organizations for the advancement of the citizenship rights and cultural development of lesbian, gay, bisexual, and transgendered people. Between 1897 and 1933, gay and lesbian groups with clubhouses and journals flourished throughout Germany and the Netherlands. As the German women's movement of the time organized around such feminine gender expectations as motherhood and moral purity, lesbians met, organized, and published under the same auspices as gay men.

After the destruction of the early movement in the Holocaust,* small gay organizations revived in Amsterdam, Copenhagen, Paris, and Los Angeles in the early 1950s. All were "low-profile" during the period of McCarthyism and the Cold War, and when the first autonomous lesbian group, the Daughters of Bilitis, was founded in San Francisco in 1955, the cautious approach of the homophiles was clear in its objectives.

With the militance generated by the black civil rights and student movements of the 1960s came a profound transformation of gay politics. Marked symbolically by the Stonewall Rebellion of 1969, when gay men and lesbians fought back a police raid on a Greenwich Village bar, the new gay liberationists did not think of themselves as a civil rights movement for a particular minority but as a revolutionary struggle to free the homoeroticism in everyone by challenging the conventional arrangements that confined sexuality to monogamous, heterosexual families.

Tensions between women and men in the movement appeared early on. Men were often ignorant of women's issues and took for granted many of the social conditions that made it possible for them to come out as gay, while lesbians needed to address fundamental problems facing all women, such as the lack of employment opportunities and violence against women, in order to gain sufficient independence to live as lesbians. Though lesbian issues tended to be greeted with coolness, if not hostility, by the feminist movement in the late 1960s, in 1970 most women's groups recognized lesbianism as an issue of concern to all, and many lesbians left the gay movement to join their feminist sisters in the early 1970s. With the rise of a culturalist school within feminist thought, lesbians acquired an important place as "women-identified women" who refused to collaborate with men, whether at home or in the public arena.

Since the mid-1970s, a New Right coalition of conservative forces has challenged feminist, civil rights, and gay and lesbian advances toward equality under a "traditional family values" banner. While most of the nations of the European Union, Canada, and Australia have passed human rights legislation banning discrimination on the basis of sexual orientation during the 1980s and 1990s, the United States has witnessed the defeat of the Equal Rights Amendment (ERA) for women, numerous referenda to repeal or block human rights laws for lesbians and gay men, and repeated attacks on the cultural expression of gay and lesbian artists and writers.

Gay liberation has given way to a series of movement groups located in workplaces, churches, ethnic communities, political parties, and recreational and social service organizations. As well, the movement has diversified with growth in rural areas, in Latin America, Eastern Europe, Asia, and Africa. Gay and lesbian groups have been major participants in the founding and advancement of community-based AIDS organizations, and in some countries the need to prevent HIV transmission has compelled governments to permit gay and lesbian people to organize for the first time.

In 1989, Denmark became the first nation to legally recognize same-sex relationships for most of the rights and responsibilities of marriage. Norway and Sweden have followed the Danish precedent. A momentum toward recognition has been building through labor union agreements, court decisions, and legal reform at the local level in other countries. In the 1990s, lesbian, gay, bisexual, and transgendered people have joined together as "queer" activists to reassert their right to participate in civil society, stimulating renewed vitality in politics, the arts, and scholarship.

References. Barry D. Adam, *The Rise of a Gay and Lesbian Movement* (New York, 1995); Mark Blasius, *We Are Everywhere* (New York, 1995); Margaret Cruikshank, *The Gay and Lesbian Liberation Movement* (New York, 1992).

BARRY D. ADAM

GENDER AND LEARNING. Women and girls learn differently than do men and boys. American feminists like Elaine Showalter argue that women and men write and read differently since the contexts of their lives are different. Nancy Chodorow argues that learning differs by gender because women and men—beginning with the ways girls and boys experience growing up—live in different cultures. Although, she suggests, girls and boys experience infancy similarly, they begin to diverge into very different paths in early childhood. Girls, she argues, grow up through a process of seeing similarities between themselves and their mothers, and they learn to value characteristics that they share with their mothers, such as nurturing, intimacy, and caring for others. Boys, on the other hand, go through a difficult period during which they develop their identities as males by how they differ from their mothers and by committing themselves to the larger public world rather than to the world of home and family. Girls' culture focuses, then, on relationships, while boys' focuses on the more impersonal public realms of work, sports, and other public activities. Exacerbating this difference, Showalter adds, in many educational settings the experiences of women and the issues that concern them are often ignored or trivialized by teachers and by curricular materials. Men and those social institutions controlled by men, she says, devalue the seriousness of women's lives. An Australian sociologist, Dale Spender adds that women as learners often have no language to describe or discuss their worlds because the language of schooling most typically reflects men's definitions of reality. Girls, then, often learn in an "alien" culture, almost as if their schooling were conducted in a foreign language.

Two important recent studies comparing girls' and boys' learning differences focus on the distinctive developmental paths taken by girls and boys. Carol Gilligan describes her investigation into the ways girls and boys and women and men use logic and reasoning to make important moral decisions. Boys, she finds, move from an early stage where they follow rules because they fear the punishment of external authorities, to a later stage where they experience themselves as independent individuals applying universal rational moral rules to specific situations. Girls, Gilligan finds, go through a different moral and cognitive developmental path. Girls are more likely to mistrust laws, external authorities, and logical rules. When girls and women are faced with difficult ethical decisions, they are more likely than boys to identify empathically with the decision, to see themselves in the situation, and to see a web of relationships that shape the moral choice. That is, rather than applying a universal rule, they look at the concrete situation and its context and try to make decisions that cause the least possible pain to everyone involved (Gilligan terms this the "ethic of care"). When Gilligan's findings are used to look at learning, one sees that girl learners are drawn to learning by involvement, exploring a situation empathically, trying several solutions, placing the learning in a web of context, and answering questions with "it depends." Boys, on the other hand, are more drawn to trusting experts, developing abstract models, searching for universal principles, and "right or wrong" answers to questions.

The second influential study on gender and learning (Belenky, Clinchy, Goldberger, and Tarule) describes the difficulty women learners experience in gaining voice. In their studies of female learners, Belenky et al. detect five developmental positions that seem to be typical of most women's movement toward voice and knowledge. Movement from one stage to the next seems to depend on the women's learning environment and support in reflecting on life experiences. The first position, silence, describes a person without voice; words and knowledge are experienced as weapons, and women deny the validity of learning from their own experience. Often, the authors discover, learners in this position exist in situations of physical or sexual abuse. In the second position, received knowing, the learner listens to others for knowledge. In this position, authority (usually seen as male) is external to the learner and is unchallengeable. The learner is defined by her lack or emptiness, while the authority possesses a surplus of knowledge that is passed on to the learner. In the third position, subjective knowing, the learner comes to see truth as something personal and private. Knowledge in this position may emerge from the learner's experience, but it does not have general applicability. In this position, the learner comes to distrust logic and analysis—often identifying them as "male approaches," because these tools seem to be used to undercut women's personal knowledge. In procedural knowing, the fourth position, the learner comes to trust the voice of reason, but a reason disconnected from the personal. Reason is seen as useful for entry to, and success in, the worlds of academe and the professions, but it is simultaneously seen as not very useful in understanding personal life. Women in this position often find themselves experiencing the worlds of work and home as completely distinct, with no overlap. Thus, strategies for developing and using knowledge in one realm are seen as inappropriate for the other. As a consequence, they often describe themselves as frauds, using tactics in which they don't believe or to which they don't commit. In the fifth and final position described by Belenky et al., the position of constructed knowing, all the voices of the learner merge. The learner concludes that knowledge depends on the frame of reference of the knower and on the context in which the knowledge is produced and used. Much like the moral agent described by Gilligan, the women learners described in *Women's Ways of Knowing* come to understand knowledge not as something abstract, universal, and unvarying but as a human product created in a certain context and valuable in terms of those it affects. The authors of *Women's Ways of Knowing* call, therefore, for a learning environment for women that enhances movement along the five positions they describe. For example, they encourage wider use of collaborative and cooperative learning situations, integrated, interdisciplinary studies, and inductive, rather than deductive, assignments. (See FEMINIST PEDAGOGY.)

While there is wide agreement today that girls and boys experience schooling differently and that they bring different needs to the learning environment, most experts also agree that schools continue to be more comfortable environments for boys and, generally, to support boys' learning more effectively. Books like Peggy Orenstein's, for instance, continue to describe many schools as hostile to girls' learning, to their sense of their own value, and of their worth to themselves and to others.

References. Mary Belenky, Blythe Clinchy, Nancy Goldberger, and Jill Tarule, *Women's Ways of Knowing: The Development of Self, Voice, and Mind* (New York, 1986); Nancy Chodorow, *The Reproduction of Mothering: Psychoanalysis and the Sociology of Gender* (Berkeley, Calif., 1978); Carol Gilligan, *In a Different Voice: Psychological Theory and Women's Development* (Cambridge, 1982); Peggy Orenstein, *School Girls: Young Women, Self-Esteem, and the Confidence Gap* (New York, 1994); Elaine Showalter, "Feminist Criticism in the Wilderness," in E. Abel (ed.), *Writing and Sexual Difference* (Chicago, 1982); Dale Spender, *Man Made Language*, 2d ed. (London, 1982).

CHERYL B. SCARBORO

GENDER AND SCIENCE is a subject that has acquired increasing prominence in the recent history of feminist scholarship and that, even today, continues to invite quite different interpretations among feminists and others. To some (perhaps many), it is understood as a subject about women in science; to others, as the science of sex differences*; and to yet others (this author included), as the study of the mutual interactions between ideologies of gender and science in the social construction of gender and science as we actually encounter these. Such differences in interpretation reflect deep differences in understandings of the meanings both of gender and of science—in particular, the extent to which each category is, on one hand, given to us by nature and, on the other hand, subject to the influence of (perhaps even constructed by) social forces. An examination of how these conceptions have varied among people and over time will, in fact, help us to explain the relatively slow emergence of this subject as part of feminist theory* proper. Simultaneously, it will enable us to identify the critical intellectual problems with which students of this subject must now deal.

In the extreme case, both science and gender are seen as purely natural categories, subject to immutable laws of development. From this perspective (which actually describes most traditional views of both science and gender), the mere juxtaposition of the terms "gender" and "science" is a reminder of the most conspicuously gender-specific fact about science— the historical absence of women from science. But although the "natural" character of science has, in general, appeared to be self-evident and uncontroversial, the same cannot be said, for any historical period, about the actual "nature" of women. Thus, to some, the absence of women from science bespeaks an inherent opposition between women's nature and the nature of science, while, to others, it is seen merely as the consequence of a residual social prejudice that bears no relation to the true nature of either women or science. In other words, depending on one's assumptions about "woman's nature," the subject of gender and science invites two readings even within this extreme case: first, as a natural opposition between women and science that warrants respect and, second, as a regrettable and remediable throwback to manifestly unscientific prejudices about women.

As feminists have become more conscious of the extent to which women are "made" rather than "born" and, accordingly, of the need to distinguish gender, a social category, from the biological category of sex, attention has turned to the social forces that have mediated the construction of women. It soon became evident that certain (mis)uses of science itself had to be counted among these social forces. With this shift in perspective, feminist scientists began to reread the subject of gender and science as an inquiry into the ways in which "biology constructs the female"—more specifically, as an inquiry into the failure of proper scientific standards in research on sex differences.

Only with a parallel shift in perspective about the nature of science did it become possible for feminists to include in their inquiry an examination of the mutual influences of ideologies of both gender and science in the construction of science itself—not only in its departure from proper standards but in its very normative values. In other words, only with the advent of an effective challenge to the traditional view of science as determined solely by exigencies of logic and experiment, a challenge that has come from recent developments in the history, philosophy, and sociology of science, have feminists been able to study the influence of gender norms on the actual historical construction of standards of "good" science. Accordingly, the subject of gender and science has now enlarged to a study of the mutually reinforcing dynamics that operate on the making of men, women, and science. A growing body of work on the historical, psychological, and scientific dimensions of these dynamics has focused attention on the deep interpenetration of the language of gender in scientific discourse and of the language of science in normative psychological discourse. In this effort, the historic conjunction between masculinity, objectivity, and autonomy ceases to be construed as a "natural" given but comes to be seen as a product of, and contributor to, social norms simultaneously dividing masculine from feminine and scientific from nonscientific. Of perhaps the greatest interest are the consequences for science of the exclusion from scientific norms of all those values that have been *culturally labeled* as feminine. Scholars have begun to explore three levels on which such consequences might be seen: first, in the selection of scientific problems; second, in the designation of "legitimate" methods; and third, in the role of tacit explanatory preferences in choices of "best" theory.

Perhaps the most critical problems facing scholars currently working in this area derive from continuing uncertainty and confusion about the nature of both gender and science. To many, gender continues to be read as synonymous with sex. To such readers, any discussion of "masculine" values in science automatically invites the supposition that women should do science differently. Not only are such readings not in accord with the intent of a scholarship aimed at the deconstruction* of the categories of masculine and feminine rather than at their reinstitution, but they are also experienced as direct threats to the political aims of women scientists who have struggled heroically to transcend such stereotypes. Alternatively, to other readers who see gender and science as purely cultural artifacts, gender appears as only one of a series of demarcators, including race, class, and ethnicity, invoked by the institution of science (one of many such social institutions) for the purposes of political domination. The most pressing questions for the subject of gender and science today are therefore twofold: What are the actual relations between gender and sex, on one hand, and between science and nature, on the other? If gender is not to be equated with sex, might it nonetheless be seen as partially rooted in nature—different from, but not entirely independent of, sex? Analogously, if science can no longer be relied on to mirror nature, can we nonetheless recognize its difference from other social institutions—deriving precisely from the ways in which science remains constrained, albeit not contained, by nature? The importance of these questions is not, however, limited to the subject of gender and science, nor does responsibility to address them lie exclusively in the domain of scholars working in this area. Rather, the relation between sex and gender has become the central question for contemporary feminist theory as a whole, just as the question about the relation between science and nature has come to reside at the center of current work in the history, philosophy, and sociology of science.

References. Ruth Blier, *Science and Gender* (New York, 1984); Ann Fausto-Sterling, *Myths of Gender*, 2d ed. (New York, 1992); Donna Haraway, *Simians, Cyborgs, and Women* (New York, 1991); Sandra Harding, *Whose Science? Whose Knowledge?* (Ithaca, N.Y., 1991); Sandra Harding and Jean O'Barr, *Sex and Scientific Inquiry* (Chicago, 1987); Evelyn Fox Keller, *Secrets of Life, Secrets of Death* (New York, 1992); Evelyn Fox Keller, *Reflections on Gender and Science*, 2d ed. (New Haven, Conn., 1995); Londa Schiebinger, *Nature's Body* (Boston, 1993).

EVELYN FOX KELLER

GENDER ROLES are behaviors and attributes expected of individuals on the basis on being born either female or male. Whereas "sex" is a biological term based on an individual's reproductive organs and genes, "gender" is a psychological and cultural term.

The gender role for females is quite distinct from the gender role for males. In Western society, to be "feminine" is to be nurturant, expressive, cooperative, and sensitive to the needs of others. To be "masculine" is to be active, aggressive, dominant, and ambitious. The distinctions have been characterized as the difference between a people orientation and an action orientation. Although "masculinity" and "femininity"* and their related traits are regarded as opposites, research clearly indicates that people possess both sets of traits in varying degrees, regardless of their biological sex. Furthermore, individual differences are far greater than gender differences with respect to all personality traits and human abilities. For example, people differ with regard to how competitive they are, but they do not differ primarily on the basis of gender.

Current gender roles probably had their origin in the division of labor prevalent in all societies. In cultures where birth control is primitive, tasks assigned to women generally have to be compatible with frequent childbirth* and nursing activities. The actual tasks assigned to women and men depend on the subsistence base of the particular society and the supply of, and demand for, labor. In industrialized societies, traditional gender roles have women concerned about the domestic sphere* and men concerned about the public sphere.* In all societies, the male role is more highly valued.

Personality traits assigned to each gender role generally stem from these traditional divisions in labor. Because of their maternal possibilities, women are supposed to develop qualities that would enhance the maternal role, such as empathy and nurturance. Because of their role as hunters, warriors, and breadwinners, men are supposed to develop qualities that would enhance performance in those roles, such as aggressiveness and competitiveness.

Gender roles are socially constructed, not biologically given. All human behavior is shaped primarily by cultural factors, in some cases in interaction with physiological predispositions. From the moment the sex of a newborn is announced, girls and boys are perceived and treated differently. As children age, parents tend to pay increasing attention to gender roles, dressing boys and girls differently, assigning different household tasks, and providing different toys. Teachers, peers, and the mass media also tend to discourage children, especially boys, from doing things viewed as more appropriate for the other sex.

The male gender role appears to be particularly rigid. During childhood and adolescence, being "masculine" involves rejecting all "feminine" behaviors and traits. Girls appear to have more leeway in their gender role, at least until puberty. At that time, however, they are supposed to concentrate on their expected role—to find a mate who will be "a good provider" and have children. For many girls, this means focusing on what males find attractive rather than on developing their own talents.

Strong conformity to traditional gender roles affects individuals on personal, relationship, and societal levels. On the personal level, traditional gender roles may be hazardous to one's health. Men have a shorter life expectancy, more accidents, and more serious illnesses than do women. Most of these gender differences can be attributed to such role-linked behaviors as risk taking, aggression, type A (compulsive, impatient) behavior, emotional nonexpression, and smoking. In contrast, women appear to suffer more from some mental health problems than do men. In particular, they are more likely to suffer from depression,* anxiety, and eating disorders than are men, and these may be related to a gender role that emphasizes appearance and inculcates a sense of helplessness in many women.

On a relationship level, women and men who conform to traditional gender roles may have difficulty relating. Since men may not have developed skills conducive to intimate interpersonal communication, the quality of their relationships with their friends, partners, and children may be poor.

The activities traditionally assigned to members of each sex may no longer be appropriate. The smaller families and longer life expectancies in modern societies, combined with the fact that many child care* responsibilities previously borne by the family* alone are now borne by society, mean that the traditional division of labor by biological sex no longer is necessary. Most women, including most mothers of young children, now are employed. However, as a result of traditional gender-role socialization of females with its lack of emphasis on career decision making, women are in the lowest-paying, lowest-status jobs. Furthermore, since our society values paid employment so much more than unpaid work, women who spend their lives or parts of their lives engaged in homemaking and child care activities often suffer from low self-esteem and self-confidence in comparison with their employed counterparts.

The traditional gender role for males also prepares men for a world that no longer exists. Men no longer are the sole breadwinners in most families, and their traditional place of dominance in society no longer is assured. Many are unprepared for the demands placed upon them by dual-worker marriages and by a changing work environment in which a woman may be their coworker or supervisor. The values underlying our major societal institutions, such as law, politics, and business, that reflect a "masculine" emphasis on competitiveness and dominance currently are being challenged.

For these reasons, change is slowly occurring in the definition of gender roles for both women and men. The modern gender role for women involves expectations for both children and a career and the development of assertive qualities along with the more traditional expressive ones. The modern gender role for men involves expectations of greater sensitivity to feelings and stronger communication skills along with traditional instrumental traits. Thus, the two gender roles have moved closer together. However, to the extent to which these roles are rigidly assigned to individuals solely on the basis of their biological sex, they may prove as restrictive as the traditional roles. The relationship between sex and gender is a problematic one, but a way must be found to recognize the reproductive differences between women and men without structuring an individual's entire personality and life around them.

Reference. Susan A. Basow, *Gender, Stereotypes and Roles*, 3d ed. (Pacific Grove, Calif., 1992).

SUSAN A. BASOW

GENDER ROLES, PRESCHOOL. Gender consciousness, like all social learning, is enhanced and intensified in a school setting. Given the opportunity to create fantasy worlds in the company of their peers, preschool boys and girls begin playing in similar ways but are attracted to distinct and separate play roles by the time they enter kindergarten. In the course of acting out a wide variety of make-believe characters, the children seek dramatic and social definitions for "boy" and "girl" with the same curiosity that governs other investigations into social and personal identity. The doll corner and block area are good places to observe the unfolding of gender roles.

In the beginning, domestic play looks remarkably alike for both sexes. Costumes representing male and female roles are casually exchanged in a flurry of cooking, eating, telephoning, and bedding down. Mother, father, and baby are the primary actors, but policemen, kittens, and even robbers often perform the same tasks. If asked, a boy will likely say he is the father, but if he were to say mother, it would cause no concern.

Behavioral differences become more apparent in the block area, where the momentum of movement and sound begins to produce a noticeable gap between the sexes. The boys zoom about, colliding and exploding in ways that have little appeal for the girls, who continue their doll corner rituals wherever they go. Both sexes build structures together, but the girls soon disperse to the art tables, while the boys remain until the buildings are toppled. We see here the first self-selected separation by sex in the classroom.

At age 4, gender specialization receives closer attention. Girls and boys still share roles, mainly in the guise of unisex pets, baby bears, and medical personnel, and continue to cook and make beds together. However, the list of he-roles and she-roles grows longer, each class developing its own inventory. In particular, the boys have begun to band together in superhero cliques whose large-scale maneuvers suit the banging-running impulses of young boys. As images of power and intrigue dominate the boys' play, the girls turn to dramatic plots that focus on female characters, adding more sisters and princesses to the mother–baby story. This continuing reenactment of family dramas most distinguishes the girls' play. Four- and 5-year-old boys and girls act out similar issues—jealousy and rivalry, friendship and contentment, fear and loneliness—but the disguises are different, and the boys prefer outer space to hearth and home.

Since the early 1970s, the causes and effects of stereotyped play among the young have been debated and cataloged. As direct connections are traced to adult mores, to biological differences, and to psychosexual stages, attempts have been made to create a school environment in which masculine and feminine roles are nearly indistinguishable. Yet the children continue, in their fantasy play, to visualize differences and act them out in stories of their own making. The persistence with which young boys and girls create separate roles in fantasy play may represent as primitive a need as the play itself.

References. V. G. Paley, *Boys and Girls* (Chicago, 1984); *Mollie Is Three* (Chicago, 1986); *The Boy Who Would Be a Helicopter* (Cambridge, Mass., 1990); *You Can't Say You Can't Play* (Cambridge, Mass., 1992); *Kwanzaa and Me: A Teacher's Story* (Cambridge, Mass., 1995).

VIVIAN GUSSIN PALEY

GENDER/SEX. Gender is a cultural construct: the distinction in roles, behaviors, and mental and emotional characteristics between females and males developed by a society. Gender is sometimes used as a synonym for *sex*, but feminists draw a clear distinction. Sex is a term that encompasses the morphological and physiological differences on the basis of which humans (and other life forms) are categorized as male or female. It should be used only in relation to characteristics and behaviors that arise directly from biological differences between men and women.

GENDER STEREOTYPES are structured sets of beliefs about the personal attributes of women and of men. (The terms "sex stereotypes" and "sex-role stereotypes" are often used interchangeably with "gender stereotypes.") Gender stereotypes are beliefs held by individuals (personal gender stereotypes) and are also shared patterns of thinking within a particular society (cultural gender stereotypes). Cultural gender stereotypes are reflected in cultural forms (e.g., television) and practices (e.g., legal system).

Gender stereotypes have been an active area of social science research for three decades. Early work on the content of stereotypic conceptions focused on the superordinate gender categories "men" and "women" and the personality traits associated with these broad groupings. More recently, researchers have taken a broader view of how people think about the sexes. Gender-stereotype targets include not only the two overarching categories "women" and "men" but also gender subtypes (e.g., "career women," "jocks"). In addition to personality traits (e.g., "Women are emotional"), the elements of stereotypic conceptions include abilities (e.g., "Men are good at math"), physical appearance (e.g., "Artistic' males have relatively slight builds and wear bulky sweaters"), behaviors, including role behaviors (e.g., "Women are more likely than men to care for children"), and occupations (e.g., "Most nurses are female").

Although men and women are not "opposite sexes" in terms of actual personality and behavior, gender stereotypes are "bipolar" that is, women and men are perceived to have opposing personal qualities. The content of beliefs about what men and women are like has most often been summarized by the terms "instrumental" (for the male stereotype) and "expressive" (for the female stereotype). Some researchers, however, feel that the core meaning of stereotypic beliefs about the sexes is best captured by the distinctions "hard–soft," "active–passive," or "agency–communion." This difference of opinion may be resolved in the near future as workers increasingly treat gender stereotypes as multidimensional. Historically, the male stereotype in American culture has comprised more positive and fewer negative attributes than the female stereotype. There is recent evidence, however, that this imbalance in the social desirability of gender stereotyping is declining or may even be reversing.

Stereotypic conceptions of the sexes are acquired by three primary means. First and perhaps most important are exposure to, and participation in, mainstream culture. For example, American children watch a considerable amount of television, which portrays men and women quite differently (e.g., men are depicted as powerful; women as peaceful). A second significant input to thinking about the sexes is contact and interaction with specific women and men. Given the general state of male dominance in American society, more men than women occupy positions of power and prestige; this means that most people have contact with men who, on average, have higher status than women. Third, the development of personal gender stereotypes is fostered by basic mental processes such as the tendency to form categories and to accentuate between-group differences.

Gender stereotypes influence information processing and overt behavior. They provide a cognitive frame of reference for the development of self-concept. That is, stereotypic conceptions of what men and women are like serve a prescriptive function by suggesting to individual women and men what they should be like. Thus, for example, the stereotypic belief that "women are not good at math" may lead individual women to avoid mathematics courses in school and to not consider careers that involve math.

Gender stereotypes also influence how we form impressions of others. Beliefs about the sexes create expectancies about specific others. These expectancies may shape what is noticed about the other, how the target's behavior is interpreted, and what is remembered about the person. The tendency is for stereotype-consistent actions to be more attended to and better remembered and for ambiguous behaviors to be interpreted in stereotype-consistent terms. However, when a perceiver has a large amount of personal information about a target, this can outweigh stereotype expectations.

Stereotypic conceptions not only influence how we think about others but also shape how we treat other people. Thus, for example, if men are stereotyped as "having leadership ability," they are more likely to be given leadership positions and have their orders complied with. Two important areas where gender stereotypes have particularly pernicious impact are the workplace (where gender stereotypes may create the expectancy that men are better suited for managerial positions, while women are "naturally" good secretaries) and therapeutic encounters (in which stereotypic male attributes are often regarded as more "healthy" than characteristics thought to be more typical of women).

Gender stereotypes are sometimes resistant to change. Beliefs about the sexes create forces toward their own fulfillment. At the societal level, gender stereotypes are pervasive in the major mediators of culture (e.g., magazines, popular music), and they tacitly influence how social institutions such as schools and the judicial system treat men and women. In interpersonal relations, our expectations that others fit our stereotypic conceptions can lead us to treat them in accord with these beliefs, making it more difficult for them to exhibit stereotype-disconfirming actions. At the level of the individual, if individuals feel that they should possess traits and abilities typical of their gender, then they are likely to develop stereotype-consistent qualities.

The foregoing does not mean that gender stereotypes are unchanging or unchangeable. As noted before, there has been an increase in the social desirability of the female stereotype. Also, specific interventions such as exposing children to nontraditional models have been shown to be effective in reducing gender stereotypes.

References. R. D. Ashmore, F. K. Del Boca, and A. J. Wohlers, "Gender Stereotypes," in R. D. Ashmore and F. K. Del Boca (eds.), *The Social Psychology of Male–Female Relations: A Critical Analysis of Central Concepts* (New York, 1986); K. Deux and M. E. Kite, "Gender and Cognition," in B. B. Hess and M. M. Ferree (eds.), *Analyzing Gender: A Handbook of Social Science Research* (New York, 1987); A. H. Eagly, A. Mladinic, and S. Otto, "Are Women Evaluated More Favorably than Men? An Analysis of Attitudes, Beliefs, and Emotions," *Psychology of Women Quarterly* 15 (1991): 203–216; D. N. Ruble and T. L. Ruble, "Sex Stereotypes," in A. G. Miller (ed.), *In the Eye of the Beholder: Contemporary Issues in Stereotyping* (New York, 1982); B. Six and T. Eckes, "A Closer Look at the Complex Structure of Gender Stereotypes," *Sex Roles* 24 (1991): 57–71.

RICHARD D. ASHMORE and FRANCES K. DEL BOCA

GENESIS. Many women are mentioned in Genesis, some with names, but are of little importance except to be instruments of perpetuating the tribe. Lamech's two wives, Adah and Zilhah, are examples; other women are mentioned to explain the origins of Israel's foes, for example, the anonymous elder and younger daughters of Lot, who conceived by their father the ancestry of the Moabites and Ammonites. Some of the women were totally absorbed in the story of their husbands' wives, like Zilpah and Bilhah, the handmaids of Leah and Rachel, respectively. Others have the same fate of being useful to the genealogy but do not even have the distinction of a name, like Cain's wife or Lot's wife. For the latter we do have a tiny blurb on her destiny: for her curiosity, she was turned into a pillar of salt standing by the Dead Sea. Noah's wife is, indeed, remarkable for her patience in enduring the enclosure of the ark for 40 days and nights. Then there are the mothers of Nephilim, who married the sons of God when "the wickedness of man was great upon the earth."

Besides these, there are three women whose stories are their very own in the Jewish Scriptures: Tamar, Dinah, and the anonymous wife of Joseph's master, Potiphar. The last named individual was the faceless and unsuccessful seducer of Joseph.

Dinah, daughter of Jacob and Leah, brought ignominy upon the tribe and shame on her brothers by her indiscreet love affairs with a prince of Canaan, the very one who was killed, along with his people, by the two sons of Jacob. Potiphar's wife and Dinah stand in contrast to Tamar, who is again mentioned by Matthew in the genealogy of Jesus. Acting according to an ancient Levirate law that entitled a woman who had lost her husband to marry the next of kin, she found herself rejected by both remaining brothers. In order to do her duty by the family in continuing its name, she seduced Judah, the father, and through him bore Perez, the ancestor of David and Jesus in the line of Judah. The story of Ruth and Naomi shows the profound effect of this ingenious woman.

The whole story of Genesis, however, focuses on the four great matriarchs: Sarah, Rebekah, Rachel, and Leah. Their respective husbands, Abraham, Isaac, and Jacob (husband of Rachel and Leah), are revered as those who gave us the knowledge of the one God, known as Yahweh, and his special providence through his promises to Abraham: a child to inherit "the promise" that would eventuate in a posterity as numerous as the stars of heaven, a land of their own, and the prediction that all nations would be blessed because of them. However, upon a closer look between the lines, it can be noted that the women were the ones who bore and protected "the child." Their hearts were attuned to the plan of God. Their one great desire was to mother the "child of promise," even though it seemed impossible at times because of age or barrenness. They taught the lesson that nothing is impossible with God.

Sarah, Abraham's most beautiful wife, had laughed when, listening behind the flaps of the tent, she heard one of Abraham's angelic visitors tell him he would return in the spring, and his wife would have a child. It was so, and Abraham named the child Isaac (meaning "She laughed") because, as Sarah said, "God had caused laughter for her." After Sarah's death Abraham purchased his first land in Canaan, a grave plot for Sarah in what is Hebron today.

Rebekah, sister of Laban, was God's answer to the prayer of Abraham's humble servant who was sent to find a wife for Isaac from Abraham's homeland. This servant had prayed for a woman whose gentle and selfless generosity matched the very loving kindness of God himself. The sign would be that the woman whom he met at a well in Mesopotamia would not only give him drink on his request but water his camels as well—a mighty task for a woman. But it was so.

Rebekah's immediate love of Isaac grew through love for the younger of her twin sons, Esau and Jacob. With a woman's insight, sharpened by divine inspiration, she contrived in a clever way to procure for Jacob the blind Isaac's blessing on his deathbed. She sensed that the younger son was more worthy to bear the promise. To protect him from his brother's revenge, Rebekah insisted that he flee back to the land of Laban and her family. She knew she would never see him again, but "the promise had been guarded." For 20 years Jacob endured the tricks of his uncle and put up with two wives, Rachel and Leah. Rachel was his beloved whom he had met at the same well from which Rebekah had drawn water many years before.

The story of Rachel and Leah's competition in bearing sons for Jacob by presenting their handmaids to him when their own wombs were barren parallels Laban and Jacob's race for the greatest prosperity. Rachel succeeded in carrying away their father's household goods to secure for Joseph the nominal inheritance of his mother's people. God's purpose through the whole story seemed to be to build up the house of Israel. And so it was. The story ends in another story, that of Joseph, Rachel's son, who saved God's family from famine by inviting them to the granaries of Egypt. In the forgiveness of his brothers who had sold him into slavery, Joseph was emulating his grandmother, Rebekah.

In the remarkable story of the matriarchs of Israel, bearing and protecting the "child of promise" run as a golden thread through the tapestry of patriarchal adventures of faith. It is prefaced in the realm of myth by the story of the woman who is symbol of all women—Eve, the mother of all. Having all the characteristics of women—intelligence, love, and curiosity—and perhaps the one weakness of believing all she heard, she is a prelude to woman's greatest glory: *hearing the Word of God, and doing it.* After the great tragedy of her son's death her resilience is, indeed, a miracle. At the birth of Seth, who took Abel's place, she exclaimed: "God has appointed to me another child instead of Abel because Cain slew him."

In Genesis we see that God has given to woman the unique privilege of bearing the child who will, with surety, crush the head of evil, though it is always accomplished through the pathway of pain.

Reference. W. Gunther Plaut, *The Torah: A Modern Commentary: Genesis* (New York, 1981).

MARIE STEPHEN REGES

GENITAL WARTS are caused by a sexually transmitted virus called human papillomavirus (HPV). The warts appear as small, painless, cauliflower-like bumps on the external genitals. Flat lesions that can escape the notice of the affected woman and her health care examiner may also occur on the cervix.

HPV is attracting more attention from the women's health community as its association with cervical cancer is increasingly defined. Although the Pap smear is not specific for detection of virus, it may detect an inflammatory process resulting from HPV or other viruses.

Genital warts usually appear two to three months after sexual contact with someone who has the condition, but symptoms may be delayed for many months. Use of the male or female condom or a flat latex barrier helps to prevent transmission of the virus.

No specific treatment exists for genital warts that become large and uncomfortable or that interfere with the elasticity of the vaginal walls. Podophyllin can be applied topically to affected tissue only, except during pregnancy, or to internal warts (urethra, vagina, rectum). Other topical treatments include liquid nitrogen, laser surgery, or 5-Fluorouracil. Repeated and frequent treatments may be needed.

HPV occurs frequently in people with HIV disease. Genital warts in women who have HIV disease are often more pronounced and more difficult to treat. Women with persistent and extensive genital warts should consider HIV testing. Because of the association of HPV with cervical cancer, women with HPV should have Pap smears every six months.

References. Abram Benenson (ed.), *Control of Communicable Diseases Manual* (Washington, D.C., 1995); Boston Women's Health Collective, *The New Our Bodies, Ourselves* (Boston, 1992); Linda Vilsa, *Body and Soul: The Black Women's Guide to Physical Health and Emotional Well Being,* Black Women's Health Project (New York, 1994).

ELAINE WHEELER

GERMAN ARTISTS (WOMEN), as was the case everywhere in Europe until the late nineteenth century, generally have painted, but only as daughters or sisters of painters in their workshops, without affixing their own names to any painting. One of the earliest exceptions known is sculptor Sabine von Steinbach (fl. c. 1300), creator of several fine statues at Strasbourg Cathedral, built by her father, Erwin von Steinbach. While some noted Italian Renaissance artists were women, the Reformation tended to relegate females to traditional occupations so that in Germany it took until the seventeenth century before autonomous women artists appear. Sybilla Merian, who had the luck to be born into a Frankfurt engraver's family and the determination to enter the Labadist sect, which freed women from traditional marital obligations, produced several volumes of etchings and watercolors. These show European and Surinam fauna and flora in amazingly aesthetic and microscopic detail; she is also said to have discovered the metamorphosis of the butterfly. In the eighteenth century, several painters' daughters such as Barbara Krafft (1764–1825) or Anna Dorothea Lisiewska-Therbusch (1721–1782) were appointed court artists after one of their works had attracted attention—in Therbusch's case, at Stuttgart and later Berlin, and in Krafft's, at Vienna, Salzburg, and Prague—where they excelled mostly as portrait painters. The most famous was Angelika Kauffmann (1741–1807), a cosmopolitan neo-classical allegorist, portraitist, and history painter. She was founding member of the London Royal Academy and a friend and protégée of Reynolds, and her beauty and artistic and musical talent fascinated Goethe, whom she portrayed in Italy.

Romantics adored women as creative spirits of almost redeeming power but took the women's creativity as homage to their own, at least as far as painting is concerned. Geniuses such as Anna Maria Ellenrieder (1791–1863), an excellent draftsperson, easily became victims of sexism and provincialism; Ellenrieder eventually ceased to paint because of chronic depression.

Not until the end of the century are women noticed again as painters, the 1880s and 1890s being the first period when art academies sporadically opened to women. After studying in Paris, Paula Modersohn-Becker (1876–1907), living in the artists' colony of Worpswede, superimposed on German naturalism the intensity of Van Gogh and Gauguin, depicting in heavy, Cézannesque strokes and bright colors the motherly simplicity of Westphalian peasant women and ruddy children. Her most daring painting is a self-portrait in the nude in which, like Frenchwoman Suzanne Valadon at the same period, she abolishes the habitual division of woman in art as *either* artist *or* model/muse, a myth perpetrated by the male establishment. Because of her early death after the birth of her child, she ranks only as a highly important precursor of expressionism, whereas Becker's senior, Käthe Kollwitz (1867–1945), became one of its significant representatives. Kollwitz was trained privately in Berlin, Königsberg, and Munich because she had been denied access to art academies. In many media, especially the older black-and-white graphic techniques (drawing, etching, lithography) that are reproduced relatively inexpensively, Kollwitz depicts the misery of wars, proletarian deprivation, and social exploitation, thus creating an art that is truly political and can be widely disseminated. She was not the only productive woman artist during the expressionist period: besides many émigré women living at one time or another in Germany, such as the Russian Marianne Werefkin (1860–1938), Gabriele Muenter (1877–1962) was an important member of the "Blaue Reiter" circle of Munich. Many landscapes painted simultaneously by both Muenter and Kandinsky permit interesting comparisons. The Bruecke group in Dresden did not produce equally important women artists.

Surrealism was an international artistic movement that inspired an entire generation of women painters, sculptors, and photographers. Sophia Delaunay-Terk (b. 1885 in the Ukraine) received her artistic training and married German art dealer Wilhelm Uhde in Karlsruhe. Later she moved to Paris, where her geometrical canvases were to rival in luminosity those of her second husband, Robert Delaunay. Together they created the "Orphist" movement, which was avidly received in Germany by Paul Klee and the "Blaue Reiter." Another creative woman from surrealist circles was the Swiss Sophie Taeuber-Arp (1889–1943), who worked as dancer and theater director as well as artist in Zurich, where Hans (Jean) Arp was attracted by her many talents. She conceived her work as a synthesis of architecture, sculpture, and painting and later collaborated with Arp and Theo van Doesburg on larger projects. In 1931, she settled near Paris, becoming a member of the group "Abstraction Création." Even better known, if not notorious, Meret Oppenheim (b. 1913 in Berlin) worked in Paris as a model of surrealist photographer Man Ray. Her felt-covered teacup entitled *Breakfast in Fur* (1936) with its quasi-Freudian ironic juxtaposition of incompatibles has become known as a rebellious act against clichés of femininity and fashion. Almost forgotten for years, Hanna Höch (1889–1978) was recently rediscovered through a retrospective in the Musée d'Art Moderne in Paris. Her incisive collages deal with machismo and the dehumanization of modern war and technology. Her later paintings are inspired by the technique of her own photocollages.

Although still not as visible as their male colleagues, postwar German women artists have been participating in every artistic movement, a few ignoring particularly feminist issues or themes, while most have formed groups supporting each other and publicizing issues of women in art. Particularly attracted to performance art have been women such as Gina Pane (b. 1939), Carolee Schneemann (b. 1939), Renate Weh (b. 1938), and Hanna Frenzel (b. 1957), treating feminist themes, consumerism, and body art. There is also a significant contemporary movement attempting to reformulate feminist aesthetics and to rewrite art history, as in the important volumes by Gisela Ecker and by Marlis Gerhardt and Renate Berger, texts that would warrant translation.

Although encyclopedias like the present one are a welcome positive manifestation of the wave of research on women in recent decades, the results so far are bound to be tentative, since much, if not most, research is still in progress on previously "invisible" women artists who were active during all periods of German art history.

References. Renate Berger, *Malerinnen auf dem Weg ins 20. Jahrhundert: Kunstgeschichte als Sozialgeschichte* (Cologne, 1982) and *Der Garten der Lüste* (Cologne, 1985); Gisela Ecker, *Feminist Aesthetics* (Boston, 1985); Marlis Gerhardt, *Stimmen und Rhythmen: Weibliche Aesthetik und Avantgarde* (Darmstadt, 1986); Germaine Greer, *The Obstacle Race: The Fortunes of Women Painters and Their Work* (New York, 1979); Joerg Krichbaum and Rein A. Zondergeld, *Kuenstlerinnen von der Antike bis zur Gegenwart* (Cologne, 1979); Roszika Parker and Griselda Pollock, *Old Mistresses, Women, Art, and Ideology* (New York, 1981).

UTE MARGARETE SAINE

GERMAN KINGDOMS OF EARLY MEDIEVAL EUROPE. During the early Middle Ages women often proved to be more learned and better in the art of writing than their male counterparts. St. Jerome, writing between 382 and 385, publicly praised women's superior intellect and addressed about one-fifth of his correspondence to women. Marcellina, the sister of St. Ambrose (340–397), wrote a number of letters to her brother. St. Augustine (354–430) received many written inquiries from women regarding biblical exegesis. Pope Gregory I's (590–604) correspondents included many women, among them Brunhild, queen of the Western Franks in Gaul. Armentaria, mother of Gregory of Tours, exchanged letters with her son. Abbesses and nuns were especially likely to be highly learned, as, for instance, Caesaria, abbess of Arles, writing about 570, and later the various female friends of St. Boniface (ca. 672/673–754), who wrote him from

England while he performed his missionary work in Germany (e.g., Egburg, Eangyth, Bugga, and Leoba, among others).

Tacitus, writing in the first century A.D., reported of Germanic women that they were believed to hold spiritual and divine power. Other sources such as Strabo mentioned women priestesses, but most of these reports were modeled on stereotypical images of barbaric women and thus are limited in their historical value. Still, Tacitus, like others, reflected verifiable aspects of religious life, although he disregarded the dominant patriarchal structure of the Germanic people.

Unfortunately, our knowledge of the times between the late Roman empire and the early German kingdoms is scarce. More concrete information is extant only from the sixth and seventh centuries onward. The early laws (e.g., the *Lex salica*, the Thuringian, Saxon, and Frisian law) excluded women from the inheritance of land, but any physical damage done to women was punished with extremely harsh measures (payments) that could lead to the total destruction of the convicted man's economic existence. In other words, Germanic women were highly appreciated and yet suppressed in patriarchal society.

Nevertheless, on a political level female members of royal families often exerted tremendous power during the period of both the Merovingians and the Carolingians. Gregory of Tours, who was consecrated bishop in 573, openly extolled the achievements of many royal women. Clovis (466/467–511), founder of the Merovingian dynasty, owed his powerful position to his mother, Basina, who had left the Thuringian king and entered a marriage with Clovis' father, Childeric (d. 482). Radegundis (518–587) divorced herself from Chlothar I, who had forcefully married her, and withdrew into the nunnery of Poitier against her husband's and the Frankish nobility's protests. Chrodechildis, who married King Clovis I in 493, convinced him to convert and thus brought the Franks under orthodox Christianity. Similar achievements are reported for Bertha of Kent (married to Ethelbert of Kent in 588) and Theudelinde, queen of the Langobard (d. 627). Brunichilde (c. 550–613), who was married to Sigebert, even assumed political control over the kingdoms of Austrasia (after her husband's death in 575) and Burgundy (in 592) and ruled for more than 30 years. Under the united opposition of the Austrasian nobility she was finally killed in 613 because of her attempts to unify her kingdom. Plectrudis, the first wife of Pippin II, tried to copy this model after her husband's death in 714 and excluded all her grandchildren, even the later famous Charles Martel, from the government. Martel, however, fled and later forced her to step down from power.

Although Charlemagne's (768–814) wives nominally lost their influence, they preserved their political power over the administration and management of the royal estates and finances. Judith, wife of Louis the Pious (778–840), not only occupied the central position at court in cultural affairs but handled most political decisions practically by herself. She even assumed the role of leader of her army in 841. In Germany in 960 Otto I placed his mother, Mathilde (895–968), second wife of Emperor Henry I, in charge of the government during his absence in Italy. Gisela, wife of King Stephen I of Hungary (ca. 959–1038), exerted tremendous influence on her husband and the country and promoted the introduction of Christianity. Nominally, this trend continued well into the High Middle Ages, but factually, royal women later lost much of their influence on public affairs, often because they came from faraway countries and had no local following in Germany.

According to St. Paul (1 Cor. 14:34ff), women were excluded from active participation in the church service. But from early Christianity on, women played a major role in administration and performed both liturgical and catechetic functions. From the fifth century their exercise of these functions was attacked, and the Synod of Orléans (533) excluded women from the church hierarchy. Although this rule was not strictly obeyed, only with the establishment of the first nunnery in 733–737 in the eastern part of the Carolingian empire (at Tauberbischofsheim, today in northern Bavaria near Würzburg) did women gain renewed access to active service within the church. Many of the nunneries and convents established all over Europe soon became famed centers of learning and culture.

The laws both of the late Roman empire and among the Germanic peoples living beyond its borders were relatively harsh toward women. In stark contrast to the post-Augustan Roman empire, where women occupied an almost equal and independent position regarding their *dos* (dowry) and their right to defend themselves in public, the Germans had quite different views toward women. Adulterous women were normally punished with the death penalty. The Burgundians extended the notion of adultery even to maidens and widows who slept with a man of their own accord. These women were treated as untouchables from then on. Characteristically the adulterous man was not punished, because, among other reasons, it was believed that his copulation did not pollute him. Whereas the pagans were convinced that women alone produced passionate desire, Christians blamed both men and women, but Roman law did not punish adulterous men either. Only from the ninth century onward was adultery considered a crime for both women and men.

Early Germanic law recognized three legitimate methods of marrying: by capture (*Raubehe*), by purchase (*Kaufehe*), and by mutual consent (*Friedelehe*). In the last, the woman's *Munt* (dowry) remained with her family. No marriage was binding without sexual intercourse, but often the first year of marriage was treated as a trial period. If the bride became pregnant, the marriage was deemed permanent. Generally, marriages were arranged by the parents (*Kaufehe*). The bride had to be a virgin; otherwise, her children were not considered legitimate and of pure blood.

According to church teaching, the only purpose of marriage was procreation, and, except when procreation was the express object, absolute purity (i.e. virginity) was required of both partners. Contrary to this teaching, in the ninth century it was publicly declared that since male chastity before marriage was rare and not expected, premarital sex was quite permissible (Third Council of Aachen in 862). However, the church firmly held the belief (see the rich *penitentials* literature from the sixth to the eleventh centuries) that even marital sex polluted the spiritual part of man. Only from the seventh and eighth centuries did the church begin to exactly define the relationships within which marriages were prohibited as incestuous. In some cases, even marriages between godparents and godchildren, who were not related through blood, were prohibited.

Whereas the Gallo-Romans practiced divorce by mutual consent and in this sense accepted equality between the sexes, the Germans did not permit women to make the decision to divorce. Only men were permitted to seek divorce. The church prohibited divorce completely during the reign of Emperor Louis the Pious (814–840), but the Franks hardly adhered to this rule. In fact, they, like most Germans and even Gallo-Romans, practiced polygamy and used female slaves as concubines. However, only the children of the official wife could inherit property. One of the common and deadly consequences of polygamy and concubinage was a form of harem fight over the relationship with the husband. The word "love" thus had practically no role in these relationships; love was rather perceived as a sensual, unreasonable, and destructive passion. New research has, however, unearthed material such as saints' lives, donations, wills, and burial inscriptions that suggest that many married couples in the early Middle Ages highly valued marital love. Whereas female saints constituted less than 10 percent of all known European saints in the sixth century, their proportion grew to 23.5 percent in the early eighth century, when the Merovingians ruled. This increase might be explainable through the large number of women's convents founded during this time. In the saints' lives (*vitae*) these holy women received special attention and gained public admiration.

Rape was severely punished, under Salic law even with death, unless the victim expressed the wish to marry the rapist, and her parents consented. Prostitution flourished among the Germanic settlers of the west, but the Visigoths severely punished freewomen caught in this business. Those who unjustly accused a freeborn woman of whoredom were punished by a large fine. Neither Louis the Pious, however, who supported the reformers of marriage laws, the Visigoths in Spain, nor the church in general succeeded in stemming prostitution, which enjoyed considerable popularity.

According to popular superstition at the time of the early Germanic kingdoms, women were the property of, or rather part of, the cosmic spirits or the infernal and nocturnal powers, as could be argued on the evidence of their menstrual cycle. The Council of Leptines in 744 condemned the opinion of many men that women surrender to the moon in order to capture the hearts of men, but this did not ease the relationship between the genders. Women were easily and often blamed for many evils in the world and thus had to be rescued from the world of wickedness to prepare them for marriage. Widows, on the other hand, were considered dangerous because of their continuous sexuality and thus were, in large part, discouraged or, in fact, even prevented from remarrying by their families. As a result, some widows become powerful figures of public life since control of the family passed on to them upon their husbands' deaths. Women in general were seen as key holders to the mystical world of the invisible and were credited with knowledge of the old lore of herbs, aphrodisiacs, potions, and other medicine (cf. Queen Isolde in the old Celtic myth *Tristan and Isolde*; see also the female relative practicing medicine in Salerno who prepares a love potion for her niece in "Les deux amants" in *The Lais of Marie de France*).

References. Werner Affeldt (ed.), *Frauen in Spätantike und Frühmittelalter. Lebensbedingunger-Lebensraum-Lebensformen* (Sigmaringen, 1990); James A. Brundage, *Law, Sex, and Christian Society in Medieval Europe* (Chicago, 1987); Edith Ennen, *Frauen im Mittelalter*. 3d rev. ed. (Munich, 1987); Peter Ketsch, "Aspekte der rechtlichen und politischgesellschaftlichen Situation von Frauen im frühen Mittelalter (500–1150)," in Annette Kuhn and Jörn Rüsen (eds.), *Frauen in der Geschichte*, vol. 2 (Düsseldorf, 1982), 12–71; Michel Rouche, "The Early Middle Ages in the West," in Paul Veyne (ed.), *A History of Private Life: 1. From Pagan Rome to Byzantium*, trans. A. Goldhammer (Cambridge, 1987), 411–549; Jane T. Schulenburg, "Saints Lives as a Source for the History of Women, 500–1100," in J. T. Rosenthal (ed.), *Medieval Women and the Sources of Medieval History* (Athens, Ga., and London, 1990), 285–320; Suzanne Wemple, *Women in Frankish Society: Marriage and the Cloister, 500–900* (Philadelphia, 1981); Susanne Wittern, *Frauen, Heiligkeit und Macht. Lateinische Frauenviten aus dem 4. bis 7. Jahrhundert* (Stuttgart, 1994).

ALBRECHT CLASSEN

GERMAN WRITERS. Modern. As in the rest of Europe, the few German women who wrote in the Middle Ages were aristocrats or nuns and often both, such as Hroswit (Roswitha) of Gandersheim, Hildegard of Bingen, and Mechthild of Magdeburg. During the Renaissance, there were women close to the humanists: Caritas Pirckheimer, Elisabeth of Brunswick-Lüneburg, and Emperor Charles V's sister Margaret of Austria.

A very interesting early baroque writer is Anna Owena Hoyen (1584–1655), who deserves more research. While little is known about her life except her struggles, she has left much poetry; for her, there is no contradiction between writing religious poetry and writing satirical attacks on certain clergymen. Catharina von Grieffenberg (1633–1694) is a major mystical baroque poet who meditates on religious subjects in a highly unconventional diction.

In the eighteenth century, women became culturally active. There are not only the theatre woman and impresario Friederike Caroline Neuber, called

"Neuberin" (1697–1760), but also the learned Luise Gottsched, the "Gottschedin" (1713–1762), who found a congenial husband to support her writing. Anna Luisa Karsch (1722–1792), who had to struggle, forged a very intense language that was the envy of male poets and anticipated the nature lyrics of Klopstock and the young Goethe. Sophie Albrecht (1757–1840) and Friederike Brun (1765–1835) are also worth mentioning.

Although the Romantics idolized women, and there were many female geniuses in their circle (Bettina von Arnim [1787–1859], Sophie von Mereau [1770–1806], Karoline von Guenderode [1780–1806], Carolina von Schelling [1763–1809], and Dorothea Schlegel [1763–1839]), their impressive creativity has been woefully undervalued (and well-nigh unpublished) to date. Two nineteenth-century writers, aloof from literary groups, have traditionally received recognition: the Austrian Marie von Ebner-Eschenbach (1830–1916), known chiefly as a writer of novellas based on traditional folklore, and Annette von Droste-Hülshoff (1797–1835), a Catholic of Westphalian nobility, known for her intensely introspective poetry.

In the twentieth century, women can be said to have finally achieved an equal place with men. During the early literary movements of the century, they are still considered the companions of relatively better known male writers, who sometimes silence their creativity; such is the case of the Ingolstadt novelist Marieluise Fleisser (1901–1974), a friend of Brecht's early years, and Claire Goll (1891–1977), whose writing underwent a crisis during Yvan Goll's relationship with poet Paula Ludwig (1900–1974). Overlooked for a long time and recently rediscovered have been Emmy Hennings (1885–1948) and Rahel Sanazara (1894–1936), companions of Hugo Ball and Ernst Weiss, respectively. Both Goll and Hennings authored autobiographical texts. The most important poets of the early part of the century are Jewish women who have combined the insights of a life of persecution, a fascination with religious themes, and a daring twentieth-century subjectivity with intense poetic experimentation: Else Lasker-Schüler (1876–1945), Gertrud Kolmar (1894–1943), Nelly Sachs (1891–1970), and Rose Ausländer (1907–1988). Hilde Domin's (b. 1912) literary criticism, especially on poetry, is equally as interesting as her poetic works. Marie Luise Kaschnitz (1901–1974), who lived in Italy much of her life, is a poet, novelist, and short story writer for whom the classical tradition is relevant. Elisabeth Langgässer (1899–1950), barred from publication during the Third Reich, has written three cycles of religious poetry, but her most important accomplishment is the novel *The Inextinguishable Seal*. Another author who was successful right after the end of the war is the Austrian Ingeborg Bachmann (1926–1973); while her modernist poetry was highly acclaimed, her prose works, for instance, *Malina*, were first condemned by male critics as "improper," only to be profusely imitated later. Ingeborg

Bachmann, in fact, is considered by many today to be the outstanding woman "classic" author of the German postwar period.

The two most important poets writing today are the highly experimental and eclectic Austrian Friederike Mayröcker (b. 1924) and the whimsical Sarah Kirsch (b. 1935), trained as a scientist, whose poetry and narrative are often imbued with magic and fairy tale, but also with harsh, contradictory reality, first that of the Democratic Republic and, since her emigration, that of the Federal Republic.

East Germany has at least three great novelists. Anna Seghers (1900–1983), exiled for many years, has movingly written about political dilemmas and the life of simple people. Her novel *The Seventh Cross* is about an early concentration camp for leftists, with the main character managing to escape. The second novelist is Christa Wolf (b. 1929), whose novels have shown that subjectivity cannot be absent from literature even at a time when the official literary ideology of the Democratic Republic prescribed a socialist realism that devalued individual psychology. Wolf's main theme is childhood (*Patterns of Childhood*, 1977) in Nazi Germany and youth in the Democratic Republic (*The Divided Heaven*, 1963; *Thinking about Christa T.*, 1968), but she has also treated the same interpenetration of political history and private fate in her long historical novella *Cassandra* of 1983 and in her novel *Kein ort. Nirgends* (1970; No Place. Nowhere) on the double suicide of author Heinrich von Kleist and Henriette Vogel, as well as in her Chernobyl text *Störfall* (1987; Out of Order), which blends essay, biography, and what might be called fantasy. Wolf has written interesting critical texts in which she attempts to come to terms with her own fiction. In a deliberately feminist vein, the third woman, Irmtraud Morgner (b. 1933), in several related novels daringly combines the life of a female troubadour with modern life and science fiction events.

The Federal Republic has a very active generation of women writers, among whom the best known are the satirist Gisela Elsner (b. 1937); the politically and sociologically oriented Ingeborg Drewitz (1923–1986); the prolific, sardonic Gabriele Wohmann (b. 1932); and the impressive Karin Struck and Verena Stefan (both b. 1947), all of whom deal in their novels with problems of female sexuality, the mother–daughter relationship, machismo, and other themes of female/feminist relevance, often blurring the traditional division between fiction and reportage.

Austria has produced a prolific generation of women, whose themes have included feminine depression (specifically, Marlen Haushofer [1920–1970]); education and daughter–parent relationships (Barbara Frischmuth [b. 1941] and Jutta Schutting [b. 1939]); and the grotesque and funny relationship between the sexes throughout the ages, for the benefit of female revolt today (Elfriede Jelinek [b. 1946]).

Although encyclopedias like the present one are a positive outcome of the wave of research on women's creativity during the last decades, so much work is currently in progress on previously "invisible" women authors of all periods that the data in this article must be considered tentative and as yet inconclusive.

References. Gisela Brinker-Gabler, *Deutsche dichterinnen vom 16. Jahrhundert bis zur Gegenwart* (Frankfurt, 1986); Heinz Puknus (ed.), *Neue Literatur der Frauen* (Munich, 1980); Jürgen Serke, *Frauen schreiben* (Frankfurt, 1982).

UTE MARGARETE SAINE

GERMAN WRITERS. Reformation through Baroque Period. With the reform of the church and the establishment of Roman law during the thirteenth century, there was a decline in women's status in Germany, so that women lost not only legal rights and the ability to hold official positions and to practice a trade within the guilds but even the possibility to acquire a full education in the liberal arts. Consequently, the following centuries saw a sharp decline in female literacy and authorship. Also, with the increasing importance of the universities since the fourteenth and fifteenth centuries, a much more rigid barrier for women's intellectual education was erected since women were not allowed to enter such institutions.

Although some people called for an educational program for girls from the time of the Reformation, these efforts died at the end of the sixteenth century. Only at the end of the seventeenth century did the movement to institutionalize basic female education gain momentum. Hence, we rarely find German female writers among the large number of poets from the fifteenth to the eighteenth centuries, although women were not illiterate altogether.

High-ranking noblewomen appear as early as in the first half of the fifteenth century as translators of French courtly literature or as patrons of courtly poets. Famous among them were Elisabeth of Nassau-Saarbrucken (1379–1456); Eleanore of Scotland, wife of the archduke Sigismund of Tyrol; and Mechthild (1419–1482), in second marriage wife of the archduke Albrecht of Austria, who created a remarkable literary circle in Rottenburg on the Neckar. The daughter of an Augsburg berger, Klara Hätzlerin (c. 1430–after 1476) gained a reputation for her work as editor and scribe of more than 200 secular and religious verses in her *Liederbuch* of 1471. She seems to have earned her living through her professional activity as a scribe and copyist.

With the Reformation the last resort for female literary productivity—nunneries and cloisters—was closed or deserted. Charitas Pirckheimer (1464–1532), however, energetically and with partial success fought for the preservation of her convent in Nuremberg. Her correspondence represents an essential part of female literature in the sixteenth century. Another epistolary author was Argula of Grumbach (1492–after 1563), who composed famous public letters in defense of early members of the reformed church and addressed them to imperial cities, dukes, and princes. Various other women who were involved in the Reformation, such as Ursula of Münsterberg (1491–after 1534), Katherine Zell (1497–1562), or Elisabeth of Braunschweig-Lüneburg (1510–1558), left important letter collections and religious treatises, along with personal accounts of their conversion to Protestantism.

In the early seventeenth century several women writers emerged at the various territorial courts. Elisabeth (1620–1697), Anna (1617–1672), and Augusta Maria of Baden-Durlach (1649–1728) composed lyric poetry and song-texts for the reformed church in Baden. Pietism helped such women as Adelheid Sybilla Schwarz (1621–1638) to express their concerns in a literary form. Schwarz was, in particular, one of the first in Germany to follow Martin Opitz's influential poetics of German language and poetry (1624), using the natural accent of prosodic speech in her own works. Also Rosamunde Juliane of Asseburg (1672–1712) was an enthusiastic pietist poetess. Both were strongly influenced by seventeenth-century French female pietists such as Antoinette Bourignon and Madame Guyon.

A truly intellectual and highly educated representative of German women poets was Anna-Maria van Schurmann (1607–1678), who composed poems in Latin, Greek, and Hebrew in addition to German. In a famous treatise (*Amica dissertatio*) she defended women's right to advanced education (1641). Anna Ovena Hoyen (1584–1655), who also excelled in her learnedness, dedicated many of her poems and songs to the Anabaptist movement. Elisabeth Charlotte, duchess of Orléans, originally Lieselotte of the Palatinate (1652–1722), wrote a highly interesting account of her experiences at the French court of Versailles in hundreds of letters to her friends and relatives in Germany. The poetry written by Catharina Regina of Grieffenberg (1633–1694) is highly acclaimed for its adamant stand against the Counter-Reformation and its expression of her strong belief in the Protestant movement. Philipp Zesen even invited her to become a member of the Rosengelsellschaft, one of the many German societies of the baroque period concerned with the purification and development of the German language.

Many other women writers such as Susanne Elisabeth Zeidler (fl.1681–1686), Margaretha Susanna of Kuntsch (1651–1716), and Anna Rupertina Fuchs (1657–1722) were active in the late seventeenth and eighteenth centuries. They predominantly dedicated their attention to lyric poetry. Christiana Mariana of Ziegler (1695–1760) was one of the first German women writers of the Enlightenment. The highest recognition as an imperial poetess was given to Sidonia Hedwig Zäunemann (1714–1740) by Göttingen University in 1738.

The first woman to be an independent writer living solely on the income of her own writing was Anna Louisa Karsch (1727–1791), who gained widespread recognition among leading contemporaries such as King Frederick II and the poet Johannes Wolfgang von Goethe. Friederike Karoline Neuberin (1697–1760), a famous actress and playwright, and Adelgunde Victorie Gottsched (born Kulmus [1713–1762]), highly acclaimed both for her participation in her husband's work on a German dictionary and for her poems, plays, translations, and letters, were the first outstanding female poets representing the postbaroque period.

There are three major problems with the history of women writers since the Middle Ages. First, since a large part of the literary work by women has not been published, it is practically impossible to assess objectively the share of female literature in the Reformation and the baroque period. Second, the literature written by women has not received sufficient attention in literary studies up to now because of the male-oriented scholarship in German literature since the Middle Ages. Third, most women writers prior to the eighteenth century composed private poetry and letters almost exclusively. Since they lacked any possibility of publication, they did not venture into plays, novels, or essays. C. M. Wieland's publication of Sophie von LaRoche's sentimental novel *The History of Lady Sophia Sternheim* in 1771 and 1772, however, constituted the beginning of a rich tradition of female literature in Germany. Today much more scholarship is focused on the history of early–modern women writers, as more women academicians have found their way into the universities.

References. B. Becker-Cantarino (ed.), *Die Frau von der Reformation zur Romantik, die Situation der Frau vor dem Hintergrund der Literatur-und Sizialgeschichte*, Modern German Studies 7 (Bonn, 1980); Gisela Brinker-Gabler (ed.), *Deutsche Dicterinnen vom 16. Jahrhundert bis zur Gegenwart* (Frankfurt, 1978); Paul Gerhard Schmidt (ed.), *Die Frau in der Renaissance* (Wiesbaden, 1994); K. M. Wilson (ed.), *Dictionary of Continental Women Writers* (New York, 1990); Jean M. Woods and Maria Furstenwald, *Women of the German-Speaking Lands in Learning, Literature and the Arts during the 17th and 18th Centuries, a Lexicon*, Repertoire zur Deutschen Literaturgeschichte 10 (Stuttgart, 1984).

ALBRECHT CLASSEN

GERMANY, 1848–1919. From the early 1840s social unrest and civil strife determined public life in the German states of the former so-called Holy Roman Empire (dissolved in 1806). The bourgeoisie aimed at participation in political affairs and the unification of Germany. When revolution broke out in France in February 1848, the Germans followed suit in March with uprisings in many states and the calling of a Parliament to bring about German unification. Parallel to these political revolutionary events in 1848, a woman's movement emerged in almost all German states. On the local and "national" level many women's unions and organizations, often pursuing specific political aims, sprang up. However, although women were soon given an observatory status in the first German Parliament, which was held in the Frankfurt Paulskirche, they did not gain an active role in poli-

tics, except for some involvement in street and barricade battles against the
armed forces crushing the revolution in 1849–1850.

The majority of employed women were in agriculture and domestic service. At the age of 13 or 14, working-class girls, having finished their basic
education, looked for jobs, but only a few were lucky enough to learn a
trade. This situation changed, to some extent, during the 1850s, when industrialization took off in Germany, and large numbers of unskilled or
semiskilled women laborers found employment in factories. Despite its bad
reputation, factory work still had many advantages over work as a servant
girl, whose economic situation and working conditions almost resembled
those of a slave. Another way out was prostitution, which witnessed a
tremendous growth in the second half of the nineteenth century in big cities
such as Berlin.

In 1875 only about 20 percent of female factory workers were married.
By 1907 this figure had risen to 27 percent, but the majority of married
women who were employed were occupied in homework for the textile
industry. Homework, however, imposed an extra burden on women that
was not adequately recognized by their husbands or by society. On the
average, married women had five children and thus already had their hands
full with heavy household chores.

In the latter part of the nineteenth century, the typewriter and compulsory elementary education opened clerical work and teaching to women.
After 1860 private commercial schools were established for girls all over
Germany. In addition, the share of women teachers at primary and secondary girls' schools increased considerably. By the turn of the century, 57
percent of all teachers in Prussia's girls' schools were women.

The General German Association of Women Teachers (*Allgemeiner
Deutscher Lehrerinnenverein*), founded in 1890 by Helene Lang, strongly
supported reforms of the school system for girls. Girls had been allowed
to take the *Abitur* (the graduating exam concluding secondary school education) externally since 1895, but only in 1908 were *Lyzeums* (secondary
schools for girls) opened. Women were officially allowed to enter the university in some southern German states around 1900, and in Prussia in
1908. One woman student had even been permitted to enter the medical
school of Heidelberg University in 1900 and to sit for exams. By 1913,
143,649 women were registered at German universities.

The increased interest of bourgeois women in social and political matters
was reflected in the creation in 1894 of the Federation of German Women's
Associations (*Bund Deutscher Frauenvereine*). The oldest member of this
federation was the General German Women's Association (*Allgemeiner
Deutscher Frauenverein*), but by the end of the century women had found
multiple ways to express their concern about education and women's employment. Since then the women's question has become a major subject of
public discussion. The most vocal representatives of the middle-class

women's movement were Helene Lange (1848–1930), Gertrud Bäumer (1873–1957), Alice Salomon (1872–1948), and Marianne Weber (1870–1950).

On the left side of the political spectrum, socialist women's groups developed from the 1880s, but under the antisocialist laws in force between 1878 and 1890 they were temporarily disbanded as illegal organizations. By 1907, 94 women's organizations with a total of over 10,000 members had been established. Despite initial hesitations, the Social Democratic Party (SPD) quickly adopted the political ideals of its women members (see Bebel) and called for suffrage for all state citizens regardless of sex. Clara Zetkin (1857–1933) and Lily Braun (1865–1916) spearheaded these efforts. By 1909, 10 percent of the total SPD membership was female. Apart from the SPD only the Progressive Party (*Fortschritts Partei*) under Friedrich Naumann admitted a leading woman activist, Marie Elisabeth Lüders (1818–1966), into its ranks.

Overall in Germany, the women's movement did not place as much emphasis on attaining the franchise as did the movements in the United States and Britain. Rather, its chief interest was in improving conditions for mothers and children. The popular literature echoed the bourgeois idyllic image of woman as "the gentle sceptre and the heart of a blissful domesticity" (*Die Gartenlaube*, an extremely successful sentimental journal; see the novels of Amalie Schoppe, Luise Mühlbach, Eugenie Marlitt, and especially Hedwig Courths-Mahler). In the early 1900s even socialist women's groups began to subscribe to some of the ideals fostered by bourgeois women's groups, especially that women's most important occupation rested in motherhood and in being a housewife.

Agitation by bourgeois and socialist groups and concern for the need for healthy mothers to raise healthy sons helped spur government recognition of the need to support the health of potential mothers with protective legislation. In 1878 women were prohibited by law from working underground or within three weeks of delivery of a baby, and in 1891 they were barred from working at night. In 1910 a law limited women's workday to 10 hours and introduced a compulsory eight-week break between childbirth and the resumption of employment.

World War I brought both improvements and severe setbacks for women. Initially, large numbers of women laborers were laid off because the textile, tobacco, and footwear industries had to cut back drastically. From early 1917 onward, however, women were sought on a large scale as wartime replacement in a wide variety of semiskilled and skilled jobs in traditionally male-dominated areas. Soon, over 700,000 women worked in the engineering, metallurgical, iron and steel, chemical, and mining industries. Yet the total number of workingwomen did not increase greatly; instead, the women's workforce relocated, thus altering the whole picture of women's social and economic roles. Fears, however, that overexploitation could deteriorate women's health and thus motivate them to leave their jobs again induced the military and the administration (which during the end of the war were almost identical) to pressure the industry to introduce the eight-hour workday. In addition, large new welfare institutions were established under the leadership of Marie-Elisabeth Lüders, head of the Prussian Women's Work Force Center in the war ministry, to provide such things as housing and health care and, above all, maternity benefits to counteract a deeply feared drop in the birthrate evident since around 1910. In this sense the war helped to heighten the status of social work, largely a woman's occupation, as a profession in the public interest. The foundation of the National Women's Service (*Nationaler Frauendienst* [NFD]) in 1914 provided the strongest expression for women's commitment to the government's war efforts, but it also reflected the state's new concern for women's welfare. The NFD was geared toward improving the cooperation between local authorities and welfare institutions to alleviate social problems conditioned by the war.

With the devastating winter of 1916–1917, the situation on the home front changed, and women increasingly demanded peace and an end to the war. The tradition of female pacifism went back several decades, however, and is best represented by Berta von Suttner (1843–1914), who had vociferously argued for peace. Her novel *Die Waffen nieder* (Put Down the Weapons, first printed in 1889) saw its last edition in 1914 just before the outbreak of the war. In 1917, the radical wings of both the bourgeois women's groups and the socialists under Clara Zetkin met with representatives of other international women's organizations—first the bourgeois women in The Hague and later the socialist women in Zimmerwald, Switzerland—to announce their opposition to the war. The era of an active and effective women's role in politics had begun in Germany.

References. August Bebel, *Women under Socialism* (1st ed., Stuttgart, 1879; 50th ed., 1909); J. C. Fout (ed.), *German Women in the Nineteenth Century: A Social History* (New York, 1984); B. Franzoi, *At the Very Least She Pays the Rent: Women and German Industrialization, 1871–1914* (Westport, Conn., 1985); Ute Frevert, *Women in German History: From Bourgeois Emancipation to Sexual Liberation*, trans. S. McKinnon-Evans in assoc. with T. Bond and B. Norden (Oxford, 1988); R.-E. B. Joeres and M. J. Maynes (eds.), *German Women in the 18th and 19th Centuries* (Bloomington, Ind., 1986); Anneliese Neef, *Mühsal eines Lebens lang. Zur Situation der Arbeiterfrauen um 1900* (Cologne, 1988).

ALBRECHT CLASSEN

GERMANY, 1919–1933 (WEIMAR REPUBLIC). When, during the last weeks of 1918, the socialists assumed power in war-torn Germany, they also instituted suffrage for women. It was, however, not the result of a long and hard-fought battle but rather an unexpected by-product of the new democratization. Over 10 percent of the delegates to the 1919 National

Assembly in Weimar were women, and women participated in local politics all over Germany as well. The turnout of women at the first elections was 90 percent, a level never reached again during the following 14 years. However, between 1919 and 1932, 112 German women were elected to the *Reichstag*, a total of between 7 and 10 percent, which was higher than the representation of women in the U.S. Congress during the same period.

In reality, however, double standards for men and women were common practice, and concrete progress on women's issues was rather limited because suffrage did not automatically give women equal rights in actual terms. Even many women politicians publicly argued against their suffrage, as, for instance, Reichstag member Paula Müller-Otfried, and on the average women voted more for the Catholic and other bourgeois parties than for the socialists. Particularly among the socialists a gender-related split on ideological questions became noticeable. Male party members perceived women as caretakers of the family and blamed women workers for undercutting men's earning potentials because of the former's low pay. Finally, they deemed political struggle to be mostly a matter of male concern. Radical women politicians such as Lida Gustava Heymann and Anita Augspurga, who, during the 1920s, fought for absolute gender equality on all levels of life, quickly alienated middle-class women and thus lost their basic support group. Despite a large percentage of women members in trade unions and white-collar organizations, which had tripled and quadrupled in the first few years of the republic, women's enthusiasm for political activities dropped rapidly during the later years. Gender patterns had thus basically not changed since the prewar years despite general improvements for women in terms of both education and work.

At the end of the war, 8 million soldiers came back from the front and demanded their jobs back. When, by February 1919, there were still 1.1 million individuals unemployed, demobilization orders stipulated that women should return to their original profession, be it the typical female occupation in the textile industry or at home. Large numbers of women, married and unmarried, were summarily dismissed in accordance with these orders. Both the trade unions and the Social Democrats only meekly protested, basically agreeing with this policy, which was designed to reintegrate the veterans into a new peacetime industry. Demobilization continued well into 1921 and took away practically all social gains women had made during the war. Again the rift between socialist and bourgeois women opened, with the latter willing to submit to the traditional and now-renewed demands that women return to the kitchen and child care, and the former protesting against this renewed misogyny.

By 1925, however, the occupational census found that there were over 1,700,000 more women in full-time occupations than in 1907. Even though the percentage had climbed from 34.9 in 1907 to only 35.6 in 1925, women now predominantly held positions in higher-income, white-collar industries and had established the role of the so-called new objective woman. But they were, nevertheless, still barred from more advanced levels, often because they lacked the education that men received and more often because the employers disliked the idea of having women in the higher echelons of the industry. Although the most visible changes in women's employment took place in retail sales, the most profound changes occurred in commerce and transportation. Whereas the total workforce in these fields increased from 3.5 million in 1907 to 5.25 million in 1925, the number of women workers increased by 82.3 percent. At the same time the percentage of women in domestic service declined from 17.1 percent to 12.5 percent.

Married women were generally expected to stay home. According to the 1925 statistics, almost all female, white-collar workers were single, and two-thirds were under age 25. Most women outside blue-collar employment left their jobs once they had married unless their husband was a farmer, a shopkeeper, or a restaurant owner, in which case they usually continued to work in the family business. In contrast, blue-collar women continued at their jobs because their husbands' income often proved insufficient to support a family. Across the board, women earned about 20 to 40 percent less than men for doing the same work. Compared to prewar levels, the wage gap had narrowed only for the skilled female worker.

Social welfare for workingwomen became a major topic among socialist women politicians. Marie Juchacz, under the aegis of the Social Democratic Party (SPD), established an organization called *Arbeiterwohlfahrt* (Workers' Welfare) in December 1919, the purpose of which was to provide assistance to all those who needed it without regard for political or religious affiliation. It provided homes for teenage girls, child care centers, soup kitchens, camps for children, care for pregnant women, and other services. Its existence was widely welcome not only because of services it offered but because it offered an area of employment for women fully in accord with traditional gender roles, thus taking away much of the tension between the sexes. Basically, it simply copied the typical bourgeois ideals from the nineteenth century and adjusted them to modern life in the industrialized Weimar Republic, showing that modern women could combine the ideal of womanhood/motherhood with that of the independent workingwoman. This institution has continued to the present and is an established part of the social welfare system of the Federal Republic of Germany.

For many women the years of the Weimar Republic saw a total transformation in terms of economics, technology, morality, and women's sexuality. The cult of youth was especially advantageous to young women. Many adopted the style of the "intellectual with *Männerschnitt*" (male hairdo; the *Bubikopf* or boyish bob). Large numbers of single women joined sports clubs and other types of organizations such as the *Wandervogel* (similar to girl scouts), *Sozialistische Arbeiterjugend* (Socialist Labor Youth), *Deutsche Turnerschaft* (German Gymnastic Association), and

Reichsverband für Frauenturnen (National Union of Women's Gymnastics).

One of many consequences of the transformation of society in the 1920s was a sharp increase in the divorce rate, from 21 per 1,000 marriages during 1901 through 1905 to 62 per 1,000 marriages from 1921 through 1925. Another consequence was the reduction in family size. The birthrate dropped even more than before the war, and the couple with two children became the norm. Although abortions were illegal, and contraceptives not easy to come by, both were in common use.

In 1925 the SPD succeeded in changing the ban on abortion. The Reichstag agreed to impose a more lenient punishment for abortion and to consider mitigating circumstances. Despite vociferous demands on the part of socialists, feminists, and other liberal groups, the criminal character of abortion was not removed. However, publications, lectures, and classes on sexuality became immensely popular. Many nationwide organizations sprang up with the open goal of spreading knowledge about abortions and, in general, improving sexual hygiene. One of the largest was the *Reichsverband für Geburtenregelung und Sexual hygiene* (Reichsleague for Birth Control and Sexual Hygiene), founded in 1928. It was estimated that by 1930 there were 1 million abortions, with 10,000 to 12,000 fatalities annually.

Theoretically, the situation of women changed considerably during the Weimar Republic. Young, unmarried women enjoyed considerable freedom and gained access to large areas of public life previously limited to men only, although on a practical level the same oppressive male standards for female roles and behaviors, particularly of married women, continued to dominate. Thus, before the dawn of Adolf Hitler and the Third Reich, women gained more rights and privileges than ever before, but the Nazi regime was soon to easily undo this progress, forcing women back into the household and the traditional role of mother. Of course, the demands of World War II would change this situation again, but ideologically the independent woman from the Weimar period was anathema to the Nazis.

References. Renate Bridenthal, Atina Grossmann, and Marion Kaplan (eds.), *When Biology Became Destiny* (New York, 1984); Gordon A. Craig, *Germany 1866–1945* (New York, 1978); E. J. Feuchtwanger, *From Weimar to Hitler* (Basingstoke, 1993); Ute Frevert, *Women in German History: From Bourgeois Emancipation to Sexual Liberation*, trans. S. McKinnon-Evans in assoc. with T. Bond and B. Norden (Oxford, 1988); Claudia Koonz, *Mothers in the Fatherland: Women, the Family, and Nazi Politics* (New York, 1987); Renate Pore, *A Conflict of Interest: Women in German Social Democracy, 1919–1933* (Westport, Conn., 1981).

ALBRECHT CLASSEN

GERMANY, 1933–1945 (NATIONAL SOCIALISM). After Hitler and National Socialism gained power in 1933, the experiences of German women were shaped by the brutal imposition of a totalitarian regime that both extolled women and suppressed their advancement. From its inception, the Nationalist Socialist German Workers' Party (NSDAP, Nazi Party) had no place for women in its ranks. At its first general meeting in early 1921 a unanimous resolution passed that stated that women could never be accepted either into the leadership of the party or into any governing committee. National Socialism viewed German women as wives and mothers who did not wish to work in factories or offices or even represent themselves in the government. A cozy home, a beloved husband, and a multitude of happy children were their only aspirations. Hitler believed in suppressing the drive for women's emancipation by emphasizing the differences between men and women and the woman's role as the preserver of the biological inheritance, domestic virtue, and even eternal morality.

The story of women in the NSDAP has several dimensions. It cannot be denied that in the 1920s there were women who found National Socialism attractive. Small numbers, attracted by its anti-Marxist philosophy and even its ultranationalist and racist ideas, joined local branches of the NSDAP. Some who believed wholeheartedly in the party proclamations became activists. Other women, however, supported the party mainly because they were concerned about foreign influence and women's emancipation and believed that what they considered positive change in the status of women would result from supporting the Third Reich.

Although Nazi women did not hold any party offices or contribute to making policies, they voted for Hitler and contributed both money and moral support to the movement. Gregor Strasser, the organizational chief of the party in the early 1930s, encouraged women to participate in the Reichstag elections. Often, a woman whose brother or husband was in the party would provide food, make uniforms, and sew flags. Others did not just follow their husbands into the party—they were quite fanatic about their involvement.

Some Nazi women were quite eager to return to traditional roles. They wanted a future where men and women would be equal but separate. Even though their work was not the same as that of the Nazi Storm Troopers (SA) or Nazi Security Guards (SS), they felt that their duties were equally important.

During the late 1920s the leaders of the Nazi women's movement spoke in public, ran campaigns and meetings, and wrote political pamphlets. Their role changed, however, in the 1930s, when there was a need for less activism and more traditionalism.

In July 1932, Hitler established a youth organization for girls, and Gertrude Scholtz-Klink, a leader of the official women's organizations in the Third Reich during the mid-1930s, tried to bring all "valuable" German women into a new group called the German Women's Enterprise. The group had limited appeal, however. It had competition from groups organized by the churches. The church groups were more appealing to German women than contrived groups supported by the party.

There were a number of women whom the Nazis featured. Among them were Magda Goebbels, the fashion-conscious wife of Joseph Goebbels, Minister of Propaganda; Leni Riefenstahl, a film director and producer who recorded the 1936 Berlin Olympics; Hannah Reitsch, a test pilot; and, of course, Scholtz-Klink, who headed the Nazi Women's Bureau, which claimed 6 to 8 million members.

The Nazi definition of the role of women actually expanded and contracted with party needs. Prior to Hitler's ascension to power, men and women worked together. Following 1933, Hitler made employed women give up jobs to return to the home and raise families. After 1936, however, when he needed them to work, he put them in factories. Because of Hitler's war preparation, the Nazis moved to improve the employment of women in the workplace. Despite all of these changing roles, however, at no time did women have any demonstrable influence over policies that affected themselves, their families, or the Nazi Party. They were not placed in positions where they wielded political power or party and state responsibility.

Women were encouraged to marry and have many children by a population policy that was the most comprehensive ever formulated by a European state. The Nazis declared that a population policy was necessary to restore the family, to encourage sexual morality, and to create a well-disciplined workforce. The Nazi state emphasized social hygiene, eugenics, and motherhood. Many women in Germany felt that, by following Hitler's population policy, they were able to contribute to the national renewal that Nazism promised.

Germany was not the only state in Europe to be concerned with population policy. Some of the actions in Nazi Germany were reflected elsewhere in Europe where incentives were given to prolific mothers, and contraception and abortion were discouraged. During the world recession of the 1930s, women were removed from the workforce and restricted in their eligibility for entrance to professions.

Nazi measures to control biology were proposed and planned from 1933 on. These included the Law for the Prevention of Hereditarily Sick Offspring; attempts to introduce the genealogical tree, which would check the blood relationships of all Germans; the euthanasia program (a policy developed to eliminate those who doctors said had physical or mental handicaps); and the establishment of the Motherhood Cross to be awarded on April 12, the birthday of Hitler's mother. The Motherhood Cross provided the woman with many children the same kind of honor as a front-line soldier.

The Nazis were strongly opposed to feminism and held that feminists were unduly influenced by both Jews and Marxists, had an unhealthy preoccupation with their sexuality, and were determined to destroy Christian-

German family life. The Nazis discouraged dieting, cosmetics, smoking, and foreign dress. German couples needed medical examinations to marry, and the fear of "hereditary defects" led to a black market in documents proving Aryan ancestry. Wives of SS men were forced to attend special bride schools. Almost 28,000 so-called undesirable women underwent forced sterilization by 1934. Aryan men were encouraged to divorce Jewish wives, and their children were taken from the mother. In 1939, it was announced that Jewish women could seek abortions, but non-Jewish women could not. Non-Jewish women who did not marry or have children were harassed. The extent of Hitler's racial policies would, of course, be implemented in what became known as the Final Solution during World War II. (See HO-LOCAUST.)

The response of the Christian faithful to racism was not uniform. A population as enormous as that of Christian women could not be socially, politically, or temperamentally monolithic. Michael Phayer states that Protestants were more tolerant toward Nazi racism than Catholics. Protestant women were more nationalistic than Catholics, which made them more receptive to National Socialism. Some Protestant women, however, also fought National Socialist ideology and the paganism it espoused. Scholtz-Klink promoted her own women's organization by playing Catholic and Protestant women's organizations against each other.

The experiences of German women living under Nazi rule varied. As pointed out in *When Biology Became Destiny*, Nazism did not begin with overt attacks against the emancipation of women. It was cloaked in extreme nationalism calling for love of the country, reduction of the unemployment by keeping women out of the workforce, and reversion of women back to the role of motherhood.

What can be said of the attitude of German women toward the racism of Hitler? A great deal of information has been derived from studying the most prominent organizations of women. Many Protestant and Catholic leaders were aware that if Germany were victorious, there would be a showdown between Christianity and the neopaganism of National Socialism. Some courageous women dared to challenge the establishment. For example, Agnes von Grone and Helene Weber both spoke out against anti-Christian elements in Nazism. Ultimately, faith, not feminism, made Nazi women reject Nazi neopaganism. Institutional and religious elements overwhelmed social factors.

While some German women conspired with the party, only a small number actually were involved in implementing Nazi policy. Despite Hitler's call for women to enter the workforce after 1937, the war production effort in Germany was not as efficient as in countries like Great Britain. Also, while a few German women consciously and actively resisted Nazism, aided its victims, and helped with the resistance, most women did neither but focused on quietly protecting their families from the intrusive totalitarian state. But all, whether party members, willing followers, resisters, victims, or just silent women trying to protect themselves and their families, were overwhelmed by the results of Nazi policies and suffered from the disasters of war, defeat, or occupation. (See also ANTI-SEMITISM; HOLOCAUST; NAZI PROPAGANDA.)

References. Renate Bridenthal, Atina Grossman, and Marion Kaplan (eds.), *When Biology Became Destiny: Women in Weimar and Nazi Germany* (New York, 1984); Joachim C. Fest, *The Fact of the Third Reich: Portraits of the Nazi Leadership* (New York, 1970); Claudia Koonz, *Mothers in the Fatherland* (New York, 1987); Michael Phayer, *Protestant and Catholic Women in Nazi Germany* (Detroit, 1990); Jill Stephenson, *The Nazi Organization of Women* (Totowa, N.J., 1981); Matthew Stibbe, "Women and the Nazi State," *History Today* (1993).

PETER M. DIMEGLIO

GERMANY, 1949–1990 (GERMAN DEMOCRATIC REPUBLIC [GDR]). With the unification of the two Germanys, 40 years of Marxist socialism on German soil came to an end on October 3, 1990. Founded in 1949, the GDR was once considered one of the leading industrial nations with the strongest economy within the so-called Eastern Bloc. As has become apparent, this was accomplished at high cost to the people and the environment.

Women constitute 52.8 percent of the total population of the GDR. According to Article 20.2 of the Constitution, women and men are equal before the law, with the advancement of women, especially in the vocational sphere, being the duty of society and the state.

Women have advanced in all areas of public life. Under the pre-1990 socialist government, they constituted about one-third of the People's Chamber. The Council of State, an organ of the People's Chamber that functioned as the head of state, included five women. The Ministry of National Education was headed by a woman, and three ministries had female deputy ministers: Electrical Engineering and Electronics, Light Industry, and Finance. Twenty-seven percent of all mayors and 51 percent of all judges (both elected officials) were women. The SED (Socialist Unity Party of Germany), then the leading party, had a 35 percent female membership, but there were no women in the Politburo, the highest organ in the party hierarchy.

Nonsexist education has been a primary goal. Girls and boys are exposed to the same curriculum, including needlework and shop as well as "participation in social production," the hours children spend each week in a factory. The educational reforms of 1965 called for a special encouragement of girls to enter technical careers. In 1985, of all full-time students at university-level institutions, 52.5 percent were women, as opposed to 24 percent in 1950.

Half the labor force is female (49.4 percent). Ninety-one percent of all women of working age are at work or in training. Young females perceive the combination of employment and family as an unquestioned fact, with their vocational success being their primary life goal. By the end of 1984, 80.3 percent of all workingwomen had completed some sort of vocational or professional training. Moreover, while women are still highly concentrated in traditionally female fields, significant changes with a continuous and clearly increasing trend have occurred. In the following occupations, for instance, women constitute significant percentages: physicians, 52 percent (1962: 28 percent); dentists, 57 percent (1962: 20 percent); and those in leading positions in the economy, 30 percent (1950: 9 percent). While female participation in agriculture decreased (1960: 60 percent; 1984: 39.4 percent) the numbers of women who completed vocational training in this area (skilled laborer to university level) dramatically increased (1960: 2.3 percent: 1984: 88.5 percent). Thus, the traditional difference in qualifications between male and female agricultural workers has disappeared. An important role in advancing women's economic and social opportunities was played by the trade union women's commissions.

Women were publicly praised and supported for being employed workers and mothers. By 1950 the Protection of Mothers and Children and the Rights of Women Acts had been adopted to guarantee women's advancement. Generous provisions for maternal care (pregnancy/maternity leave of 26 weeks, financial stipends for mothers, and paid leave from employment) and child care (for children from infants to teenagers) were made. Mothers were allowed to count each birth as one year toward their working career in the calculation of their retirement benefits; mothers of three or more children could count each birth as three working years.

While these developments overburdened women, it is important to note that the double day of women and the changes and conflicts it caused were seen as a public issue, not as the personal problem of individual women. Also supportive features, like a monthly day off for women with children and for all women over 40, have helped, although they at times reinforced, rather than changed, traditional gender roles and expectations.

Women now combine traditional knowledge gained in the domestic sphere with new knowledge of the public sphere, developing and utilizing more skills, space, and contacts than in the past or compared to men, because they are now equally at home in the home and in the world. Women's image, self-understanding, goals, and expectations of themselves and of others have changed. Accordingly, their demands on men have changed, and the divorce rate is high. Today, women perceive men as other human beings with shortcomings and vulnerabilities, not as their models or masters. Herein lies the potential to develop a new human model beyond traditional gender stereotypes, but women seem to be ahead in this process of consciousness change, and their growth represents a challenge for men to understand and accept the new female image and female perceptions of masculinity. Women's changing roles and images were frequent topics in the mass media, which represented women essentially as producers, rather than consumers. The new gender dynamics have become a prominent issue in GDR literature. The Special Council of the Academy of Science on Women in Socialist Society (founded 1964) initiated and coordinated research on the position and advancement of women.

The introduction of a market economy and adoption of a less woman-focused gender ideology will create major challenges for East German women. They are expected to suffer from especially high unemployment rates, and less supportive policies on child care will very likely make it more difficult for women to combine their productive and reproductive activities. Concerns have also been expressed over the possible adoption of the more restrictive West German law on abortion.

At the same time, this situation also provides an opportunity for women in the East and West to work freely together, utilizing Western feminist concepts and Eastern experiences and ideas.

References. Birgit Bütow and Heidi Stecker (eds.), *Eigen Artige Ostfrauen Frauenemanzipation in der DDR und den neuen Bundesländern* [Unusual Women from the East. Women's Emancipation in the GDR and the New Federal States] (Bielefeld, 1994); Council of Ministers of the German Democratic Republic (ed.), *Women in the GDR: Notes on the Implementation of the World Plan of Action on the UN Decade of Women, 1976–1985: Equality, Development, Peace* (Berlin, 1985); Dorothy Rosenberg, "On Beyond Superwomen: The Conflict between Work and Family Roles in GDR Literature," in Margy Gerber (ed.), *Studies in GDR Culture and Selected Papers from the Eighth International Symposium Society: 3. On the German Democratic Republic* (New York, 1983).

MARIA-BARBARA WATSON-FRANKE

GERMANY. Postwar and Federal Republic (FRG). The end of World War II found Germany with large numbers of men either dead (4 million) or in prison camps (almost 11 million, the last of whom returned home only in 1955), and millions of women alone faced famine, shortages of housing, disrupted medical and social services, and other problems that came in the aftermath of the military debacle (in 1946 there were 167 women to 100 men aged 20 to 30 in the western zones). During the first postwar years mostly women cleared the rubble (Trümmerfrauen) and worked to reorganize society.

The high percentage of employed women continued for a few years, although for many women survival made it necessary to go foraging for food instead of working at a job. After the majority of prisoners returned home, and huge numbers of German refugees from Eastern Europe streamed into the western zones, the number of employed women fell to 28.2 percent in 1947 (7 percent less than in 1939).

The number of divorces jumped dramatically, either because hastily arranged war marriages failed or because the returning men were not able to cope with a traditional family life or readjust to civilian existence. By 1948 the divorce rate was at 18.8 percent per 10,000, in comparison with 8.9 percent in 1939; but by 1954 the rate was reduced to 9 percent.

When the German economic miracle began in 1952, women's employment rose. In 1950, 27.1 percent of all women between the ages of 16 and 65 were employed; in 1953, 33.1 percent; and by 1980 the figure had climbed to 52.9 percent. Much of the gain was in white-collar work. In 1950 only 21.3 percent of women working in industry had white-collar jobs; in 1980, 55.9 percent did. By 1961, 36.5 percent of married women were working; by 1980, 48.3 percent were working, compared to 26.4 percent in 1950. The increase in married workingwomen triggered many heated discussions in the media about the "devastating" effects of working mothers and "latchkey children."

Actually, family life and gender relationships did not basically change in the Federal Republic until the mid-1960s. In 1960, for example, day care places were available only for one out of every three children between the ages of 3 and 6. By 1981, however, four out of five children found a place in a nursery. However, most women still took only part-time jobs, which normally required fewer qualifications and offered lower wages. Since the 1970s women increasingly continued working after marriage, even when not forced to through economic pressure.

Still, during the 1950s girls acquired, on the average, less education than boys, but this changed radically over the following 30 years. In 1960, 13.4 percent of 17-year-old boys went to advanced grammar schools (*Gymnasium*) compared to 8.7 percent of the girls. In 1979, the figures were almost equal: 20.8 and 20.0 percent, respectively. By the end of the 1980s one out of five women had graduated from the *Gymnasium*. The number of girls entering university has continuously increased. In 1960, 23.9 percent of all university students were female; in 1980, 36.7 percent; in 1986–1987, 37.9 percent. However, gender-specific study areas are still noticeable. Considerably more women than men enter the fields of education, health care, psychology, and liberal arts. In 1974, for instance, 45 percent of pediatricians were women, but only 4.5 percent of surgeons were women.

Similarly, in industry, managerial jobs remain firmly in the hands of men, whereas secretarial and menial jobs are done by women. In 1960, 64 percent of all apprentices were boys; in 1979 they still constituted 62 percent. With the computerization and automation of industry in the 1980s, women quickly experienced a decline of their market desirability. In 1980 the male unemployment rate was 3.0 percent, and the female rate, 5.2 percent; in 1985 the ratio changed to 8.6 percent (men) versus 10.4 percent (women). However, the total number of workingwomen increased from, in 1970, 7.5 million women employed either full-time or part-time, to almost 9 million workingwomen in 1985. The number of workingwomen with a specific training background increased from 38 percent in 1970 to 65 percent in 1985. Salary inequality never disappeared, however, and in the late 1980s it assumed threatening new dimensions. In 1957, industrial full-time women workers earned 45.7 percent less than men. In 1981 the discrepancy fell to 31.2 percent, but in 1988 women laborers earned, on the average, 43.9 percent; industrial employees, 53.2 percent; and white-collar workers, 45 percent less than their male colleagues.

The 1949 Constitution of the Federal Republic of Germany states that men and women are equal. Nonetheless, women's struggle to be accepted as equals continues. In 1953 all legal discriminations against women were officially dismissed from the law books. In 1958, the Equal Rights Law dropped a number of crucial male rights within the family, such as the man's exclusive right to decision making. Joint ownership of property within the family became the norm, and each partner has had, since then, the right to dispose of her or his own individual wealth.

In 1970 the first women's action group to legalize abortion was founded. In 1974 a modernized and relatively liberal abortion law (recognizing granting the first three months as a legal period for abortion) was passed by the *Bundestag* but in 1976 the Federal Constitutional Court modified the law, permitting abortion only when the mother's health is endangered, when the child would be physically handicapped, in cases of rape, or when the mother cannot raise the child for social or economic reasons. Despite protests from the Catholic Church, the medical profession, and other conservative groups, the government, controlled by the Christian Democratic party (CDU) since 1982, did not try to abolish the new abortion law because it feared a massive loss of female votes.

With the unification of East and West Germany in 1990, the Parliament passed a law allowing abortion within the first trimester, following the model of East German law. The Supreme Court struck down this law, however, and on July 14, 1995, a compromise law was passed by the Parliament. Although making most abortions except for special cases (health risk, rape, etc.) illegal, it lifted punishments for women seeking abortions and doctors performing them.

Until the mid-1950s, an increasing contingent of women politicians entered the federal Parliament. By 1957, 9.2 percent of its members were women. Then, however, a sharp decline in women's political participation occurred. By 1969, a majority of West German women saw their role in society as that of mothers and housewives. However, in that same year women voters gave the Social Democratic Party (SPD) the first victory of its postwar history, and the Action Council for the Liberation of Women (*Aktionsrat zur Befreiung der Frau*) was founded, with a radical and independent political platform on which the contemporary women's movement of the Federal Republic could be built. In the early 1970s many women's centers sprang up in most major cities, soon to be followed by women's conferences, organizations, journals and other publications, discussion groups, demonstrations, public protests against the restrictive abortion law, and so forth. In 1976 the first "woman's house" where battered wives could find refuge was built in West Berlin. This example was quickly copied, and soon there were women's houses in more than 120 German cities.

Many of the women's groups, in addition to their own goals, also engendered a vigorous political movement that, in the 1980s, channeled its resources and members into the Green Party (founded in 1979). By 1982, the Greens had won 27 seats in the Parliament, 10 of which were held by women. Since then all major political parties have been forced to adopt a number of issues from the political agendas of women's organizations. In 1985, even the conservative federal government run by the CDU initiated a party's Women Congress, while the Social Democratic Party (SPD) openly emphasized its long-standing tradition of feminist policies. In 1986, a federal ministry for women's issues, family, and health was established, and a number of new laws were put into force improving health care, child support, and job equality.

References. Elizabeth Boa and Janet Wharton (eds.), *Women and the Wende. Social Effects and Cultural Reflections of the German Unification Process* (Amsterdam and Atlanta, 1994); Angela Bogel, "Frauen und Frauenbewegung," in W. Benz (ed.), *Die Geschichte der Bundesrepublik Deutschland: Gesellschaft* (Frankfurt, 1989), 162–206; Anna-Elisabeth Freier and Annette Kuhn (eds.), *Frauen in der Geschichte: V. "Das Schicksal Deutschlands liegt in der Hand seiner Frauen"— Frauen in der deutschen Nachkriegsgeschichte* (Düsseldorf, 1984); Ute Frevert, *Women in German History: From Bourgeois Emancipation to Sexual Liberation* (Oxford, 1989); Wolfgang Glatzer, *Recent Trends in West Germany, 1960–1990* (Toronto, 1992).

ALBRECHT CLASSEN

GESTATION (PREGNANCY) is the development of the fetus* in the uterus. The period of gestation takes about 38 weeks and is divided into trimesters of three months each. The first trimester is most critical for development. The fetus is more subject to spontaneous and anomalous development during this time than it is later.

During the first eight weeks the fertilized ovum is implanted in the lining of the uterus, and through tremendous cell proliferation and diversification, the embryo develops. By the end of the embryonic stage, the rudiments of the basic organ and cardiovascular systems and body structures are established. From about the ninth week, the conceptus, which now has a recognizably human shape, enters the fetal stage. By the end of the trimester, the major organ systems are developed.

During the second and third trimesters the organ systems continue their development and diversification. The fetus, which is usually from three to less than four inches in length and one to one and a half ounces in weight at the beginning of the second trimester, averages around seven and a half pounds and 20–22 inches at birth. During the second trimester, as the fetus grows, the womb begins to swell noticeably. By around the fourth to fifth month the fetus is large enough for the mother to feel its movement ("quickening"). At about the same time, the breasts have become capable of producing milk, although they will not do so until after the birth.

By the third trimester, the uterus is quite large and feels hard to the touch. Late in the seventh month, the fetus begins to add subcutaneous fat, fleshing out the face and filling in the wrinkled skin. Braxton-Hicks contractions (painless) begin pulling and stretching the uterus, preparing it for labor and delivery. As the period of gestation nears its end, the contractions will become more frequent and intense. In the last month, two to four weeks before delivery, the fetus should assume its birth position, which normally means that its head settles into the pelvis so that the crown will be presented to the cervical opening. The action is known as "lightening" or "dropping." The period of gestation ends with parturition,* or birth.

GNOSTICISM. Images of the feminine play an important role in the mythology, theological speculation, and ritual of those religious sects that, emerging in the second century C.E. and continuing into medieval Manichaeism, are generally classified as "gnostic" (from Greek *gnosis,* "knowledge"). Gnostic sects claimed to reveal the true heavenly world (*pleroma,* Greek "fullness") to which the "spirit" or "spark of light" embodied in those who respond to the call belongs. The religious and philosophical systems of humanity may hint at this truth, but they have been perverted by the evil creator of the material world into a means of preventing humans from coming to know the true self that makes them superior to that god and his powers. Awakening from sleep or drunkenness is often used as a metaphor for receiving gnostic enlightenment.

Within the religious symbolism of gnostic groups, images of the feminine appear in three contexts: (1) as "mother" in the triad of the highest god; (2) as "wandering wisdom," a goddess figure who has become trapped with her "light power" in the world of darkness; and (3) as the soul or feminine part of an originally androgynous being who must be reunited with a heavenly male consort.

Divine Triad. Speculation concerning a divine triad of Father/Mother/Son from which all powers of the divine world emanate is often linked with platonic and neoplatonic philosophical speculation (see *Apocryphon of John; Zostrianos* and *Three Steles of Seth*). (The writings referred to in this entry can be found in James M. Robinson, *The Nag Hammadi Library in English* [San Francisco, 1977].) In order for anything to emerge out of the unknowable, transcendent absolute that is God, its radical unity must be complemented by a duality, that of the divine Mother, who is often given the name Barbelo. She is the first aeon of the "invisible spirit." Often, the neoplatonic triad of "existence, mind, and life" is situated below her in the heavenly hierarchy. Thus, Barbelo (or in some versions, which are more clearly linked to wisdom/creation speculation from Judaism, the heavenly Wisdom) is the ultimate source of all that exists.

Wandering Wisdom. Emanation of the heavenly hierarchies often takes the form of groups of androgynous beings. The divine Mother is mirrored at the conclusion of the sequence by a "youngest aeon," another Wisdom figure whose attempt to produce without a consort or whose desire for the Father results in an abortive being that must be cut off from the *pleroma*. This figure, often known as Ialdabaoth, possesses the "light" of his mother in a world that he shapes as a counterimage of the divine aeons. The story of Wisdom's fall also leaves her wandering in the "midst" outside the *pleroma* but above the world fashioned by her son and seeking aid for herself and the "light" now trapped in darkness by Ialdabaoth's fashioning of humanity. The tale of Wisdom's wandering takes on features of the mourning and wandering of such powerful goddesses as Isis as well as elements of Jewish traditions in the figures of Eve and the mysterious Norea, sister of Seth/Noah in various legends. Wisdom must be rescued by the Savior, sometimes the heavenly Human, Seth, or a Christ figure. In some cases (see *On the Origin of the World*) the spiritual Eve is the one who awakens humanity to its true, divine nature.

Soul as Feminine. Images of the soul as feminine play an important part in much ascetic and mystical writing. Stories of the soul's fall into evil hands and her wandering found in the collection of gnostic texts from Nag Hammadi could easily have been the product of orthodox Christian ascetics (see *On the Exegesis of the Soul*). The cosmological myths picture Wisdom wandering in the darkness until she can be reunited with her heavenly consort. Similarly, the destiny of the gnostic soul is reunion with a heavenly counterpart. This reunion expresses the ancient theme of the human as an originally androgynous being for whom the division into male and female and the associated torments of passion are not "natural" but a loss of an original wholeness. The weakness of the soul and its subjection to passions that trap it in the material world lead to a highly negative use of "femaleness" in gnostic asceticism (see *Thomas the Contender*). Identified with the passions she is said to cause in the male, woman, "the works of femaleness," is to be shunned. Asceticism means overcoming all such passions or desires in the soul.

These diverse images of the feminine make it difficult to assess the actual role of women either as authors of gnostic symbolism or as leaders and teachers in gnostic sects. Christian gnostic writings often appeal to the tradition of Jesus' women disciples, especially Mary Magdalene, to show that Jesus taught a gnostic wisdom different from that in the texts and preaching of the developing Christian orthodoxy. But some of the very same writings also defend the place of Mary against hostility on the part of male disciples, notably Peter (see *Gospel of Mary*). Are the opponents orthodox Christians who sought to repress the role of women as teachers and interpreters of Jesus' words? Or does the opposition originate within the gnostic circles themselves?

Opponents of gnosticism sometimes sought to slander gnostic groups by claiming that they permitted women to celebrate sacraments or allowed them as teachers. It is more difficult to assess the actual cultic role of women in gnostic circles, though a mythology that has so much emphasis on the divine feminine would presumably have women in ritual contexts as well. Would a woman have uttered the words of the heavenly Eve, Wisdom, or the divine voice in *Thunder, Perfect Mind*? Did the highest sacrament of the Valentinians, the marriage chamber (see *Gospel of Philip*), involve some form of ritual enactment? Finally, the ascetic hostility to "the feminine" seems to have been understood by some gnostics to imply that women could overcome their "feminine nature" and "become male," as in the famous conclusion to the *Gospel of Thomas* (saying 114). Asceticism in early Christianity was a critical element in freeing women from being defined as persons by their roles of subordination in the patriarchal household.

References. Elaine Pagels, *The Gnostic Gospels* (New York, 1979); Kurt Rudolph, *Gnosis* (San Francisco, 1983).

PHEME PERKINS

GODEY'S LADY'S BOOK AND AMERICAN LADIES MAGAZINE became the premier nineteenth-century women's magazine in the 1840s and 1850s, when its publisher boasted 150,000 subscribers. Although the *Lady's Book* survived well into the gilded age, its reputation was established during the first two decades of the editorship of Sarah Josepha Hale (1788–1879) from 1837 to 1877. Established in Philadelphia by publisher Louis A. Godey (1804–1878) in 1831, *Godey's Lady's Book* offered lavish embellishments (fashion plates, woodcuts, engraved pictures) but reprinted only poetry and prose appropriated without attribution from British women's periodicals. Godey recruited the 47-year-old Sarah Josepha Hale to edit *Godey's* in 1837, by purchasing and merging her *American Ladies' Magazine* (1828–1836) with his publication.

Hale continued her editorial purpose to "improve her sex" through the contents of the monthly issues of the more prosperous and popular *Godey's* by publishing the poetry, prose, and nonfiction of contemporary American authors. Hale and her publisher perfected the standard and enduring content format for the genre of popular women's periodicals: suitably inspirational poetry and unoffending fiction written by the rising class of women writers whose work supported the cult of true womanhood; instructional nonfiction to informally educate women readers in many subjects such as patriotic history and contributions of "women worthies"; and signature fashion plates and other hallmark "embellishments," as well as illustrated instructions in Victorian women's crafts and homemaking arts. Each issue concluded with Hale's monthly editorials on issues of interest to women and literary notices featuring books by and for women, Godey's own monthly notices to his gentle readers, and advertisements for mail order merchandise.

As a medium of both women's and popular culture, *Godey's* influence diminished during and after the Civil War because of rising competition, loss of its southern subscribers, and the aging of its publisher and editor. Hale retired in 1877 at the age of 90, following Godey's retirement and sale of the magazine. As a national institution, *Godey's* survived until the end of the nineteenth century, when its market and its message were supplanted by *The Ladies' Home Journal.* However, Hale's prestige as an expert on the domesticity of woman's sphere lent an uncontestable respectability to advances in women's education and employment as well as to women's involvement in benevolent activities, all of which Hale supported throughout her editorship of *Godey's.*

Although *Godey's* is remembered as a quaint publication that catered to the white, middle-class mainstream Victorian lady of leisure, under Hale's control the magazine contributed to the improvement of women's esteem, education, and employment. Her brand of nineteenth-century domestic feminism fostered general public support of mainstream women's issues, like married women's property reform. Hale's judicious application of woman's influence through a prominent national publication provided a model for successful, if conservative, women's reform that breached the barrier to women's participation in the public sphere by redefining these activities as part of their own proper woman's sphere.

References. Isabelle Webb Entrikin, *Sarah Josepha Hale and Godey's Lady's Book* (Philadelphia, 1946); Frank Luther Mott, *A History of American Women's Magazines*, 3 vols. (New York, 1930); Helen Woodward, *The Lady Persuaders* (New York, 1960); Angela Howard Zophy, " 'For the Improvement of My Sex': Sarah Josepha Hale's Editorship of *Godey's Lady's Book*, 1837–1877," Ph.D diss. Ohio State University, 1978.

ANGELA HOWARD

GONORRHEA, caused by the bacteria *Neisseria gonorrhea*, is a highly contagious, sexually transmitted disease. Women rarely have symptoms because the organism usually affects the cervix initially and is not noticed. Therefore, women are dependent on male sexual partners, who are much more likely to have symptoms (burning urination and purulent discharge from the penis), to inform them that they have been treated for gonorrhea.

If untreated, gonorrhea will spread to the internal organs. This could result in ectopic pregnancy,*pelvic inflammatory disease, and infertility, as well as possibly affecting the heart and joints (arthritis). Gonorrhea is the number one cause of persistent joint pain in persons under 45 years of age. Women are much more likely than men to suffer the complication of joint involvement (arthritis), at least, in part, because men are more likely to seek treatment before complications arise.

Gonorrhea in pregnant women increases the chance of premature labor and stillbirth. Newborns may develop serious eye infections (prevented by routine use of eyedrops), respiratory infections, pneumonia, and rectal infections. It is especially important during pregnancy that women ensure condom use by male sexual partners.

Gonorrhea is a disease of the mucous membranes; that is, it thrives in the cervix, urethra, and rectum and even in the throat. Women who have unprotected oral or receptive anal sex with a partner whom they suspect of having gonorrhea should tell their examiner to test the throat and/or anal area for the presence of gonorrhea.

Young girls may develop inflammation of the genitals (vulvovaginitis) due to direct contact with the mucous discharge from infected persons in sexual abuse.

It is estimated that a woman who has had one exposure to an infected man has a 30–50 percent chance of developing gonorrhea. After two or three sexual contacts, the risk increases to 95 percent. The high risk illustrates the importance of using condoms (male or female) as barriers.

Antibiotics by injection are used to treat gonorrhea. A concurrent infection with chlamydia occurs so frequently that oral antibiotics for treating chlamydia should be a part of the treatment regimen for gonorrhea. Sexual partners should be treated simultaneously.

Attempts to use alternative treatments or to self-treat with leftover antibiotics can be ineffective and can result in the organism's becoming resistant to usual antibiotics. It is important to get proper treatment and to complete any oral regimens prescribed (as for chlamydia). People who test positive for gonorrhea should also be tested for syphilis and should be offered HIV testing.

Even though gonorrhea is a disease of the mucous membranes, it does not appear to spread easily between women. However, in woman-to-woman sex, care should be taken to avoid oral/genital contact if gonorrhea (or chlamydia) is suspected.

Reference. Abram S. Benenson (ed.), *Control of Communicable Diseases Manual* (New York, 1995), 204–208.

ELAINE WHEELER

GOSSIP is generally a derogatory term today applied both to "idle," moralistic, and speculative talk about persons not present and to people, usually women, who engage in such talk. Its Old English form was *godsibb*, meaning akin or related, and its now archaic definitions refer to important, ritually established relations between godparents themselves or between them and the parents of the baptized person. Middle English usage designated familiar acquaintance or friends and applied to either sex, but especially to a woman's female friends invited to be present at a birth. Chaucer's Wife of Bath refers to such an intense, satisfying relationship with her female gossip. The importance of this nurturing and bonding is also implied, at least in relation to women, by Ralph Waldo Emerson in *Representative Men* (1860): "Our globe discovers its hidden virtues not only in heroes, and archangels, but in gossips and nurses."

The degradation of the term is found in the third *Oxford English Dictionary* definition, first noted in 1566: "A person, mostly a woman, of light and trifling character, esp. one who delights in idle talk; a newsmonger, a tattler." In the eighteenth century, Dr. Samuel Johnson unambiguously linked gender and a gossip in his third dictionary definition: "One who runs about tattling like women at a lying-in."

Anthropologists and sociologists have remarked on the prevalence and importance of adult women's and men's gossip in social life. It has been viewed as an informal means of teaching morality, of indirectly controlling aggression, of maintaining social control and solidarity, of covertly negotiating, of building and destroying reputations, of exchanging valuable information, of expressing sociability itself, and of offering entertainment. The powerful positive and negative potential in gossip is seen, for example, in its use by healers diagnosing and treating the social component of illness and by practitioners of malevolent witchcraft or those making accusations of witchcraft. Because gossip deals privately in particulars, personalities, and personal relationships, it is often seen as the province of those too weak or disfranchised to deal publicly with social problems and as dangerous to the official group culture.

By 1811, according to the *Oxford English Dictionary*, "gossip" was used to refer to a kind of conversation, "idle talk; trifling or groundless rumour; tittle-tattle. Also, in a more favourable sense: Easy, unrestrained talk or writing, esp. about persons or social incidents." The "less favourable" sense is influenced by deprecation of interpersonal life as frivolous, irrational, and antithetical to serious spiritual, philosophical, political, and economic pursuits. It is encapsulated in official sanctions like the biblical injunction "Thou shalt not go up and down as talebearer [later: slanderer] among thy people" (Lev. 19:16, King James 1611).

The art of gossip, which in any group requires various performance and narrative skills and involves a creative, ludic interaction, is rarely studied (except, e.g., Yerkovich). Although men certainly gossip—by any definition of the term—women's talk in Western society has become virtually synonymous with gossip and with other derogatory sociolinguistic terms also associated with women like "chatter," "prattle," "natter," "nag," and "whine." (See OLD WIVES' TALES.) Myths in oral tradition and novels, biographies, and social commentary in literary tradition have served as the measure of narration and social criticism, and much reevaluation must be done if gossip is to be viewed as equally significant storytelling. (See MYTHOLOGY.)

References. Jörg R. Bergman, *Discreet Indiscretions: The Social Organization of Gossip* (New York, 1993); John Beard Haviland, *Gossip, Reputation, and Knowledge in Zinacantan* (Chicago, 1977); Jack Levin and Arnold Arluck, *Gossip: The Inside Scoop* (New York and London, 1987); Patricia Meyer Spacks, *Gossip* (New York, 1985); Sally Yerkovich, "Gossiping; or, The Creation of Fictional Lives," diss., University of Pennsylvania, 1976.

MARTA WEIGLE

GOTHIC FICTION (1780–1830) was dominated by women writers and readers. Novels of domestic virtue, also extremely popular during this time, reinforced the roles assigned to women in late eighteenth-century English society. (See DOMESTIC NOVEL.) The gothic, however, became the expression of repressed fears and anxieties resulting from women's actual oppression in a male-dominated environment. The literary conventions these writers established reflected the ambiguity of their lives. Unwilling to jeopardize social reputation and respectability, they wrote conservative gothic novels that overtly accepted women's idealized moral virtues and social positions of legal and economic inferiority, yet within this framework they dramatized their sense of exploitation and persecution.

Horace Walpole changed the course of English fiction for 50 years when he wrote *The Castle of Otranto* in 1764 with the express intention of restoring imaginative, unreal elements to novels, which he thought had become tedious in their depiction of ordinary experience. His inclusion of the supernatural, the remote, medieval castles and ruins with subterranean vaults and secret passages, and the prolonged pursuit of an innocent heroine by a male villain became standard fare for creating a sustained mood of terror. While male writers like Matthew Lewis and Charles Maturin developed an erotic, sensational kind of gothicism, in which the reader identified with a villain-hero who eventually paid the price for his satanic indulgences and abuses of human decency, the women writers established the dominant tradition of a genteel, sublime gothic fiction where the reader identified with the female protagonist threatened and imprisoned by a male villain. In novels by Clara Reeve, "the great enchantress" Ann Radcliffe, Sophia Lee, Charlotte Smith, Regina Maria Roche, Eliza Parsons, and many others, the female protagonist was the key factor in the reader's overwhelming response to this fictional experience.

Over and over again, the central pattern of the action, often narrated in the first person, was imprisonment and escape. Emily St. Aubert in Ann Radcliffe's *The Mysteries of Udolpho* (1794) represented the typical heroine, who, left without family protection and guidance, fell victim to the greedy and tyrannical Montoni. Confined in a castle, she could rely only on her virtue to protect her against threats to her person and fortune. During all of her trials, she remained steadfast, proper, and passive; she never acted aggressively by attacking her male pursuer to free herself. Usually, the heroine's escape was provided by a miraculous turn of events, such as the discovery of true identity through a will, or by the villain's self-destruction. Her sufferings were thus rewarded by a restoration of property and a good marriage. The lengthy and emotional descriptions of settings intensified the fear of imprisonment, a feeling shared by women readers coping, in fact, with their restrictive environments. The escape was seen as a triumph of good over evil, defined in the gothic as female over male, a liberation achieved without violating the attributes that made women appealing to men, especially their naïveté, their uncomplaining passivity, and their propriety. For women writers, who might have led uneventful lives tending the hearth, with virtually no participation in worldly affairs, the lofty language of the gothic, with its focus upon natural landscapes and interior descriptions, was suitable for their talents. For their readers, the fictional experience provided a vital outlet for their own sensibilities.

Although recent recoveries of female gothics have challenged gender distinctions, this pattern has been repeated with few exceptions for over 200 years. Rare are the writers who have taken liberties with the genre: Jane Austen in *Northanger Abbey* (1818), a satire of the gothic advocating common sense in women; Charlotte Brontë's *Jane Eyre* (1847), a victory over oppression won by a deeply passionate and realistic protagonist, Emily Brontë's *Wuthering Heights* (1847), an archetypal psychological conflict conveyed in poetic gothic elements; Mary Shelley's *Frankenstein* (1818), a brilliant abandonment of the innocent heroine in favor of the villain-hero. Today, as evidenced by the thousands of "supermarket romances"* written and read by women, the formulas established between 1780 and 1830 persist in endless variation. Most recently, however, Anne Rice has earned both a popular and academic audience with innovative adaptations of vampiric fiction in her six novels thus far in *The Vampire Chronicles* (1976–1998).

References. Eugenia C. DeLamotte, *Perils of the Night: A Feminist Study of Nineteenth-Century Gothic* (New York, 1990); Kate Ferguson Ellis, *The Contested Castle: Gothic Novels and the Subversion of Domestic Ideology* (Urbana and Chicago, 1989); Coral Ann Howells, *Love, Mystery, and Misery: Feeling in Gothic Fiction* (London, 1978); David Punter, *The Literature of Terror: The History of Gothic Fiction from 1765 to the Present Day* (London, 1980); Bette B. Roberts, *The Gothic Romance: Its Appeal to Women Writers and Readers in Late Eighteenth-Century England* (New York, 1980); Ann B. Tracey, *The Gothic Novel: 1790–1830: Plot Summaries and Index to Motifs* (Lexington, Ky., 1981).

BETTE B. ROBERTS

GRASSROOTS ORGANIZING involves an organization that mobilizes individuals in a community to become the leadership cadre in formulating corrective programs. One of the noted grassroots organizations of the late nineteenth and early twentieth centuries was the Atlanta Neighborhood Union (1908), established by Lugenia Burns Hope, the wife of the president of Atlanta University. Lugenia Hope worked unremittingly to remove the blight and unhealthy living conditions in the black community that surrounded the college. She organized African American women within the community, including the wives of faculty members at Spelman and Morehouse Colleges, into a reform campaign that raised funds for a playground, kindergarten, and day nurseries. (See AFRICAN AMERICAN WOMEN [SINCE 1865].) Hope's organization divided the city into neighborhoods and then into districts. The district directors formed a neighborhood board of directors headed by an elected president, and the presidents of the neighborhoods, as members of the board of managers, governed citywide activity.

With its strength firmly grounded at the district and neighborhood level, the Neighborhood Union launched a fact-finding investigation of Negro public schools that politicized the African American community. It successfully lobbied for a new school building and higher salaries for teachers. Through the unified efforts of the Neighborhood Union, streets were paved, lights and sewers were installed, and 40 houses were replaced. Its most significant achievement was the establishment of a Health Center, which offered a clinic to treat tuberculosis and other illnesses, some nursing services, and advice on sanitation.

Between 1931 and 1932, the Health Center was enlarged to include dental and mothers' clinics for the sick. A registered nurse, a doctor, and a dentist staffed the facility, and the center examined over 4,000 persons a year.

In subsequent years communities, following the lead of Hope and the Atlanta Neighborhood Union, utilized a similar structure to improve their communities. One such community was Montgomery, Alabama. In 1949, Mary Fair Burks, head of the Alabama State College English Department in Montgomery, organized the Women's Political Council (WPC) after a personal encounter with racist treatment by the police. The membership was middle-class, consisting mostly of teachers at the college or local public schools; many were members of the Dexter Avenue Baptist Church, pastored by Martin Luther King, Jr. The group's goals in its infancy were to promote women's involvement in civic affairs by fostering voter registration education and to assist women who were victims of rape and assault. In 1949, its goals shifted to focus on challenging the bus seating policy. This transition was the result of the 1950 election of JoAnn Robinson as president. Robinson had firsthand experiences with segregated seating on buses. Under her leadership, the membership increased to 200, with three chapters in different areas of the city. From 1950 through the 1960s, the WPC became one of the most effective community-organized activist groups in

Alabama. After Rosa Parks was arrested in 1955, Robinson and WPC members organized the bus boycott. Unfortunately, the WPC began to decline after the Montgomery Improvement Association (MIA) took over the boycott, and Robinson and other professors were fired for their activist participation.

References. Mary Fair Burks, "Trailblazers in the Montgomery Bus Boycott," in Vicki L. Crawford, Jacqueline A. Rouse, and Barbara Woods (eds.), *Women in the Civil Rights Movement: Trailblazers. 1941–1965* (New York, 1990); David Garrow, "The Origins of the Montgomery Bus Boycott," *Southern Changes* (October–December 1985); Steven M. Millner, "The Montgomery Bus Boycott: A Case Study in the Emergence and Career of Social Movement," in David J. Garrow (ed.), *The Walking City: The Montgomery Bus Boycott—1955–1956* (New York, 1989); Jacqueline A. Rouse, *Lugenia Burns Hope: Black Southern Reformer* (New York, 1989).

BEVERLY W. JONES

GREECE (ANCIENT). Attitudes Toward Women are difficult to uncover in all periods of Greek antiquity since the evidence is limited and open to quite different interpretations. The wooing of Odysseus' presumed widow, Penelope, for example, is seen by some as a vestige of matriarchal institutions, while others view Penelope's position as a foreshadowing of the haremlike seclusion of women that they see in conditions of the Classical period. One can find straightforward statements, to be sure, like that of Aristotle, who maintained "the male is by nature superior, and the female inferior; and the one rules, and the other is ruled; this principle, of necessity, extends to all mankind." (See ARISTOTLE ON WOMEN.) However, even if this view prevailed throughout Greece in the time of Aristotle, a fourth-century stance does not necessarily reflect attitudes of earlier centuries.

It is not altogether artificial to examine basic attitudes during the four major chronological periods of Greek antiquity: the Bronze Age, corresponding to the third and second millennia B.C.E.; the Dark Age, extending from ca. 1150 to 750 B.C.E.; the Classical Age of the seventh, sixth, and fifth centuries; and the Postclassical period beginning in the fourth century.

Archaeological evidence has demonstrated that women enjoyed a high social status in the daily life of the Bronze Age civilization of Crete. This prominence may have stemmed from the importance of female deity and from the major role women played in religious practice. The rights of Minoan women may have included the exercise of property rights. Since Minoan culture influenced other Bronze Age civilizations, it is not surprising that artifacts from mainland Greece reflect a social status for women similar to that enjoyed by their Minoan counterparts. However, the civilization of the mainland was more than an imitation of non-Greek Crete, and the differences affected the role of women as well as other aspects of life. The religion of the first Hellenes blended male with female deity to a greater degree than did Minoan religion, thereby diminishing the role of both fe-male deity and human celebrants. Additionally, the Linear B tablets of the mainland imply exclusively male ownership of land.

There is less ambiguity about the attitude toward women in Homeric society, a reflection of Greek life in the period when the poems assumed their final form. By the late eighth century, society was founded on a patriarchal family structure in which authority resided with the male head of family. Since communal matters were decided by heads of families, women played no direct role in affairs of the early state. Yet women enjoyed high esteem: they were ennobled by their own lineage apart from that of a husband's ancestry; their cleverness and wisdom were often celebrated; and their virtues might win renown extending far beyond the walls of home and boundaries of community. In fact, women won praise for traits complementary to, but not identical with, those possessed by men. Such traits were equally necessary to the proper functioning of society but less exposed to public view.

This attitude persisted through the Classical period, when women were protected by a system of rights and duties incumbent on men, particularly fathers, husbands, and sons. Though protected and more confined to the household than males, women were not without personal rights. They were worthy of esteem, as the characters of tragedy and comedy show. Mortals like Antigone, Jocasta, Lysistrata are not weak, manipulated figures. Nor are female deities subordinate to male gods. In the Oresteia trilogy of Aeschylus, Athena completes and concludes the justice of the case against Orestes, while Apollo, Orestes' advocate, exercises a lesser power. Socrates, named by the Delphic oracle as the wisest of men, is instructed by the woman Diotima, whose name means "honored of Zeus." Diotima may have been a creation of Socrates or Plato, but the creation need not have been female. A society in which women were held of no regard would surely not create such goddesses, heroines, and instructors.

The classical Greek state was an ordered community of families and not an amorphous collection of individuals. Thus, the patriarchal structure of the individual family was transferred to the collective whole where adult males performed most of the services required for the well-being of all. Men, not women, held public office and fought to defend the state. Only in the fanciful world of comedy were women members of the assembly. Nonetheless, even among the especially patriarchal Athenians, citizenship in the fifth century required Athenian birthright from both parents, not simply the father. Ownership of property rested with the heads of families, and, thus, while an heiress might be sole inheritor to an estate, the law of many states ensured that the property would be protected by means of marriage of the heiress to a kinsman. In a few Greek states, on the other hand, women seem to have held property in their own names. Women regularly offered dedications and gifts to the gods from their own personal possessions, which, as a rule, must have been minimal. Generally, as well as being patriarchal, the Greek attitude of the Classical period was also paternalistic.

Spheres were delimited with some exactitude by the fifth century, and it was as wrong for a woman to step into the domain of men as it was for a slave to pretend to the status of a free person or for a mortal to venture into the sphere of the immortals. The sphere of most freewomen was defined by family and religion. Sepulchral inscriptions of women usually give the woman's name, that of her father, and, if married, that of her husband. Occasionally, other family members are named. Aside from family, women are often remembered as priestesses: Some 40 cults in Attica alone were served by priestesses. However, apart from service to the gods, most women did not follow occupations, and those who did were frequently associated with a family: there are many grave stele of nurses and some of washerwomen, weavers, and midwives. There were exceptions, of course, such as dancers, musicians, grocers, and vendors, but the attitude of the Classical period did not encourage many exceptions. "Your great glory," Pericles told the Athenian women in 430 B.C., "is not to be inferior to what god has made you; the greatest glory of a woman is to be least talked about by men, whether they are praising you or criticizing you" (Thucydides 2: 46).

It is interesting to remember that this same Pericles, on divorcing his Athenian wife, lived for the rest of his life with the non-Athenian Aspasia, who was much talked about and talked to for her wit and beauty. Only by an extraordinary decree was their son eventually granted citizenship. The case of Pericles and Aspasia reflects more than the force of exceptional personality. By the late fifth century, traditional values and institutions were giving way, and one result was relaxation of patriarchal paternalism. Although never enfranchised even in the Hellenistic period, women of the stamp of Olympias, mother of Alexander, wielded great power. They ruled in their own right and even led armies. However, such women were still the exceptions; neither the condition nor perception of the majority of women changed radically. Their world continued to be defined by parents, husband, and children, not armies, wealth, and intrigue. "Farewell, dearest husband. Love my children," reads the sepulchral request of one Athenian woman (*Inscriptions Graecae* II.iii: 3931). It could well be the final words of most women through the remainder of antiquity.

References. Aristotle, *Politics*, trans. B. Jowett, 520 (Oxford, 1905); Elaine Fantham, Helene Peet Foley, Natalie Boymel Kampen, Sarah B. Pomeroy, and H. Alan Shapiro, *Women in the Classical World* (New York, 1994); John Gould, "Law, Custom and Myth: Aspects of the Social Position of Women in Classical Athens," *Journal of Hellenic Studies* 10 (1980): 38–59; *Inscriptions Graecae* II.iii, J. Kirchner (ed.) (1913–1940); Raphael Sealey, *Women and Law in Classical Greece* (Chapel

Hill, N.C., 1990); *Women in Antiquity, Arethusa* 6, 1 (Spring 1973); Thucydides, *The Peloponnesian War*, trans. R. Warner (1954).

CAROL G. THOMAS

GREECE (ANCIENT). Private Lives of Women showed some change over time but greater variation according to political and socioeconomic status, urban versus rural residence, and geographical location. For the great majority of married, respectable women—regardless of status, time, or place—the home was the center of private life and the focus of daily activity.

For women of the Bronze (Mycenaean) Age, the evidence for private life is virtually nonexistent, but for the later Dark Ages and Archaic Period, Homer (eighth century B.C.) and the lyric poets (seventh–sixth centuries B.C.) provide dim outlines. Homer's upper-class women—Andromache and Penelope—spend their days weaving, tending to children, and supervising their households; they also enjoy an affectionate, mutually respectful relationship with their husbands. With Hesiod (seventh century B.C.) and Semonides of Amorgos (sixth century B.C.), the misogynic attitudes so prevalent in ancient Greece appear. While their "good wives" parallel Homer's portraits of Andromache and Penelope, their "bad" women neglect household and children in favor of attending to their appearance, eating, having affairs, and talking with other women. The assertion of independence exhibited by these "bad" women seems corroborated by the poems of Sappho of Lesbos (sixth century B.C.), which reveal a female world of intense, often erotic relationships in which women valued one another according to standards that they set for themselves. How many women devoted themselves to the male model of a good wife and what proportion exercised greater autonomy in choosing how to spend their time cannot be determined.

In the Classical Age (fifth and fourth centuries B.C.), distinctions among status, urban/rural residence, and city-state culture become more discernible. In those city-states that had developed a thriving urban center, the nuclear family replaced the larger clan as the primary social and economic unit, and the size of the group within which women could move relatively freely shrank considerably. Moreover, given the importance of citizenship and its descent through the father, the male-controlled polity often deliberately sought to strictly regulate more female sexual behavior. For free women who lived on farms, life probably continued much as Hesiod had described it in an earlier era, except for the frequent wars of the Classical Age, which called their husbands away during the growing season and often devastated their property. Warfare probably made the lives of farm women more precarious and grueling.

In Classical Athens, upper-class citizens' wives lived in near seclusion in the women's quarters of their husbands' homes and had little contact with the outside world. Always escorted by a slave or older female relative, such women ventured out only to visit the sick, attend funerals and festivals, or possibly fetch water and shop. For them, private life *was* life—motherhood, production of the family's clothing, and supervision of the household. Intimacy—both sexual and emotional—between husband and wife seems to have been minimal. Commonly regarded as legally, politically, and intellectually inferior, these women were forced to rely on their children, female slaves, and female relatives for support and companionship. In their leisure time, upper-class women probably bathed, attended to their appearance (depilation, coiffure, makeup, and jewelry), and amused themselves with pets and music; some may have read or been read to.

Middle- and lower-class Athenian citizen women led a less confined existence. Unable to afford any idleness, their husbands had considerably higher expectations for female productivity. Women were still responsible for children, clothing, cleaning, and cooking but lacked the help of more than one household slave. Lower-class women often worked outside the home, had a wider circle of friends and acquaintances, and enjoyed a greater opportunity to observe the life of the male community. However, this comparatively greater freedom may well be illusory; these women surely knew the demands of the "double day" and probably had little time for their husbands, friends, or themselves.

For the noncitizen, whether free or slave, life was hard. Most free noncitizen women were poor and had to work for wages outside the home. Some may have found a sense of solidarity and worth in trade associations to which both men and women could belong. Female slaves worked mainly as domestic drudges, and their bodies were, of course, available to their masters or to whomever their masters chose.

Spartan women appear to have enjoyed far less restricted lives than their Athenian sisters. Because the Spartan women's chief contribution to the state was seen by men as the production of sons to become Spartan warriors, Spartan women were better fed, married later (at 18 to 20 rather than 14 to 16), encouraged to exercise to stay physically fit, not confined to the house, and generally respected for their contributions to the Spartan way of life. Nor were their sexual lives so strictly regulated; Spartan women probably engaged in (and perhaps even initiated) extramarital liaisons with other Spartan men. Because their husbands were occupied year-round in military and political affairs, Spartan wives had greater responsibility and freedom in running the family's household and estate. Moreover, Spartan women could regularly count on females of inferior status to carry out the mundane jobs of housecleaning, cooking, and the production of clothing. By the fourth century, after two generations of protracted and terrible warfare, Spartan women controlled in their own right approximately two-fifths of all Spartan land and property; the old standards of self-discipline waned, and these wealthy Spartan women often invested in racehorses and lived lives of comparative luxury. Male attempts to return to the traditional ways failed; though still locked out of the military and political life of Sparta, these women had created their own society and values and maintained them in the face of strong male opposition. Spartan citizen women's relative freedom and autonomy depended, however, on the labors of thousands of nonfree men and women of servile status.

The Hellenistic Age (third through first centuries B.C.) saw a considerable easing of the male-imposed controls that had existed in city-states like Athens. After the death of Alexander the Great in 323, the eastern end of the Mediterranean was divided into three major kingdoms ruled by Macedonian-Greek dynasties, and royal women played a significant role in political and cultural life. Probably in response to these new models of female competence and power, freewomen generally began to exercise more authority and independence than had the women of Classical Athens. Moreover, frequent migration of families meant that women needed a greater measure of legal and economic competence to manage the family's affairs in a new setting or in the prolonged absences of the husband. The seclusion of women became far less common; women were relatively free to move about an urban center, to socialize with other women and their husbands, to seek divorce in an unsatisfactory marriage, and to gain an education. Finally, Hellenistic women appear to have been less restricted sexually; while adultery for women was still a potentially serious offense, extramarital liaisons and premarital sex seem more acceptable than in the Classical era, and romantic love regained a place in male–female relationships.

References. Sarah B. Pomeroy, *Goddesses, Whores, Wives, and Slaves: Women in Classical Antiquity* (New York, 1975); Sarah B. Pomeroy, *Women in Hellenistic Egypt* (New York, 1984).

VALERIE FRENCH

GREECE. Modern Greece is a Mediterranean country with Mediterranean views of honor and women's place. In this country of 10.35 million (1993 est.) population, public life is dominated by men, and the care of the home and family is still borne overwhelmingly by women. However, since the 1980s changes in gender relations have affected even remote areas of the country. In the 1990s old and new ways exist side by side. When the family walks to the taverna together or promenades, the husband walks slightly ahead, never glancing back to make sure his wife and children follow, but his wife retains her own surname and his children may carry the surname of either parent or of both. The vast majority consider a church marriage the only binding form of marriage contract, but arranged marriages are becoming rare, and rarer still is the practice of sending the bride home after the wedding night if she hasn't proved her virginity.

Article 4 of the Constitution of 1975, drawn up after the overthrow of the monarchy in 1974, promises equality of all citizens regardless of sex and equal opportunity in social, political, and economic life. When the socialist government took over in 1981, after a period of military dictatorship, it began trying to implement Article 4. High priority was given to reform of the family code and to issues such as women's social security in rural areas, motherhood and health, participation in decision making, equal employment opportunities, and international cooperation on women's issues. In 1985 the General Secretariat of Equality of the Prime Minister's Office was established.

The Family Code was reformed in the early and mid-1980s. The patriarchal family was abolished in law. Legally, partners to a marriage must decide jointly on all matters concerning their conjugal life, and each must contribute to family needs according to her or his capabilities. The age of majority was reduced to 18 for both sexes, civil marriage was allowed, and married women were given the right to acquire their own legal residence for cause.

Both partners to a marriage are legally required to retain their own surnames. Before or during the marriage ceremony they must decide, irrevocably, whether their children will bear the surname of the husband, the wife, or both. In social relations one partner may use the surname of the other as long as that spouse has no objection.

The dowry was abolished in law. However, the gift tax on property up to 5 million drachmas transferred from parents to children, male or female, was reduced by 50 percent, making it the same as the old dowry tax.

In 1982 adultery ceased to be a penal offense, and in 1984 prosecution became mandatory in cases of criminal rape. In 1986 abortion within the first 12 weeks was legalized. In 1991 legal abortions were 10.8 percent of the live birthrate.

Divorce was liberalized. Instead of the former very restricted grounds, divorce is possible by mutual consent or for serious impairment of the matrimonial bond. When there are children of the marriage, a custody agreement must be lodged with the court before the divorce is granted. Despite the more liberal conditions, divorce remains exceptional. The gross divorce rate reached a peak of 0.9 percent in 1988; in 1992 it was 0.6 percent.

Parental authority has been replaced by parental care, exercised jointly by the parents. The distinction between legitimate and illegitimate children has been abolished, and unmarried mothers are given full protection. A child born out of wedlock but recognized freely or by judicial decision has the same rights and obligations in relation to parents, inheritance, and so on as children born within a marriage.

Political Participation by women is still low, with the percentage of women in Parliament closer to that in the U.S. Congress than to Parliaments in other socialist countries in Europe. In 1987 women were 4 percent of the members of the Greek Parliament; in 1994 the percentage rose to 6 percent. (In the U.S. House of Representatives, women made up 5 percent of the members in 1987 and 7 percent in 1994.) There are also, for the first time, a few women with decision-making positions. At the ministerial level, the percentage of women in 1987 was 4.2 percent, but it declined in 1994 to 4 percent (25 women). Women are also found serving as prefects and presidents of public organizations.

Education has improved for the entire country since 1974, and illiteracy has been cut drastically. Although, in 1991, 73.5 percent of those who could not read or write were women, the illiteracy rate for women between the ages of 15 and 24 had fallen to 0.7 percent, as opposed to 8.2 percent for those over 25. For men the rates were 0.4 percent and 2.6 percent, respectively.

Education is encouraged nearly as much for daughters as for sons. In 1990 the gross enrollment rate of first- and second-level education was 99 percent for girls and 100 percent for boys. For middle-class girls, attending the university is now considered the mainstream aspiration, whereas two generations ago dowry was more important.

In the country as a whole, more men than women over age 10 have completed primary and secondary education, but in the Greater Athens area, more women have completed both primary and secondary education than have men. In both Greater Athens and Greece as a whole women make up 42 percent of those holding higher education diplomas and 28 percent of those with postgraduate diplomas.

Economic Life. From 1975 to 1983 the number of workingwomen increased by about three-quarters. In 1994 women made up about 27 percent of the adult (age 15 and over) workforce and had an economic activity rate of around 25 percent. In rural areas the rate is higher than in urban areas. According to the 1981 census, for all of Greece the women's rate was 24.7 percent; in the countryside it was 39.4 percent.

Women are concentrated in clerical, agricultural, and service occupations and earn less than men in every category of employment. There has been some improvement, with women's average wage rising from 68 percent of men's in 1970 and 1980 to 76 percent in 1990. However, many women workers in agriculture and family businesses receive no pay. Of all unpaid workers in 1990, 76 percent were women.

Women predominate in farm labor: there were 80 women for every 100 men in agriculture in 1990. In some villages women still do virtually all the farm labor: plant and harvest, tend sheep, and carry heavy loads. The government has attempted to improve conditions of women agricultural workers. Women farmworkers are granted separate pensions, independent of their husbands. Also there is free medical care for the entire farm family.

The career woman is a recent phenomenon in Greece. The separation of professions by gender has been legally abolished, and women are entering many professional fields. The more traditional career is that of educator, but the most prized jobs for women are in the civil service or government enterprises—they are overstaffed, the workload is light, and the workday ends at 2:30, so the women can come home to cook and clean. Also, it is constitutionally impossible to be fired from a civil service job. A government position has replaced the dowry as the most valuable asset a single girl can bring to marriage.

Greece has ratified the UN Convention on the Elimination of All Forms of Discrimination against Women and International Labor Convention 103 "for the protection of motherhood." (In Greece women are entitled to 15 weeks' maternity leave at full pay and cannot be dismissed while on leave.) In 1994 it joined the European Union (EU). As a member it is subject to EU laws and regulations on employment.

Changes in law and economic conditions have affected, and will continue to affect, women of all classes, but in the 1990s, as the women's low economic activity rate indicates, women's lives continued to be centered around the home and homemaking, much as they were earlier in the century. That women will plan and embark on careers is not yet a common assumption. If parents can afford it, they prefer to support their daughters until they marry, and even if the daughters get jobs, they are expected to remain at home until they marry.

Family and community pressures remain strong. Almost everyone marries, and few divorce. The number of unmarried couples is so small it is not yet measurable. For a woman the role of wife and mother is the preferred role; she bears the responsibility of caring for the home and family even if she works full-time outside the home. Her role is incomplete without a son. "May you have male children and female sheep" is a standard Greek blessing.

The strong ties that bind the family extend beyond the nuclear family to the extended family and even to nonrelatives from the native village—*patrida*. While the mother shows preference for sons over daughters, sons have strong obligations to mothers and are expected to care for them when they become old. Few old people live alone—it is the children's duty to share their home with their parents.

GREECE AND ROME (ANCIENT). Views of Female Physiology can be divided into those in which woman was seen as a radically different animal from man (represented by the Hippocratics, Greek doctors practicing in the fourth and fifth centuries B.C.) and those in which it was thought that the difference lay solely in her reproductive organs (represented by Aristotle [384–322 B.C.] and Soranus, a Roman doctor of the early second century A.D.). The former views tended to be earlier, reflecting the myth that woman had been created separately as a punishment on the "human" race, which until that time had renewed itself without her. The later assimilation of female to male physiology was influenced by dissection, first of animals and later of humans; but, as with earlier theories, the model of a woman's internal space was still predicated on the external data of breasts and menstruation and the conviction of her inherent inferiority.

The Hippocratics believed that at puberty a woman's flesh became spongier than a man's and soaked up more nourishment (in the form of blood) from her stomach than she could make use of in her small frame and "indolent" lifestyle. Her breasts became prominent because the flesh on her chest was especially spongy. The excess blood collected in her flesh until the waning moon caused temperatures to drop. The womb then drew the blood into itself from all over the body, causing heaviness in the head, pains in the legs, and so forth, until it was full, when it opened and discharged the menses. The majority of female illnesses were caused by a malfunction in this process. If the womb closed over, or its mouth turned away from the vagina, the menses either stayed and festered in the womb, ate their way out through the groin, or moved somewhere else in the body (e.g., to the lungs, where they caused consumption, or the feet, where they caused gout). They moved through the body by a passage connecting the mouth and nose with the vagina, so whenever a woman vomited or had a nosebleed, her menses were depleted by a corresponding amount. If the womb itself became too dry and empty, it could be attracted to the moister organs of the brain, heart, and liver, where it caused "suffocation" and had to be enticed back by sitting the woman on sweet-smelling herbs while administering a foul-smelling repellent to the nostrils. The same diseases that had a variety of causes in a man originated predominantly for women in the reproductive system.

Aristotle, on the other hand, stated specifically that man and woman belonged to the same species and differed only in that the man was hotter. While they were growing, children of both sexes used all their nourishment in building their own bodies. When this became less necessary at puberty, the male was able to "concoct" the residue of his nourishment into semen on account of his greater heat, whereas the female could concoct it only into menstrual blood. Women did not use up as much nourishment as men because they were not as large, strong, or active, so they produced a greater volume of residue. Accordingly, when this moved away from the chest area at puberty, it left a larger empty space to be inflated into breasts in women. The residue flowed naturally into the womb (which was held in place by tendons), where it was stored for use in reproduction or voided once a month—again with the waning of the moon. Woman was afflicted with diseases of the womb more often than any other female animal because of the amount of her menses, but they did not account for all the illnesses in her body, which in other respects was exactly like that of a man.

According to both theories, the most efficient way of keeping a woman healthy was to ensure she had regular intercourse, which moistened the womb and kept it open. Ideally, this resulted in pregnancy, which anchored the womb in place and used up the menstrual fluid, through its being either digested by the fetus or coagulating around its body. The baby was born when the nourishment ceased to be sufficient, and it fought its way out looking for food. When it began suckling from its mother, it drew the menses into the breasts, where they were converted into milk. As long as menstrual blood was being used for this purpose, a woman could not conceive. The abundant afterbirth broke down the narrow veins all over a woman's body, thereby making the drawing of blood toward the womb more comfortable when menstruation recommenced.

In the Hippocratic theory, conception took place from a mixture of "seed" emitted by both the man and woman when aroused in intercourse. The most favorable time for conception was just after menstruation, when the womb was otherwise empty. Postulating that a woman contributed seed had the advantage of explaining why a child had an equal chance of resembling either parent, but it raised the question of why a woman could not reproduce parthenogenetically. Because a father was always necessary to generate a child, Aristotle argued that he had some unique contribution to make; since the mother obviously provided the space and the material, this contribution had to be the seed of the child. Conception took place most readily when there was a minimal amount of menses present (just after menstruation) so the seed was not swamped.

Dissection and vivisection of condemned criminals in the third century B.C. showed that apart from the reproductive organs, men and women were physiologically similar, so the Hippocratic theories were rejected in favor of a more Aristotelian approach. The correspondence between male and female bodies led to the description of the female reproductive organs as the male's turned inside out: the penis became the vagina, the scrotum the womb, and the testicles the ovaries. Because regular and heavy loss of blood in men was debilitating, menstruation was viewed as an unhealthy process causing many women distress, with its sole function being reproduction. Even pregnancy was not necessarily beneficial for a woman, as it wore the body out, and Soranus could recommend celibacy as part of a healthy female regimen—which would have been unthinkable in the Greek theories.

Menopause occurred at age 45 to 50, when the excess nourishment began to be used in the production of extra flesh and, occasionally, the growth of facial hair. Apart from a few remarks in Soranus, menopausal and postmenopausal women were not treated as having any problems peculiar to themselves in the ancient gynecologies, probably because, as with prepubescent girls, they were not thought to differ that much physiologically from their male contemporaries. Primarily trying to account for a woman's monthly blood in the context of her social inferiority gave rise to the ancient cultural constructs of the female body. Once this blood ceased to flow, signaling the end of fertility, a woman's body became more like a man's and, paradoxically, less valuable.

References. Sylvia Campese, Paola Manuli, and Giulia Sissa, *Madre Materia* (Torino, Italy, 1983); Ann Hanson, "The Medical Writers' Woman," in D. Halperin, J. J. Winkler, and F. Zeitline (eds.), *Before Sexuality* (Princeton, 1989); G.E.R. Lloyd, *Science, Folklore and Ideology* (Cambridge, 1983), 58–200.

LESLEY ANN JONES

GREEK AND ROMAN ART (ANCIENT). Greek art shows women as mortals and figures from myth and allegory in sculpture and painted vases (seventh to first centuries B.C.E.). The monuments were usually made by men for male buyers; with few exceptions, they present an idealized view of women's forms and lives. Roman art in which women appear in sculpture and wall painting (first century B.C.E.–fourth century C.E.) was also made by men, but women are sometimes documented as patrons and buyers. Their representations are more varied and include not only naturalistic portraits but even, though more rarely, scenes of public life. Despite the richness of the evidence, no book has been written on the whole subject.

Greek art presents women as goddesses such as Hera, mythological figures such as Amazons, and idealized mortal women. Goddesses were shown with emotions controlled and bodies clothed in the art made between the sixth and the early fourth centuries B.C.E., but during the Hellenistic period (third to first centuries B.C.E.), both nudity (e.g., the *Venus di Milo*) and emotion appear. Stories of mythological women appear both in religious art, for example, on temples such as the Parthenon in classical Athens, and on decorated vases. These stories seldom offer clear information about the lives of real women, although they may be presented using the visual language of real life, as when mythological weddings occur.

The mortal women of Greece appear on gravestones of the fifth to the fourth centuries as deceased or mourners. On vases of all periods women are shown as wives, mothers, and servants in domestic settings or as prostitutes at parties. At home, the women weave and spin, play with children, or talk among themselves and with men. Occasionally, they appear in weddings, funerals, and religious rituals.

Both in Greek sculpture and in vase painting, women normally do not have individualized features (except for a few servants and prostitutes on decorated vases); instead, they are idealized according to the standards of beauty common in the period. In the Hellenistic period there are extremely naturalistic figurines and statues of old peasants, and images of Hellenistic queens like Cleopatra VII show individualized features, as do contemporary male portraits. In general, however, Greek art is not an especially good source of literal information about women's (or men's) lives and appearances because of its emphasis on convention and idealization.

Greek works of art indicate men's, rather than women's, ideas about beauty and social order. From myth and comparative evidence, we can assume that women produced works of textile art, but only in the Hellenistic period is there any secure evidence that a few women were considered artists. The literary sources (e.g., Pliny, *Natural History* 35, 147–148) tell about no more than a dozen women, all of whom were painters, most of whom were the daughters of artists. There is also far less information about women than about men as patrons or buyers of works of art in the Greek world, although some wealthy women are known to have given money for public monuments like temples.

Roman writings give no evidence that women were artists in the Roman world, but they do tell about women as patrons and buyers of works of art. One of the most famous examples is Eumachia, a rich woman who endowed a large public building in the Forum of Pompeii. Less splendid, but equally important, are the many examples of women who bought funerary monuments for their family members.

Roman art tends to reveal more direct information about women's lives than does Greek art. Romans seem to have preferred images that commemorated the individual's appearance, status, and activities in the world. This preference encouraged artists to provide public and private monuments that documented the real as well as the ideal and mythic worlds. Figures from myth and goddesses such as Venus appear in religious art, on tombs, and in house decoration, as at Pompeii. In addition, however, real women abound in the art of every part of the Roman empire. Highly detailed portraits of wealthy women abound, and even women without much money, many of them former slaves, paid for decorated tombstones that showed them with their families or, less often, at work, for example, selling groceries or delivering babies.

Although Roman art seems more realistic than does Greek art, it was often just as concerned with expressing gender ideals. Whether in its frequent representation of women as younger and more attractive than men or its preference for women with their families rather than in public roles, Roman art offers a strong sense of the conventions of society. The representation of the female members of the imperial family provides a last example of this sense; such women seldom appear on the decorated public monuments paid for by the Roman state, for example, the triumphal arches. When they do, though, they are either shown on coins as divine figures like Salus (the health of the empire) or shown with their husbands and children, as on the *Altar of Augustan Peace* in Rome (13–9 B.C.E.). The crossover from the private, women's realm to the public, men's world takes place in Greek art only in religious and mythological art, but in Roman art it also occurs when the emperor needs to show that his dynasty is strong and his children healthy.

References. Elaine Fantham, Helene P. Foley, Natalie B. Kampen, Sarah B. Pomeroy, and H. A. Shapiro, *Women in the Classical World* (New York, 1994); Christine M. Havelock, "Mourners in Greek Art," and Natalie B. Kampen, "Social Status and Gender in Roman Art: The Case of the Saleswoman," in Norma Broude and Mary Garrard (eds.), *Feminism and Art History* (New York, 1982), 44–77; Natalie B. Kampen (ed.), *Sexuality in Ancient Art* (New York, 1996); Diana E. E. Kleiner, "The Great Friezes of the Ara Pacis Augustae," *Melanges de l'Ecole Francaise a Rome* 90, 2 (1978): 753–785; Brunilde Sismondo Ridgway, "Ancient Greek Women and Art: The Material Evidence, *American Journal of Archaeology* 91 (1987): 399–409; Dyffri Williams, "Women on Athenian Vases. Problems of Interpretation," in Averil Cameron and Amelie Kuhrt (eds.), *Images of Women in Antiquity* (Detroit, 1983), 92–106.

NATALIE BOYMEL KAMPEN

GREEK GODDESSES, like their male counterparts, personified aspects of human existence. At the same time, they superintended the life of mortals. Not remote from the world of humans, they actively engaged in events of ordinary life. In turn, mortals demonstrated their gratitude to the deities and requested continuing succor by means of offerings and festivals, both local and international.

The six Olympian goddesses are a good gauge of the spheres under divine tutelage. Hera, wife of Zeus, was particularly a goddess of women, with marriage and the physical life of women her special preserves. The earth mother Demeter also was associated with fertility, but not human fecundity as much as that of the earth and its plant life. The domain of Athena, daughter of Zeus, included civilized life, and, in this guise, she was guardian of cities as well as patron of artisans. Just as regularly was her aid sought as leader in battle, for she was the warrior goddess and had been born fully grown from the head of her father. Not martial arts but the melting charm of love was Aphrodite's sphere, which naturally extended to include all beautiful objects capable of inciting love and marriage, one expression of love's power. Artemis' love was of another sort: associated with the wilderness, she was protectress of wild animals, especially the young. Human youth, too, were her special concern. Of all the Olympians, the sphere of Hestia may seem most limited. She was the hearth and its fire and was often not depicted anthropomorphically. A more just estimation of Hestia's role of the hearth in antiquity reflects the fact that without its warmth, the family itself would have been impossible.

The Olympians were not the only important goddesses. The Greek conception of deity was exceedingly polytheistic, so much so that it has been argued that there were more gods than humans. There were older generations of goddesses like Rhea, mother of Zeus, Poseidon, and Hera; and younger goddesses such as Persephone, daughter of Demeter, whose annual winter sojourn in Hades arrested the growth of plants. Certain female divinities were associated with special points in a person's life: gentle Hebe was the goddess as child, while Eileithyia was goddess of childbirth. Other goddesses like fearful Hecate, abetter of witches, were ever near. Nymphs, graces, muses, local deities, and embodiments of forces like the Fates abounded. Yet, in spite of the profusion, an ordering of divinity had occurred by the early Classical period. The pantheon of 12 great gods and goddesses was firmly in place in the Homeric *Iliad* and *Odyssey* when these epics were set down in written form between 750 and 700 B.C.

This pantheon included six female deities and six male. By no means simply male and female counterparts of the same domains, the Olympians were nonetheless a family over which Zeus presided as father and lord. The familial bond echoes a similar relationship among humans: during much of Greek antiquity, the extended family formed the fundamental unit of society. The family relationship of the gods has suggested a hypothesis concerning the development of Greek religion: their frequent quarrels have been interpreted as the merger of two conceptions of deity. Evidence from the Neolithic period and the Bronze Age shows that female divinity had greater visibility than male deity. Visibility may well indicate prominence in cult and conception. If so, Classical Greek belief can be seen as the joining of an Indo-European conception of a supreme male deity with pre-Greek belief founded on the primacy of divinity embodied in the female form.

Supporting this view are written records of the late Bronze Age that list several deities with names similar to gods of Classical Greece. Chief among them is "Potnia," which translates as "Mistress." Possibly Potnia represented a great mother goddess whose powers eventually were divided among several lesser deities, or Potnia may have been a title of respect for all female deities, of whom there were many, even in early periods of Greek culture.

Certainly, in the Classical period the conception of divine power was so splintered that individual deities were worshiped in different guises in neighboring villages. While all Greeks knew the primary sphere of Aphrodite to be love, in Sparta she was also honored as a war goddess. Athena, generally thought to be a virgin goddess, was designated "mother" at Elis, and the wife of Zeus was paid tribute as "widow" in Arcadia.

Along with various guises, Greek goddesses were represented in several forms. Divinity was, by the Classical period, regularly pictured anthropomorphically: gods were human in form but possessed of far greater powers than mortals enjoyed. At the same time, divinity was depicted in animal form: Athena and her owl were one and the same. The Greek myths abound with tales of goddesses assuming animal form when it was expedient to do so. Moreover, divine power was also represented by objects like Athena's aegis, Artemis' bow, or Hestia's fire: deity and symbol of deity were fused. Perhaps the three guises are tokens of three conceptions of deity, changing over time from aniconic, to zoomorphic, to anthropomorphic, with the final conception subordinating, but never eliminating, early views. Another explanation sees the composite as reflecting a worldview in which categories of existence overlap with one another rather than belonging to neatly demarcated spheres.

Modern conceptions of Greek deity most frequently emphasize human form and character. Goddesses were favorite subjects of sculptors and vase painters, whose search for the beauty of physical form may well reflect the perfect beauty ascribed to the divine figures. Goddesses were a major source of inspiration for poets and mythographers, too. However, in this sphere the divinities were not always august and solemn. Just as they represented all aspects of existence, so did they experience the full range of emotions, strengths, and weaknesses known to mortals. Goddesses could weep, sulk, and connive as well as protect, cherish, and serve as models of propriety.

As honored patrons, however, the goddesses received human respect and offerings. In private rites in the home, at local cult ceremonies, and during major international festivals, the goddesses were thanked and propitiated. They were petitioned for individual requests as ordinary as the birth of a healthy child and as embracing as the well-being of an entire city's population. The Panathenaic festival in Athens was a thank offering to the patron deity of all Athenians. Citizens and noncitizens, allies and tributaries joined to present Athena with a new cloak. Woven into the warp of the fabric was the happiness of every member of the state. Little else in human life was as important as paying proper honor to the deities. Numbered by the sage Solon among the happiest of men were Cleobis and Biton, who pulled their mother's cart over six miles to the festival of Hera at Argos when oxen were not at hand for the task. For such exemplary service, Hera answered the mother's prayer that her sons be fittingly honored. Consequently, after falling asleep, they had a most enviable death.

References. P. E. Easterling and J. V. Muir (eds.), *Greek Religion and Society* (Cambridge, 1985); W.K.C. Guthrie, *The Greeks and Their Gods* (Boston, 1950); Nicole Loraux, "What Is a Goddess?" in Pauline Schmitt Pantel (ed.), *A History of Women, vol. 1: From Ancient Goddesses to Christian Saints* (Cambridge, 1992), 11–44; M. P. Nilsson, *A History of Greek Religion*, rev. ed. (New York, 1964).

CAROL G. THOMAS

GREEK WRITERS (ANCIENT). The early Greek women writers whose works are preserved are all lyric poets. Lyric poetry, unlike epic and drama, had a ritual setting or an informal audience; it was part of women's lives, and women were composers and performers as well as audience. The most important of these poets is Sappho. She lived in Mytilene on the island of Lesbos around 630–570 B.C. (all the dates in this entry are estimates). We know almost nothing of her life. Sappho's work was collected by Alexandrian scholars into nine books. Papyrus fragments found in Egypt have restored good parts of about eight major poems; quotation provides three other long poems and many excerpts.

The major poetic form before Sappho's time was epic. Epic was oral poetry; bards learned traditional plots and formulas, which they used to improvise narrative poems on the deeds of heroes. Once writing was introduced (c. 750 B.C.), creative epic began a long, slow decline, though not before several major epics (notably Homer's *Iliad* and *Odyssey*) were recorded in writing. Sappho's poetry comes out of the same large oral background as epic. She uses the Aeolic dialect, native to Lesbos, but a polished version. Her meters and forms are derived from tradition, from hymns, laments, and work songs. But, unlike epic, Sappho's poems were sung. The meter is more fixed than Homer's, the lines shorter because the rhythm must fit the music. Sappho often used the Sapphic strophe, a four-line stanza, but also a variety of other meters. Sappho may have composed melodies for the poems or may have used traditional tunes.

Sappho's poetry has a simple loveliness that engages the hearer immediately but unfolds to reveal richness of thought and emotion. Most of the extant poems are about love between women, a love that, for Sappho, reveals itself as a sense of beauty. "The most beautiful thing is what one loves," she says, and she expresses greater desire to see Anactoria's step and sparkling smile than an awesome massing of military force (Lobel and Page, hereafter LP). As proof, Sappho adduces Helen, most beautiful (for she was everyone's choice), who chose her lover above all else. The interplay with Homer and the complex logic of the poem (Helen as paradigm for both Anactoria and Sappho) give it resonance.

Through language and image Sappho suffuses poems with fragrant, fugitive sensuousness. In 96 LP a woman in Lydia outshines her companions as the moon does the stars, the moon whose erotic magic reminds Sappho of her. The woman evoked is absent, her seeming presence a trick of vivid memory. By writing, Sappho fixes passing moments of memory (whether real or imagined) into a permanent form. Sappho is perhaps the first poet for whom the act of writing is part of the meaning of the poem. She opposes the oral tradition, with its assimilation to the typical, in her specificity of recollection, in the naming and recorded detail that escape the passing of time and of memory itself.

Yet Sappho was a singer, and her poems found their natural expression in performance. For whom did she perform? The male poets found an audience at drinking parties and political clubs. Sappho, too, must have had a set of friends; the question (most vexed) is whether they formed an organized group, a circle including young, unmarried women. On the basis of ancient remarks that Sappho "taught," scholars posit a circle whose purpose is variously imagined as religious or educational or initiatory (including initiation into eroticism). There is little evidence in the extant poems for such a circle. A two-line fragment without context says, "I will sing these pleasant things beautifully to my (female) companions" (160 LP).

The poems sometimes speak to one woman about another or use the plural "we" in reminding a woman of past friendships.

Sappho herself is elusive in the poems; the complexity of dialogue and imagined and reported speech, the often perceptible distance between poet and narrator, the dreamlike scenes and depicted intimacy with Aphrodite make locating a historical Sappho in the poems impossible.

Lyric poetry could be either monodic, sung by a single speaker, or choral, sung and usually danced by a group. Most of Sappho's extant poems are monodic. But Sappho was famous in antiquity for her wedding hymns, probably danced choral songs. No substantial fragments of wedding songs survive. Short quotations offer jocular or admiring references to the groom, laments of lost virginity for the bride. Other fragments may also come from choral songs, for instance, the ritual lament for Adonis, which belonged to a festival of Aphrodite. One fragment (44 LP), perhaps for a wedding, gives a long description of Hector's return to Troy, bringing Andromache, his bride-to-be. The meter is similar to epic hexameter, and the language more like epic than in any other poem of Sappho's.

Women poets are known from the fifth century. There was Myrtis from Boeotia. She is said to have been a teacher of Corinna and of Pindar, the composer of victory odes, but we have no evidence that would confirm this statement. No fragment or quotation attributed to her survives, just a tale of a woman's rejected love and revenge, which Plutarch says she narrated. She is mentioned by Corinna.

Corinna herself is the most problematic of the women poets. Ancient sources assign her to the fifth century as a contemporary of Pindar, but some scholars date her to the Hellenistic period (after 323 B.C.) instead. Arguments about her language and meter are not decisive either way. Papyrus finds have yielded sizable fragments of two poems, narratives of Boeotian myth, and bits of others. In a small fragment Corinna claims to sing tales for the young women of Tanagra and to make the city rejoice, so she may have written songs for women's choruses at local festivals. The meters are song meters similar to Sappho's, and the poems are in stanzas. If Corinna is Hellenistic in date, then she was a gifted archaist in a period that valued archaic poetry and local color.

Also fifth-century are Praxilla and Telesilla, the first from Sicyon, the second from Argos. Praxilla was known as a writer of dithyrambs, elaborate choral songs. One line from a dithyramb on Achilles is preserved because it illustrates the meter named Praxillean after her. Telesilla, too, had a song meter named after her. She was, according to Pausanias, "famous among women for her poetry." From the few references we may gather that she composed narratives of the gods, probably choral poetry.

Erinna, a fourth-century poet, was almost as famous in antiquity as Sappho. Her major poem, "The Distaff," said to have been in 300 hexameters, was greatly praised. About 50 broken lines of "The Distaff" have now been found on papyrus. The poem is a lament for the death of a friend, Baucis, interwoven with reminiscences of childhood and references to Baucis' wedding. A major symbol of the preserved section is the tortoise. The word is spelled in the Aeolian way in apparently deliberate reference to Sappho, who used it to refer to the lyre. The tortoise figures also in myth and in a girls' game that Erinna and Baucis played, so it serves to link the themes of childhood, marriage, spinning, death, and poetry. The Sapphic technique of rendering memory present and an imaginative meditation on the sorrows of women's lives are finely combined.

Poetry in the Hellenistic period was meant to be read by the educated. The distinction between public, political poetry, performed by men, and informal or festival poetry, which women also composed, has broken down. A favorite form now was the epigram. Three women epigrammatists, Anyte of Tegea, Nossis of Italian Locri, and Moero of Byzantium, have poems preserved in a collection known as the *Palatine Anthology*.

Most of Anyte's 20 genuine epigrams purport to be inscriptions; possibly, some were written for that purpose. Four of them, for instance, are ostensibly for the tombs of young women who died before marriage, all quite different but all through language or image referring to a Homeric scene. Anyte also has several epigrams describing pleasant places for travelers or country laborers to rest, early examples of pastoral poetry.

More unusual are Anyte's descriptive epigrams, a type that she shares with Nossis and that they may have been the first to develop. These epigrams describe genre scenes or artwork; Anyte has one of children riding a goat. While Anyte shows interest in the unremarked or inarticulate— children, animals, quiet places—Nossis is interested primarily in women. Her erotic poetry is lost, but in one epigram she is among those "loved by Cypris," while in another she asks the stranger going toward Mytilene to remember her to Sappho. Perhaps her erotic poetry was addressed to women. The epigrams we have describe women's portraits or dedications to Aphrodite. Nossis describes the portraits as true likenesses that reveal each woman's essence, whether sensuality or gentleness or wisdom. In her own style Nossis repeats Sappho's desire to fix in writing the effect of women on those near them, a woman's response to the epic "deeds of men."

Names of other Hellenistic women poets are known, for example, Hedyle. Several who lived in the third century B.C. wrote poems for various cities, perhaps on commission, or traveled to major festivals to compete in poetry contests. Inscriptions record their names. Melinno wrote a poem in praise of Rome that has survived, but we have no idea of her date. Education for women improved in the Hellenistic period, so women began to write treatises on philosophy, gynecology, and literary questions. Leontion, for instance, whose work Cicero read, was a philosopher and companion of Epicurus. Less is recorded or invented about these women than about the earlier poets. Hellenistic scholars, inevitably, sought out the "antique" poets and neglected their gifted contemporaries.

References. W. Barnstone (trans.) *Sappho: Lyrics in the Original Greek with Translations* (New York, 1965); A. P. Burnett, *Three Archaic Poets* (Cambridge, Mass., 1983); J. Duban, *Ancient and Modern Images of Sappho: Translations and Studies* (Lanham, Md., 1983); P. Jay (ed.), *The Greek Anthology and Other Ancient Epigrams: A Selection in Modern Verse Translation* (New York, 1973); G. Kirkwood, "Sappho" and C. P. Segal, "Women Poets: Corinna, Myrtis, Telesilla Praxilla," in P. E. Easterling and B. Knox (eds.), *Cambridge History of Classical Literature: Greek Literature*, vol. 1 (Cambridge, England, 1985); E. Lobel and D. Page, *Poetarum Lesbiorum Fragmenta* (Oxford, 1955); S. Pomeroy, "Technikai kai musikai," *American Journal of Ancient History* 2 (1977): 57–68; Jane Snyder, *The Woman and the Lyre* (Carbondale, Ill., 1989); E. Stigers (Stehle), "Sappho's Private World," and J. Winkler, "Gardens of Nymphs," in H. Foley (ed.), *Reflections of Women in Antiquity* (New York, 1981).

EVA STIGERS STEHLE

GYNECOLOGY/OBSTETRICS (OB/GYN). Gynecology, from the Greek words for woman (*gyn*) and reason or discourse (*logos*), is the branch of medicine that deals with the health and proper functioning of the female reproductive system.* Obstetrics, from the Latin word for midwife (*obstetric*), is the branch of gynecology that deals with pregnancy and childbirth.* To become board-certified in gynecology and obstetrics (certified by a board of gynecologists that certain standards for knowledge and competence have been met), physicians must complete a residency and pass a written examination and then, after two years of practice, have all of their hospital cases reviewed and pass an oral examination.

H

HAGIOGRAPHY. Inspirational literature that recounts the lives, deaths, and/or posthumous miracles of holy men and women; also known as saints' legends. Although similar stories have been told about the heroes of other religions and cultures, hagiography is associated, above all, with Roman Catholic Christianity between late antiquity and the Reformation. From this long period, much of it otherwise sparsely documented, thousands of hagiographical texts survive—a vast body of potential source material for feminist theologians, social historians, and other reinterpreters of the medieval past. The main problem is learning how to use this material.

Most hagiographical sources bear little resemblance to sober, trustworthy biographies—and logically so, since most hagiographers were publicists, not disinterested historians. Their central task was to glorify the memory of particular saints, usually for such practical purposes as strengthening the morale of the saint's community, attracting recruits to the saint's way of life, and drawing pilgrims to the saint's shrine. In this context, advocates of a new saint might go to some lengths to prove him or her superior, or at least equal, to earlier heroes of the faith, and advocates of earlier saints might respond by improving their own legends. Hence, the genre is full of polemical exaggerations, and legend after legend uses the same proven formulas for success—verbal commonplaces, key images, sometimes whole incidents borrowed from the Bible or from influential early legends.

What can modern scholars learn from sources like these? If we work cautiously enough, attempting to strip away all the conventional and polemical material in the legends, we may find nuggets of reliable historical detail. Donald Weinstein and Rudolph M. Bell give a large-scale demonstration of this procedure, with applications to medieval family history. Alternatively and probably with even more fruitful results, we can focus on the hagiographical elements, seeking, for example, to understand what the conventional images tell us about the assumptions and aspirations of medieval people. Some of the most interesting recent research of this kind has dealt with the issues of gender roles, sanctity, and power.

As many scholars have pointed out, the prevailing images of sanctity in late antiquity were masculine. Women were represented among the martyrs, of course, but even the martyr was envisaged as fulfilling a prototypically male role, that of athlete or warrior, which was beyond the natural capacity of women. Thus, the endurance of the female martyr Blandina, in the famous letter about the persecutions at Lyons, is depicted as miraculous: "Tiny, weak, and insignificant as she was she would give inspiration to her brothers, for she had put on Christ, that mighty and invincible athlete, and had overcome the Adversary in many contests, and through her conflict had won the crown of immortality" (Musurillo). The other great model of sanctity in this period was the monastic ascetic who withdrew from the world, renouncing all earthly pleasures and possessions to seek God alone. The conventional image of such an ascetic, like that of a martyr, was male. The strength of this gender identification is suggested by the way Jerome praises his already saintly, ascetical friend Paula when he describes her visit to desert monks in Egypt: "Her endurance [was] scarcely credible in a woman. Forgetful of her sex and of her weakness she even desired to make her abode . . . among these thousands of monks" (Jerome). There were also hagiographical romances about idealistic women who disguised themselves as men in order to join such communities of monks and achieve sainthood.

During the first two-thirds of the Middle Ages (sixth to twelfth centuries) the Western Christians most likely to become saints were bishops, abbots, monastic founders, and kings—individuals, that is, who wielded considerable power in society because of their high office and (usually) aristocratic birth. Given the emphasis on public power in this model of sanctity, it is not surprising that new female saints were even rarer than in late antiquity and likelier to be honored chiefly because they were related to male saints. But there was at least one major exception: Anglo-Saxon monastic hagiography produced some remarkably strong, positive images of abbesses who left their mark on the church. Bede's (d. 735) brief life of St. Hilda in the *Ecclesiastical History* is one example. Rudolf's life of St. Lioba (written c. 835) includes miracle stories that testify even more memorably to the kind of benevolent, world-changing power that Anglo-Saxon monks were willing to credit to holy women as well as holy men.

Turning to late medieval hagiography (thirteenth to fifteenth centuries), one finds female saints suddenly prominent. Of the new saints recognized during this period, about 30 percent were women—approximately double the percentage in the preceding centuries. Moreover, the late Middle Ages saw the multiplication of stories about the Virgin Mary, especially in her role as last resort of sinners, and a great revival of romanticized legends about early virgin martyrs like St. Margaret, St. Cecilia, and St. Katherine of Alexandria. Some of these late medieval favorites are very authoritative figures, but almost never do they recall the androgynous public authority of an Anglo-Saxon saint like Lioba. Indeed, their legends tend to dwell on virtues that sound quintessentially feminine—chastity, long suffering (whether from persecution, penitential asceticism, or illness), respect for the clergy, and compassion for unfortunates—and on such private supernatural experiences as spiritual marriages to Christ and visits from angels. Some late medieval hagiographers go so far as to suggest that being female is actually an advantage, rather than a liability, in the quest for holiness.

The late medieval emphasis on holy womanhood does not mean that some great feminist tide was sweeping through the church. In the thirteenth century, even more than the fourth or the seventh, the majority of hagiographers were celibate male clerics who had been conditioned to distrust and avoid women in general. The paradoxical attachment of such men to feminine images of sanctity has been explored, most notably by Caroline Walker Bynum, who analyzes significant uses of imagery by spiritual writers of both genders. Bynum shows that the late medieval images of female sanctity were not developed specifically to inspire and indoctrinate women, as some modern readers have supposed; in fact, they seem to have been much more important to men who were ambivalent about their own privileges and power, hence, the recurrent emphasis on those aspects of women's experience that posed the sharpest contrast to the traditional male paradigm of earthly authority and public achievements. One can see something of the same pattern in contemporary lives of male saints, a number of whom (like St. Francis of Assisi) were revered for having renounced the kinds of power that earlier medieval saints had used for the glory of God.

Even if designed primarily to meet the spiritual and psychological needs of men, however, conventional images of female sanctity undoubtedly affected the lives of women, too. Assessing their impact will be no easy task, since many of our best sources on the lives of medieval women are themselves hagiographical. But some exciting research is now being done in this area, as illustrated by the work of Bynum, Jocelyn Wogan-Browne, Barbara Newman, and numerous articles in two recent collections (Ashley and Sheingorn; Blumenfeld-Kosinski and Szell).

References. Kathleen Ashley and Pamela Sheingorn (eds.), *Interpreting Cultural Symbols: Saint Anne in Late Medieval Society* (Athens, Ga., 1990); Bede, *Ecclesiastical History of the English Nation*, trans. J. Stevens et al. (London, 1910); Renate Blumenfeld-Kosinski and Timea Szell (eds.), *Images of Sainthood in Medieval Europe* (Ithaca, N.Y., 1991); Caroline Walker Bynum, *Jesus as Mother: Studies in the Spirituality of the High Middle Ages* (Berkeley, Calif., 1982); Caroline Walker Bynum, "Women's Stories, Women's Symbols," in *Fragmentation and Redemption: Essays on Gender and the Human Body in Medieval Religion* (New York, 1991); W. H. Fremantle (trans.), Letter 108, in Philip Schaff et al. (eds.), *Select Library of Nicene and Post-Nicene Fathers of the Christian Church*, 2d series, vol. 6 (New York, 1893); Herbert Musurillo (ed. and trans.), *Acts of the Christian Martyrs* (New York, 1972); Barbara Newman, " 'Cruel Corage': Child Sacrifice and the

Maternal Martyr in Hagiography and Romance," in *From Virile Woman to WomanChrist: Studies in Medieval Religion and Literature* (Philadelphia, 1995); Donald Weinstein and Rudolph M. Bell, *Saints and Society: The Two Worlds of Western Christendom, 1000–1700*, part 1 (Chicago, 1982); Jocelyn Wogan-Browne, "Saints' Lives and the Female Reader," *Forum for Modern Language Studies* 27 (1991): 314–332.

SHERRY L. REAMES

HEALERS. See HEALTH CARE PROVIDERS

HEALTH, ECONOMICS OF. Women use more medical care on an average than men even after accounting for use of gynecological and obstetrical care. Women have about 25 percent more visits to the physician, spend 50 percent more on prescription drugs, are more likely to see a psychiatrist, and are admitted to a hospital more often. Men use more health care when they are admitted to the hospital: they stay longer. Only under the age of 5 do females use less care than males.

Women's Health Status. Do women use more medical care because they are sicker than men, or do women live longer because they use more care? Measures of women's health status as compared to men's provide a confusing answer when both physical health and emotional health are examined. Women live on average eight years longer than men, and their life expectancy has been growing at a faster rate. Women have better health statuses when clinically measured but worse health status when self-reported.

A greater percentage of women report themselves to have stress and anxiety, and a smaller proportion report feelings of positive well-being than do men. Although women are more likely to attempt suicide, more men actually take their own lives. Historically, women were reported to have more psychiatric problems, although now that new measures of psychiatric conditions include alcohol and drug abuse, the percentages of psychiatric problems are more equal across the sexes.

Medical Problems and Health Habits. Women suffer from different medical problems than men, and this may account for, or be caused by, differential use of medical care. For example, women die two to six times less often than men of behavioral-related diseases: lung cancer, emphysema, motor vehicle accidents, other accidents, suicide, and cirrhosis of the liver. An open question is, As women become more like men in their professional and pleasure pursuits and in their health habits, will women's health suffer like men's? For example, women's increased smoking and job stress may negatively affect their health.

Role in the Family. Part of the difference in the use of medical care and in health status across gender may be attributed to traditional differences in family roles by gender. An obvious and inescapable difference is that women bear the children. Additional medical expenses are incurred for women in childbearing, even in uncomplicated cases. The traditional division of labor in the home can also account for part of women's greater use of health care. If the mother does more of the child care,* then she has more exposure to the contagious diseases of children. As the traditional person in charge of the family's health, she may also seek medical care, in part, for the informational content of a visit. She can then use this information to produce the health of the rest of her family.

Women's greater use of medical care may be attributable, in part, to the fact that the wife is more likely to give care to her husband than to receive care from him. The man may substitute home care, while the woman must seek market care. The difference in the provision of home health by gender shows up in differences in the effect of marital status on health. Being married is associated with greater health for men but not for women. This is seen most vividly in elderly couples. When an elderly man's wife dies, his health declines rapidly, and he is likely to die sooner. However, the loss of an elderly woman's spouse has little effect on her health.

Insurance Coverage. In 1997 about 16 percent of the total population is without health insurance coverage. However, women are slightly less likely to have health insurance coverage and often have less extensive coverage. This occurs because women are less likely to be employed and are more likely to have jobs that do not offer insurance coverage (or provide less comprehensive coverage) and because women sometimes lose their coverage with divorce* or the death of their spouse. The "feminization of poverty"* leads to increased reliance on the public provision of coverage. Health insurance coverage increases the use of medical care. Thus, with women's slightly lower coverage it is even more dramatic to find that women use more medical care in general.

Health insurance is more costly to provide for women because women use more care. If a woman buys health insurance coverage as an individual (i.e., not through a group plan), she typically must pay more for her coverage than would a man. Often the employer charges both men and women the same premium, although it costs more to cover the woman. The pricing of health insurance by sex is part of the broader policy controversy on unisex pricing of insurance policies.

One of the reasons that women are more expensive to cover is the possibly high expenses of pregnancy. Coverage for pregnancy was often confined to married women with a family health insurance plan. However, relatively recent federal legislation mandates that the expense of pregnancy be covered without regard to marital status: it is covered as a "disability."

Special Needs of Women and Public Programs. Maternal and Child Health. In the enduring controversy about whether preventive care can actually be cost-effective, the case of maternal and child health seems to be a clear-cut cost-effective investment for the family and society. Timely provision of medical care, proper nutrition, and guidance on health habits can help both the child and the mother and prevent future, more expensive problems. Private insurance programs typically provide coverage for prenatal care and well child care. For the poor, Temporary Assistance to Needy Families (previously called Medicaid and Aid to Families with Dependent Children) often cover pregnancy-related medical expenses. It is important to note that health depends on many more things than just the use of medical care. Other factors can be vitally important, for example, health habits, sanitation, education, and nutrition. Many public programs unrelated to medical care have an important impact on health. The federally supported Women, Infant and Child (WIC) program, for example, provides important foods for eligible women and children.

Old Age. Because women live longer than men and are less likely to be married in the older ages, women are often living alone and in poor health in their old age. This can present a problem; in old age medical expenses increase, health declines, income can decline, and the ability to care for oneself decreases. This often leaves women with large expenses for medical care, including either home health care or nursing home care. The Medicare program is designed to help the elderly population meet additional medical expenses; however, it does not meet all of the expenses. Medicare covers little home health care and does not cover extended nursing home care. Thus, women with husbands in nursing homes often spend the family wealth on the husbands' care and then live in poverty.* If driven to poverty by the expenses of their dying husbands and/or their own expenses, they become eligible for Medicaid, which covers nursing home care.

Coverage for nursing home and long-term care is an increasingly important policy issue as the population ages, home care is no longer provided by the extended family, there are more single elderly women, and the costs of nursing home care rise. It is an issue of critical importance to women. Most residents of nursing homes are women. Long-term care presents a real policy problem; to cover it is extremely costly, but without it the elderly face large expenses or inadequate care. Currently, private coverage is not widely available, and public programs are inadequate.

References. Department of Health & Humanity Services website (1997); *Women's Health: Report of the Public Health Service Task Force on Women's Health Issues*, vol. 2 (Washington, D.C., May 1985): esp. 1–32.

JODY L. SINDELAR

HEALTH CARE PROVIDERS. Women have always practiced medicine. Often, though, their contributions have been overlooked because women typically practiced within the domestic setting; mothers, friends, neighbors, and even slaves provided important health care. Women also have a long tradition of practicing medicine outside their private domestic sphere as priestesses, doctors, nurses, medicine women, wisewomen, midwives, and herbalists. For example, Egyptian tomb pictures from c. 2500 B.C. show women lancing boils, circumcising babies, and operating on feet. Not surprisingly, many of the healing deities of ancient societies have feminine attributes. Thus, in Egypt, Isis was the goddess of medicine; in Greece, Artemis was the goddess of childbirth. Legends tell of Hygeia and Panacea, daughters of the god of medicine Aesculapius, as highly respected healers eventually worshiped as deities. Homeric and other classical literature, as well as biblical and Talmudic writings, attest to the prevalence and acceptance of women as healers, though few names were recorded.

Inscriptions on gravestones, particularly from the Roman period, describe women healers of later centuries. Many Greek women, both physicians and midwives, were brought to Rome as slaves in the second century B.C. Previously, Romans had relied on the domestic medicine of female relatives and friends. Over the next four centuries Greek medicine, frequently practiced by women, came to dominate Roman health care. By the third and fourth centuries A.D., other women found a commitment to healing in their Christian belief. In time much of their practice was centered in convents, where women could study medicine, nursing, and herbs. After the fall of the Roman empire, formal medical and nursing training died out in the Christianized West, except in the monasteries and convents, where monks and nuns laboriously copied and preserved ancient texts and cared for the sick. This monastic tradition continued for many centuries; some women who founded nursing orders, such as Catherine of Bologna, were even elevated to sainthood.

In the middle of the eleventh century, organized medical education was established at Salerno, Italy. Reputedly, women as well as men attended this school and taught there; more usually, women were excluded from universities of the West, which were the seats of medical education in the medieval and early modern periods. Women did care for the sick in hospitals, especially those established along the Crusaders' routes and later in growing urban centers such as Paris. However, with few trained physicians and few hospitals, the majority of the populace undoubtedly still relied on traditional domestic medicine, particularly midwifery, which had served them in the past.

By the seventeenth and eighteenth centuries, formal medical certification, such as university degrees and government licenses, increasingly inhibited women's involvement in organized medicine, since women were barred from attending the classes necessary to be certified. Yet, many people who could not afford or did not trust expensive, university-educated physicians still called in women healers. Midwifery typically remained women's work. Furthermore, in the American colonies the marked shortage of formally trained doctors required that people employed alternative, often women, healers, midwives, and apothecaries.

While these women practiced medicine, they were outside the "profession" of medicine. In the late eighteenth and nineteenth centuries, in the drive for professionalization, women practitioners were denied access to the growing numbers of schools, hospitals, and medical societies; they were pushed more to the periphery. This is seen clearly in the medicalization of parturition. Childbirth was redefined as pathologic, rather than natural; physician-managed labor was equated with safety and progress; midwives were labeled ill trained; and, later in the twentieth century, hospitals were accepted as havens for parturient women. Consequently, though in the eighteenth century midwives attended almost all births in this country, by 1910 they attended only about 50 percent, and over the next several decades midwives practically disappeared in the United States.

At the same time, two significant nineteenth-century movements—the push for woman's rights* and for health reform—coupled with developments in medical science and practice, helped open up other medical careers to women. Reformers blamed women's supposed poor health on female modesty before male physicians and insisted that the health of the nation would improve if more women became doctors. Feminists also supported women's entering medicine. Following the graduation of Elizabeth Blackwell from Geneva Medical College in 1849, hundreds of women sought medical training. By the 1880s a few previously all-male institutions admitted female students, but many continued to reject women. To provide more opportunities, all-female medical colleges were founded. When women graduates were denied internships and residencies, they founded hospitals and hired female graduates. As more schools and hospitals accepted women, the call for separate institutions diminished; many women's schools and hospitals closed or merged with men's. By the end of the century, women accounted for between 4 percent and 5 percent of U.S. physicians, a proportion that stayed fairly constant until the 1960s.

Women entered other health care occupations, most particularly nursing, in greater numbers. Before the late nineteenth century the United States had few hospitals and no nurse training schools. By the 1870s, however, partly influenced by the successes of Florence Nightingale's trained nurses in improving hospital conditions, some hospitals began to establish schools of nursing to train their workers. By 1880, 15 schools in the United States enrolled 323 and had graduated 157; by 1900, 432 schools enrolled more than 11,000 students and had graduated almost 3,500 nurses.

Today, as in centuries past, women practice medicine. According to census figures published in 1994, they constitute over 77 percent of health care workers. But, despite these figures, women do not dominate the field; in the more prestigious, powerful, and lucrative occupations their numbers are limited. While more than 94 percent of registered nurses, over 98 percent of dental hygienists, and nearly 94 percent of licensed practical nurses are women, women represent less than 20 percent of the more distinguished and influential health-diagnosing occupations. For example, they account for barely 20 percent of the physicians and less than 13 percent of the dentists. Still, since only a decade ago women accounted for less that 16 percent of physicians and under 7 percent of dentists in this country, these figures document that many health occupations have apparently begun to readjust the historic sex imbalance. Similarly, women are graduating from medical school in increasing numbers, from about 5 percent of the graduating class in 1960 to over 25 percent in 1983 to 37 percent in the early 1990s. In addition, more men are attending nursing schools, though male graduates are frequently directed away from patient care and toward administration. The trend is clear. We shall see whether the health care system can replace its sex-stratified occupational structure in the future. (See also MIDWIFERY; NURSING REFORM (U.S.).)

References. Rima D. Apple (ed.), *Women, Health, and Medicine in America: A Historical Handbook* (New York, 1990; New Brunswick, N.J., 1992); Charlotte G. Borst, *Catching Babies: The Professionalization of Childbirth, 1870–1920* (Cambridge, 1995); Leon Fink and Brian Greenberg, *Upheaval in the Quiet Zone: A History of Hospital Workers' Union, Local 1199* (Urbana, Ill., 1989); Kate Campbell Hurd-Mead, *A History of Women in Medicine: From the Earliest Times to the Beginnings of the Nineteenth Century* (Haddam, Conn., 1938) (out-of-date but still the only single source on the topic, this book must be used cautiously); Regina Morantz-Sanchez, *Sympathy and Science: Women Physicians in American Medicine* (New York, 1985); Susan Reverby, *Ordered to Care: The Dilemma of American Nursing, 1850–1945* (New York, 1987).

RIMA D. APPLE

HEALTH MOVEMENT, WOMEN'S. Women cannot have control over their lives until they have control over their bodies and their health, so understanding their own bodies and gaining a voice in health care and medical policy have been central to the women's movement.

Women call upon the health services more than men do, and health issues are a fundamental part of women's lives for a number of reasons. (1) Women live longer than men (an average of 78.3 years compared to 71.7; over age 75, there are two women for every one man), so, as elderly members of society, they have more need for medical care. (2) Normal, healthy women call upon the health services for birth control, pregnancy, childbirth,* and other services related to their reproductive organs and activities. (3) In a system based on fee-for-services, women are more likely than men to be overtreated or undertreated. There is much money to be made when products or procedures are mass-marketed to women. For example, women are more likely to have surgery, and the necessity of some surgeries can be questioned. Studies have found more than 30 percent of hysterectomies were not necessary, and cosmetic surgery, disproportionately marketed to women, is the fastest growing area of medicine. In contrast to the problem of overtreatment, women are also more likely not to have insurance coverage so may not have any insurance or adequate insurance to cover products or procedures they need. (4) The sexual division of labor means that as unpaid workers, women are responsible for the health care of children, elderly, chronically sick, and people with disabilities. The average woman now spends more years of her life taking care of older parents and relatives than taking care of children. In a situation unprecedented in history, women are now performing simultaneous roles as paid members of the labor force and as unpaid caregivers. Studies consistently show that this health issue becomes a health problem because unpaid caretakers experience significant stress and depression. (5) The health services treat men and women differently even if they present the same symptoms. Men are more likely to be given physical exams and tests. Women are more likely to be labeled as "neurotic" and given drugs. Mood-altering drugs are prescribed to women more than twice as often as to men. (6) Although men have the power in medicine and are in the decision-making positions, 75 percent of health care workers are women. In hospitals, 85 percent of health care workers are women.

Women's health movements have been made up of a wide range of individuals and groups involved in different activities and campaigns. Working for a more appropriate health care system has been a unifying issue even for women who have not consciously identified themselves as a part of the women's movement. Activities have ranged from single-issue campaigns for better local health services, to self-help groups, setting up women's health information libraries, building alliances and coalitions around women's health issues, teaching women's health courses, producing leaflets and books, and providing women-controlled health centers.

A central theme has been the recognition that much of the power of the medical profession comes from its possession and use of knowledge and information to which consumers do not have access. A primary goal of health activists has been to collect, produce, and distribute information that is accessible to women and relevant to their needs, so that women can themselves make decisions about their bodies, their health care, and their lives.

Women's health movements have identified that health systems reflect the values and priorities of society; therefore, inequalities in society get mirrored by inequalities in health and the health system. In the same way that women's health movements have analyzed and organized around the impact of sexism, much attention has also been paid to how sexism intersects with racism, poverty, homophobia, ageism, "fatphobia," and other social/cultural issues to affect the basic parameters of health, access to the health system, and culturally appropriate services being available. Specialized women's health groups, including the National Black Women's Health Project, the National Latina Health Organization, the Native American Women's Health Education Resource Center, and the National Asian Women's Health Organization, have worked to ensure that women's health activism and policy development is appropriate for a diversity of women.

Many of the issues long articulated by women's health movements received mainstream, medical system, and government attention in the 1990s. Congressional hearings in 1990 drew notice to the fact that only 13 percent of the National Institutes of Health (NIH) research budget was spent on women's health research and that almost all research was done exclusively on (white) men and then extrapolated to women. That year, NIH established the Office of Research on Women's Health, complete with funding and authority. This office is charged with three mandates: (1) to strengthen research related to diseases that affect women and ensure that NIH-supported research adequately addresses women's health; (2) to see that women are adequately represented in biomedical and behavioral studies supported by NIH; and (3) to support recruitment, retention, and reentry of women in biomedical careers. Other important governmental action to improve women's health has included the NIH Reauthorization Act, which now requires the inclusion of women and minorities in research funded by the NIH, the Food and Drug Administration's liberalized guidelines for women's participation in drug trials, the U.S. Public Health Service's establishment of a Women's Health Office in each region, and the Women's Health Initiative (a large, groundbreaking study of cancer, cardiovascular disease, and osteoporosis in women, involving more than 164,000 women at 40 sites over 15 years).

Medical schools have consciously moved toward having women make up 40–50 percent of students, but many barriers remain to having women equally involved in making the health system more appropriate. Despite increased numbers, women remain concentrated in lower-paid, lower-status jobs, and changes in the medical system mean that most physicians, male or female, have less autonomy and role in decision making than they would have had in previous decades. Whether there should be an emphasis on a women's health medical specialty or whether all practitioners should include women's health expertise in their medical specialties is a topic heavily debated.

Despite, and because of, the increased attention to women's health, women's health movements are actively addressing the issues for the next century. Instead of looking at social, economic, and political factors that affect women collectively, much of the mainstream women's health coverage is individualistic and often blames women's lifestyle decisions for their ill health. Alternative, non-victim-blaming information is still crucial. As new issues, such as violence, are addressed by the medical system, as changes in the welfare system negatively affect health, and as managed care becomes the major way to access health services, women's health movements face new challenges in working toward a health system that meets the real needs of all women.

Our Bodies, Ourselves is the classic of the women's health movement. Originally (1969) a set of notes for a women's health course, it is now a 750-page book available in many languages, adapted for many different health systems. The National Women's Health Network (514 10th Street, N.W., Suite 400, Washington, D.C. 20004) is the national membership organization that works on all women's health issues, monitors and influences policies, and provides consumer information.

Reference. Boston Women's Health Book Collective, *Our Bodies, Ourselves* (Boston, 1996).

NANCY WORCESTER

HEBREW WOMEN were members of a patriarchal culture whose recorded history in the Hebrew Bible spans approximately 1,000 years. From the patriarch Abraham and his wife Sarah in 1800 B.C.E. to the prophet Hosea and his wife Gomer in 750 B.C.E., the biblical texts show a gradual restriction of women's public and private roles.

The creation of a monotheistic patriarchal religion radically affected the status of Hebrew women. For preceding millennia, peoples of the Near and Middle East had practiced the religion of the great Canaanite goddess Asherah and her consort, a religion that revered female procreativity and fostered matrilineal descent. A system based on patrilineal descent and patriarchal control over clan property was incompatible, however, with one that promoted sexual autonomy. The Hebrew Bible charts the shift to patriarchy and the subsequent loss of autonomy of Hebrew women as they became the property of fathers and husbands.

The covenant of Abraham required the worship of one god to the exclusion of all other deities. From the outset, the covenant community was defined as male, distinguished by the sign of male circumcision. Yahweh's blessing of Abraham's seed announced the transference of procreativity from female to male. Women were included in the covenant only through the mediation of men.

Yet the shift from goddess worship to the worship of Yahweh occurred slowly. In the 400 years between Abraham and Moses, Hebrew tribes, though pledged to Yahweh, continued to worship ancient gods. Women worshiped with men in the temple and shared public feasts and celebrations. Even in the earliest period, however, the patriarchal head of the family held undisputed authority over other family members. A wife called her husband *ba'al*, or "master." Early pastoral tribes practiced endogamy— marriage within the tribes—to keep women, their future children, and property within the lineage.

The patrilineal system, which depended on knowledge of paternity and a system of laws designed to protect male prerogatives, began to appear around the time of Moses in 1300 B.C.E. The Decalogue, the first codification of Jewish law, stated clearly that woman was the property of her husband, along with his servants and his maid, his ox, and his ass (Exod. 20:17). Shortly before the Hebrew tribes invaded Canaan, Levite priests instituted laws to change the sexual behavior of Hebrew women. Levitical law denounced ancient sexual customs and devised a new system of sexual morality for women based on premarital virginity and marital fidelity, concepts alien to earlier goddess worship (Lev. 18).

Female sexuality was acceptable under the new system only when a woman was designated the property of one specific male. The female procreative ability became property, which was transferable from one male to another. A daughter lived under the authority of her father until he released her to another male. Fathers at one time could sell their daughters into slavery or prostitution, and Judges 19 and 21 suggest that a man could make wives or daughters sexually available to strangers. Marriages were arranged by male representatives of a family. The prospective bridegroom paid a "bride-price" to the woman's father to compensate him for the loss of his possession. A woman not a virgin at the time of marriage was stoned or burned to death, according to the law.

Hebrew women lived at the disposal of fathers, brothers, and husbands. If abused by male family members, women had no recourse. Tamar, who was raped by her brother Amnon, is but one example. The effects of rape on the family's status rather than the feelings of the victim were of primary concern. If a raped woman was either betrothed or married and thus the property of another man, her attacker was executed. If a virgin, the raped woman was forced to marry her attacker, whose only punishment was that he could not divorce her. A woman raped in the country was not penalized since she was out of earshot, but a woman raped in the city was executed since she could have called for help.

Hebrew women were not considered legally responsible; their vows were worthless. They could own property only if they had no brothers and married within the tribe. Israelite law required monogamy of wives; husbands were allowed as many secondary wives and concubines as they could afford. Women were not allowed to initiate divorce; men could divorce by means of a simple note. While adulterous wives were subject to the death penalty, adulterous husbands faced no legal sanction, since paternity, rather than the woman's integrity, was at issue.

Motherhood itself came to be highly regarded during the period of national formation in Canaan. Since population was needed to help settle a desert environment and replace lives lost to wars and epidemics, the primary purpose of the Israelite wife was to bear children, preferably males. When a man died childless, the law of levirate marriage required the wife to marry her brother-in-law in order to preserve patrimony. The fertile wife who stayed carefully within the confines of service to her husband and his family was deemed "virtuous" and enjoyed a measure of domestic and economic importance (Prov. 31). The Fifth Commandment ordered children to honor mothers equally with fathers. So important was motherhood that a privileged woman could claim as her own a child born to her husband's concubine. Barrenness or the failure to obtain sons brought disgrace and served as a cause for divorce.

For all its emphasis on motherhood, the Hebrew law viewed with disgust all bodily processes related to procreation. The law demanded ritual purification after menstruation, intercourse, and childbirth, functions seen as disease-related and therefore unclean. Socially isolated during her flow, a menstruating woman was considered unclean for seven days afterward. Everything and everyone she touched during that time were thought to be defiled (Lev. 15). Intercourse during a woman's menstrual period carried with it the penalty of exile (Lev. 20:18); following sanctioned intercourse, a couple was considered unclean "until the even" (Lev. 15:18). After giving birth to a son, a woman remained unclean for 40 days; after giving birth to a daughter, she remained unclean for 80 days. At the end of her ritual purification, the new mother sought certification of cleanliness from the local priest (Lev. 12).

The tradition that disparaged women's sexuality also demanded the murder of anyone who did not worship Yahweh. As part of the Deuteronomic reform in the seventh century B.C.E., Hebrew men were commanded to stone to death their wives, brothers, friends, and children for failure to worship the Israelite God (Deut. 13:6–10). According to ancient tradition, the conquest of Canaan was accomplished by the slaughter of all the men, women, and children in some 60 cities (Deut. 3:4–6). Sometimes the women were spared: regulations in Numbers specified that virgins be captured rather than slain (Num. 31:17), and Deuteronomic law encouraged the taking of any "beautiful woman" the Hebrew warriors desired (Deut. 21:10–14). If the inhabitants of a captured city returned to their former religion, they were to be killed, and their city burned (Deut. 13:12–16).

After the establishment of the monarchy in 1050 B.C.E., the practice of the ancient religion of Asherah, Ashtoreth, Astarte, or Anath and her consort Baal or El continued, despite repeated warnings and punishments from Levitical priests. Having witnessed the murder of their families and the destruction of their homes, many women taken as wives, concubines, or slaves of the invading Hebrews clung to their native worship. References to the goddess Asherah and her cult object, the asherim, which was translated in the King James version as "grove," appear over 40 times in the Hebrew Bible. The worship of Ashtoreth existed side by side with Yahwism in Jerusalem. King Solomon worshiped Ashtoreth; his many wives had "turned his heart after other gods" (1 Kings 11:4).

After Solomon's death in 922 B.C.E., when the monarchy split into the two kingdoms of Israel and Judah, women continued to worship the goddess at great cost. In the southern kingdom, Queen Maacah was dethroned by her son Asa for the crime of worshiping Asherah (1 Kings 15:13). In the northern kingdom, Queen Jezebel, the foreign-born wife of Ahab, was cruelly murdered for following the religion of her parents, the high priestess and priest of Ashtoreth and Baal in the Canaanite city of Sidon (2 Kings 9:33). Queen Athaliah, Jezebel's daughter and the only woman to rule Judah alone, reestablished the ancient religion until Hosea "put an end to all her rejoicing, her feasts, her new moon, her sabbaths, and all her solemn festivals" (Hos. 2:11).

Long after the fall of Israel in 722 B.C.E. and Judah in 587 B.C.E., polytheistic worship continued. Women in Ezekial's day wept ritualistically for Tammuz, the consort of the Babylonian goddess Ishtar (Ezek. 8:14); women of Jeremiah's era vowed openly to revere the Queen of Heaven by burning incense and making "cakes to worship her" (Jer. 44:15–19). By contrast, the religion of Yahweh excluded women from meaningful religious rituals: worship within the temple, the formation of the minyan, and reading the Torah in public.

During the Hebrew exile to Babylon in 597 B.C.E. and after the return to Jerusalem in 538 B.C.E. writings about Hebrew women became increasingly misogynistic. Hosea compared the "whoring" of his wife Gomer to the sinfulness of Israel, thus embedding negative sexual metaphors into religious thought. Prophets such as Ezekiel, Zechariah, and Ezra thought women impure, wicked, and subordinate: "From a woman sin had its beginning and because of her we all die" (Eccles. 25:24).

Although the Hebrew Bible chronicles the subordination of women within a progressively restrictive culture, biblical texts attest to a number of exceptional women. Miriam dared to reproach Moses for his exclusive claim to divine revelation. Deborah judged Israel and led in battle. Huldah, a prophet, authenticated the scroll found during the reign of Josiah. Ruth acted independently in electing to follow another woman, Naomi. Rahab saved herself and her family from death through clever strategy. Delilah and Jael successfully trapped their enemy. Despite restrictions, women found ways to resist, to bond with each other, to practice their religion, and to live meaningful lives.

Nonetheless, the majority of Hebrew women lived servile, submissive lives, dominated by a legal system that treated them as property. Rooted in the Near East and Mediterranean worlds of the fourth, third, and second millennia B.C.E., female subordination found expression in the restrictions placed on ancient Hebrew women, restrictions that became codified in the Hebrew Bible of the Jewish religion and the Greek Bible of the Christian religion.

References. Rachel Biale, *Women and Jewish Law* (New York, 1984); John Day, "Asherah in the Hebrew Bible and Northwest Semitic Literature," *Journal of Biblical Literature* 3 (1986): 385–408; Phyllis Trible, "Women in the Old Testament," in K. A. Crim (ed.), *The Interpreter's Bible: Supplementary Volume* (Nashville, Tenn., 1976), 963–966.

CHRISTINA L. BAKER

HELLENISTIC QUEENS. The period from the death of Alexander the Great (323 B.C.E.) until the Roman annexation of Egypt (30 B.C.E.), called the Hellenistic Age by historians, saw for the first time in the Greek world a number of women prominent in the public arena, a place hitherto reserved for men. These women and their activities are known from inscriptions, their faces appeared on coins, they were lauded in court poetry, and, though many contemporary or later writers deprecated their power and deplored their morals, they were often subjects of historical analysis.

The political shift from the decentralized Greek city-states in which power was typically shared by a large number of males to a hereditary monarchy in Macedon, Egypt, and Syria inevitably increased the importance of women who, because they were related to these monarchs, could be used to further political alliance by means of marriage. Such dynastic marriages increased the ability of women so placed to exert real political influence on their fathers, husbands, brothers, and sons as well as on daughters, who would, in turn, enter into politically desirable marriages. During this 300-year period the power of these women seems to have increased significantly. For example, Cleopatra VII, the last queen of Egypt, ruled independent of her male relations, and, in spite of the "bad press" she received from male writers such as Horace and William Shakespeare, can be seen from contemporary evidence to have been an astute and capable ruler.

It is significant that the two earliest Macedonian queens whose attempts to attain political autonomy have been recorded by historians, Olympias, the wife of Philip II of Macedon and the mother of Alexander, and Eurydice II, the granddaughter of Philip II, were in descent from the region of modern Albania and Yugoslavia, where traditionally women were accustomed to appearing in public and to participating in political and even military affairs. Such behaviors reinforced Macedonian custom in which women associated publicly with men, even to the extent that they sometimes accompanied them on the battlefield. Olympias and Eurydice II both desired to wield power in Macedon after the death of Alexander and employed various of Alexander's successors in their plans. While Eurydice II, who was married to Alexander's younger brother, Philip Arrhidaeus, was successful for a time, she was ultimately murdered by Olympias, who was murdered, in turn, by assassins. The recent find of a royal tomb in Macedon, which contains the body of a man, thought by some scholars to be Philip II, as well as a woman who seems to have been provided with military accoutrements, reinforces the impression of the high status and importance of these women.

Subsequent Macedonian queens are less well known; however, daughters of Macedonian nobles who were married into the royal houses of the Seleucids in Syria and the Ptolemies in Egypt made a significant impact. Two such Macedonian women, Berenice I and another also named Eurydice, were married to Ptolemy I of Egypt; the former, the mother of Ptolemy II, was reputed to have had considerable influence on him. Ptolemaic queens were distinguished at all periods for strength of character and intellect. The most famous was Cleopatra VII. She is known to have spoken seven languages and was the first Ptolemy of either sex to have learned Egyptian. She was a capable politician who, by entering into marriages with first Caesar and then Antony, effectively guaranteed the independence of Egypt from Roman rule during her lifetime and, had her son survived to adulthood, after her death. Her death confirms her intelligence and courage; she chose to die by her own hand using the bite of an asp, the symbol of Egyptian royal power, in order to deprive her Roman enemy Octavian of the chance to parade her in chains as a royal captive. She bequeathed Egypt at her death to Rome, an act that effectively forestalled further dynastic bloodshed.

The impact of these royal women is clearly seen in Egypt, where a large number of both public and private documents survive. Their names appear in official dating formulas, and cults and festivals in their honor were widespread. Hellenistic poets celebrate them equally with their spouses. Through their example, the status at least of upper-class women was substantially improved.

References. Grace Harriet Macurdy, *Hellenistic Queens: A Study of Woman-power in Macedonia, Seleucid Syria and Ptolemaic Egypt* (Baltimore, 1932, repr. Chicago, 1985); Sarah Pomeroy, *Women in Hellenistic Egypt: From Alexander to Cleopatra* (New York, 1984, rep. 1990).

SUSAN A. STEPHENS

HEPATITIS B (HBV) is a liver inflammation caused by the virus hepatitis B (HBV). HBV is transmitted in the same manner as HIV but is much more communicable. Hepatitis often causes no symptoms but may result in fatigue, headache, fever, nausea, vomiting, abdominal tenderness, and yellowing of the skin (most visible in lighter-skinned women) and whites of the eyes. The condition can remain without progression or can result in debility and even death.

A very effective vaccine is available to prevent hepatitis B and is especially recommended for health care workers (90 percent of whom are women). HBV has become so widespread that all children should be immunized against HBV during infancy. The series of three immunizations is expensive, but public health departments in many areas of the United States make it available to children.

Hepatitis is spread through contact with blood and, to a lesser extent, through contact with other body fluids, such as saliva, semen, and vaginal secretions. Therefore, HBV is easily transmissible when unclean needles are shared, when a health worker sustains a needlestick injury, or during sexual contact. Anal sexual interactions are particularly high-risk for contracting HBV.

New expensive drugs are being used to treat HBV, but prevention through vaccination and use of protective devices such as gloves and condoms (male and female) is essential.

Additional types of hepatitis continue to be identified. Hepatitis C has been found to be transmitted in a similar manner to HBV. Persons being treated with multiple drugs for HIV disease do very well in reducing the virus in their blood (and therefore improving their total health) unless they also show evidence of infection with hepatitis C. Hepatitis C seems to be a predictor of poor response to HIV treatment.

ELAINE WHEELER

HERPES GENITALIS is a sexually transmitted disease caused by a virus from the same family of viruses as chickenpox. Herpes simplex 1 causes cold sores or fever blisters, usually on the mouth. Herpes simplex 2 is characterized by red bumps, usually on the genitals, which become fluid-filled blisters. Herpes simplex 1 and 2 can occur at other body locations, depending on sexual practices. The lesions break open and eventually disappear without treatment. Twenty-five percent to 30 percent of those affected experience only one episode; the remainder, however, have recurrent episodes.

Whether a person experiences painful sores or not, once a herpes virus is in the body, it continues to exist in the nervous system. Primary infections are treated with an antiviral drug, acyclovir, which is of minimal effectiveness in recurrent infections.

In women the sores and blisters often occur in the vagina and on the cervix, where they may not be noticed, making it difficult to get timely treatment. Sores can also appear around the urethra, the clitoris, the perineum, or the anus.

Infants born vaginally to women experiencing a first infection of herpes may develop a mild, localized infection, but they can also develop a systemic infection that, in 90 percent of cases, results in neurological damage or death of the infant. The health of the infant can be preserved by cesarean birth in those mothers who have a primary infection.

Likelihood of transmission of the virus between sexual partners is greatest when the blister (vesicle) breaks open, shedding virus in the fluid. However, the virus may be present and communicable when vesicles are not evident. Use of the male or female condom is recommended when having sexual contact with others. A latex barrier should be used whenever a sore is present.

Susceptibility to the herpes viruses is associated with increased risk of cervical cancer; the mechanism and relationship are not known. Women with herpes genitalis should have Pap smears every six months to detect early cervical changes. People with HIV disease also tend to be more susceptible to herpes viruses. Herpes genitalis in women with HIV disease may be more persistent, harder to treat, and more severe. HIV testing should be recommended for women who have persistent herpes infection.

References. Abram Benenson (ed.), *Control of Communicable Diseases Manual* (Washington, D.C., 1995); Boston Women's Health Collective, *The New Our Bodies, Ourselves* (Boston, 1992); Linda Villarosa, *Body and Soul: The Black Women's Guide to Physical Health and Emotional Well Being* (New York, 1994).

ELAINE WHEELER

HETEROSEXUALITY is a sexual orientation* that manifests itself in preference for sexual partners of the opposite sex. It is considered the "norm" by Western society in general, and in most areas open deviation from that norm may be met with legal discrimination.*

HINDU GODDESSES. The concept of the female in Hinduism presents an important duality: on one hand, the goddess is fertile and benevolent, the bestower; on the other, she is aggressive and malevolent, the destroyer. A popular characterization of the goddess in all her manifestations is: "In times of prosperity she is indeed Lakshmi, who bestows prosperity in the homes of men; and in times of misfortune, she herself becomes the goddess of misfortune and brings about ruin."

Two facets of femaleness relate to this duality of the Hindu goddess. The female is, first of all, *shakti* (energy/power), the energizing principle of the universe. The Hindu notion of divinity rests upon that of *shakti*: greater power distinguishes deities from humans. Moreover, *shakti* is female. All creation and all power in the Hindu world are based on femaleness: there would be no being without the female principle, without energy and power. Femaleness is also *prakriti*, nature. Nature is the active female counterpart of the cosmic person, *purusa*, the inactive or male aspect. Whereas *prakriti* represents the undifferentiated matter of nature, *purusa* provides the spirit, the structured code. The union of spirit and matter (code and noncode, inactive and active) leads to the creation of the world in all its differentiated life forms. In female beings, *shakti/prakriti* or energy/nature dominate. This "natural energy" is, however, dangerous and accounts for the goddess as the malevolent, aggressive destroyer. When femaleness is controlled by men, the goddess is benevolent. The benevolent goddesses in the Hindu pantheon are properly married and have transferred control of their sexuality (power/nature) to their husbands.

The goddess Sita, wife of the hero/god Rama, whose story is told in the great epic *Ramayana*, is the Hindu epitome of the proper wife. She exemplifies proper wifely behavior: obediently and devotedly following her husband into forest exile for 12 years. After being kidnapped by the evil

Ravana, whom Rama finally destroys, she must prove her wifely virtue by placing herself on a lighted pyre, where she remains unscathed while the gods shower flowers upon her from heaven. Even today women who commit *sati* (burning themselves on their husbands' funeral pyres) are acclaimed as goddesses due to the internal truth-force, *sat*, that such an act embodies. (See SATI [SUTTEE].)

Yet the goddess as mother is primarily worshiped. Mothers and mother goddesses clearly represent the dual character of Hindu females. They can give and take away (whether food, love, or prosperity) from children or devotees. Moreover, mothers and mother goddesses are in control of their own sexuality; wives are not. Mothers are thought to control others (children and devotees) rather than being controlled by others (husbands).

Worship of female deities is known throughout Indian prehistory. Terracotta figurines of goddesses found in the Indus Valley date as early as 3000 B.C. Goddess worship became a significant cult in Hinduism by the eleventh century A.D. It is especially strong in the eastern and southern portions of India, those areas least influenced by the Vedic religion of the Aryan tribals who moved into, and eventually took over, northern India. The goddess of modern-day Hinduism takes many forms. As Sarawsati, she is the symbol of learning and culture. As Lakshmi, she brings good fortune, wealth, and prosperity. When she is Kali or Durga, she is both feared and respected, for she is capable of great vengeance against those who anger her. As Sitala, the goddess can cause or cure disease, particularly smallpox, chickenpox, and cholera. Most Indian villages have a *gramdevi*, a goddess of the village, who protects the village community against enemies and natural disasters.

The ideology of the goddess carries over into modern life. For example, Indira Gandhi, the former prime minister of India, was often seen as the goddess, sometimes benevolent, as at the end of the war with Pakistan for Bangladeshi liberation in 1971, and at other times malevolent, as when she sent the army into the Golden Temple of the Sikha in 1984. This ideology of the potentially powerful female has important implication for modern India for it provides validation for new roles for Indian women.

Thus, the Hindu goddess does present a contradictory duality. As the texts state: "The fearful goddess [Candika], devoted to her devotees, reduces to ashes those who do not worship her and destroys their merits" (*Devi Mahatmya*) and "For those who seek pleasure or those who seek liberation, the worship of the all-powerful Goddess is essential. She is the knowledge of the Immensity: she is the mother of the universe, pervading the whole world" (*Sri Bhagavati Tattva*).

References. Rita Gross and Nancy Falk (eds.), *Unspoken Worlds: The Religious Lives of Non-Western Women* (New York, 1980); Susan S. Wadley, "Women and the Hindu Tradition," *Signs* 3 (1977): 113–125.

SUSAN S. WADLEY

HINDUISM initially recognized women's independent religious role but then withdrew recognition gradually. It is therefore more appropriate to speak of women *under*, instead of *in*, Hinduism, as their socioeconomic status was ultimately decided by it. After sporadic and contradictory notices in the ancient texts, the topic came into focus around the fifth century B.C. Two trends were now clearly noticeable: one with more and the other with fewer options for women.

Women's education was institutionalized in the first trend. There are mentions of girl students and their hostels, a special term for women remaining unmarried for lifelong studies, women teachers of different grades, and renowned philosophers. Brahmana women studying the specialized branches of grammar and philosophy developed by famous teachers like Āpiśali and Kāśakṛtsna came to be āpiśalā and kāśakṛtsnā brahmani, that is, the students of these two teachers. Evidently, women had access to, and were established in, higher education.

Marriage for women, according to the first trend, was not obligatory: a special term indicated a maiden who was growing old in her father's house. Girls often selected their own husbands, or both parents arranged their marriage, not the father alone. Secular marriage was current, and separation and divorce were permitted under certain conditions. Second marriage, either levirate or outside the family, was not uncommon. A widow with or without children remarried or lived independently. The existence of post-puberty marriage and remarriage of women is indicated by the mention of at least three categories of sons; namely, the son of an unmarried mother, the son of a woman married in pregnancy, and the son of a remarried woman. There were also instances of polyandrous marriage and of women following matriarchal laws. There were astute women politicians, and queens are mentioned who took keen interest in the affairs of their kingdom and, if necessary, led armies on the battlefield. A woman had absolute and inalienable right over her property. Virtues like truthfulness, intelligence, kindness, courage, and so forth were considered desirable as intrinsic qualities in women.

During this period women had independent religious roles, as indicated by two sacrifices performed by women alone. One was connected with harvest, and the other one with fertility among cattle. Some mythological women performed sacrifices for their sons' welfare and husbands' victory in war. In the next stage sacrifices were performed *jointly* by husband and wife. One synonymous word for wife etymologically means one participating in sacrifices with her husband.

The second trend was almost opposite to the first. In place of ideal womanhood, it upheld *ideal wifehood*. Prepuberty marriage, which assured virginity of girls but precluded their education, was advocated. Domestic duties were glorified to the exclusion of all outside interests. Lack of women's education was deemed compensated for by living with, and serving, the husband as if he were a god. Marriage was a sacrament, and the marital tie indissoluble. Consequently, there was no divorce or remarriage for women. Women had only limited rights over their own property, and a widow had a life interest in her husband's property provided she did not remarry. Chastity of women was emphasized beyond all proportions. Male guardianship was advocated: father, brother, husband, or sons (even if minor) looked after a woman, because she was considered unfit for independence. The highest honor went to a devoted and subservient wife; the worst fate, that of being devoured by a dog, awaited a disobedient wife.

Now she lost her independent role in religion as well. As initiation ceremony and education were denied to women, they were unfit for any independent religious role. Now women could only *assist*, not participate with, their husbands during sacrifices and only if of the same caste.

The coexistence of these two trends indicates a society that was accommodating different ethnic groups with distinct cultures. Historically, economic developments, predominantly agricultural in character, brought these groups together, with the landed-interest groups wielding political and economic power in society. For religious sanctions, they were supported by the brahmanas, who were at the apex of the emerging social structure. For retention and extension of their power, they were concerned with the concentration of property in their patrilineal-patrilocal families. Therefore, a legitimate son became supremely important, as periodic offerings to departed ancestors devolved on him; this was a precondition to the inheritance of property. The second trend was ideally suited to this purpose. However, it required generating consensus at the expense of the first trend.

The task was neither smooth nor easy. From early times the virtues and the vices of women had been discussed. The pro-woman argument was that men were actually more prone to the vices ascribed to women, such as faithlessness, adultery, and fickle-mindedness. The antiwoman group, however, won the day, as the objective conditions were in its favor. The status of women was codified around the second or first century B.C., and the image of the "ideal women" was projected. The image fit in with the second trend and was useful to the dominant group. The ideal-typical women, chosen from the Hindu tradition, are Sita, Savitri, and Sati (or Parvati).

This eternal triumvirate received not only scriptural sanctions but also the recommendations of the foremost political leader Mohandas Gandhi and the social and religious reformer Vivekananda of modern times. India is proudly proclaimed as "the Land of Sita-Savitri," thus pinpointing the role of Hindu women.

Sita was the queen and heroine of the epic *Ramayana*, which supposedly has a historical basis. Unjustly insulted and with her chastity often doubted by her husband, Sita ultimately sought refuge in mother earth, from whence she had sprung. With her unquestioned loyalty to husband and infinite capacity to bear suffering, Sita's life is a saga of misfortune. If sorrow is an index to greatness, then Sita is the greatest Hindu woman. Savitri was a mythological character who brought her dead husband back to life by her steadfastness and stratagem. She is the most venerated ideal, as a part of heaven is named after her. A difficult religious ritual is dedicated to her, and women are blessed to be like her. Sati is a goddess who gave up her life because she refused to listen to the vilification of her husband. Fifty-one places where parts of her body fell when her devoted husband traveled the earth with her corpse became centers of pilgrimage. In her next life, the couple became husband and wife again.

These three ideal women demonstrate, inter alia, loyalty to husband, the tremendous power of chastity, and the eternity of the marital tie. Once married, a woman belongs to the same man forever.

In postindependence India, laws relating to Hindu women have changed considerably. The Widow Remarriage Act is more than 100 years old, but the right to divorce and the inheritance of property by daughters became legal only recently. All these measures, however, mainly benefit elite women. Moreover, since the sacred concept of marriage and inheritance remains unchanged, the impact of legal enactment is minimal. Thus, in civil marriage, god is invoked, and ancestor worship is still relevant for the vast majority.

References. Swami Nadhavananda and Ramesh Chandra Najumdar (eds.), *Great Women of India* (Almora, 1953); Prabhati Mukherjee, "The Image of Women in Hinduism," *Women's Studies International Forum* 6 (1983): 375–381; R. Shamasastry, *Kautilya's Arthaśāstra* (Mysore, India, 1951).

PRABHATI MUKHERJEE

HIV DISEASE is the collective term for states of health and illness following infection with the human immunodeficiency virus (HIV). Late stages of illness from opportunistic diseases (infections and cancers that occur due to the body's weakened defense system from the HIV virus) are called acquired immunodeficiency syndrome (AIDS).

HIV disease was first identified as a syndrome in 1981, appearing soon after exposure as a mononucleosis-like illness, self-limiting. Months or more likely years (2, 5, or 10) later, a generalized illness appears that can include swollen lymph nodes, fatigue, fever, loss of appetite, weight loss, diarrhea, and, in women, recurrent, persistent vaginal yeast (candida) infections.

HIV disease is transmitted from person to person through the bloodstream by direct or indirect contact with another person's blood. Women at great risk of HIV disease are those who use intravenous (IV) drugs and share needles. Women who have sexual intercourse with men who are needle users, especially "dirty" (shared) needles, are at great risk. Also women who have penile–vaginal or penile–anal sex with men without benefit of a barrier such as a condom (male or female) are at risk, as are women who have been the recipients of blood products or donor semen that has not been certified free of HIV virus antibodies. Women make up 90 percent of health care workers with an occupational risk of exposure to the HIV virus.

Women are more likely to contract HIV disease from men than men are from women, and women are at much greater risk of exposure to the virus when they have genital sex with men than when women have sex with women.

HIV disease affects women differentially and is increasing in women faster than in men. Women constituted only 7 percent of AIDS cases in 1985, but the percentage jumped to 18 percent in 1994. The same year AIDS became the leading cause of death for black women and the third leading cause of death in all women aged 25–44 years.

Women diagnosed with AIDS (defined as the presence of infections that occur due to the body's weakened defense system from HIV virus) are more likely to suffer multiple infections and to die sooner than men diagnosed with AIDS. Women with AIDS are more likely to be black or Hispanic (75 percent of AIDS cases occur in adolescent and adult women). Attempts to explain these findings have pointed to women's relatively lower income and limited access to health care and to intravenous drug use in communities of color.

Pregnant women with HIV disease transmit the virus to the child in 15–30 percent of births. An important study in 1994 found that mothers who are treated with AZT, an antiviral drug, reduce the rate of transmission by two-thirds. It is important that pregnant women know their HIV status so that therapy can be initiated as soon as possible and, if needed, maintained through the birthing process.

Research is currently focused on identifying factors affecting persons with HIV disease who live a long time without developing opportunistic infections (AIDS).

Treatment for persons with HIV disease is expanding rapidly to include new drug therapies. Three or more drugs may be combined and are called "drug cocktails." These combinations make it possible to reduce the amount of virus in the body to undetectable levels in some persons. Whether this means the person will maintain this level of health long-term remains to be learned. Drug therapy is expensive, however, and the issue of making treatment available to all affected persons in the United States has not been successfully addressed. A strategy for worldwide treatment is needed before the illness can be adequately controlled.

Women concerned about possible exposure to the HIV virus can be tested at confidential, low-cost testing sites available in many areas. (Contact the local health department.) Home testing through the mail has also become available. Because of the hysteria surrounding AIDS and because the groups affected are among the most socially oppressed groups in our society, women should be careful to seek testing only where it is anonymous and voluntary, accompanied with personal counseling and education. Notification of test results should be undocumented to avoid possible cancellation of health or life insurance, loss of employment, or other discriminatory actions.

"Safer sex" guidelines have become widely publicized wherever people will tolerate disclosure or frank talk about sexual behavior. Most important is the admonition that women avoid sharing needles if they use intravenous (IV) drugs and that women having sex with men who are not known to be safe from infection should require condom use (male or female). The challenge is to preserve sexual pleasure while minimizing one's risk of HIV disease and other sexually transmitted diseases.

Familial and social oppression has recently been identified as a risk factor putting women, especially women of color, at risk of HIV, hepatitis, and other sexually transmitted illnesses. Until women are heard, and our wishes are respected in relationships, and until sexual assault and abuse can be eradicated, these social factors will continue to put women at biological risk.

ELAINE WHEELER

HOLOCAUST is the murder of 6 million Jews in Adolf Hitler's "Final Solution of the Jewish problem." With the outbreak of World War II and throughout the various phases of the Holocaust, Jewish women lost all vestiges of their traditional preferred status relative to Jewish men. (See ANTI-SEMITISM.)

Einsatzgruppen are mobile killing units that functioned with the aid of local collaborators to massacre hundreds of thousands of Jews, men and women alike, in eastern Poland, the Baltic states, and a number of Russian republics. Though the women were often separated from the men on their final journey, their treatment was the same: they were ordered to undress, led in groups of 10 to the edge of a trench, and shot by firing squads of Germans with the assistance of local collaborators.

In Ejszyszki (currently part of Lithuania) in September 1941, prior to their being killed, young, pretty, unmarried women, whose names were supplied by local Poles, were called out, led to nearby bushes, and raped by German soldiers. In Libau (Liepaja), Latvia, on December 15 and 17, 1941, mothers were ordered to hold their babies against their shoulders to make them easier targets and were then murdered themselves.

Ghettos. The official leaders of the ghettos and the members of the *Judenrate* (Jewish Councils), generally German appointees, were almost all men, but records do reveal the occasional woman in an official ghetto position. For example, in Ghetto Baranovicze (today Belorussia), Mrs. Ninove was the assistant to the *Judenrat* chairman, Yehoshua Isikson. In Ghetto

Pruzhany (Polish Pruzana, today Belorussia), Dr. Olia Goldfein headed the ghetto sanitary department.

Many women, although not officially part of the *Judenrat*, were vital members of the ghetto community. Teaching in the various legal and clandestine educational systems; organizing cultural activities; and working with youth groups and in hospitals, soup kitchens, workshops, and factories, they participated actively in all aspects of ghetto existence and played an important part in the constant struggle for survival.

Certain problems that ghetto dwellers faced were specific to women: birth control, pregnancy, abortion, and the birth and nursing of babies by mothers who existed on substarvation diets insufficient for one, much less two, hungry mouths. For religious women, the German prohibition against *Mikveh* baths (the ritual purification bath that was to follow menstruation and childbirth) was another hardship. Mothers of young children had to spend virtually all their time caring for, and often hiding, their children, who were subject to seizure during the notorious children's *Aktions* (roundups) as well as the regular *Aktions* and whose presence, if discovered, could endanger the lives of other members of the family. To keep the youngsters quiet during these raids, mothers would spend large sums of money on poppyseeds and other narcosis-inducing substances, often going without food themselves.

Women did hard physical labor. In Ghetto Kovno they joined special women's workforces that slaved at building the nearby airport and at other physically demanding jobs. Such labor provided women with the chance to obtain food for their families or, if single, for themselves. Single women in Ghetto Kovno had an even smaller chance of survival than other women and searched desperately for male protectors. Many formed fictitious unions that sometimes became lifelong marriages.

Being part of a family was also dangerous, however. The great sense of responsibility family members felt for each other spelled doom for many, since it could involve great personal sacrifice and often prevented young people from abandoning their families and trying to escape. Fear of German retaliation against their families also delayed Jewish armed resistance. Only when their families were decimated, and the final destination of the Jews became clear, did armed resistance become a reality. (See HOLOCAUST, Resistance.)

Though their lives were more precarious than men's in the ghetto, women and girls who managed to escape the ghetto had a better chance of survival than men did because there was no telltale sign such as circumcision to set them apart from the rest of the population. Some Jewish boys living on the Aryan side were disguised as girls so that they would not be betrayed by their circumcision.

Concentration Camps. The first concentration camp for women was opened on May 15, 1933, at Ravensbrück, north of Berlin. Ravensbrück's administrative structure was similar to that of other camps: The camp commandant, guards, and administrative staff were males. They were assisted by 150 female supervisors, SS *Aufseherinen*. About 3,500 SS women trained as supervisors at Ravensbrück before being sent to other camps.

At Auschwitz, the largest camp in the concentration camp universe and the one that served as a processing center for many of the others, the women's section (*Frauenabteilung*) was established in 1942. The first group to be imprisoned there consisted of 999 German women from Ravensbrück and an equal number of Jewish women from Poprad, Slovakia. "Old-timers" from this group were among the cruelest and most hated of Auschwitz's *Stubhovas* and *Blokhovas* (female inmates who served as barracks supervisors).

In the vast kingdom of the camps, the women who survived the initial selections at Auschwitz and elsewhere were mainly young women, without children, in their late teens and early 20s. Upon arrival at Auschwitz, mothers with young children were sent to the left, to the gas chambers. "Older" women (including those in their 30s and 40s) and pregnant women (who were rarely able to pass the nude selections) were also sent to the left. Dr. Gisela Perl, an inmate doctor, terminated the pregnancies of many of those who did pass in order to save their lives. Not surprisingly, when liberation finally came, male survivors were found to outnumber the women and to be older as well.

A rare exception to the policy of death for pregnant women occurred in one of the Kaufering camps where, in December 1944, apparently on a whim, the Germans established a *Schwanger Kommando* (pregnancy unit). During the winter of 1945, despite all the usual horrors of camp life, seven women managed to give birth to healthy babies there.

Pregnancy was not the only gender-specific problem faced by women in the camps. Brutal medical experiments, including sterilization, were performed on them by doctors like Professor Carl Clauber, who initiated such experiments in Ravensbrück and later continued them in the notorious Block no. 10 in Auschwitz. Women were also forced to join camp brothels for the entertainment of German troops and the camp elite. There was even an all-woman orchestra at Auschwitz under the direction of Alma Rose, Gustave Mahler's niece. As described by Fania Fenelon, they played at selections, executions, and as accompaniment to those on their way to the gas chamber.

At the camp at Salaspils, Latvia, a stone monument in the form of a colossal female figure is now the camp's symbol, in honor of the young girls so brutally violated by the Germans and their collaborators.

Despite the horrendous conditions—death, disease, starvation, slavery, and torture—inmates supported each other and formed "camp sister" relationships that sometimes endured beyond the camps as well. Often life itself depended on such friendships.

Some women were able to maintain their faith, improvising prayers, lighting "candles" on the eve of holidays, fasting on Yom Kippur, and abstaining from eating bread on Passover, despite their ceaseless hunger.

Education also remained a concern for many. In Bergen Belsen, where families and individuals with foreign passports were kept in a separate camp for eventual exchange for Germans stranded in Allied territory, mothers attempted to educate their children. Bronia Koszicki, for example, paid with her meager bread rations for her sons' private lessons.

Women sang, told stories, and even gave theatrical performances in order to overcome the brutal realities of ghetto and camp life. Art was produced under impossible conditions, sometimes with stolen materials and often at the risk of the artist's life. Such works were later to serve as eyewitness accounts of every phase of ghetto and camp life.

Helga Weissova-Hoskova was deported as a teenager to Terezin. Her drawings, which she managed to bring with her after liberation, illustrate daily life in Terezin. Though virtually unknown, Esther Luria's drawings provide a moving account of life in Ghetto Kovno. The drawings of Violette Rougier (née Lecoq), a non-Jew who was sent to Ravensbrück for her participation in the French Resistance, graphically depict the brutal conditions in that camp and help the viewer to comprehend why fewer than one-third of the 132,000 women sent there survived. (See FRENCH RESISTANCE.) Mme. Rougier's drawings are powerful, first-rate historical documents that were used as evidence in the Hamburg war trials.

What Mme. Rougier did in her drawings another French Resistance fighter, Charlotte Delbo, achieved in the plays she wrote based on notes she took while in Auschwitz and Ravensbrück. One of these plays, *Who Will Carry the Word*, has been translated into English and has an all-woman cast.

Holocaust Historiography. The portrayal of women in the Holocaust is based on male-oriented records written mostly by men. Israeli historiography does portray women as equal comrades among the groups who used physical resistance, but it fails to examine issues and aspects unique to women. The extreme vulnerability of Jewish women—not just in the camps, ghettos, and hiding places, where most were confined but even in the partisan bases, where the rape and sexual abuse of young girls and women were common, is nowhere recorded in the detail that the subject warrants.

There are some very fine diaries written by Jewish girls, like the teenaged Anne Frank, Gertrude Schneider, Sarah Fishkin, and Eva Heyman, and by Jewish women, such as Ruth Leimarson-Engelstern, Tova Draenger, and Naomi Schatz-Weinkranz. They are essentially private in nature, telling of the inner lives and family experiences of their writers.

Nazi women are underrepresented in the literature of the Holocaust, for only minor female offenders appeared in the postwar trials. In the Nuremberg trials there was only one female defendant, a former doctor at Auschwitz. Ilse Koch (known as the Bitch of Buchenwald) was a study in human barbarism who committed such atrocities as making lampshades from human skin. Yet it required several trials before she was convicted, for her legal status was merely that of the wife of Karl Otto Koch, the commandant of Buchenwald.

Properly used, oral history could greatly enhance Holocaust historiography in general and the portrayal of women in particular. However, oral history has been shunned by most establishment Holocaust historians, and by now, the relatively small number of mature women who survived the Holocaust has all but died out. Their memories are now beyond retrieval, taking with them our ability to better understand the Holocaust through the eyes of those who represented 50 percent of its victims.

References. *Amit Woman*, March–April 1989, New York (whole issue); Yaffa Eliach, *Hasidic Tales of the Holocaust* (New York, 1982); Fania Fenelon, *Playing for Time* (New York, 1979); G. Tillion, *Ravensbruck* (Paris, 1988); Z. Lubetkin, *In Days of Destruction and Revolt* (Naharia, Israel, 1980).

                                                                    YAFFA ELIACH

HOLOCAUST. Resistance to the enslavement and death of Jews in Nazi Germany's "Final Solution" was carried out by women and men.

Women among the Righteous Gentiles. Many of the righteous non-Jews who fought to save the lives of Jews in Nazi-occupied Europe were women. In a society where large segments of the population collaborated with the Nazis or watched in silence, they chose to assume responsibility for being their brothers' and sisters' keepers. A few are mentioned here as representative of these outstanding women, who came from a wide range of countries, religious denominations, social strata, educational backgrounds, political ideologies, and age groups. All that they had in common was the commitment to save human lives, even in the face of danger to their own.

In Lithuania, Sofia Binkiene (1902–1984) rescued Jews of the Kovno ghetto. Anna Borkowska (d. 1988) was the mother superior of a small cloister of Dominican sisters near Vilna. For a brief period of time she sheltered 17 of Vilna's Jewish Resistance fighters in her convent. She smuggled the first four grenades into the ghetto for the resistance and taught Abba Kovner how to use them. She was arrested in 1943, and the convent was closed.

Elizabeth Abbey (1882–1951?) was a German Quaker who taught history at the Luisen girls' school until she was dismissed in 1933 for anti-Nazi views. She later provided Jews in Berlin with false identity papers and helped them cross the border to Switzerland.

Mrs. Bikeviczowa was an illiterate Catholic peasant woman who lived in the small village of Libednik, Poland. For the crime of attempting to save Jews, she was betrayed by her neighbors and murdered (along with the Jews) by members of the *Armia Krajowa*, among them her own son.

Matylda Getter (d. 1968) was mother superior of the Warsaw branch of the Order of the Franciscan Sisters of the Family of Mary. She sheltered scores of Jewish children fleeing the Warsaw ghetto and returned them to their relatives after the war.

Hanna Van Der Root was a Dutch rescuer of Jewish children. Took Heroma was another Dutch rescuer, whose strong sense of moral obligation led her to risk her own safety and that of her husband by hiding Jews in their home in Dordrecht. After the war Took Heroma became involved in the political education of women and other social issues and was eventually elected to the Dutch parliament, where she served for 17 years.

Jewish Women Who Organized Rescue Attempts. Women were members of the various public committees that attempted to rescue Jews from Europe. One of these Jewish leaders was Gisi Fleischmann (1897–1944), a Zionist activist in Slovakia, one of the founders of the Working Group, which attempted to rescue Slovakian Jewry. In March 1942, the Working Group tried to stop deportations by bribing Adolf Eichmann's representative in Slovakia. Lack of funds made this and other rescue attempts very difficult. On September 28, 1944, Fleischmann was arrested, and in October she was deported to Auschwitz, where she was gassed upon arrival. Recha Sternbuch of Switzerland was another of the women who aided rescue attempts, working on behalf of Orthodox Jews.

Jewish Women as Partisans and Members of the Resistance. Not being circumcised, female Jewish freedom fighters could move more freely on both sides of the ghetto wall than their male comrades and were often used as couriers. They held significant positions in the partisan movement and were among the organizers of many major uprisings. A significant number of rank-and-file female partisans and Resistance fighters were in combat fighting units as well as supporting ones. There were also older women, mothers, and children living in the partisan family camps who were noncombatants protected by the partisans.

Haika Grossman (b. 1919), a member of the Bialystok ghetto's antifascist cell, was also an organizer for the underground. Posing as a Polish woman, she traveled on many missions to other ghettos and, along with five other women also posing as Poles, brought crucial assistance to fellow partisans in cities and forests. She participated in the Bialystok ghetto uprising in August 1943.

Zivia Lubetkin (1914–1976) was a member of *Dror* (*Freedom*) of *HeHalutz HaLohem* and a leader in the Jewish underground in Poland. As one of the founders of the Jewish Fighting Organization (ZOB), she was instrumental in determining its character and policy. During the Warsaw ghetto uprising of April 1943, Lubetkin was in the command bunker at 18

Mila Street. She escaped through the sewers and later joined the Polish uprising of August–October 1944.

In Ghetto Vilna, Rozka Korczak (1921–1988) and Vitka Kempner-Kovner were two of the female members of the underground who favored armed resistance. Eventually, they left the ghetto to join the autonomous Jewish partisans in the forest of Rudnicki.

In Berlin, in the clandestine, underground, anti-Nazi *Baum Gruppe*, which was composed mainly of Jews, there were several women: Marianne Baum, the wife of Herbert Baum, and Edith Frankel and Lotte Rotholz, both of whom were arrested and sent to Auschwitz, where they died. In the French underground, German-born Jewish activist Marianne Cohen (1924–1944) saved scores of Jewish children by smuggling them out of occupied France to safety in Switzerland.

One woman who has become a symbol of the courage and moral strength displayed by countless others whose names are lost to us is the poet Hannah Szenes (1921–1944). An émigré to Palestine from Hungary, she enlisted in a special Palestinian Jewish unit of the British army and was parachuted into Nazi-occupied Europe to rescue prisoners of war and organize the Jewish resistance. Captured in Hungary, she was tortured, and her mother's life was threatened, but she refused to translate the radio transmission code used by members of her operation. Szenes was executed by a firing squad.

Resistance in Concentration Camps. As individuals and as members of the Resistance, women played a significant role in several concentration camp uprisings. On October 23, 1943, a young woman who arrived in Auschwitz on a transport from Bergen Belsen grabbed an SS man's pistol and shot two SS officers in the disrobing room adjacent to the gas chamber. She has served as the model for a number of accounts in the literature of defiance. One of the most dramatic escapes from Auschwitz involved the Jewish woman Mala Zimetbaum and her Polish friend Edward Galinski, who were later caught and publicly executed on September 15, 1944. Another instance of female courage in Auschwitz is the uprising on October 7, 1944. Members of the Auschwitz *Sonderkommando* organized an armed uprising with the help of young Jewish women workers at the Union Werke ammunition factory. Under the leadership of Roza Robota, the women smuggled gunpowder into the camp. Several of them were arrested and severely tortured, but they refused to betray the others. On January 6, 1945, a few days before the camp was evacuated, Roza Robota, Ella Garter, Estusia Wajsblum, and Regina Sapirstein were hanged.

References. W. Bartoszewski and Z. Lewin, *Righteous among Nations: How Poles Helped the Jews, 1939–1945* (London, 1969); J. Campion, *In the Lion's Mouth: Gisi Fleischmann and the Jewish Fight for Survival* (Baltimore, 1987); Chaika Grossman, *The Underground Army: Fighters of the Bialystok Ghetto* (New York, 1988); H. D. Leuner, *When Compassion Was a Crime* (London, 1966).

YAFFA ELIACH

HOME ECONOMICS (also DOMESTIC SCIENCE) is a profession devoted to the development and application of scientific rules for home management, consumerism, child development, and nutrition, as well as cooking and sewing.

Formal instruction in the domestic arts began in the early nineteenth century, when private seminaries for girls were anxious to prove that education would enhance, rather than threaten, female domesticity. Catherine Beecher, Lydia Maria Child, and others reinforced that message through domestic self-help books for American housewives. Beecher's *Treatise on Domestic Economy* (1841) argued that homemaking was a demanding profession, requiring skill, efficiency, and precise training.

Domestic education remained in the home or in private schools until land-grant colleges in Iowa, Kansas, and Illinois established home economics programs for women students. They were regarded as practical companions to the agricultural programs for men.

The period 1880–1910 saw growth and self-definition for "home economics." A number of social concerns, coinciding at the turn of the century, made Americans particularly receptive to the claims of home economics advocates. The first was concern that industrialization and urbanization were destroying traditional home life. Alongside that worry was nativist concern that the millions of immigrants pouring into America were insufficiently educated in sanitation, consumer protection, and household management to establish stable, healthy homes. Also, consciousness of the new "germ theory" and a new enthusiasm for science, medicine, and technology meant that Americans sought to preserve the traditional family in a highly sanitized, modernized context. Finally, underlying all of these concerns was a deep anxiety about the place of American women and the effect of education on women's role in society. Many worried that the declining marriage rates and birthrates among educated women and the increasing employment opportunities for women in the cities meant that women were defying the laws of nature in refusing to assume their biologically destined roles as wives and homemakers.

All of these concerns were addressed and appeased by the home economics movement that came to prominence between 1880 and 1910. Ellen Swallow Richards (Massachusetts Institute of Technology), Marion Talbot (University of Chicago), Helen Kinne (Columbia University), and Caroline Hunt and Abby Marlatt (University of Wisconsin) were in the vanguard of the academic forces that joined with the American Household Economics Association and the General Federation of Women's Clubs to promote the synthesis of scientific research and household management for improved health, efficiency, and economy. Leaders of the movement expressed confidence that cities could be civilized, immigrants Americanized, and educated women domesticated with systematic exposure to the principles of home economics. For all its modern, scientific thrust, then, the early home economics movement was quite conservative in its social goals and its attitude toward gender roles.*

The first efforts at national coordination were the Lake Placid Conferences, 1899–1909. The first conference agreed on the name "home economics," in preference to "domestic arts," "domestic science," or even "euthenics." Subsequent conferences dealt with school curricula, teacher training, and community service. In 1909, the conferees decided to affiliate more formally as the American Home Economics Association (AHEA).

In its first 75 years, the membership of the AHEA grew steadily from just over 800 in 1909 to over 9,000 in 1935 to over 50,000 by the early 1980s. Paralleling that growth has been steady growth in home economics education in the United States, from elementary schools to universities. Throughout these years, the American home economics movement has had to deal with two fundamental conflicts over goals and strategies: whether to offer narrow training in specific skills or a broad education in the science and philosophy of home management and whether to train women for the traditional role of wife and mother or for a professional career as a home economist. Attitudes have ebbed and flowed with general currents in American society. In the 1920s and 1930s, for example, collegiate home economics focused on job opportunities for women as home economics teachers, nutritionists, and textile experts. Later, in the 1940s and 1950s, there was greater focus on courses in marriage, family relations, child development, and consumer science on the assumption that students would soon marry and become managers of their households. Since the 1960s, there has been a switch back to preparation for professional jobs as social changes and women's increased desire and need for economic independence increased demand for consumer advocates, child care specialists, nutritionists, and family relations experts.

Contemporary home economics has abandoned its original hostility to feminism* and has sought to adapt its goals to those of modern American women. Though the field is still stigmatized by its historical advocacy of female domesticity, the fact remains that home economics has been an important avenue of economic and professional mobility for many American women.

References. M. N. Carver, *Home Economics as an Academic Discipline* (Tucson, 1979); B. Ehrenreich and D. English, *For Her Own Good: 150 Years of the Experts' Advice to Women* (New York, 1978); H. Pundt, *AHEA: A History of Excellence* (Washington, D.C., 1980); Laura Shapiro, *Perfection Salad* (New York, 1986).

VICTORIA BISSELL BROWN

HOME INDUSTRY. Also known as domestic industry, cottage industry, the putting-out system, and protoindustry, home industry refers to gainful employment at home in the manufacture of articles for the market. Originally, artisans, or craftsworkers, of both sexes typically performed their labor in a home workshop, with the aid of family members, servants, apprentices, and other helpers. Only a small percentage of people who lived in urban centers engaged exclusively in artisanal labor. More commonly, home industry served to supplement agricultural labor and allowed the rural working classes to make productive use of time not allocated to outdoor work. Typically, raw materials were brought to the workers' homes by distributors, or "middlemen," employed by distant manufacturers; and sometime later finished articles were collected, and wages were paid based on piecework. Articles commonly produced in the home included pins, nails, scythes, clogs, chains, furniture, household linen, lace, garments, and various clothing accessories. With the growth of national and international markets during the early modern period (the sixteenth through the eighteenth centuries), opportunities for home industry expanded. Men, women, and children participated; increasingly, such earnings allowed young people to gain economic independence and thereby to marry at earlier ages than before.

By the late eighteenth and early nineteenth centuries, changes in the location and organization of manufacturing and distribution, the introduction of new sources of power, the invention of new tools and machines, and the development of improved transportation systems combined to shift production in some industries (led by textiles) from home to factory. With notable exceptions, such as weaving in parts of Germany, cabinetmaking in France, and cigar rolling in the United States, by the mid-nineteenth century men began to work away from home, and home industry became gender-specific, that is, women's work.* An increasingly refined division of labor followed the breakdown of manufacturing processes into smaller and smaller tasks that took less and less skill. Fewer skilled workers and more "little hands" could be employed, for lower wages. Men employed in workshops and factories often organized against competitors, including female, unskilled, and homeworkers (whose lower overhead and unrestricted hours allowed them to undercut workshop labor prices). Children increasingly fell under compulsory education laws that limited their service as homeworkers. Women working at home, however, continued to provide a major source of labor. Whether bound to home by responsibility for dependent children or for ill or aged relations, by reasons of their own health, or by social norms that required "respectable" married women to remain at home, most working-class and significant numbers of middle-class women still had to make financial contributions to family subsistence. They constituted a ready labor supply for manufacturers in seasonal industries, especially for garment makers in expanding ready-to-wear industries. Homeworkers could be employed, at minimal overhead cost, for long hours in times of press and let go in "dead seasons." Some women, often daughters of artisanal workers, served apprenticeships or worked in shops for years to learn skills that enabled them to earn good wages at home; the artificial-flower makers of Paris constitute one example. By the early twentieth century, however, most homeworkers in garment making, jewelry assembly, and other home industries were women of little skill or training forced to take whatever work they could find.

Isolated from each other, homeworkers rarely attempted to organize for higher wages or better working conditions and continued to labor for less than subsistence wages, often in conditions that shocked social reformers; they dominated the labor force of the "sweatshops" that raised social consciences and led to international conferences and some regulation by legislation (often poorly enforced) in the early twentieth century. "Protective" labor legislation, instituted in many industrial countries between the 1880s and 1930s, usually bypassed homeworkers; indeed, by restricting the employment of women in factories, it often intensified the sexual division of labor whereby highly organized, largely male factory workers improved their wages and working conditions, while unorganized, largely female workers continued to constitute a marginal workforce with minimal benefits. In many urban centers today, including London, Los Angeles, Paris, and Toronto, large numbers of women continue to do homework in the garment and other industries. (See PROTECTIVE LEGISLATION.)

References. Lourdes Beneria, *The Crossroads of Class and Gender: Industrial Homework, Subcontracting, and Household Dynamics in Mexico City* (Chicago, 1987); Eileen Boris, "Regulating Industrial Homework: The Triumph of Sacred Motherhood," *Journal of American History* 71 (1985): 745–763; Eileen Boris, *Home to Work: Motherhood and the Politics of Industrial Homework in the United States* (New York, 1994); Marilyn J. Boxer, "Women in Industrial Homework: The Flowermakers of Paris in the Belle Epoque," *French Historical Studies* 12 (1982): 401–423; E. Hope, M. Kennedy, and A. de Winter, "Homeworkers in North London," in D. L. Baker and S. Allen (eds.), *Dependence and Exploitation in Work and Marriage* (London, 1976), 88–108; J. H. Quataert, "Combining Agrarian and Industrial Livelihood: Rural Households in the Saxon Oberlausitz in the Nineteenth Century," *Journal of Family History* 10 (1985): 145–162; J. W. Scott, "Men and Women in the Parisian Garment Trades: Discussions of Family and Work in the 1830s and 1840s," in P. Thane, G. Crossick, and R. Floud (eds.), *The Power of the Past: Essays for Eric Hobsbawm* (Cambridge, England, 1984), 67–93.

MARILYN J. BOXER

HOMELESSNESS in the 1980s reached its greatest extent since the depression,* and for the first time women and children were visible among the homeless. To the old picture of the homeless white male alcoholic was added the picture of the bag lady, the teenage runaway or throwaway soliciting on the streets of major cities, and the family group eating in a soup kitchen. Another new element was the rising minority population among the homeless.

The number of homeless, who are present in every corner of the country, can only be estimated. The Department of Housing and Urban Development (HUD) in the mid-1990s operated on the basis of 600,000 homeless at any given time. In 1988, around 44 percent of those using shelters were African Americans and 10 percent were Hispanic. About 14 percent of shelter users were single women; 40 percent were members of family groups; and 30 percent were members of one-parent families. Many, probably most, of the one-parent families were headed by women. A 1984 Boston study estimated that 84 percent of the homeless families in that city were female-headed.

The homeless can be classified as the chronically disabled (e.g., mentally ill, chemically addicted), those homeless because of personal crises (e.g., family violence, divorce or desertion, health problems), and those homeless through economic causes (e.g., unemployment, loss of welfare benefits, lack of affordable housing).

Although those suffering personal crises account for 40 percent to 50 percent of the homeless, because their homelessness is usually temporary, their percentage at any given time is small. Perhaps as many as a third, with wide variations across the country, are homeless for economic reasons. The steady decline in unemployment in the 1980s and 1990s from a high of 10.8 percent in 1982 did not bring a proportional decline in homelessness, especially among women. Homeless women are likely to have been victims of child abuse and/or battering as adults. Most have little education and no work skills. Those capable of holding jobs usually lack the skills required for jobs other than low-skill service jobs with wages too meager to pay the rent in most cities where a continuing decline in rental housing for both single and family occupancy has resulted in serious rent inflation. Without a support network, homelessness is almost inevitable. The children are likely to lack food and are probably not attending school. About half have developmental disorders or suffer depression.

The number of women homeless through chemical addiction is growing, but the leading cause of homelessness among single women is mental illness.* From 1955 the number of mental patients in state institutions fell as legal reforms mandated the release of patients whose illness could be controlled by psychotropic drugs and tightened requirements for admission to mental institutions. Unfortunately, very few of the mental health centers that were to care for all the mentally ill, except the few who were a danger to themselves or others, were built, and, even where they are available, there is no mechanism to assure that, once released from the hospital, the patient will go to a center for continued treatment. Further, there is little or no effort to train and place former patients in jobs so that they can function in society; and there is very little possibility of channeling those in the community in need of it into treatment if they do not seek it themselves. Those who voluntarily commit themselves to hospitals are released as soon as possible. A woman with mental health problems who does not have a strong support network is at risk of joining the ranks of the homeless.

The homeless, except for those in single room occupancy (SRO) "welfare hotels" and transition houses, spend their days on the streets, looking for work, scavenging, panhandling, or just constantly moving. They spend their nights in emergency shelters; in public parks, streets, and alleys; in subways and bus and train terminals; under bridges; under stairwells or in other hidden niches of public buildings to which they can gain access; in abandoned buildings; or in their own cars.

As the number of homeless grew, shelters run by religious and other charitable organizations were grossly inadequate. Local and state governments responded in varying degrees. New York, Philadelphia, and Chicago, for instance, have "right to shelter" ordinances, guaranteeing shelter space to any who need it. In Houston, on the other hand, the law forbids local public funding.

The federal government first responded in the early 1980s through the Federal Emergency Management Agency (FEMA) and since 1987 has played an increasingly important role. The Stewart B. McKinney Homeless Assistance Act of 1987, with amendments passed in 1988, funds diverse spending programs through several departments and agencies of government.

In 1987 FEMA established the Emergency Food and Shelter Program, and HUD set up a competitive grant program, Emergency Shelter Grants (ESG). Between 1984 and 1988, through combined private and government efforts the number of emergency shelters increased from 1,900 to 5,400, with bed capacity rising from 100,000 to 277,000. (Average occupancy rose from 70,000 to 180,000.)

Funding for McKinney Act programs has continually increased, going, for instance, from $283 million in 1990 to $1.1 billion in 1995. Also, in 1993 HUD addressed the federal government's fragmented approach to the problem of homelessness with a consolidated plan, the Continuum of Care. Communities seeking HUD competitive grants must create their own "continuum of care" plans for long-term development.

Under HUD's Continuum of Care are four programs: (1) The Emergency Shelter Grant (ESG) Formula Program provides funds to convert buildings for use as emergency shelters and for food and consumable supplies (beds, bedding, etc.) needed for the shelters. (2) Supportive Housing Program (SHP) provides transitional housing with the supportive services needed to move persons or families from homelessness to independent living. It also has a permanent housing component for people with disabilities. (3) Shelter + Care provides permanent housing and services for people with disabilities. (4) Section 8, Moderate Rehabilitation Single Room Occupancy (SRO) Housing provides funds to rehabilitate buildings (e.g., an old hotel or

Young Men's Christian Association [YMCA]) to supply permanent housing in SRO apartments. Supportive services are optional. In 1996 every state received at least one grant through these programs.

HUD's consolidated approach has shifted the focus from emergency to transitional and permanent housing and greatly increased the supportive services component of its programs. In 1987 HUD's ESG program limited the amount that could be used for support services to no more than 15 percent. Since then the focus has shifted to services to help the homeless achieve self-sufficiency.

Although private and public aid, both short-term emergency aid and longer-term help to move the homeless to self-sufficiency, have all increased substantially since the early 1980s, homelessness remains a problem, and the change in welfare laws may help increase that problem in the future. Further, the policy issues in the care and treatment of the mentally ill and the chemically addicted have not been resolved. Continued federal and state support of affordable housing and social programs for counseling, aid, health care, and the education and training of the homeless will continue to be needed for the foreseeable future.

References. Barnard-Columbia Center for Urban Policy, *The Continuum of Care: A Report on the New Federal Policy to Address Homelessness* (Washington, D.C., 1996); Jim Baumohl (ed.), *Homelessness in America* (Phoenix, 1996).

HOMOPHOBIA is fear of homosexuality.* This term was given prominence in 1972 by George Weinberg and has since been used to refer to a wide range of negative attitudes, feelings, and behaviors toward homosexuals and homosexual activity evidenced on both individual and societal levels.

On the societal level, homophobia is a component of heterosexism, the belief that heterosexual activity is superior to homosexual activity. Like sexism, racism, and ethnocentrism, heterosexism is a form of social prejudice based mostly on misconceptions and stereotypes. Unlike discrimination* based on race, sex, or national origin, discrimination based on sexual orientation is not specifically prohibited by federal civil rights laws. Thus, in most states, homosexuals can be fired from their jobs, not hired for certain positions, discharged from the military, denied housing and custody of children, and arrested for engaging in private consensual sexual activity between adults, solely on the basis of their sexual orientation.*

Whereas nearly all cultures are heterosexist, cultures vary in the degree to which homosexuals and homosexuality are feared. In a number of cultures, male homosexuality during youth or adolescence is socially acceptable or even encouraged (e.g., among a number of African tribes and the Mohave Indians); in the United States, homosexuals are nearly totally rejected and stigmatized. Male homosexuality is more often culturally proscribed or sanctioned than female homosexuality, in part, because female homosexuals are less frequently thought of as sexual and partly because a female still can become pregnant even if not sexually attracted to men. Another reason for the greater stigma attached to male homosexuality is that rejection of the male heterosexual role can be viewed as a rejection of status privileges, whereas rejection of the female heterosexual role can be viewed as a rejection of a subordinate status. It is also the case that in the United States males are socialized more rigidly than females and define their role by denying all qualities and behaviors that are vaguely feminine. Thus, sexual relations with another man threaten the rigid gender lines drawn by the culture.

On an individual level, homophobia is related to a range of personality characteristics typical of prejudiced individuals: authoritarianism, conservative support of the status quo, and rigidity of gender roles* and gender-role attitudes. These attitudes appear to be acquired particularly easily by men as part of their gender-role socialization, which produces a generalized fear of femininity.* More men than women think homosexual relations should be prohibited, but this may relate to the fact that most people think of males when they hear the word "homosexual." It also may relate to the rigidity of male socialization and to the higher status males have in the culture.

Homophobia and heterosexism operate as social control mechanisms for both women and men to keep them in "their place." Heterosexuality is "compulsory" in our society, and rebels are punished (Rich). If one deviates from traditional gender-role behavior, one runs the risk of being labeled a "dyke" or lesbian, if one is female, or a "queer" or "faggot," if one is male. Such labeling can cause one to lose credibility, friends, jobs, housing, and advancement opportunities. It can also subject one to harassment and physical violence, as in "queer baiting" and "queer bashing." Since homosexuals are so stigmatized, many people cling to traditional gender-stereotyped behaviors in order to avoid giving anyone the opportunity to suspect their sexual orientation. Such social control was evident in the women's movement in the 1970s, when there was much concern about lesbians* being "too" visible and vocal in the movement, thereby "threatening" the success of the movement's objectives. Lesbianism, in particular, threatens traditional social arrangements since it belies the patriarchal belief that women need men for their happiness and protection. Consequently, nearly all feminists who are vocal are subject to accusations of lesbianism.

Such is the power of homophobia in our society that many homosexuals have internalized these attitudes and act them out in self-denying and frequently self-defeating ways. As long as societal homophobia exists, and being thought a homosexual is a major stigma, many people, both gay and straight, will restrict their behavior and their lives to try to ensure societal acceptance.

References. A. Rich, "Compulsory Heterosexuality and Lesbian Existence," *Signs* 5 (1980): 631–660; George Weinberg, *Society and the Healthy Homosexual* (New York, 1972).

SUSAN A. BASOW

HOMOSEXUALITY is a term coined in 1869 to refer to sexual relationships among persons of the same sex.

Though women have loved and lived with women, and men with men, in societies around the world and in ancient and modern times, the ways in which these relationships have been recognized (or suppressed) have varied immensely by time and place. In societies as widely separated as Melanesia, Amazonia, Central Africa, and western Egypt, it has been common for many (sometimes all) males to have homosexual relations for at least a part of their lives. In these societies, sexual relations between older and younger males are thought to be part of the experiences of parenting and growing up. Best known to Western society is the classical heritage from Greece and Rome, where adolescence was a time when young men left their biological families to become lovers of adult men. Sexuality was but one element of an affectional and educational relationship.

With women's experiences so often left out of the historical record by patriarchal societies, less is known about female bonding, but the writings of Sappho from ancient Greece did give the name of the island of Lesbos to love between women. (See LESBIANS.)

Anthropological research shows, as well, the existence of gender-mixed persons among many of the native peoples of North and South America, Polynesia, Indonesia, and eastern Siberia. The *berdache* of North America and *mahu* of Polynesia included men who took on aspects of women's dress and work, and it is known that female *berdaches* sometimes married women, and male *berdaches*, men.

In societies where homosexuality is both universal and obligatory, it makes little sense to talk of homosexual persons, but in Western societies there has been a strong tradition of sharply differentiating between "homosexual" and "heterosexual." At least as early as the seventeenth century (and probably before) there is evidence of a homosexual underground in the European capitals, where men could meet, court, and make sexual contact with one another. From these origins has emerged the modern gay world, which is organized not unlike an ethnic group with its own bars and neighborhoods, newspapers and churches, recreational and political groups.

For women, the development of lesbian networks is more recent. Lacking the financial independence and public mobility of men, some women formed "romantic friendships" without abandoning family participation.

Only with the growing independence of women in the twentieth century could some choose to create women-only households and public places of their own and thus form a lesbian subculture.

The process has not been easy, and lesbians and gay men have suffered centuries of persecution at the hands of church and state through banishment, imprisonment, torture, and even execution. Periodic governmental campaigns have resulted in the murder of dozens, sometimes thousands, of homosexual people, as in fifteenth-century Venice, eighteenth-century Holland, early nineteenth-century England, and Nazi Germany. Today homosexual acts between consenting adults are legal in most jurisdictions around the world, with the notable exception of the USSR and half of the states of the United States and Australia, as well as in theocratic nations such as Iran, Israel, and Ireland. Romania and Cuba have also conducted active campaigns of persecution in recent history. On the other hand, places that have actively moved to prohibit discrimination* on the grounds of sexual orientation include Norway, France, Ontario, Quebec, Wisconsin, and New South Wales, as well as a number of cities in the United States and Canada.

In the 1970s and 1980s, research on gay and lesbian people has emerged from the grip of moralistic and pathological frameworks to explore the dynamics of apparently gender-free relationships in comparison with heterosexual arrangements. Recent scholarly work shows that lesbians tend toward egalitarian bonding and value sexual fidelity, while gay men often successfully combine a primary love relationship with sexual pluralism. Studies by Karla Jay and Allen Young and by William Masters and Virginia Johnson have pointed toward high levels of versatility in sexual roles and techniques and of mutual sexual understanding among same-sex couples.

Despite some easing of homophobic attitudes in recent times, the decision to express homoerotic feelings and carry them through to loving and living with same-sex persons continues to be experienced as an important status passage. Called "coming out," the affirmation of one's own emotional life still entails, for most gay people, a willingness to brave the incomprehension or censure of families, coworkers, neighbors, employers, and friends. Though homosexuality is often experienced as a crisis of adolescence when peers are dating and marrying, many homosexuals come out later in life, sometimes after years of heterosexual marriage and denial. Recent studies have punctured the myth that growing old gay leads to inevitable loneliness. There is no lack of evidence of happy and productive lives among older gay people who tend to have developed extended circles of supportive friends.

Today there is some organized gay presence in almost every city of Western Europe, North America, and Australia, which can be reached simply by looking up "gay" in the local telephone directory. A perusal of any gay/lesbian newspaper reveals a wealth of activities centering around sports, education, politics, religion, and self-help. Larger cities offer such gay-oriented professions and services as law, medicine, travel, accommodation, and restaurants. Gay and women's bookstores are bursting with novels, plays, and recordings that have flowed from the gay cultural renaissance of the modern era.

In 1981, the hitherto unknown disease of acquired immunodeficiency syndrome (AIDS) became known, causing, in its first five years, more than 12,000 deaths, the majority of which occurred among gay men. Though some sought to exploit the disease to attack the civil liberties of gay people, and governments were slow to respond, organizations have sprung up in gay communities to offer support to those afflicted by the epidemic, to push for research funding, and to counsel everyone to practice "safe sex" to stop the epidemic.

Today lesbians and gay men have succeeded in carving out a limited social space where they can "be themselves" but remain vulnerable to the depredation of heterosexist forces.

References. E. Blackwood, *Anthropology and Homosexual Behavior* (New York, 1986); P. Blumstein and P. Schwartz, *American Couples* (New York, 1983); J. Weeks, *Coming Out* (London, 1977).

BARRY D. ADAM

HORMONES secreted by the glandular (endocrine) system control and regulate growth, the reproductive cycle, and other physiological processes. The hypothalamus, the part of the brain just above the pituitary gland, releases hormones that regulate the pituitary (the main endocrine gland). The pituitary gland releases hormones with various functions, including the regulation of the reproductive cycle through the stimulation of egg and sperm development and hormone production in the ovaries and testes. Other endocrine glands include the thyroid, parathyroids, adrenal, pancreas, and ovaries in women and testes in men.

In chemical composition almost all hormones are either amino acids (chiefly proteins and polypeptides) or steroids (compounds based on a carbon ring nucleus). Steroids are produced by the adrenal cortex, ovaries, and testes (and also by the placenta, which is composed of endocrine tissue, during pregnancy). There are four families of steroids: androgens, estrogens, progesterone, and corticosteroids. Androgen, estrogen, and progesterone, the "sex steroids," are responsible for the physical and physiological differences between men and women. (See also PUBERTAL DEVELOPMENT; REPRODUCTIVE SYSTEM.)

HOUSEWIFE (HOMEMAKER) is a married woman who works within her own home serving the needs of her own family* and who is not a member of the paid labor force. Because the work she does is not legally an occupation and is not waged, it tends to be discounted. Although her work differs in many respects from work in the paid labor force, it is of economic value to the family. The standard of living that can be achieved from the income of a one-earner family that includes a housewife can go considerably beyond that attained by the same income earned by the combined efforts of husband and wife.

The housewife's work is recompensed not in money but in sharing whatever level of economic support her husband's earnings make possible and in sharing her husband's status. The level of the housewife's "pay," then, has no necessary relation to the kind, amount, or quality of the work she does. With the availability of technology and the unavailability of paid domestic workers, except for the very wealthy, housewives of all socioeconomic levels perform much the same basic duties. The "pay" may very well vary in inverse proportion to the amount of work done. Housewives whose husbands earn less or who have more children will usually have to work harder and enjoy fewer luxuries than those who have few children or whose husbands earn more. Further, the quality of the housewife's work is irrelevant to her status. The best housewife and the worst get their status from their husband, not from their own accomplishments.

The housewife has no set hours of work but is on call 24 hours a day, seven days a week. She has no job description; the work consists of whatever needs to be done. There is no necessary order for doing housework, and most jobs can be postponed or put off. Housework is almost always done in isolation from other adults. Loneliness and lack of adult companionship are two drawbacks that encourage many women to consider a return to the paid workforce.

A considerable part of the housewife's time and energy is spent shopping for goods for household consumption and in further preparing the purchases for family use. Personal services to family members also constitute a significant part of the housewife's tasks. A large number of her chores are low-skill, monotonous, and repetitive and for immediate consumption. Her work tends to be taken for granted and is more likely to be noticed when it isn't done than when it is.

The housewife's access to economic support for the services she performs does not depend entirely on the husband's income but also depends on the economic arrangements of the individual household. In some cases, the housewife is the fiscal agent for the family, managing all family finances. Or she may have a household allowance, set with more or less collaboration between husband and wife, from which she supplies personal and household needs, or she may have the use of charge accounts and joint bank accounts. In other cases, the housewife may be put in the demeaning position of having to ask her husband for all moneys needed, even inconsiderable sums.

Emotional and sexual services are a regular, legitimate part of the job. On the emotional satisfaction derived from the marriage its success or failure and its continuation or dissolution are most likely to depend. However, in an era in which divorce* is easy and acceptable, a marriage may be ended not because of dissatisfaction with the housekeeping, nurturing, or sexual services performed but because the affection of one of the partners has shifted. Although it might be either party, the husband has much more opportunity to find new sources of affection and sexual gratification than does the housewife.

When there are preschool children in the home, the work of the housewife fills her days and sometimes her nights. But after the youngest child reaches school age, the time needed for housework begins to decline. The job of the housewife ceases to be a full-time occupation. Many housewives turn to volunteer work, but, increasingly, more of them enter or reenter the workforce. In 1988, the number of married women in the United States who were housewives was still almost 50 percent of the total, but fewer of them and fewer in the future will be housewives for their entire married lives.

The occupation of housewife carries high economic and physical risks. The housewife is vulnerable to impoverishment upon the death of her husband or as a result of divorce. Feminist efforts to obtain Social Security payments for divorced housewives who were married less than 20 years and mandatory survivor benefits in pension plans met with success. Social Security credit independent of the husband's account and provision of equitable economic support for displaced homemakers are among issues of continuing concern. The housewife's dependent position in relation to a husband who is the sole earner of the family makes her liable not just to economic risk at the dissolution of the marriage but to economic, emotional, and physical risks during the marriage. Police response to family violence and the establishment of crisis centers, safe houses, and support groups for battered women are also feminist concerns.

References. B. R. Bergmann, *The Economic Emergence of Women* (New York, 1986), ch. 9; A. Oakley, *The Sociology of Housework* (New York, 1974).

HOUSEWORK is work done for the care and maintenance of a home and its occupants. This service may include child care* as well as the provisioning of food, clothing, and household items, doing laundry, and cleaning and maintaining the home. The duties are traditionally "women's work,"* and except for very wealthy families, most or all of them are done as unpaid labor by family members, primarily by the wife/mother of the family.

The multitude of tasks involved in housework covers the entire range from low-skill to high-skill work. However, most of the essential services are monotonous and repetitive, the product of the labor being almost immediately consumed (prepared food, made-up beds, cleaned dishes, etc.). The work is not counted as part of the gross national product and, since it is unpaid, is not as highly valued as paid labor. When it is paid, the personal services required and the working conditions make it a low-paying, low-status job.

Technology took much of the production for household consumption and the heavy manual labor out of housework. By increasing standards for all classes and putting some work back into the duties of the middle-class wife/mother (e.g., laundry), it has largely erased differences in the general nature of housework done by middle- and working-class wives/mothers and has increased the monotonous and repetitive nature of much of that work.

Reformers interested in maintaining the patriarchal family system have tried at various times to give housework a different name in an attempt to raise its status. In the early twentieth century the terms *"domestic science"* and *"home economics"* were tried. In the period after World War II *"homemaking"* became the preferred term. The status was unaffected. Utopian and feminist theorists have proposed various schemes for making housework, including child care, communal or completely professional. The utopian communities of the nineteenth century generally made the work communal, but it was still done by the women.

Women who prize traditional feminine values and enjoy cooking, sewing, and other skills involved in housekeeping prefer housework to work in the paid labor force. There are, however, many women who do not enjoy or have an interest in those skills. The assumption that women have a "natural" inclination for housework and "are good at it" is deeply embedded in the patriarchal system of gender-role segregation. Since destroying that myth threatens the work roles of men in the home, it is not a myth that will be easily demolished.

HUMAN CAPITAL THEORY first appeared in a special issue of the *Journal of Political Economy* in 1962 on "Investment in Human Beings." It was preceded by papers by Jacob Mincer and Theodore W. Schultz and was followed by a book by Gary S. Becker. Human capital theory has flourished ever since at the University of Chicago and elsewhere. If its success is to be judged by the impact it has had on scholarly work, not only in economics but in the other social sciences as well, it has been quite spectacular. A vast empirical literature, testing its predictions and implications, has succeeded in confirming many of both. Its very success, however, has caused some of its more enthusiastic proponents to go beyond taking credit for contributing to our knowledge of human behavior and come perilously close to claiming that they can explain all of it. These extreme claims are particularly misplaced when it comes to differences in the economic status of women and men or different racial and ethnic groups.

As its very name suggests, human capital theory is essentially an extension of the idea of physical capital. Just as businesspeople invest in new plants and equipment today in order to increase productive capacity and obtain greater returns later, so there is investment in people that does not result in present satisfaction but in future returns, pecuniary and otherwise. Examples are expenditures, of time as well as money, on education and training,* job search, migration, better health, more and "higher quality" (i.e., better trained and more highly educated) children. Such items had earlier, for the most part, been treated as "consumption goods." They were viewed primarily as influencing well-being directly, not as a means of raising future income. Thus, the new approach was genuinely innovative and provided the foundation for a massive and successful research program.

Both the strengths and the weaknesses of the human capital approach are well illustrated by the way it has been used to explain the male–female earnings gap. Beginning with the premise that individuals and their families decide to invest in themselves today in order to achieve higher returns later, it is reasonable to assume that both the quantity and the type of human capital accumulated will be influenced by the amount of time the person expects to spend in the labor force.

As Jacob Mincer and Solomon W. Polachek argue, men who normally work for pay all of their adult lives will tend to make greater investments in human capital than women who are likely to be in the labor force intermittently. Hence, men are more inclined to become physicians, while women are likely to become nurses. Similarly, women will be more reluctant than men to acquire skills that atrophy rapidly when not used. Hence, women are more inclined to become social workers, while men may become physicists. Further, time spent out of the labor force directly reduces the amount of work experience women have in general and with a given employer in particular. An extensive survey of studies of the earnings gap that take such factors into account (Treiman and Hartmann) showed that the most thorough studies explained not quite half of the differential; the record of more recent studies is somewhat better (Blau and Ferber). It is, however, equally important to note that they still leave more than one-third of the differential unexplained, raising the possibility that some of that may be caused by discrimination.*

Thus, human capital theory helps us to understand why women earn less than men. It also has useful policy implications, for it suggests that women can improve their situation by acquiring more and different kinds of education, training, and experience. At the same time, there is no justification for ignoring a variety of other factors that stand in the way of economic equality for women (and other groups) that call for different remedies.

More generally, there is reason to question the single-minded focus of the most dogmatic adherents of human capital theory on economic rationality, which suggests that all persons in full knowledge of available alternatives and outcomes make choices so as to maximize satisfaction. It is also assumed that these choices are always freely made. Hence, differences in occupations, earnings, marital status, fertility, and even health are viewed as the result of voluntary decisions.

Similarly, the contention that all "widespread and/or persistent human behavior can be explained by a generalized calculus of utility-maximizing behavior" (Stigler and Becker) needs to be critically examined. It represents a very narrow view of a complex world, ignoring the potential importance of traditional attitudes, social pressures, and institutions in influencing human behavior. All these may themselves have been shaped by economic conditions in an earlier time, but they tend to last long after they have outlived their relevance. They can constitute significant constraints on the choices individuals make. The emphasis on voluntary choices particularly tends to underestimate the extent to which persons confronted by less favorable options, say, because of their race, sex, or social background, are likely to be caught up in a circle of unfavorable feedback effects.

A well-balanced view, fully recognizing that the extent to which people are willing to use resources to enhance their own productivity has much to do with their earnings potential, also acknowledges that in a world where all individuals are not born equal, where markets are imperfect, and where uncertainty abounds, many other factors influence the outcome. Thus, for instance, it is important to recognize that, in large part because of lingering traditional values, boys and girls are socialized differently, and, according to much available evidence, continue to face substantially different opportunities in the labor market. It is equally important to recognize that labor market discrimination—when two equally qualified individuals are treated differently solely because of a personal characteristic such as sex, race, religion, or disability—may help to explain occupational segregation* and male–female earnings differentials. Further, the expectation of discrimination would, in turn, be likely to influence the decision on how much human capital to accumulate.

The issue whether or not to accept the broadest claims of human capital theory is an important one from a practical point of view. The theory lends itself all too readily to explaining inequality in a way that amounts to blaming the victim. Poverty* is the result of insufficient investment. Women earn less in the labor market because they tend to specialize in homemaking—never mind that they supposedly specialize in homemaking, in large part, because they earn less in the labor market.

Such premises naturally encourage complacency and comfortable acceptance of the status quo. There is no reason, however, to reject the valuable insights the theory has to offer or the increased knowledge the related active research program continues to provide. The basic idea that families can and do invest in their children and that persons can and do invest in themselves in ways that enhance their earning power need not be combined with acceptance of the implications suggested by the most extreme proponents of human capital theory. It can, in fact, be used to support policies that would more nearly equalize the opportunity to make such investments and the rewards for making them, once the unrealistic assumption that equal opportunity already exists is discarded.

References. Gary S. Becker, *Human Capital* (1964; 3rd ed., Chicago, 1993); Francine D. Blau, Marianne A. Ferber, and Ann Winkler, *The Economics of Women, Men, and Work*, 3rd ed. (Englewood Cliffs, N.J., 1997), 191–194; Jacob Mincer, "Investment in Human Capital and Personal Income Distributions," *Journal of Political Economy* 66 (1958): 281–302; Jacob Mincer and Solomon W. Polachek, "Family Investments in Human Capital: Earnings of Women," *Journal of Political Economy* 82 (1974): S76–S108; Theodore W. Schultz, *The Economic Value of Education* (New York, 1961); George J. Stigler and Gary S. Becker, "De Gustibus Non Est Disputandum," *American Economic Review* 67 (1977): 76–90; Donald J. Treiman and Heidi I. Hartmann (eds.), *Women, Work, and Wages: Equal Pay for Jobs of Equal Value* (National Research Council, Washington, D.C., 1981).

MARIANNE A. FERBER

HUMOR has emerged as a very significant force in recent battles over the redefinition of female and male roles, stereotypes, and interactions in American culture. Humor is not a peripheral or inconsequential force in shaping and expressing thoughts and images. Through various media, humor, satire, and joking are often the primary means for communication on contentious topics such as race, sex, gender, and conflict between groups. The use of humor as a weapon of attack or defense is not a new phenomenon. Over a century ago, Freud identified the hostile joke as one of the three forms of humor (the others being obscene jokes and innocent jokes).

Humor is a complex and interesting form of discourse. Its exemption from many of the rules of logic, taste, etiquette, and fair play that apply to other forms of communication makes humor a particularly potent weapon in intergroup conflicts, especially in ideological wars of words and images. Through humor all of the most vicious aspersions and damaging stereotypes against racial, religious, gender, and other minorities have been circulated throughout history. Those who control humorous communication and define what is "funny" are able to launch verbal and symbolic barrages at other groups or individuals with virtual impunity. If called into account for their verbal aggression, they quickly retreat behind the "only joking" defense, usually combined with the "don't you have a sense of humor?" offense.

Throughout the history of human societies dominant groups have controlled (or at least tried to control) the land, the institutions, the wealth, and the citizens of those societies. Key to their control over people, land, and privileges is their control of the ideas and symbols that shape human thoughts and actions. Control over the ideas and images is generally achieved through domination over the major institutional purveyors of discourse and symbolic displays (e.g., government, religion, education, mass

media, and popular culture). Until recent decades in American society all
of these sources for the massive dissemination of ideas and symbolic displays were virtually in total control of white males.

The humor that emerged from these male-dominated and patriarchal institutions has generally portrayed women as both physically and intellectually incompetent (e.g., Lucille Ball, Gracie Allen, or the early Goldie
Hawn). They were also portrayed as promiscuous sex objects for the pleasure of men (Mae West, Marilyn Monroe, or Daisy Mae). Alternatively,
females were comedically displayed in deprecating caricatures of all that is
"wrong" with women (e.g., Phyllis Diller or the females of W. C. Fields or
Marx Brothers movies). From the routines of "baggy pants comics" of
vaudeville to the most currently popular "blond jokes," the universal punch
line asserts that women are valued only for providing sex or that they are
incredibly stupid.

Recently, women have gained at least some influence and inclusion in
virtually all areas of American culture and institutions. As a consequence
female voices and female perspectives are being heard much more frequently in all forms of public discourse. From movies, music, books, television, and politics the wit and humor of women have become a significant
(albeit a minority) presence. Women comics have taken advantage of these
opportunities to question or ridicule patriarchal assumptions of male supremacy and the central importance of males to society. While patriarchal
humor and ideology have portrayed men as sexual athletes, masterful and
indispensable to women, antipatriarchal humor paints a very different picture of men. From the perspective of antipatriarchal humor, men are child-
like ("Psychoanalysis is easier for a man because when it comes to returning
to his childhood, he doesn't have far to go"); emotionally underdeveloped
("While women have radar dishes that seek out, and focus on, a wide range
of emotions, men have those rabbit-ear antennas with aluminum foil
wrapped around them. They pick up only the main channels—pain and
orgasm"); useless to women ("A woman without a man is like a fish without a bicycle"); sexually maladept and inconsiderate ("The lovemaking was
fast and furious. He was fast, and she was furious"); slobs ("If a single
man drops his socks on the floor, he'll wait until he is married for his wife
to pick them up for him"); useless around the house ("The only benefit of
having a man around the house is that the added weight on the couch
discourages burglars from stealing it"); drunkards ("He saw a sign that
said "Drink Canada Dry"—so he moved there"); or worse ("They just were
not compatible. She was a Libra, and he was an asshole").

In addition to the opportunities to launch attacks on male pretensions
of God-like supreme importance, antipatriarchal humor affords the opportunity to assert that, indeed, *women* are the superior gender: "They have
discovered something that can do the work of three men—one woman,"
"Remember that Ginger Rogers did everything Fred Astaire did—back-

wards and in high heels;" "A woman's place is in the house—and in the Senate."

Recent television shows also reveal a shift in the balance of buffoonery. On popular shows such as *The Simpsons, Tool Time,* and *Men Behaving Badly,* the leading male characters are portrayed as inept, practically useless, and out of control. The leading women in this genre of comedy are shown as sane, wise, and more in control.

We should not, however, conclude that women now dominate humor or that most gender humor now makes men the butt of humor. Between November 1993 and March 1994, this author recorded 698 stand-up comedy acts from television (mostly from the Comedy Network). Of these, only 98 (less than 15 percent) featured female comedians.

Furthermore, humor or ridicule is still a major weapon unleashed against women who would challenge patriarchal domination and seek power and independence. A prime example of this is the barrage of ridicule aimed at Hillary Clinton from the moment she emerged as an influential figure in American politics and culture. For her refusal to confine her efforts to the traditional female role of domestic labor (e.g., baking cookies) she became the object of scorn in political cartoons, stand-up comedy routines, and barbershop and barroom witticisms. These "Hillary" (or "Billary") jokes portray the First Lady as being power-mad, unfeminine, and unattractive. Many of these jokes also assert that President Bill Clinton is not a "real man" because he has allowed Hillary to assume such power and independence. Examples of "Billary" jokes include (1) How did Bill first meet Hillary? In high school they dated the same woman; (2) How did Bill first meet Hillary? In high school they dated the same man; (3) At Christmastime the president entered the White House carrying a present he had gotten for Hillary. The marine guard at the door asked, "What have you got there, sir?" The president replied that he had gotten a puppy dog for Hillary. The marine guard replied, "Hell of a good deal, sir."

Humor reveals the topics or issues at the forefront of public concern or attention at a particular point in social history. It also reveals the prevailing sentiment or perspectives on these topics. The present proliferation of gender humor indicates the importance of the changing roles of men and women in modern American society. In previous generations humor was almost entirely performed by males and represented a male perspective. Today feminists and other proponents of gender equality are making effective use of humor as a means to deconstruct patriarchal ideologies and sexist stereotypes. At the same time, antifeminists and defenders of patriarchy continue to use humor to resist these challenges to male domination of women and society.

References. Philip Auslander, "Brought to You by Fem-Rage: Stand-up Comedy and the Politics of Gender," in Lynda Hart and Peggy Phelan (eds.), *Acting Out: Feminist Performances* (Ann Arbor, 1993); Regina Barreca (ed.), *Last Laughs: Per-*

spectives on Women and Comedy (New York, 1988); Eileen Gillooly, "Review Essay: Women and Humor," *Feminist Studies* 17 (1991): 473–492; Robin Morgan, *Dry Your Smile* (New York, 1987).

CHARLES E. CASE

HYPERGAMY/HYPOGAMY. Hypergamy is a marriage system in which the woman "marries up." The preferred marriage is one in which the woman marries a man of a higher social class. The man should not marry a woman of higher status, nor should a woman marry below her status. This system is found in conjunction with hierarchical societies and with the dowry* as the only form of marital payment, as among the higher castes in India and in Renaissance Italy. The wife's family,* by giving a dowry that tends to become extravagantly high, may hope to improve its rank and social position or to make politically advantageous connections. The upward movement of women from lower social strata means that there will be an excess of women at the top. The high cost of dowries also means that families will not be able to, or will be very reluctant to, dower more than one daughter. Female infanticide, forcing daughters into the cloister, and polygamy are among the methods used to decrease marriageable women at the top. In the lower social classes there may be a scarcity of marriageable women.

Hypogamy is the opposite of hypergamy. In this system the desired marriage is one in which the man marries up. Such hypogamous marriages appear frequently among the heroes of the Greek legends. In modern hypogamous marital systems high marital payment in the form of bridewealth benefits the maternal lineage, as hypergamy benefits the paternal.

I

ICELANDIC WRITERS. Women belong to an ancient and rich literary tradition with roots in the Old Norse culture. The oral tradition in poetry can be traced to women's culture, particularly to such activities as healing and prophesying. The main poetic genres were visions and incantations, but there were also dreams, work songs, laments, and poems on healing. The most important remnants of the Old Icelandic oral tradition are the Eddic poems. This loose collection of poetry, composed before the eleventh century and preserved in a manuscript dated from c. 1270, is characterized by fantastic stories of mythological figures, supernatural events, and a heroic world. (*Edda* means great-grandmother and can etymologically be related to óðr, or ode.) Many of the poems abound in female experiences such as giving birth, embroidering, doing laundry. They describe feelings of love, betrayal, mourning, and abandonment. Some are women's monologues; others, dialogues between women. In *Sigurdrífumál* (The Monologue of Sigurdrifa), a woman is teaching a man healing verses. *Oddrúnargrátr* (The Lament of Oddrun) is a dialogue between a woman in labor and a midwife who shares her own sorrows. In *Grottasongr* (The Song of Grotti) two slave women are singing as they work at an enormous millstone called Grotti, grinding out death and destruction to their suppressors. *Völuspá* (The Vision of the Sibyl), the most celebrated poem of Old Icelandic literature, has traditionally been interpreted as a poem about the apocalypse of the pagan culture—or the end of the world in general. However, the powerful image of the sibyl sinking into the earth after giving over all her knowledge to Odin symbolizes a more specific apocalypse: that of women's culture.

A similar story of appropriation can be seen in the myth in which Odin steals the mead of poetic inspiration from a giantess by tricking her. The story appears in Snorri Sturluson's *Edda* (c. 1230), a textbook of poetics in which young men are encouraged to learn the metaphors of the ancient oral tradition for use in their courtly verses. This work culminated a process beginning with the coming of Christianity (c. 1000) and then literacy by which poetry was taken out of the realm of women's culture and transferred to what became the first Icelandic literary establishment: the schools, the scribes, and the monasteries. At the same time, the thirteenth century marks the rise of the Icelandic sagas, an anonymous, but overtly masculine, genre emphasizing feuds and battles. Of special interest is the famous *Laxdœlasaga* (The Saga of the Laxdale Dwellers) because of its great interest in women's life. A curious female perspective runs through the story, frequently suppressed by the genre's demand for masculine action and enterprise.

Up until the nineteenth century specific women poets are mentioned only sporadically in literary sources, and the few surviving poems by women are fragmented. Nevertheless, women's literature survived for centuries in oral form alongside the dominant canon of men. Their genres were the more flexible ones: ballads, lyrics, occasional poems, folk songs, and folktales. When women attempted a genre with strict metrical rules, they tended to parody the genre.

The first literary work published by an Icelandic woman was the book of poems *Stúlka* (1876; A Lass), by Júlíana Jónsdóttir (1838–1918). In many of her poems she writes about women—their hard work and powerlessness, often parodying the masculine tradition with irony and grotesque imagery. Her strong awareness of being a woman in a patriarchal world, also expressed in the title of her book, is typical of Icelandic women writers up to the present day.

Unlike their counterparts in many other countries, early women writers in Iceland generally did not attempt fiction, perhaps because of the strong tradition of the sagas. The first to do so was Torfhildur Hólm (1845–1918), who experimented with historical novels based on the lives of eminent Icelandic bishops. Her first novel, *Brynjólfur Sveinsson biskup* (1882; The Bishop Brynjólfur Sveinsson), is not only the first Icelandic novel by a woman but also the first historical novel in modern Icelandic literature. Despite their originality, these novels are artificial and uneven. In her short stories, the first examples of this genre by a woman writer, she explores various aspects of woman's rights.

Around the turn of the century a group of women writers emerged who developed a new form of þulur (cantos), a genre of oral litany characterized by fantasy and fragments of folk songs. The þulur express women's feelings and the clash between dreams and cold reality. The most prominent figure in this group was Unnur Benediktsdóttir Bjarklind (1881–1946), better known as Hulda (the fairy or hidden one). In addition to her contribution to the þulur genre, she became the main proponent of symbolism. Praised, but misinterpreted in her own time, she had an enormous literary output.

Her first book of poems, *Kvæði* (1909; Poems), contains powerful metaphors of nature that suggest the oppressed condition of women. Also associated with this group is Ólöf Sigurðardóttir (1857–1933), who published two books of poetry entitled *Nokkur smákvæði* (1888, 1913; Some Short Poems). Her work has an explicit feminist perspective, challenging the patriarchal society by examining women's desire for independence, love, and creativity. Her prose fragment *Hjálpin* (c. 1887; Help), the first example of narrative filtered through the consciousness of a single character, reveals the anguish of a woman trapped in marriage.

The period from 1920 to 1950 saw the development of the novel among several women writers who were some of the most prolific of this century. Kristín Sigfúsdóttir (1876–1953) wrote novels and short stories about the exploitation of women, forced marriages, disillusionment, illness, and death. However, like many other women writers, she tends to end her works in reconciliation, concealing their rebellious content. The many novels and short stories of þórunn Elfa Magnúsdóttir (b. 1910) focus on the condition of women and the conflict between career and family. Ragnheiður Jónsdóttir (1895–1967), known as an author of children's books, has written psychological novels, significant in their use of ambiguity to expose the deceptive surface of daily life. The enormously prolific Guðrún Árnadóttir frá Lundi (1887–1973) wrote romances about rural life. Her best-sellers established a genre that has attracted numerous women writers up to the present day.

Overshadowed during this period by fiction, women's poetry began to show important changes around 1950. The first signs of modernism can be seen in the pointed satire of Halldóra B. Björnsson (1907–1968), published in *Ljóð* (1949; Poems). The real breakthrough occurred with Vilborg Dagbjartsdóttir (b. 1930), most explicitly in her third book of poems, *Kyndilmessa* (1971; Candlemass). Her innovations, springing from an overtly feminist point of view, consist of colloquial language and images of daily life. These features, along with the blending of fantasy and ordinary reality as well as the use of unexpected points of view, characterize contemporary women's poetry. This style is apparent in the surrealistic epigrams of þóra Jónsdóttir (b. 1925), as well as in the poems by Nína Björk Árnadóttir (b. 1941), þuríður Guðmundsdóttir (b. 1939), and Ingibjörg Haraldsdóttir (b. 1942).

The highly original short stories of Ásta Sigurðardóttir (1930–1971), collected in *Sunnudagskvöld til mánudagsmorguns* (1961; Sunday Night to Monday Morning), mark the breakthrough of modernism not only in women's prose but in Icelandic prose in general. In a new literary language they describe women and other outsiders, with their utter alienation and fears that border on paranoia. The novels and short stories of Jakobína Sigurðardóttir (b. 1918) describe the clash between rural life and urban culture from a socialist point of view. The lyrical novels and short stories of Álfrún Gunnlaugsdóttir (b. 1938) portray women fleeing from a threatening environment. One of the most original writers in recent decades is Málfríður Einarsdóttir (1899–1983). Her prose fragments, published when she was in her 70s, mix fantasy, memoirs, philosophy, lyricism, and grotesque imagery to create a strange and unreliable world. A similar mixture of genres is seen in the works of Steinunn Sigurðardóttir (b. 1950). The nonchalant tone with which she juxtaposes lofty themes and ordinary phenomena like sexual relationships results in farcical, but incisive, statements about life. The most celebrated woman writer in Iceland today is Svava Jakobsdóttir (b. 1930). Her novels, short stories, and plays reflect women's search for identity as ordinary reality is transformed through surreal and grotesque metaphors of fantasy and horror. Her first collections of short stories, especially *Veisla undir grjótvegg* (1967; Feast by a Stone Wall), are some of the most revolutionary works in contemporary Icelandic literature.

HELGA KRESS

IMAGES OF BLACK WOMEN. Black feminists have always been concerned with the oppressive images and objectification of black women. According to K. Sue Jewell, black women have been depicted as Mammies, Sapphires, and Jezebels. It could be argued that there is some accuracy in each of these images. Black women have historically worked as domestics (Mammy), been strong and assertive (Sapphire), and been forced into sexual servitude (Jezebel). This kernel of truth makes these images so insidious and plausible. However, these images are a distortion of black women's positive attributes, such as their nurturance and assertiveness.

In response to these images some black women may restrict their behavior, dress, and mannerisms to correspond with these caricatures. Conversely, other black women may alter their behavior for fear of reinforcing these images. Following are the possible psychological implications of these images.

Mammy. This image originated in the South during slavery. Mammy was depicted as a self-sacrificing domestic servant who happily performed her duties with no expectation of emotional compensation. If this image is internalized, it may leave contemporary black women vulnerable to role strain—that is, strain caused by the expectation that they can effortlessly perform multiple roles without getting their personal needs met.

Physically, Mammy was depicted as an obese woman who nurtured herself and others with food. This image may contribute to eating disorders. For example, among economically disadvantaged women bingeing may provide a socially appropriate way of coping with stress or emotional deprivation. The eating disorders of overweight black women may go unrecognized because their physical appearance is consistent with the image of the fat Mammy. Conversely, the Mammy image may represent poverty and powerlessness to upwardly mobile black women. As a result, weight restriction may be used in order to distance themselves from this image (Thompson).

Mammy's dark complexion represents the pain concerning physical appearance. The value placed on skin color began in slavery, when lighter-complexioned blacks were granted preferential treatment. Regardless of complexion, black women may confront the legacy of "color consciousness." For example, "feelings of resentment and anger about the possibility that one is too dark or too unattractive to males are just as common as feelings of guilt and shame about the possibility that one has enjoyed unfair advantages because of lightness of skin color" (Neal and Wilson).

Sapphire was portrayed in the 1940s Amos and Andy television show as the hostile wife of Kingfish. This image has implications for how black women's anger is expressed. Acting out the Sapphire image may take the form of "telling it like it is." At times this may be appropriate and effective. However, it becomes problematic when aggression is used to mask feelings of vulnerability or when behaviors that are consistent with this image (e.g., angry confrontation, verbal abuse) are embraced as the only acceptable means of expressing anger. In contrast, some black women may avoid the expression of anger for fear of reinforcing the Sapphire image.

Jezebel. During slavery white slave owners exercised almost complete control over black women's sexuality and reproductive capacity. The sexually promiscuous Jezebel image arose in order to justify this sexual exploitation. Based on this image, "the Black female came to be viewed as a legitimate (culturally approved) victim of sexual assault" (Williams). This leaves black women more vulnerable to forced sexual encounters while simultaneously making it difficult for them to seek help (Foley).

Mammy, Sapphire, and Jezebel are not simply historic icons. They continue to have implications for the psychological functioning of black women. The challenge is to develop an "oppositional gaze" toward these images (hooks). That is, these images must be critically examined and redefined in ways that empower black women.

References. P. H. Collins, *Black Feminist Thought* (Cambridge, Mass., 1990); L. Foley, "Date Rape: Effects of Race of Assailant and Victim and Gender of Subjects on Perceptions," *Journal of Black Psychology* 21, 1 (1995): 6–18; b. hooks, *Black Looks: Race and Representation* (Boston, 1992); K. Sue Jewell, *From Mammy to Miss America and Beyond* (New York, 1993); P. Morton, *Disfigured Images: The Historical Assault on Afro-American Women* (New York, 1991); A. Neal and M. Wilson, "The Role of Skin Color and Features in the Black Community," *Clinical Psychology Review* 9 (1989): 323–333; B. Thompson, *A Hunger So Wide and Deep* (Minneapolis, 1994); C. West, "Mammy, Sapphire, and Jezebel: Historical Images of Black Women and Their Implications for Psychotherapy," *Psychotherapy* 32, 3 (1995): 458–466; L. Williams, *Race and Rape: The Black Woman as Legitimate Victim*, Unpublished manuscript, University of New Hampshire, Family Research Lab, 1986.

CAROLYN M. WEST

IMAGES OF WOMEN IN AMERICAN LITERATURE. In 1975, when Cheri Register identified the "image of women" approach as "the earliest form of feminist criticism and . . . thus the most fully developed, having already produced its own hardcover texts," critical interest had already shifted. As Toril Moi pointed out 10 years later, the "image" approach— "the search for female stereotypes in the work of male writers and in the critical categories employed by male reviewers commenting on women's work"—gave way about 1975 to analyses of works of women writers.

Earliest among "image" studies in American literature was Leslie Fiedler's, which delineates two stereotypes—the light (spiritual) and the dark (sexual) heroine. Feminist studies developed rapidly in the 1960s. Katharine M. Rogers, tracing literary misogyny from Judeo-Christian and classical to modern time, cites numerous examples from American literature. Mary Ellmann observes that "thought by sexual analogy" permeates Western culture. Ellmann shows how male writers and critics attribute to women characteristics such as formlessness, passivity, instability, confinement, piety, materiality, spirituality, irrationality, and compliancy and identify women as "incorrigible figures," such as the shrew and the witch. Kate Millett's *Sexual Politics* gained popularity among both academic and general readers, partially, at least, because it analyzed images of women as sex objects in works by two of the decade's most controversial American writers—Henry Miller and Norman Mailer—and did so with an authoritative aplomb that made four-letter words critically respectable.

During the 1970s journal articles, anthologies, and collections of essays expanded the "image" tradition. Kimberley Snow and Wendy Martin applied the "image" approach specifically to American literature. Anthologies (Ferguson; Murray; Pearson and Pope) revealed the inadequacy of negative and ideal stereotypes and thus the need to examine works by both men and women. Two collections of essays (Cornillon and Springer) pointed the same way. Susan Koppelman Cornillon criticized the "unreal" female characters in works by both men and women, challenged the techniques of modernist writers and formalist critics, and called for new ways of reading and writing literature.

The earliest images of women in American literature by men picture woman as evil and frivolous. Thomas Weld's description of Anne Hutchison in his introduction to the second edition of John Winthrop's *A Short Story of the Rise, reign, and ruine of the Antinomians . . . and the lamentable death of Ms. Hutchison* (1644) employs satanic and serpentine imagery and finds her murder by Indians at Hell-gate providential punishment. Nathaniel Ward's *Simple Cobler of Aggawam* (1647) satirizes the Puritan woman preoccupied with fashion, labeling her "the epitome of nothing."

Eighteenth-century writers continue the pattern but focus more directly on woman's sexuality. Benjamin Franklin's treatment of his mother and of

Deborah Read (*Autobiography*, 1868) reveals how minimally he regarded them. His satires also illustrate his sexist attitude, except when he allows his garrulous widow Silence Dogood and the promiscuous Polly Baker to voice his criticism of the double standard regarding sexual morality and property rights. His "Old Mistresses Apologue" (1926) reduces a woman to sex object. John Trumbull's *The Progress of Dullness* (1772–1773) satirizes women as clothes trees, gossips, and readers of Samuel Richardson's sentimental novels.

When Americans begin writing novels, the virgin turns whore, falling prey to the wiles of the rake. Abandoned, she dies in childbirth, while the rake loses not a degree of social status. In the first American seduction novel, William Hill Brown's *The Power of Sympathy* (1789), stories of seduction fit into each other like Chinese boxes, the outermost dissolving when the would-be seducer repents, only to learn that the woman he loves and now wishes to marry is his sister by his father's early philandering. Although the heroine resists seduction, she dies, appalled at the near incest.

A variation on the seduction theme emerges in Charles Brockden Brown's gothic novels. Believing that higher education and financial independence would raise women's status, Brown introduces such ideas into his works. Constantia, the central female character in *Ormond* (1799), well educated and financially secure, resists Ormond's advances and kills him when he attempts rape, though, as in others of Brown's novels, the woman merely reacts to circumstances.

The image of the fallen woman persists in the nineteenth and twentieth centuries, the heroine suffering either ostracism or death. Nathaniel Hawthorne's Hester Prynne wears her scarlet letter to her grave, and Zenobia of *The Blithedale Romance* (1852), fallen in grace and fortune, takes her own life, as does the blemished heroine of Stephen Crane's *Maggie, a Girl of the Streets* (1893). In the twentieth century Ernest Hemingway's Catherine Barkley (*A Farewell to Arms*, 1957), like her predecessors, dies after childbirth, punished for her affair with Frederic Henry.

Generally, women characters play small parts in nineteenth-century fiction by men, except as stereotypes or as symbols. The women intended as wives and mothers in Washington Irving's stories fail even in those roles. Dame Van Winkle, described as a termagant, never appears to prove or disprove the label; Katrina Van Tassel, whose wealth and beauty beguile Ichabod Crane, slips from his grasp. Not all of James Fenimore Cooper's women are "sappy as maples and flat as a prairie," as James Russell Lowell describes them in "A Fable for Critics" (1848). Child-maidens, such as Alice Munro in *The Last of the Mohicans* (1826) and spirited, self-sacrificing, and conventional young women such as Elizabeth Temple in *The Pioneers* (1823), enjoy limited action, but Cooper prematurely kills off independent, strong, and sexual Cora of *The Last of the Mohicans*.

Premature death—either literal or figurative—is, in fact, commonplace for women in nineteenth-century works by men. Light and dark heroines so assigned include Hawthorne's Priscilla and Zenobia of *The Blithedale Romance* and Hilda and Miriam of *The Marble Faun* (1860), Herman Melville's Yillah and Hautia of *Mardi* (1849), and Lucy Tartan and Isabel of *Pierre* (1852). Ironically, in *Pierre*, the hero, characterized throughout the novel by female imagery, suffers an untimely death. Edgar Allan Poe's maidens, with the exception of Rowena and Ligeia, seldom appear in pairs, but whether they represent ideals of beauty (Helen), intelligence (Ulalume), or sexuality (the wife in "The Black Cat"), they meet death early. Virgins in Melville's "The Tartarus of Maids" (1855) appear destined to be worn out either as millworkers or as childbearers. Some of the girls and women created by Mark Twain, who idealized the female as the guardian of home and culture, survive; others do not. Roxanne, the strong, passionate black woman of *Pudd'nhead Wilson* (1894), for example, disintegrates as a person and is sold down the river by her son.

The mature woman or mother figure in the early nineteenth century usually remains in the background, supporting and protecting husband and children, guarding the morals and asserting that things will turn out right. At mid-century Walt Whitman, sometime champion of sexual equality, errs blatantly when attempting to exalt women with the remark: "There is nothing greater than the mother of men." As the century wanes, however, the mother becomes overly protective and rigidly moralistic, as illustrated by the hypocritical, drunken Irish mother in Crane's *Maggie*, who self-righteously drives her daughter into the streets. Marginally, she resembles the bitch figure that emerges as the century ends.

Three stereotypes of women appear in Henry James' *The Bostonians* (1886): the clairvoyant young woman, the lesbian, and the spinster reformer. Verena Tarrant, exploited by her parents as a public speaker and "sold" to Olive Chancellor, eventually finds her "true nature" in marriage to Basil Ransom. Olive Chancellor, the wealthy feminist reformer, who seems to have personal as well as political designs on Verena, loses out to Ransom. Miss Birdseye, a venerable spinster past her prime as an abolitionist, succumbs, like Verena, to the wills of stronger people.

Toward the end of the century, William James delineates the Bitch Goddess Success, an image that in various forms continues into the twentieth century. Martha Banta points out two forms—the bitch of conscience (moral tyranny) and the bitch of avarice (the greed to possess). *The Portrait of a Lady* (1881) and *The Wings of the Dove* (1902) provide examples of both. Trina Sieppe in Frank Norris' *McTeague* (1899) combines the two forms. In Theodore Dreiser's novel *Sister Carrie* (1900), Carrie Meeber represents the "sweet" bitch, luring men to her as she rises to success unmindful of the wrecks she leaves behind.

Cultural changes brought about by the first wave of the feminist movement and later aggravated by the social impact of World War I led to the development of the new woman, one who seeks suffrage, increased sexual freedom, and a career. Male writers quickly reflected this change. Scott Fitzgerald's flapper of *This Side of Paradise* (1920) develops into a variety of bitch figures—the golden Daisy Faye Buchanan (*The Great Gatsby*, 1925), who lures Jay Gatsby to his death; Brett Ashley of Hemingway's *The Sun Also Rises* (1926), who continually teases Jake Barnes and wrecks the life and art of the young bullfighter Romero; Margot Macomber of Hemingway's "The Short Happy Life of Francis Macomber" (1938), who shoots her husband fatally; the mindless, heartless Faye Greener of Nathanael West's *The Day of the Locust* (1939), who destroys father, friends, and acquaintances as she tries to ease her own despair; and Mrs. Lillian Taylor, the black matriarch in Chester Himes' *The Third Generation* (1954), who, through her emulation of white culture, drives her doctor husband to poverty, her sons to self-destruction and crime, and herself to prostitution.

Not all women in twentieth-century novels by men are aggressive. Characters such as Dorothy in *The Fifth Column* (1938) and Maria in *For Whom the Bell Tolls* (1940) continue to represent passive servants. Examples of formlessness—soft body, soft mind—include Doris Hollis in Hemingway's *To Have and Have Not* (1937) and Elena Esposito in Norman Mailer's *The Deer Park* (1955).

Twentieth-century mother figures come in various forms, none favorable. William Faulkner's creations are either cold mothers—Mrs. Compson of *The Sound and the Fury* (1929)—or earth mothers—Lena Grove of *Light in August* (1932) and Eula Varner of *The Hamlet* (1940). Destructive mothers akin to the bitch figure include the deadly "Mommy" in Edward Albee's *The American Dream* (1961) and the comically destructive mother in Philip Roth's *Portnoy's Complaint* (1969). Black mothers range from the passive mother in James Baldwin's *Go Tell It on the Mountain* (1951), who submits herself and her children to her husband's violence, to the nagging mother in Richard Wright's *Native Son* (1940).

The most stark image to emerge in the twentieth century is woman as sex object. Promiscuous characters like Candace and Quentin Compson in Faulkner's *The Sound and the Fury* and Temple Drake in his *Sanctuary* (1931) combine whore and bitch, provoking violence and hatred in male characters that make past misogyny seem mild. The works of Henry Miller, such as the *Tropic of Cancer* (1934), *Tropic of Capricorn* (1939), *Plexus* (1949), *Sexus* (1953), and *Nexus* (1960), contain seemingly endless images of woman as cunt, sewer, whore, and bitch. Kate Millett characterizes Mailer as a "prisoner of the virility cult" who sees and depicts sex as war and war as sexual. Quoting extensively from his works, she illustrates his view of women primarily as recipients of male aggression, a salient example being Rojack's impregnating, then sodomizing Cherry, the maid, after having strangled Deborah, his wife.

In the mid-1970s critical interest generally shifted from the "images" approach in works by men to the study of women writers and a literature that would more accurately reflect women's experiences and model their possibilities. Even so, occasionally, an "images" analysis appears, taking a new direction. Kristin Herzog examines women, African Americans, Native Americans, and other ethnics in works by Hawthorne, Melville, W. W. Brown, and Martin R. Delany, as well as in the epic *Dekanawida* and other Native American narratives. Although Carol Fairbanks focuses on images created by women writers, the introduction to her work describes male-created images of women, ranging from the reluctant to the courageous, used as foils to magnify male heroes. Kali Tal depicts both Asian and American women. The Asian, extremely objectified and uncomplicated, emerges as whore, "inscrutable lover," or "will-less mistress" useful for pleasure. Americans, difficult, troublesome, untrustworthy, appear most often as betrayers, though sometimes as therapeutic objects. Sylvia Barack Fishman, employs the original "images" approach—examining the immigrant, the Jewish mother, and the American Jewish princess in works by Henry Roth, Herman Wouk, and Philip Roth—before shifting to works by women.

References. Martha Banta, "They Shall Have Faces, Minds, and (One Day) Flesh: Women in Late Nineteenth-Century and Twentieth-Century American Literature," in Marlene Springer (ed.), *What Manner of Woman* (New York, 1977); Susan Koppelman Cornillon (ed.), *Images of Women in Fiction* (Bowling Green, Ohio, 1972); Mary Ellmann, *Thinking about Women* (New York, 1968); Carol Fairbanks, *Prairie Women: Images in American and Canadian Fiction* (New Haven, Conn., 1986); Mary Anne Ferguson (ed.), *Images of Women in Literature* (Boston, 1973); Leslie Fiedler, *Love and Death in the American Novel* (New York, 1960); Sylvia Barack Fishman, *Footprints: Changing Images of Women in American Jewish Fiction* (Hanover, N.H., 1992); Kristin Herzog, *Women, Ethnics, and Exotics* (Knoxville, Ky., 1983); Wendy Martin, "Seduced and Abandoned in the New World: The Image of Women in American Fiction," in Vivian Gornick and Barbara K. Moran (eds.), *Women in Sexist Society* (New York, 1971); Kate Millett, *Sexual Politics* (New York, 1969); Toril Moi, *Sexual/Textual Politics* (London and New York, 1985); Michele Murray (ed.), *A House of Good Proportion* (New York, 1973); Carol Pearson and Katherine Pope (eds.), *Who Am I This Time?* (New York, 1976); Cheri Register, "American Feminist Literary Criticism: A Bibliographical Introduction," in Josephine Donovan (ed.), *Feminist Literary Criticism* (Lexington, Ky., 1975); Katharine M. Rogers, *The Troublesome Helpmate* (Seattle, 1966); Kimberley Snow, "Images of Women in the American Novel," *Aphra* 2 (Winter 1970): 56–68; Marlene Springer (ed.), *What Manner of Woman* (New York, 1977); Kali Tal, "The Mind at War: Images of Women in Vietnam Novels by Combat Veterans," *Contemporary Literature* (Spring 1990): 76–95.

LUCY M. FREIBERT

IMAGES OF WOMEN IN ENGLISH RENAISSANCE LITERATURE. This subject culminates in the image of Milton's Eve in the epic poem *Paradise Lost*. Although Milton's Eve comes, in the mid-seventeenth century, at the end of the Renaissance in England, her image builds upon, and perpetuates, Renaissance antifeminist commonplaces, while it also questions and undermines them.

Milton emphasizes Eve's subordinate position in his description of Adam and Eve in Book 4: "For contemplation he and valor formed, /For softness she and sweet attractive grace; /He for God only, she for God in him" (11.296–299). Eve herself articulates and generalizes that subservience: "God is thy Law, thou mine; to know no more/Is woman's happiest knowledge and her praise" (11.638–639). When she rebels against her secondary position, she separates herself from Adam in their Edenic tasks and thus is vulnerable to Satan's temptations.

Yet Milton's Eve also embodies some of the Protestant reformer's ideas about companionate marriage. Eve's sinfulness is not hers alone. While she falls tempted by Satan, Adam falls out of desire for her love. Eve's influence leads to the couple's mutual education. Through her pleas to Adam for forgiveness, Adam learns of the need for reconciliation and mercy, the Christian teaching of Milton's epic. As the mother of humankind, Eve learns that "by me the Promised Seed shall all restore" (12, 1.623). When the poem ends, Adam and Eve are "hand in hand" as they meet the world all before them. Although Milton's Eve becomes a more complex figure than her first presentation in *Paradise Lost* suggests, the dominant impression of woman's representation in Milton's poetic career and corpus remains that of a subordinate, shadowy figure.

When the Renaissance in England was at its height, in Edmund Spenser's Elizabethan world, the great epic poet of the 1590s presents images of women that contrast with the shadowy or negative women of Milton's epic poem. While antifeminist views of female nature are embodied in the allegorical Error in Book 1 of Spenser's *The Faerie Queene*, other females throughout the epic serve to celebrate women.

In part because Spenser's poem was written in praise of his own Queen Elizabeth, the positive images of women range widely. They include the gentle, yet forceful, Una, whose cry, "Fie, fie, faint harted knight" (1. ix. 465) shocks the feeble Redcrosse Knight into action against the temptations of Despair. In the third book of *The Faerie Queene*, the virtue of Chastity is exemplified through the woman warrior Britomart. In this portrait, Spenser tells Queen Elizabeth that he is disguising praise of her, his own queen, since explicit celebration would be inadequate: "But O dred Soveraine/ Thus farre forth pardon, sith that choicest wit/ Cannot your glorious pourtraict figure plaine/ That I in colour showes may shadow it,/ And antique praises unto present persons fit" (3. i. 23–27).

Throughout her reign, Queen Elizabeth provided a strong, positive image of a woman, through which poets from Peele's play, *The Arraignment of Paris*, through William Shakespeare's *Henry VI*, Part 3 found opportunities to create dominant roles for woman. Yet Queen Elizabeth herself perpetuated some of the misogynist stereotypes that haunted her at her accession in 1558, in such tracts as John Knox's *Blast of the Trumpet against the Monstrous Regiment of Women*. Queen Elizabeth ruled through her own alienation from her womanliness. She ruled as the Virgin Queen, continuing the idea of chastity as the norm and replacing in her still newly Protestant country the lost ideal of the Virgin Mary. The artifice of her costuming and the artfulness of her speeches both contributed to her power.

During Elizabeth's reign from 1558 to 1603, positive images of women include the female characters of Shakespeare's comedies, like Rosalind of *As You Like It* and Beatrice of *Much Ado about Nothing*. After James I's accession, however, the Jacobean theater explored female characters who achieved tragic, heroic stature, like John Webster's *The Duchess of Malfi*. In her closet drama, *The Tragedy of Mariam*, Elizabeth Cary explored the dilemmas facing strong women. In addition, in this later period of the Renaissance, such women writers as Elizabeth Grymeston, the author of the *Miscelanea*; Lady Mary Wroth, the author of the poetry and prose epic romance *Urania*; and Amelia Lanier, the author of a poetic defense of Eve, became creators of rich images of women, which we are only now beginning to recover.

References. Mary Beth Rose (ed.), *Women in the Middle Ages and the Renaissance: Literary and Historical Perspectives* (Syracuse, 1986); "Women in the Renaissance," *English Literary Renaissance* 14 (1984): 253–439.

NONA FIENBERG

IMAGES OF WOMEN IN MEDIEVAL DRAMA represent those regarded as important agents in Christian history. The Virgin Mary and female saints played central roles in the drama of salvation enacted in hundreds of plays of biblical history and saintly deeds during the later Middle Ages. As vehicles for divine power and intercessors for human sinners, these holy females are so important that one can speak of a "feminization" of late medieval piety that is reflected in the drama.

Although all plays draw on the large body of exegetical, apocryphal, and folk material to interpret the women's actions, principles of selection also reflect the ideology of the social group producing the play as well as ideologies implicit in different dramatic genres. As the place of women in these ideologies varied, so images of women in the plays could vary widely.

The earliest and most widespread scenes with women characters were enactments of the angel's announcement of Christ's resurrection to the three Marys at the tomb (the *visitatio sepulchri*). We call these scenes "liturgical dramas," but since they usually took place within the celebration of the Easter matins office, were sung in Latin, and acted by and for clerics, they are more appropriately regarded as liturgical expansions than as "drama." The gender of the three Marys is unimportant, for they are spiritual icons, representing all worshipers who seek Christ.

However, in a number of Easter plays, usually from the fourteenth or fifteenth century and in the spoken vernacular, the three Marys who come to anoint Christ's body are referred to as "weeping women." Attention is drawn to their gender by a spice merchant who, like a quack apothecary, promises that the ointments he sells them will act as aphrodisiacs or cosmetics to heighten their erotic appeal. One of the three Marys, Mary Magdalene, was especially associated in medieval drama with female sexual misconduct. She was portrayed as a beautiful, vain, and lecherous young woman who abandoned her worldly sins and became an example of Christ's mercy to those who demonstrated true penitence and ardent love of him.

In some scenes, the Marys are greeted with scorn when they bring news of the Resurrection to the apostles; Peter, Thomas, and others scoff that they cannot believe women's words since everyone knows that women love to spread idle tales. The function of this dramatic denigration of women is to critique conventional wisdom and worldly status. Just as the first announcement of Christ's birth was given to poor shepherds, so the first news of his Resurrection comes to women who are socially inferior. The devotion of the Marys or the exemplary penitence of Magdalene represents possibilities outside the normal structures of life, but possibilities available to all in their spiritual or social condition. Within the context of late medieval communal festivity, plays with gender symbolism expressed alternatives to the status quo.

Other representations of the Marys in drama might emphasize the theme of female kinship. In apocryphal legend Mary Salome and Mary Jacobi were said to be half sisters to the Virgin Mary through earlier marriages of their mother, St. Anne. The cult of St. Anne, part of popular piety of the fifteenth century, celebrated the female lineage of Anne and her daughters. Plays in which the kinship of these "holy women" is emphasized often are connected to lay devotional groups with largely female membership.

Cycles and passion plays produced for an urban bourgeoisie in which male civic and craft guild patronage predominated tended to portray biblical women as wives, workers, and neighbors. Many scenes of Joseph and Mary demonstrated proper marital relations as described in contemporary conduct books, while Noah's wife and the wives of other characters like the spice merchant, Pilate, or the smith who made the nails for the Crucifixion provided comic examples of disordered female behavior. Mary Magdalene's sister Martha—who in monastic and mystical literature had represented the less elevated "active life" of service in the world (whereas Mary represented the "contemplative")—now took on status as the busy housewife who entertained the men of God and gave alms. Martha earned salvation not by rejecting the world but by using its goods properly, with pious economy. She could be a role model not only to the housewife but to her bourgeois husband as well.

Eve as archetypal disobedient female is always portrayed with women's weaknesses of vanity, manipulativeness, irrationality, and perversity in plays of the Fall. The image of Eve in the medieval drama draws on anti-feminist satires, while the portrayal of Mary, who redeems humankind from the effects of the Fall, draws on a corresponding literature of pro-feminist praise.

Although the typical medieval morality play casts a male as protagonist, at least one from Holland portrays a girl who is seduced into a Faustian pact with the Devil. The virtues and the vices are often female in the morality tradition, whose iconography is indebted to the visual arts.

Despite the variety and importance of female figures in medieval drama, acting was, with few exceptions, an activity only for males until the Renaissance. When a play was performed in a convent, the nuns took all the parts, male and female. In the late fifteenth century, too, dramas produced by the urban bourgeoisie occasionally cast young women, daughters or wives of important men in town, in female parts. Otherwise, female roles were probably filled by young men whose pubertal changes were still taking place, about age 18–20 in this period of later maturation.

KATHLEEN ASHLEY

IMAGES OF WOMEN IN RESTORATION AND EARLY EIGHTEENTH-CENTURY DRAMA vary widely from classic antifeminist stereotypes to tough-minded portraits of women confronting complex problems in a society that grants them no genuine authority.

At the beginning of the period, the Restoration belle is a self-assured, independent, and witty young woman reluctant to give up the pleasures of single life. She likes the city and its freedom to come and go, to select her acquaintances and pastimes, to feel, in a way, free. Harriet in Etherege's *The Man of Mode* (1676) epitomizes the type. In a milieu where cleverness is the ultimate virtue, only she possesses the sangfroid and intellectual strength to hold her own in verbal combat with the libertine hero. Harriet shares Dorimant's pleasure in the control and conquest of the love chase, but ultimately she differs from other women whom Dorimant pursues in the self-control and wit that allow her to hold out for marriage. Though the witty belle may be libertine in attitude, unlike the beau, she must be chaste in action.

Excused some from this stricture are young country girls, who, like amoral animals, are free from the pretenses of society. Brought to town by a jealous old husband, Margery Pinchwife in Wycherley's *Country Wife* (1675) does not conceal her pleasure in the omnivorous Horner's advances. The "natural" Miss Prue in Congreve's *Love for Love* (1695) freely proclaims, "Now my mind is set upon a Man, I will have a Man some way or other" (5.1). However, most women unable to control their sexual needs are fair game for ridicule. Their names proclaim their image: Lady Cock-wood in Etherege's *She Wou'd if She Cou'd* (1668), Mrs. Loveit in Etherege's *The Man of Mode* (1676), Mrs. Termagant in Shadwell's *The Squire of Alsatia* (1688), Mrs. Wittwoud in Southerne's *The Wives' Excuse* (1691), and Lady Wishfort in Congreve's *The Way of the World* (1700). The wits ridicule those who are unable to suppress sexual desires beneath a mask of prudery or who fail to maintain a predatory coolness and so allow themselves to be victimized. A superannuated belle like Lady Wishfort is ridiculous for not realizing that she is no longer a beauty, yet she is also pathetic, trapped in a society that compels her to paint on the bloom of youth.

Judging from the couples they see around them, many young women in Restoration comedy do not expect much from marriage. Alithea, though otherwise the brightest woman in *The Country Wife*, feels obliged to marry her foolish suitor because she mistakes his self-absorption and negligence for genuine love and trust. But more often, aware of the real consequences of loveless marriages of convenience, women seek to marry someone not only attractive but also perhaps compatible. To this end countless heroines engage in witty "proviso scenes." In the most famous of these scenes (in *The Way of the World*), Millamant tries to carve out with Mirabel ground rules for daily coexistence to ensure her "dear liberty" before allowing that she "may by degrees dwindle into a wife" (act 4). Taking the lead that other women such as Catherine Trotter, Mary Pix, and Delarivière Manley will follow, Aphra Behn makes noticeable how stock elements of the marriage plot exploit women by reassigning the commonplaces: in *The Rover* (1677) the sentimental idealist on married love is the prostitute Angellica Bianca, not the virtuous, but tough-minded, Hellena. In this and a series of later plays Behn demonstrates the ways standard marriage plots do the culture's work to keep women in their place.

By the 1690s playwrights turn their attention from public courtship to the private consequences when couples wed without choosing carefully. Generally, husbands cope with unhappy marriages by philandering or gaming; without legal or economic protection, women had fewer options. In Colley Cibber's notorious *Love's Last Shift* (1696), Amanda's husband Loveless, absent for 10 years, returns only when he believes her dead. After enduring what the epilogue calls his being "lewd above four acts," this patient wife finally reclaims him on his terms with a variation of "the bed trick." Discovering that the delightful woman in bed is not a courtesan but his disguised wife, Loveless vows to reform, praising "the chaste Rapture of a Vertuous Love" (act 5). (An unconvinced Sir John Vanbrugh followed up on the Amanda/Loveless story later that season in *The Relapse*.) More often, wives—such as Lady Easy in Cibber's *The Careless Husband* (1704) and Mrs. Bellamant in Henry Fielding's *The Modern Husband* (1730)—rely on the strength of their virtue and forbearance to retrieve wayward husbands.

Particularly telling, however, are the images of unhappy wives in plays that offer no easy solutions. In Thomas Southerne's *The Wives Excuse* (1691), Mrs. Friendall holds off tempting advances while covering for her lascivious and mean-spirited husband. But at play's end, when Friendall is discovered in bed with Mrs. Wittwoud, the Friendalls agree to part, granting Mrs. Friendall a separate maintenance. He is pleased with his new freedom, but she recognizes her position: "The unjust world . . . condemns us to a Slavery for Life: And if by Separation we get free, then all our Husband's Faults are laid on us. . . . I must be still your Wife, and still unhappy" (act 5). Lady Brute in Vanbrugh's *The Provoked Wife* (1697) and Mrs. Sullen in Farquhar's *The Beaux' Stratagem* (1707) face, in some ways, a harder condition: their husbands, unlike the loathsome Mr. Friendall, are merely bored and boring. Though Mrs. Sullen is promised a "divorce" that will allow her to remarry, an option not available to women in the audience, Lady Brute's circumstances remain unresolved at play's end.

The portrayal of women in tragedy of the period is apparently far removed from these quotidian problems. In spectacular heroic drama, women often fit simple cultural stereotypes: Lyndaraxa and Almahide in Dryden's *Conquest of Granada* (1670–1671) and Nourmahal and Indamora in his *Aureng-Zebe* (1675) offer variations on standard contrasts between the manipulative seductress and the long-suffering wife. But the latter image of woman—as the civilizer whose noble love attempts to turn man's drive for power toward socially acceptable goals—gains increasing prominence. As Jaffeir says to his wife, Belvidera, in Otway's *Venice Preserved* (1682), "Oh Woman! lovely Woman! Nature made thee/To temper Man: We had been Brutes without you" (act 1.1).

With growing frequency, women characters begin to dominate tragedy that is moving toward pathos. Following the lead of such plays as Otway's *The Orphan* (1680), Banks' *Vertue Betray'd* (1682), and Southerne's *The Fatal Marriage* (1694), Nicholas Rowe produced what he called "she-tragedies," centering on the undeserved distresses and domestic woes of their heroines: *The Fair Penitent* (1703), *The Tragedy of Jane Shore* (1714), and *Lady Jane Grey* (1715). Modern readers admire the spirited Millwood, in George Lillo's *The London Merchant* (1731), who says she learned from men that money secures one from contempt and dependence. "You [men] go on deceiving and being deceived, harassing, plaguing, and destroying one another," she tells her accusers, "but women are your universal prey" (act 4.2). Yet contemporary audiences prized the play's Maria Thorowgood, who dutifully suffers "generous distress" when her beloved is revealed as a murderer. Like the good women trapped in bad marriages in comedy or bereft maidens like Indiana in Steele's *Conscious Lovers* (1722), good-natured Maria Thorowgood is the image of woman that carries into the great novels of the eighteenth century.

References. Paula R. Backscheider, *Spectacular Politics: Theatrical Power and Mass Culture in Early Modern England* (Baltimore and London; 1993); Jacqueline Pearson, *The Prostituted Muse: Images of Women and Women Dramatists, 1642–1737* (New York, 1988); Mary Anne Schofield and Cecilia Macheski, *Curtain Calls: British and American Women and the Theater, 1660–1820* (Athens, Ohio, 1991).

SUSAN K. AHERN

IMAGES OF WOMEN IN ROMANTIC PERIOD LITERATURE are most commonly thought of in terms of the poetry of men (Blake, Wordsworth, Coleridge, Byron, Shelley, and Keats) and prose fiction by such men and women as Mary Shelley, Austen, and Scott. The images of women in the poetry of the great Romantics contrast significantly with the depiction of women in prose fiction. In the first, we see the female in terms of male aspirations and desires; in the second, women characters are generally more developed human beings.

Typically, the Romantic poet-persona seeks the ideal in terms of sexual union with a mysterious and elusive female, who often turns out to be a reflection of his desire for self-fulfillment. Because the poet considers this often-exotic female as the Other and, primarily, in terms of his own male ego, women appear as idealizations, not individuals. This pattern emerges in Shelley's *Alastor* (1816) and in Keats' *Endymion* (1818), with variations such as Coleridge's Abyssinian maid and her magical dulcimer in "Kubla Khan" (1816). But if the female represents the object of the male quest, she also threatens the male as the femme fatale, who, like Keats' belle dame, seduces and destroys the pale knight and is thus blamed for the failure of imaginative vision. In the most narcissistic and nihilistic form of the quest, the desired female is the quester's sister, and the incestuous relationship is doomed to failure. We see this pattern in Byron's *Manfred* (1817), where we learn that Astarte had been destroyed by her brother's love, a supreme form of self-love. Although presumably without incestuous longing, in "Tintern Abbey" (1798) Wordsworth looks into his sister Dorothy's wild eyes and sees, not her hopes and fears, but his own "former self."

Also in Romantic poetry nature is depicted in female terms in opposition to male powers of imagination. Blake envisions nature as the deceptive goddess Vala, and Wordsworth, although a worshiper of nature, also reveals the darker shades of her power and influence in such works as the Lucy poems and the "Intimations Ode" (1807). Individual women in Wordsworth's poetry often become subsumed in nature and its processes so that they have no voice, no identity apart from the male poet's perception of nature: Lucy dies and is "rolled round in earth's diurnal course / With rocks, and stones, and trees" ("A Slumber Did My Spirit Seal").

Readers have noted the particular association between nature and motherhood in Wordsworth's poetry, generally concluding that Wordsworth sought the guardianship and protection in nature that he lost with the death of his mother when he was a young child. Wordsworth perceptively describes the natural process of the mother–infant bonding in a noted passage in Book 2 of *The Prelude* (1850).

Although a male-centered solipsistic vision prevails in much of the poetry, the Romantics also strive to place male–female relationships in the context of the fundamental human rights and freedoms inspired by the French Revolution. In *America* (1793), for instance, Blake dramatizes the intrinsic relationship between political and sexual liberation; following Mary Wollstonecraft's *Vindication of the Rights of Woman* (1792), he sees the analogy between political and marital tyranny. In a renovated world, the "doors of marriage are open," and females glow "with the lusts of youth" (15:19, 15:22). Like Wollstonecraft, Blake sees female liberation also liberating men from the self-destructive relationships based on power and jealousy. Shelley, despite the contradictions in his own life and art, also claims in his *Defense of Poetry* (1840) the "abolition of personal and domestic slavery" and the "emancipation of women" to be the highest hopes for humankind.

The Romantic poets do, on occasion, acknowledge and even criticize their own self-absorption, but one of the strongest critiques of Romanticism comes from Mary Shelley, daughter of Mary Wollstonecraft and wife of the poet. In the character of Victor Frankenstein, Mary Shelley reveals the dangers of egotistical self-absorption, even when accompanied by genius. The more caring, sociable, and "human" monster (identified by some readers as feminine), created and destroyed by Frankenstein's ego, challenges the justice of Frankenstein's ambition. But *Frankenstein* (1818) is full of unresolved problems, and Mary Shelley seems both to condemn and to desire Frankenstein's God-like creative powers.

The Romantics generally aspired to the great masculine, prophetic tradition of Miltonic poetry, in which the male bard as God-like creator sought the inspiration of his female muse. Such a concept of creativity and authorship excluded the female writer, as Mary Shelley suggests in the introduction added to the 1831 edition of *Frankenstein*. But the relatively new form of the novel was congenial to women both because of its "newness" and because the female writer could focus on the moral and ideological issues arising out of daily life and basic human relationships and institutions.

Jane Austen, of course, knew that she had been excluded from a male tradition. She has Anne Elliot argue in *Persuasion* (1818) that "men have had every advantage of us in telling their own story. Education has been theirs in so much higher a degree; the pen had been in their hands" (Chapter 23). Through close and sympathetic portrayal of characters like Anne

Elliot, Emma Woodhouse (*Emma*, 1816), and Elizabeth Bennet (*Pride and Prejudice*, 1813), Austen presents women who change and develop as they discover knowledge of themselves and their social world. We sometimes see her women characters through men's eyes, but we are almost always allowed to focus on the heroine's developing consciousness.

In his historical novels, Scott presents a wider panorama of society than does Austen, focusing less on a developing consciousness than on the larger forces and movements of society. In so doing, he creates a variety of male and female characters, ranging in social class from royalty to low-life criminals. Generally speaking, Scott is more successful in depicting native Scottish characters—often peasantry who speak in dialect—than ladies and gentlemen. While Scott's ladies are often as stiff and conventional as their language, his lower-class women have a flesh-and-blood liveliness. A good case in point is Jeanie Deans (in *The Heart of Mid-Lothian* [1818]), who refuses to save her innocent sister's life by telling a lie in court but undertakes a solitary and dangerous journey on foot to London to obtain a royal pardon. Behind Jeanie's courage lies the Scottish Presbyterian tradition, perhaps narrow-minded and at times fanatical but asserting itself in Jeanie as an absolute moral standard.

Despite the working generalizations between poets and novelists, we should acknowledge that the images of women across genres are as varied as the authors themselves. The Romantic period constitutes less a consistent school of thought than a historical span that includes such diverse writers as Byron and Austen. Even within the work of individual authors, often unresolved and contradictory images of women abound, revealing the ambivalent attitude toward women and their place in late eighteenth-century and early nineteenth-century culture.

References. Sandra M. Gilbert and Susan Gubar, *The Madwoman in the Attic* (New Haven, Conn., 1979); Margaret Homans, *Women Writers and Poetic Identity* (Princeton, 1980); Barbara Schapiro, *The Romantic Mother: Narcissistic Patterns in Romantic Poetry* (Baltimore, 1983); Irene Taylor and Gina Luria, "Gender and Genre: Women in British Romantic Literature," in Marlene Springer (ed.), *What Manner of Woman* (New York, 1977), 98–123.

JUDITH W. PAGE

IMAGES OF WOMEN IN VICTORIAN LITERATURE are often stereotypic reflections of social realities in nineteenth-century Britain. The middle-class ideal of womanhood was a domestic one; the Victorian woman is seen as daughter, wife, and mother, with qualities men deemed suitable for the fulfillment of these roles. The highest manifestation of this ideal is "the angel in the house," a label derived from a poem written by Coventry Patmore between 1854 and 1860, extolling married life and the model wife, a competent manager of domestic affairs and an exemplar of all the moral virtues.

Charles Dickens consistently reflects the image of the angel in the house. In *David Copperfield* (1849–1850), Agnes Wickfield is the paradigm of this stereotype. She has control of the management of her father's household, her mother being dead, and she wears at her waist a basket containing the house keys. This image of Agnes is combined with the picture of her ascending the staircase, the light from a stained-glass window shining behind her. The image of the saintly woman pervades the novel; to the end, David sees Agnes as "ever pointing upward . . . ever directing me to higher things!" (Chapter 60). The role is repeated in Esther Summerson, the domestic and moral anchor of *Bleak House* (1852–1853), whose emblem also is the basket of household keys. Esther is a model female—modest, loyal, self-sacrificing, caring, subordinate to men and nurturing of children.

Women who fall short of the domestic ideal do so because they are incompetent in some way to fulfill the role of housekeeper, wife, and mother; they lack the moral qualities considered essential for the role, or they are psychologically unsuited to the passive, subservient character demanded by it.

Dickens presents many ineffectual angels. Often they are childish women like David Copperfield's wife, Dora, prized for her innocence and sweetness in spite of her very real deficiencies as housekeeper and wife. Generally Dickens treats such characters tenderly, torn between their attractive feminine qualities and their serious inability to manage for their husbands. Sometimes, however, he uses the indifference to good household management as a metaphor for a warped social vision and misplaced priorities. Mrs. Pocket (*Great Expectations*, 1860–1861) buries herself in the peerage, ignoring her children. Mrs. Jellyby's establishment in *Bleak House* goes to ruin, and her family is neglected as she sets her sights on philanthropy in Africa. Setting these irresponsibilities against the larger themes in the novels, Dickens implies that such women should be attending to their domestic duties.

Frequently, the angel in the house role is too limiting for independent-minded women of intelligence and spirit. In *Jane Eyre* (1847) Charlotte Brontë's heroine complains bitterly of the "restraint" and "stagnation" of the domestic role (Chapter 12). In *Middlemarch* (1871–1872) George Eliot demonstrates the limitations of the traditional female role for Dorothea Brooke and Rosamond Vincy. Dorothea had hoped to be her husband's "lamp holder" (Chapter 5) by helping him with his scholarly work. Limited by her female education, Dorothea does not presume to do such work on her own, but she is frustrated when Casaubon is incapable of sharing it with her. Like Jane Eyre, Dorothea Brooke is both psychologically and intellectually unsuited to find contentment as the passive household angel.

Rosamond Vincy is, typically, educated to be ornamental. Her "accomplishments" and her delicate, blond beauty make her attractive to a variety of suitors but do not prepare her for the realities of married life, nor do they give her that spiritual dimension that a woman was expected to possess as if it were genetic. Her husband, Lydgate, expected her to be the angel in his house, gracing his life and assisting him in his career by being a careful manager and a sympathetic retreat from his worldly troubles. Lacking the practical education, common sense, and strength of character to fulfill Lydgate's expectations, Rosamond makes him and herself miserable as they struggle with their problems. His stereotypical view of womanhood is as much to blame for their unhappiness as she is.

Generally, aggressive women, old or physically unattractive women, women desiring to do traditionally masculine work, and unmarried women of a certain age are considered anomalous and inherently unfeminine. These characters sometimes are given a wider scope than the traditional heroine, their idiosyncrasies freeing them from the conventional role. Wilkie Collins' Marian Halcombe, the dark and unattractive sister in *The Woman in White* (1860), is resourceful, brave, and intelligent. She is given "manly" virtues to compensate for her lack of beauty. While men treat her as an intellectual equal, Marian is not an example of the "new woman" found in the later novels of the period. She has no ambitions to do men's work or to claim rights denied to her because of her sex.

Elizabeth Gaskell creates a sympathetic picture of elderly widows and old maids in *Cranford* (1851–1853), showing clearly the pressure of financial constraints on women with no men to provide for them. The genteel poverty and sexual paranoia of the Cranford ladies are handled with light comedy, but other novels provide a darker picture of women without men. George Gissing's pathetic Madden sisters (*The Odd Women*, 1893) show the desperation of husbandless females and the suffering of those who marry only to fulfill social expectations or to find financial security.

Some female characters fail morally. In Thackeray's *Vanity Fair* (1847–1848) Becky Sharp is conniving and ambitious; she manipulates men, and her sexual behavior is suspect. Skilled at many kinds of household management, she does not employ her domestic skills for the comfort of husband and child. Thackeray makes Becky amusing and interesting, but he also makes it clear that she is no model for his female readers. His most damning indictment is her lack of concern for her young son; a bad, unloving mother is an unnatural woman.

Few Victorian heroines are like Becky Sharp. Most fallen angels are portrayed as victims of adverse social circumstances or unscrupulous men. Female sexual purity is so fixed in the Victorian mind that few nineteenth-century novelists treat its lapses realistically. Most, like Charles Dickens, sentimentalize fallen women. David Copperfield's childhood playmate, Little Emily, is lured away by the magnetic villain Steerforth. Seduced and abandoned, Emily is saved through the help of another fallen woman, Martha, a stereotypical prostitute with a heart of gold. While Elizabeth Gaskell's *Ruth* (1853) may be seen as a plea for a single standard of sexual morality, her handling of the fallen woman echoes the sentimental view; Gaskell endows Ruth with superhuman virtues of forgiveness and self-sacrifice, almost canonizing her with a saintly death.

Traditionally, the obverse of the saintly angel is the dark femme fatale, the dangerous fiend-woman who both charms and destroys men. Few mainstream Victorian novelists present this figure, although shadows of her haunt the sexual nightmares of the period. Normally passionate women such as Jane Eyre must wrestle to reconcile their strong sexual feelings with the conventional view that good women did not experience sexual pleasure. Brontë balances Jane's intense feelings with heavy doses of propriety, and she provides a hideous analogue for passion gone wild in the character of Rochester's mad wife, Bertha.

Comedy is a safeguard for the novelist who wishes to present a sexually attractive female. Anthony Trollope's Madeline Vesey-Neroni (*Barchester Towers*, 1857) is a flagrant flirt; the beautiful Madeline flatters, insinuates, and tempts. While protesting her lack of heart and her unfeminine love of manipulation, Trollope softens her image by making her a humorous adversary to the pompous, power-hungry Mrs. Proudie and the hypocritical Mr. Slope. He further restricts her power to do real harm to the good men of Barchester—enticing as she is—by confining her to her invalid sofa.

Later in the period, novelists began treating women realistically. George Meredith satirizes the male desire for a wife who perfectly reflects the husband's ego. In *The Egoist* (1879), Clara Middleton escapes marriage to a hopeless male chauvinist. Thomas Hardy's *Tess of the D'Urbervilles* (1891) illustrates the consequences of false male images of women and the sexual double standard. Tess is a victim not only of rape but of her husband's view that she is irreparably tainted by it. Angel Clare's inability to excuse Tess and her own acceptance of his view of her are at the heart of their tragedy.

Novels of the period present many examples of women for whom the Victorian ideal is a contining—sometimes deadly—trap. Jane Eyre, Dorothea Brooke, Tess Durbeyfield, and scores of their sisters show that the image was not resisted without physical, social, or psychological peril. The suffering women experience for their nonconformity reveals the potency of the image in the nineteenth century.

References. Susan Fraiman, *Unbecoming Women: British Women Writers and the Novel of Development* (New York, 1993); Sandra M. Gilbert and Susan Gubar, *The Madwoman in the Attic* (New Haven, Conn., 1979); Barbara Hardy, *Forms of Feeling in Victorian Fiction* (London, 1985); Carolyn Heilbrun, *Reinventing Womanhood* (New York, 1979); Judith Mitchell, *The Stone and the Scorpion: The Female Subject of Desire in the Novels of Charlotte Brontë, George Eliot, and*

Thomas Hardy (New York, 1994); Martha Vincus (ed.), *Suffer and Be Still* (Bloomington, Ind., 1972).

SHARON LOCY

IMMIGRANT WOMEN are always numbered among the persons voluntarily seeking new homes or work in the United States. Over 14 million women crossed U.S. boundaries in the 100 years after 1860, and another 4 million entered in the following 20 years. Still, women's representation varied considerably from group to group and across time. Their exact experiences resembled neither those of immigrant men nor those of native-born American women.

Prior to 1880, most immigrant women came from Northern and Western Europe in numbers only slightly lower than for men of similar backgrounds. These women were both settlers, traveling to cheap American land in family groups, and labor migrants, seeking work in growing American cities.

As migration to the United States peaked in the latter nineteenth century, both the origins of immigrants and women's representation changed. Demands for unskilled male labor was growing, while in the female labor market clerical work—scarcely open to non-English speakers—fueled growth. Not surprisingly, women made up only one-third of immigrants from Southern and Eastern Europe prior to World War I. The migration of Chinese and Japanese women was further harshly restricted by discriminatory legislation (see Evelyn Glenn). Still, famine and pogrom did not discriminate on the basis of sex: Irishwomen outnumbered men during these years, and almost as many female as male Jews left their ghettos in Eastern Europe (see Diner; Weinberg).

Immigration restrictions of the 1920s changed migration patterns, in part, by giving priority to the relatives of immigrants already living in the United States. Women always took special advantage of provisions for family reunification. Since 1930, women and children have made up two-thirds of immigrants entering the United States. Moreover, as migration levels began to climb again after 1965, the newest immigrants from Asia, the Caribbean, and Latin America continued to demonstrate the disproportionate attraction of the United States for women: female majorities are now the rule, not the exception.

While marriage and family reunification have probably provided most women with the incentive to migrate to the United States, the desire to work cannot so easily be separated from these concerns. Most women who entered the United States needed to work at some time in their lives. Still, foreign-born women have held jobs in relatively limited sectors of the U.S. economy. Domestic service was of greatest importance in the nineteenth century, attracting young, unmarried women from Ireland, Scandinavia, and Germany. Even today, women from Latin America and the Caribbean are employed disproportionately in household work and child care, especially if they lack proper visas. Factory work generally and textile and garment production in particular have also remained important employers of women immigrants. Ninety years ago, Italian, Jewish, and Polish women sewed garments; today, Mexican and Asian women work in sweatshops that are little changed from the past. (Today, however, immigrant women are no more likely to work for wages than are the native-born.) Some immigrant women are extremely well educated. Women's migration has created a virtual brain drain of health care workers from some parts of the Third World like the Philippines and the Caribbean.

Immigrant women and men brought with them attitudes toward work, family responsibilities, and sexuality that often seemed at odds with native U.S. middle-class ideals. Whether these traditions encouraged female autonomy, self-support, and celibacy or sexual unions outside marriage; or submissiveness, early marriage, and high fertility, the immigrant woman has always attracted special and alarmed attention from native-born Americans. During the Progressive Era, her image was that of a backward conservative, a resister of "Americanization," a breeder of inferior children, and a potential prostitute. However, it was also that of the helpless victim of American employers and thus the logical beneficiary of protective legislation and educational or welfare programs teaching American cooking, cleaning, and childrearing standards.

Reality, of course, was more complex. Women banded together as workers, as welfare workers for their ethnic communities, as members of religious groups, and—more rarely—as activists for woman's rights. Responsible as they normally were for child rearing (and thus, for much cultural transmission), immigrant women probably did experience culture conflict and culture change in a manner quite different from that for men. Quarrels between parents and daughters over proper womanly behavior were common; for daughters the claim to one's own wage, leisure time, and choice of a husband were typical goals. While some immigrant mothers encouraged their daughters to Americanize and themselves welcomed life in the United States as an escape from patriarchal limitations, others built communities that could support their efforts to pass on older traditions. For today's immigrants—predominantly women from Third World countries—the process of adaptation is further complicated by the complexities of race in a multiethnic society.

References. Hasia Diner, *Erin's Daughters in America* (Baltimore, 1983); Kathie Friedman-Kasaba, *Memories of Migration: Gender, Ethnicity, and Work in the Lives of Jewish and Italian Women in New York, 1870–1924* (New York, 1996); Donna R. Gabaccia, *From the Other Side: Women and Gender in Immigrant Life, 1820–1990* (Bloomington, Ind., 1994); Evelyn Glenn, *Issei, Nisei, Warbride* (Philadelphia, 1986); Louise Lamphere, *From Working Daughters to Working Mothers* (Ithaca, N.Y., 1987); Vicki Ruiz, *Cannery Women, Cannery Lives* (Albuquerque, N. Mex., 1987); Maxine Schwartz Seller (ed.), *Immigrant Women* (Philadelphia,

1980); Sydney Weinberg, *The World of Our Mothers* (Chapel Hill, N.C., 1988); Judy Yung, *Unbound Feet* (Berkeley, Calif., 1995).

DONNA R. GABACCIA

IMPOSTOR PHENOMENON is an internal experience of intellectual phoniness that seems to be prevalent among high-achieving persons, with particularly deleterious effects on women. The term was first used by Pauline Rose Clance and Suzanne Imes in a 1978 paper describing their clinical findings among high-achieving women. It is an emotionally debilitating condition characterized by persistent and unwarranted anxiety about achievement, dread of evaluation, fear of failure and exposure, inability to internalize success, and lack of enjoyment of accomplishment and achievement. Research using Clance and Imes' original construct as well as a scale to measure impostor phenomenon behavior, which Clance developed in 1985, is ongoing. Results at this point indicate that the impostor phenomenon is more prevalent among women whose educational or other achievements surpass expectations based on their family or cultural milieu. In most studies, men are found to identify themselves as suffering from impostor feelings as readily as do women. Clance has recently suggested that, although men may acknowledge the presence of impostor phenomenon characteristics at rates comparable to their acknowledgment by women, women's achievements may be affected more and affected more adversely by these feelings than are men's. This is due, in part, she hypothesizes, to sex-role stereotyping in child rearing and other cultural practices, which leads women to denigrate their achievement needs and to become hyperresponsible in meeting the nurturance needs of others.

References. S. M. Chrisman, W. A. Pieper, P. R. Clance, C. L. Holland, and C. Glickauf-Hughes, "Validation of the Clance Impostor Phenomenon Scale," *Journal of Personality Assessment* (1995); P. R. Clance, *The Impostor Phenomenon: Overcoming the Fear That Haunts Your Success* (Atlanta, 1985); P. R. Clance, D. Dingman, S. Riviere, and D. Stober, "The Impostor Phenomenon in Interpersonal Social Contact: Origins and Treatment," *Women and Therapy* 15, 4 (1995): 79–96; P. R. Clance and S. A. Imes, "The Impostor Phenomenon in High Achieving Women: Dynamic and Therapeutic Intervention" (1978); C. Cozzarelli and B. Major, "Exploring the Validity of the Impostor Phenomenon," *Journal of Social and Clinical Psychology* 9 (1990): 401–417.

PAULINE ROSE CLANCE and MAUREEN O'TOOLE

INCEST is prohibited by law in all states of the United States (although a few states do not have laws *specifically* prohibiting incest). While legal definitions of incest vary considerably, in most states incest statutes forbid marriage or sexual intercourse between blood relatives, regardless of age (American Bar Association). Because of the narrowness of the legal definition, many cases of incestuous abuse are prosecuted under the broader child sexual abuse laws, according to which sexual activity between children and adults—including genital touching and sexual intercourse—is a crime in every state. While states differ in their definitions of a child, most use 16 years of age as the criterion.

Researchers do not feel bound to accept the legal definition of incest. Although there is no consensus among them regarding the best definition of this crime, most include sex acts between blood and nonblood relatives (whether of the same or opposite sex) ranging from vaginal and anal intercourse to milder acts such as sexual kissing. Some researchers also include noncontact experiences such as genital exhibition or sexual propositions. The term "incestuous abuse" is used here to distinguish exploitative incestuous acts from mutual nonexploitative sex play between relatives of approximately the same age.

With the emergence of the second wave of feminism in the late 1960s in the United States, increasing numbers of incest survivors started talking about their abuse. The percentage of women who have ever been incestuously abused in the United States is unknown. The best estimate comes from a study based on face-to-face interviews with a multiethnic probability sample of 930 adult female residents of San Francisco in 1978 (Russell). Defining incestuous abuse as any sexually exploitative contact or attempted contact between relatives, 16 percent of these respondents, or one in every six women, admitted having experienced at least one incident of incestuous abuse before the age of 18.

Only four cases of incestuous abuse (2 percent) in this study had been reported to the police, and only one had resulted in a conviction. With the mandatory reporting laws now in effect, the percentage of cases that are reported today is likely to be much higher. (Every state now requires doctors, psychologists, teachers, and certain others who work closely with children to report all suspected cases of child sexual abuse to child protective services or to law enforcement agencies.)

Four-and-a-half percent of the surveyed women disclosed having been sexually abused by a father, 4.9 percent by an uncle, 2.0 percent by a brother, and 1.2 percent by a grandfather. The prevalence rates for incestuous abuse by female relatives were strikingly low, with female perpetrators constituting only 5 percent of all the incest perpetrators.

The prevalence of incestuous abuse for boys has consistently been found to be much lower than for girls. For example, in the largest national epidemiological study conducted in the United States (n=2,626), only 1.8 percent of boys reported having been incestuously abused. Eight percent of girls reported such abuse—a rate more than four times higher (these statistics were extrapolated from Table 2, Finkelhor).

It is widely believed that incestuous abuse is more prevalent among the lower classes and among people of color. However, David Finkelhor and Larry Baron report that "studies have consistently failed to find any black-white differences in rates of sexual abuse" (69). The same applies to social class (67).

Studies invariably show that a preponderance of incest perpetrators are male, while the vast majority of incest victims/survivors are female. Most male and female incest survivors are abused by males (Russell and Finkelhor). This suggests that male sexual and sex-role socialization likely plays a key role in causing incestuous abuse. For example, men are reared to prefer partners who are younger, smaller, more innocent, more vulnerable, and less powerful than themselves. It follows that children would be more sexually attractive to men than to women. In addition, males are expected not only to take the initiative but also to overcome resistance.

Incestuous abuse is a crucial social problem because of the large number of victims, the acute suffering that often occurs at the time of the abuse, and the long-term damage that often results. Research, such as that reviewed by Angela Browne and David Finkelhor, has repeatedly found a history of incestuous abuse to be associated with adult mental health impairments, including "depression, self-destructive behavior, anxiety, feelings of isolation and stigma, poor self-esteem, a tendency toward revictimization, and substance abuse" (Browne and Finkelhor, 162). Sexual maladjustments and difficulty in trusting others are also widely reported. Such behavior as running away from home, prostitution, alcoholism, drug addiction, and delinquency is also common.

One of the most alarming and well-established long-term effects is the tendency of incestuously abused children to be revictimized later in life. According to Browne and Finkelhor, impaired self-esteem, self-protection, and trust make "victims vulnerable to abusive individuals or unable to anticipate dangerous sexual situations" (also see Russell, 157–190).

A few incest survivors interviewed in Russell's study describe the long-term impact of the abuse on their lives in the following excerpts (12):

Sexually I was very messed up for a long time. I feel that I could have ended up in a mental hospital from the experiences. . . . It will affect me forever. (Stepfather–daughter incest, age 9)

I can't seem to get over it. It's so deep-seated, even now at 43 I'm still affected. (Attempted rape by brother-in-law, age 16)

Everything that's happened to me since in my life has been a result somehow of that experience. (Stepfather–daughter incest, age 14)

I think now that all men are out there for what they can get. You can't even trust your own brother. (Brother–sister incest, age 16)

I went completely inside myself. . . . There probably isn't one area it hasn't touched. (Father–daughter incest, age 15)

Most knowledge about the psychological characteristics of incest perpetrators is still based on the very small percentage of apprehended and/or incarcerated cases. These men and boys cannot be considered representative of undetected perpetrators. Therefore, the value of theories generated by studying them is very limited.

Feminism has revolutionized our understanding of violence and sexual abuse of females. Besides helping incest survivors to disclose their experiences without fear of blame, feminist theorists recognize how gender inequality, embedded in patriarchal institutions like the traditional family, promotes incestuous abuse. In her groundbreaking book, for example, Judith Herman wrote, that "a frankly feminist perspective offers the best explanation of the existing data [on incestuous abuse]. Without an understanding of male supremacy and female oppression, it is impossible to explain why the vast majority of incest perpetrators . . . are male, and why the majority of victims . . . are female" (3). Herman indicts the patriarchal family as fostering incestuous abuse. She points out that when fathers perceive themselves as bosses and their wives and children as duty-bound to serve them, the daughters are at risk of father–daughter incest. Efforts to combat incestuous abuse therefore require a radical transformation of the patriarchal family into a family based on equality—whether the adult caregivers are heterosexual, bisexual, lesbian, or gay. To achieve such a shift is a daunting task.

Recently, a movement has emerged that denies the validity of retrieved memories of forgotten incestuous abuse reported by many adult survivors. This movement has become a serious threat to incest survivors because once again their experiences are being discredited, and their voices silenced. Although there are many convincing cases in which false memories of incestuous abuse have been induced by authority figures, particularly therapists, the false memory movement grossly exaggerates their prevalence.

Just as Freud maintained that most of his female patients' reports of incestuous abuse were fantasies, many future reports of incestuous abuse may come to be dismissed as instances of false memory. While movements against rape and woman battery exist in the United States, the lack of a comparable incest survivor movement increases the likelihood of such dismissals. This situation may be due to many members of the mental health profession individualizing, pathologizing, and depoliticizing their incest clients. Effective prevention requires understanding the social and cultural causes of incestuous abuse and getting beyond a tunnel-vision preoccupation with individual survivor treatment issues.

References. American Bar Association, *Child Sexual Abuse and the Law* (Washington, D.C., 1981), 52; Angela Browne and David Finkelhor, "Initial and Long-Term Effects: A Review of the Literature," in D. Finkelhor (ed.), *Sourcebook on Child Sexual Abuse* (Beverly Hills, Calif., 1986); David Finkelhor, "Early and Long-Term Effects of Child Sexual Abuse: An Update," *Professional Psychology: Research and Practice* 21, 5 (1990); David Finkelhor, "The International Epidemiology of Child Sexual Abuse," *Child Abuse and Neglect* 18, 5 (1994), 412;

David Finkelhor and Larry Baron, "High-Risk Children," in D. Finkelhor (ed.), *Sourcebook on Child Sexual Abuse* (Beverly Hills, Calif., 1986); Jean Goodwin, *Sexual Abuse: Incest Victims and Their Families* (Boston, 1982); Judith Herman, *Father–Daughter Incest* (Cambridge, Mass., 1981); Eleanore Hill, *The Family Secret* (Santa Barbara, Calif., 1985); Janis Tyler Johnson, *Mothers of Incest Survivors* (Bloomington, Ind., 1992); Toni McNaron and Yarrow Morgan (eds.), *Voices in the Night* (Minneapolis, 1982); Diana E. H. Russell, *The Secret Trauma* (New York, 1986); Diana E. H. Russell and David Finkelhor, "The Gender Gap among Perpetrators of Child Sexual Abuse," in *Sexual Exploitation* (Beverly Hills, Calif., 1994); Vernon Wiehe, *Sibling Abuse* (New York, 1990); Melba Wilson, *Crossing the Boundary: Black Women Survive Incest* (Seattle, 1993).

DIANA E. H. RUSSELL

INDIA. Ancient. The history of women has been reconstructed mainly on the basis of textual and, to some extent, inscriptive material, in the composition and transmission of which women played little part. The inherent bias of our sources obviously limits our understanding considerably.

The tendency to view the history of women in early India as one of continuous decline has been modified by the recognition that the situation may be more complex, with regional variations being significant, and that prescriptive texts, on which much historical analysis is based, do not necessarily have much validity.

Our earliest sources, the *Vedas*, suggest that women participated in some tribal assemblies; however, other political units excluded women from participation. References to women rulers are virtually absent, with those who wielded power directly doing so only under exceptional circumstances. Thus, Krpī (fourth century B.C.), who is known only in Greek records, is supposed to have ruled a small state in northwest India after her husband's death and to have led a heroic resistance to Alexander, organizing women under her. Gautamī Balaśrī (first century A.D.) wielded power on behalf of her son and grandson, and Prabhāvatī Guptā, as regent between A.D. 365 and 440, used her father's genealogy instead of her husband's.

In myths and legends, the young, beautiful, scheming wife who goads the good, but aging, monarch into evil is a recurrent stereotype (e.g., Daśaratha's wife Kaikeyī in the epic *Rāmāyana* and the emperor Aśoka's wife Tissarakkhā in Buddhist literature), probably reflecting prevalent attitudes toward women who aspired to political power in a male-dominated society. Apart from employment as personal attendants and perhaps as spies, women did not occupy administrative posts.

Besides being solely responsible for housework, women participated in weaving and various agricultural operations. Lower-caste women probably assisted their husbands, for they, unlike high-caste women, were held responsible for their husbands' debts. However, we do not hear of women heads of craft guilds or merchant caravans. At least some women controlled economic resources, as is evident from donations to Buddhist monastic

orders by housewives, washerwomen, and daughters of artisans and traders. This contrasts markedly with prescriptive literature, which treats
women as items of property, entitled only to *strīdhana* (literally, women's
wealth; generally, clothes, jewelry, and utensils).

Women slaves are referred to in the earliest texts and were initially much
more common than men slaves. They were probably used for household
work, pastoral activities, domestic crafts, and agriculture. In addition to a
strenuous routine, they were subjected to sexual violations as well.

With the emergence of the caste system (*varṇa*) consistent attempts were
made to link that institution with the gender hierarchy. This meant greater
restrictions on high-caste women to ensure the "purity" of the highest
castes through the production of legitimate offspring. Purity gradually came
to imply restrictions of movement, clothes, and communications with others and became especially severe for widows. However, *satī* (burning a
widow on her husband's funeral pyre) was not common during this period.
(See SATI [SUTTEE].) Often, relations between the castes were expressed
in terms of the gender idiom, with the higher caste being equated with the
masculine, and the lower with the feminine principles.

Given the importance of birth in defining caste, attempts were made to
establish an ideal system of marriage in which the father gave away the
bride along with gifts (dowry) to a groom of the same caste but different
clan (*gotra*). However, as many as eight forms of marriage were recognized,
though not necessarily approved. These included marriage by mutual consent, rape, and the giving of bridewealth. In many of the condemned forms,
the role of the mother was as important as that of the father, if not more
so. Approved forms of marriage were recommended for the higher castes.
This would suggest that the caste system was linked to patriarchy, with
each probably serving to reinforce the other. Ultimately, both led to the
ideal of woman as dependent on her father, husband, and son, respectively,
in her youth, middle, and old age.

In the priestly ideal, keeping a daughter unmarried beyond puberty was
viewed as more and more sinful with the passage of time, as the loss of
each menstrual cycle was the equivalent of killing an embryo. However,
both popular and classical literature refer to mature women marrying men
of their choice. While the priests recognized physiological and social reproduction as the major goals of marriage, other considerations may have
governed actual alliances. Political matchmaking is clearly evidenced as
early as the sixth century B.C., when Bimbisāra, ruler of south Bihar, married three princesses from different states, thus consolidating his position.

The attitude toward female sexuality, especially in religious literature,
appears to be ambiguous. On one hand, the link between women and reproduction was recognized and reiterated through ritual; on the other,
women were regarded as potentially polluting, often being bracketed with
the lowest caste, the *śūdras*. They were regarded as untouchable during

menstruation and childbirth and at all times posed a threat to the *brahmacārin* (male initiate), a celibate engaged in acquiring ritual learning. Women were regarded as evil by religious reformers such as Buddha and Mahāvira.

The attitude toward prostitutes reveals similar ambiguities. The earliest references are from the eighth through sixth centuries B.C. Priestly literature is almost consistently hostile to the prostitute, whose presence was, however, required on certain ritual occasions, especially for fertility cults.

That Vedic ritual postulated the need for sons to perform funeral rites for their fathers has been commonly regarded as sufficient explanation of the low status of women within Hindu society. Further, while the presence of the wife was required in most sacrifices, she had no independent ritual status. Common rites of passage such as naming the child, the first haircut, and so forth were performed silently for the daughter, but *mantras* (prayers) were used in the case of the son.

With the advent of Buddhism, women were allowed to enter nunneries. This proved an outlet for much pent-up creativity, which is reflected in the *Therigāthā* (songs composed by nuns). Both rich and poor women, including ex-slaves, embraced the ascetic ideal cheerfully. However, women did not enjoy equality, nuns being explicitly subordinated to monks. Other heterodox faiths such as Jainism also recognized women saints, although women were commonly regarded as a source of temptation.

With the growth of the cult of individual devotion (*bhakti*) within Hinduism, we find references to women saints such as Avvaiyār and Karaikkāl Ammaiyār (fifth century A.D.) who were renowned as much for their worldly wisdom as for their unwavering faith. Significantly enough, while women had no access to Vedic literature, the epics and the *Purāṇas*, which received their final shape during this period, were open to them. The religious doctrine of these texts was markedly different from the Vedic sacrificial cult, and it is likely that it represents an attempt to unite diverse regional cults, possibly including popular cults specific to women, into one uniform tradition.

Women do not seem to have had access to brahmanical (priestly) ritual learning, the right to which was theoretically reserved for men of the three highest castes. However, it is likely that they received training in traditional crafts and skills. Moreover, the compositions of women scholars and poets such as Ghoṣā (a Vedic seer) and references to women such as Gārgī and Maitreyī, who participated in philosophical discussions during the sixth century B.C., would suggest that some women at least were literate. Nevertheless, they were exceptional, and by the fifth century A.D., plays conventionally portray women and lower-caste men as unable to speak Sanskṛt, the language of the literate elite.

References. A. S. Altekar, *The Position of Women in Hindu Civilization*, 3d ed. (Delhi, 1962); U. Chakravarty, "The Rise of Buddhism as Experienced by Women,"

Manushi 8 (1981): 6–10; U. Chakravarty and K. Roy, "In Search of Our Past: Problems and Possibilities for a History of Women in Early India" (paper presented at the Symposium on the Social Role of Women in Indian History, Indian History Congress, 1986); R. S. Sharma, *Perspectives in the Social and Economic History of Early India* (New Delhi, 1983).

KUMKUM ROY

INDIA. Medieval Period (1206–1765). As the ruling class in most of medieval India was Muslim, the position of women in the imperial courts, the most powerful being those located in Delhi, was informed by the values of medieval Islam. This meant that apart from notable exceptions like the famous Razia Sultana, a Muslim queen who ruled over the Delhi sultanate (1206–1526) from 1236 to 1240, women of the court were housed in imperial harems, sealed off from the society at large. During the Mughal period (1526–1765), the imperial harem consisted of thousands of women—there were 5,000 in the time of Emperor Akbar (1565–1605)—divided in different sections and overseen by chaste matrons known as *daroghas*. The complex as a whole was overseen by a governess called the *hakima* and guarded by eunuchs who were similarly organized in a carefully arranged hierarchy. Although contemporary Muslim writers were loath to write about the harem and its inmates, seventeenth-century European travelers like the physicians Niccolao Manucci and Francois Bernier did gain guarded access to the Mughal harem and subsequently filled their memoirs with the gossip and rumors that swirled around it. Indeed, the aura of mystery that surrounded the harems of India, along with those of contemporary Iran and Turkey, seems to have contributed significantly to the formation of European attitudes about Islamic civilization in general, according to which women were seen as objects of sensual delight for "Oriental despots."

Mughal harems, however, were far more than domiciles for the objects of pleasure-seeking kings or, indeed, of complex political intrigue. Many harem women came to exercise great influence on the court and participated in the politics of the time. This tradition began with the founder of the Mughal empire, Babur (r. 1526–1530), whose wife, Maham Begam, sat by her husband on the throne of Delhi. Mumtaz Mahal, wife of Emperor Shah Jahan (r. 1627–1658), for whom the famous Taj Mahal was built, was entrusted with the custody of the Royal Seal, meaning that all state documents passed through the imperial harem. Moreover, recent research has brought to light a number of edicts that leading women of the harem issued directly and with their own seals, pertaining to such affairs of state as the disposition of grazing lands, the collection of land revenue, and the appointment of high imperial officers and local collectors. Indeed, it was probably on account of the extensive influence of Indian women in the Mughal harem that Emperor Akbar instituted a liberal religious policy accommodating Indians into his political system.

The institution of the harem in medieval India grew out of concrete political and social realities rooted in Islamic and Indian culture. For one thing, the lack of primogeniture in Islamic civilization meant that there was no clear principle of succession on the death of a male ruler. On such occasions, different wives of the ruler often promoted their own children in anticipation of inevitable succession disputes, which explains why harems became the foci of intense political intrigues. Second, Indo-Muslim harems grew up as a result of the practice of taking the daughters or other close relatives of conquered kings as tokens of the latter's submission to the political authority of the victorious conqueror. Throughout India the dominant marriage pattern was and is hypergamous, according to which women are given in marriage to socially superior castes or clans. Therefore, the practice of placing the women of defeated Hindu princes in the harem of a Muslim ruler was both socially and politically logical, for it neatly symbolized the superior social rank of the Muslim ruling class according to Indian conceptions of social order.

The loss of political sovereignty by Hindus in the thirteenth century had profound implications for non-Muslim women, as it did for non-Muslim society generally. Prior to the Muslim invasion of India, Hindu *rajas* had traditionally been responsible for guarding and maintaining social relations, especially India's hierarchically arranged caste system. But with the advent of Muslim invasions and the loss of the Hindu king, there occurred a mixing of pure and impure castes that resulted, from the brahminical perspective, in social chaos. Deprived of Hindu *rajas* who were responsible for maintaining social order, Hindu society devised other techniques for preserving that order: (1) the formulation of elaborate marriage codes so that marriage itself was elevated as the primary act by which rank could be maintained, (2) the rigidification of the caste system in general, and (3) the seclusion of Hindu women. Thus, it seems due to a dynamic *within* Hindu society and its response to the Muslim invasions that the Islamic institution of purdah, by which Muslim women were segregated from the common crowd, was adopted by Hindus. (See PURDAH.)

In the countryside, the medieval period also witnessed a general withdrawal of women from agricultural field operations and their economic confinement to the home. For example, in seventeenth-century Bengal, women used to join men in transplanting paddy (rice), in reaping and spreading it to dry in the sun, and in husking it. With the deepening of Islamic influence after the seventeenth century, however, the division of labor became increasingly polarized along gender lines, so that today in Muslim areas only men perform field operations—the transplanting, reaping, and spreading of paddy—while only women do the husking, which is considered a domestic chore.

At the same time, the long-term trend toward the domestication of women seems to have indirectly promoted the peaceful expansion of Islam in parts of the subcontinent. It is probably axiomatic among agrarian societies that to the extent that field operations are monopolized by men, they become increasingly irrelevant as agents in cultural transmission. Moreover, to the extent that women are confined to the household, which is the domain of young children, they acquire preponderant influence in this respect. In South India from the seventeenth century on, village women sang folk songs known as *chakki-namas* or *charkha-namas* while performing household chores such as grinding grain, spinning cotton, or rocking babies to sleep. These songs adapted the subtle vocabulary of Islamic mysticism, or Sufism, to everyday household tasks and in this way allowed a specifically Islamic worldview, with its own values and vocabulary, to penetrate village households. Children thereby imbibed Islamic conceptions and values from nearby household women.

References. Richard M. Eaton, *The Rise of Islam and the Bengal Frontier, 1204–1760* (Berkeley, Calif., 1993); Richard M. Eaton, "Sufi Folk Literature and the Expansion of Indian Islam," *History of Religions* 14 (1974): 117–127; S.A.I. Tirmizi, *Edicts from the Mughal Harem* (Delhi, 1979).

RICHARD M. EATON

INDIA. Modern. British and American Women in India had three major roles during the nineteenth and twentieth centuries: memsahibs, missionaries, and social and political activists. Memsahibs were the wives of British officials and were generally characterized as narrow-minded women dedicated to transplanting English institutions to India. Recent scholarship has emphasized how their socialization in England and in India channeled them into the task of buttressing English culture in an alien environment and how their living situation in India created physical and emotional dislocation. The memsahibs lacked intellectual stimulation, challenging work routines, and supportive networks of female friends and relatives, especially at crucial events such as childbirth. They also experienced long separations from their children, who generally went to England for their education.

During the 1820s, male missionaries began to bring their wives to India. These women were expected primarily to provide examples of Christian family life and only secondarily to do educational work in the *zenana*, or women's section of the homes of Westernized Indians. Gradually, daughters of missionaries and other single women came as full-time missionaries. Roman Catholic nuns and Protestant women worked at all levels of female education, and the Protestants founded major women's colleges such as Isabella Thoburn in Lucknow, Kinnaird in Lahore, and Madras Christian. In 1870, Clara Swain (1834–1910) went to Bareilly, United Provinces, and became the first woman physician to do medical work among Indian women. Her pioneering efforts in medical education for Indian women were more firmly grounded when Edith Brown (1865–1956) established a medical school at Ludhiana, Punjab, and Ida Sophie Scudder (1870–1960) started another at Vellore in South India. Both Swain and Scudder were American graduates of the Women's Medical College of Pennsylvania.

By the 1860s the condition of women in India had attracted the concern of British women social activists who were not missionaries. Mary Carpenter (1807–1877) and Annette Ackroyd Beveridge (1842–1929) went to India in 1866 and 1872, respectively, to establish secular schools for Indian girls. Both collaborated initially with Indian men belonging to the Brahmo Samaj, a rationalist Hindu reform society based in Calcutta.

Margaret Noble (1867–1911), an Anglo-Irish educational reformer, arrived in India in 1898, drawn by Swami Vivekananda, who was a follower of Ramakrishna, a Bengali priest who preached a mystical devotion to God combined with social activism. As Sister Nivedita ("she who has been dedicated") of the neomonastic order of Ramakrishna, she assumed the lifestyle of an orthodox Hindu woman and opened a school for girls in Calcutta. After the death of Vivekananda in 1902, Nivedita expanded her activities to include writing about Indian culture for Westerners and working with young Bengali political radicals during the nationalist agitation protesting the British partition of Bengal in 1905.

Annie Besant (1847–1933), Margaret Cousins (1878–1954), and Dorothy Jinarajadasa were other British women who were attracted to India because of their religious interests as Theosophists and who stayed to work for Indian nationalism and with Indian women. Coming to India in 1893 ostensibly to study the *Vedas*, Besant quickly became involved in social and political reform. She promoted the Central Hindu College and supported self-rule for India through her newspaper, *New India*, and her Home Rule League. The zenith of her political career occurred in 1917, when she was arrested for her anti-British political activity and was elected as the first woman president of the Indian National Congress. But after Mohandas Gandhi emerged in 1918 with his confrontational program of civil disobedience, Besant, as a foreigner committed to gradualism, faded into political obscurity.

Margaret Cousins, an Irish suffragist, accompanied her husband to India in 1915. By 1917 she was organizing a deputation of Indian women led by Sarojini Naidu to petition British officials for an extension of the franchise to Indian women. They achieved some success when Indian provincial legislatures granted the vote to limited numbers of women during the 1920s. In collaboration with Dorothy Jinarajadasa, an English suffragist married to a Sri Lankan Theosophist, Cousins organized the Women's Indian Association, based in Madras, in 1917 and edited its English-language journal, *Stri Dharma*. By 1926 Cousins was calling for an all-Indian conference on women's education. Its meeting in 1927 led to the formation of the All India Women's Conference (AIWC), which had much broader objectives. Indian women were dominant in the AIWC, but Cousins remained a tireless worker for it both in India and abroad and was elected its president in 1936.

Cousins also provided a link between Margaret Sanger (1884–1966) and Indian women. After much debate the AIWC first passed a resolution on birth control in 1932. When Cousins arranged for an invitation to attend the 1935 AIWC meeting, Sanger undertook an extensive tour of India to publicize birth control through contraception during an era when Indian women were criticized for speaking in public on this topic. Sanger even visited Mohandas Gandhi, who argued that abstinence was the only moral means to limit conception. Sanger returned to India in 1952 and 1959 to promote the International Planned Parenthood Federation, and by then Indian women, especially Dhanvanthi Rama Rao (b. 1893) and Avabai Wadia (b. 1913), had become major crusaders for family planning.

Other British women went to India to work primarily for Indian independence and incidentally for Indian women. Madeleine Slade (1892–1982), who took the name of Miraben or Sister Mira, became a close personal follower of Gandhi and worked in village and *harijan* or "untouchable" uplift programs. Agatha Harrison (1885–1954), an early social worker in England and China, was an intermediary between Indian nationalists and British officials in London. Although Miraben was not active in women's organizations, Harrison attended annual sessions of the AIWC whenever she was in India and helped Indian women to make political contacts when they visited London.

Thus, British and American women in India had varying contacts with Indian culture and Indian women. Memsahibs were the most incorporated into the imperial enterprise and had the most formal relationships with Indian women, usually through purdah parties confined to women only or social work organizations. Missionary women had more direct interaction through their proselytizing and educational and medical institutions. Single missionary women as well as secular British teachers and physicians enjoyed significant professional opportunities in India because of the existence of female seclusion. Although they also provided role models of professional women for Indian women, they enjoyed easier access to professional opportunities in education and medicine because of their nationality than did their Indian peers. Finally, independent women activists such as Sister Nivedita and Margaret Cousins attempted to participate in, and interpret to Westerners, Indian culture and politics. The lives of British and American women reveal complex patterns of complicity with, and resistance to, the imperial structure as well as ambivalent efforts to achieve professional and personal autonomy and cross-cultural understanding.

References. Antoinette Burton, *Burdens of History: British Feminists, Indian Women, and Imperial Culture, 1865–1915* (Chapel Hill, NC, 1994); Nupur Chaudhuri and Margaret Strobel (eds.), *Western Women and Imperialism: Complicity* *and Resistance* (Bloomington, Ind., 1992); Kumari Jayawardena, *The White Woman's Other Burden: Western Women and South Asia during British Rule* (New York, 1995); Margaret McMillan, *Women of the Raj* (London, 1988); Barbara N. Ramusack, "Catalysts or Helpers? British Feminists, Indian Women's Rights, and Indian Independence," in Gail Minault (ed.), *The Extended Family: Women and Political Participation in India and Pakistan* (Columbia, Mo., 1981), 109–150; Barbara N. Ramusack and Antoinette Burton (eds.), "Feminism, Imperialism and Race: A Dialogue between India and Britain," special issue of *Women's History Review* 3, 4 (1994).

BARBARA N. RAMUSACK

INDIA. Modern. Marriage and Family. India is the world's second most populous nation, with as many languages and as much diversity in food and other aspects of culture as in all of Europe. Marriage and family patterns also vary widely by ethnicity, religion, caste, village-urban residence, education, occupation, and social class.

Indian family law, rather than being uniform for all citizens, has different provisions for each religious community. Hindus (83 percent of the population) are governed by the Hindu Marriage Act of 1955 and its subsequent amendments. (See HINDUISM.) Muslims (11 percent of the population) are governed by Islamic family law. (See ISLAMIC LAW.) Christians, Sikhs, Parsis, Jews, and other minority religious communities as well as tribal groups are governed by specific regulations. This pluralistic system of family law, while offering respect for the customary marriage and family practices of different religions, castes, and tribes, sometimes conflicts with the constitutional guarantee of equal rights for women and governmental policies designed to improve women's status. For example, while requiring monogamy for Hindu, Christian, Parsi, and civil marriages, India has retained the Koranic prerogative for Muslim men to marry up to four wives, even though many Muslim nations have passed laws restricting polygyny.

A Hindu man has a religious duty to arrange the marriages of his children within their caste (*jati*), and most marriages are still arranged. Most Indians enjoy romantic tales of "love marriages" but respect their families' ability to find appropriate spouses for them and point to high divorce rates in Western countries to demonstrate the failure of love as the basis for marriage.

Unmarried adults (women at 18 and men at 21) have the legal right to select their own spouses, whether of the same or a different caste, and to have civil marriages registered with the state. Although still a tiny percentage, such love marriages are increasing. Even in arranged marriages most women are given an opportunity to meet a potential groom and to decline an offer of marriage.

Age at marriage varies greatly by education and social class. A university-educated, high-caste man typically is not considered eligible for marriage until he is suitably employed, by which time he may be over 30. Educated women of the same class usually marry in their mid-20s. By contrast, lower- and lower-middle-class women ordinarily marry in their teens; the average age at marriage for all Indian women is 17, and for men 22.

Among the higher Hindu castes, a bride's family is expected to provide a dowry commensurate with the education, earning potential, and social standing of the groom. The financial burden of providing dowry, especially if a family has several daughters, is one reason the birth of a daughter is considered inauspicious. The Dowry Prohibition Act of 1961 makes it illegal to ask for dowry and to either give or receive money or goods in consideration of the marriage but "takes care to exclude presents" given at the time of marriage. Thus, dowry, which previously was agreed upon formally by both families, has been replaced by the uncertain expectation of gifts and not infrequently by disappointment on the part of the groom or his family. Dowry murders, in which a new bride's sari "accidentally" catches fire while she is cooking and burns her to death in retaliation for a dowry that is deemed insufficient, have occurred with increasing frequency. Women's groups in India have mobilized to protest dowry murders and police inaction in prosecuting them, but the number of convictions remains minuscule.

A Hindu woman typically leaves her parents' home at the time of her marriage and goes to live with her husband in the joint family headed by his parents. She is expected to show respect to her husband's parents and siblings and to take directions from her mother-in-law in cooking and household work. She has relatively low status until after the birth of her first son, for a son must make offerings to the family ancestors after his father's death. An older married woman, with married sons and daughters-in-law to help her run the household and with grandchildren to adore, is considered to be in the prime of her life.

Ideally, a Hindu man resides with his parents through their lifetimes. Land and other property ordinarily are divided among the sons sometime after their father's death. The timing of the partition varies somewhat by religion, caste, and the extent and nature of joint family holdings. Hindu daughters now also have a right to inheritance, but they usually are expected to waive the right to land and property in return for gifts at the time of their marriages.

Although the ideal of the patrilineal joint family is strongly held, an ethnographer studying household composition typically finds fewer than half the households in a village or urban neighborhood to consist of a married couple living with their married son(s) and their families. This may be explained, in part, by the relatively short life expectancy in India (54 in 1981), resulting in the fathers of many married men having died long before their own sons are old enough to marry and thus making a patrilineal joint family an impossibility for the years until a son marries. Even when father and son are both alive and married, extenuating circumstances may result in their living apart. Rural men often migrate to the city in search of employment, leaving their families in the village. Similarly, educated, middle-class men may find better employment opportunities and move to another city or even another country with or without their wives and children and without any sense of "breaking" the joint family as long as the move is made for economic reasons, with parental blessings and with money being sent back to the "joint" family. Although squabbles among the women in joint families are legendary, most women share with their husbands the desire to maintain a joint family. A wife living with her husband and children in a nuclear family may have greater independence, more power in household decision making, and more time alone with her husband, but she may also miss other women with whom to share child care and housework and may feel lonely and vulnerable apart from the family network of support.

Divorce by mutual consent after a year's legal separation has been permitted for Hindus since 1976, and divorce on a limited number of grounds has been available for Hindus, Christians, and Parsis for longer periods. Under Islamic family law, a husband may divorce his wife unilaterally, but a wife has only limited grounds for divorce. Divorced women are stigmatized, and very few Indian women are legally divorced, although de facto separations are not uncommon. Divorced women often lose custody of their children, as children belong to their father's patrilineage. Although Muslim women may remarry, opportunities for Hindu, Christian, and Parsi women to remarry are few.

The Widow Remarriage Act of 1856 legalized remarriage for Hindu widows, but the religious belief that a wife remains married to the same husband through many lives, reinforced in this life by the loss of custody of her children as well as the loss of rights to maintenance from her husband's household if she remarries, keeps the number of remarriages by widowed Hindu women to a minimum. Remarriage is less restrictive for Muslim women, although children are still presumed to belong to their father's family. Rates of remarriage are increasing for both divorced and widowed women, but mainly among young, childless women.

References. Indian Oxygen, *India: A Statistical Outline* (New Delhi, 1987); Devaki Jain, "India: A Condition across Caste and Class," in Robin Morgan (ed.), *Sisterhood Is Global* (Garden City, N.Y., 1984), 305–310; Pauline Kolenda, *Regional Differences in Family Structure in India* (Jaipur, 1987); Rama Mehta, *Divorced Hindu Woman* (Delhi, 1975); D. Pathak, *Hindu Law and Its Constitutional Aspects*, 4th ed. (Delhi, 1986).

MARY JANE BEECH

INDIA. Modern. Women in Development is an issue that came into prominence in the latter half of the 1970s as a result of a growing concern that

economic growth-oriented policies often either leave out women as beneficiaries or have a negative impact on women. In India, as elsewhere, an
increasing number of research institutes and public-policy groups have begun to advocate that attention be given to the impact of development projects on women, that women be included as direct project beneficiaries,
that women be involved in the planning and implementation of projects,
and that census and other statistics on women be improved in order to
facilitate women-oriented project planning and impact analysis. Two major
institutes in India are the Centre for Women's Development Studies in New
Delhi and the Research Unit on Women's Studies at S.N.D.T. Women's
University in Bombay. In New Delhi, feminist organizations such as Saheli
and the Manushi Trust are important activist groups concerned with the
entire range of woman's rights problems in India, including the impact of
development policies on women.

One of the key issues in making development plans more helpful for
women is income generation. Although purdah (veiling and seclusion of
women) prevents many women of propertied households from working in
public at wage labor, millions of others work daily at agricultural tasks, in
factories, and in cottage industries (doing piecework at home). (See PUR-
DAH.) In addition to working for wages, rural and urban Indian women
are the primary caretakers of the household. Traditional development strategies have done little to offer laboring women more stable employment,
better working conditions, or fair wages—women are typically paid a fraction of what men receive for doing the same work. The mechanization of
food crop production and processing has led to decreased employment opportunities for women in most cases. An increase in employment for
women in tailoring for the export clothing market has brought with it very
low rates of pay, deplorable working conditions, and little job security.
Multilateral organizations such as the International Labor Office (ILO)
have become sensitive to these employment problems of women and, along
with groups in India, are promoting improved options and conditions for
women workers through activities such as organizing 2,000 women lace
workers in south India into cooperatives.

Although recent decades have brought dramatic improvements in health
throughout much of the developing world, high rates of infant and child
mortality, maternal mortality, and malnutrition among women are still to
be found in India. India is one of the few countries of the world where
men have a longer life expectancy than women. In north India, the preference for sons is so strong that far better care is taken of infant boys than
infant girls. One result of differential feeding and health care is that girls
have mortality rates twice as high as those of boys in certain northern areas.
Other reports indicate that Indian women of childbearing age have had
higher mortality rates in the 1980s than in previous decades. Yet other
studies document increased levels of malnutrition among women and girls.

The benefits of urban-based improvements in medical technology and health care are not being directed toward poor and rural females, but increased attempts to reach women with simple medical care and preventive measures are being made. Decentralized maternal and child health programs run through primary health care centers in local areas and staffed by local auxiliaries provide greater ease of access for rural women and children than large hospitals in the urban areas. In spite of such programs, health workers find that families make little effort to take "unwanted daughters" to nearby health centers for treatment. Even with sufficient motivation, poor women generally cannot spare time from labor or money for a short bus trip to get to the primary health care center.

Just as Indian women generally receive lower wages than male workers and have lower rates of survival and worse health than males, they also are likely to be less literate than males and less often are educated to levels equivalent to those of males. According to 1981 census figures, the male literacy rate in India is 47 percent, while the female literacy rate is 25 percent. Regional differences are important, with male–female disparity in literacy being the least in the southern state of Kerala and the greatest in the northern state of Rajasthan. Illiteracy among women is higher in rural than urban areas and higher among poor, unpropertied groups. Over the past few decades, literacy rates have risen throughout India, but recently the rate of change has begun to decline for females. Efforts to promote female literacy include nonformal education projects through which adult women learn basic literacy skills as well as incentive plans that involve cash or grain remuneration to households that send daughters to school.

In spite of startling achievements by some Indian women in government, higher education, and professions such as medicine and law, the vast majority of Indian women are significantly deprived of equal standards of welfare when compared to their male counterparts. In the wider society, in the village, even within the household, females have a lower status than males. If the broad goals of development include equitable improvement in life chances for all, then improving the status of women in India should be taken as an overriding target of all development projects.

References. Devaki Jain, *Women's Quest for Power: Five Indian Case Studies* (New Delhi, 1980); Madhu Kishwar and Ruth Vanita (eds.), *In Search of Answers: Indian Women's Voices* (London, 1984); Barbara D. Miller, *The Endangered Sex: Neglect of Female Children in North India* (Ithaca, N.Y., 1981); Maitrayee Mukhopadhyay, *Silver Shackles: Women and Development in India* (London, 1984).

BARBARA D. MILLER

INDIA. Modern. Women in Politics (British Period). By the mid-nineteenth century much of India was under British control. When the ruler of Jhansi, a small state in central India, died leaving only his young wife and adopted son as heirs, the British moved to annex the state. Three years later, during the Great Mutiny of 1857, the *sepoys* (Indian soldiers employed by the British) mutinied and murdered the entire European population of Jhansi. When the British army arrived to take revenge, the Rani (Queen) Lakshmi Bai joined the mutineers. She led her troops against the British and perished fighting. A heroic figure who has since been celebrated in song, drama, and legend, she became the symbol of Indian womanhood fighting for freedom.

Following the formation of the Indian National Congress in 1885, a number of women from the families of the founding members appeared at the annual sessions. When the congress met in Bombay in 1889, there were ten women in attendance. By the following year, in Calcutta, Swarnaku-mari Ghosal and Kadambini Ganguli attended as official delegates, and in subsequent years women attended and contributed to the program by singing patriotic songs.

Women's entry into agitational politics began when the British decided in 1905 to partition the state of Bengal for greater administrative efficiency. The protest movement centered on the boycott of foreign-made goods and the exclusive use of *swadeshi* (Indian-made) goods. At this time many women took a vow to avoid using foreign goods for the sake of the motherland.

Only in the first decade of the twentieth century did an infrastructure (leaders, women's organizations, and the integration of women into existing political organizations) make possible women's full-scale entry into the nationalist movement. Three leaders became extremely important at this time. Madame Cama, a Parsi from Bombay, moved to Europe in 1907 and there created an Indian national flag in green, yellow, and red bearing the words *Bande Mataram* (Hail to the Motherland). Annie Besant, born in London, became a Theosophist and adopted India as her home. By 1916 she had set up the Home Rule League and established an antigovernment newspaper called *New India*. Arrested and interned by the British, she was released in 1917 and elected president of the Indian National Congress. Sarojini Naidu studied in England, wrote poetry, and by the early years of the twentieth century was speaking at sessions of the congress about Hindu–Muslim unity, female education, and women's status. She played a major role in the emerging women's organizations and in 1918 moved the resolution in the congress that women be given the franchise on the same terms as men. Her long service in the nationalist movement made her the most prominent political woman in India in the first half of the century.

The return of Mohandas K. Gandhi to India in 1917 was perhaps the single most important event in terms of encouraging women's involvement in politics. Preaching a nonviolent form of rebellion, Gandhi urged mass involvement and particularly encouraged women to bring their skills to this movement. By 1921, Besanti Devi, Urmila Devi, and Suniti Devi (women from the household of the prominent congressional leader C. R. Das) had joined the young men who were selling *khaddar* (homemade cloth) on the streets in defiance of a government ban. Their arrest, the first arrest of women for political activity, galvanized the city and the nation.

The civil disobedience campaign began in March 1930 with Gandhi's march to the sea, and although women were not included in the march, they met Gandhi at every stop along the way. When Gandhi reached Dandi, he unveiled a program for women that included the boycott and picketing of foreign cloth and liquor shops, teaching spinning and selling *khaddar*, and continuous propaganda. Gandhi regarded women as far more suitable for these activities than men, primarily because of their patience and ability to suffer. Moreover, he believed there would be less violence if only women picketed. There were demonstrations all over India, but those in Bombay were the most spectacular in terms of women's involvement, and because of this they became the primary focus of news media attention.

At the same time that women were acting in harmony with the program proposed by Gandhi, a number of women were convinced a more radical approach was necessary. Acting mainly in Bengal, young women (many of them students) joined the secret revolutionary organizations and accepted the proposition that brave and sacrificing acts were necessary to arouse the people against the British. In 1931 Santi Ghosh and Suniti Choudhury assassinated the district magistrate of Comilla, East Bengal. In Chittagong, Pritilata Waddedar led a band of young men in an armed attack on the European club. Not long after this event Bina Das attended her own college convocation ceremony in Calcutta and shot at (but missed killing) the governor of Bengal. While relatively few young women were involved in these events, many were involved in the day-to-day activities of the revolutionary movement.

In India's small towns and villages, the women who participated in the political movement did so with the males of their families and with little consciousness of a women's agenda. Nevertheless, there were many brave village women who stepped forward to rally the crowd or lead the picketing.

The 1935 India Act not only increased the franchise but also gave Indians the equivalent of home rule. This act included reserved seats for women (something that most women's organizations had agitated against), and a number of women prepared for political office. With the advent of the Quit India campaign in 1942, many women came forward to offer individual *satyagraha* (truth force) and court arrest. Others joined the underground movement that produced antigovernment propaganda, and still others became involved with the more radical alternatives to Gandhi's program for winning freedom from the British.

When Subhas Chandra Bose, the Bengali leader who had broken with Gandhi and begun cooperating with the Axis powers, formed his Indian National Army in Singapore, he included a women's regiment. The Rani of Jhansi brigade, under the command of Colonel Lakshmi, was designed, recruited, and trained to participate in combat for the liberation of India. However, Rangoon fell before any of these women were actually engaged in combat.

With the end of the war and the formation of the Constituent Assembly, women once more took their place in politics. Both elected and appointed to the Constituent Assembly, they joined in working out the details of India's new government.

References. Vijay Agnew, *Elite Women in Indian Politics* (New Delhi, 1979); Geraldine Forbes, *Women in Modern India* (Cambridge, 1996); Manmohan Kaur, *Role of Women in the Freedom Movement, 1857–1947* (New Delhi, 1968); Madhu Kishwar, "Women and Gandhi," *Economic and Political Weekly* 20 (October 5, 12, 1985); Gail Minault, "Purdah Politics: The Role of Muslim Women in Indian Nationalism, 1911–1924," in Hanna Papanek and Gail Minault (eds.), *Separate Worlds* (Delhi, 1982).

GERALDINE FORBES

INDIA. Modern. Women in Politics (1947–1985). The participation of women in politics began with the movement for India's independence. In part as a result of their contribution to the nationalist cause, the Constitution adopted soon after independence accorded women equal rights under the law and explicitly prohibited discrimination on the grounds of sex (Articles 14 and 15). The Constitution also provided for universal adult suffrage (Article 326), and women have thus been active participants in every Indian election.

Some women have attained powerful political positions; generally, these have been women of considerable economic means and, often, of prominent political families. Foremost among them has been Indira Gandhi, the daughter of Jawaharlal Nehru (and no relation to the nationalist leader, M. K. Gandhi), who served as prime minister from 1966 to 1977 and again from 1980 to 1984. She first gained the post when bosses of the ruling Congress Parliamentary Party selected her to complete the term of the deceased incumbent, Lal Bahadur Shastri; they believed that she would be easily controlled and that her family background would guarantee the party continuing popularity and legitimacy. The party bosses were right on the latter count but dead wrong on the former. Indira Gandhi emerged as the most powerful politician in postindependence India, splitting the party, isolating the bosses who brought her to power, and then winning resounding victories on her own.

However, in June 1975, Gandhi was brought to her knees by a series of political movements criticizing her government as corrupt and ineffective and a High Court decision that Gandhi was guilty of illegal election practices and must resign. Declaring an emergency, Gandhi suspended most civil liberties and imprisoned over 100,000 political opponents. In 1977 she allowed a parliamentary election, and her party was defeated. In the 1980 election, however, after the mismanagement of the Janata Party government that replaced her, Gandhi was again returned to office.

Indian women have also served in both houses of Parliament and in the state legislatures, been governors and chief ministers of states, and served at the national level as ambassadors and cabinet members. However, despite the achievements of an elite few, women as a whole are underrepresented throughout India in both appointed and elected positions, they have minimal power within the parties, and they participate in elections as candidates and as voters with less frequency than men. Still, the rates of participation overall are higher than one might expect, given the low status of women in India and their low educational level.

Since the first general election in 1952, the percentage of women voters has grown, but it has still not equaled that of men. As of 1980, 48 percent of all those registered to vote were women. However, of those who actually went to the polls in the 1980 parliamentary elections, only 43 percent were women; in 1984, 44 percent were women.

Participation varies according to several economic and cultural indicators. Even more than is the case with men, the participation of women increases with educational level, urban location, and income. Among Hindu women, those of the highest castes are more likely to participate politically than those of lower castes. Hindu women, as a whole, are more active political participants than Muslim women.

The percentage of women members of the Lok Sabha, the elected house of the Indian Parliament, has ranged from a low of 2.8 percent in the first, 1952, election, to a high of 8.5 percent in the 1984 election; the average percentage of women members has been 5.6 percent. This compares favorably to many Western industrialized countries. In 1984, for example, women were less than 5 percent of both the U.S. Congress and the British House of Commons.

Below the national level the percentage of women in government declines. Women have averaged just about 4 percent of the membership of state legislative assemblies and, despite legal requirements for their participation, less than 2 percent of the membership of village governments.

Since the 1970s there has been an explosion in the number of women's organizations, some of them attached to political parties and others autonomous, lobbying for women's interests. With some success, they have sought greater legal protection for women against violence, particularly rape and dowry-related deaths. (See DOWRY, Dowry in India.) Less successful has been the struggle for a uniform civil code that would remove family law from its present jurisdiction under religious law and instead subject marriage, divorce, and inheritance to civil control; this effort, which would presumably enhance women's legal rights within all religious groups, has met the most resistance from some within the Muslim community.

Reference. Mary Fainsod Katzenstein, "Towards Equality? Cause and Consequence of the Political Prominence of Women in India," *Asian Survey* 18 (May 1978): 473–486.

LESLIE J. CALMAN

INDIA. Modern. Women's Movement (British Period). Nineteenth-century social reformers in British India had campaigned against social practices like widow's immolation (sati), female infanticide, child marriage, and purdah. (See PURDAH; SATI [SUTTEE].) One remedy for ameliorating women's position, apart from social legislation, was considered to be education. The issue of female education sparked a debate on the best kind of education to be given women. As the twentieth century began, the most significant authorities on women's education regarded service to the family as the basic tenet of women's education. This precluded the possibility of a woman's regarding herself as an independent entity. The entry of a woman into politics was not considered a possibility. Essentially, a woman was a mother, and her joy came from serving others. Hence, what was encouraged and what women chose were service-oriented education like medicine and teaching. Against this backdrop of the home as the woman's primary world, one should view the women's movement that emerged.

Given such constraints, it is not surprising that the women's deputation that met in 1917 with E. S. Montague, the secretary of state for India, presented him with a memorandum of demands that initially included only better facilities for education and improved health and maternity services. The demand for the same franchise rights as would be granted to men was included after these women were told that Montague was meeting only with deputations that wanted to discuss political issues. The Women's Indian Association was formed in 1917, and the All India Women's Conference, formed in 1926 by Indian women and their Western supporters Annie Besant and Margaret Cousins, continued to illustrate this dichotomy between service and politics. The All India Women's Conference, at its birth, was positive that it would take up only health and education issues. However, it was inevitable that other issues like child marriage, divorce, and inheritance could not be left untouched. Eventually, these issues and others like birth control, abolition of the Devadasi system of dedicating girls to the temples, prostitution, and the employment of women in industry were taken up by the movement for discussion and action. Their points of view were disseminated through journals such as *Stri Dharma*, the organ of the Women's Indian Association; pamphlets; branch organizations; and yearly conferences. What was characteristic was that while there were differences of opinion, they resisted communal divisions. In fact, the women's organizations demanded uniform civil legislation. They registered their protest against the Hindu Code Committee that was set up, arguing that it should be called the Indian Code Committee and should deal with all the different communities. They demanded a comprehensive act, not piecemeal legislation.

On the political front, the women's organizations took a firm stand in demanding adult suffrage, rejecting separate electorates and the reservation of seats for women. By 1926, all the provincial legislatures had opened their doors to women. By 1932, many women had successfully contested seats on equal terms with men in municipalities, corporations, and academic bodies of universities. When women began functioning as legislators, many in the movement had to define this activity as service to the nation, to be differentiated from what they termed "party politics."

Given these circumstances, participation in the national movement for freedom had to happen within the narrow concept of service and sacrifice. While those who participated claimed the nation was now their home, others felt that the issues of women would be left behind if their activities were to shift to another front. Mohandas Gandhi, the leader of the national movement, himself did not envisage any radical alteration in the status of women. He chose picketing liquor shops and foreign cloth shops as the work to be done by women. The choice of liquor and foreign cloth was an excellent strategy. The effects of both—drunkenness and unemployment—affected the home directly. Moreover, the causes were popular enough to draw unexpectedly large numbers of women to picket, burn foreign cloth, organize demonstrations, and go to jail with their children. The rough, hand-woven cloth called *khadi* and the spinning wheel, or *charka*, became living symbols largely through the efforts of women. At this point of history, there was the feeling that the women's fight for freedom was subsumed in the national fight for freedom. At the end of the British period it seemed as if the women's movement had achieved what it had set out to achieve. Hope was in the air.

Reference. Kamaladevi Chattopadhyay, *Indian Women's Battle for Freedom* (New Delhi, 1983); papers presented at the Second National Conference on Women's Studies, Kerala University, Trivandrum, April 9–12, 1984.

                                                                    C. S. LAKSHMI

INDIA. Modern. Women's Movement (1947–1985). India's achievement of freedom in 1947 ushered in an era of hope. A policy of planned social change was to be realized through development based on a mixed economy, and the Constitution proclaimed gender equality, ending, at least formally, the subordination of women. The Central Social Welfare Board (CSWB) was created in 1953 to improve and expand existing welfare programs by providing financial assistance to voluntary organizations. Not only did the number of organizations dependent on CSWB proliferate, but many of them, which were involved in target-oriented programs, lost their earlier dynamism and sensitivity to women's issues. In rural areas organizations established as part of community development catered to the needs of upper-caste women or existed only on paper.

Thus, up to the 1960s, activities in women's organizations were marked by a dull uniformity. Most carried on cultural activities reinforcing traditional values or ran craft classes. The more serious ones promoted income-generation activities for needy women. The preindependence umbrella organization, the All India Women's Conference, was exhausted after its vigorous struggle to bring fundamental legal changes in marriage and property rights for women. Its hundreds of branches carried on stereotyped activities affecting primarily upper- and middle-class urban women. Its leadership, satisfied with juridical equality, on many occasions was co-opted into various power positions. Thus, the vast number of women who had poured into the arena of freedom before independence slipped back into their old grooves. Women leaders forged no links with the wide mass of women.

The period from the late 1960s was marked by growing economic crises, rising prices, and generalized discontent in rural and urban areas. Women participated actively in struggles of the rural poor, tribals, and the industrial working class, as in the militant Naxalite movement against the landlords, corrupt police officials, and rural rich, powerful particularly in West Bengal, Andhra Pradesh, Bihar, and Kerala. In these wider movements, women's issues, such as wife beating, alcoholism, and rape, were occasionally highlighted. Middle-class urban women were active in the anti–price-rise movement.

By the early 1970s, while mainstream women's organizations remained silent and acquiescent, politically aware women were involved in the larger economic struggles. The patriarchal organization of these movements, however, raised some very basic issues about women's role and the recognition of their contribution in these struggles. These issues have since been taken up by new women's groups.

The International Women's Year initially vitalized some established women's organizations and a few women academics. The report of the Committee on the Status of Women revealed the stark reality of the unequal status of women. Evidence of the adverse sex ratio, widening illiteracy, declining economic and political participation in formal organizations, and the growing spread of the dowry system eroded the earlier complacency of Indian society. (See DOWRY, Dowry in India.) The emergence of autonomous women's groups marks the beginnings of the second phase of the women's movement in India. These groups provide an alternative pattern of working for women's causes. They are independent of any political party, though some members have political affiliations and political perspectives. The Western feminist movement—its literature and its style—has affected them, though issues and strategies are, of course, different. Many members claim to be socialist feminists. Nearly 400 delegates from almost all parts of India participated in the National Conference on Perspectives for Women's Liberation in Bombay in December 1985, representing over 100 groups. These groups are very different from the established women's organizations. The members come from middle-class, educated urban society and belong to all shades of political ideology. They are young, very often unmarried, and informal in demeanor. They strongly oppose hierarchically structured organization and have adopted the collective as their model. These groups have acquired names that suggest feminist solidarity or woman power.

These new groups have taken up issues like atrocities against women, rape, alcoholism, wife beating, dowry harassment and murder, family violence, problems of workingwomen, traffic in women, oppression of Dalit and minority women, media distortion of women's image, personal laws, health issues, and problems of women in slums. Priorities vary by region.

Various strategies are used, depending on the issue, to mobilize public opinion. They use pamphlets, leaflets, and petitions and organize protest rallies, sit-ins, and demonstrations. They also organize street-corner meetings, street plays, skits and songs, and poster exhibitions. Newsletters in regional languages and journals have been started to reach out to larger numbers of people. There are special-interest feminist groups working in the fields of health, media, law, violence against women, book production, and so forth.

Nearly a decade of the women's movement has brought to the surface some important issues. One is the relationship between women's groups and other organizations involved in socioeconomic struggles of the poor. Second, support to individual women stepping out of the oppressive family system has to be provided by the women's groups. Further, how are structures, methods, and intragroup dynamics to be devised to achieve an egalitarian character? Feminism is a frequently debated issue. Does the Indian–Asian sociocultural system have a place for feminism of the Western type? Societies having experienced colonial rule find themselves in a situation in which modern industrial development is not a boon. The sheer struggle for survival, the high level of illiteracy, and the hold of obscurantist social practices make the mass of women absolutely helpless and often apathetic in the fight against gender discrimination and patriarchal oppression. Thus, for the Indian feminists, linkage between women's issues and wider movements becomes crucial.

The period of the quiet 1920s seems to be over. Not only have new women's groups with youthful dynamism, a different style of working, and a women's perspective on various issues emerged, but developments have also vitalized established women's organizations, some of which are beginning to be sensitive to women's subordinate status.

References. Neera Desai and Vibhuti Patel, *Indian Women: Change and Challenge* (Bombay, 1985); Jana Everett, *Women and Social Change in India* (New Delhi, 1979); Devaki Jain (ed.), *Indian Women* (New Delhi, 1975).

NEERA DESAI

INDIAN WRITERS. Though the literary tradition of India has been dominated by men, there have always been women who were an integral part of it. The earliest religious literature, the *Vedas*, contains hymns composed by women. In medieval literature, there have been well-known female ascetics in both north and south India, for example, Āṇṭāḷ, Mahādevi Akkā, Lalded, Jana, Sahaja, and Mīrābāi, whose songs of love and devotion are still sung. The historical records also tell us of women bards who composed original verses as well as kept the genealogies for the queens of medieval India. However, the phenomenon of women writers who, on the literary scene in large numbers, make an impact is entirely modern.

India is a land of many languages, and each language has its own literature, which is marked by its own individuality. However, the totality is undeniably Indian. Although India is split in many religions and divided into different climates, regions, and lifestyles, the different literatures share the same dreams and concerns. This commonality is nowhere more obvious than in the writings of the women. Whether the language is English or Bengali, Hindi or Tamil, the women writers show a certain unity of ideas because their concerns are unique.

The rise of modern Indian literatures generally took place simultaneously in the early nineteenth century. Later on, the schools and the colleges educated young generations of Indians who grew up with the same textbooks and similar curricula. An urban middle class began to emerge with a voracious appetite for literature in its own language. The writers abandoned religious and erotic poetry in favor of new genres, like fiction, which became popular in every modern Indian language.

This development provided an easy opportunity for women writers because they had their own oral traditions, which were particularly suited to the spoken, narrative form. The stories in the oral tradition were of a domestic nature, focusing on interpersonal relationships between family members, a woman's work inside and outside the house, and her place in the general scheme of things. Interestingly, these are the very concerns that dominate women's writing in the modern period.

Earlier, the women, especially the female saints and ascetics, sang of love and devotion to God. Most of them were considered unconventional because they did not follow the role given to them by society; they were outside the mainstream and strongly criticized the restrictions placed on them by Indian society. This spirit of rebellion and a preoccupation with the problems of women are other characteristics of women writers in the twentieth century.

The first writers to make a name for themselves in modern times came from well-educated, progressive, and elite families. It was natural that they chose English as their language.

Toru Dutt (1856–1877) was educated in Europe and knew French and

English well. Her first book, A *Sheaf Gleaned in French Fields, Verse Translations and Poems*, was published in Calcutta in 1876 and attracted wide attention for its originality, vigor, and selection of themes. However, Toru Dutt died in 1877, thus cutting short a promising career as a poet. Her posthumous volume of English poems, *Ancient Ballads and Legends of Hindustan*, appeared in 1885, containing poems on various topics, including her own impending death. Sarojini Naidu (1879–1949) began her writing career at an early age. Her first volume of poetry, *The Golden Threshold*, came out in 1905, *The Bird of Time* in 1912, and her third *The Broken Wings*, in 1917. However, after her first meeting with Mahatma Gandhi, the poet went into the background, and the active freedom fighter emerged. The main theme of her poetry is romantic love and yearnings. Her poetry does not have a variety of emotions nor a wide range of subjects; its dominant note is joy, and it is filled with exuberance of life.

The two women writers who are well known and well established in postindependence Indian literature in English are Kamala Markandaya (b. 1927) and Anita Desai (b. 1937). Both of them introduced in their well-written and well-constructed novels the phenomenon of being women in modern India. Kamala Markandaya's early novels focused on the economical and sociological problems, for example, hunger and poverty (*Nectar in a Sieve*, A *Handful of Rice*), East–West encounter (*Some Inner Fury*), and the clash between the new and old ideas (*Silence of Desire*). Anita Desai, from her first novel, *Cry, the Peacock*, chose the psychological complexities of human personality, the delicate balance needed in family and interpersonal relationships (as in *Fire on the Mountain, Clear Light of Day*). Anita Desai has not shunned the violent aspects of life, and, therefore, alcoholism, arson, rape, suicide, and murder are all present in her writing.

Though highly acclaimed for the literary quality of their work in the English-speaking world, the women writers in English hold only a marginal appeal for the general Indian reading public. Their influence is also minimal. Women writers in Indian languages enjoy large readership. In their writing one finds the rawness of emotions and harsh realities of life. Their writing is a true mirror of modern society, its progress, and the changes that have affected women's lives.

Another interesting characteristic of this writing is that most of the women writers share a bond with each other whether they are writing in Tamil, Bengali, Punjabi, Urdu, or Hindi. There is a certain continuity of themes and ideas. Indian womanhood, in all its variety, is the center of their universe. There has been no theme that touched the life of a woman that we do not find included. The oppression of the woman, whether as a prostitute or as an economically dependent wife, was a recurrent theme in the 1950s.

However, the most remarkable phenomenon of the later writing is the emergence of a new woman. She has the courage to break the traditions, she may not be highly educated but can earn a living for herself, and, above all, she can make a decision about her own life. Her lot may not be enviable, but at least she has fought for, and gained, equality with men. Many of the novels portray women in the process of discovering themselves and their potentialities.

Fiction remains a popular genre, and most of the writers have developed their own style, ranging from poetic and romantic to analytical and minimalistic.

Some of the well-known women writers are Amrita Preetam (Punjabi); Ashapurna Devi, Mahashweta Devi, and Anurupa Devi (Bengali); Kandanika Kapadika (Gujrati); MK Indira and Anusuya Shankar "Triveni" (Kannada); Kausalya Devi Kodoori (Telugu); Ismalt Chugtai and Qurratul Ain Hyder (Urdu); Mahadevi Verma, Usha Devi Mitra, and Krishna Sobti (Hindi); and Kusumavati Deshpande (Marathi). Some of these are poets as well.

Amrita Preetam and Mahadevi Verma have received the Gyanpeeth Award, a prestigious award given to one Indian writer every year as a recognition of the writer's genius and his or her contribution to Indian literature.

USHA NILSSON

INDIAN WRITERS. Devotional Poets in Hinduism include the Tamil-speaking Āṇṭāḷ (ninth century C.E.) and Kāraikkāl Ammaiyār (c. eighth century C.E.); Mahādevi Akkā, who wrote in the Kannada language (twelfth century C.E.); and the princess Mīrābāi (sixteenth century C.E.), who composed in Hindi. Very little historical information is available about their lives, but from later hagiographical literature and legends, certain common patterns are discernible. The women are portrayed as falling in love with the deity at a young age, rejecting earthly marriage or barely tolerating an unhappy married life, being initiated by a male saint, defying social norms, composing poems that express a passionate romantic love for God, and eventually "merging" or "becoming one" with the Lord enshrined in a holy place.

Most of the poets did not aspire or live up to "traditional" norms incumbent on women by the code of the lawgiver Manu (first century C.E.). Rather than get married and beget children in this life, they longed to be wedded to, or continually serve, the god they were in love with. In cases where they were actually married to a human being, they still asserted their first loyalty to the deity and sometimes left their husbands to seek a spiritual life despite stern social disapproval. Abandoning societal norms, which enhanced family honor and provided a well-defined and secure social role, some saints sought the company of groups of other devotees, frequently male. The piety and poetry of these saints were greatly admired, and some of the saints were enshrined in temples and worshiped after their deaths, but women poets were *not* considered suitable role models for Hindu women in earthly life. Honor and fidelity to one's husband were perceived as governing values for most Hindu women. Only in the realm of devotion to God were the women saints held to be models whose passion could be selectively emulated. None of the saints was regarded as a guru or formal instructor who could initiate other devotees.

The songs of women saints are similar to many works of male devotees who were part of the medieval devotional (*bhakti*) movement in India. The poems contain themes of "bridal mysticism"; verses are addressed to the deity cast in the role of the lover, but the poems are not generally explicitly erotic. In Hindu *bhakti* poems, God was frequently portrayed as the "supreme male," and *all* human beings were women in relation to him. Therefore, even male poets sometimes spoke from the stance of a woman pining for "her" divine lover. Female poets, however, never identified themselves in a male role. The women poets (as well as some male devotional poets) long not so much for liberation from this life (*moksa*), considered to be a classical Hindu norm, but for a passionate union with the Lord. Many verses are spoken from the stance of a girl separated from her lover, and these are the most poignant in all the collections. Occasionally, a poet may identify herself as a cowherd-girl in a myth connected with Krishna and speak in her voice. In times of separation, some poets like Āṇṭāḷ sent birds and clouds as messengers to the God-lover, to convey their love for him. Mīrābāi and Āṇṭāḷ describe dreams in which the Lord came as a bridegroom and took their hands in marriage; other verses speak of ecstatic unions between the deity and the saint.

Āṇṭāḷ's poems were canonized and became part of daily and annual home and temple liturgy for the Śrīvaiṣṇavas. The poems of Mīrābāi, Mahādevi Akkā, and the fourteenth-century Kashmiri saint Lallā are sung by congregations of pious worshipers. Many of the poems have been set to music, and sometimes the correct melody is mentioned in the text of the verse by the composer. Unlike the Sanskrit *Vedas*, the most sacred Hindu scripture, which could be recited only by male members of the highest ("priestly") class of society (*brāhmaṇas*), the poems of the women devotional poets were in the vernacular. Anyone, regardless of caste or sex, had the authority to chant or sing them.

The poems of Mahādevi Akkā, Kāraikkāl Ammaiyār, and Lallā are addressed to the god Śiva. Āṇṭāḷ's passion is directed toward Viṣṇu, and Mīrābāi addresses her poems primarily to Krishna, an incarnation of Viṣṇu. Critical editions of the poetry are not always available, and while Āṇṭāḷ's poems (totaling 173 verses) have been critically edited, and the canon fixed, estimates on Mīrābāi's poems range from 103 to 590 songs.

References. A. J. Alston, *The Devotional Poems of Mīrābāi* (New York, 1980); Dennis Hudson, "Bathing in Krishna: A Study in Vaiṣṇava Hindu Theology," *Harvard Theological Review* 73 (1980): 537–564; A. K. Ramanujan, "On Women Saints," in J. S. Hawley and D. Wulff (eds.), *The Divine Consort* (Berkeley Calif., 1982), 316–324.

VASUDHA NARAYANAN

INDONESIA comprises around 13,000 islands, about 180 million inhabitants, and a wide variety of ethnic groups. The relatively high position of women in traditional society can be attributed to several factors—a low level of urbanization and state control, slow penetration of the world religions, and a bilateral kinship system that also favored endogamous marriage. Females were actively involved in the rural economy, especially in rice growing, and enjoyed considerable economic independence as food producers and market traders. Tenth-century Javanese inscriptions show that village women entered into contracts, incurred debts, owned property, and were prominent in communal decision making. While adultery was condemned, premarital sex was tolerated, and unsuccessful unions were easily dissolved. Women also took leading roles in indigenous rituals and acted as spirit mediums. Such individuals were normally postmenopausal, since, although female fertility was respected, sexuality itself was considered a powerful and potentially dangerous force.

The belief that female sexuality needed to be controlled became more prominent with the arrival of the world religions. From around the eighth century C.E. Indian influence was particularly noticeable among the elite of Java and Bali. Hinduism and Buddhism clearly articulated the notion of female inferiority in religious life and male political dominance. This pattern was further encouraged by the expansion of Islam from the fourteenth century. Though women remained much freer in village society, where monogamy was the norm, upper-class men usually took more than one wife and commonly had many concubines. High-ranking females led a more secluded life, with premarital chastity strictly enforced and the ability to initiate divorce greatly limited. Nonetheless, strict purdah and veiling were never adopted. Wellborn women were still able to maintain considerable economic independence and political influence, particularly in the negotiation of marriage alliances.

In the seventeenth and eighteenth centuries most of Java and key areas in other Indonesian islands came under the control of the Dutch East India Company. Women were less able to compete in long-distance trade, and the introduction of cash crops combined with Chinese penetration into the peddling trade adversely affected female ability to maintain an independent income. The growing presence of foreign men, Chinese and Europeans, and the rise of port cities like Batavia (modern Jakarta) brought a rise in con-cubinage, an expanding demand for female domestic slaves, and an increase in prostitution. Male authority was also promoted among the small number of Indonesians who became Christian as a result of proselytizing by Eur-opeans. However, women were attracted by the Christian prohibition against taking a second wife and the possibility of appealing to Dutch-run courts for legal redress in marital disputes.

The nineteenth century saw the expansion of Dutch colonial control, most obviously on Java. While all peasants suffered with the colonial stress on cash crops, Javanese women may have survived better than men because they were able to sell household produce to supplement their income from agricultural work. However, males were preferred as laborers in crops other than rice, and female plantation workers were employed in low-ranking, time-consuming, and poorly paid tasks. To some extent the Indonesian "housekeepers" of European males can be seen as cultural brokers, but this did not mean improved status, since they had no legal rights. The spread of European middle-class values among educated Indonesians fostered the ideal of domesticity, encouraging women to withdraw from the workforce.

Indonesian women occasionally emerged as leaders in anti-Dutch con-flicts, and a few have been officially entitled National Heroines. The most enduring expression of female concerns, however, came from a wellborn Javanese, Raden Kartini (1879–1904), whose letters to Dutch friends pro-tested against the lack of access to educational opportunities, polygamy, and arranged marriages. She is honored as a National Heroine on Kartini Day (April 21).

In the early twentieth century the nationalist movement encouraged some aristocratic Indonesian women to mobilize around gender issues. The new political organizations through which they expressed their views expanded to incorporate middle-class women. While these women's groups were pri-marily concerned with equipping females for traditional roles as housewife and mother, with training in housekeeping, dressmaking, and child care, they did provide a forum for opposition to polygamy, child marriages, and forced unions. Under their aegis schools were established for girls, and periodicals were published.

During the 1920s women's organizations became more political, and the major nationalist groupings all formed women's branches. Women also joined the Indonesian Communist Party (PKI), and several were imprisoned by the Dutch following the abortive 1926/1927 communist uprising. But the primary concern of all anticolonial groups was political independence, and "women's issues" were given only passing attention. Women were told that their organizations should give priority to the nationalist struggle.

The concentration on nationalist, rather than feminist, concerns was also due to the potentiality for disagreement between secular and religious women's organizations. The most important Islamic religious organization was Aisyiyah, the women's arm of the Muslim modernist movement Muhammadiyah. Though Aisyiyah's leaders were also concerned with female education, marriage reforms were sensitive because they appeared to conflict with Islamic law. Whereas discussion of feminist issues often caused divisions between women's groups, they were largely united in endorsing the nationalist cause. In the 1930s women were politically active in the independence movement, and a number were jailed or exiled. One Dutchwoman was finally elected to the Volksraad, a deliberative body including both Dutch and Indonesians, in 1935. From 1941 suffrage for Indonesian women was introduced for municipal councils, but any progress was prevented by the outbreak of World War II.

From 1942 to 1945 the Japanese invaded and occupied Indonesia. All prewar women's groups were dissolved, and the Japanese promoted new mass organizations that provided military training for young women. At the local level, women's organizations were required to produce and distribute food to the occupying Japanese army. The numbers remain speculative, but as many as 10,000 Indonesian women may have been forced to provide sexual services to Japanese military as *jugun ianfu*, or comfort women.

Following the Japanese surrender, the Dutch sought to reimpose their colonial regime, despite Indonesia's declaration of independence. In the Indonesian resistance women's units played an important role caring for wounded soldiers, organizing kitchens, serving as couriers, and conducting literacy classes. The 1945 Constitution was a significant document, giving Indonesian women legal equality with men, but only after the Dutch departure in 1948 was Indonesia able to institute an independent government. Eighteen women were elected to the 257-member Parliament in the 1955 elections. Nonetheless, opposition to marriage reform from Islamic leaders meant that it was impossible to reach agreement on measures that would give greater protection to women and end practices such as polygamy. The economic position of women also showed little improvement. Discrimination in wages was rampant, despite a 1957 law that stipulated equal pay for equal work.

Without the bonding of the nationalist struggle, fissures began to appear in the women's movement, accentuated by the economic and political chaos of the early 1960s. Women's Islamic groups retreated from political matters, but the communist-linked women's organization, Gerwani, actively campaigned against discrimination in wages and employment. Issues such as inequities in marriage and sexual violence received less attention. Although lower-class membership of Gerwani grew, many Indonesian women were not comfortable with its political activism. Meanwhile, army leaders were disturbed at the growing communist strength. In 1965, following allegations of a planned coup, they took control of Indonesia's government.

The Communist Party was banned, with Gerwani coming under particular attack.

Under what is officially termed the "New Order" government led by President Suharto, policies relating to women have been coordinated by the ministry of state for the role of women. Stress has been not on political involvement but on women as educators of children and guardians of the family. An important tool in spreading this message is the government-sponsored Family Welfare Association (PKK). Some advances have been made. It is noteworthy that the resurgent Indonesian Islam has not moved against women, who have equal rights of divorce and fair access to marital income. A 1974 law restricted polygamous marriage so that Muslim men can take a second wife only under stringent conditions. In rural areas, the successful family-planning program has helped reduce domestic burdens, and although two-thirds of illiterates are women, the literacy rate among girls has improved markedly. Nonetheless, the majority of Indonesian women are still disadvantaged in relation to men. Female vocational training remains directed toward traditional pursuits such as teaching and health care. Young Indonesian women employed in factories have helped fuel Indonesia's current economic growth, but their wages remain low, the opportunities for advancement negligible, and implementation of workers' rights halfhearted. Rural women have found that mechanization has closed many traditional avenues for supplementing income. Political activism among women is also low. Less than 6 percent of the highest echelon of civil servants are females, and women as a group exert minimal influence in political, religious, literary, or artistic life. There is little possibility of major change unless the government begins to promote a new kind of Indonesian woman.

References. Jutta Berninghausen and Bridgid Kerstan, *Forging New Paths: Feminist Social Methodology and Rural Women in Java* (London, 1992); *Kartini Centenary: Indonesian Women Then and Now* (Melbourne, Monash University, 1980); Elsbeth Locher-Scholten and Anke Niehof (eds.), *Indonesian Women in Focus: Past and Present Notions* (Leiden, 1992); Claudine Salmon, "Essai de bibliographic sur la question féminine en Indonésie," *Archipel* 13 (1977): 23–36; Laurie J. Sears (ed.), *Fantasizing the Feminine in Indonesia* (Durham, N.C., 1996); Jean Gelman Taylor, "Kartini in Her Historical Context," *Bijdragen tot de Taal-, Land-en Volkenkunde* 145 (1989): 295–307; Cora Vreede de Stuers, *The Indonesian Woman: Struggles and Achievements* (The Hague, 1960).

BARBARA WATSON ANDAYA

INFANT ABANDONMENT. Women in different societies, cultures, and times have sought ways of coping with an unwanted child for whom they could not, or would not, provide. Although the problem of the disposition of unwanted infants usually had been associated with increased industrialization and urbanization, recent work has shown that the problem was both a rural and urban one that transcended geographical and national boundaries and existed since ancient times.

From antiquity through the Middle Ages, by placing unwanted babies in conspicuous places, parents abandoned their children, but not to die. Parents abandoned their babies as an alternative to infanticide to alleviate their poverty, to preserve the patrimony from a partitive inheritance, or to "correct for gender" and deformities. Child abandonment most often was the feasible form of family limitation in situations of poverty during the Roman era. In the eleventh and twelfth centuries, a period of prosperity, mention of child abandonment appeared less frequently; during the subsequent periods of economic decline during the later Middle Ages, abandoned children again became a problem.

Institutionalized, regulated systems of infant abandonment arose in the late Middle Ages in Italy and southern France and spread northward throughout most of Europe. The Catholic Church established foundling homes, equipped with a rotating turnstile, in which a cradle swiveled so that a person could deposit a baby in the half facing the street and then turn it so that the baby rotated inside. Infants remained in the institutions only a few days and then were sent out to wet nurses in the countryside. The ideological justification for the establishment of foundling homes was to prevent the deaths of those infants through infanticide. Nevertheless, in the eighteenth and nineteenth centuries, abandoned infants had a likelihood of death more than triple that of nonabandoned infants; between 60 and 90 percent died. By the nineteenth century, national and local governments assumed the direction of the foundling institutions and determined policy toward infant abandonment.

Both married and single mothers gave up their children to the foundling institutions. Their decisions to abandon were affected by several factors: the availability of the institutions and the ease with which mothers could abandon their infants; the magnitude of the stigma of having an out-of-wedlock child; the family economy, affecting the ability to keep and rear a child; the availability of other options of child care, including kin networks, charity, and welfare; and the ease with which parents could later reclaim their children. In Spain, until the 1790s about half the abandoning mothers were married and abandoned their children because of poverty. During the nineteenth century, Paris and Milan represent the two extremes in the proportion of married women who abandoned their children. The majority of babies left at the foundling institution in Milan were legitimate, but only between 5 and 15 percent of those abandoned in Paris were babies of married women. In Russia as many as one-third to one-half of the abandoning mothers were married, until the 1891 reforms excluded virtually all children of married women from the foundling institutions. In Madrid and Milan during the eighteenth and nineteenth centuries, parents could easily reclaim their abandoned children, which helped make infant abandonment an option for married women feeling the pinch of poverty that a newborn might bring. Mothers usually abandoned infant boys and girls in equal proportions. Generally, a high illegitimacy rate, an acute rate of rural-to-urban migration, the prohibitive poverty of the mother, and permissive government policies contributed to staggering rates of infant abandonment.

In nineteenth-century Europe there were two models of dealing with unwanted infants: the Protestant model used in Britain and the Catholic model of foundling institutions adopted by the French, Spanish, Italian, and Russian governments. The British permitted single mothers to seek child support from the father of the child and provided poor relief for some women and their infants. Alternatively, many British women avoided poorhouses and parish or governmental poor relief by sending their infants directly to "baby farms," where the mothers paid other, predominantly rural, women to care for their babies. A mother rarely expected the return of her child. In the Catholic model, unlike the Protestant approach, women, in effect, abandoned their infants to the state. The secular government took over the former obligation of traditional Catholic charity. Rarely did women abandon babies on the street or on doorsteps in any European country. When child adoption became possible (such as it had been in the United States), and when social welfare became more widespread in the twentieth century, infant abandonment was no longer a major issue. (See also WET-NURSING.)

References. John Boswell, *The Kindness of Strangers: The Abandonment of Children in Western Europe from Late Antiquity to the Renaissance* (New York, 1988); Rachel G. Fuchs, *Abandoned Children: Foundlings and Child Welfare in Nineteenth-Century France* (New York, 1984); Volker Hunecke, *I trovatelli di Milano: Bambini esposti e famiglie espositrici dal XVII secolo* (Bologna, Italy, 1988); David L. Ransel, *Mothers of Misery: Child Abandonment in Russia* (Princeton, 1988); Joan Sherwood, *Poverty in Eighteenth-Century Spain: The Women and Children of the Inclusa* (Toronto, 1988).

                                                                        RACHEL G. FUCHS

INFANTICIDE is the killing of an infant under one year of age. Infanticide has been, at least for some infants, tolerated, condoned, or even encouraged from the Stone Age to the present by peoples in every stage of cultural sophistication.

In many societies there is a period after birth before the newborn is considered fully human. During this period of a day (before nursing begins), a week or two (before the child is named or publicly recognized by the father), or even as long as three years (as among the Amahuaca of Peru), destruction would not be considered the killing of a person.

For infanticide to be condoned or tolerated, it must be committed for reasons and by means that are acceptable to the community. Poverty,* real or relative, of the family* or the community is the leading cause of infanticide. Killing newborns has been a widely accepted way of limiting family size in societies without safe and proven methods of contraception. In some cases families are not to exceed what the community decides is "normal size."

Killing infants whose presence will overburden the mother, hence, jeopardize other family members or the entire community, is sometimes mandatory. Among migrating people, the death of a child born too late in the season to stand the rigors of a migration or born before an older sibling is out of its mother's arms may be required. Infants are also killed to increase spacing between children, allowing the others more chance of survival. One or both pairs of twins or an infant whose mother dies as a result of childbirth* may be murdered.

Mentally or physically defective infants may be killed out of fear that the deformity is hereditary, that the child is a "changeling" or the work of the devil, or that the mother will be blamed or out of the need not to "waste" food and care on poor risks for survival. The killing of neonates in modern maternity hospitals may have stemmed from the belief that the "quality of life" in store for the child makes life not worth living. However, advances in prenatal diagnosis and fetal surgery as well as the legalization of abortion have reduced some of the ethical and legal problems involved in decisions on anomalous infants. (See REPRODUCTION, ETHICAL ISSUES IN.)

Infants are also killed for political reasons, such as infant sacrifice for the good of the community or elimination of possible rivals, and for reasons not usually condoned by society, such as killing the children of rival wives or concubines or killing one's own offspring because they are not wanted by a new sexual partner or because they are illegitimate. The legalizing of abortion may have reduced, but has not eliminated, the murder of newborns by unwed mothers.

Historical and anthropological evidence indicates that where infanticide is condoned or tolerated, it is often directed against female infants more than male infants. "Ideal" sex ratios favor males. In Rome an early law is supposed to have required citizens to keep all sons and the firstborn daughter. In China the ideal ratio of boys to girls was 5 to 2. In patrilineal societies, where poverty or relative poverty is a cause of infanticide, females do not add to the patriliny* but take wealth from it for dowries. Especially where hypergamous marriages (in which women marry up) are common, and dowries tend to become excessive, female infanticide is likely to be practiced.

Although Buddhism and Taoism opposed infanticide, it was widely practiced in poorer districts of imperial China, directed against girls. The efforts of the People's Republic to limit families to one child have again brought reports of female infanticide. In India female baby killing was tolerated into the nineteenth century. Daughters were so devalued that they were sometimes accepted as punishment for sins of the past life. No longer condoned, female infanticide has been replaced in some parts of India by "underinvestment" (deliberate undernourishment and insufficient care), leading to excessive female mortality. Female infanticide, sometimes required by tribal custom in ancient Arabia, was condemned by Mohammed but continued to be practiced among Bedouins until modern times. In some areas of the Middle East, too, it has been replaced by "underinvestment."

In Europe, infanticide was tolerated until the advent of Christianity. Thereafter, the level of frequency and of toleration varied according to area, time period, and status of the perpetrators. Evidence of infanticide directed primarily against females is so scattered for the ancient and medieval periods that some scholars deny that there was more killing of female than of male infants. Although there is too little evidence to conclusively prove the case, the little demographic evidence from Greece and Rome and the few registers from medieval villages that show evidence of badly skewed sex ratios *all* show an unnaturally large number of boys in comparison to girls (Coleman). In Renaissance Florence, where dowries were high, and demographic records more plentiful, a higher incidence of female infant deaths can be documented (Trexler).

Except when done by public agents, most deaths, overt and covert, are by passive means, chiefly abandonment. So in Sparta state officials threw anomalous infants over a cliff; elsewhere in Greece unwanted infants were usually abandoned in the wild to starve or be killed by wild animals. In the Amazon infants are left under a tree in the rain forest; in the desert, buried in the sand; in the Arctic, left on the ice; in the neonatal intensive care unit, put in a room in an out-of-the-way corridor. Sometimes they are left where there might be hope for their survival, as at hospitals and churches. "Overlaying" is thought often to have been a covert form of infanticide. (But many cases of "overlaying" may actually have been crib deaths—see Johnson.) In different areas of Europe from the sixteenth through the eighteenth centuries, parents could murder their infants by sending them to wet nurses. Infants are also killed by intentional neglect. Leaving the infant in dangerous situations, to be killed by "accident," was especially common in the nineteenth century. Today most infanticide has been replaced by "underinvestment," greatly increasing the child's chance of death in early childhood.

Almost all murder of infants is done by parents (or surrogate parents), alone or through accomplices. The mother is the most likely agent. Abject poverty or overwhelming stress may prevent her from relating to her baby. Fear of blame because of the child's deformity or its sex and fear of shame and stigma because of the child's illegitimacy are frequent causes for a mother's getting rid of her newborn.

During the Middle Ages infanticide usually came under the jurisdiction of the church courts, which could not dispense capital punishment. Not until the early modern period did civil governments begin to take an interest in prosecuting cases of infant deaths, for which the death penalty was given into the nineteenth century. Prosecution of offenders was marked by biases regarding sex, class, and marital status: only certain types of people were ever tried or punished. Fathers of murdered infants were never tried; married mothers, seldom. Wet nurses were not tried—unless the child lived. In Florence returning the child before it was 30 months old could result in a fine or a whipping. The unwed mother and the poor and the old (accused as witches) were tried and convicted. The unwed mother had little chance of acquittal unless she could show evidence, such as the preparation of clothing, that she was planning to raise the child.

In patriarchal society infanticide has been directed against female infants, committed primarily by women, and until the late twentieth century, only women, almost always marginal women, were punished for it.

References. E. Coleman, "Infanticide in the Early Middle Ages," in S. M. Stroud (ed.), *Women in Medieval Society* (Philadelphia, 1976), 47–70; G. Hausfater and S. B. Hrdy (eds.), *Infanticide: Comparative and Evolutionary Perspectives* (New York, 1984); M. P. Johnson, "Smothered Slave Infants: Were Slave Mothers at Fault?" *Journal of Southern History* 47 (1981): 493–520; W. A. Langer, "Infanticide: A Historical Survey," *History of Childhood Quarterly* 1 (1974): 353–365; R. C. Trexler, "Infanticide in Florence: New Sources and First Results," *History of Children Quarterly* 1 (1973): 98–116.

INFERTILITY affects between 10 and 15 percent of women. In addition, about 20 percent of pregnancies end in miscarriage. In the past the major solution to childlessness was adoption, but the number of babies available for adoption has decreased substantially. This and the development of new reproductive technologies mean that infertility is often construed as a medical condition for which women seek (and are expected to seek) medical solutions.

Infertility has many causes, including genetic factors, environmental hazards, infections, and hormonal imbalance, but it is often not possible to pinpoint a "cause." Identified in roughly equal proportions are male problems (low number of sperm, antibodies), female problems (failure to ovulate, blocked tubes, endometriosis* [the accumulation in the pelvic cavity of tissue from the uterine lining]), and incompatibility between sperm and the woman's reproductive system.

Men's fertility is examined by means of one major test, the semen test, and the major treatment is donor insemination (DI). Semen from a (usually anonymous) donor enables women to bypass a man's infertility. In contrast, treatments for women are more extensive, ranging from antibiotics for infections, to hormone therapy to induce ovulation, and to in vitro fertilization (IVF) and related therapies. The development of IVF has increased the visibility of infertility, although the high costs of treatment limit its availability, and its low success rate means that it is a solution for the less than one in five women who conceive and give birth to a live baby. Hormone therapy is often employed in IVF to induce multiple ovulation, increasing both the success of IVF and the potential risks of high doses of hormones and the risks of multiple pregnancies and births.

Most women still become (and expect to become) mothers, although they have fewer children than their grandmothers did. Motherhood is no longer linked to economic survival for women in the developed world, although this is not always the case for women in other cultures and historical periods. There are, however, strong links between fertility and a woman's social position in many families and communities. Childless women (whether because of infertility or by choice) are marginalized and stigmatized by being described as "desperate," "deviant," or "unwomanly."

Problems in conception may mean that women remain childless or become mothers only after a delay. For some women infertility means having fewer children than they would like and challenges notions of families as comprising two or more children. Infertility may disrupt women's (and men's) plans and hopes for themselves and their relationships. Women's sense of themselves as "women" is often linked to becoming or being mothers, which provides women with an identity, purpose, and a sense of belonging.

Adjustment and coming to terms with infertility are a complex and unfolding process: women commonly report feelings such as grief, shock and anger, failure and inadequacy, and loss of control over their lives. For some women these feelings focus on infertility and medical solutions, but for others they focus on the threatened loss of identity as mothers and the lack of a relationship with a child. However, infertility is not always problematic, especially when viewed over the life span. How women make sense of infertility is also related to the value of children and motherhood within communities and on women's personal circumstances that provide them with identities that do not depend on their relationship with a child or children.

References. Peggy A. Field and Patricia B. Marck (eds.), *Uncertain Motherhood: Negotiating the Risks of the Childbearing Years* (Thousand Oaks, Calif., 1994); Mardy S. Ireland, *Reconceiving Women: Separating Motherhood from Female Identity* (New York, 1993); Mary-Claire Mason, *Male Infertility: Men Talking* (London, 1993); Carolyn M. Morell, *Unwomanly Conduct: The Challenge of Intentional Childlessness* (New York, 1994); Annette L. Stanton and Christine Dunkel-Schetter (eds.), *Infertility: Perspectives from Stress and Coping Research* (New York, 1991); Michelle Stanworth (ed.), *Reproductive Technologies: Gender, Motherhood and Medicine* (Cambridge, U.K., 1987).

ANNE WOOLLETT

INTELLIGENCE QUOTIENT (IQ) is a measure of intelligence derived from performance on one of several available standardized tests. Originally,

IQ scores were computed by dividing an individual's mental age by his or her chronological age and multiplying by 100. (Mental age refers to one's mental development relative to others'; thus, a child with a mental age of 9 performs on an intelligence test at the level of the average 9-year-old.) Today scores on most tests are based on their deviation from (distance above or below) the average score of a normative group, with this average usually set by convention at 100. Psychological opinion is divided on the extent to which these scores reflect genetic versus environmental influences on mental ability.

Critics of IQ tests have argued that test items tend to be biased in favor of white, urban, middle-class individuals. They have also observed that cultural values can affect attitudes toward taking the test, motivation, comfort in the testing situation, and rapport with the test giver. Efforts have been made to construct reliable and valid, culture-fair tests that eliminate group differences in performance, but on the whole they have been disappointing.

On the most widely used intelligence tests, average female and male scores do not differ, but this is by design. On early versions of the Stanford-Binet Intelligence Scale, the first standardized IQ test in the United States, girls scored higher than boys at every age up to 14. Psychologists were reluctant to conclude that girls were intellectually superior to boys. Instead, in the 1937 revision of the test, psychologist Lewis Terman eliminated sex differences once and for all by simply deleting items that favored one sex or adding items favoring males. Other tests have followed similar procedures.

Although the sexes do not differ in average performance, over the years several writers have proposed that males as a group are more *variable* than females in intellectual ability, that is, are overrepresented at both the low and high ends of the scale. (See VARIABILITY HYPOTHESIS.) Historically, this notion has sometimes been used to argue that training females for intellectually challenging professions is a waste of educational resources. It is true that a somewhat greater proportion of males than females score at the lower end of the IQ scale, possibly because boys are more vulnerable than girls to congenital defects and early illness and head injury. However, evidence for a *general* difference in variability or for a greater proportion of males at the high end of the spectrum has been plagued by methodological problems and is considered weak by most feminist and mainstream psychologists.

The original purpose of IQ tests was to predict school achievement, and for both sexes, modern tests do this fairly well, especially when supplemented by other sorts of information. However, IQ scores are less than accurate in predicting achievement outside the classroom, where educational preparation, motivation, and opportunity are critical determinants of occupational success. Even intellectual giftedness does not ensure such success if other factors conspire to limit it. In 1921, Stanford University researchers began to study a cohort of children in the top 1 percent of the IQ score distribution. Most of the boys grew up to achieve prominence in professional or managerial fields. In accord with social expectations of the time, most of the girls grew up to be homemakers. Those employed outside the home overwhelmingly went into lower-status occupations.

Related research finds that females are more likely than males to show a decline in IQ after grade school. Traits traditionally defined as "masculine," such as assertiveness and independence, seem to promote intellectual development in both sexes. It is not yet clear whether sex-role changes during the 1970s and 1980s have reduced or eliminated sex differences* in patterns of intellectual development as measured by IQ tests.

Currently, static descriptions of how well individuals or groups do on IQ tests are giving way to analyses of the problem-solving strategies used by high and low scorers. This shift in emphasis may eventually lead to insights about why the sexes, although they do not differ in average IQ test performance, do sometimes differ slightly on tests of specific skills, such as verbal or mathematical ones. It should be noted, however, that such differences account for only a small proportion of the overall variance in test scores and cannot explain existing occupational disparities.

References. E. E. Maccoby and C. N. Jacklin, *The Psychology of Sex Differences* (Stanford, Calif., 1974); P. Sears and A. H. Barbee, "Career and Life Satisfactions among Terman's Gifted Women," in J. C. Stanley, W. C. George, and C. H. Solano (eds.), *The Gifted and the Creative: A Fifty-Year Perspective* (Baltimore, 1977).

CAROLE WADE

INTERNAL LABOR MARKET is a unit within a large organization to which a specific set of rules and procedures relative to wage rates and promotion paths is applied. Men have been found concentrated in internal labor markets with opportunities for promotion and high pay, while women's internal labor markets are characterized by dead-end jobs paying low wages. Even when they enter the same internal labor market, job tracking may be very different for men and women with similar credentials.

INTERNATIONAL COUNCIL OF WOMEN (ICW) was founded in 1888 by a group of American and British women, led by May Wright Sewell, Susan B. Anthony, and Francis Willard, to "provide means of communication between women's organizations of all countries" without violating "the independence or methods of work" of any of them (Constitution of 1888). Forty-nine delegates from eight countries attended the first meeting. Today, the ICW represents 70 national councils.

Since the goals of the organization were to promote international cooperation, Sewell devised a constitution broad enough to enable women of various political and social persuasions to join. Equally broad bylaws enabled individual countries to establish all-encompassing national women's councils. The first Quinquencennial World Congress of Women, held in Chicago in 1893, brought together over 600 women. When the Austrian and Hungarian National Councils joined at the Third Congress (Berlin, 1904), the council idea spread to Central Europe. In the years before World War I, to women's rights priorities (the primary stumbling block to unity) was added the problem of national heterogeneity within a single political system. The issue became especially acute when Norwegian insistence on a separate council was opposed by the Swedish Council in 1905. The ICW then excluded from its programs "political and religious questions of a controversial nature affecting the inter-relationship of two or more countries." After World War I, the ICW adopted the state principle: only national councils representing independent states could participate formally in its proceedings. The ICW remains aloof of the nationality question.

Officers and the board of the ICW are elected, without regard to nationality, at the triennial international congresses by official delegates of national boards. Observers from nonmember states, such as the USSR and Eastern European nations, may be invited but cannot vote. In 1963, the headquarters of the ICW was permanently moved to Paris; prior to that the headquarters was located in the home country of the president.

In its early years ICW stressed equal access to schools and training programs, equal pay for equal work, state-supported maternity leaves and benefits, protection of workers, and the development of machinery and programs to alleviate the drudgery of housework as well as to promote better working conditions for domestic workers. In the 1920s, ICW standing committees worked closely with the League of Nations, especially in matters of health, welfare, peace, racial equality, and the rights of national minorities. The Joint Committee of Major International Organizations, which was interested in education for peace and founded at the suggestion of the ICW in 1925, laid the basis of much of the work after World War II in the areas of exchanges, international understanding, and the revision of textbooks. The committee itself was disbanded in 1946, when the United Nations was founded.

Many of the activist women of the ICW perished in World War II, and many of those of Eastern Europe perished in its aftermath. However, the work of the ICW was renewed with the liberation of Europe in 1944. It became one of the original nongovernmental organizations affiliated with the United Nations (UN) with a consultative status. ICW pursued the same work in the UN as it had in the league, focusing on welfare, refugees, health, and education programs. The ICW works with the UN through its standing committees. The ICW liaison officer was instrumental in creating the Conference and Committee of Nongovernmental Organizations (NGOs) in consultative status with various UN agencies such as the Food and Agriculture Organization (FAO); the United Nations Educational, Scientific, and Cultural Organization (UNESCO); and the United Nations Children's Fund (UNICEF).

Through the 1960s, the membership of the ICW expanded to include many African and Asian countries, and the organization became directly involved in programs of economic development in those areas. The stress ICW placed on the involvement of women in development was picked up by the United Nations in its 1973–1983 Decade of Women. The ICW continues its programs of providing vocational training in new occupations and promoting facilities needed by women.

The triennial congresses of the ICW are characterized by an increasing representation of non-Western women. The avoidance of any discussion of political issues endows it with greater agreement than is usually the case in international gatherings. Many of the non-Western councils receive government subsidies but apparently maintain their independence nonetheless. Western national councils lost much of their vitality to the newer women's organizations that emerged in the 1970s.

Standing committees have been formed to meet the needs of the time. The first two, Peace and International Arbitration and Press, and Finance and Law, were founded in 1899. In 1986 the committees were Arts and Letters; Child and Family; Economics, Education, Environment, and Habitat; Health; Home Economics; International Relations and Peace; Laws and the Status of Women; Mass Media; Migration; Social Welfare; and Women and Employment.

Since national councils are very loosely composed, statistical information on the number of women involved is not available. An overview of the ICW is given in the International Council of Women's *Women in a Changing World: The Dynamic Story of the International Council of Women since 1888* (London, 1966). The available archival and published materials on the ICW have been deposited in the Paris headquarters of the ICW, and significant materials on the organization are located at the Library of Congress in Washington, D.C., and the United Nations Library in Geneva, Switzerland.

MARTHA BOHACHEVSKY-CHOMIAK

IRAN. Traditionally, in Iran, as in other Middle Eastern countries, the established social paradigm maintained that women should be confined to household activities and to the rearing of children, while men should engage in activities outside the house. The division along gender lines was enforced by seclusion, the veil, and the legal subordination of women to men, practices that were enshrined in the religious law or *Shari'ah*. However, generally only women of the upper and middle classes observed strict seclusion—poorer women had to work and go to market to buy food and other goods. Furthermore, seclusion did not prevent women from exercising influence beyond the physical boundaries of the household.

Despite seclusion, women contributed to culture, politics, education, and the economy, as is attested by references to their role in dynastic politics, in the textile and carpet industries, and in agriculture. Women also participated in many urban riots, as when prices of staple goods went up suddenly, or when they responded to the call of religious leaders to defend moral standards threatened by the government and its representatives. Important examples include the role women played against the tobacco concession, which in 1890 gave a British subject full monopoly on the purchase, sale, and export of all tobacco grown in Iran, and in the Constitutional Revolution of 1905–1911.

In the late nineteenth century, the belief in maintaining a strict separation along gender lines began to erode. The impetus for change came initially from Iran's increased involvement in world markets. As knowledge of European civilization spread among the Iranian elite—intellectuals and officials—they became convinced of its superiority and desirous of emulating European ways, including the treatment of women. Gradually, the traditional role of women began to be questioned by a growing segment of the elite, who encouraged younger women in their households to receive modern education. This generation of mainly upper-class women pioneered the enlightenment of more traditional women through education and the press.

The efforts of the Pahlavi rulers, Reza Shah (1925–1941) and Muhammad Reza Shah (1941–1979), to build a strong central state following European models, facilitated further change in women's traditional role. Although both rulers were hostile to participatory democracy, they believed that a modern state must end the isolation of women. The process of women's entry into the public arena, slow at first, gathered momentum in the 1960s. The state tried to integrate women into the social, economic, and educational life of the country in order to achieve more rapid economic growth. The regime also desired to appear more progressive to offset rising accusations of repression by internal opposition groups, particularly intellectuals, and other groups in the West. Pressure for change also came from women with modern education, whose numbers began to grow rapidly in this decade.

The regime took the initiative to pass the Family Protection Law in 1967 and its amendment in 1973. Although these reforms did not grant women rights equal to men's, they extended the franchise to women and improved women's rights within marriage and divorce and at work. However, the regime's efforts met with serious criticism. The secular activists branded these efforts as cosmetic and inadequate. The growing religiously oriented opposition groups denounced them as morally corrupting and aimed at undermining Islamic values. The growing rapprochement between the regime and U.S. policies widened the scope of opposition, ultimately resulting in revolution in 1979.

The causes of the 1979 revolution are complex and beyond the scope of this brief discussion. A crucial factor in the demise of the regime was the quadrupling of oil income in the early 1970s, which enabled it to speed up Western-inspired reforms. However, some of the reforms were positive. For example, the economic expansion created greater employment opportunities, including opportunities for women. Moreover, the number of women attending high school and university rose rapidly.

But the vast majority of the population, whose lifestyle was governed by religious values, became increasingly hostile to these reforms and considered them a threat to their way of life. Even women who benefited from the new employment opportunities were repelled by the regime's arrogance and widespread corruption. To silence growing dissent, the regime engaged in greater repression.

The involvement of the clergy, led by the highly respected Ayatollah Khomeini, a staunch critic of the Shah, turned hundreds of thousands of traditional men and women against the regime. Their participation in the revolution, along with radical leftist and nationalist groups, succeeded in overthrowing the Shah's regime.

The Shah was not replaced with a more liberal democratic regime but by the Islamic Republic, under leaders hostile to many of the changes during the twentieth century. With popular support from the majority of the traditional sectors of society, the new Islamic Parliament began to roll back some of the reforms that they viewed as contradictory to the *Shari'ah*, particularly those that had affected women's traditional role. High on the list was imposing an Islamic code of dress, or *hijab*, which made the covering of a woman's hair and body mandatory, and the abolition of the Family Protection Law. Women were encouraged to assume their traditional roles as homemakers and mothers. Although women were barred from becoming judges in compliance with the direct decree of the *Shari'ah*, the regime did not ban women from the labor force entirely; the exodus of many professionals after the revolution protected women's employment in the private sector and in public sector jobs such as education and health.

Although the vast majority of traditional women had opposed many of the Western-style policies of the shah, they did not approve the repeal of the 1967 Family Protection Law or the attempt to discourage women from working. Many, including some who traditionally had worn the veil or had adopted it as a symbol of opposition to the Shah, were angered by its forced imposition.

The regime's effort to alleviate women's sense of betrayal at the outcome of the revolution and to respond to the rising pressure from women for change in their status did not begin until the end of the Iran–Iraq War in 1988. The high rate of male casualties during the eight-year war with Iraq and the urgent need to rebuild the shattered economy were equally important in forcing the regime to revise its gender ideology in order to draw more women into the workforce.

For example, the regime changed its attitude from pro-natalist to pro-family planning and lifted the ban on the sale and distribution of contraceptives. Similarly, restrictions that segregated men and women in the workforce have been slowly eroding. Women are also being hired in greater numbers in the civil service—30 percent of government employees are women. In addition, restrictions against women's entry into law schools were relaxed following the change in the regime's attitude about employment of women in the legal profession. The barriers against women judges were lifted, although only in 1997 were a few women allowed to occupy this position. Many of the provisions of the abrogated 1967 Family Protection Act have also been restored.

Developments since the 1979 revolution reveal that the public perception of women began to change radically. The most important has been the great political awakening of the majority of women. Before the revolution traditional women did not pay attention to politics or participate actively. But they are taking part in the political process in great numbers. The increase in the number of women representatives in the Iranian Parliament, from 4 in the first (1984–1988) to 17 in the fourth (1996–2000), is a sign of this trend.

The women deputies come from traditional backgrounds and firmly believe in the values taught by Islam. They wear the *chador*, a full-length, loose, often black cover inside and outside the Parliament. However, they have publicly denounced many of the laws passed by the regime as contrary to Islam. They effected changes to create greater opportunities in education and employment and helped with the passage of an Islamic Family Protection Law in 1995. In 1997, the payment of alimony was indexed to the rate of inflation in order to protect the purchasing power of divorced women.

Their demand for improving women's condition has been supported by a new crop of Islamic feminists who publicize their views in writing, in books and magazines. Their arguments in favor of ameliorating the condition of women are made in the name of making society more Islamic, which they believe promotes justice for all. They acknowledge that Islamic societies in the past have discriminated against women, but they attribute these inequities to deviations from Islamic teachings. They blame women's disadvantages in the *Shari'ah* on the fact that the law was interpreted in the past by men.

Muslim feminists hold that Islam as a religion accommodates the needs of women better than any other religion. For example, they point out that, initially, Muslim women had greater freedom to participate in the social life of the community. Moreover, they believe that women's legal and economic independence has been safeguarded in the *Shari'ah* from interference by their male relatives. They mention Islamic marriage, which is a contract between consenting partners, and the bride-price, which is payable to the woman before the consummation of the marriage, as proof of women's capacity.

The presidential elections in 1997 offer additional evidence that the events of the past two decades have fundamentally altered the public perception of the role of women. The participation of the majority of Iranian women of voting age led to the victory of Seyyed Muhammad Khatami, who based his campaign, in large part, on greater civil liberties and better conditions for women.

The president acknowledged the importance of the women's vote by keeping his pledge. Although fear of opposition from conservative members of Parliament kept him from choosing women as members of the cabinet, he selected Masumeh Ebtekar, a 36-year-old university professor, as one of his six deputy-presidents. The appointment was not a token gesture, such as heading the office of women's affairs, but a substantive post as the head of the Environmental Protection Agency, where she would have many men as subordinates. Although many barriers remain before women, the trend set into motion by the new president shows that the Islamic Republic finally is paying serious attention to women's needs and their power.

References. V. M. Moghadam, "Women's Employment Issues in Contemporary Iran: Problems and Prospects in 1990s," *Iranian Studies* 28 (1995): 3–4, 175–203; Guity Nashat, "Women in Pre-Revolutionary Iran: A Historical Perspective," in Guity Nashat (ed.), *Women and Revolution in Iran* (Boulder, Colo., 1984), 5–37.

GUITY NASHAT

ISLAMIC LAW is presently applicable in contemporary nation-states primarily in the sphere of personal and family law, the Islamic law of crime and tort, commerce and contract, procedure and evidence, and so forth, having been largely replaced by codes drawn from other sources. Even when defined to comprehend only personal and family law (the sphere of law that touches most profoundly on women), the term "Islamic law" is very imprecise and must be considered at several levels.

There is, first, the law of the Koran, a work considered by Muslims to be the revealed word of Allah. There are verses in the Koran that appear to be predicated on the equality of men and women (e.g., 33:35), and there are verses that appear to be predicated on the superiority of men over women in some particular respect or context (e.g., 2:282). Equality of women was not in the seventh century the issue that it has become in the twentieth century, and the improvement that Muhammad attempted to introduce in the status of women must be judged and appreciated in the context of his time. In this perspective the reforms of the Koran were far from inconsiderable: female infanticide was condemned as equivalent to murder; obtaining the consent of the woman to marriage was stressed; marriage was placed on a more permanent basis; and *mahr*, or bride-price, was converted to a dower paid to, and the property of, the woman herself;

women's rights to own and to inherit property were recognized and confirmed; the process of divorce was regularized; and casual divorce was disapproved.

Second, during the two or three centuries following the death of Muhammad, the law of Islam was cast in its classical form by scholars who interpreted and analyzed the extant material. The Koran being far from a complete or concise legal manual, the scholars had recourse to extra-Koranic material. The most important extra-Koranic source became the sayings and doings of Muhammad during his life on earth. These anecdotes of the Prophet's life were collected in the Hadith literature, which became a source of Islamic law second only to the Koran itself. More important, a human element was introduced in the equation as human minds worked to interpret and expound the divine will and purpose. Several schools of law arose during this time: Islam split into Sunni and Shia branches, and within each branch different schools followed their respective interpretations of the law. (The Sunni branch accounts for approximately 90 percent of the present Muslim population; four distinct schools of Sunni law survive.)

The divergent interpretations reached by the classical scholars may be illustrated by considering the question of a woman's right to the dissolution of her marriage. All schools of law permit the woman to approach the *qadi* (judge) for a divorce, but they vary considerably in regard to the precise grounds on which a divorce may be granted. Classical Hanafi Sunni law allowed the woman to obtain a divorce in the absence of her husband's consent on only two grounds: the husband's inability to consummate the marriage or the fact that the husband had become a missing person, and 90 years had elapsed from the date of his birth (putative widowhood). The Maliki Sunnis allowed a woman to divorce on several additional grounds, including cruelty, desertion, failure to maintain, affliction with a dangerous disease, or insanity.

During the period when the classical scholars were filling in the gaps and putting their gloss on the Koranic law, the rights of women were severely cut back. The reforms of the Koran in the sphere of woman's rights were arguably too revolutionary for their time—or at least for the men of their time. Thus, for instance, the Koran clearly states (2:241, Yusuf Ali's translation): "For divorced women/ Maintenance (should be provided)/ On a reasonable [scale]./ This is a duty/ On the righteous." There is nothing here to imply that the obligation to provide maintenance to a divorced wife is limited in time or that anything other than the woman's remarriage should automatically bring the right to receive such maintenance to an end.

The Koran also introduced a "waiting period" (*idda*) following a divorce during which the woman is prohibited from remarrying. The original purpose of *idda* was, first, to allow the spouses (essentially the husband, because both pronouncement and revocation of *talag* [repudiation] lay in his hands) time for reconsideration and possible reconciliation. Second, *idda* serves to prevent confusion of paternity by allowing time to ascertain whether the divorced woman is pregnant; if she is found to be pregnant, her *idda* continues until the pregnancy has terminated. *Idda*, then, is a period of three months (three menstrual cycles) or, if the woman is pregnant, until delivery; a divorced woman is prohibited from remarrying until her period of *idda* has concluded.

The classical scholars decided that the maintenance referred to in Sura 2:241 (quoted before) subsisted only for the duration of the *idda* period. This, of course, places a woman in a much more vulnerable position (particularly given the husband's right of unilateral divorce) and makes it much easier for a man to discard his wife than the Koran arguably intended.

Third, as the religion of Islam spread into new lands, converts carried over into their new faith their existing social patterns and customary practices. The interaction of pre-Islamic custom and Islamic law was occasionally to the benefit of women. Thus, the Malaysian custom of *harta sapencharian*, according to which a wife is entitled on dissolution of the marriage by death or divorce to between one-third and one-half of the property acquired through the joint efforts of the spouses during the subsistence of the marriage, carried over and became integrated with Malaysian Muslim law, although it has no precedent in orthodox Islamic law. More commonly, however, custom served to deny women rights recognized in Islam; for example, the custom of denying women rights of inheritance, particularly when the property involved is land, which is found in many agrarian communities, was not discontinued by converts to Islam, in spite of the right of succession explicitly conferred upon women by the Koran.

Finally and most important in the modern world, individual nation-states have altered, reformed, and reinterpreted the classical law by decree, statute, and/or judicial decision. Again, the question of the woman's right to obtain divorce may be taken as illustrative. Hanafi law was extremely restrictive in this regard; virtually all Hanafi countries have given the wife greatly enhanced rights of petitioning for dissolution of her marriage, frequently drawing on Maliki interpretations to justify these reforms. (A very useful book on contemporary Muslim law is by Mahmood; this volume brings together in English translation the relevant legislation of several countries; the 1972 edition is out of date and a new edition is scheduled to appear shortly.)

The situation is, even today, confused by the dichotomy between law (meaning here the legally enforceable law of the relevant state) and custom (meaning here both non-Islamic custom and practices deriving from Islam but contrary to the reformed and/or modernized law of the state). Informants not infrequently make statements such as the following to investigators: "According to Muslim law, a woman does not inherit in the presence of a son or brother." "According to Muslim law, a woman has no right to divorce." The first statement is directly contrary to both Koranic law and contemporary state law; the second, even assuming the informant to be a Hanafi Sunni, is contrary to contemporary legislation applicable to Hanafi countries.

In a social setting where female illiteracy is high, and women are, to a greater or lesser degree, secluded and dependent on male support and protection, it is not surprising that women are often uninformed concerning their legal rights and/or reluctant to assert them. To this extent, the position of Muslim women is a social, rather than a strictly legal, problem; changes in the law enhancing the rights of Muslim women will be of little benefit as long as women are not in a position to claim and assert rights that are already theirs. This is not to say that reform is not urgently necessary; it must, however, be recognized that changes in the law will not of themselves automatically solve the social problem.

The recent upsurge in Muslim self-confidence, frequently expressed in a conservative or fundamentalist emphasis, has again brought the women's issue to the forefront. Partly this is a reflection of the fact that in the contemporary world the application of Muslim law is more or less confined to the arena of family law, and, partly, it is a reflection of the male tendency to see the "purity" of society as being symbolized by women and ensured by restrictions on women.

The need of the moment is to go back to the original source, the Koran, leaping over the interpretations and interpolations of the classical scholars, and to derive an interpretation that is relevant and appropriate to the present age. It is extremely important that Muslim women scholars play a leading role in this task; this time, the work of interpretation must not be left in the hands of men alone. The basis for hope and optimism lies in the fact that Muslim women are increasingly devoting themselves to this challenge. (Watch for the forthcoming works of Dr. Riffat Hassan.)

It may help put the Muslim situation in perspective to note that in June 1986 the Irish Republic held a referendum on a constitutional amendment that would have permitted divorce on very restrictive grounds (the amendment lost); and in July 1986 the Synod of the Anglican Church considered again the question of whether to ordain women priests (again procrastinating and voting to delay taking a decision). The arguments used by representatives of the Catholic Church who oppose divorce on any grounds, like those used by representatives of the Anglican Church who oppose the ordination of women, are not unanalogous to those employed by their conservative brothers in Islam.

Reference. Tahir Mahmood, *Family Law Reform in the Muslim World* (Bombay, 1972).

LUCY CARROLL

ITALIAN ARTISTS (FIFTEENTH THROUGH EIGHTEENTH CENTURIES). Before the Renaissance women artists are found in convents or in workshops where, usually as wives or daughters of a master, they contributed to the shop's production. By the fifteenth century, however, as artists strove to promote art to the level of music and poetry and themselves from craftpersons to professionals, convents were no longer cultural centers, and guilds were banning or restricting employment of women, even wives and daughters.

The few known fifteenth-century women artists were nuns. Most is known about the abbess Caterina dei Vigri (St. Catherine of Bologna) because of her sanctity, not her art. Her painting seems untouched by the changes sweeping the artistic and intellectual world of Renaissance Italy. In the sixteenth century the Florentine abbess Pautilla Nelli was the most gifted of a handful of nun-artists, but her fresco *The Last Supper* in the Church of St. Maria Novella shows that she, too, lagged behind current developments in art, and the strict enclosure of convents under the Counter-Reformation cut them off even further from the artistic and literary movements of the day. Although there will continue to be nun-artists, from now on, professional women artists are almost always laywomen.

Women artists worked within certain limitations. Training was still done in workshops, but male students now traveled all over Italy to seek out the best teachers. In some cities artists joined together to share the costs of models for private drawing sessions. With rare exceptions, women could not travel freely in search of instruction, nor could they attend a drawing class with men without ruining their reputations. To study male nude models was, of course, out of the question, leaving women seriously hampered in their ability to paint figures.

Another serious limitation was a restricted market. Italy, unlike the Netherlands, did not have a substantial middle class of individuals interested in buying art to decorate their homes. Most art was public art—altar pieces, official portraits, ceilings, overdoor panels—commissioned by princes of church or state and other very rich patrons and made according to their specifications from a limited range of subjects in history, mythology, religion, and allegory—the kind of art for which women were not trained. Most Italian women artists did portraits and plant and animal pictures.

Generally, the attitude toward women artists was friendly, if patronizing. Until the eighteenth century all women artists were described as attractive, and praise concentrated on their virtue, charm, and fulfillment of domestic duties. In discussions of their art, the platypus effect was often evident (the wonder is not that she paints well but that a woman can paint at all). However, if women vied for, and received, the lucrative public commissions, resentment could result, as in the case of Properzia di Rossi (c. 1490–1530) of Bologna. (Bologna was a center of female humanism with a tradition of women artists that went back to Santa Caterina and continued through Elisabetta Sirani.) Rossi began as a carver of fruit stones (peach, cherry, etc.), delicate carving suitable for women. When, c. 1520, she moved on to sculpture, she entered a male monopoly. Her reputation was ruined by the slanders of a jealous artist after she won a commission for several figures for a church facade.

Most women professional artists were daughters of artists, and most married, usually, other artists. A few continued active after marriage, in some cases becoming the economic mainstay of the family, but for most, marriage ended or seriously curtailed their careers. Some daughters of artists were overshadowed by their more famous fathers or brothers. Marietta Tintoretto (1551–1590), daughter of Jacobo Tintoretto, worked on backgrounds of her famous father's composition but was also a popular portraitist.

The Bolognese Lavinia Fontana (1552–1614), on the other hand, was one of the several women whose success exceeded their fathers'. She achieved fame as a portraitist when quite young, and when she moved to Rome, her portraits commanded very high prices. After she married, she supported the household. Her husband helped her with backgrounds and domestic duties. She expanded beyond portraits to larger works, altar pieces, and other religious works.

A large number of the women artists who have been recorded were noted, like Fontana, for their precocity. Fede Galizia (1578–1630), daughter of painter Nunzia Galizia, by her late teens had an international reputation. Although that reputation was based on her portraits, she also did religious paintings and was among the earliest Italian still-life artists.

The most famous woman painter of the sixteenth century, Sofonisba Anguissola (1532/1535–1625) was the daughter not of a painter but of a nobleman and was a phenomenon of her age. From an artistically talented family (three of her sisters were also artists until death or marriage interfered), Sofonisba was a child prodigy whose fame soon spread beyond Italy. She was invited to the court of Philip II of Spain (1559), where she became court painter and had gifts lavished upon her, including a royal dowry when she wed a Sicilian nobleman c. 1570. Four years later she returned to Italy as a widow, remarried, and settled in Genoa, where royalty, aristocracy, artists, and intellectuals flocked from all over Europe. The adulation paid her must have encouraged other women to enter art. She is also important as an innovator. In addition to portraits, including a large number of self-portraits, she did "conversation pieces," group portraits in which the figures are engaged in some activity, usually domestic—the origins of genre painting.

Although women were generally trained by their father or another family member, sometimes nonrelatives were hired to teach them as well. In the case of Artemesia Gentileschi (1593–1652/1653) this practice had disastrous effects. Gentileschi is one of the outstanding painters of the seventeenth century, an important baroque artist who helped spread the new Caravaggesque realism to Florence, Genoa, and Naples. Yet she is best remembered for the 1612 rape trial of the man hired to teach her, Agostino

Tassi. He was eventually acquitted, even though, to make sure she told the truth, her evidence was taken under torture. Her greatest works are biblical, and mythological scenes centered on strong female characters such as Judith, Esther, Lucretia, and Cleopatra. She did several paintings of Judith and Holofernes, a popular subject at the time. Her earliest-known rendition of the subject, perhaps influenced by her rape, is the violent, bloody *Judith Beheading Holofernes*, in which Judith has just thrust the sword through Holofernes' neck. Her third, *Judith and Her Handmaiden*, showing Judith and her servant, with Holofernes' head in a basket, preparing to flee the camp, is often considered her greatest painting. She was one of the first women to paint female nudes. The subject of Suzanna and the Elders was popular with male artists, but Gentileschi's treatment is very different from theirs. Her almost completely nude Suzanna is frightened and cowers away from the two lecherous old men leaning over her.

Elisabetta Sirani (1638–1665) died unmarried at age 27, but by that time she had completed a large body of work, taught a large number of women students in her own studio, and made a lot of money. The precocious daughter of a Bolognese artist, she became the sole support of her family after her father's health prevented his continuing to paint. Not satisfied with doing just portraits, she gained important commissions for religious paintings and thereby aroused jealousy in her male rivals. When they accused her of having men, including her father, paint her pictures, she invited a group to watch her paint a portrait, which she did in one sitting. She also did biblical and history scenes featuring heroines, but her slender, gentle women are far different from Gentileschi's vigorous heroines.

Among other seventeenth-century women artists are Sister Lucrina Fetti (given name Guistina; fl. c. 1614–c. 1651) of Mantua, who was taught by her more famous brother Dominico and who did portraits of her convent's patrons, the Gonzagas, and religious compositions for the convent and the church of Sant' Orsola; and Giovanna Garzoni (1600–1670), from Ascoli Picena, most interesting today for her studies of plants, insects, and small animals. In the accuracy of their detail they foreshadow the work of Maria Sibylla Merian. (See GERMAN ARTISTS.)

Eighteenth-century Venice produced the enormously popular rococo painter Rosalba Carriera (1675–1757), whose works are found in major museums throughout the world. In her early 20s she developed the pastel portrait and spread its popularity. She never married, and she cared for her mother and sisters, whom she taught to paint. After her father's death in 1719, she went to Paris to paint Louis XIV (then 10 years old) and created a demand for pastel portraits that lasted into the nineteenth century. In 1720 she became the first woman elected to the French Royal Academy in almost 40 years. In 1730 she was invited to the Hapsburg court and spread the popularity of pastel portraits to Vienna. Her portraits are meant to flatter, not reveal character. However, the superficiality reflects the values of the age. Her self-portraits display her ability to interpret the personality of the individual through the face.

Little is known of other Italian women painters of the eighteenth century. Marianna Candide Dionigi (1756–1826) painted landscapes in oils and wrote a book on landscape painting before she turned her interest to archaeology.

Giulia Lama (c. 1685–after 1753) was a highly talented late-baroque painter and one of the first women to paint male nudes. She did some very large altarpieces in neomannerist style for churches in Venice, an achievement that may account for the resentment of male artists toward her. She is also among the first women artists to have negative comments made about her looks.

The discovery of women artists that began with the second wave of feminism in the late 1960s continues. The basic spadework is completed, but a definitive history of Italian women artists is still to be written.

References. Elsa Honig Fine, *Women and Art* (Montclair, N.J., 1978); Ann Sutherland Harris and Linda Nochlin, *Women Artists, 1550–1950* (New York, 1976); Karen Petersen and J. J. Wilson, *Women Artists* (New York, 1976); Chris Pettys, *Dictionary of Women Artists* (Boston, 1985).

ITALIAN WRITERS (SEVENTEENTH AND EIGHTEENTH CENTURIES). In seventeenth-century Italy, women's literary output changed both in quantity and in character. The cultural splendor of the Renaissance courts had gone, as had the secular literary enclaves and the publishing trade they had fostered. We would look in vain for the social sanctuaries of female emancipation that existed in the sixteenth century. As a consequence, the greater part of the writing done by women in the baroque age deals with religious subjects, organized in neat generic categories and according to the moral and theological teachings of the Counter-Reformation church.

With the loss of their political freedom to Spain, the Italian states surrendered the trade and banking supremacy to the Northern Europeans. A new conservative economy, based on land property, had tragic consequences for the female population as, increasingly, more girls were, at birth, destined for the convent, in order to spare reduced and unproductive family holdings.

Convents became centers of social and cultural life. To edify and to entertain, the nuns, who were among the best-educated women of their time, wrote religious plays, poetry, and prose. We know the names of many authors, but their works remain mostly unresearched. Of the literature produced in seclusion, outstanding are the letters of Sister Celeste Galilei (1600–1634), not only for their historical value—they were addressed to her father, Galileo, and dealt with family and convent matters—but also for their vivid descriptions of people and activities around her, of the comforts and discomforts of monastic life, and for their direct and graceful style, remarkably free of the rhetorical excesses typical of baroque prose.

Galilei's good-natured acceptance of fate has its counterpart in the polemical stance of Sister Arcangela Tarabotti (1604–1652). Her works constitute the strongest denunciation of women's condition in her times. The underlying argument of *Antisatira* (1644; Antisatire) and of *Difesa delle donne* (1651; Defense of Women) is that the relative position of men and women in this world ought to be decided in the natural light of reason and that female dignity is fully consistent with religious beliefs. *La semplicità ingannata*, earlier titled *Tirannia paterna* (1654; Simplicity Deceived or Paternal Tyranny) is a study of the social and psychological causes of women's confinement, while *Inferno monacale* (Nuns' Hell) describes the effects of convent life on the unwilling nun. Sister Arcangela was not the first woman of the period to defend her sex. In *Il merito delle donne* (1600; Women's Merit), Moderata Fonte (1555–1592) had organized her arguments in the form of a dialogue. In *La nobiltà e l'eccellenza delle donne* (1600; Nobility and Excellence of Women), Lucrezia Marinella (1571–1653) used the form of the treatise; these last two works were new in arguing that women's position of inferiority was the result of the constraints imposed on them by a male society.

Lucrezia Marinella also wrote historical and mythological epic poems. Throughout the century, the epic remained the most prestigious genre and an acceptable one for women to cultivate. Among those who contributed to it are Maddalena Salvetti Acciaiuoli, Angela Scaramuccia, Barbara Albizzi, and Margherita Sarròcchi.

Many women were acclaimed as female wonders of learning. The most celebrated was Elena Cornaro Piscopia, of a Venetian aristocratic family, who was a poet, was conversant in many languages, and was a philosophy graduate of the University of Padua. A woman of learning also was Sara Copia Sullam, author of a letter entitled *"Manifesto"* (1621), in which she rebutted Baldassarre Bonifacio, a priest, who had accused her of denying the immortality of the soul. The letter is dedicated to her father, who had answered for her orthodoxy before the elders of the Venetian ghetto where she lived.

In the theater women could still enjoy some freedom of movement and lifestyle. Of Laura Guidiccioni Lucchesini only the oratorio *Rappresentazione di Anima e Corpo* (1600; Play of Soul and Body) has come down to us. Other works by her, now lost, were *Disperazione di Fileno* (1590; Fileno's Despair), *Satiro* (1591; Satyr), and *Il gioco della cieca* (1594; Blind Man's Bluff). They were set to music by Emilio Del Cavaliere and are reputed to have been the very first examples of opera. Isabella Andreini, celebrated poet and star of the *Commedia dell'Arte*, died on a tour of

France in 1604. Following in her footsteps came Margherita Costa, acclaimed opera singer in Italy and abroad, author of satirical sonnets and of burlesque love lyrics.

Women's massive reentry into the field of lyric poetry occurred at the end of the century. In 1690, to counteract the extravagance of baroque taste and promote a classically restrained style, a new academy, called Arcadia, was founded in Rome. Others followed in imitation everywhere in Italy. They fostered an affectation of refined feelings and a taste for artificial pastoral settings, at the center of which stood a female creature of coy flirtatiousness and rococo delicacy. Extraordinary is the number of women poets, mostly from the aristocracy, who wrote in the Arcadian fashion and were admitted to the academies. In general, however, their poetry kept closer in sobriety of content and expression to sixteenth-century Petrarchism than did the men's. The best known of these women poets is Faustina Maratti Zappi (c. 1680–1745), as much admired for her talent as adored for her charm and sensuous beauty. Her poems, formally and thematically correct, occasionally show the emotions of a woman severely tested by life. The poetic output of the indomitable marchioness Petronilla Paolini Massimi was, on the other hand, directly inspired by autobiographical events suggestive of a gothic novel. A pre-Romantic fascination with ruins and lugubrious landscapes is noticeable in the pastoral poems of Prudenzia Gabrieli and in the historical odes and romances of Diodata Saluzzo Roèro (1774–1840), while *Arcadia* still triumphed with Angela Veronese (1779–1847), whose poems have a graceful musicality and are full of flowers, shepherds, and shepherdesses. Among the most celebrated poets of the day were Maria Maddalena Morelli and Teresa Bandinetti Landucci, who improvised verse on a given topic at public events organized in palaces and in auditoriums.

By the second half of the eighteenth century the cultural life of many Italian cities revived. Private salons, hosted by cultivated ladies of the upper classes, became meeting places for intellectuals and literati. The limits of their education were discussed and extended. Diamante Medaglia Faini drew a plan of study for girls that included mathematics, politics, and the experimental sciences. Many women gained entry in professional fields normally reserved to men. The old quarrel about the relative capacities of the sexes had been revived in 1727, when Aretafila Savini Rossi felt compelled to debate G. A. Volpi on women's intellectual powers and when, in a Latin speech, Maria Agnesi upheld their right to education. Such debates were gallantly settled in favor of the aristocratic women present. When Giustina Renier Michiel translated Shakespeare and filled five volumes with the history of Venetian festivals and traditions, she seemed to exercise a prerogative of her aristocratic class.

Middle-class women began modern literary careers. Luisa Bergalli (1703–1779), friend of the Carriera sisters, supported herself and her family in Venice by writing tragedies, comedies, and melodramas and by providing producers and publishers with translations. She also edited a comprehensive anthology of women poets and the collected work of Gaspara Stampa. To Elizabetta Caminèr Turra (1751–1796) goes the credit of being the first woman journalist in Italy. She was the founder and sole editor of *Nuovo giornale enciclopedico*. She also wrote a great number of theatrical adaptations and pedagogical texts for the young.

References. J. De Blasi, *Le scrittrici italiane dalle origini al 1800* (Florence, 1930); N. Costa-Zalessow, *Scrittrici italiane dal XIII al XX secolo* (Ravenna, 1982); G. Conti Odorisio, *Donna e società nel Seicento* (Rome, 1979); Rinaldina Russell (ed.), *Italian Women Writers* (Westport, Conn., and London, 1994).

RINALDINA RUSSELL

ITALIAN WRITERS (FROM THE NINETEENTH CENTURY). In Italy the end of the eighteenth century saw the first revolutionary movements aimed at the establishment of more modern regimes; at the beginning of the next century, the long struggle for the unification of Italy began and was achieved in the decade 1860 to 1870. Women participated with their writings and their money; many also fought on the barricades. In Naples, Eleonora Fonsèca Pimentel, poet and journalist, was imprisoned as a conspirator, sided with the Republicans in 1799, and, upon surrender, was executed with them. Isabella Trivulzio di Belgioioso wrote about the 1848 uprisings in Milan and Venice. She also embarked on advanced social experiments and described the conditions in which women lived in Italy and abroad. The connection between the form of government and the current regimes was theorized by Maria Giuseppina Guacci, and it was effectively illustrated in her memoirs by Henrietta Caracciolo, who, until Garibaldi's troops entered Naples, had been unsuccessful in her efforts to renounce the veil.

After the unification of the country, women writers graduated from political and social tracts to creative literature. In fiction, their output was consistent with the realism of the post-Romantic novel that depicted the depressed living conditions in the countryside. The first true realist writer was, in fact, a woman, Caterina Percoto (1812–1887), whose stories about the underprivileged in her native Friuli are free from the sentimentality and the paternalism that mar much of the European regional literature. In Naples and in Rome, Matilde Serào fought her way to a commanding position in the male world of journalism and left a masterpiece of nineteenth-century reportage in *Il ventre di Napoli* (1884; The Bowels of Naples). This is a collection of articles skillfully organized and written in rebuttal to a statement made in Parliament about the necessity of cleaning the poor districts of Naples by "disemboweling" the city. Of Serào's huge fictional production, the best stories are "La virtù di Checchina" (1884; Checchina's Virtue), "Telegrafi dello Stato" (1884; State Telegraphs), "Scuola normale femminile" (1885; Women Teachers' College), and *Suor Giovanna della Croce* (1901; Sister Giovanna of the Cross), all stories of women, of their hardships, courage, and weaknesses. An accomplished writer of fiction was Anna Zuccari Radius, better known by the pen name of Neèra. In Milan, where she spent most of her life, she earned the admiration of good society by becoming a professional writer without losing her femininity. Of her 18 novels, the most successful and significant are *Teresa* (1886), the story of a woman sacrificed by her family to her brother's right to a full education and life, and *L'indomani* (1890; The Day After), a pitiless analysis of a middle-class marriage from the wedding ceremony to the birth of the first child. Greater critical recognition went to the prolific Sardinian writer Grazia Delèdda, who in 1926 became the second woman to be awarded the Nobel Prize in literature. The conflicts that had arisen in Sardinia between medieval social structures and a new economic reality were instinctively and skillfully transformed by Delèdda into tales of innocence, sin, and expiation and were played out with inexorable inevitability in a landscape that seemed magical and foreboding.

Serào, Neèra, and Delèdda declared themselves against the militancy of the feminist movement, out of either conviction or the need to safeguard themselves against unwarranted hostility. Many, however, were the women whose work was directly inspired by the movement and by the social turmoil that the new country was experiencing at the turn of the century. Maria Antonietta Torriani, alias Marchesa Colombi, informed the public about the condition of workingwomen in her novel *In risaia* (1878; In the Rice Fields). A polemical thrust is also found in her books *La gente per bene* (1877; The Upright People) and *Un matrimonio in provincia* (1885; A Small-Town Marriage). E. Ferretti Viola's *Una fra mille* (1878; A Woman among a Thousand) created a scandal and brought about a parliamentary debate. Anna Franchi fought for divorce and in old age wrote *Cose di ieri dette alle donne di oggi* (1946; Things of Yesterday Told to the Women of Today). The most celebrated feminist writer of Italy is, deservedly, Sibilla Aleramo. When it was published in 1906, her autobiographical book *Una donna* (*A Woman*, 1906) created a sensation in Europe. It is the story of a young provincial wife who becomes progressively aware of women's oppressed condition in society and who, in the end, gives up her husband and child to live in the capital as a feminist writer.

In poetry, women were influenced by the decadent trends that dominated literary circles of the late nineteenth and early twentieth century. Contessa Lara (1849–1896), Regina di Luanto (1862–1914), and the younger Amalia Guglielminetti (1885–1941) were femmes fatales in life and in literature. They expressed their languid or aggressive sensuality in backgrounds of opulent interiors and in suggestive art nouveau imagery. In the

the Italian code was, in some ways, more progressive than the French, it nevertheless represented a step backward for women of the northern regions of Lombardy and Venice, which had been regulated by the more enlightened Austrian code before unification.

Single women enjoyed the most equality with men under the Pisanelli Code. As opposed to the feudal pattern, daughters inherited equally with sons. Both sexes came of age at 21, and, until married, women could freely choose their place of residence, seek employment, and control their own property. Dowries were no longer required before marriage, which was now a civil, rather than religious, ceremony. (See DOWRY, In Western Societies.) Only if pregnant were single women at a distinct disadvantage, for the law forbade paternity suits except in the cases of rape or violent abduction.

Once married, women lost most of their legal independence. A wife had to assume her husband's name and live where he chose. Under the doctrine of *autorizzazione maritale* (marital authorization), which had previously been abolished in Lombardy and Venice, a wife could own property but needed her husband's consent for any major transaction such as taking out a mortgage, bequeathing gifts, or opening a bank account. The code modified another traditional doctrine, that of *patria podestà* (paternal authority), so that mothers could theoretically become the head of the family and regulate the affairs of minor children. In practice, women exercised this right only during the prolonged absence of the father as a result of separation, desertion, emigration, or a penal sentence of over one year. As in the Napoleonic Code, the grounds for marital separation were markedly unequal, and the difficulty for women of escaping the control of their husbands was especially significant in the absence of divorce. A husband could demand separation after the simple adultery of his wife, but he himself could not be challenged unless he flagrantly and publicly maintained a concubine for an extended time.

Both single and married women were politically disfranchised. Although Lombard and Venetian women had formerly enjoyed the right to vote in local "administrative" matters, after 1865, Italian women could not exercise administrative or national "political" suffrage, hold governmental office, act as notaries, or even serve as witnesses to civil acts.

The passage of the Civil Code aroused lively debate and severe criticism among supporters of women's emancipation. Many women had been active in the movement to unify Italy and expected better treatment by the new liberal state. Most followed the lead of Guiseppe Mazzini in working for a new Italy free from sex and class inequalities. Both the first phase of the Italian women's movement of the late nineteenth century and the second wave beginning in the 1970s made legal reform a primary goal. In 1877 women gained the right to witness civil acts; in 1919 they gained more control over their property and access to the profession of law; in 1945 they received the vote at all levels; and only in 1975 did they finally receive equality within the family.

References. Judy Jeffrey Howard, "The Civil Code of 1865 and the Origins of the Feminist Movement in Italy," in B. B. Caroli et al., *The Immigrant Woman in North America* (Toronto, 1978), 14–22; Paolo Ungari, *Storia del diritto di famiglia in Italia* (Bologna, 1974).

MARY GIBSON

ITALY. Law for the Protection of the Labor of Women and Children. In 1902, the Italian Parliament passed the first protective legislation for workingwomen and children. The origins of the law lay in an earlier proposal of 1897 designed by socialist women from Milan and published in *Avanti!*, the newspaper of the Italian Socialist Party. For the protection of adult women, the socialists demanded an eight-hour day, a limitation on dangerous and unhealthy work, a ban on night work, and maternal leave for a month before and after childbirth. In 1901, the Female Union (*Unione Femminile*), an organization of both bourgeois and socialist feminists, petitioned Parliament for similar legislation.

Meanwhile, the government presented a less far-reaching proposal to Parliament at the end of 1900; over socialist objections, this version became law on June 16, 1902. It limited the workday of adult women in industry to 12 hours, including 2 hours for meals and rest; guaranteed a one-month maternity leave after childbirth; and recognized the right of mothers to breast-feed after returning to work. To facilitate inspection, industries were required to notify the government of the names of all female employees. Enforcement of the law, however, was lax because of the paucity of state inspectors and the resistance of many employers. As early as 1905, Parliament amended the law to try to increase compliance and placate employers. Further amendments banned night work for all women in 1907 and three years later established a Maternity Fund (*Cassa della Maternita*), which gave lump sums to female industrial workers at the birth of each child.

The issue of protective legislation for adult women divided Italian feminists and prompted a historic debate between two prominent crusaders for female emancipation: Anna Maria Mozzoni and Anna Kuliscioff. The veteran emancipationist Mozzoni, who had always argued for sexual equality on the basis of the inalienable natural rights of all human beings, rejected the law as equating women with children in need of protection. According to Mozzoni, the law would limit women's right to work and deny them access to the factory floor, where their common experience had made them conscious of their own dignity and strength as women and as workers. The law simply served the interest of employers who, now that the textile industry was declining, wanted to push women out of the labor force by appealing to motherhood and the preservation of the race.

Kuliscioff replied that women, as mothers, must be protected from overwork, which weakened and endangered the future of the human species. As a doctor, Kuliscioff was especially sensitive to improving the appalling working conditions of lower-class women. She also argued that working-class men would benefit since they would no longer have to compete with women who accepted such terrible conditions; with these words she echoed the position of the Socialist Party, which preached that improving men's wages and returning women to the home would strengthen society. Most feminists, whether socialist, bourgeois, or Catholic, sided with Kuliscioff. The passage of the protective legislation of 1902 ushered in an era of moderation among feminists of all ideological tendencies. They increasingly argued for improvements in the status of women on the basis of their mission of motherhood rather than natural rights.

References. Maria Vittoria Ballestrero, *Dalla tutela alla parita: La legislazione italiana sul lavoro delle donne* (Bologna, 1979); Claire LaVigna, "The Marxist Ambivalence toward Women: Between Socialism and Feminism in the Italian Socialist Party," in Marilyn J. Boxer and Jean H. Quataert (eds.), *Socialist Women* (New York, 1978), 146–181; Maria Luisa Zavattaro, "La disciplina giurdica del lavoro femminile durante gli ultimi cento anni," in *Società Umanitaria, L'emancipazione femminile in Italia* (Florence, 1961), 129–169.

MARY GIBSON

ITALY. Women's Movement (1860–1914). The origins of the Italian women's movement date back to the *risorgimento* (the struggle for the unification of Italy, c. 1815–1860). Earlier, in the eighteenth century, only a few isolated voices—like that of Rosa Califronice in her *Brief Defense of the Rights of Women* of 1794—called for the extension of equality before the law to women. The *risorgimento*, however, which evolved through phases of secret organizing and then war, drew liberal and democratic women together and gave them valuable political experience. Expecting to be rewarded for their patriotic work, these women were disappointed when the first civil code of united Italy, passed in 1865, subordinated married women to their husbands and limited suffrage to men.

To combat the inferior position of women in Italian civil and political life, women first organized informally around a series of often short-lived journals. In 1872, Aurelia Cimino Folliero De Luna founded *La Cornelia*. Directed toward upper-class women, it dealt with the need for reform in education, the professions, and family law until it ceased publication in 1880. More influential and long-lived was *La Donna*, directed by Gualberta Alaide Beccari from 1868 until 1891. The center of the most significant emancipationist network of those years, *La Donna* tried to appeal to working-class as well as middle- and upper-class women. It promoted the ideal of the "citizen mother" who, as an independent and educated woman, would pass down to her children a love for the new Italy. The role of citizen mother was not limited to bourgeois women who remained in the home but also encompassed all wage-earning women, who deserved the right to work outside the home. These early emancipationists had some limited success: in 1874, the universities were opened to women; in 1877, women gained the right to witness civil acts; and in the 1880s, male high schools and teacher-training colleges began to admit women.

The most prominent and outspoken of these pioneers for woman's rights, Anna Maria Mozzoni, initiated the first official emancipationist organization. In 1881 in Milan she founded the League to Promote Female Interests. Interclass in orientation, the league sought equality in law, education, and work. It paid special attention to the large numbers of working-class women who had recently entered the rapidly expanding textile industry and received wages that averaged one-half those of male workers. Basing her emancipationist philosophy on the argument that all human beings had natural, inalienable rights, Mozzoni encouraged women of all classes to work together to fight sexual discrimination. In the 1890s, a group of local Leagues to Protect Female Interests, modeled on Mozzoni's original organization, sprang up throughout Italy. *Vita femminile* served as the bulletin for these leagues from 1895 to 1897.

A profound shift from what one Italian historian has called "radical emancipationism" to "moderate feminism" occurred in the 1890s. During this decade, Mozzoni's model of interclass leagues gave way to a profound division between socialist and bourgeois feminism. With the creation in 1892 of the Italian Socialist Party, most socialist women withdrew from organizations devoted solely to the "woman question" and constituted themselves as sections within the party or the working-class Chambers of Labor. Under pressure from the party, socialist feminists increasingly subordinated women's rights to the economic struggle against capitalism. Anna Kuliscioff, the leading socialist feminist, argued that bourgeois women pursued only their class interest at the expense of working-class women. The advent of socialist society would bring justice and equality to both female and male workers. Yet, like many of her colleagues, Kuliscioff did not turn her back on all women's issues but campaigned vigorously for protective legislation and the vote for women.

Meanwhile, bourgeois women began forming national associations such as the National Council of Women in 1903 and the National Suffrage Committee in 1904. Both increased their influence by affiliation with larger, international organizations: the International Council of Women and the International Suffrage Alliance, respectively. The strength of the bourgeois women's movement was most evident at the first national congress of Italian women held in 1908 in Rome. It was attended by over 1,400 women, including the delegates of 70 feminist and female charitable societies. In many ways, this congress, by its emphasis on welfare, education, and protection of the family, exemplified the retreat of Italian feminism from the radical egalitarianism of Mozzoni. Increasingly, feminists saw women and men as equivalent rather than equal and women's maternal role as the basic justification for both protection and rights. The congress was progressive, however, in its long discussions of the need for female suffrage and in its reaffirmation of the value of lay education. In response to this latter resolution, Catholic feminists withdrew from the National Council of Women and formed their own separate organizations.

The second decade of the twentieth century found Italian feminists still organizationally split between bourgeois and socialist wings but united in the pursuit of female suffrage. In 1913, Italian women were again disillusioned by Parliament when it passed a bill extending the vote to all men but excluding women. The war interrupted the suffrage campaign by setting a new national agenda. Although the outbreak of hostilities did not represent the death knell of Italian feminism, it encouraged bourgeois women to move to the right under the influence of nationalist propaganda and the splintering of socialist solidarity during the debate over intervention. While feminism survived the war, it was forcibly suppressed in the 1920s, when Mussolini outlawed all nonfascist women's political groups; ITALY. Law for the Protection of the Labor of Women and Children. (See also ITALY, Civil Code of 1865.)

References. Franca Pieroni Bortolotti, *Alle origini del movimento femminile in Italia, 1848–1892* (Turin, 1963); Franca Pieroni Bortolotti, *Socialismo e questione femminile in Italia, 1892–1922* (Milan, 1974); Annarita Buttafuoco, "Condizione delle donne e movimento di emmancipazione femminile," in Giovanni Cherubini (ed.), *Storia della società italiana*, vol. 2, part 5, *L'Italia di Giolitti* (Milan, 1981), 145–185; Judy Jeffrey Howard, "Patriot Mothers in the Post-Risorgimento: Women after the Italian Revolution," in Carol R. Berkin and Clara M. Lovett (eds.), *Women, War, and Revolution* (New York, 1980), 237–258.

MARY GIBSON

ITALY, 1911–1926. Women's organized activities and concerns reflected the Italian political spectrum and the events that culminated in fascist dictatorship.

Early in the century Italian women, like those in most Western countries, advocated improved education, access to all professions, full legal capacity, and protection against sexual exploitation, with suffrage the overriding issue. Between 1904 and 1911, a Pro-Suffrage Committee, including representatives of the CNDI (Consiglio Nazionale Donne Italiane), an umbrella organization federated with the International Council of Women, and benevolent associations, such as the Unione Femminile Nazionale, actively campaigned for suffrage.

Women were active members of the Socialist Party, the largest and strongest opposition party. Socialist men, striving for universal male suffrage, distrusted the woman suffrage movement, which in their view might be part of a strategy to preserve the power of the liberal bourgeoisie. Socialist women shared these misgivings but also resented the patronizing misogyny among men in their own party.

Socialist women were often active in the Pro-Suffrage Committee at the local level. However, the alliance between socialist and middle-class women fell through in 1911 when middle-class organizations advocated gradual women's suffrage, mirroring current male suffrage. By then rightist tendencies were appearing among middle-class groups as some of their leaders rallied to the nationalist movement that supported the war to gain control of Libya (1911). The women's movement was further divided concerning Italy's intervention in World War I and cooperation with a government at war. Following the bourgeois–socialist split at the International Women's Conference in The Hague in 1915, socialist feminists who were still cooperating in local chapters of the Pro-Suffrage Committee pulled out, and the committee became an instrument for propaganda and support for the war effort.

In the war and the immediate postwar period the gap seemed to widen between middle- and working-class women. Socialist women, in the Unione Femminile Socialista, a separate organizational network within the party, were active in the strikes and antiwar activities that punctuated Italian life, especially in 1917–1918. After the war, the Sacchi Law (1919) met most of the bourgeois feminists' demands, establishing married women's full property rights and access to professions and careers (with the exception of the military, the judiciary, and the high bureaucracy), while working-class women took to the streets in large numbers, protesting women's layoffs and the rise in the cost of living and supporting land reform.

In Italy, as elsewhere, the war produced a broadening consensus for women's suffrage, and the opportunity was there for the women's movement to build a wider cross-class base. The socialists were pivotal at this stage. They endorsed the franchise (universal male suffrage had been introduced in 1913) but, split over the 1917 Soviet Revolution, failed to make suffrage a political priority. The Chamber of Deputies voted for women's suffrage in 1919, but the Senate had not approved it before the legislature was prematurely dissolved in 1921. A divorce bill was also introduced in 1919 but failed to win sufficient support from the Socialist Party, while it triggered violent reactions by Catholics and the new women's groups that had been founded for the defense of the family inside Catholic Action, such as the Unione Donne di Azione Cattolica (1919). In 1922 the CNDI dropped support for divorce to appease right-wing nationalists within the organization.

The 1921 elections brought three newly founded parties into the parliamentary arena: the Popular Party, the communists, and the fascists. The Popular Party, attempting to organize Catholics on a democratic platform, was careful to avoid any stand that might contradict the church in matters concerning the family and its role in society.

As for the communists, a number of young and dedicated women leaders filled its ranks after the split from the socialists (1921). While attention was being given to woman's double shift and the socialization of housework, eyes were turned to Soviet Russia and to the debates on the "woman's question" inside the Communist International. To these young revolutionaries, the domestic women's movement appeared outdated, if not outright compromised, by its relations with conservative and reactionary politics.

Fascist women, who were largely upper-class and often from large land-owning families, were few in number until 1923, when nationalist women merged into the Fascist Party. The 1921 statutes of the party confined women to a separate women's structure, the Fasci Femminili. Nationalist women, organized inside the Italian Nationalist Association, were quite visible and vocal in these crucial years. Their basic ideological tenets were "women's return to the home" and "separate spheres for men and women." On these grounds they had the support of Catholics, who clearly discouraged woman's work outside the home. Middle-class feminists did not confront outright this right-wing ideological campaign. Claiming neutrality in the face of the fascist attacks on the Left and its institutions, they could hardly conceal the antisocialist and "antiparliamentarian" feelings that they shared with conservatives. Only a minority held antifascist and pacifist views and advocated reforms such as divorce. In fact, following Benito Mussolini's takeover of the government in 1922, the CNDI kept relying on Mussolini's promises in the matter of suffrage. However, when, in 1923, the government introduced a proposal for women's vote in local elections, only special categories of women—the literate, war widows, and mothers of war dead—were to receive the franchise. (This mock legislation was passed in 1925.) Also in 1923, a decree "relieved of duty" all civil employees, mostly women, who had been hired after May 1915 (war widows and women breadwinners were excepted).

Between 1923 and 1926 women were gradually barred from offices and significant chairs in both public and private secondary schools. Following the passage of the "emergency laws" that tightened fascist control in 1926, socialist and communist women were exiled or imprisoned, and middle-class organizations were either dissolved or forced to accept fascist-approved leadership.

Reference. Franca Pieroni Bortolotti, *Femminismo e partiti politici in Italia (1919–1926)* (Rome, 1978).

MARGHERITA REPETTO ALAIA

ITALY, 1922–1939 (Fascism). Paradoxically profoundly traditionalist and totalitarian, the fascist regime sought to control and intervene in all aspects of human life (private and public) and to mobilize the masses and build popular support for its policies. At the same time, the regime failed to challenge the economic status quo and reinforced the traditional social order and gender roles. Policy toward women combined these aspirations but was most successful when it adhered to traditional values. Service to the nation was dictated by gender. Women, viewed by fascist theorists like Fernando Loffredo and Nicola Pende as inferior intellectually and physically, contributed to the state by bearing and rearing children. They provided the cohesive bond in the family, thereby reinforcing social stability. At the same time, they served the larger purposes of fascism by offering sons for the cause of Italian expansion.

Actual policies were the products of pressure from veterans to displace females from the employment market; traditionalist, especially Catholic, thought on the role of the family; the widespread fears of population decline and stagnation that gripped Europe in the interwar period; and, finally, fascist totalitarianism, which was spurred during the 1930s by depression and war. The subordination of the individual to the nation intensified after 1938 in formal measures in defense of the race and against the Jewish community.

The earliest fascist statements regarding women, in the movement's 1919 program, promised full political equality and were either holdovers from Mussolini's leftist past or borrowed from futurist political manifestos. They rapidly disappeared under pressure from returning veterans. Equally illusory was the right to vote in administrative elections that Mussolini granted in 1925 to certain categories of women. Local democracy was abolished in 1926 and with it women's limited franchise.

Demographic fears shaped policy. The regime sought to encourage early marriage and large families: in 1926 a special tax was levied on single people, and in 1929 preference was given in state employment to men with children. Marriage loans, subsidies for large families, and housing preferences were also instituted between 1929 and 1934. Many of these regulations were also adopted in other countries, but the fascists used them to compensate families for state-imposed wage cuts. The ideal fascist woman was honored by the Day of the Mother and Child on December 24, established in 1933 as an annual celebration. Women were mobilized to support fascist imperialism. When sanctions were imposed because of Italian aggression in Ethiopia, the "Duce" (Mussolini) called on women to donate their gold wedding bands to the struggle. They were also encouraged to abandon foreign styles and expensive imports; the slim and elegant bourgeois woman was depicted as the useless opposite of the ideal of fascist motherhood.

After 1925 the Opera Nazionale Maternita ed Infanzia (ONMI), a semipublic agency, provided direct assistance to mothers and small children. In a country plagued by an excessively high infant mortality rate, the ONMI was useful but lacked adequate funding. The ONMI was flanked by the *fasci femminili* (women's groups), which were founded in 1921. The women's *fasci* were involved in welfare activities and in the supervision of female youth groups. By 1934, almost 1.350 million individuals participated in the *donne fasciste* for adults, the *giovane fasciste* for young girls, and the *massaie rurali* for peasant women. The fascists also went to great efforts to eliminate female competition from the marketplace. The 1923 Gentile Educational Reform banned women from teaching in certain disciplines and in predominantly male schools, the 1933 regulation set a limit on women's right to compete in state employment examinations, and a sweeping 1938 decree limited female employment in both state and private enterprises to 10 percent. At the same time, the fascists used seemingly progressive social legislation, such as a 1934 law on maternity benefits for women employees, to increase the cost of female labor.

The impact of fascist repression fell hardest on the working class, especially on poor women. However, the fascists had only limited success in encouraging larger families or early marriage. Fascism narrowed the horizons for countless women with its incessant emphasis on a limited female role, yet the regime never banned women from the universities. Moreover, wartime mobilization nullified many of the restrictions on female employment. Fascism succeeded best when it reinforced the socially conservative doctrines of other institutions such as the Catholic Church. Its policies toward women probably slowed certain demographic trends but could not reverse disincentives to large families. Nor could the fascists enforce their policies against the employment of women in a society in which females were forced to leave the home out of economic necessity.

References. Lesley Caldwell, "Reproducers of the Nation: Women and the Family in Fascista Policy," in David Forgacs (ed.), *Rethinking Italian Fascism: Capitalism, Populism and Culture* (London, 1986), 110–141; A. De Grand, "Women under Italian Fascism," *Historical Journal* 19 (1976): 947–968; Victoria De Grazia, *How Fascism Rules Women: Italy, 1922–1945* (Berkeley, Calif., 1992); Emiliana Noether, "Italian Women and Fascism: A Reevaluation," *Italian Quarterly* (Fall 1982): 69–80; Perry R. Willson, *The Clockwork Factory: Women and Work in Fascist Italy* (New York, 1993).

ALEXANDER DE GRAND

ITALY, 1943–1945 (Partisans). Following the removal of Benito Mussolini from power in July 1943, the negotiation of an armistice with the Allies by a new Italian government, and the German occupation of most of Italy, a formal, organized resistance movement emerged in September 1943. Until May 1945, when the northern area was liberated, and the war ended, this movement engaged in a struggle against the Germans and what remained of the fascist regime.

Some 200,000 Italians took part in the Resistance; among them were 55,000 women, who were recognized as partisans or patriots. There are two sides to the story of women's participation in the Resistance. On one hand, it was crucial to the success of the effort; on the other, this activity represented the first formal, mass mobilization of women acting in the public sphere and thus had a significant impact on women's experience, expectations, and status.

The Resistance, focused for the most part in the territories north of Rome, was directed by Committees of National Liberation (CLNs), made up of members of center-to-left opposition parties (the communists, Action Party, socialists, and Christian Democrats in particular). Partisans were organized in formal military brigades, smaller sabotage and action squads, support, propaganda and information services, and groups directing civilian demonstrations. Leadership was, at least initially, in the hands of already active, experienced, political men and women.

Even before September 1943, women had shown their discontent with the failures of fascism and the disastrous effects of the war and occupation by engaging in demonstrations and strikes demanding *pane e pace* (bread and peace). Leaders, recognizing the need to bring women formally into the Resistance, appealed to them, encouraging and supporting more concrete organization to give direction to their rebellion.

Women participated in all branches of Resistance activity; the majority of those listed as partisans were active in the GAP or SAP, while a smaller number were enlisted in the formal military brigades, and some commanded units and had military rank. Eventually, a number of exclusively female battalions were created, and women were particularly responsible for supplying the provisions and medical services for all partisans. All units of the Resistance had attached to them *staffette*, or couriers, a service usually provided by women, and they often became the most publicized heroines of the struggle.

Each of the political parties directing Resistance activity either created or expanded its own women's organizations and sought women members, as its general vision of a new, progressive and democratic Italy required an expansion of the electorate. Most important in organizing women were the *Gruppi di difesa della donna* (GDD), the first unit of which was founded in Milan in November 1943 by already politically active women. Created initially to support the partisans, the GDD very quickly became advocates of an improved and more equal position for women. By the end of the war GDD membership was estimated at 70,000. In September 1944, in Rome (which had by then been liberated), another women's organization emerged: the Union of Italian Women (UDI). Founded by primarily communist and socialist women, UDI was to be an ongoing mass organization, and by the end of the war it had absorbed most GDD sections. The Christian Democrats responded by building their own "flanking group," the Center of Italian Women (CIF). Both organizations remained active in the postwar years.

During the Resistance the women's organizations had begun to articulate demands for emancipation; among them were the right to vote, election to political office, legal equality, and equal pay for equal work. In the new Constitution of the postwar republican government these were formally granted. Women had also stressed their separate, natural, maternal, and nurturing roles, hoping to have these recognized as public functions with appropriate institutional support. This was not to be the case, as political parties and their leaders saw stable family life as crucial to the reconstruction of Italy, had limited resources to support social maternity and child care, and, in general, viewed the Resistance activity of women as extraordinary since women's "natural" place was in the home. The result was that many constitutional provisions reinforced the subordination of women in marriage and the private family. Thus, though Resistance activism propelled women into nontraditional activities and brought legal and political advances, it would be more than two decades before women's emancipation became feminist liberation.

                                                                  JANE SLAUGHTER

ITALY. Removal of Fascist Legislation began in June 1944, when the first free government under Allied occupation repealed the decree barring women from offices and chairs in institutions of secondary education and, in January 1945, gave women the vote by decree. The Constitution for the new Republic of Italy, issued in 1947, established the principles of equality of all citizens, equality between spouses, equal pay for equal work, equal political rights, and equal access to careers, jobs, and professions.

The language of the Constitution reveals a compromise among different ideologies. Catholic insistence that woman's role in the family was an inherent feature of the female that had to be considered when defining woman's rights can be seen in several articles. Article 37 on woman's right to work defines her role in the family as essential, and Article 29 hedges parity between spouses "within the limitations needed to guarantee the unity of the family."

Fascism had actively discriminated against women in matters of education, pay, and access to jobs and careers. The Sacchi Law of 1919 had listed offices and careers from which women were barred. Using this as a basis for further discrimination, between 1933 and 1939 laws authorized public and private employers to establish sex-segregated policies in hiring and job classification. In 1938 the fascist government established a 10 percent maximum for female employment in public and private jobs. Guidelines followed in 1939, listing as "especially suited for women" jobs as secretaries, clerks, sales help, cashiers, switchboard operators, and the like. Pay ranges were set on the basis of sex. Wages of women were 30 percent to 50 percent lower than men's.

After 1945, gradual revisions of hiring and promotion policies took place, but the action was so casual and incomplete that women had to fight for their constitutional right to equality. They began by challenging the ban against women jurors. Between 1951 and 1956, hundreds of appeals against jury discrimination were filed with the high courts, which, for the most part, interpreted the Constitution conservatively. Finally, in 1960, the Constitutional Court overturned the exclusions of the 1919 Sacchi Law, paving the way for a 1963 law repealing all discriminatory legislation and giving women access to all careers, professions, and public offices. Active campaigning by organized women, ratification of the European Economic Community Treaty (1957), and high court rulings brought about a 1960 comprehensive agreement between employers' associations and unions, paving the way for a pay system based on the principle of equal pay for equal work. (See EUROPEAN UNION [EU] LAW.)

Women's inferior position in law on matters pertaining to family, sex, and procreation antedated fascism. Major changes in the criminal code in 1930 worsened women's position. It made the wife's adultery a more serious crime than the husband's and restated protection for the "crime of passion." It retained the "marriage of reparation" by which an offer of marriage (if consented to by the woman) led to the acquittal of a rapist. Dissemination of birth control information was made a crime, and the abortion law was made more severe.

The repeal or reform of these laws was slow and highly controversial. Women were divided. Organized Catholic women, though, in many cases, not insensitive to the need of changing archaic laws, were unwilling to challenge Catholic conservatism on such issues. The repeal in 1958 of laws on state-controlled prostitution was the first successful attempt to change legislation that repressed woman's individual and sexual freedom. It remained, however, an isolated instance until 1970, when divorce was finally permitted. Thereafter, rewriting of family law won increasing backing across a wide political spectrum. In 1971 the ban on birth control information was overturned by the Constitutional Court. Under intensified pressure by organized women, new laws based on equality within the family were finally passed in 1975. Specific legislation provided birth control education and access to birth control devices through a public network of family planning centers. Abortion was legalized in May 1978 after three full years of political battles and successfully survived a repeal referendum in 1981.

Between 1979 and 1980, criminal code provisions on rape and sexual violence came under scrutiny. Women's groups, after a national grassroots campaign, introduced a "people's initiative" reform bill in 1980. Bills were also introduced by all political parties, but, because of controversy spurred by some features of the women's project, as of 1991 the legislation had not been passed. In 1981, the acceptance of attenuating circumstances for "crimes of passion" was finally wiped from the books.

References. Annamaria Galoppini, *Il lungo viaggio verso la parità* (Boulogna, Italy, 1980); Maria Michetti, Margherita Repetto, and Luciana Viviani (eds.), *Udi: Laboratorio di politica delle donne* (Rome, 1984).

MARGHERITA REPETTO ALAIA

ITALY. Since 1970. Equality of Italian men and women was guaranteed by the 1947 Constitution, but the bitter political divisions and economic hardships of the reconstruction years were not conducive to the basic reforms needed to implement that equality. With a few exceptions (maternity leaves [1950] and repeal of the prostitution laws [1958]), major legislation removing discrimination and reforming the law in matters related to family, divorce, birth control, abortion, and equal employment opportunity were not enacted until the 1960–1980 period.

As elsewhere, the 1970s witnessed the birth of grassroots feminism. Feminist groups, which were strongly anti-institutional, criticized the Left for its failure to alter gender roles in family and society. The 1974 referendum on the divorce law (passed in 1970) was a watershed. Large numbers of women had their first experience of feminist activism in the successful campaign to retain divorce. In the years that followed, despite reciprocal criticism, the Unione Donne Italiane (UDI) (founded after World War II by women affiliated with the Left) and feminist groups drew closer in the struggle to legalize abortion (finally voted in 1978). On the other hand, this issue widened the gap between the movement and organized Catholic women.

In the 1980s the women's movement was deinstitutionalized. The UDI in 1982 dissolved its organizational structure and became an umbrella organization for a variety of local and single-issue groups. This was only part of a larger diaspora as the movement fragmented, with independent groups active in large and small towns. Changes in women's lives set new priorities: many of the new movements are oriented toward self-promotion and self-improvement.

Among Catholic women, older organizations like the Centro Italiano Femminile (CIF) lost their centrality to new ones. Long-lived associations moved from neighborhood charity work to programs to combat world poverty and hunger. Managerial skills and international involvement often characterize churchwomen's activities: a woman chairs one of the most important commissions for the laity instituted by Vatican Council II. On the issue of women's position in the church, the ground is being shifted from power sharing to changes in the nature of the church's mission, by which the very issue of hierarchy would be made meaningless.

Cultural activities make up a lively and significant part of the women's movement in the mid-1980s. More than 100 centers, managed exclusively by women, collect and preserve local history of women and organize libraries, seminars, conferences, and exhibits. Women's bookstores provide critical links in the network. Two scholarly journals, *Memoria* and *DonnaWomanFemme* (*DwF*), and a monthly magazine, *Noi Donne*, founded in 1944 and associated with UDI, are distributed nationally.

Women are 52 percent of the electorate. They account for 10.2 percent of the members of Parliament following the 1987 elections (the highest percentage since 1946). They constitute 1.9 percent of mayors and 35 department heads in local administration. Only 7.5 percent of women in the civil service hold executive posts. Of 547 department heads, 5 are women.

Labor force participation has increased from less than 32 percent in 1977 to 35 percent in 1985, with more women in the workforce in north and central Italy (36 percent) than in the south (31 percent). They also constitute 58 percent of the unemployed. Women make up over 37 percent of the service sector, 23 to 24 percent in agriculture, and 22 to 23 percent in manufacturing. On the whole, they are in the less-skilled and lower-paying jobs. According to the 1981 census, 88 percent of elementary school teachers, but fewer than 35 percent of university faculty, are women; they make up 63 percent of the nurses but only 21 percent of specialists and 15.9 percent of general surgeons. Women account for only 13 to 14 percent of entrepreneurs and self-employed professionals but over 67 percent of workers in family-owned and -operated business (where the overlap between the role of housewife and extra-domestic worker is constant). Married women make up well over half the women in the labor force, and their number is on the increase. However, the return of women to the labor market after child rearing is still not a highly visible trend in Italy.

Women's progress in education has been constant since the reform of mandatory education in 1963. By 1981, female illiteracy had dropped to 3.8 percent (for males it is 2.2 percent). In the 1980s, over 49 percent of postmandatory high school students are girls, and 44 percent of university graduates are women. However, female participation in education leading to technical jobs or university curricula that will lead to careers in the scientific professions is low. The majority of women who do concentrate in mathematics or scientific fields go into teaching. In medicine, almost 38 percent of the students were women in 1983–1984.

Italy has the lowest birthrate in Europe (9.9 per 1,000 inhabitants in 1988): the average number of children per woman is below the replacement level. Surveys indicate that use of birth control devices is limited; the abortion rate, though still in the high-average bracket, appears on the decrease: 299.4 per 1,000 live births in 1988 as compared to 385.5 in 1983. Data are based on legal abortions, that is, performed in health institutions according to the 1978 law, but it is estimated that some 1,000 are performed outside the law.

Divorce rates, though considerably lower in Italy than in most industrialized countries, has been on a slow increase: from 0.2 per 1,000 inhabitants in 1980, 10 years after it was first introduced (1970), it has grown to 0.5 in 1988 (the European average was 1.6). Separations, which grew consistently in 1970–1980, are also on a slow increase. Following the European trend, the marriage rate has been steadily dropping over the years: from 7.4 per 1,000 inhabitants in 1970 to 5.5 in 1988.

According to the 1981 general census, out of 1.25 million single-parent families, well over 1 million were headed by women, three-quarters of them widows. Paid maternity leave before and after childbirth was extended in 1971 to all workingwomen, paralleling legislation in all European Economic Community (EEC) countries, and it has been further improved by judicial decrees of the Constitutional Court. (See EUROPEAN UNION [EU] LAW). However, budget cuts, growing costs, and inefficient administrations (often the case in the south) have resulted in very slow growth in services such as child care. Child care was established as a national service network in 1971, but its availability varies widely. Thus, in Naples in 1983, only 2 percent of children under 4 years were covered by day care as compared to 10 percent in Milan and 27 percent in Bologna. Day care quality is generally good, and there are waiting lists everywhere.

Equal Opportunity legislation was enacted in 1977; in March 1991, a law was passed implementing European Community guidelines on positive action. It provides incentives for private employers and public agencies who carry out positive action projects and calls for the central administration as well as regional government to draft positive action plans within a year. The law enlarges the concept of discrimination, placing the burden of proof on the employer in antidiscrimination suits.

The interest in gender issues in Italian society remains high. According to EEC opinion polls, feminist concerns have taken root in mainstream ideologies.

References. Margherita Repetto Alaia, "La condizione socio economica della donna in Italia," in *Le società in transizione: italiani e italoamericani negli anni ottanta* (Acta of the Balch Institute Conference, Philadelphia, October 11–12, 1985) (Rome, 1985), 158–181 (English ed. forthcoming); Giulietta Ascoli et al., *La questione femminile in Italia dal '900 a oggi* (Milan, 1979); Lucia Chiavola Birnbaum, *Liberazione della donna: Feminism in Italy* (Middletown, Conn., 1986); Yasmin Ergas, "1968–1979: Feminism and the Italian Party System: Women's Politics in a Decade of Turmoil," *Comparative Politics* 14 (1982): 264.

MARGHERITA REPETTO ALAIA

J

JAPAN. Ancient Period (to A.D. 1200). Women possessed strong religious and spiritual power, ruled on their own authority, and held significant rights in economic life, sexual relationships, and marriage. Japan's emulation of sophisticated patriarchal Chinese ideals and institutions in the sixth to eighth centuries A.D. provided a legal and ideological framework for the diminished status of women, but the decline was gradual, leaving a great gap between law and practice for many centuries.

Fertility was central to native Japanese beliefs. The creative powers of female and male deities show relative parity in the origin myths, but the female sun deity, Amaterasu, became the ancestral deity of the imperial line and progenitrix of the Japanese people.

In prestate Japan, where the concept of rule was inextricably linked to communication with deities and other forces of nature, women were recognized as legitimate rulers. A Chinese chronicle recorded an unmarried priestess-ruler, Himiko, as ruling a kingdom in Japan before A.D. 297. Replacing a male ruler who had created chaos, Himiko conducted diplomacy in her own name while occupying herself with magic and sorcery. Himiko's 13-year-old female relative replaced a male king who had succeeded her but failed to bring peace. According to Japan's own chronicle (*Nihon shoki*, compiled in A.D. 720), a semilegendary female ruler, Jingū, ruled for 70 years after the death of her husband-emperor in A.D. 200. This formidable shamanistic ruler led expeditions against Korean kingdoms while pregnant.

The tradition of female rule continued for almost two centuries after the adoption in the sixth and seventh centuries of Chinese institutions that excluded women from bureaucratic offices. Beginning with Suiko (592–628), the first Japanese ruler to use the title *tennō* (emperor), six women occupied 8 of the first 16 imperial reigns: Kōgyoku (642–645), Saimei

(655–661, same person as Kōgyoku), Jitō (690–697), Gemmei (707–715), Gensei (715–724), Kōken (749–758), and Shōtoku (764–770, same person as Kōken). Scholars have commonly claimed that female sovereigns were passive intermediaries, filling a vacancy to secure the throne for the line of the deceased sovereign. However, with the exception of Kōgyoku/Saimei, all ruled actively, and most had no designated male successor for whom to keep the throne.

The centralized *ritsu-ryō* (penal and civil codes) government of the seventh and eighth centuries codified imported patriarchal principles into the written law requiring patrilineal transmission of property and the household headship (to be occupied by the main wife's oldest son). The relationship between husband and wife was to be comparable to that of father and child. There was no penalty for a wife's accidental death during a beating by her husband, but husband beating was punishable by 100 blows and by execution if he should die. A wife was liable for divorce on six grounds: barrenness, adultery, unfilial behavior to parents-in-law, talkativeness, kleptomaniac habits, or jealousy. A husband could be divorced if he was absent more than two years (three if childless). Upon marriage the wife's property was joined to the husband's, and, upon her death, it passed to their children without reverting back to her natal family. A divorced wife could take her property with her.

These provisions, which assumed a Chinese-style patrilocal and patrilineal social base, remained largely impracticable due to Japan's strong matrilocal and duolineal tradition. In marriage, the wife's residence was central: a husband visited or moved into it, sometimes as the son-in-law. Patrilocal marriage was the exception. In the Nara (710–784) and the Heian (794–1185) periods, marriage was a flexible practice requiring no official contract or registration. After a woman received a man for three nights, her family accepted him as her husband by offering symbolic rice cakes in the "Third Day Ceremony." Divorce occurred when he stopped visiting or moved out of her house. Both continued to hold possessions independently, and, upon divorce, the husband took his property out of his wife's residence. Conspicuously absent were the separation of the woman from her natal family and her transfer into an unfamiliar patriarchal household.

Matrilocal arrangements, however, did not imply matriarchy or gender equality, as overenthusiasm has led some scholars to claim. Polygamy among the elites, which was noted as early as Himiko's time, constrained women's position. It was not uncommon for a Heian noble to have many wives, perhaps living with one and visiting the others. Marital customs made it easy for a man to initiate divorce, although women also took the initiative on occasion. In a "visiting marriage," female independence was combined with the anxiety of waiting for the husband to show up.

In the Heian period, aristocratic clans used marriage politics to gain de facto political power, as did the Fujiwara, who successfully married their daughters into the imperial line, thus exerting great influence on future emperors raised in the maternal household.

In the palace milieu, imperial wives and female attendants swelled in number. Enjoying immense luxury, court women cultivated aesthetic tastes that were valuable assets in the refined games of court politics. Their physical mobility was restricted by their own sense of elitism and contempt for matters outside the court—religious institutions excepted.

From the ninth to the twelfth centuries, court women established Japanese literary traditions and wrote Japan's seminal classics. They wrote in the Japanese syllabary (*kana*), which is far more suited to expressing sentiments than Chinese, which was used by men for official documents.

Commoners practiced polygyny and polyandry until about the eighth century. The communal songfests, held in conjunction with the fertility celebrations at such times as seeding and harvesting, were frequent settings for open sex. Women and men were free to engage in sexual relationships regardless of marital status.

In agriculture, before the spread of livestock, sexual division of labor did not necessarily imply inequality in the social values of female and male labor. Men tended to work on fields distant from home, where they tilled and irrigated rice paddies and harvested crops. Women worked closer to home, where they husked rice to be paid as tax, planted millet and wheat as well as rice, cut grass, and harvested. But male labor gained greater prestige as the management of livestock and instruments of reclamation became male prerogatives in the ninth and tenth centuries. The *ritsu-ryō* government formally differentiated the economic worth of the sexes by allotting females two-thirds of the male portion of the state's land and exempting them from military service. Women were the primary producers of textiles, and they headed production units for sake and pottery that were used for both practical and ceremonial purposes.

Women of all propertied classes held firm economic rights through inheritance. In their own names, women received loan seeds and bought and sold land. Heian female aristocrats, like the males, amassed land commended to them by lesser landholders who sought the tax exemptions that their prestige could provide.

In the earliest periods Japanese women held public authority, economic power, and spiritual prestige. Their exclusion from the political structure after the eighth century articulated the male-dominant ideology of the centralized state. However, women's economic power was still ensured by their strong position in inheritance, and indigenous beliefs gave them a high and charismatic position. However, the gradual diffusion of Confucianism and Buddhism tended to degrade female biological functions, spreading ideas of female pollution and spiritual inferiority. By the Heian period, women were forbidden to enter certain sites sacred to Buddhism and were relegated to secondary positions in Shinto office hierarchy. (See CONFUCIANISM; BUDDHISM.)

References. William McCullough, "Japanese Marriage Institutions in the Heian Period," *Harvard Journal of Asiatic Studies* 27 (1967): 103–167; Chieko Irie Mulhern (ed.), *Heroic with Grace: Legendary Women of Japan* (New York, 1991); Hitomi Tonomura, "Black Hair and Red Trousers: Gendering the Flesh in Medieval Japan," *American Historical Review* 99 (1994): 129–154; Patricia Tsurumi, "The Male Present versus the Female Past: Historians and Japan's Ancient Female Emperors," *Bulletin of Concerned Asian Scholars* 14 (1982): 71–75; Haruko Wakita, "Marriage and Property in Premodern Japan from the Perspective of Women's History," *Journal of Japanese Studies* 10 (1984): 77–99.

HITOMI TONOMURA

JAPAN. Feudal Period (1185–1886). Women enjoyed an initial period of considerable independence but lost personal rights as society placed increasing emphasis on military values and Confucian principles. Japan's "feudal" age lasted nearly seven centuries over the duration of three warrior governments (*bakufu*). In the first half of Kamakura rule (1185–1333), the prevailing custom of female property rights was upheld in the law (the Jōei Shikimoku, 1232) and in verdicts concerning inheritance disputes.

A daughter held secure rights to the family property before and after marriage. Marriage was generally patrilocal, but a woman maintained a strong tie with her natal family and kept property separately from her husband's, though grants from husbands were common. Widows could act as the functional head of the house, freely apportioning the husband's land or designating the next household head. Children generally followed the patrilineal descent, but often women (whether married or not) legally adopted daughters or sons to whom to bequeath their property.

Women's property rights also entailed feudal (local peacekeeping and military) obligations via the *bakufu*-awarded *jitō* (steward) title attached to land grants. Women came to hold the *jitō* title usually through inheritance of land, though a few received it directly from the *bakufu*.

Women's "public" role as *jitō* deteriorated in the fourteenth century as the natal family gradually restricted bequests to daughters, whose portion could "leak" to the husband's side through her children descending in his line. Women's military capacity was also delegitimated during the national emergency caused by the repeated threats of Mongol invasion (1274 and 1281), which demanded actual fighting, and the subsequent period of disorder saw each warrior house consolidating its territories under the most able male. By the mid-fourteenth century, women had been reduced to a dependent status and were mere recipients of sustenance income from the household head.

Popular Buddhist movements of the Kamakura period (the Pure Land, True Pure Land, Nichiren, and Ji sects) offered equal access to salvation regardless of sex, status, or occupation and won many female adherents, who contributed great material support. However, in Shinto, female shrine attendants (*miko*) had lost much of their charismatic role of ancient times and now occupied secondary positions in the established structure or became itinerant priestesses. (See JAPANESE RELIGION.)

Because laywomen were also barred from full participation in Shinto ceremonies, they were denied full membership in village communities whose political and economic life centered around the local, exclusively male, shrine association (*miyaza*). Peasant women held inheritance rights until the seventeenth century and contributed to the shrine's fisc or treasury by donating land, but their community status was recognized via an affiliated male.

The weakened Muromachi *bakufu* (1336–1572) allowed the growth of provincial lords (*daimyō*), and warfare became endemic. Devoid of economic independence, warrior-class women primarily served to produce offspring for the husband's house (*ie*). Motherhood received high social esteem, but so did "feminine virtue," understood as chastity and obedience. The ever-present threat of turncoats and broken alliances fostered the practice of "strategic marriages"—the exchange of females as hostages or spies. Oda Nobunaga, the first of the "Three Unifiers," for example, married his younger sister Oichi to the Azai in 1563 but 10 years later destroyed the Azai, sparing Oichi and her daughters while killing the sons.

Some wives of warrior leaders attained tremendous political power. Hōjō Masako (1154–1225), the wife of Japan's first shogun (Minamoto no Yoritomo), was called the "nun shogun" after taking the tonsure, and Hino Tomiko (1440–1496), the wife of the eighth Ashikaga shogun (Yoshimasa), influenced shogunal succession and built her own commercial empire.

Merchant and artisan women, compared to warrior-class women, lived a life of greater latitude and independence, enjoying divided inheritance in commercial property and benefiting from the rapid commercialization in late medieval times (fourteenth through sixteenth centuries). In the *za* (trade and handicraft associations) of ash (used for dye), fans, *obi* (the kimono sash), and salt in Kyoto, among others, some women seized monopoly privileges and passed them from mother to daughter.

The centralized Tokugawa regime (1600–1868) built a peaceful society based on a four-status hierarchy (samurai-warriors, peasants, artisans, and merchants), each with its proper Confucian behavioral code. The principle of female inferiority cut across status lines and was disseminated by moralistic works such as *The Greater Learning for Women (Onna Daigaku)*, commonly attributed to Kaibara Ekken (1630–1714). As women were born with five blemishes (they were disobedient, inclined to anger, slanderous, jealous, and stupid) and lacked the intellect to make independent judgments, they were to live a life of "Three Obediences": to parents before marriage, to the husband in marriage, and to a son in old age.

The *bakufu* and domain codes articulated this principle, which was differentiated in severity by status, with the greatest constraints imposed on women of the samurai class (about 7 percent of the population), whose role was reproduction for the husband's lineage. Marriage was contracted between two houses with the permission of a feudal superior. A wife's adultery was a crime punishable by death, while polygamy was common for husbands. The husband held the right to keep the wife's dowry upon her death and to divorce. For a wife, refuge in a "divorce temple" was the only means to divorce, and even an unauthorized sojourn away from her husband was an infraction. The *bakufu* formalized the previous era's hostage system and kept *daimyō*'s wives permanently in the capital (Edo, today's Tokyo), where the *daimyō* resided in alternate years with his retinue. The law did offer wives a measure of protection against physical abuse: execution for killing a wife in a beating and exile for pawning a wife.

Women of the lower classes had more freedom than did those of the warrior class. Widows and daughters of the peasant class sometimes held the house headship, though only as intermediaries for male relatives. Peasant women married relatively late (early 20s) and practiced abortion and infanticide to maintain a relatively small and sex-balanced household that valued girls for providing labor at home or income as hired hands. Merchants commonly placed the family's primary holding with the daughter and took in a son-in-law. Authorities emphasized diligence for peasants and humility for merchants rather than sexual morality and met adulterous acts with leniency since they had insignificant consequences for the state.

In marked contrast to ancient times, Tokugawa society regarded female-specific biological functions, such as menstruation and childbirth, as defilements. Chanting of the "Blood Bowl Sutra" to save women from hell became popular, while occupations associated with *Shintō* purity, such as sake brewing, turned into strictly male professions.

The shogunate's measures of social control extended to popular entertainment, cutting short centuries of female contributions to the performing arts as singers, dancers, and storytellers. In the late sixteenth century, Izumo no Okuni, a self-claimed priestess, captured a large audience with her quasi-religious dances and songs and eventually founded female Kabuki theater. The authorities viewed female Kabuki, which admittedly contained elements of prostitution, as injurious to public morals, and proscribed it repeatedly beginning in the 1620s.

Concurrently, the autonomy of prostitutes was undermined by licensing certain persons and districts: Yoshiwara in Edo, Shinmachi in Osaka, Shimabara in Kyoto, and other "legal" quarters. However, there remained a larger number of unlicensed practitioners liable for punishment: for example, a bathhouse owner whose bath women prostituted illegally was crucified in 1637.

Tokugawa society was unquestionably patriarchal, but it offered women some degree of leverage. Despite the "Three Obediences," widows held considerable power and rarely "obeyed" the son. Women had access to education, if less so than men, at home or in temple schools (*terakoya*). As with Tamura Kajiko (1785–1862), a textile dealer's daughter who established her own school, women of upper- and middle-level merchant families were particularly well educated. Samurai-class women had no economic independence, but those who served as attendants in the shōgun's or *daimyō*'s household received regular salary and benefits.

References. Chieko Irie Mulhern (ed.), *Heroic with Grace: Legendary Women of Japan* (New York, 1991); Hitomi Tonomura, "Women and Inheritance in Japan's Early Warrior Society," *Comparative Studies in Society and History* 32 (1990): 592–623; Haruko Wakita, "Marriage and Property in Premodern Japan from the Perspective of Women's History," *Journal of Japanese Studies* 10 (1984): 77–99.

HITOMI TONOMURA

JAPAN. Post-Meiji Period (from 1886). Japanese women collectively have initiated, provoked, and absorbed a history of animated discourse spurred, in part, by the early Meiji (1868–1912) slogan, "Women are people too." Today the debate continues, focused now on the issues of antifemale sexism in the workplace and the ramifications of the Equal Employment Opportunity Law, which was passed in April 1986.

The attitude of early twentieth-century society is summed up by the phrase "Taishō Democracy," for the Taishō period (1912–1926) ostensibly was liberal and democratic. But not for women, however, who were banned from political participation as a result of the Peace Police Law (Article 5), which was operative from 1900 until its abolishment in October 1945. (See JAPAN, Security Police Law.) (Two months later, women were enfranchised to be elected to public office and to vote, a right exercised for the first time in April 1946.) The state's ideologues propagated a cult of sanctified motherhood informed by the "norm" of hegemonic patriarchy, in which married women effectively were confined to the altruistic role of "good wife, wise mother."

Male-defined maternal altruism, however, presupposed affluence and sexually satisfied husbands. Young single women from impoverished rural and urban families were sold to brothels that flourished in major urban centers, which were disproportionately populated by single and apparently lecherous men. During the years of the Taishō Democracy, the number of female prostitutes, licensed and unlicensed, burgeoned and is estimated to have reached 178,000 by 1925. Under government auspices, tens of thousands of girls and women were sold to brothels overseas to serve as sex objects for Japanese troops. Known as *karayuki*, they preceded the indentured prostitution of up to 70,000 Korean girls and women during the Pacific War (1937–1945). A law forbidding female prostitution became operative in 1958, but organized pimping continues to flourish. The intertwining of patriarchy and militarism in the first half of this century thus strangled the realization of human and civil rights for women, belying the courageous efforts of Japanese feminists.

The patriarchal cult of motherhood was premised on the conflation of sex roles based on biological capacities and gender roles based on sociohistorically constructed notions of appropriate behavior. Consequently, the defiant arrival of the Japanese flapper—the *moga* (*modan garu*, or modern girl)—with her bobbed hair, plucked eyebrows, manicured nails, Euro-American outfits, and unabashed penchant for drinking, smoking, and cruising, challenged the arbitrariness of the sex/gender system. (Short hair for women had been banned in the early Meiji period, although activists flouted this decree and its symbolic message.) Regardless of whether individual *moga* viewed the personal as political, collectively they symbolized an alternative to the "good wife, wise mother" role.

Accompanying the "modern girl" was the "new workingwoman" (*shin-shokugyō fujin*), for whom employment was also a means of postponing an inevitable arranged marriage. Unlike her foresisters and contemporaries from impoverished villages whose coerced labor supplemented their families' budgets and fueled the silk and cotton industries, the "new workingwoman" was an urbanite of many labels, all diminutive: "gasoline girl," "shop girl," "one-yen taxi girl," "bit-part girl," "mannequin girl," and the oxymoronic "girl boy," who waited on tables. Graduates of Tokyo Women's College (1918) were nicknamed "Marx girl" on account of the political (not home) economy courses offered there. Japan Women's College (1901), however, did offer "bridal training" classes, and by 1928 there were about 730 finishing schools for young women.

Real girls between the ages of 10 and 15 worked alongside women in the textile mills, where they were underpaid, brutalized by sadistic foremen, and crippled by the tubercular climate. Despite the Factory Act of 1911, revised in 1926, the workday in busy periods remained about 15 hours, 3 hours over the limit. Mannequin girls, on the other hand, earned more than male white-collar workers for the glamorous task of posing rigidly for several hours in store windows. The growth of the industrial and commercial sectors in the early twentieth century created divergent avenues of employment (many exploitative) for single women in particular. The vast majority of women continued to labor in agriculture, the married among them acting as unpaid assistants to their farmer husbands.

The idealization of motherhood was tenacious enough to forestall the mobilization of female laborers during the Pacific War (1937–1945). Between 1940 and 1944, the number of women in the civilian labor force averaged only 40.5 percent of nonmilitary workers (only 5.5 percent higher than in 1930), despite the accelerated conscription of young men in 1942 and 1943. Moreover, they were paid less for their work than their male counterparts—even in 1987, the earnings of female workers averaged 53 percent that of males. (In place of female workers, the state redeployed male workers from nonessential industries and conscripted male and some female students, older men, and Chinese and Korean laborers.) Forty percent of these workingwomen were unmarried and ranged in age from 15 to 24 years.

Despite the creation of a women's volunteer labor force early in 1944, female workers continued to be regarded as temporary help. The single women among them were encouraged to marry and thereby fulfill their national destiny, a message echoed by the Greater Japan Women's Association, which was formed by government decree in 1942 with the forced merger of women's associations. Women were not drafted for combat service, although they were trained, on a neighborhood basis, to wield bamboo spears in preparation for an American invasion. An exception was the Lily Brigade, a volunteer fighting corps of mostly female students, which was annihilated in the battle for Okinawa.

Like the *karayuki*, many war widows faced humiliation and ostracism as victims of gossip about their sexual appetites. Moreover, an average of 13 percent of all women born at the outset of the Pacific War remained unmarried, largely due to the war death of otherwise available grooms. In contrast, an average of 4 percent of Taishō-born women remained unmarried. Since a "normal" woman is a married woman, single women continue to face social, political, and economic discrimination. Organizations such as the *Dokushin Fujin Renmei* (League of Single Women, 1967) and *Onna no Hi* (Women's Movement, 1979) lobby on their behalf for tax reductions, increased Social Security benefits, and access to government housing and bank loans. Presently, there are at least 143 women's organizations representing women from a wide range of political and socioeconomic backgrounds, including lesbians, atomic bomb victims, convicts, widows, battered wives, and single parents (both unwed and divorced).

Unlike its American counterpart, the Japanese postwar Constitution (1947) guarantees equal rights for women (Article 14). This progressive reform was implemented through the efforts of American women serving with the Occupation and their Japanese female colleagues. Despite this provision, wife and mother remain a woman's unequal and primary gender roles. Two-thirds of the 33 percent of women who continue in academe beyond senior high school attend two-year colleges and major in home economics, education, and cultural studies, in that order. These are subjects that ultimately will enhance their marriageability. (The first women's studies curriculum was introduced at Ochanomizu Women's College in 1979.)

The Equal Employment Opportunity Law passed in April 1986 ensures women—who collectively constitute over 50 percent of the workforce—

equal opportunity with men in all stages of employment, from recruitment to retirement. However, the actualization of this law by male-oriented corporations is lagging, in part, because violators are not penalized. A 1990 poll of 1,286 female office workers conducted by the Sendai Bar Association revealed that 84 percent of the women surveyed have not experienced improved working conditions since the enactment of the law. Working conditions vary according to the size of the company, and female employees at large companies especially are forced to assume significant overtime work. Female part-time workers, most of whom are married and work to supplement their budgets, are especially exploited. Neither the employment law nor the Constitution takes into account the low ascribed status of the female sex, which is a socially constructed (and therefore deconstructible) handicap. Japanese women will continue to demand recognition from men in their society that "women are people too."

References. R. Atsumi, "Dilemmas and Accommodations of Married Japanese Women in White-Collar Employment," *Bulletin of Concerned Asian Scholars* 20 (1991): 54–62; G. L. Bernstein (ed.) *Recreating Japanese Women, 1600–1945* (Berkeley, Calif., 1991); M. Hane, *Peasants, Rebels, and Outcasts: The Underside of Modern Japan* (New York, 1982); T. S. Lebra, *Japanese Women: Constraint and Fulfillment* (Honolulu, 1984); Merry I. White and Barbara Maloney (eds.), International Group for the Study of Women, *Proceedings of the Tokyo Symposium on Women* (Tokyo, 1979).

JENNIFER ROBERTSON

JAPAN. Security Police Law (1905–1945) strictly regulated political activity in Japan from 1900 to 1945. Article 5 of the law prohibited women (along with military men, policemen, the clergy, public and private school teachers, and persons deprived of their civil rights) from joining political organizations; it also barred women (along with minors and those deprived of their civil rights) from even attending political meetings. The restrictions on women had appeared earlier in the Law on Associations and Meetings of 1890 and were probably based on German and French precedent (although German and French limits on women's rights of association had been relaxed by the time the Japanese legislation was drafted).

By 1900 the Ministry of Internal Affairs, which was responsible for drafting and enforcing the law, was prepared to drop the ban on women's attendance at political meetings, but the House of Peers opposed the ban's being lifted. Most Peers were simply offended by women's public activities, but more sophisticated Home Ministry officials hoped to replace politics, which they considered disruptive, with a constructive agenda for women, which included household production, savings, the education of children in scheduling and other forms of industrial discipline, and nonpartisan patriotic organizations.

Women's right to attend political meetings was passed by the House of

Commons in 1907 and 1908 but not accepted by Peers until after the New Woman's Society had lobbied for it from 1919 to 1922. In response to the New Woman's Society and other groups favoring women's political rights, in 1931 the government of Prime Minister Hamaguchi Osachi tried to grant women the right to join political organizations and also to vote in local elections, but the House of Peers balked, and the movement for women's political rights disintegrated in an atmosphere of military crisis after the Manchurian Incident later the same year. The prohibition of women's membership in political organizations remained in effect until 1945. It was selectively enforced, and especially during the 1920s women did join feminist and other political organizations. Nevertheless, the law swallowed much of the energy of the woman suffrage movement and probably restricted the movement's scale even as the electorate expanded to include all adult men by 1926. (See also JAPANESE WOMEN'S MOVEMENT.)

References. Sharon Nolte, "Women's Rights and Society's Needs: Japan's 1931 Suffrage Bill," *Comparative Studies in Society and History* 28 (1986): 690–714; Sharon Sievers, *Flowers in Salt: The Beginnings of Feminist Consciousness in Modern Japan* (Stanford, Calif., 1983).

SHARON H. NOLTE

JAPANESE AMERICAN WOMEN DURING WORLD WAR II were second-generation women of Japanese descent, the majority of whom spent time in concentration camps during the war. In this period, "Japanese American women" referred to second-generation Japanese women (Nisei) exclusively, as first-generation immigrants (Issei) had been prohibited by law from gaining citizenship, and the third generation (Sansei) were not yet into their teens.

On February 4, 1942, five months after Japan bombed Pearl Harbor, President Franklin D. Roosevelt signed Executive Order 9066, giving authorities the power to remove all persons of Japanese ancestry from the West Coast because of "military necessity" and to place them in remote camps in interior areas of the nation. For Nisei women and for all Japanese Americans involved, this was the single most wrenching episode in their lives both physically and psychologically. Later, they would be unrelenting in their efforts to extract an apology and compensation from the government, for this act that had abrogated their rights under the Constitution and subjected them to three years of exile from their homes.

For years, anti-Japanese sentiment had been a fact of life on the West Coast, as amply evidenced by housing segregation and the 1924 laws that barred immigration from Japan and prohibited alien Japanese from becoming naturalized citizens or owning land.

This situation had become increasingly volatile during the years preceding World War II, fueled partly by the aggressive wars of expansion by the militarists in Japan, partly by powerful agricultural interests on the West

Coast that felt threatened by the inroads made by the Japanese, and, in good part, by race-baiters. These various forces, ignited by the bombing of Pearl Harbor, culminated in the forcible removal of the Japanese from the West Coast.

Of the 110,000 persons sent to concentration camps, 71,986 were citizens. Nearly 15,000 of these were Nisei women between 15 and 30 years of age and densely clustered around age 17. Although they had no way of knowing it, they would spend an average of one and a half years confined there.

In addition to those incarcerated, a few Nisei women were scattered in spots around the country to which their families had fled on hearing rumors of being herded into camps. In addition, a few had lived outside the "military areas" before the war and thus were not affected by evacuation orders.

For the most part, the Nisei woman was bilingual and bicultural. She teetered on a precarious line between her dual identities as a Japanese and as an American. But she had learned very early the survival technique of adaptability and moved in both worlds with a certain amount of facility. At the same time she was speaking Japanese to her mother while performing her female duties in the home, she might be thinking of her date that evening with a zoot-suiter who would take her to a jitterbug palace.

When the evacuation orders were handed down, the entire Japanese population on the West Coast was swept into temporary Assembly Centers, set up at such facilities as racetracks, fairgrounds, and livestock exposition buildings. By the end of 1942, they had all been transferred to 10 Relocation Centers in remote regions across the country in California, Arizona, Wyoming, Colorado, Utah, and Arkansas.

"Bewildered" best describes the Nisei woman's state of mind at this juncture. Young, politically naive, and unaccustomed to challenging authority, she flowed with the tide of events, following the elders' counsel to make the best of a bad situation.

The new camps typically consisted of 36 or more blocks, each block having 12 tar-papered barracks measuring 20 by 120 feet and partitioned into six units. The rooms were equipped with one hanging lightbulb, army cots and mattresses, and a potbellied wood stove. The community toilets, washroom, and showers were located in the center of the block, along with the laundry room and mess hall.

The entire complex was operated like a city, headed by a project director with a staff of Caucasian aides who headed the various departments in which the evacuees worked.

Evacuees settled into their new environment with amazing dispatch. Life took on a curious sense of normalcy as schools, variety stores, hospitals, barbershops, beauty shops, and even credit agencies were set up in each camp. Newspapers, typed on stencils and reproduced, kept inmates abreast of the camp happenings.

Nisei women enrolled in the high schools, took clerical jobs, or worked in the hospitals. A few taught school. Another few took jobs as domestics for the Caucasian administrators. Caring for infants or infirm parents generally fell to Nisei women. (Issei parents were on the average 33 years older than the Nisei women, and, though some were still hardy, many were not.) Water had to be carried in from the laundry room for baths and other daily rituals, and the laundry toted there had to be washed by hand. Each chore, even obtaining meals, required a trip outside the living quarters.

For leisure time there were dances, arts and crafts classes, libraries, sports, and old movies. These provided some lift from the dull routine and sense of aimlessness that soon began to pervade the camps.

Evacuees had barely settled into their new environment when they were recruited to fill the nation's acute labor shortage and were given temporary leave from camp to work on farms. It should be noted here that plans for a more permanent resettlement of evacuees outside the West Coast had been put into motion even before the evacuation was completed. This effectively mitigated the charge that the Japanese had posed a security threat. As a matter of fact, no disloyal act had been charged to any Japanese American before the evacuation, nor would it ever be.

Among the first to take permanent leave were college students. Included in their number were many Nisei women, some of whom had been deprived of the opportunity for college, partly because they had not yet come of age but also because their needs and aspirations in the family were usually superseded by those of the males. The students were closely followed by individuals who could not take the cramped camp life and felt that almost any treatment on the outside was preferable to confinement. These groups tested the waters of the war-inflamed public. While some ugly incidents did occur, on the whole the evacuees were received with tolerance, if not enthusiasm.

Next to venture out were those of high employability and without family responsibilities. Among these were secretaries and stenographers. Many took jobs as domestics and then went on to factory or office work when the opportunity arose. It should be noted, however, that if an English-speaking member was needed at the family's home base in camp, usually the female remained behind.

Meanwhile, in what surely has to be regarded as incredible under the circumstances, the army began to draft all eligible Nisei men from the camps in early 1943. Two combat teams had previously volunteered from among Nisei in the camps and in Hawaii to establish a record of loyalty. They were apparently doing so to the satisfaction of the War Department.

Then, in July 1943, Japanese American women were recruited for service in the Women's Army Corps (WAC). Approximately 50 women answered the initial call, serving as AIR-WACs at various air bases in the country, in medical detachments, at army recruiting, and in the Military Intelligence Schools as typists, clerks, and researchers.

In January 1945, as Japan was breathing its last breaths in the war, the evacuation orders were rescinded. By this time only half the 110,000 inmates remained in camps. They had resettled in cities like Chicago, Denver, Minneapolis, and New York. Nisei women were working as secretaries, nurses, and domestics, attending college, tending babies, or working in garment factories.

One woman, Mitsuye Endo, represented by lawyer James Purcell, lent her name to a landmark case that argued that the War Relocation Authority had no right to detain loyal American citizens in Relocation Centers. The Supreme Court ruled in her favor on December 18, 1944.

At war's end, most Nisei women returned to the West Coast to take up a life interrupted by three years of exile.

After many years of lobbying by Japanese Americans, a government commission was established in 1980 to study the "wartime relocation and internment of civilians." They found that the broad causes for the detention were "race prejudice, wartime hysteria, and the failure of political leadership." In 1988, Congress passed the Redress Bill, which required payment of $20,000 together with a letter of apology from the president to all Japanese Americans who had been interned. By 1995, most of those eligible had received the redress payments.

References. Mei T. Nakano, *Japanese American Women: Three Generations 1890–1990*, 4th ed. (San Francisco, 1995); U.S. Commission on Wartime Relocation and Internment of Civilians, *Personal Justice Denied* (Washington, D.C., 1982); Michi Weglyn, *Years of Infamy: The Untold Story of America's Concentration Camps* (New York, 1976).

MEI T. NAKANO

JAPANESE RELIGION and women have been closely connected in Japanese civilization since the nation's mythological origins. Shamanistic folk religion, Shinto, Buddhism, Christianity, and the new religious cults of the nineteenth and twentieth centuries have found in women their most numerous and dedicated supporters. For its part, religion in Japan has sometimes provided justification for improving the status of women and, at times, has endorsed prevailing views of women's inferiority.

Shamanism and Shinto. In ancient Japan women held a high place in folk religion and Shinto. They had a major role in agricultural rites because their procreative power was viewed as sacred. Women shamans (*miko*) spoke in the name of the divine beings that possessed them and banished malignant spirits. Some, like the semilegendary Himiko and Jingū, even became rulers. With the rise of the Yamato clan in the fourth century, the sun goddess Amaterasu Ōmikami became the principal deity in Japan's native religion of Shinto. Imperial princesses functioned as priestesses at major shrines of Amaterasu.

In villages the central role of women in folk religion and Shinto eroded over time. Buddhism reinforced indigenous taboos against the blood pollution of women and led to their exclusion from certain sacred places or events. Males became the nucleus of Shinto rituals, with females as their assistants. The function of women shamans in folk religion became passive, with a male Buddhist priest or mountain ascetic interpreting their utterances. An 1873 governmental ban on their activity was lifted after World War II. Today women shamans serve mainly in rural areas.

*Buddhism.** Viewed as a means of strengthening imperial power, Buddhism quickly obtained the patronage of Japan's ruling elite after its entry from Korea in the sixth century. Under official sponsorship Zenshin-ni, the first nun (*ama* or *bikuni*), studied Buddhism in Korea for two years. Empresses and court ladies proved to be generous patrons of Buddhism. Empress Kōmyō (701–760) sponsored charitable institutions for the poor and the sick and was instrumental in establishing government temples and nunneries in every province. By the Heian era (794–1185), elite women regularly attended religious ceremonies and made retreats at temples. Many became nuns at some point in their lives. Taking Buddhist vows did not necessarily mean a total break with secular affairs. Some continued to administer landholdings and occasionally resumed political activity, as in the case of Hōjō Masako (1157–1225), the "nun shogun."

Buddhism became a religion of the masses during the Kamakura period (1185–1333) as new sects preached universal salvation as accessible even to women. In fact, the founder of the Jōdo Shin sect, Shinran, is known as the monk who married. His wife, the nun Eshin, and his daughter, the nun Kakushin, actively propagated the sect. The refuge temples (*kakekomidera*), certain convent temples established during this era, gave hope to abused wives by granting them sanctuary and a divorce after a period of temple service. Throughout the premodern period, itinerant nuns helped spread Buddhist beliefs. Then as now, laywomen joined groups (*kō*) that collected money to support temples and shrines and organized pilgrimages. Buddhist nuns today constitute about one-third of the Buddhist ministry.

Christianity. Christianity first came to Japan in the mid-sixteenth century. Attracted by its teaching on monogamous marriage and salvation as accessible to all, female converts joined from every social class. One of these, Hosokawa Gracia (1536–1600), is still cited as the model of a virtuous and valiant samurai wife.

With the reintroduction of Christianity in the late 1800s, missionaries took the lead in providing educational opportunities for girls at mission schools. Converts who became prominent educators included Tsuda Umeko (1865–1929), a pioneer in studying abroad and founder of Tsuda

College, which prepared women for economic independence as English teachers; Yasui Tetsu (1870–1945), Japan's first woman college president; and Hani Motoko (1873–1957), the first female newspaper reporter in Japan and the founder of a progressive school. Christian women spearheaded such social reforms as the movement to end legalized prostitution (1886–1956). Today, organized activity for women includes branches of the Young Women's Christian Association, the Salvation Army, and more than 90 congregations of Catholic sisters.

New Religious Cults. Women played prominent roles in the new religious movements that arose outside organized Shinto and Buddhism in the nineteenth and twentieth centuries. Several founded new sects. Nakayama Miki (1798–1887), known as "Beloved Parent" by her followers, started Tenrikyō; the prophetess Deguchi Nao (1837–1918) founded Ōmoto; noted for her faith healing, Kotani Kimi (1901–1971) cofounded Reiyūkai; and Kitamura Sayo (1900–1967), who would wear a man's suit for her public appearances because of the rough and unconventional language of the deity that spoke through her, began Tenshō Kōtai Jingū Kyō. Each one had the distinctively shamanistic traits of exposure to great physical and spiritual adversity, possession by a personal deity, personal charisma, the powers of healing and divination, and an outpouring of "revealed" writing.

References. Carmen Blacker, *The Catalpa Bow: A Study of Shamanistic Practices in Japan* (London, 1975); Kasahara Kazuo (ed.), *Nihon Joseishi* (History of Japanese Women), vols. 2, 3, 5, 6 (Tokyo, 1973); Junko Oguri and Nancy Andrew, "Women in Japanese Religion," in Gen Itosaka et al. (eds.), *Kodansha Encyclopedia of Japan*, vol. 8 (New York, 1983), 256–257.

MARGIT NAGY

JAPANESE WOMEN'S MOVEMENT organized the effort to understand and change conditions affecting all Japanese women and is conventionally dated from the founding of the Bluestocking Society in 1911. The founder, a young writer named Hiratsuka Raichō (Japanese names are given with the surname first), planned simply to create a journal in which women could portray their own experiences but soon took up the cause of protective legislation for mothers. Swedish feminist Ellen Key's works were translated in the society's journal, *Bluestocking*, along with the works of American anarchist Emma Goldman and British psychologist Havelock Ellis. Hiratsuka's nucleus of a few dozen literary women quickly expanded to 300 members, and their first journal issue, printed in a run of 1,000 copies, prompted an astonishing 3,000 letters from women who asked advice on marital problems, submitted manuscripts, or sought employment with the journal. Clearly, there was an avid audience waiting to discuss women's problems. The themes in *Bluestocking* were quickly taken up by general-interest magazines with circulations in the tens of thousands. What made the founding of the Bluestocking Society a turning point was its rejection of male leadership, its broad definition of the "woman problem," and its ability to reach a small, but influential, audience.

However, the Bluestocking Society was not the beginning of feminist theory or politics in Japan. During the 1880s, two upper-class women, Kishida Toshiko and Fukuda Hideko, spoke up for equal rights under the auspices of the Liberal Party. In the same period women and girls working in textile factories staged strikes and walkouts. After the turn of the century the social democratic Commoners' Society, including women but under the leadership of men, demanded political rights for women and blamed the oppression of women on the capitalist system.

All these activities met with harassment from the police. The Security Police Law of 1900 prohibited women from joining political organizations or even attending political meetings. (See JAPAN, Security Police Law.) Other legal barriers included the civil code, which permitted a married woman to own property but not to manage it, and the restriction of most higher education to men. More generally, both law and custom sanctioned family unity under men's authority. Defining women's role as "good wives and wise mothers," government officials sponsored conservative groups such as the Patriotic Women's Society, which skyrocketed to half a million members during the Russo-Japanese War (1904–1905). The society was scorned by the feminist avant-garde but was still important in aiding soldiers' families and in legitimating women's participation in public affairs.

Meanwhile, the Women's Christian Temperance Union, founded in 1886 by Yajima Kajiko and Mary C. Leavitt, campaigned against prostitution and concubinage. Its branch society in Osaka became the first women's organization to demand woman suffrage, and the national union formed a suffrage auxiliary in 1921 under Kubushiro Ochimi and Gauntlett Tsune. However, the union's emphasis on moral reform restricted its agenda.

In 1919 Hiratsuka and journalist Ichikawa Fusae formed the New Woman's Society, which won minor legislative victories in the passage of laws abolishing the ban on women's attendance at political meetings and prohibiting the marriage of men with venereal disease. Within three years the group had disbanded, but its veterans went on to lead nearly every feminist cause of the 1920s, an era of high politicization. Simultaneous movements on behalf of workers and tenant farmers legitimated activism and made alliances possible. Ichikawa emerged as the symbolic and tactical leader of the suffrage movement; she also worked for the International Labor Organization (and, after World War II, served populist causes in the House of Councilors for many years). She headed the political bureau of the Tokyo Federation of Women's Organizations, a landmark in the organization of Japanese women. The federation distributed milk and conducted research on the damages caused by the Great Kantō earthquake of 1923; as its members discovered their potential power, they took up the issues of prostitution, protective legislation for women workers, educational advancement, and political rights as well. Ichikawa, however, was convinced of the need for a single-purpose suffrage organization and founded the League for Women's Suffrage in 1924. The group gained about 2,000 members, published a monthly journal, and campaigned in the election of 1928 for men who favored woman's rights.

The largest organization favoring woman suffrage was the All-Kansai Federation of Women's Organizations, which represented some 3 million women in the Kyoto-Osaka-Kobe triangle and stressed social service. The most radical were several proletarian women's organizations led by women such as Yamakawa Kikue and Akamatsu Tsune. Since the police hounded them, and the male Left was ambivalent toward women's organizations, the proletarian women's groups were small and short-lived, but Yamakawa and Akamatsu became prominent in left-wing politics after World War II. The National Association of Women Primary School Teachers also supported suffrage, along with Christian and Buddhist girls' groups.

The peak of the suffrage movement came in 1931, when the government sponsored a bill for local women's suffrage, which passed the House of Commons but was overwhelmingly defeated in the House of Peers. At the same time the cabinet continued earlier efforts to build conservative and patriotic women's organizations such as the Greater Japan Federation of Women's Societies, which was run by male officers chosen from the Ministries of Education and Internal Affairs.

Government-sponsored organizations swamped feminist organizations during the period of militarism and war, 1931 to 1945, and women's political rights were hardly mentioned. Very few women unambiguously opposed militarism, but new research is needed to determine who actively supported militarism and who tacitly acquiesced while continuing earlier efforts for social welfare. Veterans of feminist and suffrage organizations had founded national alliances to abolish prostitution (1923), to protect consumers (1928), to promote birth control (1930), and to secure welfare legislation on behalf of mothers and children (1934). Governmental policy was vigorously pro-natalist, and a welfare bill for mothers and children passed in 1936. Despite limited gains in social welfare, most women experienced the war years as characterized by regimentation, separation from family members, bereavement, hunger, and, finally, defeat.

The Allied Occupation (1945–1951) considered the low position of Japanese women one aspect of feudalism and militarism, and occupation authorities quickly inaugurated women's equality in a new Constitution and in laws guaranteeing equal rights in political participation and the family and equal pay for equal work. These provisions were in advance of American law at the time and also in advance of what most Japanese women dared to claim. More immediate concerns were national poverty, children's education, and family harmony at any cost to the individual.

The most successful occupation reforms were voting rights and the encouragement of voluntary associations. The voting rate of Japanese women has regularly surpassed that of Japanese men since 1968 and remains one of the highest in the world. In 1970 the five largest women's organizations had 15 million members and showed remarkable clout on issues of consumer and environmental protection. Typically, these organizations have focused on the enhancement of a woman's separate sphere in the home and the welfare of the whole society rather than on woman's autonomy. Since 1970 a small minority of veteran activists and critical young women has asserted a new feminism attacking the fundamental concept of separate men's and women's spheres.

References. Sharon H. Nolte, "Women's Rights and Society's Needs: Japan's 1931 Suffrage Bill," *Comparative Studies in Society and History* 28 (1986): 690–714; Susan Pharr, *Political Women in Japan: The Search for a Place in Political Life* (Berkeley, Calif., 1981); Sharon Sievers, *Flowers in Salt: The Beginnings of Feminist Consciousness in Modern Japan* (Stanford, Calif., 1983).

SHARON H. NOLTE

JAPANESE WRITERS (CLASSICAL). Japanese women writers played a major role in creating their culture's classical, elite literary tradition. Although their significance lessened greatly in later centuries, around the turn of the second millennium A.D., women writers enjoyed preeminence unparalleled in any other premodern literary tradition worldwide.

The first compendium of poetry in Japanese, the *Manyōshū* (The Collection of Ten Thousand Leaves), compiled mid-eighth century A.D., includes significant verses by women from the earliest periods. *Genji Monogatari* (*The Tale of Genji*), often called the world's first novel, was the work of a woman. Women were viewed as the natural and appropriate creators of literature in the native Japanese vernacular. This position is clearly evidenced by an ironic contrast to Western literary tradition: the oldest extant example of Japanese narrative prose by an identifiable author is the *Tosa nikki* (Tosa Diary), a literary diary created by a man who wrote in the guise of a woman.

Several sociological factors help account for the prominence of women among the earliest Japanese authors. Mythological and historical evidence indicates the significant position of women in early periods of the culture. In *Kojiki* (712; The Record of Ancient Matters), a mythopoetic account of origins, the central deity is Amaterasu, the sun goddess, who is presented as the ancestor of the Japanese ruling house. The oldest foreign record of an encounter with people in the Japanese islands is a Chinese account describing a tribe led by a woman called Pimiko.

The overwhelming influence of political and religious systems and cultural values imported from the Asian mainland gradually brought a decline in the position of women, but one such cultural system, the Chinese system of writing and its subsequent adaptation in Japan, was crucial to the formation of literature in Japan and directly affected the role of women as writers. Prior to Chinese contact Japan had no written language, but by the fifth century written Chinese was already becoming well established in Japan, its function being, in some ways, analogous to that of Latin in Europe. It was the language of official written discourse in the realms of politics and religion. Following the Chinese Confucian model, women were excluded from official participation in politics, and though a few did learn some Chinese, they were discouraged from demonstrating such knowledge.

By the ninth century an indigenous Japanese writing system called *kana* was developed. It used a relatively small number of simplified Chinese characters to represent sound alone, detached from meaning. *Kana* made it possible for the first time to write in pure Japanese vernacular rather than in Chinese. *Kana* writing was used by both sexes to record poetry, and the written exchange of poems was an important part of social discourse and courtship among the aristocracy. As the classical poetic tradition developed, many of the characteristics of the earliest poetry of women—the expression of personal, private emotions and a predominantly melancholy tone—came to dominate the formal Japanese poetry of both men and women.

Literary diaries were the most common form of classical women's writing. The earliest of these is *Kagerō nikki* (Edward Seidensticker [trans.], *The Gossamer Years*). Written by a woman known to us only as "the mother of Michitsuna," it covers the years 954 to 974 and is a virtual autobiography recounting the author's unhappiness over her husband's diminished affection after his attentions shifted to a later secondary wife.

Another sort of diary is *Makura no sōshi* (The Pillow Book) by Sei Shōnagon, a woman in court service. Completed shortly after the year 1000, it takes the form of a collection of notes, lists, and comments, rather than a chronological diary or journal. The personal voice of Sei Shōnagon, witty and acerbic, contrasts strikingly with the self-pitying attitude of Michitsuna's mother. *Makura no sōshi* is still judged one of the greatest masterpieces of literary style in the Japanese language, and its random essay form became a mainstay of later literary writing by men.

Among all the writing by premodern Japanese, male or female, undisputed pride of place goes to *Genji Monogatari*. Like Sei Shōnagon, but about a decade later, its author, Murasaki Shikibu, was also in service as a tutor to an imperial consort, apparently having achieved this position because of her established literary reputation.

Genji Monogatari is a vast work of narrative fiction, rather than a diary, more than 1,000 pages in English translation. Completed early in the eleventh century, it depicts an imaginary court of about a century earlier and centers around the amours of the idealized male hero, the prince Hikaru Genji, "Shining Genji." Its later, darker chapters shift, after the prince's death, to the amorous lives of two younger men, each a pale, partial reflection of Genji.

Though the work was read by both men and women, its primary audience was the women at court. It was written serially and circulated chapter by chapter, apparently read aloud and discussed among the women. For this audience *Genji Monogatari* must have been both diverting and soberingly instructive in its depiction of many aristocratic female characters of varied personality. As in women's literary diaries, more outward social and political concerns scarcely appear. The psychological intensity of women's passion, the negative power of jealousy, and the importance of personal taste and grace are its major concerns. Despite vast cultural differences, the book has an extraordinary feeling of modernity and accessibility.

The canon of classical Japanese literature includes about a half dozen other significant diaries and works of fiction by women. The last important flowering of the women's courtly literary tradition came some 300 years after *Genji* in the diary entitled *Towazugatari* (The Confessions of Lady Nijō). Written by an imperial concubine, it describes both her years at court and her later life when she became an itinerant nun after falling out of favor. Not only is she writing in the tradition of earlier courtly women diarists, but also she shows instances in which court activities were modeled on scenes in *Genji Monogatari*.

The decline of the court, the rise of other genres of literature and drama, and the gradually declining social position of women in subsequent centuries shifted literary preeminence away from the brushes of women writers. Only in modern times has writing by Japanese women begun to regain significance.

References. *The Manyōshū*, trans. Nippon Gakujutsu Shinkokai (New York, 1965); Murasaki Shikibu, *The Tale of Genji*, trans. Edward G. Seidensticker (New York, 1964); "A Tosa Journal," in *Classical Japanese Prose*, trans. Helen C. McCullough (Stanford, Calif., 1990); *Kojiki*, trans. Donald L. Philippi (Princeton, 1969); *Gossamer Years*, trans. Edward G. Seidensticker (Rutland, Vt., 1964); *The Pillow Book of Sei Shonagon*, trans. Ivan Morris (New York, 1967); *The Confessions of Lady Nijō*, trans. Karen Brazell (Stanford, Calif., 1973); Donald Keene, "Feminine Sensibility in the Heian Era," *Landscapes and Portraits* (New York, 1971); Ivan Morris, *The World of the Shining Prince, Court Life in Ancient Japan* (New York, 1964).

SUSAN MATISOFF

JAPANESE WRITERS (MODERN). In the closing years of the Meiji era (1868–1912), Japanese women began to reemerge as major writers after centuries of comparative silence. Despite their brilliant performance as writers during the Classical age, women's active participation in the national literature had reached its nadir in the Tokugawa age (1603–1867), at least in part because the Tokugawa ethic supported the masculine samurai code and the enforcement of Neo-Confucianism's definitively subordinate position for women within the social hierarchy.

Two late Meiji figures, the short story writer Higuchi Ichiyō (1872–1896) and the feminist poet Yosano Akiko (1878–1942), symbolize the changing opportunities for women in the new age. Higuchi, whose tragically short life culminated in four years of intense literary activity, in her fiction captures the force of traditional roles as they conflict with the personal aspirations of characters, many of whom are drawn from the fringes of the then-fading pleasure quarters of the Yoshiwara. Her writing fully reveals the still-existent constraints that Japanese society placed upon women. Yosano's poetry, in contrast, is the product of a career spanning a life of social activism and of feminism with a strong maternalistic bent. Taken together, the two writers, both of whom rank among the greatest practitioners of their respective genres, foreshadow the level of achievement and the persistent themes and concerns that recur in the works of ensuing generations of women.

Women's writing has tended to be marginalized by the readiness of Japan's largely male critical literary establishment to consign it to a separate category of "women's-style writing" (joryū bungaku) and to label it as privatized and emotional. However, any consideration of the actual works themselves shows the great variation and scope of twentieth-century Japanese women's writing.

Although women suffered from a de facto exclusion from many important literary circles (the bundan), especially those centering around major universities to which women were not yet admitted, they found more hospitable ground and support in a few social and literary movements and institutions sympathetic to feminist concerns. One of the earliest of these was the feminist literary magazine Seitō (Blue Stocking), which was founded in 1911 by Hiratsuka Raicho (1878–1971) and which published works by leading women writers, including Yosano and Okamoto Kanoko (1889–1939), the latter of whom was another exponent of maternalism in both her poetry and her prose. Although the magazine, which ceased publication in 1916, existed for only the last two years of the Meiji and the first four of the Taishō (1912–1926) periods, its emphasis upon the individual creative energies of women prepared the ground for the more economic- and class-oriented expression of feminist concerns by women writing within the proletarian literary movement. The left-wing literary magazines and circles that sprang up in the Shōwa (1926–1989) decades of the 1920s and 1930s became a seedbed for writers of socialist and anarchist political convictions, many of whom were to have illustrious careers in the postwar years. Writers such as Hirabayashi Taiko (1905–1972), Miyamoto Yuriko (1899–1951), and Sata Ineko (b. 1904) underwent imprisonment because of their political beliefs, with Miyamoto's confinement continuing throughout the war years. The social consciousness evident in the works of enormously popular writers such as Hayashi Fumiko (1903–1951) and Ariyoshi Sawako (b. 1931) is clearly in sympathy with the economic and class issues advanced in left-wing circles. Enchi Fumiko, perhaps the leading "recognized" woman prose writer and literary aesthetician of the postwar period, began her prewar career as a left-wing playwright. In poetry, too, a proletarian consciousness is expressed in the works of such powerful writers as Ishigaki Rin (b. 1920) and Ibaragi Noriko (b. 1926); poets maturing in the postwar years, such as Kōr Rumiko (b. 1932), Tomioka Taeko (b. 1935), who is also a novelist of note, and Atsumi Ikuko (b. 1939), combine concern for feminist issues with a perspective on Japan's postwar demoralization and materialism.

The exclusion of women from most other established critical and literary circles had the effect of fostering a cross-generic and cross-movement solidarity among the writers themselves through such organizations as the Women Writers Association (Joryū bungakushakai), which awards a coveted literary prize. Published anthologies of prizewinning stories reveal an impressive range of stylistic and thematic treatment. In poetry, too, women have continued to produce works in an amazing range. The postmodern cosmopolitanism of novelists like Kurahashi Yumiko (b. 1935) and of poets like Tada Chimako (b. 1930) represents a final intellectual challenge to stereotypes of suitable and appropriate styles and themes in women's writing. So, too, do the eroticism and violence of the poetry and fiction of Kanai Mieko (b. 1947), who sprang from the revolt against society of the 1960s generation.

Lack of translation remains a major obstacle to world recognition of the power and variety of works by Japanese women. Although increasing numbers of translations into English have begun to appear, the bulk of the work by these and other women writers, work of high literary value, remains untranslated. The full range of the resurgence of women's writing can only be suggested here, but the twentieth century has become a second great age of Japanese women writers and rivals the early glory of classical Japan (Heian, late eighth through twelfth centuries), which first gave rise to the concept of "women's writing."

VICTORIA V. VERNON

JAZZ. Beginnings through 1950s. Not until 1987 did the U.S. Congress, in a concurrent resolution by both houses, express appreciation of jazz "as a rare and valuable national American treasure to which we should devote our attention, support and resources to make certain it is preserved, understood and promulgated." The rich contributions of women to this only recently recognized art form are just beginning to be acknowledged and researched.

Spirituals. Spirituals are precursors of jazz, black American religious folk music appearing in the southern states in the early 1800s, sung by male and female Christian slaves, in unison or two-part harmony, expressing suffering and prayers in slow laments or shouting hopes in lively jubilee songs. Both the laments and the jubilee songs reveal African characteristics also pervading blues, jazz, and gospel: intense emotional expression, spontaneous improvisation, a strongly syncopated rhythmic sense enhanced with hand clapping or foot stomping, and a call-and-response form. These African elements are melded with the 4/4 time and basic harmonies of the European diatonic scale, which slaves heard in the secular and sacred music of American whites in the early nineteenth century. From 1871 to 1878 spirituals were introduced throughout the United States and Europe by the Fisk Jubilee Singers, four young men and five young women.

Ragtime. Ragtime is piano music, fusing the syncopations of jubilee songs with the musical structure of marches (three, four, or five thematic sections and modulating interludes), flourishing 1895–1920. "Raggy" (syncopated) tunes for dancing were played by blacks on fiddles and banjos even in antebellum times; by the 1880s raggy music, played by brass bands and orchestras, ushered in the era of the cakewalk, 1897–1900, the dance craze that captured the United States and Europe. Among the six or seven published cakewalk composers is one woman, Saddie Koninsky, with her "Eli Green's Cakewalk," 1896. By the late 1890s this raggy, syncopated style came to be particularly identified with piano music called "ragtime" (first piano rags published 1897). Played by black men in bordellos and sporting houses of the South and Midwest, popularized by piano rolls, commercialized by Tin Pan Alley, published in sheet music in million-copy lots to be sold in the new "five-and-ten-cents stores," ragtime was soon taken over and genteelized by middle-class white women to play at home on their new pianos. (Sales of inexpensive uprights, perfected by the late 1880s, averaged around 300,000 per year in the first two decades of the twentieth century.) Among the millions of white, female piano players of rags, a few also composed and published rags: May Aufderheide, who wrote at least six rags, two of which were standards with New Orleans jazz bands; Gladys Yelvington; Julia Lee Niebergall; Adeline Shepherd, who wrote a hit rag that William Jennings Bryan used in his 1908 campaign for the presidency; Louise V. Gustin; Nellie M. Stokes; Irene Giblin; Irene Cozard; Maude Gilmore; Ella Hudson Day; Nina B. Kohler. Most versatile of the female rag composers was Muriel Pollock, who wrote songs and theatrical scores as well. Most creative of the piano-roll artists in the period 1918–1928 was Edythe Baker. Interest in ragtime, revived in the 1970s by the movie *The Sting*, was sustained through the 1980s by ragtime festivals, clubs, and newsletters. Outstanding contemporary female ragtime pianists include Molly Kaufman, Kathy Craig, Yvonne Cloutier, Jo Ann Castle, "Sister Jean" Huling, Mary Green, Joan Reynolds, and Virginia Tichenor Gilseth.

Traditional Jazz. An improvised, 4/4 music, based on a melody with set harmonies, traditional jazz appeared about the turn of the century, a blending of jubilee and ragtime syncopations with the call-and-response form and individualized sounds of the blues (see BLUES), played by instruments from marching bands (cornet with melodic lead, clarinet with counter-melody, trombone as lowest voice of this trio), with other instruments for rhythm (piano, drums, banjo, guitar, bass, or sousaphone). By 1915 the word "jass," later "jazz," replaced the term "ragtime" to designate this syncopated music.

The two most important female bandleaders in early jazz were also pianists. Lovie Austin toured in vaudeville, leading Lovie Austin & Her Blues Serenaders, and recorded extensively. Lillian Hardin Armstrong, pianist, composer, vocalist, and arranger, led bands, some all-male, some all-female, and also worked in King Oliver's band, where she met and married Louis Armstrong, 1924. She recorded the classic Hot Five sides with him in 1927. Lee Morse, vocalist, led Lee Morse & Her Blue Grass Boys, sometimes using a western cowboy yodel to enliven her jazz.

A third long-active pianist and blues shouter but not a bandleader, Billie Pierce, with her trumpeter husband, DeeDee, accompanied Ida Cox on tour, worked the tent circuit, and played with the Preservation Hall Jazz Band in New Orleans. The female band pianist with the longest continuous career in traditional jazz is Jeannette Kimbal, who began about 1923 with the Papa Celestin Band and continued to play for over 65 years.

Swing. Beginning in the mid-1920s and continuing into the 1950s, swing was played by big bands, usually 13 to 15 members (five reeds, five brass, piano, bass, drums), utilizing written arrangements, including rhythmic riffs and a call-and-response between the brasses and reeds for the large ensemble, limiting improvisation to soloists.

Female vocalists were featured with most swing bands: Ivie Anderson, with the Duke Ellington Orchestra for 12 years, and Mildred Bailey, the "Rocking Chair Lady," part Indian, the first nonblack woman to absorb the blues style successfully, who sang with Paul Whiteman and Benny Goodman and co-led a band with husband, Red Norvo ("Mr. and Mrs. Swing").

The supreme Billie Holiday, "Lady Day," with a highly individualized style, riding off the beat, composing unique songs, recorded more than 350 records, protested against racial hatred in her famous song "Strange Fruit," and sang with the bands of Benny Goodman, Teddy Wilson, Count Basie, and Artie Shaw.

Helen Humes, master of blues, ballads, jazz, rhythm and blues, bop, and pop, sang with Count Basie 1938–1942 and with the Red Norvo trio. Maxine Sullivan, with a relaxed, but swinging, cool jazz, style, worked with Claude Thornhill, with her husband, John Kirby, and in clubs and festivals until her death. Lee Wiley sang on radio with Paul Whiteman, with the Dixieland groups of Eddie Condon, with Pee Wee Russell, and with Jess Stacy's big band. Helen Forrest was featured with Artie Shaw, Benny Goodman, and Harry James and with singing star Dick Haymes on a long-lasting radio series. Anita O'Day, considered one of the top 10 female jazz singers by critic Leonard Feather, was featured with the Gene Krupa band, with Stan Kenton, and with Benny Goodman and influenced later jazz singer June Christy, who followed O'Day with Stan Kenton.

Two all-woman big bands starred in this period, one all-white and feted in the press, one racially integrated and ignored by all but the black press. Female bands and orchestras had appeared as early as 1884, but the first to earn national fame was Ina Ray Hutton and Her Melodears, led by the "Blonde Bombshell of Rhythm," pianist and gyrating vocalist Hutton, who later led other all-female and all-male bands.

The International Sweethearts of Rhythm, the first racially integrated women's band, was the hottest female jazz band of the 1940s and the most enduring (1938–1955). They made a "Swing Battle of the Sexes" tour with the Fletcher Henderson band, were broadcast by shortwave to every theatre of war, and played for domestic black troops and for troops in Europe. By 1947 key players of the group, Ernestine Tiny Davis, trumpet, and Vi Burnside, tenor sax, withdrew to form their own women's bands.

Several other women's bands, both black and white, functioned during World War II, but only Eddie Durham's All Star Girl Orchestra was in a class with the Sweethearts. Pianist and blues singer Georgia White led a female band in Chicago and later worked with Big Bill Broonzy, recording about 100 songs.

Outstanding jazz instrumentalists of the swing era include several pianists. Norma Teagarden alternated leading her own band with playing piano in brother Jack Teagarden's band. The child prodigy Hazel Scott, pianist and vocalist, was noted for jazzing the classics. Barbara Carroll, composer and pianist, led a trio, then continued as soloist into the 1970s. Dorothy Donean worked as a hot jazz pianist/entertainer.

One of the all-time great jazz musicians is Mary Lou Williams, pianist, composer of over 350 pieces, arranger, and bandleader. In the John Williams band by age 15, in four years she was "The Lady Who Swings the Band," soloist, arranger, and composer with Andy Kirk's Twelve Clouds of Joy. She made arrangements for Benny Goodman, Louis Armstrong, Cab Calloway, Tommy Dorsey, Glen Gray, Earl Hines, and Duke Ellington. She arranged her "Zodiac Suite" for the New York Philharmonic and performed it with them—the first jazz musician to appear with a major symphony; she played her "Mary Lou's Mass" in St. Patrick's Cathedral, New York City, the first jazz played in a nonblack church; and she was awarded a full professorship by Duke University, perhaps another first.

Among many excellent female instrumentalists, Valaida Snow, trumpeter, singer, and dancer, stands out. She played with Earl Hines in Chicago, in revues in London and Paris, and in bands in Russia, Germany, the Near East, the Far East, Stockholm, and Copenhagen, was imprisoned in a Nazi camp, then resumed her career in the United States. Marge Hyams, able vibist with Woody Herman in 1944–1945, the year his band was voted "best swing band" by *Downbeat*, led combos, then joined the George Shearing combo. Mary Osborne played guitar, recording with Mary Lou Williams, Coleman Hawkins, and Ethel Waters, led combos, and played with Jean Wald's all-female orchestra; with Russ Morgan; with Joe Venuti; and on a long-running radio show. Melba Doretta Liston, jazz trombonist, composer, and arranger, toured with Dizzy Gillespie, Count Basie, and Billie Holiday, later led her own all-female quintet, and wrote arrangements for Mary Lou Williams and others. The first woman elected to the Songwriters' Hall of Fame, lyricist Dorothy Fields, collaborated for her greatest jazz successes with composer Jimmy McHugh. Unlike the vocalists and pianists of swing, who are given due credit in jazz histories, the outstanding female instrumentalists have been almost completely ignored.

Gospel. Strongly rhythmic and emotional black American religious music, gospel is the modern form of the spirituals, differing from the swinging syncopations of jazz and the blues only in the subject matter of the gospel lyrics, based on the Christian religion. That important difference led many churches at the turn of the century to forbid their congregations to join in "sinful" secular music. As a corollary, most jazz musicians did not play hymns or spirituals in clubs. Although Mahalia Jackson, "queen of the gospel singers," as a child loved to listen to the records of Bessie Smith and Ma Rainey, she refused ever to sing the blues and only after much persuasion agreed to sing gospel music outside the church in jazz festivals and concerts. In contrast, Sister Rosetta Tharpe, accompanying herself on guitar, gladly made gospel famous in the 1940s in nightclubs and with record hits, but the sad price of her success was a virtual shunning by the Holiness church congregations. Other well-known gospel singers were Clara Ward and Roberta Martin.

Although the differences between sacred and secular black music have been emphasized by the churches, the musical style of these two strands of development is the same. A strikingly different musical style began to appear in black music in the early 1940s. (See JAZZ, Modern Developments.)

References. Rosetta Reitz, Liner Notes for Records in Women's Heritage Series 1980–1987, Rosetta Records, 115 W. 16 St., New York, N.Y.; Eileen Southern, *The Music of Black Americans: A History* (New York, 1971).

JEAN KITTRELL

JAZZ. Modern Developments. In the bop years 1940 to 1948 and the "cool" years 1949 into the 1960s, musicians moved toward a more sophisticated style: from familiar harmonies and singable melodies to unexpected dissonances and melodic phrases difficult for listeners to remember; from impelling two- and four-beat rhythms inviting toe tapping, hand clapping, and dancing to subtle, nondanceable rhythms; from traditional or big band instrumentation to smaller groups, often without piano, using non-traditional instruments; from "rebop," to "bebop," to "bop," to "cool jazz," to "modern," to "progressive," to "new."

The incredible Ella Fitzgerald, the "First Lady of Song" among jazz singers for more than half a century beginning in the 1930s, with a virtuoso range and command of intonation, mastered a variety of styles, swinging to fame with "A Tisket a Tasket" and the band of Chick Webb (which she led for a year after his death), brilliantly scat singing in bop style in the 1940s, evolving her own jazz ballad style. She toured nationally and internationally with Jazz at the Philharmonic 1946–1950, then with her own groups through the 1980s.

Singer-pianist Sarah Vaughn, first with Earl Hines, then as bop vocalist with Billy Eckstine, rose to international fame as a soloist with unique piano styling and innovative vocals, performing in over 60 countries and appearing with major U.S. symphony orchestras. Roberta Flack continued the same demanding dual performance of vocals with keyboard accompaniment. Pianist Marilyn McPartland developed a style much richer harmonically and melodically than that of ragtime or stride piano. She presides over a weekly national public radio series, begun in 1979.

Singers continue to outnumber instrumentalists among present-day female jazz musicians. Nancy Wilson, major star throughout the 1960s, touring the United States, Europe, and Japan, now appears on television as singer, actress, and host. Odetta, a big woman accompanying her big voice with guitar, considers herself a folksinger who does not attempt to distinguish folk ballads from blues, work songs, and popular music. Cleo Laine, one of the greatest living jazz singers, displays astonishing originality, an incredible range, agility of movement from lower to higher registers, and a variety of musical styles.

International superstar Aretha Franklin epitomizes the artistic and popular fusion of jazz, popular music, blues, gospel, and soul, with six gold LPs and 14 gold singles, each signifying 1 million records sold, a fusion continued by Tina Turner and Diana Ross.

The innovations of modern jazz disturbed performers and devotees who preferred earlier jazz forms. (See JAZZ, Beginnings through 1950s.) A traditional jazz revival, begun in San Francisco in 1939, continued into the 1990s through jazz clubs that had memberships almost completely white and that supported concerts, newsletters, and festivals featuring traditional bands and female vocalists, predominantly white, often strongly influenced by Bessie Smith, vocalists like Barbara Dane, Pat Yankee, Carol Leigh, Joanne ("Pug") Horton, Jean Kittrell, Ruby Wilson, Jan Sutherland, Terrie Richards, Paulette Pepper, and Banu Gibson.

The bifurcation between modern and traditional jazz is obvious in the production of American and European jazz festivals and publications, which generally feature either traditional or modern jazz but not both.

Although earlier forms of jazz, especially the blues, were the progenitors of rock in the 1960s, and all blues bands and festivals proliferated in the 1980s, most bands from the 1950s on preferred the modern style of expression, leaving to a minority of traditional bands the early forms. (See BLUES.)

Most major female jazz musicians from the 1950s to the present, however, more flexible than band units, are neither extremely avant-garde nor simply traditional. They defy categorization into such separate stylistic modes and make irrelevant most fine distinctions among jazz, popular music, folk music, gospel, rhythm and blues. They fuse past and present, combining modern harmonies and syncopated rhythms, continuing the emotional passion of the blues and the joy of jubilee songs.

References. Sally Placksin, *American Women in Jazz, 1900 to Present* (New York, 1982); Eileen Southern, *The Music of Black Americans: A History* (New York, 1971). See also the monthly publication *The Mississippi Rag* (ed. and pub. by Leslie Johnson, Minneapolis).

JEAN KITTRELL

JEWISH FEMINIST THEOLOGY is two-pronged: criticizing the laws, texts, and institutions of male-defined Judaism and constructing Jewish expression for women's religious and social experiences. The feminist critique uncovers a structure within Judaism in which men function as subjects and women as "other," outside the normative practices and the positions of power of the community. A feminist reading of Jewish texts shows that women enter into *halakhic* (legal) discussions of Jewish religious practices only when they affect the course of a man's life—for example, in marriage or divorce. The specific experiences of women's lives are otherwise generally ignored by the prescribed religious practices (e.g., no blessing for childbirth). Images of femininity as dangerous to men and to religious sanctity have flourished beginning in biblical literature and continuing until the modern period (e.g., Isaiah 3).

Pressure from the feminists has led to recent eliminations of many barriers to women's full participation in Judaism, such as the ordination of women rabbis. In calling for such changes in women's role in Judaism, some feminists see no contradiction between feminism and Judaism's hidden, but genuine, intentions. According to this position, the equality of women and men is intended by Judaism's prophetic teachings of justice and by the devotion to God that underlies Talmudic law. This intention has not been realized during the course of Jewish history for sociological, not theological, reasons, they argue.

A more radical position contends that women should not lead Jewish lives based on male models but should rather create their own religious expressions and, in particular, bring about a revolution in Jewish language. Women's religious expressions should be rooted not in the authority of male rabbinic systems but in identification with the historical experiences of Jewish women. Increasing numbers of feminists insist that incorporating female language, especially about God, is the key to transforming women from "other" to "subject." The type of female imagery to be used is important, since traditional Jewish descriptions of God's femininity (e.g., passive and receptive, as in Jewish mysticism) reflect male imagination, not women's experiences. Addressing God as She or Goddess raises the question of whether Jewish feminists are giving a new name to the traditional God of Jewish patriarchy or evoking a Goddess of the ancient world, who was worshiped, according to the Bible, by many ancient Israelites. Some feminists call for reviving ancient Jewish women's rituals, such as the celebration of the New Moon as a women's holiday or the Yiddish prayers created in Europe by men and women for women's use. Others urge new types of religious services, incorporating movement and improvisation. Central to Jewish feminist theology are new, woman-centered interpretations of biblical texts, particularly the writing of feminist *midrashim* (commentaries) about female biblical figures, and the recovery of historical Jewish women's experiences.

References. Blu Greenberg, *On Women and Judaism: A View from Tradition* (Philadelphia, 1982); Susannah Heschel (ed.), *On Being a Jewish Feminist: A Reader* (New York, 1976).

SUSANNAH HESCHEL

JEWISH WOMEN. Middle Ages. At this time Jewish women lived in prosperous urban Jewish communities of the Islamic world and in smaller Jewish enclaves in France, Germany, and England. Because rabbinic law, codified c. 600 C.E. in the Babylonian Talmud, ordained a comprehensive structure for Jewish life, Jews everywhere shared common institutions, systems of governance, and religious and social practices. These included the separation of women from the public sphere and emphasis on their home-based roles as wives and mothers. In addition to rabbinic ordinances, local environment played a vital role in the way in which Jewish social and family life developed, leading to sharp divergences in practice and custom between the Islamic (Sephardic) and Christian (Ashkenazic) milieux.

Jews in the Sephardic setting, mirroring elements of Muslim practice, preferred to confine women to domestic pursuits. Wives often contributed financially through needlework, however, and the least fortunate worked in the marketplace. In this Arabic-speaking environment, girls were given Arabic names indicative of beauty or good fortune. Women were married quite young, usually to older men. Marriage, which was often a way for a man to forge business alliances or elevate his social status, was an economic contract to which the husband contributed a marriage gift, while the bride brought a larger dowry of capital and goods. The marriage contract (*ketubah*) protected the wife's welfare and rights and in case of divorce (not uncommon in this middle-class environment) required the return of her dowry. Among Sephardic Jewry, polygamy was permitted (although uncommon) until the twentieth century. Women were rarely learned, although a few exceptions are known, but many were pious, achieving religious merit by acts of charity or facilitating study for their husbands and sons. Beyond a few letters, no literary works can be attributed to these women.

In Christian Western Europe, Jewish communities, suffering under onerous constraints, were small and cohesive. Marriage for both girls and boys took place at 12 or 13, in order to establish new and secure economic units and to circumvent sexual temptation. Marriage was considered the normal state, and matches would generally be found for everyone. Marriage contracts specified good treatment for the bride and required the return of her dowry in case of divorce (which was rather rare in this milieu). In 1000 C.E., the foremost rabbinic authority of Germany forbade polygamy for Ashkenazic Jewry and ruled that no woman could be divorced against her will. Women's notably high dowries brought them status and active participation in the family economy, and they frequently took the initiative in business matters, with moneylending, perforce, being the common occupation. Licoricia of Winchester, a businesswoman in thirteenth-century England, had direct dealings with the king and court and contributed a significant amount toward the rebuilding of Westminster Abbey. Occasionally, Jewish women in the Christian world, usually from families of the rabbinic elite, were relatively learned. Rabbis' daughters or wives, such as Dolce of Worms (d. 1196), often instructed other women and led them in prayer. Jewish women were loyal to their people and beliefs; Jewish and Christian Crusade chronicles record an overwhelming female willingness to die as martyrs with their families rather than convert to Christianity.

The everyday life of Jewish women was probably similar to that of Christian women of the gentry or urban middle class, although Jewish women had no recourse to convents where female spirituality and learning might flourish. In the late Middle Ages a devotional literature (*tehinnot*) began to develop for women, and some women left autobiographical and homiletical testaments (ethical wills). The best known is *The Memoirs of Glückel of Hameln* (trans. M. Lowenthal [New York, 1977]). Written in the seventeenth century, this fascinating document reflects many of the values and concerns of medieval Jewish women.

References. Judith R. Baskin (ed.), *Jewish Women in Historical Perspective* (Detroit, 1991); S. D. Goitein, *A Mediterranean Society: The Jewish Communities of the Arab World as Portrayed in the Documents of the Cairo Genizah*, 3 vols. (Berkeley, Calif., 1967–1978).

JUDITH R. BASKIN

JEWISH WOMEN. 1500–1800 were simultaneously an enduring testimony to traditional Jewish piety and eloquent challengers by both example and word to their status in classical Jewish law (*Halakha*). Divided among many countries and cultures, Jewish women in early modern Europe nevertheless shared a common religious tradition. This tradition along with the institutions established to enforce and safeguard it clearly delineated their rights and responsibilities as well as the many restrictions on their lives, whether in France, Germany, England, and Holland or in Hungary, Austria, Italy, Poland, and the Ottoman Empire.

Excluded from the intellectual life of the community, restricted to a peripheral role in its spiritual life, and barred from positions of leadership or authority, Jewish women were expected to devote themselves to the care of the home. This could and often did include managing the family business, thereby permitting the husband to devote himself exclusively to study. Revered and respected within these confines and protected financially by access to their dowry and socially by the cohesiveness of the communities, Jewish women successfully sustained the life of their families. Husband, brother, and father sustained the world of law, learning, and prayer, thanking God daily for making them neither gentile, slave, nor woman.

Throughout the early modern period, Jewish communities enjoyed extensive autonomy. Permitted to adjudicate civil cases according to Jewish law, rabbis and lay leaders exercised considerable authority and significant disciplinary powers. These could be used to protect the legal rights of women, for example, to ensure that a widow received the amount specified in her marriage contract and the capital worth of her dowry. Disciplinary authority could also serve, however, to confine women's activities and punish "deviant behavior." Corporative autonomy also facilitated the creation of numerous Jewish charitable institutions, whether to care for the poor, bury the dead, visit the sick, or provide for orphans. Through these, women could contribute to the well-being of community members.

If the Jews enjoyed the privilege of living according to their particular laws and customs, they also suffered from oppressive taxes, geographical restrictions, and significant limitations on their economic activities. While individual Jewish men accumulated vast fortunes as purveyors, bankers, and traders, the majority remained confined to a life of poverty and petty trading. The wives and daughters of the wealthy court Jews of Germany and Austria took advantage of their access to the non-Jewish world by dressing in the latest fashions and learning the language and literature of the country in which they lived. Unfettered by any formal religious education, they could be more receptive to non-Jewish culture than their husbands or fathers. Their less affluent sisters, however, interacted with the non-Jewish world primarily in the markets, where they traded used clothing or peddled their wares. One need only turn to the seventeenth-century ethical writings of Glückel of Hameln, a mother of 14 and a businesswoman of great acumen, to appreciate the determination, spiritual strength, practical wisdom, and enduring insecurity and insularity that characterized these women's lives.

Predictably, sources pertaining to the individual lives of Jewish women are rare. Those that do exist, however, testify to an unexpected diversity considering the pervasive influence of Jewish law and the social, religious, and intellectual barriers separating Jews from their fellow countrymen. The variations one finds in the lives of Jewish women not merely reflect significant differences of location and class but also reveal that throughout this period individual Jewish women exercised leadership, engaged in intellectual debate with non-Jewish luminaries, and challenged rabbis and lay leaders by successfully turning to non-Jewish courts of law. Sara Copia Sullam, a seventeenth-century Venetian poet, singer, and composer, who was well versed in Greek philosophy and the classical languages and was considered "dear to men of taste as well as to those who understand and cultivate Italian poetry," proudly and successfully defended her faith before the Italian poet Ansaldo Ceba's entreaties to convert. Rozette of Alsace, the widow of a wealthy eighteenth-century banker, defied the male members of her husband's family, the community authorities, and the local non-Jewish courts by successfully pleading her case before the Metz Parliament. As a result she inherited her husband's vast wealth and almost succeeded in destroying the juridical autonomy of the Metz Jewish community.

Most richly documented is the participation of Jewish women in the salons of eighteenth-century Berlin. For a brief, but intense, moment, social class, intellectual brilliance, and the ideals of German *Aufkalrung* (enlightenment) permitted women like Rahel Varnhagen, Dorothea Mendelssohn, and Henriette Herz to capture the minds and hearts of Germany's brightest young men. (See SALIONÈRE.) Having successfully rebelled against their tradition and their status, however, these women found little spiritual satisfaction or religious significance in the Judaism offered by the reformers. All formally converted to Christianity.

"The wife is content," the eighteenth-century Jewish philosopher Solomon Maimon asserted, "if only in return for her toils she becomes in some measure a partaker of her husband's fame and future blessedness." This simple description may have characterized the ambition of many Jewish women in early modern Europe; it hardly suffices for the whole story.

References. Deborah Hertz, *Mixed Company: The Jewish Salons of Eighteenth-Century Berlin* (New Haven, Conn., 1987); M. Lowenthal (ed. and trans.), *The Memoirs of Glückel of Hameln* (New York, 1977); Solomon Maimon, *An Autobiography*, Moses Hadas (ed.) (New York, 1967), 17.

FRANCES G. MALINO

JEWISH WOMEN. From the Eighteenth Century living in Western, Central, and Eastern Europe and the United States acquired increasing access to education, both secular and Jewish; to career opportunities; to secular political leadership; and to increased participation in religious study and ritual. The modern period in Jewish history is generally dated from the beginnings of political and social emancipation in Western Europe during the eighteenth century, which gradually extended eastward to Central and Eastern Europe. The impact of these developments on women's lives and the question of whether history written from women's perspective would date modernity differently has yet to be explored by historians (Hyman and Cohen). No comprehensive history of Jewish women in the modern period in any geographical area has been written, and even recent standard texts of Jewish history by Salo Baron and Robert Seltzer barely mention women's existence. Jewish women in North Africa and Palestine experienced fewer changes in their lives during the eighteenth, nineteenth, and twentieth centuries until the mass migrations to France and Palestine in the twentieth century.

Modernity's effects on the lives of Jewish women are ambiguous. While introducing new options, both secular and religious, modernity also meant the end of many religious practices central to women's traditional Jewish culture and a decrease in women's control over areas of communal responsibility as Jews increasingly left rural and village life for middle-class existence in urban areas. Synagogue reforms, including the elimination of the separate women's section from non-Orthodox synagogues, led to some equality of participation in synagogue services but also brought an end to the autonomy and leadership exercised within the women's section. Similarly, urbanization brought charity under the control of men, who distributed it through large organizations; this meant that women suffered a loss of power and prestige, since in village life charity had been in the hands of women, affording them a vehicle for social influence. However, modernity has seen a shift in Jewish identity from objective factors—the degree of ritual observance—to subjective factors—the emotional identification with family celebrations. Thus, modernity's shift from synagogue to home as the center of Judaism has brought an increase in women's control over Jewish identity formation through family-centered religious practices (see Kaplan).

Education in secular matters was traditionally not forbidden to women, and Jewish parents of wealthier classes frequently engaged tutors to teach their daughters foreign languages, literature, music, and the arts. This secular education seems to have enabled Jewish women to assimilate more easily than men. The famous salons run by Jewish women in Berlin in the late eighteenth and early nineteenth centuries represent the first formal intellectual bridges between Jews and Christians. However, Jewish education—training in Hebrew—was traditionally denied Jewish women, thus barring them from the study of Jewish texts, including the Bible, the Talmud, and their commentaries, which had, over the centuries, formed the core of Jewish men's intellectual discourse. Traditional Jewish education for girls first became widespread in the modern period as religious schools were opened to counter tendencies toward assimilation. By the 1980s the major non-Orthodox rabbinical schools in the United States and England were ordaining women rabbis.

Secular leadership became impossible for Jewish women in the modern period as Jews were increasingly emancipated from political and social disabilities in Europe and the United States. Jewish women figure importantly in movements of political change (e.g., Rosa Luxembourg and Emma Goldman) and social welfare improvement (e.g., Lilian Wald and Bertha Pappenheim). Within the Jewish community women became leaders of Reform Judaism in England (e.g., Lily Montague) and of secular and Zionist women's organizations (e.g., Sadie American and Henrietta Szold). Women also became important figures in the development of modern Hebrew and Yiddish literature (e.g., Leah Goldberg and Kadie Molodowsky).

References. Charlotte Baum, Paula Hyman, and Sonya Michel, *The Jewish Woman in America* (New York, 1975); Paula Hyman and Steven M. Cohen, *The Jewish Family: Myth and Reality* (New York, 1986); Marion Kaplan in Paula Hyman and Steven M. Cohen, *The Jewish Family: Myth or Reality* (New York, 1986).

SUSANNAH HESCHEL

JEWISH WOMEN. Rabbinic Attitudes toward Women were first expressed in the Mishnah, a law code based on centuries of scriptural interpretation and daily practice, compiled by like-thinking scholars (rabbis) in the early third century C.E. Ultimately, the Mishnah, enlarged with generations of commentary (the Gemara), evolved into the Talmud, which became the basic text of Jewish life, governance, and religious practice from the sixth to the twentieth centuries. While the rabbis believed that the Talmud authoritatively interpreted biblical revelation, it is unknown which of its numerous laws and ordinances were actually in effect at the time they were recorded. Thus, rabbinic views of the relation between male and female may reflect an ideal vision rather than a contemporary reality. Nevertheless, these attitudes became the guidebook and practical pattern for ensuing forms of Jewish life.

Rabbinic Judaism, like many conservative societies, places women at a severe disadvantage in the legal, religious, and social realms of life. Since rabbinic Judaism emerged from a patriarchal tradition, woman is considered only as she falls under male control and provides for male needs. As long as women fulfill male expectations, they are revered and honored. Rabbinic literature is not lacking in words of praise for the supportive, resourceful, and self-sacrificing wife, nor is there a lack of concern for a woman's physical and emotional needs and welfare. Moreover, historically, efforts were made to ameliorate some of her worst legal disabilities. All good for the woman, however, is predicated on her remaining a separate and subordinate entity.

Woman's dependent status can be illustrated in a number of ways. In a court of law women are generally unacceptable witnesses; in this instance, as a number of others, women are consigned to the same category as slaves and children. In terms of religious observance, women are exempt from most regular obligations, especially those bound to be performed communally at specified times: these include prayer and study, which was itself seen as a form of prayer. As a consequence, women are excluded from religious activities that take place in the public sphere and from those endeavors, particularly intellectual pursuits, that confer social and religious status. It has been suggested that women are exempt from time-linked commandments because of family responsibilities that might prevent their regularly fulfilling them. This may have some validity, but the exemption of women from the most central activities of Jewish life is also a profound statement of rabbinic Judaism's view of woman as a being separate from man and deficient in religious capacities and needs. Since women are denied religious personhood together with males who are in some way incomplete, damaged, or dependent, they join the category of those who are denied access to sanctity because they diverge from normal male completeness. One of the most revelatory indications of rabbinic Judaism's male-centered system of reality is still a part of traditional Jewish practice. This is a threefold prayer that men recite daily, thanking God for not making them a gentile, a slave, or a woman.

Woman's otherness from man is stressed throughout rabbinic literature. While women are credited with more compassion and concern for the unfortunate than men, perhaps as a result of their maternal roles, they are also linked with witchcraft, wantonness, licentiousness, and sexual abandon. Despite biblical examples of vigorous and resourceful women and in the face of influential and admirable women of their own times, the rabbis generally diminish women's abilities and qualities in their scriptural exegeses, general comments, and personal anecdotes. Thus, Beruriah, the wife of the second-century sage Rabbi Meir, and virtually the only woman described by the Talmud as learned in Jewish law, is transformed in some traditions into an adulteress and a suicide.

Some recent scholarship has approached rabbinic Judaism's attitudes toward women from an anthropological stance, employing the concept of public and private domains to explain the sharp dichotomy created between men and women. The distinction between culture and nature, in which culture is assigned to men and perceived as both separate from, and superior to, women's realm of nature, is also useful: when they are defined almost exclusively in terms of their natural—that is sexual—functions, which are often frightening or threatening to men, women appear anomalous and must be separated. Indeed, rabbinic Judaism is very anxious to circumscribe, defuse, and control the sexual attributes of the female as both polluter and temptress. Thus, a perception of women as unclean, due to menstrual and postpartum discharges, is fundamental to the rabbinic separation of women, for the unclean woman is a potential source of pollution to male holiness. Not only sexual relations but any physical contact between husband and wife are prohibited for nearly half of each month until the wife has been ritually purified of her periodic uncleanness. Similarly, women are also dangerous to men through the stimulation of sexual desire. If the menstruating woman should not enter the synagogue at all (according to some views), the nonmenstruating woman must sit separately and out of sight so that men will not be distracted from their prayers by her enticing presence. The rabbinic remark that woman is "a pitcher full of filth with its mouth full of blood, yet all run after her" (Babylonian Talmud Shabbat 152a) is in its own terms less an opinion than a statement of fact. In rabbinic Judaism's worldview, a woman incarnates her disturbing and anomalous differences from men and therefore must be maintained in a specific and limited realm of the ordinary where her fearful powers will be under male control.

References. Judith R. Baskin, "The Separation of Women in Rabbinic Judaism," in Y. Y. Haddad and E. B. Findly (eds.), *Women, Religion and Social Change* (Albany, N.Y., 1985); R. Biale, *Women and Jewish Law* (New York, 1995); Judith Hauptman, "Feminist Perspectives on Rabbinic Texts," in L. Davidman and S. Tenenbaum (eds.), *Feminist Perspectives on Jewish Studies* (New Haven, Conn., 1994), 40–61.

JUDITH R. BASKIN

JUDGES in the United States have long been dominated by white, middle-class male lawyers with strong local connections. Because of the high visibility of U.S. Supreme Court Justices Sandra Day O'Connor and Ruth Bader Ginsberg, many people don't realize that there are proportionately far fewer women judges than there are women legislators. For example, in 1995, although more than 20 percent of state legislators were women, only about 10 percent of state court judges were women.

There are two important questions related to women in judicial office: why are there so few women judges, and do women judges make any difference?

It has always been, and remains, more difficult for women than men to succeed in attaining and retaining high political office in the United States. It has been even more difficult for women to attain judicial office than other public office for several reasons. First, women judges must meet high standards of education and experience to be eligible for judicial office. Aspirants must have graduate law degrees; often, successful candidates must also have from 5 to 10 years or more of legal experience. Second, judges are selected in complicated ways that make women judicial candidates dependent on their ability to build strong professional and personal reputations among the mostly male and often conservative legal circles that influence judicial selections. Third, the qualifications needed to build such reputations are generally based on the career paths to the bench followed by male judges. Yet, women lawyers as a group do not follow the same career paths as white males. For example, women are much less likely to hold partnerships in large, corporate law firms, a common route to federal judicial office.

The eligible pool theory explains the lack of women judges by the fact that relatively few women lawyers possess the same educational, political, and career credentials held by men who successfully attained the bench. Thus, the small percentage of women judges is not due to gender bias but is simply a reflection of the small eligible pool of women. There are two flaws in this theory. One, although it does account for part of the under-representation of women on the bench, it does not account for all, and it does not explain the wide range from state to state in the gender composition of their courts. Two, so long as the traditional male career patterns remain the standard for judgeships, the eligible pool of potential women judges may appear smaller than it actually is.

Studies of the backgrounds of federal lower-court judges appointed by all presidents since 1976 clearly indicate that women are more likely to be younger, less politically active, and engaged in public service law than traditional male appointees. The reality is that career opportunities for women lawyers have been more plentiful in the public sector than in the private sector. Yet, there is no reason to believe that practicing corporate law better prepares a lawyer to be a judge than practicing law as a public defender. It seems that one key to increasing the number of women judges may be to take into account gender differences in career patterns in evaluating women's qualifications for office.

The impact of an expansion of traditional standards for judicial qualifications based on a historical male model can be seen in the federal courts. Changing attitudes by just four U.S. presidents (Carter, Reagan, Bush, and Clinton) dramatically altered the gender composition of the federal bench and increased the number of women judges from 5 in 1976 to 120 by July 1994. Prior to President Carter's term of office, only 8 women had ever served as federal judges in the entire history of the United States. Carter deliberately encouraged women to apply and took some of the "old boy" political influence out of the nominating process by establishing merit nominating commissions with both men and women members. Carter went on to appoint 11 women to the U.S. Appeals Courts and 29 to the District Courts. Although Reagan disbanded the nominating commissions and did not appoint as many women judges as did Carter, he made history by appointing the first woman to the Supreme Court. President Bush continued this new tradition, and by 1992, when President Clinton took office, women constituted 11 percent of the federal bench. Clinton in only two years raised the ratio of women to 14 percent and appointed a second woman to the Supreme Court. By all accounts, these federal court women judges have been as good as, or better than, their male colleagues in performing their judicial duties.

Unfortunately, no such dramatic change has taken place in the gender composition of the state court system, although the number of women judges has increased considerably. Accurate counts of state court women judges, especially limited jurisdiction judges, are very difficult to come by due to a lack of centralized record keeping. A rare 1996 study found a 54 percent increase in the number of women general jurisdiction trial court judges from 1987 to 1996. However, this sizable increase in numbers represented only a 1.2 percent increase in women's share of the states' general jurisdiction trial court benches because of the large increase in the total number of such judges in the same time period. In 1987, 20 states had never had a woman supreme court justice. By 1992, 39 women sat on 32 state supreme courts, and only 10 states had never had a woman supreme court justice. In 1991, Minnesota became the first state to have a female majority (four of seven justices) on its supreme court. In 1997, Michigan became the second state, although by that time Minnesota had lost its female majority due to a retirement.

Since the 1980s there have been important changes in the gender composition of the legal profession. As a consequence of changing public attitudes and broader opportunities for women, more women are going to law schools. In 1980, only 8 percent of lawyers were women; by 1992, that figure had risen to 19 percent. With women's law school enrollments approaching 50 percent, the percentages of lawyers who are women will continue to increase, although there will still be a time lag for those desiring judicial office to acquire the requisite professional experience. In 1979, a National Association of Women Judges was founded to push for increased appointments of women judges and to assist women lawyers in running judicial campaigns. By 1995, its membership included both justices O'Connor and Ginsberg and over half of the other women judges in the country. With the many illustrious federal and state court women judges as role models, we can presume that many more women lawyers will aspire to the bench. Thus, the numbers of women judges will no doubt continue to increase steadily, perhaps even dramatically, if changes are made in the selection processes.

What difference will such an increase in women judges make in the operation of our courts? A new field of feminist jurisprudence argues that a significant increase in women lawyers and judges will have a profound impact on the law because of their personal, gendered experiences in our sexist society. For example, the first woman on the U.S. Supreme Court, Justice Sandra Day O'Connor, has told of her difficulties in establishing her legal career. When she graduated from Stanford Law School near the top of her class, the only job offered her in California was as a legal secretary. The second woman on the Supreme Court, Justice Ruth Bader Ginsberg, has written of the "chill wind" that blew against her and the few other women in law schools in the 1960s, making them feel unwelcome.

If women, as a consequence of these kinds of experiences, bring to the bench a different set of attitudes or perspectives on legal issues than do their male colleagues, they should decide these issues differently. The relatively small number of women judges, their dispersal across the country, and the relatively short time most have been in office create problems for researchers trying to determine if these gender differences exist. In 1993, a special issue of *Judicature* brought together the most recent research on this question. The thrust of the findings, from a variety of courts, supported the position that women judges are making a distinctive contribution to our legal system in areas involving issues of gender fairness. It does not appear that women judges have a special and distinct perspective on all types of cases that reach the courts. However, it certainly does appear that the presence of women judges could help to counterbalance any one-sided perspectives of an all-male bench in areas such as divorce, domestic violence, juvenile justice, damages, and sentencing. Particularly in new and still-developing areas of the law such as woman's rights, where precedent may be an inadequate guide, indications are that our new women appellate judges may help break new ground.

Reference. "Women on the Bench: A Different Voice?" *Judicature* 77, 3 (November–December 1993).

ELAINE MARTIN

JURORS. Women jurors were almost unknown until well into the twentieth century. Under common law, adopted by the American colonies, jury service was restricted to males. In 1879, the U.S. Supreme Court sanctioned this practice, saying that while states could no longer restrict jury service to whites due to the passage of the Fourteenth Amendment, they could continue to restrict it to males (*Strauder v. West Virginia*, 100 U.S. 303 1879).

During the nineteenth century efforts to include women on juries were sparse and short-lived. In 1870 Wyoming became the first state or territory to permit women to serve as jurors. It did so because transient male jurors were unwilling to convict lawbreakers. This experiment ended after three court terms when the judge who had initiated it resigned in 1871 and was replaced by a judge opposed to woman suffrage. Washington Territory assumed that the obligation to serve on juries followed from suffrage. This assumption and the resulting practice of mixed juries survived a court challenge in 1884, but three years later the territorial court reversed its position and excluded women from territorial juries. In 1896 Utah became the first state to include women on juries. Of the 15 states that extended full suffrage to women prior to the passage of the Nineteenth Amendment, only 5 also permitted women to serve as jurors.

Even after the Nineteenth Amendment in 1920 extended the right to vote to women, many states continued the practice of all-male juries. Opposition to women jurors centered around the following arguments: (1) jury service would cause women to neglect their homes and families, (2) women would be embarrassed or upset by the material that they would encounter in courtrooms, (3) jury service would unsex women, (4) women jurors would have difficulty comprehending complex legal arguments, and (5) sequestering female jurors would be difficult. By 1942 only 28 states permitted women jurors. Fifteen of these allowed women to claim exemptions not available to men. The 1957 Civil Rights Act required that women be included on federal jury lists; however, it did not affect state practices. In 1961 the U.S. Supreme Court upheld a Florida statute that required women to register with the clerk of court if they wished to be included in jury lists (*Hoyt v. Florida*, 368 U.S. 57 1961). The Court's rationale was that women's family responsibilities would make jury service a hardship. Since most women could be expected to take advantage of an automatic exemption, the state was justified in requiring those who wished to serve to register.

By 1973 all 50 states permitted women jurors, but 19 provided them exemptions not available to men. As a result, jury lists tended to underrepresent women severely. In 1975 the U.S. Supreme Court held that the practice of excluding women who did not specifically indicate their willingness to serve on juries was unconstitutional because it deprived the accused of a jury drawn from a cross-section of the community (*Taylor v. Louisiana*, 419 U.S. 552 1975). In 1979 the Supreme Court overturned an automatic exemption for women jurors but indicated that a gender-neutral child care exemption would be permissible (*Duncan v. Missouri*, 439 U.S. 357 1979).

The inclusion of women on jury lists does not necessarily result in their representation on jury panels. During their voir dire (an examination of prospective jurors to ascertain that they are competent and objective) attorneys have an opportunity to question prospective jurors and challenge those they believe biased. During this process women are often asked questions about their spouses, their spouses' occupations, and their family life that are not posed to men. In addition, trial practice books frequently provide advice based on sex-role stereotypes. For example, lawyers are advised to avoid women jurors if their clients are women because female jurors tend to be harsher on members of their own sex but to seek women jurors if their clients are attractive young men. Female jurors are also portrayed as unpredictable and tenderhearted, thus good jurors for the defense in criminal cases and for the plaintiff in civil cases. However, since housewives are unaccustomed to handling large sums of money, lawyers should avoid women jurors if their clients are seeking large damage awards.

Research on the relationship between gender and juror performance is limited and somewhat mixed. Nevertheless, it yields a few generalizations. Both male and female jurors tend to favor litigants of their own sex. There appears to be no support for the notion that women jurors are acquittal-prone; in fact, women jurors seem more likely to convict. Finally, female jurors have been found to participate less in deliberations, to be selected to serve as foreperson less frequently, and to be less likely to be judged influential by other jurors.

Reference. A. R. Mahoney, "Women Jurors: Sexism in Jury Selection," in L. Crites and W. Hepperle (eds.), *Women, the Courts, and Equality* (Beverly Hills, Calif., 1989).

JILDA M. ALIOTTA

K

KIBBUTZ is a collective community in Israel (there are currently about 270 such communities). Equality and democracy are among its basic values. To meet these values, it has developed a unique social structure. All major household services are provided by the community: meals are cooked in the communal kitchen and served there; clothes are cleaned, mended, and ironed in the communal laundry; and children are looked after in the children's houses. Thus, many of the traditional household chores are recognized as legitimate full-time work. Women and men are economically independent of each other. All women belong to the workforce. Economic rewards are equal to all and are independent of the work or prestige of one's occupation. Women receive the same economic rewards as men, and a single parent receives the same family supplement for children as a couple receives. Between 40 and 50 percent of the participants in the governing bodies of the kibbutz are women, but they are almost completely absent from boards of economic control.

From the 1950s, two processes that might affect equality between the sexes have become apparent. First, as a result of a growing division of labor, almost all workers in child care, laundry, and kitchen are women, while most of the agricultural and industrial workers are men. Second, the family has become increasingly important in kibbutz communities, as manifested in a higher rate of childbirth, a high rate of marriage, and a relatively low divorce rate. Institutional changes have also occurred. Children sleep in their parents' houses in all the kibbutzim but one, although formerly they slept in children's houses, where they received care and schooling.

A third dramatic process occurred in the mid-1980s. The kibbutz communities suffered from the economic crisis in Israel, and processes of economic decline started. Measures taken to overcome these processes have often affected gender equality by limiting the possibilities of people in nonmanagerial and noneconomic positions (mostly women) from entering into managerial positions and participating in economic decision making.

While the kibbutz social structure was to abolish inequalities, its apparent inability to do away with the sexual division of labor has put it in the center of many studies. Attempts were made to answer four fundamental questions from the kibbutz experience:

1. What are the main sources of sex-role division? The answer to this question deals mainly with the issues of nature versus nurture. On one hand, the failure of sex-role equality on the kibbutz is claimed as support for arguments based on the natural disposition of women to gravitate toward natural female roles; on the other hand, it is maintained that the kibbutz cannot be taken as a test case because of the unfinished nature of its "revolution." On this view, the kibbutz has managed to absorb women in both male and female occupations at one time or another but has still failed to incorporate men into traditionally female occupations.

2. Does sex-role division necessarily lead to inequality between the sexes? Equal opportunities to enter all jobs and offices in the kibbutz exist, although there is always social pressure on women and men to enter the jobs that are perceived to be the responsibility of their gender. This leads to strong pressure on women to continue working in nurturing and service jobs and to a vicious circle that reinforces the sexual division of labor. These jobs carry almost the same prestige as any other nonmanagerial jobs of the same skill level. The most prestigious jobs, however, are in top management and are usually held by men.

3. Does the growing importance of the family lead to inequality? Studies dealing with the division of labor within the family household found that there is little sexual division of labor. This may be changed as children's sleeping quarters have been moved to their parents' houses.

4. Why did the economic prosperity and the high technology not bring about more gender equality? How would the recent economic crisis affect gender equality? Studies showed that when society does not put gender equality as a goal by itself, it will not occur as a by-product of other changes.

Kibbutz members, particularly women, have continuously sought solutions to problems occasioned by the sexual division of labor. Discussions related to this topic date back to 1910, when the first kibbutz was created. An important convention was held in 1966 to deal with the work and political activity of women. In 1982 a united effort to change the situation was made by the two largest kibbutz federations, which established a joint Department for the Advancement of the Equality between the Sexes. One of the measures taken to cope with the situation that resulted from the mid-1980s economic crisis in Israel was a cutback in the central bodies of the kibbutz federation. One of the first departments considered obsolete was the Department for the Advancement of the Equality between the Sexes. At the beginning of the 1990s personnel and budgets were cut back, later the departments were shut down, and some of their functions were passed to other departments, and others were abandoned.

The kibbutz has achieved much in promoting women's equality, but it still has a long way to go. The experiment of the kibbutz brings up questions and solutions that are a fertile ground for the development of feminist theories and practice. Some of the issues it has addressed are the feminization of poverty, economic independence of women, collective child rearing, and the role of community in family life.

References. M. Palgi, "Women in the Changing Kibbutz Economy," in *Economic and Industrial Democracy* 15 (1994): 55–73; M. Palgi, J. Blasi, M. Rosner, and M. Safir, *The Israeli Kibbutz Tests the Theories* (Philadelphia, 1983); E. Ben Rafael and S. Weitman, "The Reconstruction of the Family in the Kibbutz," *European Journal of Sociology* 21 (1984): 1–27.

                                                                    MICHAL PALGI

KOREA. Modern Period. *The Women's Movement* emerged from the first school for women, the Ewha Hakdang (school), founded in 1886, where young Korean women not only learned to read and write but also were introduced to the concepts of political, religious, and personal freedom. On March 1, 1919, a large number of female students and women all over the country participated in the nationwide uprising against Japanese colonial domination. Thereafter, Korean Christian women educated in mission and church schools acted as a main force in anti-Japanese political activities during the Japanese colonization period of 1910 to 1945.

Women's Studies. Ewha Womans University (EWU), successor to the Ewha Hakdang, today leads Korea in feminist education and research, as Korea leads Asia. EWU inaugurated the first women's studies course in 1977; later established a Department of Women's Studies with a master's program; and in the mid-1990s launched a Ph.D. program. In 1984 the Korean Association of Women's Studies was established, and by 1989, 61 colleges and universities were offering women's studies courses. As of 1995, 11 universities, both coeducational and women's, had women's research centers. The Korean Women's Research Institute of EWU established the Asian Center for Women's Studies, which published the first issue of *Asian Journal of Women's Studies* in 1995.

New Women's Movement. Second-wave feminism developed in Korea concurrently with the political and social movements of the 1970s. Women who participated in direct collective actions in the student, labor, democratization, and national unification movements that began in the 1970s founded autonomous women's groups in the 1980s, such as the Korea Women for Equality and Peace (1983), the Korea Women's Hot Line (1983), and the Korea Women's Association for Democracy and Sisterhood (1987). In February 1987, a few months prior to the June Revolt, an umbrella organization, the Korea Women's Associations United (KWAU), composed of over 20 member organizations, was formed.

Defining the Korean women's movement as part of the larger, nation-wide, mass-oriented human rights and democratization movement, KWAU has striven to achieve women's liberation, national unification, and democratization simultaneously through coalition strategies. Their coalition work has made women's agendas visible in the broader political arena by mobilizing a substantial number of women for direct actions (e.g., the first protest against the police use of tear gas against student protesters in the 1980s).

In order to promote consciousness-raising* and solidarity among women of various backgrounds, KWAU inaugurated the annual Korean Women's Conference on World Women's Day, March 8, 1985. In 1987, KWAU initiated the Woman of the Year Award to a woman or a group for contributing toward women's liberation. The first award was given to a former student activist and union organizer, Kwon In Sook, who filed suit against a police officer, Moon Kwi Dong, at the Inchon Local Court on the charge of police rape. Her decision to reveal the police rape was one of a series of events triggering the June 1987 Revolt, which brought about a constitutional change allowing general presidential elections.

Alternative Culture Movement. The women's movement has also been characterized by the emergence of alternative/feminist cultural movements such as Another Culture (1984), which emphasizes a partnership between women and men to create an alternative culture. Feminist work and criticism in the 1980s helped to create an alternative women's culture through artistic expressions of women's experiences from women's perspectives. Women artists, musicians, dramatists, and ritual and dance performers organized the Society for Feminist Culture and Art (1992). Being Ourselves, the first organized group of lesbians in Korea, and the Korean Network for Women, Environment and Sustainable Development were formed in 1995.

Sexual Discrimination. The Korean women's movement has started to challenge practices in the workplace such as the prohibition against, or hindrance of, women workers and union organization; public policies that discriminate against women in employment opportunities, advancement, and retirement; and violence against women in the household, the workplace, and the larger society.

Since the 1980s ad hoc committees composed of women's and other social movement groups have worked together informally in a series of sex discrimination cases. The first case that prompted their coalition work was the police rape of a female political student-prisoner arrested in 1984. A committee of 11 women's organizations brought a charge against the minister of internal affairs and the chiefs of Chongyangree and Sodaemun police stations.

Other committees include the Association of Women's Organizations for the Elimination of Early Retirement at Age of Twenty-five for Women

(1985), the Special Committee for the Legislation of a Special Law against Sexual Violence (1992), and the Joint Committee on the Sexual Harassment Case of a Seoul National University Research Assistant (1993). This 1993 case, brought by a committee of university students and 27 women's organizations, was the first sexual harassment case in the workplace in Korea. In 1995, Women in Solidarity for the 20% Ratio System to Increase Women in the National Assembly was founded by 56 women's organizations to prepare for the June local elections.

Violence against Women. In the 1990s, violence against women has been one of the top priorities of the women's movement. Violence against women includes sexual assault (both date rape and marital rape), women battering, incest, sexual harassment, trafficking in women (prostitution and sexual slavery), and pornography. A series of women's organizations were founded to oppose sexual violence, such as the Korean Council for the Women Drafted for Sexual Slavery by Japan (1990), the Korea Sexual Violence Relief Center (1991), the Crisis Center against Sexual Violence (1993), and the Counseling Center for Family and Sex opened by the Women's Association for Democracy and Sisterhood. The Korea Women's Hot Line initiated the Committee for Legislation on Gender Violence. Later, for a national campaign, KWAU member organizations formed the Special Committee for Legislation on Sexual Violence.

The Korean economic miracle under the authoritarian military regimes of the 1960s and 1970s resulted in continued expansion of the sex industry in Korea. Because of media exposure of the allegedly high rate of HIV positive prostitutes in the Asian sex tourist industry, there has been an increased demand for young "virgin" girls. The shortage of supply of young girls for the ever-expanding sex industry has been one cause of the increased use of violence, such as luring and kidnapping, to secure recruits. In 1995, it was estimated that there were approximately 6,000 women and young girls in Korea in virtual imprisonment, being locked into "involuntary" prostitution.

Peace and National Unification. Korean feminists, in coalition with foreign feminist activists and researchers concerned with military prostitution, have been involved with resistance against the presence of the U.S. military and foreign interferences that hinder Korean national unification. The 1992 violent sexual assault and murder of Yu Keum Hee and other acts of violence by U.S. military personnel against Koreans have ignited the anti-American movement in recent years. Protesters demand a revision of the existing Status of Forces Agreement and the withdrawal of U.S. military forces from Korea.

The 1995 rape of an elementary school girl by three American soldiers in Okinawa caused an uproar in Korea against both the United States' and Japan's 50-year-long militarization of Okinawa. These incidences of military violence against women raised consciousness among women in Korea,

Okinawa, and Japan and made them recognize the connection between Japan's military "comfort women" (sex slaves drafted by Japan during World War II) and American military violence against the poor, neocolonized women in Korea and Okinawa. By realizing the interconnection between militarism, commodification of female sexuality, racism, and class oppression, the movement to oppose violence against women in war and peace has become the focal point of Korea's women's movement.

KWAU member organizations have been in the forefront in planning and participating in a series of annual meetings on "Women and Peace in Asia" held since 1991, where Korean women from North and South Korea and from Japan have opened a dialogue on women's responsibilities in achieving Korean national unification and peace in Asia. A historic meeting of groups of ordinary citizens from North and South, authorized by the two governments for the first time since the division of Korea in 1945, was held in Pyongyang in 1992. At this meeting, four South Korean and four North Korean military "comfort women"/sexual slavery survivors burst into tears, embracing each other after sharing their stories.

"Comfort Women"/Sex Slaves. At an international conference on "Women and Tourism" held in 1988 by the Korean Church Women United, one of the member organizations of KWAU working on the issue of sex tourism and prostitution since 1970, Professor Yun Chung-Ok, the pioneer researcher on the "comfort women," presented the first research report on the issue since the end of World War II. Her report galvanized participants from all over the Asian and Pacific region, helping to launch the Asian Women in Solidarity for "Comfort Women" Movement in 1992.

The issue of Japan's military "comfort women"/sexual slavery confronts women's sexual oppression in its totality by relating it to the structures of colonial, military, state, race, and class oppression. In the 1990s, the Asian Women in Solidarity for Japan's Military "Comfort Women"/Sexual Slavery Movement has become the cutting edge of the emerging global feminist movement against violence against women.

Reference. Alice Yun Chai, "Integrative Feminist Politics in the Republic of Korea," in Lois West (ed.), *Nationalist Feminisms* (New York, 1997).

ALICE YUN CHAI

KOREA. Traditional Period. At some time between the first century B.C and the fourth century A.D., Korean society, which had been organized into loose tribal federations, was reorganized into several states. The earliest description of Korea from this period is in the *Wei-chih*, a third-century Chinese history that includes observations recorded by troops sent to Korea to reclaim Chinese colonial posts. This eyewitness account describes the northern peoples as more developed socially and politically than those in the south. The Puyŏ people who settled along the Sungari River in Manchuria and the Koguryŏ people in southern Manchuria and the northwestern part of the Korean peninsula were close to achieving statehood. The Puyŏ practiced uxorilocal marriage (marriage in which husbands reside with the families of their brides). The Puyŏ and the Koguryŏ both practiced polygamy and enforced strict laws against jealous women. The *Wei-chih* is less informative on the Korean peoples inhabiting the southern part of the peninsula, saying very little about their social structure. They are described as still being organized into tribal federations; they, too, soon achieved statehood.

Political structures in Korea stabilized into what is known as the Three Kingdoms: Koguryŏ in Manchuria and the northern peninsula, Silla in the southeast, and Paekche in the southwest. Buddhism was introduced sometime in the fourth century, and all three kingdoms embraced it as a state religion. (See BUDDHISM.) To promote centralization, the three kingdoms also adopted from China a basic Confucian bureaucratic structure. The adoption of a Confucian bureaucracy did not affect indigenous social structure, which was a rigid class society based on birth. This was particularly true of Silla, which conquered Koguryŏ and Paekche and unified the peninsula in 668.

Silla observed what is known as the system of bone rank. The bone rank was the level of aristocratic rank, which determined one's education and official post. What is noticeable about the Silla bone rank system was that children's bone ranks were determined by both parents' bone ranks in equal measure. Though only men were allowed a public life in most instances, in the royal succession, class superseded gender. Thus, there were three female rulers in Silla who were the last of their bone rank. The throne passed to them before passing to males at the next level of bone rank. In fact, among the aristocracy, succession, inheritance, and surnames often seem to have passed through daughters' descendants. Marriage custom in the Silla included polygamy and endogamy.

The Koryŏ dynasty (918–1392) adopted a more elaborate Confucian bureaucracy as well as a civil service examination. Confucianism, however, remained confined to the political sphere, while Buddhism maintained its popularity in the religious sphere. The rigid class structure and the small ruling elite, within which power was perpetuated, remained intact, though status now came to depend on official post. Women were excluded from public life altogether, and royal succession was limited to the male line. Women did continue to play an important role in the domestic sphere. In private life, women enjoyed a fair degree of freedom and independence. Families of royal consorts, for instance, exerted a great influence on politics. Among aristocratic and official families, a daughter received an equal share of inheritance. Marriage was uxorilocal. Thus, a daughter and her husband played a role at least as important as that of her brothers in matters concerning her natal home. As men were allowed to have several wives, this sometimes resulted in visiting husbands. Divorce and remarriage were common. In the case of divorce, both spouses had an equal claim on children. A woman was permitted to be a head of household. Presumably, women were allowed to pursue religious vocations, but information is sparse—not a great deal of literature from this period is extant. Love songs produced toward the end of the Koryŏ depict passionate women.

The Chosŏn dynasty (1392–1910) was founded on Neo-Confucian ideology, and the dichotomy that allotted Confucianism to the public/political sphere and Buddhism and indigenous social customs to the religious/private sphere was no longer acceptable. From its inception, the Chosŏn government engaged in full-scale social engineering to transform Korea into a Confucian normative society. This required restructuring the family system along patrilineal and patriarchal lines. Confucian funereal and mourning rites were adopted, as was ancestor worship. (See CONFUCIANISM.)

Native Korean customs concerning women were gradually changed. Equestrianism among women, which had been common, was now forbidden. Women were also prohibited from associating with men who were beyond a certain degree of kinship. Uxorilocal marriage became less frequent. Remarriage of *yangban* (the hereditary upper class from which the bureaucracy was staffed) women virtually ended by the sixteenth century. Women could no longer be heads of household, and, in the case of divorce, they lost all claim to their children. Those customs that granted daughters rights equal to those of sons lasted longer. Contrary to Confucian norms, which required that male descendants perform ancestral rites, daughters shared ritual duties on a rotating basis. Daughters also continued to enjoy equal inheritance. By the mid-seventeenth century, however, daughters were losing ground in their rights to property and ritual heirship, and the adoption of an agnatic kin when there were daughters became widespread. One native custom that persisted through the adoption of patriarchy was the contribution that a woman's status made in determining that of her descendants. In the case of the *yangban* family, only children by a legal *yangban* wife became full-fledged *yangban*. Children of commoner or slave concubines, however illustrious their father may have been, were not full-fledged *yangban* and were discriminated against within the family and in public life.

In the realm of popular religion, women dominated. Shamans were predominantly women, and, unlike China, where male shamans presided over important rites, in Korea female shamans were in charge of every aspect of shamanistic ritual.

The Chosŏn period also produced women poets, painters, and writers. The Korean alphabet was devised in the fifteenth century, and while elite males continued to write in classical Chinese, women wrote in Korean. The first substantial autobiography written in Korean was written by a woman in the early nineteenth century, and it is one of the major classics of Korean literature.

Reference. Sandra Mattielli (ed.), *Virtues in Conflict* (Seoul, 1977).

JAHYUN KIM HABOUSH

L

LABOR, ORGANIZED (TO c. 1888, U.S.). The relationship between organized labor and women began with early industrialization in the Northeast. Many women worked as factory girls in textile mills in New England and even more worked at home for systems of outwork production in boots and shoes, garments, and hats throughout the northeastern states. The experiences of working for wages under the time discipline of factory life contrasted sharply with the female experience of unpaid household production for family subsistence before 1820. A dual model of appropriate work for women took shape in the early nineteenth century: the unmarried factory girl and the homebound wife who occasionally supplemented family income with paid work.

Women's involvement in labor protest started as early as the opening of the first factories. (See WORKER MILITANCY.) New England textile operatives conducted strikes against low wages in 1821, 1824, and 1827, while the turnouts in Lowell, Massachusetts, in the 1830s and 1840s marked the emergence of the first labor union organized and led by women workers. These early women's organizations cooperated with workingmen's associations that were active in the 1840s. Sarah Bagley of the Lowell Female Labor Reform Association edited *The Voice of Industry* and organized political activity among workingwomen in support of a 10-hour day. To justify their rebelliousness, New England textile operatives, like many protesting artisans and mechanics in the 1840s, identified with the rights won by their forebears in the American Revolution, specifically by evoking their status as "daughters of freemen." Many female industrial workers throughout the nineteenth century called on their common experience of womanhood to complement their sense of class consciousness.

Labor protest and organization were more difficult for women outworkers who worked for low wages in their homes in isolation from other workers. Most remained passive, but some shoe workers in Essex County, Massachusetts, and outworkers in New York City, Philadelphia, Newark, and other northeastern cities complained vociferously about working conditions and low wages and organized protests. Whether they worked at home or in the new factories, the economic relations of early industrialization influenced the work and lives of many nineteenth-century women.

Most women's employment was in light industries that made cotton and woolen textiles, garments, shoes, hats, collars, paper, and carpets and printed books and newspapers. Their work was characterized by a sexual division of labor that for many of them meant low wages, low status, and poor working conditions. Patriarchal values in the family and the factory combined to direct working girls into temporary unskilled work with low wages and little future. Women seldom experienced formal apprenticeships and could not depend on the craft customs of male workers. Their status as temporary workers without skills seemed to threaten male jobs and resulted in the exclusion of women from trade union activity except when male unionists wished to control their presence in the industrial workplace. The family wage, one of the major goals of nineteenth-century trade unions, did not include the wages of workingwomen but rather applied to all male workers, whether married or unmarried.

In industries where the sexual division of labor prevented competition between men and women over work, cooperative relations often developed. In these situations, women workers in the textile, collar-making, parasol-making, bookbinding, shoemaking, and carpet-weaving industries developed and led their own organizations. The disruptive impact of Civil War casualties and westward migration on marriage forced many women reluctantly into the labor market and, after the war years, created a diverse female labor force that included self-supporting women and female heads of families as well as young, single factory girls and wives who returned to the workforce during times of depression. Balancing work, family responsibilities, ethnic ties, and gender expectations, some of these women fought to build their own unions, pursued power for female interests within the national labor movement, and developed connections with the woman's rights movement.

In the National Labor Union of the late 1860s and the Knights of Labor in the 1880s, women members organized committees on women's work. They made common cause with women in different industries and regions and debated the importance of suffrage and temperance. As Knights of Labor, carpet weavers, textile workers, and shoe stitchers formed alliances on the community and national levels to gain power and representation for workingwomen. Within the Knights, however, two different and conflicting ideological positions on workingwomen limited the effectiveness of these efforts. The first was a moral critique of industrial capitalism based on the values of family life and domesticity. Women's natural sphere remained the home, not the workplace, and although women were welcome in the Knights' assemblies, they were expected to leave the workforce after marriage. The second position was a general commitment to equal rights for workingmen and workingwomen. Equality of rights was championed by women workers in the textile and shoe industries in the Northeast who fought for representation for women in the Knights and for autonomous female assemblies. In 1886 they persuaded the Knights to appoint Leonora Barry, a hosiery worker from New York, to investigate the conditions of workingwomen and encourage their organization. After 1886, however, many of these activists left the Knights for trade union organizations that later joined the American Federation of Labor.

References. Mary H. Blewett, *Men, Women, and Work: The Study of Class, Gender, and Protest in the Nineteenth-Century New England Shoe Industry* (Urbana, Ill., 1988); Thomas Dublin, *Transforming Women's Work: New England Lives in the Industrial Revolution* (Ithaca, N.Y., 1994); Susan Levine, *Labor's True Woman: Carpet Weavers, Industrialization, and Labor Reform in the Gilded Age* (Philadelphia, 1984); Theresa Anne Murphy, *Ten Hours' Labor: Religion, Reform, and Gender in Early New England* (Ithaca, N.Y., 1992); Carole Turbin, *Working Women of Collar City: Gender, Class, and Community in Troy, 1864–86* (Urbana, Ill., 1992); David A. Zonderman, *Aspirations and Anxieties: New England Workers and the Mechanized Factory System, 1815–1850* (New York, 1992).

MARY H. BLEWETT

LABOR, ORGANIZED (MODERN, U.S.), and women have had a limited and strained relationship for the past century. From the 1890s to the present, an increasing, but relatively small, percentage of women workers have joined trade unions. In 1900 only 3.3 percent of women wage earners belonged to unions. Eighty years later, almost 16 percent of workingwomen were members of the labor movement as compared to 29 percent of workingmen. Women's relatively low union representation has been attributed to the organization and policies of American trade unions, the composition of the female workforce, and the structure of the labor market. These reasons are integrally intertwined.

In the early twentieth century, women were inhibited from participating in the American labor movement because of the exclusionist policies of trade unions and the gender-segregated nature of the American labor market. The American Federation of Labor (AFL), which dominated the labor movement from its founding in 1886 until the establishment of the Congress of Industrial Organizations (CIO) in 1935, primarily represented skilled, white, male workers who came originally from Northern and Western Europe. These AFL members were chiefly employed in transportation, communications, mining, construction, metalworking, and shipbuilding. In contrast, women, blacks, and immigrants from Southern and Eastern Europe were barely represented in the trades of the federation. Women worked in largest proportions in the very occupations that were weakest in labor organization among men. In 1910, for example, more than 56 percent of women wage earners worked in the fields of domestic and personal service, trade, professional service, and the clerical occupations, but in that year fewer than 17 percent of men were employed in the same groups. Only in the clothing, textile, and shoe industries did significant numbers of women have an opportunity to join labor organizations.

There is a controversy among scholars about women's attitudes toward trade unions in the era of the AFL. Some historians argue that women were not interested in union membership because they typically worked only until marriage, when they would withdraw from the labor force until or unless their husband's earnings were diminished or terminated by layoffs, work accidents, or in the event of desertion, illness, or death. Other specialists focus on the adverse effects of union policies on women's participation in the labor movement. The AFL refused to grant separate charters to groups of women who were excluded from all-male unions on the grounds that individual organizations had the ultimate authority for setting their admission policies. Women foundry workers, streetcar conductors, coal miners, and barbers, among others, were barred from joining unions in their fields. When women entered industries with strong craft traditions, union men protested their hiring, struck against women's employment, and invoked or sponsored protective legislation to bar women from working in the same fields or on the same terms as men.

Only in industries where women were employed in large numbers did male unionists accept women's admittance to their organizations and then only reluctantly in order to protect their own economic interests. Last, even when the AFL unions professed a commitment to organizing women, little was done to realize the goal. The AFL left the task of organizing women to the National Women's Trade Union League, a coalition of middle- and working-class women that had only limited success in dealing with the AFL unions. Even in the most progressive city labor federations, there was a profound and persistent suspicion that women wage earners would break strikes, rob men of their jobs, and undermine union wage scales. Women who entered nontraditional jobs during World War I lost their positions after the war, at least, in part, because AFL unions promoted sexual and racial segregation in the American labor force.

The Congress of Industrial Organizations, founded in 1935, was a federation of affiliated industrial labor unions that organized workers in the mass-production industries. Originally established within the AFL, it was independent of the craft federation from 1938 to 1955. The CIO was officially against sex and race discrimination. Although it initially organized the automobile, steel, and rubber industries, which employed few women, it also organized the textile, meat-packing, and electrical industries, where large numbers of women worked. As a result of CIO unionization campaigns, women became organizers, rank-and-file union leaders, stewards, committee members, convention delegates, and union officers. Most female union activists were single and tended to be inspired either by left-wing political ideologies or by the commitment of their family members to the labor movement. Despite women's gains under the CIO, they were unrepresented at conventions and almost entirely excluded from the national offices and policy-making decisions of most CIO unions.

Like the AFL unions, the CIO advocated equal pay for equal work as a way of preventing the substitution of women for men at lower wages. Since women did not usually perform the same work as men, few women benefited from the equal wage policy. During the extreme labor shortage of World War II, however, women who filled men's jobs earned men's wages for the duration of the war. The CIO's commitment to the seniority principle tended to depress women's occupational opportunities. In practice, seniority meant that women, who were usually the last hired, were the first to be fired in the event of labor force reductions. The CIO unions did not always even defend the job rights of experienced women workers. Some contract agreements prohibited the employment of married women and required single women to resign upon marriage. The labor unions also insisted on classifying jobs as male or female, with separate wage rates and seniority agreements that limited women's job opportunities. The CIO shared responsibility for reinforcing occupational sex segregation and women's inferior position in the labor force, even though it improved the conditions of labor and wages for those women covered by its collective bargaining agreements.

The principal constituency of the CIO and the AFL has been blue-collar workers. Even in 1940 the blue-collar sector employed just over 20 percent of women wage earners. In contrast, most workingwomen were employed in white-collar occupations, fields that were only briefly and halfheartedly organized by the CIO in the 1930s and 1940s. Not until the 1970s did trade unions actively organize the white-collar sector.

The most important source of growth in the labor movement since World War II has been unionism among public employees. This trend has brought increasing numbers of women into unions and professional associations that bargain collectively. An unprecedented 40 percent of women wage earners in the public sector (principally in the fields of education, health, social service, and public administration), many of whom are professionals, are represented by collective bargaining units, more than twice the proportion for women workers as a whole. The same percentage of women workers as men workers in the public sector are unionized. As a result of union membership, women have assumed leadership roles in their organizations and brought to the fore issues of particular concern to them.

The increased presence of women workers in public sector labor organizations can be attributed to three factors. Since the mid-1960s unions of public workers have undertaken concerted efforts to expand membership beyond their traditional blue-collar base to include white-collar workers as well. Moreover, the civil rights and women's liberation movements helped legitimate public sector workers' desire for collective representation. An even more fundamental factor has been the dramatic rise in married women's labor force participation since 1950. By 1980, married women with spouses present and school-age children were as likely as single women to be employed outside the home. As permanent members of the workforce, women have been more concerned about their job opportunities, security, and benefits. They consequently have increased their participation in local union activities, achieved election to local and national union offices, and secured employment as union staff members.

Equal pay for work of comparable value, popularly known as comparable worth or pay equity, has been the most important women's issue to emerge from activities of the public sector unions. Comparable worth is aimed at solving the problem of women's low wages, which stems from the persistence of occupational sex segregation. Under comparable worth, women's and men's wage rates would be computed on the basis of such job requirements as skill, training, level of responsibility, and mental and physical exertion. Pay disparities between men and women—which are largely attributable to an artificial sexual division of labor that clusters women workers in lower-paying jobs—would be overcome by demonstrating the comparable worth of numerous kinds of jobs throughout each employment hierarchy. Women could anticipate large pay increases under this reclassification of work.

The women's liberation movement of the 1970s resulted in a number of challenges to the American labor movement. Women wage earners in many fields sued their employers and their unions for denying them equal pay for equal work as well as access to nontraditional jobs. Women also founded two organizations to improve their conditions of labor. The Coalition of Labor Union Women, established in 1974, has brought new visibility to women union leaders within the labor movement, while the group 9 to 5, organized first on a local basis in 1973, has concentrated on the problems of unorganized office workers. The surge in workingwomen's organizations ironically occurred just a few years before the dramatic economic downturn of the early 1980s, which considerably weakened the traditional manufacturing core of labor movement strength. The future of the labor movement depends now, as never before, on the organization of white-collar workers in the public and private sectors. In practical terms, that means the organization of women into collective bargaining units, a challenge that trade unions have only begun to meet. (See also WORKER MILITANCY.)

References. Nancy Schrom Dye, *As Equals and as Sisters: Feminism, the Labor Movement, and the Women's Trade Union League of New York* (Columbia, Mo.,

1980); Maurine Weiner Greenwald, *Women, War, and Work: The Impact of World War I on Women Workers in the United States* (Westport, Conn., 1980); Ruth Milkman (ed.), *Women, Work and Protest: A Century of U.S. Women's Labor History* (Boston, 1985); Barbara M. Wertheimer and Anne H. Nelson, *Trade Union Women: A Study of Their Participation in New York City Locals* (New York, 1975).

MAURINE WEINER GREENWALD

LABOR FORCE PARTICIPATION consists of active employment or actively seeking employment in the paid labor force market. Any individual 16 years of age or older who is currently employed (i.e., working for pay at least one hour in the last week) or who is currently unemployed (i.e., actively seeking employment in the last four weeks) is classified as "in the labor force." Labor force participation (LFP) is usually expressed as a rate:

$$\frac{\substack{\text{Labor Force} \\ \text{Employed + Unemployed}}}{\text{Employed + Unemployed + Out of the Labor force}} \times 100$$

This rate is the percentage of the population engaged in paid labor market activities. The formula has been changed twice, in 1940 and in 1983. Prior to January, 1, 1983, the denominator was the civilian noninstitutional population (i.e., military workers were not included). Before 1940, the concept of labor force was not used. Instead, individuals were classified as "gainfully employed" according to their "usual occupation." Statistics have been adjusted to make them comparable over time.

Women uniformly have lower labor force participation rates than men (in 1993, 57.9 percent and 75.2 percent, respectively); however, there are vast differences in rates among different subgroups of women. Until the mid-1980s, African American women always had higher LFP rates than white women; however, by 1990 this trend had reversed. In 1993, white women's LFP rate was 58.0 percent; African American women, 57.4 percent; and Hispanic women 52.0 percent. Married women have lower LFP (59.4 percent) than single women (66.4 percent).

Although data prior to 1940 are not strictly comparable to today's estimates, a consistent picture has emerged. Female LFP has been increasing since the turn of the century. While popular belief holds that the labor shortages created by World War II served as a catalyst for bringing women into the labor market, this dramatic influx of women into the paid labor market has antecedents at the beginning of this century. In fact, much of the rising LFP in the last two decades represents a return to pre–World War II patterns. The long-term growth trend in female LFP was temporarily interrupted by the high fertility years following World War II (creating the baby boom), when LFP rates were far below historic trends.

The century-long upward trend of women's LFP is explained by changes in the pre-1900 labor market that had inhibited females from paid employment. In 1900, 17 percent of white and 42 percent of black women were in the labor force; however, only 2 percent of white married women were in the labor market. In part, this was a response to very low wages of married women, 30 percent less than those of single white women.

One reason for low levels of female LFP was that few jobs were available, since women were confined to employment in only a few occupations and industries. Usually, this employment resembled the tasks women performed in household production. Before the large demand for women clerical/secretarial workers, a large proportion of women were employed as domestic servants or in the clothing industry.

Fertility and household production were other factors that inhibited labor force participation. In 1900, a woman averaged about 4 children in her lifetime; today the average is 2.07. (See CHILDREN, Their Effect on Labor Supply.) Also, in 1900 over one-third of all women lived on farms in homes resembling "small cottage firms." Most women's production was here rather than in the paid labor force. Thus, during this period, the workingwoman was not the "average woman." In contrast to today, workingwomen* at the turn of the century tended to have less education, to be married to men with low or nonexistent incomes, or to be immigrants.

Between 1900 and 1920, the picture began to change. There were increases in women's wages, opportunities for employment, and levels of education attainment. This period also saw rapid increases in urbanization, as well as in the long-term decline in women's fertility.

Women's wages increased 16 percent faster than men's during this period. Much of this economic change and the increase in school completions can be attributed to the emergence of clerical employment, for which increased education was necessary.

The decline in fertility decreased the time spent in child rearing, enabling women to substitute paid employment for home production. At the same time, the movement of our economy into a more urban industrial base facilitated women's entrance into the paid labor market by moving them from the rural and "cottage firm" environment into the industrial centers where paid employment was available.

While changing socioeconomic factors facilitated women's increasing labor force participation, the increase varied throughout this century and among sociodemographic groups. Labor force participation rates increased by 10 percent (18.7 to 29.4) during the first 40 years of this century, by 11 percent (29.4 to 40.7) during the next 20 years, and by about 17 percent (40.7 to 57.9) since 1960. These aggregate patterns mask dramatically different subgroup patterns. Between 1920 and 1940 participation rates of young males aged 25 to 34 rose from 16.5 percent to 33.3 percent (a 17 percent increase). At the same time participation rates for women aged 45 to 54 increased by only 10 percent (from 12.5 to 22.5). For the next 20 years (during the years of high fertility) this age pattern reversed, and labor force participation for women under 35 actually declined, while participation rates for women over 35 increased dramatically. After 1960, the earlier age patterning resumed but on a much larger scale. In 1993, nearly 75 percent of women aged 25 to 34 were employed (nearly a 100 percent increase over 1960).

Educational and occupational patterns also have shifted over time. Although female LFP rises with education, between 1940 and 1970 the largest influx of women into the labor force occurred among less educated women. This trend then reversed itself, with the more highly educated increasing their participation more rapidly. By 1993, nearly universal participation existed for individuals with four or more years of college (94.3 percent for men and 81.3 percent for women). As educated women entered the labor force, and discrimination against female employment decreased, female occupational employment shifted. Although 19 percent of women are still employed in administrative support positions (with over 75 percent of this occupation being female), an increasing number are professionals or managers (27 percent in 1993 as compared to 16 percent in 1970).

These trends left female LFP patterns closely resembling men's, although at a lower level, by the 1990s. In fact, the trend of increasing female labor force participation contrasts with the declining male labor force participation (due to earlier retirement and decreasing African American male participation). Thus, the trend is toward equalization in rates. While the aggregate differential between male and female participation stood at 36.4 percent in 1970, by 1993 the differential had closed to 17.3 percent. By 2005, a differential of only 11.4 percent is projected.

References. Barbara R. Bergmann, *The Economic Emergence of Women* (New York, 1986); Frances D. Blau and Marianne A. Ferber, *The Economics of Women, Men and Work* (Englewood Cliffs, N.J., 1992); Victor R. Fuchs, *Women's Quest for Economic Equality* (Cambridge, 1988).

NAN L. MAXWELL

LACTATION is the secretion of milk from the breast. During pregnancy, glandular tissue of the breast develops an increased number of ducts ending in sacs called alveoli. The alveolar cells absorb water and nutrients from the bloodstream and, under the stimulus of the hormone prolactin, begin the synthesis of the nutrients into milk components. Before birth the synthesis is not complete but produces colostrum, a milklike liquid but without milk fat. After birth the abrupt drop in sex steroids allows the completion of the synthesis, and within two or three days the milk "comes in." Another hormone, oxytocin, triggered by suckling, enables the milk to flow from the alveoli to the nipples. As long as nursing continues, suckling triggers the release of prolactin and oxytocin and the production and flow of milk. As the baby is weaned, prolactin secretion and milk production decrease.

Human milk is the best food source for human babies. For the first four to six months, it can supply all of the nourishment needed, is more digestible than formula milk, and transfers maternal antibodies to the infant. Immunization is highest during the first few weeks. For many women who are able to breast-feed, the experience is highly satisfying. It also allows the uterus to return to normal size more rapidly, allows the body to expel excess fluids and tissues, and makes it easier to lose the weight gained in pregnancy (it takes approximately 1,000 calories a day to produce milk).

La Leche League International (9616 Minneapolis Avenue, Franklin Park, IL 60131), founded in 1956, through its manual *The Womanly Art of Breastfeeding*, information sheets, and local chapters offers information, individual counseling, and support groups for women who wish to nurse.

LANGUAGE. See COMMUNICATION; SEMIOTICS AND FEMINISM

LATIN AMERICA is a kaleidoscope of complexity and diversity; assembly lines produce cars in the midst of home industries producing handicrafts; street vendors in native dress sell their wares in front of modern supermarkets; the latest disco songs are played by people speaking only Indian languages; modern cities are surrounded by miserable shantytowns.

Suffrage. Post–World War I feminists believed social change could be achieved only if women were politically empowered. Opposition to their vote, based on fear that women would be unduly influenced by the Catholic Church and that they would support conservative policies, was formidable. The very idea that women were capable of reaching decisions on national affairs was difficult for many to accept.

Among the earliest franchised to vote was Puerto Rico, in 1932. In the next election Puerto Rico sent 113 women to the House of Representatives. Maria Louisa Arcelay-Rosa, one of the earliest proponents of day care systems, improved working conditions, and progressive managerial techniques, was elected a representative. In 1936 Maria Martinez de Perez Almoroty was elected to the Senate. Within a 30-year period, 39 of 77 municipalities elected women mayors. Cuban women were franchised in 1934. (See CUBA.)

Emancipation came to Brazil in 1932, after a 15-year struggle. Unlike earlier pioneers, feminists demanded some of the rights of men of their own class, not change for all women. The majority of Brazilian women did not vote. Omitted from leadership positions, many remained behind the scenes in a male-dominated society. (See BRAZIL WOMEN'S MOVEMENT.)

Argentina got the vote in 1947, a year after Perón was elected. From 1911 to 1946, 15 separate suffrage bills had been defeated by the Senate, but Perón's bill was approved overwhelmingly. Perónist populist ideology emphasized dignity of the worker, including women.

In Chile the feminism movement started in 1915 with the formation of the first secular women's group, the Women's Reading Circle. Upper-class

Club de Senoras became the principal agitator for the feminist movement during the 1920s. Between 1920 and 1940, several short-lived groups worked for woman's rights, notably, the National Council, which included only educated, well-to-do women. The First National Congress in 1944 began a more diversified movement, and the Federation of Women's Organizations embraced all political ideologies. Suffrage was obtained in 1949, ending the movement.

In Peru, 1911–1915, Maria Alvarado almost alone fought for women's suffrage, forming the first woman's organization, Feminine Evolution in 1915. In the early 1920s, a few others joined in working for suffrage. The National Council of Women was founded in 1924, but members disagreed on suffrage and even civil code reforms to grant married women equality. Alvarado was jailed, then exiled in 1925, ending women's agitation for rights. The vote was granted in 1955, catching most women by surprise. It was considered a gift.

In Uruguay in the 1910s, a few women's rights groups were formed. In 1916, the National Council for Suffrage urged abolition of white slave trade. In 1919, a purely suffrage organization, Uruguayan Alliance of Women's Suffrage, was active. The franchise was achieved in 1932.

Ecuador in 1929 was the first Latin American country to franchise women. This was done with no women's movement in evidence. Paraguay was the last to achieve the vote in 1961.

Mexican feminists, middle-class suffrage supporters, emphasized the *soldadaras'* (female soldiers') contribution to the formation of the revolutionary state as reason for granting suffrage but did not obtain the vote until 1958. In the revolution, women journalists, propagandists, and political activists were sometimes forced to work in demeaning jobs for the army; but aiding in revolutions did not guarantee full integration, equality, or participation in national affairs.

Most countries gave suffrage after the 1950s (Mexico, Bolivia, Colombia). Trujillo of the Dominican Republic and Odrio of Peru gave the vote to enhance their political image. Opposition to electoral participation or running for office remained high. This inertia in incorporating women into the political arena is, in part, responsible for the limited present performance. Women have, however, cast decisive votes in critical elections, as for Perón in Argentina and Allesandrio in Chile.

Feminism. Secular women's organizations appeared in the 1830s and 1840s. The public service–oriented Company of Mary and Sisters of Charity brought about the civil codes of 1870 and 1884, which expounded the ideals of increased family and economic rights for women. The first feminist congress in Yucatán saw 700 women at Peon Contreros Theater. As elsewhere, schoolteachers dominated, but the vote was never discussed.

In Argentina in the late eighteenth and early nineteenth centuries, women began to emerge from seclusion, organized cultural gatherings modeled on

French salons, and held parties to raise money for charitable and cultural causes. In 1789 women raised funds for construction of printing works to train and employ orphans; women volunteers supervised the printing works and continued to raise funds for maintenance. Women philanthropists helped found the National Theater and supported the arts, there being 20 to 30 women culturally active in Buenos Aires. By the latter half of the eighteenth century, as in France and Britain, government had to assume relief for the poor that traditional Catholic charities could not meet. Co-operation of church and state built hospitals, founding homes, and work-houses. Progressive thinkers concerned about useful occupations for upper-class women urged increase in philanthropic work and inclusion in the day-to-day operation of new hospitals. These volunteers were not in decision-making roles (nuns did this unless there were priests available). Participation was considered not only a religious obligation but a civic responsibility.

President Rivadavia of United Provinces established the Benefecent Society, which was funded by the state as a secular women's charity organization. The Society of Beneficence, 1823–1948, was designed to establish and run elementary schools for girls but grew to encompass all social services for women and children. Late nineteenth-century male reformers who wanted to modernize Argentina took up the issue of education for women. In the late nineteenth century socialists tried to organize women workers. The Argentine Socialist Party, organized in 1896, was an outspoken supporter of woman's rights, including suffrage and legal equality.

The Argentinian Association of University Women espoused socialist ideology: education, suffrage, legal equality, physical fitness, a single standard of sexual morality. It attacked prostitution and called for changes in divorce laws and property rights. In the 1920s the Women's Rights Association tried to organize across class, religious, and political lines (11,000 members). The 1926 New Civil Code incorporated many of their demands, with attention to suffrage. They did not succeed, however, in integrating women across class lines.

Second Wave Feminism. Stimulated by conferences sponsored by private and government institutions through the 1970s, women's studies have become an important topic in Latin American social science. Most scholars engaged in such research do not consider themselves feminists and resent being seen as such. Women's studies did not stem from a vigorous women's liberation movement. Not until 1979 did women's liberation movements emerge in countries like Brazil, Colombia, and Mexico. Argentina's budding feminist movement was cut short by a military coup in March 1976. The single most important characteristic of present research on women throughout continental Latin America is its perspective of structural dependency. The principal objective of work on women by social science is to analyze Latin American social formation.

In the past decade, few Latin American societies appear to have developed even a modest level of feminist activity. Small pockets of activity exist in almost every large Latin American city, but they are isolated and beleaguered. One organization in Colombia deals with women's issues but is more broadly committed to agrarian issues. Venezuela has a women's group, a government women's commission, and a women's movement within its Socialist Party. Since the early 1970s several consciousness-raising and a few study groups have met in Mexico City. Organized feminist activity exists within the leftist parties and unions, all united chiefly around the issue of abortion.

Women's Progress. In the mid-twentieth century, women's status rose somewhat through use of the ballot, holding electoral and appointive office, and entrance into universities, professions, the labor force, and business in greater numbers. Notable women appointed to office include Chilean Gabriela Mistral, special ambassador to the League of Nations and the United Nations, and Rosaria Castellanos of Mexico and Carmen Naranjo of Costa Rica, ambassadors to Israel. Brazilian and Argentine women professionals outnumbered men but were not in positions of decision making or responsibility.

Less progress has been made in family relationships, divorce, double standards, and the workplace. In Mexico, as in many other Latin American societies today, the family is founded on the unquestioned, absolute supremacy of the father and the necessary and absolute self-sacrifice of the mother. Cuba and Nicaragua have made giant strides in abolishing gender discrimination in law and practice. In Nicaragua women have been integral to the process of social transformation since the inception of the revolution. Following the Sandinista victory, they have been incorporated at every level of new government and had voice in all programs for social, economic, and political reconstruction.

Economic. Throughout the modern period, governments have viewed intensive industrialization as a panacea for progress. More often than not, this has resulted in growth without progress. Rising inflation and stresses resulting from increased population were not adequately addressed. Structural and institutional changes have not accompanied industrialization. The gap between rich and poor has widened in spite of the steady growth of the middle class. Some have met problems of modernization by repression. By 1975, three-fourths of governments were dictatorships. Immigration (especially to the United States) and transnational workers (*maquiladorasi*) are common phenomena.

Family planning and population control have also been perceived as a progressive solution to poverty, along with industrialization. In Puerto Rico sterilization predominates as a means of control. With the highest rates in the world, 35 percent of women of reproductive age are sterilized (compared with 30 percent in the United States). Between 1950 and 1970, the total fertility rate was reduced by 48 percent, with tacit sanction by the government, which failed to promote other contraceptive means at a time when female employment shifted from home to factory. A clear relationship existed between sterilization and incorporation of women into the workforce.

Optimism generated in the 1950s by prospects for rural commercial development and by green revolution agricultural production came to an end in the 1970s. In the last three decades, rural unemployment, migration to cities, and marginalization of rural women for technological and economic benefits of development have increased rapidly in many countries of Latin America. Import substitution policies as a strategy for development led to rising foreign debt. To acquire foreign exchange to improve balance of payments, encouragement of export-oriented agriculture led to food scarcity. Purchasing food from abroad to ease food scarcity perpetuated a vicious circle of dependency and poverty.

The green revolution also led to a higher concentration of agricultural resources in the hands of capitalist entrepreneurs—agricultural labor became migrant. Consequently, women's agricultural work shows a relative decrease in all countries and an absolute decrease in many.

Reference. Elsa M. Chaney, *Supermadre: Women in Politics in Latin America* (Austin, Tex., and London, 1983).

LATIN AMERICAN ARTISTS (TWENTIETH-CENTURY). Many well-known women artists of the twentieth century have had a formal education in the arts. They attended schools of art in their countries and also went to art institutes in France and the United States, receiving instruction from famous painters and sculptors. Returning to their homeland, these women introduced the new art trends, such as cubism, surrealism, and expressionism, that expressed reality in a different way.

The new European art trends were adapted to Latin American reality, resulting in unique art expressions and particular personal styles. European surrealism, for example, became a reality in Latin America, where artists and writers found what Cuban writer Alejo Carpentier called magical realism. This magic reality is present in the exuberant nature of the Latin American tropical landscapes and, among other things, in the richness of Latin American myths, folklore, and cultures. Women artists of Latin America were also socially aware and were determined to express themselves strongly as women with progressive ideas. Although there are many excellent women artists in Latin America, here only a few representative ones can be mentioned.

Tarsila do Amaral (1886–1973) and Anita Malfatti (1896–1964), both from São Paulo, were among the pioneers of modern art in Brazil. Amaral studied art in Paris from 1920 to 1922, first at the Academy Julien and later with Emile Renard. At home and abroad she became involved with modernism, cubism, and primitivism. In her search for authenticity and

Brazilian themes, she visited different parts of Brazil and observed the festivities and the people. Nativistic themes are portrayed in *The Negress* (1923), *Abaporu* (1928), and *Antropofagia* (1929). The latter two are also examples of "tropical surrealism," that is, the representation of the exuberant vegetation of the tropics in a surrealistic way.

Malfatti studied expressionist painting with Lovis Corinth in Germany and became interested in cubism in New York. In December 1916 she exhibited her paintings in São Paulo. This was the first exhibit of modern art in Brazil and one of the first in Latin America. She caused a scandal with paintings such as *The Woman with Green Hair* (1916) and *The Man of Seven Colors* (1917), which demonstrated her position against the traditional expression of reality.

Maria Martins (1900–1973), Djanira da Mota e Silva (b. 1914), and Lygia Clark (1920–1988), all Brazilian, also had an impact on modern Latin American art. Martins studied painting in Paris in 1930 and sculpture in Belgium under Oscar Jasper in 1939. She cofounded the Fundação do Museu de Arte Moderna do Rio de Janeiro. Her sculptures, also an example of tropical surrealism, show the immense flora of the Brazilian jungle.

Mota e Silva is a primitivist whose paintings re-create scenes from daily life and folklore. She has also done religious paintings mainly inspired by saints. Some of her works are *Tea Plantation in Itacolomi* (1958) and *Saint Peter and the Station of the Cross* (1943).

Lygia Clark, a member of the neoconcrete movement and cofounder of the Brazilian Neo-Concretist Association (1959), studied art in Rio de Janeiro and Paris (1950–1952). She also taught at the Sorbonne, Paris, from 1970 to 1975. Her sculptures are essentially "abstract constructivist." Some of her sculptures are *Space Bird, Project for a Planet*, and *Fantastic Carriage*.

Another influential figure in Latin American contemporary painting was Frida Kahlo (Mexico, 1907–1954), who was married, off and on, to the famous painter Diego Rivera. Their association lasted some 25 years. Most of Kahlo's paintings are autobiographical, expressed in a surrealistic and fantastic way. Her paintings show an obsession with pain and death and a strong attraction to eroticism, aggression, and procreation. The obsession with pain and death in her poetry can be explained, in large part, by her health problems. When she was a child, she had polio and, as a teenager, was in an accident that left physical and emotional scars. Some examples of her many paintings are *The Two Fridas* (1939), *Self-Portrait with Diego in My Mind* (1943), and *The Broken Column* (1944).

Tilsa Ysuchiya (Peru, 1932–1984) was inspired by the Indian cultures of her native land. After studying at the School of Fine Arts of Peru (1954 to 1959), she studied at the Sorbonne and attended classes at the École des Beaux Arts in Paris. Her works are based on her imagination and on

Quechua legends and myths, all combined in a fashion reminiscent of dreams or a surrealism of Indian motifs. Representative paintings are *Myth of the Tree* (1976) and *Myth of the Woman and the Wind* (1976).

Beatriz Gonzáles (Colombia, b. 1936) studied fine arts and art history at the University of the Andes and in 1966 studied graphics in Rotterdam. In *The Last Table* she represents da Vinci's *The Last Supper* on a large coffee table. *The Parrots* (1986) expressed a political message. It is a 40-foot frieze oil painting on paper that shows the heads of the Colombian president and his advisers, arrayed and colored like parrots.

Raquel Forner (b. 1902), Noemi Gerstein (b. 1910), Alicia Peñalba (b. 1918), Sarah Grilo (b. 1921), and Marta Minujín (b. 1943) are distinguished Argentinian artists.

Forner studied art at La Academia Nacional de Bellas Artes of Buenos Aires and in Paris from 1929 to 1930. She is a cofounder of Cursos Libres de Arte Plástico, the first private academy of modern art in Argentina. She has painted a Space series, an Astrobeings series, and an Astronauts series. Gerstein and Peñalba have distinguished themselves as sculptors. Gerstein is attracted to metallic constructions, as, for example, her *Constellation* (1963), in which she used small tubular segments. Peñalba won the International Sculpture Prize at the sixth biennial exposition of São Paulo. In her earlier work she made totemlike structures inspired by primitive sources, but her more recent compositions are asymmetrical. These latest ones suggest motion in space. An example is *Absent* (1961).

Sarah Grilo and her husband, José Antonio Fernández Muro, became leaders of the abstract movement in Argentina. Sarah was a self-taught artist. After coming to New York in 1962, she included in her painting signs, graffiti, letterings, and numerals. Examples of that period are *Charge* and *Inferno*, both of 1964.

Marta Minujín came to New York on a John Simon Guggenheim Memorial Fellowship. There she excelled as a multimedia artist of international renown. She has staged environmental "happenings," transient artistic events, and has done experiments in interactive and dynamic art. For example, in *El batacazo* (The Long Shot) there are smells, sounds, and sights.

María Luisa Pacheco (1919–1982) studied in her native city of La Paz, Bolivia, and from 1951 to 1952 in Madrid with Daniel Vázquez. In 1957 she established her home in New York. She was three times awarded a fellowship by the John Simon Guggenheim Memorial Foundation and has won many national and international awards. She has used themes from her native land in cubist, expressionist, and abstract styles.

Amelia Peláez (Cuba, 1897–1968) from 1927 to 1934 studied art in Paris at the École des Beaux Arts, École de Louvre, and under Russian artist Alexandra Exter. She was the first Cuban painter to be an advocate of contemporary art in her country. She searched for a syncretic style: modern, personal, and Cuban. An example of her work is *The Hibiscus* (1943).

Finally, Myrna Báez (Puerto Rico, b. 1931) studied art in the Academia de San Fernando, Madrid (1957). She expresses social criticism in her art, as, for example, in *Barrio Tokyo* (1962), a scene of poverty.

References. Erika Billeter et al., *Imagen de México. La aportación de México al arte del siglo XX* (Dallas, 1988); Luis R. Cancel et al., *The Latin American Spirit: Art in the United States, 1920–1970* (New York, 1988); Gilbert Chase, *Contemporary Art in Latin America* (New York, 1970); Halliday T. Day and Hollister Sturges, *Art of the Fantastic in Latin America, 1920–1987* (Indianapolis, 1987).

AMALIA MONDRÍQUEZ

LATIN AMERICAN WRITERS. See BRAZILIAN WRITERS

LATINA is a term referring to women of Spanish-related origin groups: Mexican American (Chicana), Puerto Rican, Cuban, Central and South American living within the United States. In order to understand the life demographic portrait of Latinas, it is first necessary to draw an overall portrait of the Latino population (males and females). The specific societal conditions of Chicanas or Mexican American women are highlighted.

The Latino population in the United States has been increasing significantly for the last 20 years. Latinos increased by 61 percent between 1970 and 1980 and 53 percent between 1980 and 1990. According to the U.S. Census Bureau, Latinos numbered 22.4 million in 1990. Their number reached 27 million in 1994. Demographic projections indicate continued and steady growth rates: in 1990, 1 in about every 10 Americans was Latino; it is estimated that by 2050 1 of every 5 Americans will be Latino. High birthrates and steady immigration, particularly from Central and South America, account for such population growth. Within the Latino population, Mexicans continue to be the largest group, followed by Puerto Ricans and Cubans. Latinos continue to be concentrated geographically in 10 states, with California and Texas having 54 percent of all Latinos.

Significant differences in socioeconomic indicators persist between the Latino and the total population. Latino unemployment rates continue to be consistently higher: the 1993 Latino unemployment rate was 11.9 percent compared to 7.1 percent for non-Latinos. The occupational distribution of employed males differed between Latinos and non-Latinos, with Latino males more likely to be concentrated in low-paying and less stable occupations. While non-Latino males cluster in managerial and professional occupational levels, Latino males are concentrated as operatives and service workers. The median income of Latino families continues to be consistently lower than that of non-Latino families. From 1981 to 1991, the difference between the median family income of Latinos and non-Latinos ranged from $11,000 to $14,000. Not surprisingly, poverty rates for Latino families and non-Latinos reveal important differences. Latino families are more likely to live below the poverty level than non-Latino families (26.2 percent and 10.4 percent, respectively). In 1992, individual Latinos (29.3 percent) were also more likely to live below the poverty level than non-Latinos (9.6 percent). Although Latinos make up approximately 9 percent of the total population, more than one in every six persons living in poverty (18 percent) is Latino. Tragically, 40 percent of Latino children under 18 years of age are living in poverty, in contrast to 13 percent of non-Latino children. The Census Bureau figures reveal that while Latino children represent 12 percent of all children living in the United States, they represent 21 percent of all children living in poverty.

Although some sectors of the Latino population have experienced higher levels of educational attainment since the 1970s, Latinos, in general, continue to lag behind the rest of the United States. Most Latino adults have completed fewer years of education than non-Latinos. In 1990, 31 percent of Latinos (25 years and over) had less than a ninth grade education, in contrast to 9 percent of the total population. In 1991, fewer than half (44 percent) of all Mexican-origin persons (25 years and over) had completed high school, in contrast to 80 percent of non-Latinos. About one-quarter of the Latino population (25 years and older) have at least some college education, while almost half (46 percent) of non-Latinos have some college education. Latino high school dropout rates remained around 40 percent between 1972 and 1990. During the same period, the dropout rates for whites and African Americans showed consistent improvement. In 1991, 8 percent of non-Latino whites did not complete high school. The percentage of African Americans who dropped out of high school (14 percent) in 1991 had declined by 7 percent since 1972. Educational progress for the Latino population appears to be at a standstill, and, in some areas, educational attainment levels are actually declining.

Within the Latino population, Puerto Rican families are the most likely to live below the poverty level, have the lowest median income, and have the highest number of children living in poverty. Almost 41 percent of all Puerto Rican families were maintained by women. About two-thirds (66 percent) of the Puerto Rican families in poverty were female-headed families.

The Cuban population is most likely to have higher levels of educational attainment, higher earnings, lower poverty rates, and a larger percentage of men and women in professional and managerial occupations. Chicanas are two times more likely to have jobs in the service sector than Cuban women. Cuban women have a higher mean income than either Chicanas or Puerto Rican women.

Looking more closely at the largest Latino group, the Mexican-origin or Chicano population is concentrated in the five southwestern states of Arizona, California, Colorado, New Mexico, and Texas, with approximately 85 percent of all Chicanos(as) living in these states. Their family size continues to be larger than that of both the total population and all other Latino groups in the United States. In 1991, 27 percent of all Mexican-origin families lived below the poverty level, followed by Puerto Ricans (36 percent). Poverty levels for both Latino groups are increasing, while that of the total population remains relatively constant at about 11 percent. The occupational distribution of the Mexican-origin population differs from that of the total population. It is concentrated largely in the blue-collar and low-paying service occupations. Women are concentrated in technical work and sales, similar to females in the total population. Mexican-origin women, however, experience marked differences from other women, with only 14 percent of Chicanas located in managerial and professional occupations in comparison to 28 percent of non-Latinas. Similarly, 25 percent of employed Chicanas are found in the service sector in comparison to 18 percent of non-Latinas. Lastly, the proportion of Chicanas in the operative, fabricators, and laborer occupational categories (16 percent) equaled twice that of non-Latinas (7 percent).

Differences persist between the median earnings of Chicanos(as) and the total population. In 1991, the median earnings of Chicanos ($18,186) represented 61 percent of the median earnings of the male population ($29,418). Chicanas earned 45 percent ($9,260) of that of the total female population ($20,550). Both groups of women earned less than their male counterparts.

Various reasons have been offered to explain the nature and degree of labor force participation among Latinas. One of those most frequently cited to account for the more limited entrance of Latinas into the paid labor force is their higher fertility rates. Some theories claim that their higher fertility rates force Latinas to leave the labor force and also cause employers to become more reluctant to hire them. Another explanation stresses the role of Latino cultural patterns that are believed responsible for socializing women to value their roles as wives and mothers over their role as wage earners. Such values block Latinas from seeking outside employment and hinder those women who are in the labor force from pursuing options tied to job advancement. In addition, researchers have shown that labor force participation is dependent on a wide range of other societal factors. Low levels of education and work experience are frequently cited as major factors contributing to the specific patterns of labor force participation of Latinas.

Current feminist research stresses the role of social structural discrimination and the persistently limited upward occupational mobility of Latinas. A distinction is made between the primary and secondary labor market. Jobs in the primary labor market are better paid, have greater security and benefits, and have a greater potential for career advancement. These positions are held primarily by white males and, to a lesser extent, white females. The secondary labor market consists of low-paying jobs with less security and limited opportunity for advancement. Historically, women and people of color have been concentrated in the secondary labor market.

Limited access to all levels of education, particularly postsecondary education, remains one of the most critical problems facing Latinas in the United States. In one of the few studies on Latinas and education, Maria Chacón points out that "of all the major population groups [Chicanas] are the poorest, and most underrepresented in higher education." Studies have also emphasized the gender-specific stress factors that contribute to the higher attrition rates among Chicanas. Chicanas share such stress factors with other women of color. Chacón's study concluded that Chicanas in college face specific difficulties in comparison to their male counterparts and white women. Chicanas reported spending more hours attending to domestic responsibilities than males with the same marital status. Such responsibilities included child care, household chores, and care of elderly relatives. In addition, Chicanas reported receiving less emotional support for their educational aspiration from their parents than their brothers or other male relatives received. These factors had a negative impact on the academic performance and progress of Chicanas. Since the majority of Chicanas—and Latinas in general—are of working-class origin, they also experience stress due to financial problems and insecurities. Latinos and Latinas identify financial problems as a significant stress factor during their college years. As the number of Latinas gradually increases in institutions of higher education, the need to formulate and implement policy recommendations aimed at the retention of Latinas will take on additional urgency.

Throughout the United States, Latinas will continue to face difficulties based on race, class, and gender. Although Latinas experience problems similar to those of white women, many issues take on added dimensions as a result of the intersection of race, class, and gender that produces a matrix of domination responsible for limiting the life chances of Latinas. Historically, Latinas have formed organizations, both national and local, in an effort to improve their daily life circumstances. For example, Chicanas established the Comision Femenil Mexicana in 1970. Its main project was the creation of the Chicana Service Action Center, which addressed welfare rights and unemployment in Los Angeles. The Mexican American Legal Defense and Education Fund established the Chicana Rights Project to address the specific needs of Chicanas. In addition, numerous conferences have been organized by Latinas to discuss their problems and formulate policy recommendations. Although limited improvements have been made, Latinas will continue to face a difficult road ahead as they continue to work for a better future for themselves and their communities in American society.

Statistics cited were obtained from the U.S. Bureau of the Census, *The*

Hispanic Population in the United States: March 1992 (20–465RV) and *Hispanic Americans Today* (P23–183).

References. Maria Chacón, *Chicanas in Postsecondary Education* (Stanford, Calif., 1983); Teresa Córdova et al. (eds.), *Chicana Voices—Intersections of Class, Race and Gender* (Austin, Tex., 1986); Alma M. García (ed.), *Chicana Feminist Thought: The Essential Writings* (New York, 1997); Alma M. García, "The Development of Chicana Feminist Thought, 1970–1980," *Gender and Society* 3 (1986): 217–238; Adela De La Torre and Beatriz Pesquera (eds.), *Building with Our Hands: New Directions in Chicana Studies* (Berkeley, Calif., 1993).

ALMA M. GARCÍA and TOMÁS JIMÉNEZ

LEARNED HELPLESSNESS. A number of psychologists have speculated about the role of helplessness and hopelessness in depression,* but Martin Seligman formulated the learned helplessness theory of depression. The concept of learned helplessness evolved out of a series of experiments with dogs on the effects of prior Pavlovian conditioning on later learning. Dogs subjected to inescapable shock later demonstrated a failure to initiate voluntary attempts to escape. The theory was tested with humans, and it was postulated that depressed persons believe they have little control over important outcomes in their lives and, thus, do not attempt to exercise control. Learned helplessness theory contends that the basic cause of all the deficits observed in helpless animals and humans after uncontrollable events occur is the expectation that in the future they will not be able to control outcomes.

This theory of depression has affected psychotherapeutic treatment of women, since women are more frequently diagnosed as depressed than men and since this theory has influenced treatment approaches for depression. The learned helplessness theory recognizes the importance of a sense of powerlessness and its possible impact on mood, and it also concedes that helplessness can be learned in response to certain environmental contingencies. However, the "problem" of learned helplessness is still viewed as residing within the individual, and, by implication, the solution lies in treating the individual.

Theorists make several recommendations for therapeutic interventions based on the learned helplessness theory. For instance, therapeutic strategies that undermine the expectation that goals are uncontrollable and unattainable should be effective in reversing the depressive feelings (Beach, Abramson, and Levine). A number of specific strategies have been presented: reversing an individual's expectations of no control; facilitating a change from unrealistic to more realistic goals; decreasing the importance of unattainable goals; and reversing an individual's expectations that other people have control over his or her goals. Basically, if the cause of learned helplessness and depression is hypothesized to be the expectation that responding will be ineffective in controlling future events, then the basic therapeutic effort should be to change this belief to one in which the individual believes that responding will be effective and that anticipated bad events will be avoided. The focus of these treatment models is thus on altering the depressed individual's *expectations* or *goals*.

What is missing from these perspectives, however, is a recognition of the individual's circumstances. For women and other disfranchised persons, ignoring these circumstances can be tantamount to prescribing acceptance of limited control or institutionalized powerlessness. For example, if a single mother of three children reports depression and a sense of helplessness, her depression may be the result of a realistic sense of powerlessness resulting from, for instance, limited occupational opportunities and inadequate facilities for child care. To attempt to modify her expectations or goals without recognizing the actual limitations under which she is operating may lead to a minimization of the difficulties she is facing. That is, treatments derived from the learned helplessness theory of depression focus on the expectations or beliefs of the individual, for the most part, ignoring situational factors.

If the learned helplessness model recognizes that environmental contingencies can influence one's beliefs about future expectations, it seems appropriate to also understand that these contingencies may be stable elements of an individual's circumstances and thus may have a pervasive influence on an individual's outlook. An individual's attributions that outcomes are stable may not be an indication of a cognitive aberration but rather may be an accurate appraisal of his or her circumstances. It is essential that mental health professionals recognize and take into consideration the multiplicity of factors that may be contributing to an individual's distress.

The learned helplessness theory has made some valuable contributions toward the understanding of depression: it explains some of the beliefs and behaviors of depressed persons and even provides experimental evidence as to how beliefs about helplessness are acquired. In this respect it furthers our recognition of factors that may contribute to depression in women. However, it is important, especially when women and disfranchised persons are being treated, not to neglect the role that situational factors may play in supporting a sense of helplessness.

References. L. Y. Abramson, M.E.P. Seligman, and J. D. Teasdale, "Learned Helplessness in Humans: Critique and Reformulation," *Journal of Abnormal Psychology* 87 (1987): 40–74; S.R.H. Beach, L. Y. Abramson, and F. M. Levine, "Attributional Reformulation of Learned Helplessness and Depression: Therapeutic Implications," in J. F. Clarkin and H. I. Glazier (eds.), *Depression: Behavioral and Directive Intervention Strategies* (New York, 1981).

                                                                        MARY KAY BIAGGIO

LEARNING. See GENDER AND LEARNING

LEISURE TIME (U.S.). Women's use of leisure time has been historically defined in relation to household and work obligations, prevailing ideologies about women's appropriate sphere of action, and the expansion of the leisure and entertainment industries.

In the premodern American colonies, leisure was understood not as a separate sphere of activity but as intertwined with the rhythms of the day and seasons. Quilting bees, huskings, and barn raisings were among the activities in which work, recreation, and sociability were mingled. Leisure was not sex-segregated ideologically but grew out of the work roles of women and men. In villages and towns, shared labor such as spinning, laundering, berrying, and attending at childbirth* were occasions for women's sociability. Depending on the degree of settlement, visiting was a primary form of leisure, reinforced by women's customary practices of borrowing and bartering. In the larger towns and cities of the late eighteenth and early nineteenth centuries, commercial entertainment such as taverns and theaters were part of an informal, heterogeneous public life with relatively little segregation by sex and class.

Urbanization and the changes wrought by capitalism, especially the rationalization of the workday and increased separation of home and workplace, profoundly altered the sexual division of leisure in the nineteenth century. Leisure became increasingly stratified by sex, class, and race. Men's recreation, based in commercial and voluntary organizations such as saloons, militias, and fraternal orders, excluded women from many forms of social life. Victorian notions of respectability and purity also proscribed female participation in public recreation. At the same time, the household and women within it became culturally identified with leisure and rest, a realm apart from the competitive market and workplace. Despite the widespread mythology of the leisured woman, in reality only a small elite could employ enough servants to free women of child care and household duties. Women's leisure continued to be intertwined with household labor and kinship relations, but it was increasingly homosocial in character, particularly among middle-class wives. For working-class and black women, the pressing demands of survival left relatively little time or opportunity for leisure.

By the 1890s, new ideas about women's roles and the growth of the entertainment industry expanded women's leisure activities. The "new woman" not only represented the movement of women into education, employment, and political activity but symbolized an expanded social life. Active sports such as bicycling and tennis became popular among young middle-class women, while working-class adolescents sought pleasure and autonomy in dance halls. Leisure entrepreneurs tamed and refined formerly male-oriented entertainment, such as music halls and variety theaters, for the new female audience. In the early twentieth century, new forms of mixed-sex leisure, including dance palaces, motion pictures, and amusement parks, expressed and legitimated an emergent ideology of companionate social relations between the sexes. The image of the "family that plays together" was later reinforced by the advent of radio and television.

Still, gender divisions remain one of the most salient characteristics of leisure. Women more often report leisure activities that involve socializing and are located at home, church, and clubs. Moreover, women do not experience leisure as a sphere separate from "obligatory" time as men do; housework* and child care* overlap with the family's leisure hours. Most significant is women's loss of leisure time with the expansion of female labor force participation* since World War II and the consequent legitimation of the "double day" for working wives. Since the 1920s, men's overall working hours, in employment and at home, have risen only one-half hour per week, while women's have increased five hours. Ironically, while women's housework produces goods and services used in the family's leisure, their employment has enabled many men to labor fewer hours in support of their families and has given them increased leisure time.

References. R. A. Berk and S. F. Berk, *Labor and Leisure at Home* (Beverly Hills, Calif., 1979); K. Peiss, *Cheap Amusements: Working Women and Leisure in Turn-of-the-Century New York* (Philadelphia, 1986).

KATHY PEISS

LESBIAN LITERATURE boasts a long, but sporadic, history in Western civilization and texts. Before the late 1800s, most topically "lesbian" literature was written by men; however, only texts authored by women, particularly lesbians, are classified as lesbian literature per se. The first lesbian author appeared in antiquity: celebrated lyric poet Sappho of Lesbos (b. 612 B.C.E.) addressed love poems to female friends. Her poetic fragments prompted the eponymous designations for "female homosexuality," "sapphism" and "lesbianism."

After Sappho, Western lesbian literature suffered a long drought. Widespread illiteracy and oppression of women from classical times until the late Middle Ages limited women's textual production, publication, and preservation—and lesbian texts would have been suppressed on religious and sociopolitical grounds, if written at all. John Boswell observes only a few minor instances of lesbian textual matter during the post-Classical millennium covered by his sweeping history.

Romantic ballads addressed to women and believed composed by female troubadours in early medieval France are extant. The Italian-born French writer/scholar Christina de Pisan included Sappho's and Hippolyta's biographies in her 1405 "feminary," *The City of Ladies.* The ecclesiastical investigation of Sister Benedetta Carlini, an early seventeenth-century nun described in Vatican evidence uncovered by Judith Brown, confirms that historical lesbian activity occurred and was categorized as "sodomy," sexual sin, when officially documented.

European Renaissance and Enlightenment references to lesbian behaviors, mostly in men's legal, medical, and pornographic writings, generally display marked ignorance of anatomical and social realities, treating lesbianism as overly masculine women's illicit attempt to achieve male prerogatives. Among other English-language writers (the focus henceforth), Shakespeare capitalized on the dramatic potential of female transvestism and mistaken identity, occasionally penning scenes of female–(fe)male romance fraught with lesbian overtones, for example in *Twelfth Night*.

In her landmark historical study Lillian Faderman launches an exhaustive documentary survey with the sixteenth-century French male libertine poets, who advanced that the ongoing erotic/pornographic tradition of fantasy lesbian relations was designed to titillate male readers. Faderman argues that women's passionate "romantic friendships" spanning the eighteenth and nineteenth centuries were an accepted social phenomenon linked with, but not identical to, lesbianism, yet she perceives women's romantic writings to be precursors of twentieth-century lesbian literature.

For example, Mary Wollstonecraft's autobiographical novel *Mary: A Fiction* (1787) describes romantic friendship's trials and tribulations. The loving letters American poet Emily Dickinson wrote to her sister-in-law Sue Gilbert exhibit the extreme emotions and florid verbiage of protolesbian texts of the mid-1800s. Henry James' 1885 novel, *The Bostonians*, definitively portrays late Victorian "Boston marriage." This middle-class, independent-living arrangement, adopted by such "spinster" couples as writer Sarah Orne Jewett and Annie Fields, provided a socially approved bridge between the accepted excess of nineteenth-century romanticism and the sexologically suspect "new woman" lesbianism of the twentieth century.

In the early 1900s, discretion was the byword of nascent lesbian literature. Cigar-smoking American imagist poet and critic Amy Lowell composed lush verse using a male persona, including poems for her female love objects; Lowell engaged in discreet, Boston, marriagelike domesticity. So did novelist and reputed lesbian Willa Cather, who had spent her youth as cross-dressing "William." Cather drew *My Ántonia* (1918) and other tomboyish protagonists from a masculine point of view, her male narrators effectively disguising her lesbian subtexts.

Paris expatriate Gertrude Stein—the best-known lesbian author since Sappho—depicted fin de siècle romantic friends under the stylistic influence of Jamesian psychorealism in her first novel, *Q.E.D.* (1903). Stein soon developed her characteristic modern, "cubist," coded-lesbian style, as in the long, slyly erotic 1915 poem "Lifting Belly." Stein's self-absorbed *Autobiography of Alice B. Toklas* (1933) immortalized her wifely "companion"; they hosted a legendary post–World War I artistic salon. Natalie Barney's "Amazonian" salon gathered Paris' most creative lesbians: French novelist Colette, American poet H. D. (Hilda Doolittle), *New Yorker* journalist Janet Flanner, and others.

In an astonishing efforescence during the 1920s and 1930s, lesbians seemingly dominated the female ranks of modernism. Margaret Anderson and Jane Heap edited *Little Review*; Sylvia Beach published Joyce's *Ulysses* (1922); Edna St. Vincent Millay's play *The Lamp and the Bell* (1921) masked lesbian matter in a fantastical setting. After her parodic *Ladies Almanack* (1928), Djuna Barnes released *Nightwood* in 1936 to effusive praise from modernist hierophant T. S. Eliot. Two English novels published in 1928 proved more significant: Virginia Woolf's ambisexual *Orlando* (a paean for Vita Sackville-West) and Radclyffe Hall's *The Well of Loneliness*. Despite being banned in England and briefly subject to U.S. censorship, Hall's gloomy tome became the lesbian bible for over four decades.

Cross-dressing "John" Hall tapped her own life and contemporary psychology to fashion Stephen Gordon, *The Well of Loneliness'* main character. Stephen constitutes a definitive invert, the mannish, lesbian type sexologist Havelock Ellis classified as "the third sex." Hall's fictional apologia sought public sympathy for congenital inverts unable to resist lesbianism because these "women" were actually men trapped in female bodies, attracted to essentially heterosexual, "normal" feminine women. Hence, the "well of loneliness" in doomed lesbian sexual mismatches.

Hall faced little serious competition midcentury. The Great Depression ground down upon lesbian literature. Gale Wilhelm's fine, but slim, novel *We Too Are Drifting* (1935) proffers a cynical vision not unlike Hall's. Jane Rule has remarked that unusual decadence and elegance limited the popular success of Barnes' *Nightwood*. In the late 1930s and 1940s, Nancy Drew mysteries rose to enduring popularity among youthful lesbians, disdaining Drew's boyfriend but relishing her independence. World War II materials shortages restricted "leisure" publishing. Hall's novel was still being read by virtually every U.S. lesbian.

McCarthyism tarnished 1950s prosperity, but easy postwar life permitted a new literary medium, lesbian pulp fiction. The cheap "drugstore paperbacks" with garish covers cast lesbians as sexually voracious, socially deviant women hurtling toward bad ends, unless "saved" by a man. Like soft-core porn, lesbian pulp novels assumed men's heterosexual moral sensibilities, but 1950s lesbian readers had limited options, as Barbara Grier's book reviews in the Daughters of Bilitis organ *The Ladder* (1956–1972) indicated. Ann Bannon attained an enduring lesbian readership with her "Beebo Brinker" pulp series, while Claire Morgan authored a more highbrow work, *The Price of Salt* (1958), but everyone still read Hall.

Lesbian textuality trod water. In 1964, Canadian Jane Rule published her first deft, if sexually oblique, novel, *Desert of the Heart* (interpreted as

Desert Hearts, a 1980s lesbian film classic); 1965 brought Violet Leduc's ambivalent *La bâtarde*. However, *A Place for Us* (1969) created a sensation. Under the pseudonym "Isabel Miller," Alma Routsong self-published this historically based novel after commercial houses refused the positive, sometimes erotic tale. Retitled for mass marketing, *Patience and Sarah* (1973) was widely read by "women's libbers," but everyone, even lesbian-feminists, still read Hall.

The "second wave" feminist movement of the late 1960s and early 1970s sparked the greatest explosion of lesbian writing since the 1920s, and the movement benefited from a symbiotic backdraft of lesbian-feminist periodicals and women's publishing houses. Established poets, such as Andrienne Rich, and newer voices, such as Audre Lorde, Alta, and Judy Grahn, could reach women nationwide. In the watershed year 1973, Jill Johnston's nonfiction *Lesbian Nation* became required reading, as did novels *Patience and Sarah*, Monique Wittig's *The Lesbian Body* (translated from the French), and June Arnold's *The Cook and the Carpenter* (her *Sister Gin* followed in 1974).

Most importantly, in 1973, Daughters, Inc. published activist-poet Rita Mae Brown's first novel, *Rubyfruit Jungle*. Lesbians anointed Brown's autobiographical picaresque their new bible, and mainstream Bantam picked up the title in 1977. Protagonist Molly Bolt cracked jokes through her tomboyish childhood and strained adolescence, enjoyed pansexual adventures, and came of age as a lesbian-feminist filming a documentary of her truculent mother. Humorous, woman-identified *Rubyfruit Jungle* easily supplanted Hall's tragic saga, reflecting lesbianism's improved social standing.

The lesbian literary juggernaut extended throughout the 1980s into the 1990s. Anthologies on every imaginable topic overran bookstores. Aging belletrist May Sarton, novelist Alice Walker, and poets Minnie Bruce Pratt and Gloria Anzaldúa accomplished mainstream successes based on merit, rather than novelty; Walker's smash best-seller *The Color Purple* (1982) became a hit movie. Bonnie Zimmerman details this literary heyday, describing how feel-good myths and coming-out stories gave way to varied, more maturely realized works.

The personal overshadowed the political by the early 1990s. "Sex-positive" glossy magazine *On Our Backs*—edited by television talk show "sexpert" Susie Bright—and lesbigay quarterly *Out/look* elbowed *Sinister Wisdom* and *Common Lives, Lesbian Lives* on coffee tables. Historian Joan Nestle revived butch/femme; sex radical Pat Califia championed s/m erotica. Alison Bechdel's syndicated comic strip *Dykes to Watch Out For* has chronicled a generation, à la Doonesbury. Jeanette Winterson and Sarah Schulman established themselves as cutting-edge novelists; French-Canadian Nicole Brossard and Americans Cherry Muhanji and Judith Kaplan ran toward the postmodern; and Dorothy Allison's harrowing first novel, *Bastard Out of Carolina* (1992), was a National Book Award finalist.

Lesbian literature had "arrived"—again. But the major news on the eve of the twenty-first century was the meteoric rise of lesbian "genre fiction." Joanna Russ pioneered women's sci-fi in the 1970s; Marion Zimmer Bradley's mainstream fantasy novels, some showcasing lesbian "Free Amazons," have attained cult status. Katherine Forrest has led the van of lesbian mystery writers since the 1980s, along with Barbara Wilson, though Sara Paretaky's straight private investigator V. I. Warshawsky dominated the early 1990s. Lynn Andrews and Australian Anna Livia generated notable lesbian sci-fi/fantasy, while Jewelle Gomez's *Gilda Stories* (1991) assured that lesbian vampirism may never die.

During the twentieth century, Western lesbian literature has progressed from covert to classical, from déclassé to consciousness-raising* to commercial, paralleling the social fortunes of lesbians and lesbianism. Print media still inform lesbian culture, even as the Internet expands textual horizons.

References. Shari Benstock, *Women of the Left Bank: Paris 1900–1940* (Austin, Tex., 1986); John Boswell, *Christianity, Social Tolerance, and Homosexuality* (Chicago, 1980); Lillian Faderman, *Surpassing the Love of Men* (New York, 1981); Jeanette Foster, *Sex Variant Women in Literature* (Tallahassee, 1985 [1958]); Barbara Grier, aka Gene Damon, *Lesbiana: Book Reviews from The Ladder, 1966–1972* (Tallahassee, 1976); Jane Rule, *Lesbian Images* (New York, 1975); Bonnie Zimmerman, *The Safe Sea of Women: Lesbian Fiction 1969–89* (Boston, 1990).

PENELOPE J. ENGELBRECHT

LESBIAN MOTHERHOOD is the condition or institution of being a mother when the woman defines herself or is labeled as a lesbian. Because homosexuality* is stigmatized behavior, it is difficult to estimate the number of lesbian mothers in the population, though researchers have agreed that there are at least several hundred thousand and possibly as many as 2 or 3 million in the United States. Lesbian mothers include women who have become mothers through widely varying circumstances: in heterosexual marriages; by means of adoption; and outside marriage by means of heterosexual intercourse or artificial insemination by donor.

While some lesbian mothers remain legally married to the fathers of their children, the majority are probably divorced or never married; from a legal point of view, most are "single" despite the fact that they may be involved in long-term relationships with women partners. This means that they share many problems also experienced by other "single" mothers and female heads of household. These include low income (often linked to difficulties collecting child support payments), housing discrimination, problems locating adequate, affordable child care,* and stress derived from performing parental roles without assistance from another adult.

At the same time, lesbian mothers are especially vulnerable to some problems less frequently faced by heterosexual mothers. Most significant among these are legal challenges to child custody. Lesbian mothers are likely to be viewed as "unfit" by judges solely because of their sexual orientation* and therefore try to avoid custody litigation whenever possible. In many cases, this leads them to compromise with former husbands about child support and other paternal obligations, thereby exposing themselves and their families to more severe financial problems than they might otherwise encounter. Cases have been documented in which former husbands have explicitly demanded such compromises in exchange for agreements not to challenge custody. Some recent research also indicates that fear of custody disputes may be a major source of anxiety for many lesbian mothers, even when such disputes have not occurred.

Probably the majority of lesbian mothers had their children during marriages, in many instances before recognizing their sexual orientation. For self-defined lesbians who wish to become mothers, both pregnancy and adoption may be difficult to achieve. An increasingly visible group of lesbian mothers become pregnant through artificial insemination, either using semen donated by a friend or a person contacted through an intermediary or using semen obtained from a sperm bank or similar service. If a known donor is used, there is some risk that he may later seek visitation or even custody rights. Artificial insemination by donor, on the other hand, entails no legal obligations for the donor and is entirely anonymous. It may be expensive, however, and some physicians may be unwilling to provide the service for unmarried women or for lesbians. For similar reasons, lesbians usually encounter difficulties qualifying as adoptive parents.

Another issue of concern to lesbian mothers is the effect of their stigmatized sexual orientation on their children. Some women, sharing the values of the wider culture, prefer that their children develop a heterosexual orientation and take measures that they feel will encourage their children in that direction. For others, concern centers around the reactions of other children and the possibility that they will tease or harass children whose mothers are known to be lesbian. Both of these concerns, as well as anxiety about custody litigation, may lead mothers to be secretive about their lesbianism.

Much of the literature on lesbian mothers has concerned psychological outcomes for children, particularly the impact of lesbianism on sexual orientation. Virtually all research has shown that maternal homosexuality has no effect on children's later sexual proclivities. Rather, a substantial body of research indicates that children of lesbian mothers fare no differently than children of other single mothers.

There is also a growing literature on lesbian mothers themselves. This has included personal accounts by lesbian mothers, especially of experiences with custody litigation, and a number of practical guides to becoming mothers or to dealing with the legal complexities of lesbian motherhood. A significant legal literature, aimed both at attorneys representing lesbian mothers and at judicial audiences, also has emerged. More work remains to be done in a number of key areas, including the long-term experience of children conceived through artificial insemination and the implications of changing mores on the legal problems faced by lesbian mothers.

References. N. D. Hunter and N. D. Polikoff, "Custody Rights of Lesbian Mother: Legal Theory and Litigation Strategy," *Buffalo Law Review* 25 (1976): 691–733; J. Jullion, *Long Way Home: The Odyssey of a Lesbian Mother and Her Children* (San Francisco, 1985); E. Lewin, "Lesbianism and Motherhood: Implications for Child Custody," *Human Organization* 40 (1981): 6–14; C. Pies, *Considering Parenthood: A Workbook for Lesbians* (San Francisco, 1985).

ELLEN LEWIN

LESBIANS are women who choose other women as affectional and sexual partners and who identify themselves as lesbians. In doing so, they break with deep-seated cultural assumptions about heterosexuality,* suffer the social consequences of this identification, and create through this sense of difference a community with a distinctive approach to everyday life.

While lesbians are usually defined (and define themselves) in relation to an erotic response or choice, many understand their lesbianism as a specific political commitment centered in their interests in woman-identification and women's political challenge to patriarchal institutions and mythology.

The word "lesbian" itself derives from the Greek Isle of Lesbos and a colony of female homosexuals associated with Sappho of Lesbos, c. 600 B.C. The term "lesbian" was redefined positively with the advent of the feminist and gay liberation movements of the 1960s and 1970s. Some lesbians now describe themselves as gay, female homosexuals, or dykes. The author Alice Walker has coined the term "womanist"* to describe female bonding among black women.

Lesbian identity derives from social definitions and categorizations that are grounded in specific historical and cultural conditions. "Coming out" is a process of recognition and self-awareness of oneself as a lesbian. This process is not linear but includes most, if not all, of the following: the realization of erotic interest in women, sexual experiences with women, strong emotional attachments to women, involvement and membership in a lesbian subculture, and transformation of identity. Many women on the route to a lesbian identity deny and repress their desires, interests, and connections to women.

There are lesbians of every race, economic background, age, and religious and political affiliation. Yet lesbians are often invisible. Lesbian invisibility results both from others' denial of the possibility and existence of women-identified relationships and women-centered sexuality as well as from deliberate efforts on the part of lesbians to keep their sexual identity unknown. Lesbians who are members of ethnic communities and racial minorities in the United States often keep their identity unknown to maintain important ties with those communities despite homophobia.*

Lesbians suffer problems similar to those of other women with regard to economic and legal discrimination,* the lack of control over reproduction, limited representation in the major social institutions, violence against women, and ideologies prescribing "proper womanhood" promulgated by religion, the psychological profession, and the media.

But lesbians, as a consequence of their sexual identity, have additional problems as well. They are excluded from legal protection in housing, employment, military service, adoptions, and child custody. Their relationships do not have the economic and social supports of heterosexual married couples. Lack of legal protections and negative cultural attitudes often result in lesbians' denial of their identity to coworkers, friends, or family members. For example, though the vast majority of lesbians are self-supporting and must rely on their own labors for survival, they anticipate discrimination at work; some portion do lose their jobs; and very often these fears and experiences force lesbians to limit their workplace contacts with colleagues and to keep their identity secret.

Crucial to lesbians' survival are their extended family* of friends. These friendship networks support lesbians through major and minor life events, provide the context for kinlike rituals at holiday times, and serve as the source of new lover relationships. Lesbian relationships hold the potential for a unique pairing of equals; however, they, too, must grapple with issues of autonomy and dependence and disparities in couples of age, income, religion, or class.

Many lesbians are mothers of children from heterosexual marriages. Lesbian mothers share with other single women the problems of low income, limited housing, and child care* options. Lesbian mothers, however, also fear child custody battles in which their sexual identity might be used to declare them "unfit mothers." In the 1980s, other lesbians were able to choose to have children through artificial insemination by using formal sperm banks or informal networks of friends willing to donate sperm.

The development of explicitly public and feminist-identified lesbian communities has occurred recently. Between the 1920s and World War II, most lesbians were either isolated or participated in the "homosexual underground" of bars and social clubs in urban bohemian quarters. World War II altered the lives of lesbians who joined the military by advancing their economic independence and fostering the development of urban meeting grounds at which other lesbians could be found. The cultural milieu of the 1950s exercised considerable pressure on lesbians to marry, and the political persecution of the Cold War/McCarthy era resulted in serious repression of sexual minorities and political dissidents. Nevertheless, Daughters of Bilitis was formed in 1955 as an organization focused on providing support for lesbians and educating the general public about the "normality" of these women. Most lesbians in the 1950s chose to survive either by being "obvious dykes" who appeared manly to others and worked in jobs traditionally defined as masculine or by being "superladies" who chose to "pass" as heterosexual women.

The black civil rights movement of the 1960s was the prototype for the early women's and gay liberation movements. The new movements emphasized lesbian and gay pride, the importance of "coming out" and not being invisible, and the positive assertion of rights to end sexual and political oppression. Lesbians have complicated relationships to both the feminist movement and the gay liberation movement.

The 1970s lesbian communities were motivated by feminist politics. Lesbianism was seen as a choice for women in a sexist world. Women's independence from men and the importance of female identification, bonding, and loyalty to other women were encouraged. Lesbian separatism, the repudiation of, and withdrawal from, male society, was a particular organizational and political strategy that emerged in the early years of lesbian community development. Though not embraced by most lesbians, it was a necessary ingredient in the formation of an alternative feminist culture. The issue of separatism caused conflict within the women's movement and among lesbians themselves. More recently, serious conflict has emerged concerning class and race among lesbians and the extent to which the primarily white and middle-class lesbian communities attend to racism and economic difference. The 1980s saw considerable controversy among lesbians about sexual practice and sexual pleasure.

Some of the most enduring features of lesbian communities are cultural: the creation of presses, publications, and music that assert the distinctiveness of lesbian experience and offer a portrayal of lesbians' lives that makes sense to them. Books about lesbian sexuality, written by lesbians, were published in the early 1980s. Lesbians have also created for themselves and other women coffeehouses, bookstores, and self-help health and other projects in most small and large cities across the country.

References. T. Darty and S. Potter (eds.), *Women-Identified Women* (Beverly Hills, Calif., 1984); C. Moraga and G. Anzaldua (eds.), *This Bridge Called My Back: Writings by Radical Women of Color* (Watertown, Mass., 1981); C. Pies, *Considering Parenthood: A Workbook for Lesbians* (San Francisco, 1985); J. P. Stanley and S. J. Wolfe (eds.), *The Coming Out Stories* (Watertown, Mass., 1980).

BETH E. SCHNEIDER

LETTERS ON THE EQUALITY OF THE SEXES (1838) is the first in-depth philosophical discussion of woman's rights by an American woman, Sarah Moore Grimké. In the *Letters*, Grimké made a far-reaching examination into the conditions of the lives of women in the United States and around the world. She analyzed the laws affecting women; the inequities women faced in education and employment; the specific injuries suffered by female slaves; and the subjugation of women by men, especially in marriage. Most important, in the *Letters* Grimké provided a biblical justification for the liberty and equality of women as moral and autonomous beings.

Grimké and her sister Angelina Grimké (Wald) were prominent speakers on the abolitionist circuit at a time when it was considered inappropriate and immoral for women to speak in public. They were both acclaimed and condemned for their activism. The most vicious attack came in the form of a pastoral letter from the Council of Congregationalist Ministers of Massachusetts, which denounced their behavior as unwomanly and un-Christian. Sarah Grimké wrote the *Letters*, originally published as a series of articles in the *New England Spectator* in 1837, in direct response to the charges raised against her and her sister in the pastoral letter. She argued that God made no distinction between men and women as moral beings and that whatever was morally right for a man to do was also right for a woman.

The most significant contribution of the *Letters* to feminist thought is Grimké's demonstration of a scriptural basis for the equality of the sexes. Taking scriptural verses that for centuries had been used to demonstrate the *inequality* of the sexes, Grimké provided new interpretations that supported the essential equality of women and men. Specifically, she argued that the biblical account of creation showed (1) that both male and female are created in the image of God, and thus there can be no difference between them; (2) that God gave man and woman dominion over all other creatures, but not over each other; and (3) that woman was created to be a helpmate to man, *like unto himself.* She interpreted the story of Adam and Eve in the Garden of Eden as showing that since both ate the forbidden fruit, both sinned. Thus, though both women and men fell from innocence, they did not fall from equality. She also used notions from the New Testament, such as the idea that there is no male or female but only one in Christ, to demonstrate the equality of the sexes.

Grimké provided an important analysis of marriage in the *Letters*. She expressed concern that in marriage women were deprived of their moral autonomy. Women defined themselves before marriage solely in terms of attracting a future husband and after marriage in terms of fulfilling their husbands' needs. Moreover, the laws regarding married women, which deprived women of property and contract rights and of their very legal existence through the notion of coverture, assured women's moral dependence. Grimké argued as well that the functionalist attitude of husbands toward their wives—that wives were instruments of domestic comfort and physical pleasure rather than moral and intellectual companions—furthered the destruction of woman's autonomy and sense of self-worth.

In her analysis of woman's economic status and role, Grimké pioneered not only the notion that every vocational sphere should be open to women but also the notion of comparable worth—that a laundress who works as long and as hard as a wood sawyer should be paid equally with him. Atypical of many feminist tracts of this era, the issues addressed in the *Letters* were not confined to the concerns of white, middle-class women. Grimké was well aware of, and expressed concern for, the exceedingly hard labors of working-class women. Nevertheless, she was firmly entrenched in the nineteenth-century, middle-class cult of domesticity and consistently maintained that women must not abandon their special responsibilities in the home.

The *Letters* also contain many expressions of feminist sisterhood. Grimké paralleled the condition of degradation and subjugation of white, middle-class American women with those of female slaves and working-class women in the United States and with women in Europe, Asia, and Africa. In the *Letters*, though Grimké did not show a strong conception of the positive foundations of female solidarity, she did give clear expression to a notion of female bonding through common suffering.

References. Sarah M. Grimké, *Letters on the Equality of the Sexes and Other Essays*, ed. and intro. Elizabeth Ann Bartlett (New Haven, Conn., 1988); Gerda Lerner, *The Grimké Sisters from South Carolina: Pioneers for Woman's Rights and Abolition* (New York, 1971).

ELIZABETH ANN BARTLETT

LEVIRATE is a marriage law or custom by which the widow and a brother (or failing a brother, the nearest male kin) of the deceased husband may or must marry. The dead husband is presumed to continue his duties to his wife and children, and any progeny by the brother are considered to be the children of the deceased.

The custom existed widely in ancient western Asia (e.g., among the Israelites, Hittites, Assyrians) and is found in Polynesia, Central Africa, the Americas, and elsewhere. In some societies (e.g., Israelites, Malagasy), the law prescribed brother–widow marriage only if the deceased husband had no sons. In Deuteronomy (25: 5–10) only the first son was considered the son of the deceased.

Interpretations vary. Some see the practice as an aspect of patrilineal inheritance, although not all societies with the custom are patrilineal. Others point to its social utility in providing a system for the maintenance of widows and orphans or to its significance in providing heirs to perform rites and sacrifices for the deceased.

LIBRARIANSHIP. Although the existence of libraries can be traced as far back as the ancient cultures of Sumer and Egypt, modern American library service derived a great deal from England. Probably the first university library was established in 1638, when John Harvard left 400 volumes to the college that was renamed after him. Social libraries (libraries in which members bought stock) and circulating libraries (libraries that charged users rental fees) began in the 1700s. Public libraries came into existence in the nineteenth century, with the Boston Public Library (opened in 1845) being one of the earliest large public libraries.

It appears that the earliest librarians were men. In fact, because some of the social and circulating libraries catered to popular taste (not necessarily literary quality), "[t]he use of these libraries by women went so far as to raise serious doubts about the propriety of teaching the feminine sex to read" (Shera, 37). In 1853, the first convention of librarians was held in New York. It was attended by 82 *men* ("librarians, educators, authors, and clergy") (Gates, 87).

Women soon entered the field of librarianship, however. When Melvil Dewey established the first library school in 1887, the majority of students were women. Dewey recruited women into the profession, partially because of economics. Since library resources and funds were limited, Dewey and other leaders in the library movement saw the employment of women as a way to save money. Well-educated women could be employed for less money than men, and since librarianship was one of the few professions open to them, women were content to settle for this inequity (Schiller).

For years, a majority of librarians have been female. In 1994, 84.1 percent of the nation's librarians were women (*Statistical Abstracts*, 411). Of the 4,363 students reported to have graduated from 48 reporting accredited library and information science programs in 1994, approximately 2,450 were women. Of these graduates, 1,496 women and 322 men began careers in library positions (Zipkowitz).

Although there continues to be a salary gap between female librarians and their male counterparts, the gap appears to be closing. The average beginning salary of the 1994 graduates just mentioned was $28,065 for women, while it was $28,182 for men. The median was $26,000 for women, compared to $27,000 for men. A 1992 salary survey of the Association of Research Libraries' (ARL) university librarians (not including those in law and medical libraries) found that women were making about 8 percent less pay than men in ARL member libraries ("ARL Librarians," 18). Similarly, a Special Libraries Association (SLA) report issued in 1993 found that women's salaries in special libraries have increased by 27 percent since 1990 and by 165 percent since 1976, while for men they increased 19 percent since 1990 and 129 percent since 1976 ("Women Gaining," 110–111).

Despite the fact that most librarians are women, a majority of the top management positions are filled by men. The ARL survey found that of the 103 top directorships in ARL libraries, 60 percent were held by men, although women made up 60 percent of the ARL professional workforce. In the ARL libraries, the salary margin narrows as women advance up the career ladder; the average salary for female academic library directors is $98,989, or 2 percent less than the $100,981 for men. The SLA survey finds the standard librarian/information specialist nearing salary equity ($36,567 median for men versus $35,480 for women), while the median salary for managers was $46,150 for men versus $42,000 for women.

References. "ARL Librarians Average $42,144," *Library Journal* 118, 5 (March 15, 1993); J. K. Gates, *Introduction to Librarianship* (New York, 1968); A. R. Schiller, "Sex and Library Careers," in M. Myers and M. Scarborough (eds.), *Women in Librarianship: Melvil's Rib Symposium* (New Brunswick, N.J., 1975), 11–20; J. H. Shera, *Introduction to Library Science* (Littleton, Colo., 1976); *Statistical Abstracts of the United States 1995* (Washington, D.C., 1995); "Women Gaining in SLA's 11 Biennial Salary Survey," *Library Journal* 118, 18 (February 15, 1993); F. Zipkowitz, "New Directions for Recent Grads, *Library Journal* 120, 17 (October 15, 1995) 26–33.

CHERYL BECKER

LIENU ZHUAN is the title of a collection of biographies of notable Chinese women compiled by the Confucian scholar-official Liu Xiang (77–6 B.C.E.). Published at a time when Confucianism* had just become the state orthodoxy, the text was meant to give women a stake in the Confucian enterprise by praising those women who contributed to the strengthening of the moral fabric of society and denouncing those who weakened it. The present shape of the text dates from the thirteenth century and comprises eight chapters with 15 biographies per chapter. Each of the first six chapters is devoted to a particular "type" of woman. The first six are of virtuous types, namely, "exemplary mothers," "worthy and astute women," "benevolent and wise women," "women of propriety," "women of sexual integrity," and "women of superior intellect." The women in Chapter 7 are "licentious and depraved women." Chapter 8, not of Liu Xiang's hand but added sometime later, consists of a miscellany of model women.

The virtuous women, in their decisive actions and bold speeches, show themselves to be fully conversant with, and faithful to, Confucian teachings, often more so than the men in their lives. As mothers and wives, they dispense advice at every turn, not just in the domestic sphere but in the political sphere as well. Some excel in the use of subtlety in reforming their wayward husbands or sons, while others mince no words in denouncing behavior they consider unacceptable. Some of the women are more taken up with their sense of their own personal honor and are ready to die if necessary to protect that honor from any hint of disgrace. The "bad" women, in contrast to these virtuous women, are interested only in their own pleasure and think nothing of the moral consequences of ensnaring men with their beauty. The fall of nations is blamed on these selfish, licentious women.

The importance of this text lies first in its presentation of such a large number of lively, articulate, and astute women for praise in the Chinese sociopolitical realm (even if it was for their contributions to the moral life of men) and second, for setting a precedent for collecting biographies of women. All subsequent dynastic histories and local gazetteers included virtuous (but not depraved) women in their biographical sections. Later editions of the *Lienu zhuan* often were illustrated and updated with women of subsequent dynasties.

Reference. Albert O'Hara, *The Position of Women in Early China according to the Lieh Nu Chuan, the Biographies of Chinese Women* (1945; repr. Taipei, 1971).

M. THERESA KELLEHER

LITERARY CRITICISM. Feminist, analyzes texts with respect to the ideology of gender. In its preoccupation with how women in particular are represented in the system of gender relationships, feminist literary criticism may also share characteristics with other kinds of criticism, such as Marxist, neohistoricist, psychoanalytic, poststructuralist, cultural, and multicultural criticism. Its scope encompasses all world literatures and is not limited to the canonical genres of fiction, poetry, and plays.

Feminist literary criticism emerged in the United States in the 1960s, although its precursors can be found in the self-reflexive comments of women writers who discuss their circumstances as literary producers. Virginia Woolf, the first modern feminist critic, provides a more direct impetus to feminist critical activity in her explorations of woman's economic, artistic, sexual, political, and educational position in a society characterized by patriarchal dominance. Simone de Beauvoir's monumental study *The Second Sex* (1949; United States, 1952) signals the emergence of a contemporary, interdisciplinary, theoretical discourse on women. Beauvoir's claim, "One is not born, but rather becomes, a woman" (*The Second Sex*, 1974, 301) has assumed even greater resonance in feminist work today.

The activity of feminist criticism occurs in various nonevolutionary forms in the latter half of this century. Kate Millett represents feminist criticism's initial activity: the exposé and critique of women's representation in works by male authors in the literary canon. More than an obvious "first phase," this strategy of rereading, also epitomized in Judith Fetterley, marks an important dimension of feminist critical activity and has become increasingly developed and particularized through the contributions of reader-response and poststructuralist criticism.

The work of recovering, reassessing, and reissuing lost and forgotten texts by women writers, a major enterprise within feminist literary criticism, has resulted in rich discoveries of writers whose analyses of sex, race, class, and sexual orientation challenge conventional delineations of "the literary" with respect to genre, author, subject matter, and style. The publication lists of the Feminist Press, Kitchen Table Women of Color Press, Naiad Press, and series such as New York University Press' "Cutting Edge" and Columbia University Press' "Between Men—Between Women" in the United States, of *des femmes* in France, and of Virago and Verso in England demonstrate the feminist effort to subvert received notions of literary critical tradition. These texts contribute significantly to investigations of writing signed by women, as well as being useful in efforts to document relationships between women writers.

A number of works characterize this interest in women's writing and writing about women. Ellen Moer's *Literary Women* was one of the first important considerations of a women's literary tradition. Sandra Gilbert and Susan Gubar present a provocative and controversial theory of female creativity. These and other critical studies illustrate the benefits of what Elaine Showalter terms "gynocritics" or "the study of women *as writers* . . . the history, styles, themes, genres, and structures of writing by women, the psychodynamics of female creativity, the trajectory of the individual or collective female career, and the evolution and laws of a female literary tradition" (248). Showalter contrasts "gynocritics" with what she regards as the "ideological" mode of *"feminist reading"* or the *"feminist critique,"* which "offers feminist readings of texts which consider the images and stereotypes of women in literature, the omissions and misconceptions about women in criticism" (245), as well as considerations of woman-as-sign in discursive systems. Showalter's view, relying on an essentialist conception of gender, has been broadly challenged, particularly for its exclusions.

The circle of activity needs to be drawn ever larger to encompass various feminisms often reflective of divergent interests and emphases. Some of the more pressing issues within contemporary feminist literary criticism are represented in the landmark dialogue between Peggy Kamuf and Nancy Miller. Kamuf's piece can be viewed as one of the initial challenges to the essentialism that is taken by some as characteristic of feminist work in the 1970s. This debate forms a major preoccupation of contemporary feminist literary criticism. The issues are elaborated in Fuss and Butler. The attack against essentialism, on the nominalization of woman/women, reflects current poststructuralist understandings of representation, particularly the role of language and the authority of experience, as well as of identity politics, inclusive of sexuality, gender, race, class, and other similar category descriptors.

Several varieties of feminist criticism deserve special mention. Feminist literary scholarship concerned with psychoanalysis has gained impressive strength, offering feminist rereadings of Freud and Lacan, of canonical authors and texts, and of works by women writers. Critical writing addressing African American literature and culture offers a rich area of study. Many early works (Roseann P. Bell, Bettye J. Parker, and Beverly Guy-Sheftall; Barbara Smith; Cherrie Moraga and Gloria Anzaldua; Gloria T. Hull, Patricia Bell Scott, and Barbara Smith) retain their currency. They have been supplemented by an impressive array of more specific monographs that focus, in the main, on groups of African American women writers and on diasporic cultural-aesthetic relationships.

Various other alliances (postcolonial studies and queer studies in particular) are resulting in exciting new directions for feminist criticism. Gayatri Chakravorty Spivak's work represents just such a complex convergence as she probes the intersections of feminism, Marxism, poststructuralism, and racism from the standpoint of the postcolonial speaker. Lesbian and queer studies evidence explosive levels of activity, warranting extended discussion of their own. Notable recent works are by Laura Doan and Karla Jay. Feminist literary criticism of the past decade suggests an even broader range for investigating the significant relation of gender to social institutions, as we continue to explore the complex nexus of exclusion, in order to supplement, challenge, and rewrite the terms upon which past literary critical activities have been based.

References. Roseann P. Bell, Bettye J. Parker, and Beverly Guy-Sheftall (eds.), *Sturdy Black Bridges: Visions of Black Women in Literature* (New York, 1979); Judith Butler, *Gender Trouble* (New York, 1990); Judith Butler, *Bodies That Matter* (New York, 1993); Simone de Beauvoir, *The Second Sex*, trans. and ed. H. M. Parshley (New York, 1974); Laura Doan (ed.), *The Lesbian Postmodern* (New York, 1994); Diane Elam and Robyn Wiegman (eds.), *Feminism beside Itself* (New York, 1995); Jane Gallop, *Around 1981: Academic Feminist Literary Theory* (New York, 1992); Judith Fetterley, *The Resisting Reader* (Bloomington, Ind., 1978); Diana Fuss, *Essentially Speaking* (New York, 1989); Sandra Gilbert and Susan Gubar, *The Madwoman in the Attic: The Woman Writer and the Nineteenth-Century Literary Imagination* (New Haven, Conn., 1979); Gloria T. Hull, Patricia Bell Scott, and Barbara Smith (eds.), *All the Women Are White, All the Blacks Are Men, but Some of Us Are Brave: Black Women's Studies* (Old Westbury, N.Y., 1982); Karla Jay (ed.), *Dyke Life* (New York, 1995); Karla Jay (ed.), *The Lesbian Erotic* (New York, 1995); Karla Jay and Joanne Glasgow (eds.), *Lesbian Texts and Contexts: Radical Revisions* (New York, 1990); Peggy Kamuf and Nancy Miller, *Diacritic* 12 (1982): 42–53; Elizabeth Meese, *(Sem)Erotics—Theorizing Lesbian: Writing* (New York, 1992); Kate Millett, *Sexual Politics* (New York, 1971); Trinh T. Minh-Ha, *Framer Framed* (New York, 1992); Ellen Moer, *Literary Women: The Great Writers* (Garden City, N.Y., 1977); Cherrie Moraga and Gloria Anzaldua (eds.), *This Bridge Called My Back: Writings by Radical Women of Color* (Watertown, Mass., 1981); Elaine Showalter, "Feminist Criticism in the Wilderness," in Elaine Showalter (ed.), *The New Feminist Criticism: Essays on Women, Literature, and Theory* (New York, 1985); Barbara Smith (ed.), *Home Girls* (New York, 1983); Gayatri Chakravorty Spivak, *In Other Worlds* (New York, 1988); Patricia J. Williams, *The Alchemy of Race and Rights* (Cambridge, 1991).

ELIZABETH A. MEESE

LOCAL COLORISTS are writers of the latter nineteenth and early twentieth centuries whose work is characterized by use of authentic local settings, regional dialects and characters, and historically accurate details of custom and habit. Their vision—especially in the early period of the New

England school—was of a rural matriarchy that was counterposed to industrialism and Calvinism, which were seen as patriarchal systems inimical to women. Thus, their fiction often presents strong women characters in preindustrial milieux and focuses on rural women's cultural traditions and practices, some now largely forgotten, such as herbal medicine. The form the local colorists favored was the short story, although there are a few notable local color novels, for example, Harriet Beecher Stowe's *Minister's Wooing* (1859), *Pearl of Orr's Island* (1862), and *Oldtown Folks* (1869).

The women's local color story in the United States derived from the "village sketch" tradition pioneered in the 1820s by an Englishwoman, Mary Russell Mitford (1787–1855). Her focus was on eccentric personalities caught in humorous predicaments, and her sketches, which were enormously popular, were filled with specific local detail.

In this country the local color tradition may be distinguished from the other dominant women's literary tradition in the nineteenth century, sentimentalism or domestic realism, more recently labeled "woman's fiction" by Nina Baym. Local color literature was much closer to realism in its use of authentic character and local detail and in its avoidance of hyperbolic rhetoric and idealistic and romantic plot (all features of sentimentalism).

Caroline Kirkland was one of the first American women writers to develop realist literature. In her preface to *A New Home—Who'll Follow?* (1839), which describes pioneers' experiences in Michigan, Kirkland states that she is consciously emulating Mitford's sketches. But Harriet Beecher Stowe (1811–1896) was the first to formulate the classic American women's local color story with several New England "sketches" published in the 1830s. The first novel by a black woman, *Our Nig* (1859), by Harriet E. Wilson, which is set in New England, is an interesting hybrid that reflects a local color and sentimentalist influence along with that of the black slave narrative.

The other pioneer of the women's local color movement was Rose Terry Cooke (1827–1892), whose stories are set mainly in Connecticut. The best of these are collected in *Somebody's Neighbors* (1881) and *Huckleberries Gathered from New England Hills* (1891). Probably the greatest of the New England local colorists was Sarah Orne Jewett (1849–1909), whose *Country of the Pointed Firs* (1896), set in Maine and focusing upon a powerful rural matriarch, is considered a classic of American literature. The other major New England local colorist was Mary E. Wilkins Freeman (1852–1930), whose *Humble Romance and Other Stories* (1887) and *New England Nun and Other Stories* (1891) include several masterpieces of the genre.

Other women who wrote important northeastern local color works include Elizabeth Stuart Phelps (Ward) (1844–1911), Alice Brown (1857–1948), Celia Thaxter (1835–1894), Constance Fenimore Woolson (1840–1894), Harriet Prescott Spofford (1835–1921), Elizabeth Oakes Smith

(1806–1893), Annie Trumbull Slosson (1838–1926), Esther B. Carpenter (1848–1893), Harriet Waters Preston (1836–1911), Alice B. Neal (1827–1863), Elsie Singmaster (1879–1958), Margaret Deland (1857–1945), and Helen Reimensnyder Martin (1868–1939). The latter three set their material primarily in Pennsylvania. Peripheral to the local colorists were the women humorists Frances Whitcher (1813?–1852) and Marietta Hoxley (1836–1926).

The local color tradition was transported to the South by Mary Murfree (1850–1922), whose *In the Tennessee Mountains* (1884) is considered her most important work, and Grace King (1851–1932) of Louisiana. Kate Chopin (1851–1904), whose work, like King's, is set in the Delta region, is the best known of the southern regionalists. Her novel *The Awakening* (1899) is now regarded as a feminist classic. Other important writers of the southern school include Katherine McDowell (1849–1883) and Ruth M. Stuart (1849–1917).

Alice Cary (1820–1871) was among the earliest to set their works in the Midwest. The midwestern tradition included Mary Catherwood (1847–1902), Alice French (1850–1934), and Zona Gale (1874–1938) in her early works, such as *Friendship Village* (1908). Mary Hallock Foote (1847–1938) treated the Far West.

Later writers such as Willa Cather (1873–1947), Ellen Glasgow (1873–1945), or Mary Austin (1868–1934), who set their material in specific regions, are not considered local colorists because their work lacked what Edith Wharton called the "rose-coloured" tint associated (in many cases incorrectly) with the nineteenth-century school.

References. Nina Baym, *Women's Fiction* (Ithaca, N.Y., 1978); Josephine Donovan, *New England Local Color Literature: A Woman's Tradition* (New York, 1983); Lina Mainiere (ed.), *American Women Writers: A Critical Reference Guide*, 4 vols. (New York, 1979–1982).

JOSEPHINE DONOVAN

LOCUS OF CONTROL is a theory of individual differences in expectancies for control. The theory states that people learn, through rewards and punishments, to hold certain expectations as to control over the events of their lives. Persons holding internal locus of control beliefs expect personal control over their lives. Those holding external locus of control beliefs place the expectancy for control outside themselves, on luck, fate, chance, or powerful others (Rotter).

Early work with the locus of control construct tended to overgeneralize the concept by labeling people "internals" or "externals," and a great deal of research demonstrated the social, emotional, and psychological superiority of "internals." Hanna Levenson, among others, questioned this either/or conceptualization of locus of control. She thought it possible to believe both in the power of luck and in individual effort. Levenson further pointed out that many people believe that not only luck and fate but also powerful other people control their lives. She developed a scale to measure the internal and two external dimensions (chance and powerful others) of the locus of control concept.

P. Gurin et al. also objected to the mental health assumptions attached to an internal locus of control. They argued that when outcomes are positive, feelings of internal or personal control are more likely to result in positive mental health. However, when outcomes are negative, an internal locus of control can result in self-blame and self-hatred. Gurin et al. also pointed out that for some groups an external locus of control may be more healthy, especially if that external view acknowledges the role of society in determining personal outcomes. Among their sample of low-income blacks, they asserted, it is probably more realistic to acknowledge the societal constraints on individual behavior; racial and economic discrimination* limits personal control. Gurin et al. thus introduced an additional external dimension of locus of control, "system's blame," and demonstrated the healthy consequences of such external beliefs for the politically and economically disadvantaged.

A similar process has been demonstrated with feminists. Feminists were found to be internal on personal control but external on ideological measures and more critical of the system as responsible for women's inferior status in society. Externality for this group was shown to be related to involvement in the feminist movement, a result similar to that found for blacks: involvement in social and collective action for blacks was positively related to a belief in system's blame. Thus, an awareness of systematic factors controlling one's outcomes, especially when coupled with internality on the personal control dimension, seems to motivate one to try to change the system.

A number of studies have found women in general to be more external in their locus of control than men. Self-esteem and sex-role socialization* are cited as possible determinants of the extent of internal-external locus of control. Women with higher self-esteem and less rigid sex-role socialization tend to be more internal in their locus of control. This difference is important in that women with a more internal locus of control are also found to be higher achievers and are probably more assertive. Among recent college student samples, however, there tend to be fewer sex differences in locus of control beliefs.

The locus of control concept has generated a rich body of literature and many questionnaire-format instruments with which to assess locus of control beliefs. In addition to the several general assessment instruments, specialized instruments have been developed to assess locus of control with regard to health, achievement, affiliation, and so on. Current theorists point out the need to include a measure of the value of the reinforcement. Presumably, the extent to which one values health, for example, the more internal or personal will be the expectancy to control health-related behaviors.

References. P. Gurin, G. Gurin, R. Lao, and M. Beattie, "Internal-External Control in the Motivational Dynamics of Negro Youth," *Journal of Social Issues* 25 (1969): 29–53; Hanna Levenson, "Multidimensional Locus of Control in Psychiatric Patients," *Journal of Consulting and Clinical Psychology* 41 (1937): 397–404; J. Rotter, "Generalized Expectancies for Internal-External Control of Reinforcement," *Psychological Monographs* 80 (1966): 1–28.

PATRICIA D. ROZEE

M

MACHISMO, or male dominance behavior, has been defined as both universal and particularly Hispanic. Francisco J. Santamaria writes that "machismo" refers to the vulgar expression of manhood and virility. It is a derivative of "macho," which, according to Santamaria, means a man who has much energy or is very brave or of strong character. It also means superiority in size and strength, among other attributes. Machismo is defined in the *Simon and Schuster International Dictionary: English/Spanish, Spanish/English* as male chauvinism, exaltation of masculinity, and hemanship.

Although machismo has been considered a Hispanic phenomenon, Gloria Canino (117–118) has observed that it also is a social class phenomenon among low-income Anglo groups that show the same type of male dominance. Machismo can be found in other cultures as well as the Hispanic.

Different theories attempt to explain machismo. The psychoanalytic theory focuses on men's use of sexual attitudes to prove their superiority over women. The macho man creates an illusion of superiority that is maintained by dominating others who are weaker than he, especially women. The penis is a symbol of his power.

Mexican writer Octavio Paz said that machismo is a mask that Mexican men wear in order to hide insecurities and fears. That mask of strength and superiority is a way to protect themselves from the lack of a well-defined identity. Paz thinks that this is a result of historical events in Mexico dating from the Spanish conquest to recent times. One of these historical events is related to *the Malinche*. She was a Mexican Indian and lover of Spanish conqueror Hernán Cortés. Mexicans have been struggling for generations between a rejection of the Indian who gave herself to the Spaniard and a rejection of the Spaniards who conquered them. Samuel Ramos has given a similar interpretation. He uses Alfred Adler's psychoanalytical ideas to interpret machismo as a defensive reaction to the Spanish conquest and a rebellion against authority.

Another theory views machismo as a product of socialization that is received at home during the early years. This socialization creates different roles according to gender. Simone de Beauvoir explained this differential socialization: the girl is taught to be passive, to learn how to please her husband and to be loyal to him, to stay at home, and take care of the children and housework. The boy is taught to be aggressive and to conquer the world beyond the walls of the house. The world of the woman is limited, thus, to her home, while the man moves in an ample space. He is the authority, while she is the "good girl" who obeys. While de Beauvoir was not talking about machismo but rather about differences between the sexes, it follows that when society encourages such extreme differences in behavior, machismo may easily develop. (See *SECOND SEX, THE.*)

These extreme differences in behavior are encouraged in Hispanic society, especially in small towns where almost everybody knows each other and, for that reason, tries to maintain a good reputation. Hispanics give great importance to the concepts of *honor* and *honra* (honor, virginity). Because the woman is considered weak and vulnerable to sexual assault, her male relatives (brothers, father, and husband) are very concerned about protecting her *honra*. If she loses her *honra*, her male relatives lose their *honor* (honor, reputation as a protector). In order to keep his honor, the man tries to protect the women of his family. Ways to protect the woman are to limit her space and supervise her actions. If the woman is young, a *chaperona* accompanies her when she has a date with a boyfriend.

There are negative and positive qualities attributed to the macho man. Among the negatives is promiscuity, because manhood is shown in the number of women conquered. If the macho man has money, he may have a second household with its own mistress. That second home is known in Spanish as *la casa chica* (the small home). Other negative qualities are the high consumption of alcoholic drinks and the violent repayment of insults. Fighting is seen as proof of masculinity and is a way to demonstrate power. Another negative quality, which may be considered a positive one, is the suppression of suffering in public. Macho men do not cry because that is considered a sign of weakness.

Among the positive qualities can be mentioned courage, bravery, and loyalty to friends. The macho man keeps secrets, even when beaten, to protect friends and does not show that he is suffering pain. He can also be aggressive when needed: to defend his honor, the honor of a friend, or the *honra* of a woman. Finally, the macho man provides for his family out of a strong sense of duty.

References. Gloria Canino, "The Hispanic Woman: Sociocultural Influences on Diagnosis and Treatment," in R. Becerra et al. (eds.), *Mental Health and the Hispanic American* (New York, 1982); R. E. Cromwell and R. A. Ruiz, "The Myth of

Macho Dominance in Decision Making within Mexican and Chicano Families,"
Hispanic Journal of Behavioral Sciences 1, 4 (1979): 355–373; Simone de Beauvoir,
The Second Sex, trans. H. M. Parshley (New York, 1974); O. Giraldo, "El ma-
chismo como fenómeno psicocultural" (Machismo as a Psychocultural Phenomenon), *Revista Latinoamericana de Psicologia* 4, 3 (1972): 295–309; Octavio Paz,
The Labyrinth of Solitude: Life and Thought in Mexico, trans. Lysander Kemp
(New York, 1950); Samuel Ramos, *Profile of Man and Culture in Mexico* (Austin,
Tex., 1962); Francisco J. Santamaria, *Diccionario de Mejicanismos* (Daly City, Calif., n.d.); Marcela Lucero Trujillo, "The Terminology of Machismo," *De Colores*
4, 3 (1978): 34–42; Rosendo Urrabazo, *Machismo: Mexican American Self-Concept*
(diss., Berkeley University; can be obtained through the Mexican-American Cultural
Center, San Antonio, Tex.).

AMALIA MONDRÍQUEZ

MACON, COUNCIL OF. A national synod of the Frankish clergy con-
voked by King Guntram in 585. According to Gregory of Tours (*History
of the Franks.* VIII. 203), at the meeting a bishop, unnamed, put forward
the proposition that women were not included in the term "man." His
opinion was refuted, confirming that women had souls and, therefore, were
spiritual equals with men.

That the issue could be raised and seriously discussed at the council
shows the persistence of attempts to give women a separate definition from
men and to deny them a similar destiny. The church, at the same time that
it continued to look on women's spirituality as somehow of a lower order
than men's, remained consistent in its insistence on basic spiritual equality.

MAGAZINES, FEMINIST. Explicitly feminist magazines in the United
States date from shortly after the 1848 Seneca Falls Women's Rights Convention, though earlier magazines printed feminist work; for example, the
Philadelphia *Lady's Magazine* in 1792 published selections from Mary
Wollstonecraft's *A Vindication of the Rights of Women.** In a cultural
climate with most popular magazines for women endorsing and representing a conservative, separate spheres mentality, domesticity, fashion, and
consumerism, the new magazines met a small, but eager, niche in the periodical marketplace.

In the 1840s, Margaret Fuller edited and contributed to the transcen-
dentalist *Dial*, which published her "The Great Lawsuit: Man vs. Men.
Woman vs. Women," among other feminist writing.

Suffrage magazines published the proceedings of suffrage conferences
and news of the movement, along with literature and discussion of reform
and social issues. *The Lily* (1849–1856), first edited by Amelia Bloomer,
advocated dress reform and woman suffrage and provided the first publication for Elizabeth Cady Stanton. The monthly *Genius of Liberty* (1852–
1854) was published from Cincinnati, the *Pioneer and Woman's Advocate*
from Providence, and the *Woman's Advocate* (1856–1860) from Philadel-

phia, the first magazine to be owned, edited, typeset, and printed by women and to focus on the rights (and wrongs) of working-class women. Boston's *Una* (1853–1855), founded by Paulina Wright Davis, specifically set out to counter the period's ladies' magazines, offering an alternative of suffrage news, legal and political issues, education, and literature. *Sibyl: A Review of the Tastes, Errors and Fashions of Society* (1856–1864) was the journal of the National Dress Reform Association and advocated women's voting rights, arguing that women, like black Americans, were enslaved. *The Revolution* (1868–1870) was edited by Susan B. Anthony and Elizabeth Cady Stanton. During Reconstruction, *The Revolution* promoted voting rights for black and white women; equity for working-class women; and marriage, divorce, and dress reforms. The Chicago *Agitator* (1869), the *Woman's Campaign* (1872), the *Ballot Box*, later the *National Citizen and Ballot Box* (1876–1881), the Chicago *Sorosis* (1868–1869), the Nebraska *Woman's Tribune* (1883–1909), the Oregon *New Northwest*, the Denver *Queen Bee* (1879–1896), and *The Farmer's Wife* give some indication of the national coverage of suffrage and women's issues. At the most radical extreme was *Woodhull and Claflin's Weekly* (1870–1876), which championed woman's rights and free love.

Later in the suffrage movement, the weekly *Woman's Journal* (1870–1917), edited by Lucy Stone and Henry Blackwell, became the chief periodical for the U.S. National Woman Suffrage Association (1870–1890) and then the National American Woman Suffrage Association. It was among the most highly subscribed, if more conservative, of the suffrage journals. Suffrage periodicals continued to appear, replacing earlier journals or adding to the mix: the *Woman's Tribune*, based in Washington state from 1889; the *Woman's Column* (1888–1904), a livelier version of the *Woman's Journal*, edited by Alice Stone Blackwell until she became coeditor of the *Journal*, *Progress* (1902–1910) from Ohio; and the state suffrage organization newsletters, for example, the *New York Suffrage Newsletter* (1899–1913). In addition to the suffrage periodicals, the growing women's club movement produced a number of journals, some with a feminist slant, and specialized journals for independent women—for example, the *Business Woman's Journal* (1889–1896)—gained audiences and shared commentary on issues like dress reform.

In England, Bessie Rayner Parkes and Barbara Boudichon established in 1858 the *English Woman's Journal*, a wholly women's concern focused on stories of exemplary women, women's employment, and literature. In 1888, Louisa Lawson, an active suffragist, created *Dawn*, the first feminist periodical in Australia. The *Freewoman*, edited by Dora Marsden from 1911, and its successors—*The New Freewoman*, edited by Harriet Shaw Weaver from 1913, and the *Egoist*—pioneered the use of advertising to subsidize their publications and radical suffrage politics. *Time and Tide*, a London journal organized by Lady Rhondda, introduced in the 1920s a regular evaluation of government policies on women's issues.

While there were no wholly feminist African American magazines, *Ringwood's Afro-American Journal of Fashion*, the first (1891) illustrated periodical by and for black women, contained a biographical section edited by feminist activist Mary Church Terrell. In the 1920s, the *Negro's World's* women's page under Amy Jacques Garvey followed a feminist, woman's rights agenda.

The "woman question," suffrage activities and arguments, women's education and roles in public life, and various reform movements (marriage, divorce, property and wage rights, dress, sports) also held a consistent and relatively prominent place in general, mainstream periodicals of the nineteenth century: *The Atlantic Monthly, Putnam's*, the *Republic*, the *Knickerbocker*, the *Arena*, the *North American Review, Scribner's*, the *Nation*. Most of the subscribers to general and women's, as well as feminist, magazines were women, but that did not determine the general magazines' position on suffrage or on other women's issues, as it was felt that women themselves were hardly unanimous in their views.

Charlotte Perkins Gilman's *The Forerunner* (1909–1916) and Emma Goldman's *Mother Earth* introduced a new level of feminist analysis in the magazines. *The Forerunner* was largely written by Perkins Gilman herself, from editorials through three serialized novels.

The Ladder (1956–1972), the first lesbian magazine in the United States, founded by the Daughters of Bilitis and based in San Francisco, is notable for its book reviews. *The Ladder* was followed by *Amazon Quarterly, a Lesbian Feminist Art Journal; Sinister Wisdom: A Journal for the Lesbian Imagination in the Arts and Politics; Lesbian Contradiction: A Journal of Irreverent Feminism; Focus: A Journal for Gay Women; Out*; and a number of other magazines.

Starting in the late 1960s, a plethora of feminist magazines developed across the United States. The literary magazines *Aphra, Primavera*, and *Black Maria*, and others like *13th Moon, Conditions, Chrysalis, Quest, Spare Rib, Calyx, Conditions*, the *Woman's Review of Books* and *off our backs* are just a few of those that succeeded, often under consensus group editorships. Ethnic feminist magazines include the Chicana *Encuentro Feminil*, the Native American *Namequa Speaks*, and the Jewish *Bridges*.

Not until the 1970s did feminist magazines become popular, mainstream periodicals. *Ms.* magazine (1972–), first edited by Gloria Steinem, was launched as an organ of the women's movement and in support of the Equal Rights Amendment. In its 25+ years of publication, *Ms.* has undergone several transformations, focusing on personal and family issues in the 1980s after it was sold by its feminist founders and then, in the 1990s, eschewing advertising and raising its subscription price to become a substantive quarterly, with topical special issues.

The establishment and growth of women's studies as an academic field have brought numerous feminist scholarly journals. General interdisciplinary journals—*Feminist Studies, Women's Studies International, Interna-*

tional Journal of Women's Studies, NWSA Journal, Signs—have established the field, and *Signs*, among others, has published its germinal scholarship, for example, Adrienne Rich, "Compulsory Heterosexuality and Lesbian Existence." *Sage: A Scholarly Journal on Black Women* has published topical special issues, for example, "The Diaspora" and "Artists and Artisans," and is a major source for scholarship on black women.

Also prominent since the 1970s are disciplinary journals with a specific focus on feminist analysis or on the scholarship on women. Almost every discipline has at least one such journal, for example, *Hypatia, a Journal of Feminist Philosophy*, the *Journal of Women's History, Tulsa Studies in Women's Literature, Women and Literature, Women and Therapy, Women and Politics, Gender and Society, Affilia: Journal of Women and Social Work, Psychology of Women Quarterly*. General-interest academic journals throughout the disciplines have also published special topic issues focused on women or on feminist studies in the discipline; some do so annually.

References. David Doughan and Denise Sanchez (eds.), *Feminist Periodicals, 1855–1984* (New York, 1987); Frank Luther Mott, *A History of American Magazines*, vols. 1–4 (Cambridge, 1930, 1938, 1957).

CAROL KLIMICK CYGANOWSKI

MAGAZINES, WOMEN'S (NINETEENTH-CENTURY), in both Britain and America tended to reinforce the status quo, though their content and readership changed to reflect changes in society. Early in the century, the typical reader of women's magazines was a member of the upper classes, seeking light entertainment to fill her leisure time. The most popular British periodicals at this time were the "society" or "quality" journals such as *The Lady's Magazine or entertaining companion for the fair sex* (1770–1847), *The Ladies' Monthly Museum* (1789–1847), and *La Belle Assemblee* (1806–1847); these three shared identical content from 1832. Supposedly devoted to the improvement of readers' minds and the encouragement of virtue, they generally included reader-written sentimental poetry and romantic fiction with titles such as "The Fatal Fortnight" or "Secrets of the Confessional," sheet music, needlework patterns, question-and-answer pages dealing with love and family, etchings of the latest Paris fashions and detailed descriptions of clothing worn by court beauties, and—before about 1825—exchanges on current issues and some national and international news. But even limited treatment of public affairs largely disappeared from such magazines as the increasingly powerful ideal of the devoted wife and mother, untainted by knowledge of the world, led to greater emphasis on the "womanly virtues" of propriety, innocence, and docility. More space was devoted to fashion as clothing became more elaborate; women's magazines became an important source of information on appropriate dress for women of the nouveau riche. The fiction took on a more sober tone, and there was less reader involvement. The intellectual level was generally lower than in women's magazines of the previous century.

Of a somewhat higher caliber was the first long-running women's magazine in America, Sarah Josepha Hale's *Ladies' Magazine and Literary Gazette* (1828–1837). Though known as "the American lady's magazine," it differed significantly from its British counterpart in its more realistic fiction, its absence of fashion features, and a good deal of editorial content advocating improved education and legal status for women. Mrs. Hale went on to edit the enormously popular *Godey's Lady's Book* (1830–1898). Together with its competitors and imitators, *The Ladies' Companion and Literary Expositor* (1834–1844) and *Peterson's Ladies' National Magazine* (1842–1898), *Godey's* exerted strong influence on national tastes in literature, home furnishings, and domestic life. Many outstanding writers of fiction and poetry, including Poe, Hawthorne, Longfellow, and Stowe, were published in the major women's magazines, though these same writers sometimes decried the frivolity and sentimentality of the magazines' usual material. Serious-minded American women could find suitable intellectual fare in *The Ladies' Repository and Gatherings of the West* (1841–1876), one of several magazines out of Cincinnati; associated with the Methodist Episcopal Church, the *Repository* reviewed some of the best new literature and offered intelligent, in-depth essays on literary and religious topics.

Social and economic upheavals in midcentury broadened the content of women's magazines on both sides of the Atlantic. The reform-minded editor Camilla Toumlin, for example, described for the upper-class readers of *The New Monthly Belle Assemblee* (1848–1870) the terrible living and working conditions of the seamstresses and shop girls who slaved to produce the fashions glorified in the magazine's own pages. The better American magazines also took up social causes such as temperance and public health but tended to avoid the subject of woman's rights and often opposed women's suffrage. It was thus left to smaller feminist publications such as the British *Woman's World* (1866–1869) to challenge the cult of domesticity. The Langham Place feminists published *The Englishwoman's Journal* (1858–1865) to encourage greater employment opportunities for women, but even they found the suffrage issue too controversial to cover. The first wave of American feminism produced magazines such as Amelia Bloomer's *The Lily* (1849) and Mrs. E. A. Aldrich's *The Genius of Liberty* (1852–1854), later published as a regular feature in *Moore's Western Lady's Book*. Lucy Stone's *Woman's Journal* (1870–1917) provided a weekly voice for the suffrage fight. However, the readership for such magazines was relatively small.

In the latter part of the century, a revolution in printing technology and marketing techniques—particularly the acceptance of advertising as a major component of every magazine's content and cash flow—combined with an increase in literacy to encourage the creation of affordable magazines for middle-class women with few or no servants and limited income. Setting the pattern was Samuel Beeton's *The Englishwoman's Domestic Magazine* (1852–1881), a monthly offering guidance on domestic economy, courtship advice, information on hygiene and nursing, and such innovative features as paper dress patterns, as well as the usual mix of fashion and fiction. Of course, the more expensive and sophisticated fashion magazines continued to flourish, such as Beeton's society weekly *The Queen* (1861–) or the American *Harper's Bazaar* (1867–1913), which combined light, entertaining essays and features with extensive fashion coverage. But the dominant magazines were clearly the many low-cost, practical monthlies for the home-centered woman, a good number of which have survived to the present day. Best known in America are *McCall's Magazine* (1873–), *The Ladies' Home Journal* (1883–), and *Good Housekeeping* (1885–), which provide thorough, scientific information on gardening, cooking, sewing, interior design, and child care to housewives who increasingly viewed themselves as professionals. By 1900, *The Ladies' Home Journal* would have a circulation of over 1 million subscribers, greater than any other American magazine.

The last two decades of the century saw enormous growth in the magazine industry; in Britain alone, 48 new women's magazines were founded between 1880 and 1900, and the diversity of the new publications reflected the increasing diversity of women's lives. Magazines were designed for women of various age groups, social classes, educational levels, and occupational groups. Particularly interesting to the feminist scholar are those designed for workingwomen, such as the *Woman's Gazette, or news about work* (1875–1880), later titled *Work and Leisure* (1880–1893), which included information on job opportunities as well as fiction and light entertainment. In America, a *Business Woman's Journal*, completely owned and managed by women, was published in the 1890s. But, for the most part, the important women's magazines of the nineteenth century focused on concerns seen as appropriate to "woman's sphere" and encouraged the maintenance of this separate sphere. Advertisers found the traditional home-centered woman to be an excellent customer for their clothing, cosmetics, and household products, and so they preferred to patronize publications that would not lead women to question their functions as consumers and caretakers. While the women's magazines did a great deal toward defining household management as a trade requiring skill and intelligence and helped women to develop those skills, they did very little to help and often directly hindered the movement toward opening other trades for women and defining womanhood in less restrictive ways. (See also *GODEY'S LADY'S BOOK AND AMERICAN LADIES MAGAZINE*.)

References. About American magazines: Helen Woodward, *The Lady Persuaders* (New York, 1960). About British magazines: Irene Dancyger, *A World of Women: An Illustrated History of Women's Magazines* (Dublin, 1978); Cynthia Leslie White, *Women's Magazines 1693–1968* (London, 1970).

NAOMI JACOBS

MALE CHAUVINISM was a term used frequently in the late 1960s and early 1970s to designate a male mind-set, a blatant, often bellicose glorification of male superiority that basically denies women identity as human beings. To the male chauvinist, "Man" is not generic but identical to "man." Woman is "other."

Chauvinism, from Nicolas Chauvin, a French soldier who idolized Napoleon, means a kind of blind and exaggerated patriotism that glories in its country's show of military strength. The U.S. Communist Party is credited with having broadened the usage of the word during the 1940s to include blatant racist and sexist attitudes and beliefs (Treichler and Kramarae, 243).

Reference. P. Treichler and C. Kramarae, *Feminist Dictionary* (Boston, 1985). 243.

MAMMARY GLANDS (BREASTS) are modified sweat glands present in both males and females. Under the influence of estrogen and progesterone, the glands in young girls begin to grow and develop during puberty. (See PUBERTAL DEVELOPMENT.) Further development takes place during pregnancy under the influence of the hormone prolactin from the anterior pituitary gland as well as increasing levels of estrogen and progesterone. The association of the breasts with the reproductive system is indirect and functional. They secrete milk for the nourishment of the infant. Each mammary gland is a skin-covered elevation positioned over the chest muscles usually over the second to sixth rib. Just below the center of each mammary gland is a pigmented protruding *nipple* surrounded by a pigmented circular *areola*. Smooth muscles within the areola and nipple cause the nipple to become erect when stimulated.

Internally, each gland consists of 15 to 20 lobes of glandular tissue arranged radially around the nipple. Each lobe terminates in a single *lactiferous duct* that opens onto the nipple. The lobes are separated and surrounded by adipose tissue. The amount of adipose tissue determines the size and shape of the breast. There is considerable variation due to genetic differences, age, percentage of body fat, or pregnancy. Size of mammary glands has nothing to do with the ability of a woman to nurse an infant or with the amount of milk produced.

FRANCES GARB

MAMMOGRAPHY. See CANCER

MANAGEMENT. Women have exercised basic management functions since the beginning of history, but, with a few exceptions, they have been executives in major U.S. corporations only since the 1940s. Since then, technological advances, rising education levels, and demographic, attitude, legal, and social changes have led more women into nontraditional careers, including management. In 1997, 43–46 percent of all U.S. managers were women.

Though the percentage of women in management has climbed steadily, two concerns are the misleading nature of numbers and the shortage of women at top levels. Women classified as managers/administrators include many with lower-level positions such as restaurant and bar managers. Of the four women who are chief executive officers (CEOs) of Fortune 1,000 firms, two own the companies, and one took over after her husband's death. Only one was promoted through the ranks.

Only 5 percent of top executives of major U.S. firms are women, and in 1993, 9 percent of executive vice presidents of Fortune 1,000 firms were female. By the mid-1990s, 81 percent of Fortune 1,000 firms had women within two tiers of the CEO, and 44 percent had women who reported directly to the highest position.

As women advanced, more were asked to serve on corporate boards of directors. About 6 percent of newly elected board members were women in the 1970s, but many were considered tokens. In the mid-1980s, 4 percent of board members of major U.S. firms were women, and by 1990, 56 percent of all boards had at least one female member. In 1994, however, only 2 percent of corporate boards, which average 13 members, had three or more female members.

White female managers' annual median income was only 66 percent of the comparable figure for white male managers in 1992. Among managerial women, blacks earned 103 percent of whites' pay then, but Hispanics' median salaries were 93 percent of their white counterparts'. In 1995, 50 of the 2,500 best-paid officers of Fortune 500 firms were women, up from 29 in 1994 but still representing just 2 percent of the best-paid officers. In 1996, the total compensation of the highest-paid American woman was about one-ninth that of the highest-paid man.

The glass ceiling, a term coined in 1987, is a transparent, but impermeable, barrier excluding women from top corporate jobs. Despite its visible cracks, most agree that the glass ceiling remains intact. Obstacles preventing large numbers of women from cracking it are (1) stereotypes, perceptions, and expectations, (2) lack of appropriate types of experiences, (3) inhospitable organizational culture and climate, and (4) unsupportive organizational structures and practices.

Senior executive women recently ranked male stereotypes of females as the most important barrier to women's ascent to top positions. Some people still believe that women are less logical, objective, or managerially competent than men. Others think they will be unwilling to travel, make tough decisions, or work long hours. Women leaving executive posts rarely quit paid employment, and senior women are less likely to have children than their male counterparts. Nevertheless, the assumption that women will want less responsibility during childbearing years sometimes is an excuse for excluding them from the highest echelons.

Managerial women and men are similar in behaviors, abilities, values, commitment, and overall effectiveness. Their tendency to use autocratic or democratic leadership differs, however, with male managers being more likely to make unilateral decisions, characteristic of an autocratic style. Female executives are more democratic, favoring participative decision making. Studies of actual managers revealed no gender-based difference in their propensity to use task or interpersonal styles, but laboratory research showed that women were more likely to use the latter, which stress the importance of human interaction. Task styles, on the other hand, are oriented toward work accomplishment.

Some studies view female managers more positively than males. Research relying on supervisory, self-, or subordinate input found that women were rated higher on communication, empowerment, feedback, decisiveness, ability to facilitate change, and planning. Nevertheless, a 1995 Gallup poll showed that 54 percent of American women and 37 percent of American men preferred to work for a male boss. A similar 1993 poll put those percentages at 44 and 33, respectively, which signals some backsliding, particularly in women's preferences.

Besides stereotypes, people have gender-related expectations of women. They must be assertive but not pushy, decisive but not overbearing, compassionate but not "soft." Their behavior cannot be considered too stereotypically "masculine" or "feminine."

The second major barrier to women's attaining top corporate positions is the belief that they lack appropriate experience. Two-thirds of Fortune 1,000 chief executives said that women had insufficient experience to head major U.S. corporations, but only 29 percent of executive women surveyed agreed. Perhaps the debate is not over the amount of experience but the type. Women still are concentrated in staff or advisory positions, which, historically, have not led to the top. Until recently, executive women may not have had access to critical developmental assignments, including troubleshooting, turnaround, or divisional start-up experience.

Organizational culture and climate form the third barrier that slows executive women's career pace. Arguably, the most important cultural barrier is top executives' greater comfort with those similar to themselves. This feeling can influence selection decisions at high levels where competence is assumed, and "fit" receives more weight. The inclination of white males, predominant in CEO positions, to hire "clones" can harm women and minorities desiring advancement.

Other culture/climate barriers are real and/or perceived lack of acceptance in informal structures, discrimination and harassment, constant performance pressure, and backlash. Despite improvement in the business climate, some executive women feel that they are not as readily included in business-related social activities as are men. Some feel that they receive less coaching, political advice, and sponsorship associated with mentoring than their male colleagues. In the 1990s, however, white women, but not women of color, have obtained mentors at about the same rate as men.

Discrimination poisons the work environment. It still harms women and minorities and offends all who believe in fair treatment. Male CEOs ranked it first in a list of reasons that more females are not top executives, and 27 percent of a sample of managerial women called sexism the greatest impediment to their career progress. Sexual harassment, an illegal form of sex discrimination, remains common in organizations, and almost 60 percent of executive women report having experienced it. A power imbalance can cause this problem, and managerial women lack clout compared to CEOs, a few of whom may feel threatened by females' moving into previously male enclaves.

Many executive women perceive constant performance pressure. Others' unceasing challenge of their credentials exhausts them, and they must expend extra energy to maintain enough power and visibility to do their jobs.

The final culture/climate barrier is backlash. Some who would be shocked to think that they may have enjoyed unearned privilege now feel relatively disadvantaged. The attitude of some white males who are angry about their perception of losing jobs or promotions to minorities and women can create a difficult workplace atmosphere for aspiring females.

Unsupportive organizational structures and practices, including lack of managerial accountability for diversity, ineffective recruitment, difficulty obtaining performance feedback, and differing promotion criteria, impede women's career progress. A Center for Creative Leadership study published in 1995 linked lack of accountability and inadequate incentives for developing diversity to shortages of women and minorities in management. Firms' failure to recruit candidates for top posts from sources likely to include underrepresented groups was another obstacle.

Accurate performance feedback is crucial for anyone wishing to advance, yet executive women are less likely to get it than their male peers. Some male CEOs remain uneasy with female colleagues, which may explain their reluctance to share performance-based information. The tendency to promote men based on potential and women based on previous performance also poses a challenge. Women must have a solid achievement record, whereas men with less stellar performance may be promoted based on perceived potential.

All aspiring women face the challenges described so far, but women of color see a concrete ceiling where Caucasian women see glass. Concerns of the former include race-based stereotypes, lack of role models and mentors, and biculturalism, which occurs when people forced to operate in one culture at work and in another at home experience stress.

Interestingly, career/family balance issues, gender-based pay disparities, and reluctance to relocate typically were not cited as barriers to women's advancement. Collectively, however, challenges women face in their quest for top positions seem daunting. But if the Berlin Wall fell, the glass ceiling can break. Some pioneers already have shattered it.

Senior executive women in U.S. firms are similar in race and educational levels. Ninety-one percent are Caucasian; 3 percent, African American; 3 percent, Asian/Pacific Islander; and 1 percent, Hispanic. Nearly two-thirds of senior managerial women have earned a bachelor's degree. High-ranking executive women are 13 percent more likely than male counterparts to be unmarried, and over 50 percent of senior female executives are childless as compared to 3 percent to 5 percent of the comparable male group.

Women who have cracked the glass ceiling attribute their success to an early career change from staff to line jobs, luck and timing in being assigned to crucial projects, visibility, help from higher levels, and budgetary experience. Over 90 percent of a group of executive women said they excelled in supervisory roles, which they assumed within their first three years of employment. They accurately identified what their firm valued and attracted widespread top support based on exceptional performance.

Early in their career, women breaking the glass ceiling showed entrepreneurial initiative, attended to the organization's culture, and demonstrated effective job performance, which gave them credibility. Women reaching top rungs also set priorities, managed time well, adopted a style that made male peers comfortable with them, and had much physical stamina. Those who were married had supportive spouses.

Countervailing trends will affect how rapidly women become top leaders of major U.S. corporations. On one hand, increasing numbers of women in the workforce, their rising education levels, and the tumultuous business environment could open doors for relative corporate newcomers, including women. Female leaders might bring new perspectives to traditional organizations, giving them a competitive edge. On the other hand, fear of backlash could reduce organizations' commitment to diversity, harming upwardly mobile managerial women.

Executive women's turnover rate, which is 12 percent higher than that of male peers, may either speed or slow their climb to CEO positions. High-ranking women rarely leave corporations to return home. They depart to gain flexibility and control, achieve a better match with their core values, escape an inhospitable culture, or start their own businesses. Numbers in the last category have risen rapidly. In 1996, for example, 78 percent more women-owned firms existed than in 1987.

In the short run, women's corporate exodus will delay females' advances into highest corporate echelons. Fewer women with the necessary qualifications to become CEOs will remain. In the long run, however, women who quit corporations to start firms may create opportunities for managerial women. Today's women-owned small businesses may become to-morrow's corporations and may develop cultures hospitable to females.

Though more women probably will assume top posts, their automatic ascent is not guaranteed. The "pipeline theory," which states that it is only a matter of time before women are represented equally as top executives, has been discredited. Anyone needs about 25 years of experience to become CEO, but appropriate types of experience are crucial.

Male CEOs do not believe females will move into high posts quickly. Only 18 percent surveyed in a 1992 *Fortune* study thought a woman would lead their firm in 20 years. This could reflect resistance to change, however, since a Catalyst study predicted that women's representation in top management would rise to 15 percent within a decade.

Despite concern that a younger generation of men may view younger women as competitors for scarce positions, Jill Barad, Mattel's CEO, is optimistic. She believes that the next generation, which has grown up seeing women in various roles, will view the sexes as business peers and will contribute to the glass ceiling's final demise.

References: Nancy J. Adler and Dafna N. Izraeli, *Competitive Frontiers: Women Managers in a Global Economy* (Cambridge, U.K., 1994); Margaret Foegen Karsten, *Management and Gender: Issues and Attitudes* (Westport, Conn., 1994); Judy B. Rosener, *America's Competitive Secret: Utilizing Women as a Management Strategy* (New York, 1995); Susan Vinnecombe and Nina L. Colwill, *The Essence of Women in Management* (New York, 1995).

MARGARET FOEGEN KARSTEN

MANNERS, NOVEL OF. The novel of manners, which developed in the nineteenth century, portrays with detailed realism the social customs, conventions, traditions, mores, and shared habits of a given social group at a particular time and place and explores as well as demonstrates the powerful control that these social constructs exert over characters in the novel.

Because it focused attention on the domestic arena and its emotional impact on the fictional characters, the novel of manners naturally attracted women writers. Many of these writers, however, did not succeed and wrote a type of fiction called the novel of sensibility or sentiment, which stressed the intensity of the characters' emotional responses frequently beyond the limits of the rational. Some excellent women writers of novels of manners also wrote novels of sentiment or satires of such novels. It is important to note that the true novel of manners examines objectively the impact of social gestures and constructs on characters with attention to verisimilitude in an attempt to assist the intellect more than the heart in grasping social and psychological profundities.

One of the most successful writers of novels of manners was Jane Austen. Not only was Jane Austen (1775–1817) a novelist of manners, but her novels gave definition to the genre by bringing to culmination the artistic structure (including the perfection of an objective narrative technique infused with irony, wit, and perspicacity) and themes of the mainstream eighteenth-century novel. She wrote her major works in a remarkably short time. Her first novel, *Sense and Sensibility*, appeared in 1811, *Pride and Prejudice* in 1813, *Mansfield Park* in 1814, and *Emma* in 1816.

Austen's novels exhibit a constant maturation of theme and artistry, but her first publication, *Sense and Sensibility*, deserves special attention. Even though the compositional history of this novel is not clearly known, the earliness of this work within her oeuvre is undebatable, and yet, as her biographer Elizabeth Jenkins states, *Sense and Sensibility* "was obviously prepared for press when Jane Austen's powers were approaching their zenith" (64).

Centuries of belief in sex-role differences had stipulated that the female was the seat of emotional life in complement to the male's rationalism. Sensibility developed into a complex concept that is only very generally defined as an overindulgence in emotion. Sensibility contrasts with rationalism as a guide to discovering the laws that regulate human and metaphysical relations. A fine sensibility often felt contempt for cities, formal gardens, and conventional society and loved such things as wild landscapes, if viewed according to the dictates of picturesque beauty. Historically, women were so aligned with sensibility that, as they became writers of fiction and analyzers of manners, they quite naturally wrote about emotions and emotional issues. The assignment of emotions and feelings to one sex and rationalism to the other had enormous ramifications, all very important to the novelists of manners and to none more than to Jane Austen, who early and clearly saw the split between sense and sensibility as a major theme. Her determination to objectively and realistically depict these social constructs and their effects on character and situation gave the genre most of its themes and artistry. Readers have often failed to appreciate Austen's opposition to the values of her society, as well as her detailed examination of a society that markets sexual feelings and "other kinds of feelings too; the feelings for nature, for religion, for the poor, and for learning and art. . . . If love is affected, so also may be pity, enthusiasm, piety, and admiration" (Hardy 41). Perhaps the largest failure of appreciation of Austen's work is the lack of understanding her most important theme: "insistence that sense and sensibility must work together" (76).

Jane Austen showed her genius by exploring this complex issue in her early novel *Sense and Sensibility*. Even though the novel approaches the directness of a tract on the subject at times, critics were years determining that the heroine is the sister who so clearly stands as the representative of "sense," rather than the sister who represents "sensibility." Critics were even less ready to see Austen's major theme: the need for sense and sensibility to work together in balance and in both sexes and a further need for social constructs to support this cooperation. The importance of this novel to Austen and the tradition of the novel of manners cannot be over-estimated. Understanding this split between mind and feelings has been crucial to the historical attempt to remove the restrictions from the lives of women, especially the barriers into those areas of life most highly valued, the greatest barrier being the belief that women do not have adequate rational capacity to be educated. Austen referred several times to *Sense and Sensibility* as her unforgettable child. Its themes certainly inform those of the rest of her fiction and, thereby, the definition of the novel of manners.

Austen's novels are often criticized for what is seen as a too narrow range of interests. She concentrates on the country life among the upper middle class in southern England near the end of the eighteenth century to the exclusion of interest in even major national and international events. On the other hand, Austen is the subject of almost unbroken praise for the complex portrayal of what she called "the delicacy of mind," captured only by a supreme concentration on looking and listening. Many critics and readers go further to praise Austen's moral concerns, which they feel give her themes the highest significance. She is further praised by feminists for what Ellen Moers calls Austen's "deep concern with the quality of a woman's life in marriage" (107); other critics note her depiction of society's lack of concern for unmarried women. All of these concerns informed the development of the novel of manners.

Among Austen's precursors were Fanny Burney (1732–1840) and Maria Edgeworth (1768–1849). Three of Burney's novels were novels of manners: *Evelina* (1778), *Cecilia* (1796), and *Camilla* (1796). Although all three have many of the characteristics of Austen's major novels, *Cecilia* is least susceptible to being classified as a novel of sentiment. At the same time, Wilbur L. Cross describes *Evelina* as "the novel in which we move from the old to the new manners" (94). Cross also remarks, "Before Fanny Burney, the novel of manners had been cultivated exclusively by men" (95). Austen paid Burney homage by taking from her works the title and theme of *Pride and Prejudice*.

Maria Edgeworth wrote novels of manners that exposed false sentiment and frivolous nonsense in fashionable London society (e.g., *Belinda* [1801]). Edgeworth spent her childhood in England but moved to Ireland, a set of circumstances that allowed her to write fiction contrasting the manners of two societies (*Ennui* [1809]; *The Absentee* [1812]) and thus create the international novel.

Among novelists following Jane Austen was Elizabeth Gaskell (1810–1865), who wrote various kinds of novels, but her subject was always women. Several of her novels, including *Cranford* (1853), *North and South* (1855), and *Silvia's Lovers* (1857), are aptly called novels of manners. In all her novels, characters struggle to understand their social circumstances and moral obligations.

Charlotte Smith (1749–1806), Elizabeth Inchbald (1753–1821), Frances

Trollope (1780–1863), Susan Ferrier (1782–1854), Catherine Gore (1799–1861), and Harriet Martineau (1802–1876) are other women novelists of the period who worked in the genre.

Later in the nineteenth century, certain works by the realist George Eliot (1819–1880), such as *Middlemarch* (1872), *Daniel Deronda* (1876), and *Mill on the Floss* (1860), mark her as an important recorder and analyst of social manners. Harriet Beecher Stowe (1811–1896) wrote short novels about New England that are explorations of the society of the region. Sarah Orne Jewett (1849–1909) wrote almost all short fiction, but it concentrates on the intense and subtle ways society's manners and conventions dominate people. Kate Chopin's *The Awakening* explores the manners of Creole society in the South and its various methods of controlling characters' intentions and actions. Later yet is the novelist of manners Edith Wharton (1863–1937). Wharton's province was upper-class New York society, and her fiction depicts and contrasts the manners of both the old and new moneyed families, and American and European manners. Wharton's novels share with other novels of manners a moral concern for the characters as well as for the effects of moral and immoral behavior of the societies involved.

References. Jane Austen, *Sense and Sensibility*, ed. James Kingsley, intro. Margaret Ann Doody (Oxford, 1990); Marilyn Butler, *Jane Austen and the World of Ideas* (Oxford, 1975); Wilbur L. Cross, *Development of the English Novel* (London, 1899); Barbara Hardy, *A Reading of Jane Austen* (New York, 1979); Elizabeth Jenkins, *Jane Austen* (New York, 1949); Ellen Moers, *Literary Women: The Great Writers* (Garden City, N.Y., 1977); LeRoy W. Smith, *Jane Austen and the Drama of Woman* (New York, 1983); Tony Tanner, *Jane Austen* (Cambridge, Mass., 1986); James W. Tuttleton, *The Novel of Manners in America* (Chapel Hill, N.C., 1972); Merryn Williams, *Women in the English Novel, 1800–1900* (New York, 1984).

GLORIA STEPHENSON

MARIANISM is the Christian cult of the Virgin Mary. Mythological antecedents and religious cults dedicated to female figures (goddess or goddesslike) abound in both prehistory and history throughout the world. Cults parallel to that of the Christian Mary exist in such varied traditions as classic Greek and Roman, Hindu, ancient Egyptian, and Japanese. For example, Mary intercedes, Persephone-like, on the part of the dead; exists prior to God (Christ) like Gaia, Cybele, and Demeter; and remains a virgin uncommitted to marriage bonds like Athena and Artemis. The Hindu goddesses Devi, Durga, Kali, and Lakshmi share some traits with Mary; however, the Hindu manifestations incorporate both compassionate and frightening aspects, while Mary has only the former. The mother/son imagery shows up in the Egyptian representation of Isis and Horus. Mary may be compared in some ways with the Japanese Sun Goddess Amaterasu.

The cult dedicated to Mary grew out of the renewed interest in the earthly world and the individual as well as the religious reform that characterized the twelfth century in Western Europe. Additionally, the emphasis on the Crucifixion and the suffering of Christ led to a new focus on his humanity. As a result, the Byzantine emphasis on his human mother, Mary, spread to Western European Christianity. The Cistercian monks wore white in honor of Mary's purity as a virgin and established "lady" chapels meant for the adoration of Mary in hopes of her intercession with God. One of the abbots in particular, Bernard of Clairvaux, was instrumental in spreading devotion to Mary as Virgin and Mother. In both art and literature, Mary functioned as a powerful and positive symbol of unity between God and human and between male and female.

A striking change in literary and artistic representation occurred during the thirteenth century, when the cult of the Virgin reached its zenith. Mary became exemplum rather than symbol, more "real," a problematic change for the status of women. For example, the poets and troubadours of the courtly tradition in literature frequently mixed references to the Virgin and the Lady, the sacred and the profane, resulting in the still-extant references to "Our Lady," meaning Mary. In art, her physical/mother aspects became more pronounced. Concurrently, the Catholic Church restricted the role of women and emphasized the male authority hierarchy based on the traditional view of woman as Eve (physical being), who caused the fall of humanity by acting on her own. Therefore, the subordination of woman to man punished her for original sin and prevented future sin by restricting her independence. St. Thomas Aquinas formally defined the subordination of marriage as the proper realm for women (besides consecrated virginity).

During the fourteenth and fifteenth centuries, because of these changes and the Franciscan interpretation of the cult (the use of the Holy Family concept in reaching the laity), Mary gained an even stronger mother image. As the laity became obsessed with Mary, the ideal virgin/bride/mother, the church itself became concerned about the cult's undermining male religious and social authority. Emphasis on Mary mother-and-son rather than father-and-son threatened to reverse gender roles. For the most part, the hierarchy dealt with its fears of the cult by considering Mary an exception, emphasizing her purity even to her intact hymen before, during, and after childbirth and the lack of putrifaction of her body after death. Yet even this stress did not allay clerical fears of female sexuality: nuns may have used the metaphor of Christ as lover, but priests and monks always looked to Mary as mother.

Though the cult no longer influences the majority of Catholic countries to the extent that it once did, it still wields considerable influence. The medieval vitality of Mary as role model and of Mary and motherhood continues in the Iberian peninsula and Latin America; for example, the Mexican cult of the Virgin of Guadalupe and the Luzo-Brazilian cult of

Nossa Senhora de Fátima. In the United States, Pat Driscoll adapted the cult when she wrote "Daring to Grow," a 1975 essay extolling the pregnant Mary as a contemporary role model. (See also EVE AND MARY.)

References. Margot I. Duley and Mary I. Edwards (eds.), *The Cross-Cultural Study of Women* (New York, 1986); Joan M. Ferrante, *Woman as Image in Medieval Literature* (New York, 1975); Naomi Goldenberg, *Changing of the Gods* (Boston, 1979); Arvind Sharma (ed.), *Women in World Religions* (Albany, N.Y., 1987).

DEBRA D. ANDRIST

MARITAL PROPERTY is property acquired during marriage. To achieve a more equitable distribution of property at divorce, all common-law property states except Mississippi classify certain property acquired during marriage, regardless of title ownership, as spousal or marital property, subject to division at divorce.* Like community property* in community property states, traditionally, marital property includes all earned income, savings, interest, dividends, all returns on investments, and property purchased with that income (e.g., home, automobile). Traditionally, it does not include property brought to the marriage or property acquired through inheritance or certain gifts received after marriage. Today divorcing couples are likely to have relatively little of their wealth invested in the traditional forms of property and more in "new property" such as pensions, insurance, professional degrees, and intangibles such as goodwill built up in a business or future earning capacity. States vary widely in their acceptance of this "new property" as marital property. As yet very few include intangible assets.

The advantages of the marital property concept and the growing awareness that marriage is an economic partnership to which both parties contribute led to the idea of extending the concept to the entire marriage, not just to divorce settlement. The Uniform Marital Property Act (1983), a model law that states may adopt, establishes marital property within the common-law property system. It recognizes marriage as a partnership to which each spouse makes an equal contribution and in which each has an equal share. Its marital property laws are based on laws in community property states, but common-law features are also incorporated. The spouses share ownership of marital property throughout the duration of marriage. Management, however, is by whichever spouse holds the title. In 1984 Wisconsin became the first state to adopt a marital property system based on the Uniform Marital Property Act.

MARRIAGE is a legally and socially sanctioned institution that has existed in every society but under widely different forms. It is, generally speaking, an approved sexual relationship, in almost all cases between one or more women and one or more men. There are instances of legally approved same-sex marriages, but they are rare.

Marriage provides the basic unit for the procreation and rearing of off-spring, the sexual division of labor, production and consumption, and ful-filling personal needs of affection and companionship. Through a legally sanctioned marriage offspring acquire legitimacy and the rights that go with legitimacy, including inheritance rights.

The relationships within marriage are, to a large extent, governed by the laws, customs, and mores of the community. Choice of partner, work roles, rights to children, division of authority, dissolution of marriage, remar-riage, and division of inheritance are all regulated, at least to some degree. Incest taboo is universal, but the proscribed degrees of kindred differ. Only parent–child sexual relations are universally condemned. Sexual division of labor is also universal, but "men's work" and "women's work" are not everywhere the same. Authority in patriarchal societies (in which the vast majority of people have lived for at least the last 5,000 to 6,000 years) resides ultimately in the male, although the extent of subordination of fe-males has varied widely over time and place.

The condition of subordination in America and Europe in the nineteenth century was such that marriage reform was a priority of the feminist move-ment that began in midcentury. Some gains were made, but marriage re-form remains a major concern of second-wave feminism. Some feminists think that the abolition of marriage and the family is the only solution to women's subordination. Others think that reforms in education, institu-tions, and attitudes can turn marriage into an egalitarian relationship. (See also FAMILY; FAMILY [AS A SOCIOECONOMIC UNIT].)

MARRIAGE PENALTY (MARRIAGE TAX). A married couple, both of whom are employed, pay more income tax than an unmarried couple, both of whom are employed. Under U.S. income tax law, married couples must pay tax on the sum of their income. Since the income tax is progressive, the tax will be higher on the combined income of two people than it would be if the incomes were taxed separately. The difference is called the mar-riage penalty or marriage tax.

A two-earner couple, however, pays less tax than a single person would pay on an income equal to the couple's combined income. Also penalized are single parents. Households headed by currently unmarried mothers (or fathers) are not taxed as leniently as households headed by a couple, only one of whom receives income. The tax rate for single heads of household is between the single person and the two-earner married couple rates. The marriage penalty has the effect of encouraging unmarried employed couples to remain unmarried and unwaged housewives to remain out of the labor market.

MASCULINITY/MASCULINITIES. Women's studies have rendered mas-culinity problematic to pose a fundamental challenge to patriarchal norms.

Traditionally, only the subordinated "other" has been marked by the category that creates the hierarchical division. Thus, just as in a heterosexist culture only the sexual orientations of lesbians and gays are seen as requiring causal explanations, and in a racist society race or ethnicity is seen as a property only of individuals marginalized by their race or ethnicity, so patriarchal thinking sees only women as defined by their gender. As Simone de Beauvoir wrote, "A man would never get the notion of writing a book on the peculiar situation of the human male" (xvii).

In classical dialectical fashion, women's studies seized upon the validity of Beauvoir's observation and developed it to such an extent that it undermined itself and is no longer true. Masculinity has been denaturalized so that its social construction has become visible, and there now exist numerous and varied analyses of "the peculiar situation of the human male."

In its simplest, indeed oversimplified, form, feminist analyses of masculinity simply insist that men as well as women are gendered beings, always simultaneously insisting that gender marks not just difference but hierarchy, that is, power or patriarchy.

Power relations exist not just between the genders but within each gender as well. The concept "masculinities" has emerged as an important tool in analyzing the various dimensions of power that constitute the male side of gender relations.

While men as a group hold patriarchal power over women as a group, subgroups of men also hold various degrees of power relative to other subgroups of men. Men as well as women are hierarchically ordered along lines of race, class, sexual orientation, ethnicity, age, religion, physical appearance, able-bodiedness, and various other categories. Men engage in forms of competitive bonding that both solidify and threaten patriarchal solidarity among them. The concept of "masculinities" is paradigmatically deployed not merely to categorize a range of differences among men but to further conceptualize these differences as contestations over differing shares of patriarchal privilege. The makeup and relative hierarchical positions of these differences vary greatly over time and place. To date many of the most sophisticated analyses that manage the difficult task of holding simultaneous foci on both masculinity as men's domination over women and masculinities as relations of domination and subordination among men have emerged from gay studies and have focused on the constructions and significance of male bodies, joined very recently by an emerging literature on black men that shares significant features. Women's studies have understood the structural analogy "woman:nature=man:culture" as a foundational patriarchal construct and demonstrated how our culture maps this construct onto its mind/body dualism, to the great detriment of women. As a corrective, just as they have moved to demonstrate that women are also intellectual beings and makers of culture, they now move to show how men are also thoroughly embodied beings.

Similar to an earlier analogous phase in the development of women's studies, the shift from the earlier monolithic "masculinity" to the more nuanced "masculinities" has emerged over the last decade in the literature of what has come to be called "men's studies"* (sometimes "pro-feminist men's studies" or "the critique of masculinity"). It is indebted to the sociological concept of "hegemonic masculinity," itself indebted, in turn, to Italian Marxist Antonio Gramsci's concept of "hegemony." Gramsci's innovation in Marxist theory was to conceptualize domination not merely, or even primarily, as based on force or coercion, as Marx and those in the tradition following him had understood it, but rather as rooted in much more subtle and insidious fashion in the cultural milieu and ethos of a society. This was the mechanism by which the ideas of the ruling class became the ruling ideas of the era, an idea that Marx had suggested but had not further developed. Domination is, at least partly, a discursive practice, as the point might be put today.

Understanding gender as power means that masculinities are also patriarchies. While some fear that women's studies' examining men and masculinities as part of its ongoing investigation of gender represents a retreat from its antipatriarchal theory and practice, this development should rather be understood as an integral part of its academic and political agenda. For leaving masculinity/masculinities uninterrogated, allowing "gender" to continue to function as a euphemism for "women," thereby maintaining women's otherness, fundamentally embodies patriarchal thinking.

Reference. Simone de Beauvoir, *The Second Sex*, trans. H. M. Parshley (New York, 1953).

HARRY BROD

MASOCHISM is a term introduced by ethologist/sexologist Richard von Krafft-Ebing (c. 1901) in reference to sexual "perversions" detailed in the novellas of Leopold von Sacher-Masoch (b. 1836). The writings of Sacher-Masoch regularly featured the sexual subordination of men to women. Krafft-Ebing used the term to describe the phenomenon wherein the individual derives sexual gratification by being completely and unconditionally subjected to the will of a person of the opposite sex, deriving sexual gratification from enslavement, humiliation, and abuse.

Krafft-Ebing introduced the term to the sexology literature, but it was left to Sigmund Freud and his followers, specifically Helene Deutsch and Marie Bonaparte, to make it a permanent feature of psychological discourse on women. They transformed the theme of Sacher-Masoch's novellas (subordination of men to women) into a metaphor for male neurosis, but an innate feature of psychological femininity.* Freud located masochism in his larger theory of *thanatos* and *eros*, death and life drives. His theory outlined three types of masochism, *moral, erotogenic,* and *feminine.* In his paper "The Economic Problem of Masochism" Freud distinguished the three: the first was a norm of behavior, the second a condition imposed on sexual excitation, but the final, feminine masochism was "an expression of feminine nature." For males, masochism is linked, in part, to unresolved feelings of guilt that only pain can alleviate. Part of the source of this guilt, Freud theorized, was the wish to be beaten by the father, a wish to have a "passive female relation to him." For women, however, masochism was a natural extension of their biological experience of coitus and childbirth. Freud's disciple, Helene Deutsch, concluded that women are naturally masochistic. She noted that much of what is pleasurable to women (sex and motherhood) is, indeed, painful. The distinction between the tolerance for pain and the enjoyment of it was not addressed in these theories.

It was left to psychoanalysts interested in sociocultural factors of personality to connect women's social subjugation to their "desire" to be dominated by men, to their "innate" masochism. In the early 1930s, psychoanalysts Clara Thompson and Karen Horney each located instances of so-called masochism in the structural constraints on female sexuality and behavior. Thompson called it "an adaptation to a circumscribed life" and noted that Freud based much of his theory of feminine masochism on his therapy with passive male homosexuals. Horney saw the cultural influences on women as so powerful that some degree of masochism was seemingly inevitable.

It is interesting to note how Sacher-Masoch's erotic vision of male subordination has become so completely subsumed into a theory of feminine psychology. Both the professional and the public mythology that women secretly, manipulatively, or unconsciously enjoy abuse remains—to the extent that the concept of masochism has become a foundation of clinical theories about female personality and, specifically, about abused women. The enjoyment/endurance argument persists to this day.

Current research into woman abuse, female personality development, and mental illness* continue the controversy. Researchers in woman abuse and victimization, such as Lenore Walker and Paula Caplan, have sought to counter the myth of women's masochism. Walker traces women's endurance of physical abuse to both social conditioning and the cumulative effects of defenselessness and emotional exhaustion. Caplan has traced women's endurance of victimization to its roots in the female role in society and the institutionalized right of men to abuse women. The very question "why does she stay?" tends to presuppose that a woman chooses to endure abuse, that she, indeed, has *real* choice.

The vast body of recent empirical research on woman abuse finds no evidence for unconscious masochism. The last study to seriously entertain the masochism hypothesis as an explanation was published in the early 1960s. Since the 1970s, the majority of writers in the field have devoted their energies to refuting the masochism hypothesis, and empirical evidence provides little support for the assumption that masochism has any role in women's endurance of abusive relationships.

In modern psychiatry, the word has evolved from a description of a sexual perversion to a categorization of a persistent pattern of self-defeating behavior. Still, however, it has remained a "feminine" characteristic and has come to be applied to self-sacrifice, even to altruistic behaviors, particularly as they are practiced by women. In 1985, the American Psychiatric Association (APA) proposed a new category for its manual of clinical diagnosis (DSM III): "Masochistic female personality disorder." Assailed by feminists and therapists for being sexist in name and victim-blaming in spirit, the APA revised the name to "Self-defeating personality disorder." Although feminists, therapists, and researchers remain uncomfortable with its implications, the category has been added to the revised appendix of the new manual, and "self-defeating" behavior has become the newest metaphor for enduring domination and the newest way to imagine that women enjoy it.

References. P. Caplan, *The Myth of Women's Masochism* (New York, 1985); K. Horney, *Feminine Psychology* (New York, 1967); C. Thompson, *On Women* (New York, 1964); L. Walker, *The Battered Woman* (New York, 1979).

ALYSON L. BURNS

MATERNAL INSTINCT is a presumed biological readiness, desire, or ability to mother. Speculations about such an instinct go back to ancient times and have figured predominantly in scientific theories since the time of Charles Darwin. In the late nineteenth and early twentieth centuries, such leading psychologists as William James, William McDougall, and G. Stanley Hall argued that women have a special need and ability to protect and care for the young. Theorists linked this maternal "instinct" to women's purported emotionality and tendency to focus on the immediate and concrete. Even in the behaviorist era that followed, when the idea of instinct fell into disrepute, many psychologists continued to refer to innate motherly feelings or abilities.

In recent years, formal instinct theories have not found wide acceptance in academic psychology. However, the assumption of a biological basis for maternal behavior has figured in psychological speculations on the importance of perinatal "bonding" between mother and child (for which there is no empirical support) and in the evolutionary theories of ethologists and sociobiologists. Sociobiologists consider a human maternal instinct to be a predictable response to the facts of procreation: since males can impregnate many females, but females can transmit their genes to only a limited number of offspring, females are assumed to be more willing to protect their genetic investment in any given child.

In traditional conceptualizations, an instinct is an adaptive, complex, genetically programmed behavior pattern performed without learning by all appropriate members of a species in the presence of a specific stimulus. Such fixed patterns are well documented in many nonhuman animal species. Thus, a spider will spin an intricate web without being taught to do so, and a wolf will howl in a certain way even if it has never heard the howl of another wolf. However, contemporary scientists generally agree that fixed, automatic patterns of complex behavior do not exist in human beings. Certainly, none of the hundreds of behaviors that go into infant and child care emerge automatically in all women.

More recent approaches to instinctive behavior emphasize biological *predispositions* to engage in certain behaviors under given conditions rather than fixed behavior patterns. Again, ethological work has established the existence of such predispositions in nonhuman species, including, in many, a maternal predisposition to nurture the young. The clearest examples are in lower animals. For example, after female rats give birth, they ordinarily respond to their young by nursing, building a nest, and retrieving pups that wander off. In contrast, male rats typically have nothing to do with newborns and may even attack them. After a few days of contact, males will lick and retrieve the young, but they still do not feed them or build nests. Virgin female rats also take longer than new mothers to show parental behavior. Hormones may influence maternal behavior in female rats postpartum; when virgin females are injected with blood plasma from rats that have recently given birth, their maternal behavior reportedly begins sooner than it otherwise would.

Evidence from higher animals, however, is far less clear. Moreover, many biologists and social scientists question the common practice among ethologists of generalizing from animal to human behavior. They observe, too, that not all animals are alike. Ethologists looking for a maternal instinct have tended to concentrate on species in which parental sex differences* are obvious and follow human stereotypes, for example, baboons and rhesus monkeys. But in many other species males play an active part in infant care. Male mice help care for their young, some male birds take turns sitting on eggs and feeding new hatchlings, and male wolves aid in feeding by regurgitating food. Male owl monkeys, titi monkeys, and marmosets carry infants around, handing them over to their mothers only for nursing.

Other problems plague theories of maternal instinct. For example, equating an instinct with a predisposition or with readiness makes the concept difficult, if not impossible, to evaluate scientifically, since then it is not susceptible to disconfirmation. If the predicted behavior occurs, one can argue that conditions were right for its emergence. If it does not, one can argue ad hoc that conditions must have been wrong; the instinct exists but has not been activated. In addition, arguments for a maternal instinct have difficulty explaining the many examples of neglectful, cruel, and even murderous behavior by human mothers toward their children. In tribal cultures that practice or condone infanticide,* it is often the mothers who kill their infants. In the eighteenth century, middle- and upper-class European women commonly sent their offspring to live with wet nurses under conditions that almost ensured an early death. During the Victorian era many women abandoned or killed their illegitimate children rather than face scandal.

Historically, reliance on instinct as an explanation of parental behavior has discouraged empirical investigation of fathering and of male responses to children. However, researchers have begun to fill the gaps. They find that in the United States, fathers of newborns are as likely as mothers to hold their babies, rock them, talk to them, smile at them, and look directly at them. They are also as competent as mothers in handling them. Women do tend to react more enthusiastically than men to unfamiliar infants, but there is evidence that males suppress their responses in public in accordance with social norms. While it is likely that unlearned responses to the young do exist in both sexes, the specific conditions under which such responses emerge or fail to emerge remain to be determined.

In the meantime, popular belief in a maternal instinct continues to have far-ranging social and personal consequences, including pressure on women to procreate, feelings of guilt in women who wish to, or must, remain childless, feelings of inadequacy in women who mother, acceptance by both men and women of women's greater responsibility for children, and lack of social and economic supports for child rearing.

References. S. Shields, "To Pet, Coddle, and 'Do For': Caretaking and the Concept of Maternal Instinct," in Miriam Lewin (ed.), *In the Shadow of the Past: Psychology Portrays the Sexes* (New York, 1984); C. Tavris and C. Wade, *The Longest War: Sex Differences in Perspective*, 2d ed. (San Diego, 1984), esp. pp. 68–71, 159–163.

CAROLE WADE

MATH ANXIETY, a fear of mathematics and a conviction that one does not understand math, has never understood it, and never will understand it, was first studied by researchers in the mid-1970s. Both women and men have math anxiety, but more women seemed to have it than men, and women avoided mathematics more than men. From high school, females took relatively fewer math courses and consistently scored lower than males on standardized mathematics tests from about the age of 14.

In the mid-1970s, as women students were being urged to enter nontraditional fields such as the physical sciences and engineering, there was growing concern about the overall decline of interest in mathematics (13,723 fewer bachelor's degrees in mathematics were awarded in 1981 than in 1971) and particularly about the decline in test scores on nationally used standardized tests.

Research mounted, and workshops and special programs for the "math-anxious" were started. Special programs geared specifically toward women were sponsored by women's colleges, women's centers, affirmative action offices, and university mathematics and engineering departments. Some researchers concluded that the major problem for women was not math anxiety but math avoidance. However, the National Mathematics Assessment tests in 1978 and 1982, which distinguished scores on the basis of the amount of mathematics taken, continued to show that girls outperformed boys by a slight margin until age 14, but from age 14, boys outperformed girls by about three percentage points (National Assessment of Educational Progress).

Sociobiologists talking about visual spatial perception and brain lateralization credited the differences in ability to genetic differences in men and women. Feminist mathematicians, sociologists, and psychologists found abundant environmental evidence to explain the differences. From birth, girls are encouraged to be less independent, less adventurous than boys. Gender-specific toys and games encourage passivity in girls and movement, interest in speed, and eye-hand coordination in boys. Parents often accepted poor performances from daughters that they would not tolerate in sons; some deliberately discouraged their daughters from taking advanced math programs.

The school experience also discouraged mathematical achievement in girls. In class girls were often called upon less than boys, not encouraged as much to perform well, and treated more leniently when they failed. Textbooks used in mathematics classes were highly sexist. When they did not completely ignore girls and women, they presented the worst possible stereotypes, insulting and denigrating to women.

Researchers also found that a major difference between boys and girls who do not like math is that once girls passed the minimum requirements, they were free to avoid math courses, but boys very often were not—the careers they aspired to (or their parents intended them for) required mathematics. Among girls, math avoidance was a greater problem than math anxiety.

Another factor cited was the pressure on girls, once they reached adolescence (the time that their math scores drop), to not compete with boys academically and to pay more attention to being popular than to getting good grades. Peer pressure might lead a girl to stop trying to get good grades in math or not to take any math beyond 10th grade geometry.

By the mid-1990s women still took less mathematics in high school and college than men, more women disliked mathematics than men, and girls still scored lower in mathematics on national tests such as the college boards and Scholastic Aptitude Tests (SATs). Nevertheless, there was impressive improvement. Sexism* is less pervasive in textbooks, and more parents and teachers encouraged girls to take math courses and to perform well in them. In 1992 more girls reported being advised by parents, teachers, and counselors to take math courses than boys did. More women are taking more math courses in high school and college. In 1994 more female high school graduates (68.1 percent) had taken algebra than male graduates (64.7 percent), and the percentage of boys who took calculus (9.4 percent) differed by only 0.3 percent from the percentage of girls (9.1 percent). The rise in the number and the percentage of women graduates in engineering and the physical sciences has been conspicuous. The percentage of women graduates in engineering rose from 0.8 percent in 1970 to 12.5 percent in 1985. In the physical sciences, women's share of earned doctorates rose from 5.6 percent in 1970 to 16.2 percent in 1985. Of the degrees given in mathematics, in 1970 women earned 37.4 percent of the bachelor's degrees and 8.4 percent of the doctor's; in 1995 their share had increased to 47.8 percent and 27.5 percent, respectively (all statistics are from the Center for Education Statistics, *Digest of Education Statistics, 1996* [Washington, D.C., 1997]).

The number of women in fields that require competence in calculus or advanced mathematics is still low when compared with the numbers in traditional fields that require little or no mathematics, but present trends indicate that more high school girls realize mathematics is vital to their futures and that the gap in mathematics achievement is continually narrowing.

Reference. National Assessment of Educational Progress, *Third National Mathematical Assessment: Results, Trends and Issues* (Washington, D.C., 1983).

MATING AND DATING GRADIENT, an informal process for defining an appropriate field of marriage-eligibles, helps to ensure that higher-status females are more likely to date and therefore to marry higher-status males than lower-status males. The dating and mating gradient was first described by Williard Waller, then a sociologist at Pennsylvania State University, in an article published in 1937.

In the United States, marriage* is a more important determinant of the social position of women than of men; women tend to take on the social status of their husbands, while the husband's social status is more determined by his occupation, income, or wealth. Marriage and the dating process that leads to marriage thus tend to be more important for women (and their parents) than for men. Cultural norms prescribe that women should strive to move up the status hierarchy (or at least to remain stable) through their mate selection.

Waller and other family sociologists argue that dating as a process for mate selection first emerged alongside modernization, especially after World War I, in the United States. The institution of dating weakens the traditional family control of its children's mate selection. The dating and mating gradient developed to limit children's choices of dating partners and thus to increase the likelihood that children would choose an "appropriate" (from the family's perspective) mate.

As Waller first described it at Pennsylvania State University, the dating and mating gradient operated within the Greek fraternity and sorority system. Each fraternity and sorority had a prestige ranking on campus. Students dated in accord with the ranking: members of high-prestige sororities dated only members of high-prestige fraternities. A key object in dating was to reassert one's status by showing off the high ranking of one's date. Waller argued that this "dating gradient" operated primarily in casual dating rather than in marriage-oriented dating. Later research found that serious, marriage-oriented dating followed the same patterns Waller had described for casual dating.

Ira Reiss, in further explorations of the gradient, argued that the dating patterns of a group follow the social-class origins of the group so that dating facilitates endogamous marriage (people marry people of similar social characteristics). That is, young people date in accordance with their parental social class, race, religious, and ethnic backgrounds. A series of studies supported this argument. Parents usually want their children to marry someone of a similar (or higher) social class; campus dating systems unintentionally achieve this because of the ways in which they reflect parental social class. Little work has been done with noncampus dating patterns, but sociologists argue that the concern for endogamy is widely distributed among American families.

The dating and mating gradient is a primary method used by middle-class American families to get their daughters married to the "right" man. Operating primarily on college campuses, it is an institutionalized way for preserving class endogamy* by narrowing dating choices to a field of eligibles composed of persons of the same class, ethnic, religious, and economic stratum.

References. I. L. Reiss, *Family Systems in America*, 3d ed. (New York, 1980); J. F. Scott, "Sororities and the Husband Game," *Trans-Action* 2 (1965): 10–14; W. Waller, "Rating and Dating Complex," *American Sociological Review* 2 (1937): 727–737.

ALLEN SCARBORO

MATRIARCHY is a system in which women rule. J. J. Bachofen, John McLennon, and Lewis Henry Morgan theorized that all societies passed through a matriarchal period before the development of herding and agriculture (as opposed to hoe culture). Morgan (followed by Engels) believed that herding and agriculture, by enabling men to accumulate property, brought about patriarchy* and the subjection of women. Other evolutionary anthropologists denied that there had ever been a matriarchal period.

By the early twentieth century anthropologists began to distinguish between matrilineal descent, matrilocal residence patterns, and rule by women. In the general movement of British and American anthropologists away from general evolutionary theories toward functionalism, matriarchal theories were no longer considered viable.

The idea of matriarchy has been revived by some feminist anthropologists and by some cultural and socialist feminists. They do not, however, see matriarchy as a female version of patriarchy but as an egalitarian society in harmony with nature. They cite the newly recognized importance of gathering in the economy of foraging societies, the widespread worship of mother goddesses, and evidence from female burials as indications that women occupied a different and higher place in prehistoric society. Other feminists believe male dominance has been universal and dismiss matriarchy as wishful thinking. Even as wishful thinking, however, matriarchy has served as an important symbol. Women utopian writers, philosophers, and poets have used the concept to construct their vision of the future.

References. J. J. Bachofen, *Das Mutterrecht* (1861); Friedrich Engels, *Origin of the Family, Private Property, and the State* (1884); John McLennon, *Primitive Marriage* (1865); Lewis Henry Morgan, *Ancient Society* (1877).

MATRIFOCALITY is a term usually applied to a culture system in which the mother has the major responsibility for the economic and social well-being of the family. The father is often absent or, if present, plays a weak role in domestic life. Black Caribbean family groups and the separate units of compound polygamous families in some areas of Africa are cited as examples of matrifocality. In the United States matrifocality is associated with poverty.* The term has also been used to describe British working-class family life, in which there is a strong division between the domestic sphere,* where the mother is the dominant figure, and the public sphere,* where the male has authority.

MATRILINY is a lineage system in which kinship and descent are traced through the female. Although there are many variations among matrilineal societies, in general, women are responsible for the care of the children, and adult males have authority over women and children; however, that authority is divided, the father-husband having authority over the nuclear family and a male of the mother's family, most likely the brother or oldest son, having authority over the lineage.

Although matrilocality* is thought to have been a necessary, but not determining, precondition for the original appearance of matriliny, matrilineal societies are not necessarily matrilocal. Either can exist without the other. (The Hopi are both matrilineal and matrilocal; the Trobrianders of the South Pacific are matrilineal and patrilocal.) Today less than half of the matrilineal societies are also matrilocal.

Survivals of matriliny in later patriarchal-patrilineal societies (as the Hebrew and the Bronze Age Greeks) have been found. At present, matrilineal societies are scattered over the world with concentrations in Africa, the Pacific, and North America. They are most common in the Pacific Islands and among American Indians of the eastern grasslands and the arid South-west.

Reference. D. M. Schneider and K. Gough (eds.), *Matrilineal Kinship* (Berkeley, Calif., 1961).

MATRILOCALITY is a residence pattern in which a married couple settles with or near the wife's family. Matrilocality may have been a precondition for the development of matrilineal descent, but each can exist without the other (e.g., matrilocal residence in patrilineal neo-Babylonia). The Hopi and the Apache are examples of matrilocal societies.

MEDICALIZATION OF MOTHERHOOD. See MOTHERHOOD, SCIENTIFIC

MEDICINE, WOMEN IN. See HEALTH CARE PROVIDERS

MEDIEVAL WOMEN. Daily Life of Religious was carefully regulated to ensure an unvarying routine. Within a few centuries of its composition in the mid-sixth century, the Rule of St. Benedict became the norm for most Western European nuns (*moniales*), sometimes called Black nuns because of the color of their habit, the dress that identified them as religious. Traditionally, the first monastery for Benedictine nuns is said to have been founded by Scholastica (c.480–c.543), Benedict of Nursia's sister, at Plombariola, a few miles away from her brother's monastery for monks at Monte Cassino. But actually, the history of women's adoption of the Benedictine Rule is still unclear, and Scholastica's existence has even been questioned.

While Benedictine nuns and monks followed the same rule with virtually no gender-specific requirements, some rules were written especially for women, and these reveal different expectations for female and male religious. One of the earliest such rules in Western Europe was Caesarius of Arles' *Regula an virgines* (513); the rule St. Clare of Assisi wrote in 1252 is the first known to have been composed by a woman. In general, rules for women required stricter enclosure within the monastery walls than rules for men. However, none of the rules written especially for women ever attracted many followers. Women were more likely to adopt rules designed for men, as did the Cistercian women (the White nuns) of the twelfth and thirteenth centuries. The reactions of the men to the women who imitated their way of life are one of the current issues in scholarship. Some scholars have emphasized the official discouragement men gave their female imitators, while others stress the informal cooperation of women and men.

The nun who joined a Benedictine monastery made three promises: stability (of residence), obedience (to her abbess), and a conversion of her life (*conversatio morum*). She spent approximately four hours a day in communal prayer. There were seven designated times for prayer, the "canonical hours" (*horarium*) of the "Divine Office": Matins (said during the night), Lauds (at daybreak), Prime, Terce, Sext, None, Vespers, and Compline (before retiring). During the Divine Office, the nuns read or sang psalms from the Old Testament (the Hebrew Bible), lessons (primarily Scripture readings), hymns, and set prayers like the Our Father.

Private prayer and individual religious experiences did not become the focus of religious life until the later medieval ages, and even then the majority of prayer time was spent in the oratory reciting the Divine Office. In contrast to the Sacraments, for which a priest was necessary, the Divine Office could be said by the nuns on their own, in a manner identical to that of the monks.

Called to choir by their sacristan ringing a bell, the nuns prayed in antiphonal fashion, rotating among themselves the position of leader. Some question whether the nuns actually read the Latin during the Offices, suggesting instead that they memorized the psalms. In any case, the time spent in choir was central to religious life, so much so that the Benedictine Rule called the Divine Office the *opus dei*, literally, "the work of God."

The other two main activities of the day were manual labor (*opus manuum*) and spiritual reading (*lectio divina*). Labor, either physical or mental, was considered essential to the well-being of the individual woman as well as necessary for the common good. For most nuns, "labor" meant copying and embellishing manuscripts or sewing and decorating garments. Some women labored by serving in particular offices, such as the cellaress (in charge of the storeroom) and the portress (keeper of the gate to the monastery). The degree of responsibility the nuns had for preparing their own food varied, but in many houses they rotated among themselves the responsibility for cooking and serving their meals of bread, two cooked dishes (primarily vegetables), and wine, ale, or water. When the nuns ate in their refectory, one of them, the designated "weekly reader," read to the others, who ate in silence.

In the earlier Middle Ages, women sometimes labored in the fields and farms belonging to their monastery, but this became increasingly rare and finally impossible when strict enclosure for women was universally mandated in Pope Boniface VIII's bull *Periculoso* in 1298. According to the episcopal hierarchy, increased seclusion would benefit the nuns, who would be freer to concentrate on prayer. Some feminists have argued instead that rigorous closure had negative effects on the women: it curtailed the activities open to them, their education suffered, poor monasteries became even poorer, and the abbesses lost authority to men on whose aid they were increasingly forced to rely.

Even though some scholars question how widespread literacy actually was among nuns, feminists have generally praised the emphasis on reading within the monastery. Christian religious women were virtually the only literate women of the medieval period. A female teacher or *magistra* instructed the novices, the women seeking to enter the monastery. Nuns were expected to read manuscripts from the monastery library, which included books of Scripture and writings of monastic and church leaders. Although letters of advice to nuns assumed that they would be particularly interested in lives of earlier Christian women, the nuns were able to study the entire tradition. Among the nuns who composed literature of their own were Hrotsvit of Gandersheim (tenth century), Elisabeth of Schonau (1129–1165), and Gertrude the Great of Helfta (1256–1301/2). Illiterate women also joined monasteries; from the twelfth century on, many of them became "lay sisters," performing manual labor instead of reading.

The feminist critique of medieval monasteries for women has often focused on the question of the women's independence from men. Since Sacraments requiring a priest's service were essential to religious life, nuns always had to find priests willing to provide them with the eucharist, extreme unction, and burial. From the twelfth century on, confessions were increasingly made to the clergy. As strict enclosure became the norm, the women had to hire men to perform the necessary labors outside the monastery. To solve these problems, some monasteries of women included religious men as integral parts of their community: monks or canons to serve as priests and administrators, and lay brothers to perform manual labor. Sometimes the abbess or prioress ruled over both sexes (as in some eighth-century Anglo-Saxon houses and at twelfth-century Fontevrault); other times men were in charge (as with the twelfth-century Gilbertines). While some scholars lament women's need to make arrangements including men, others praise the nuns' creative adaptation to the circumstances that confronted them.

Feminist scholars have been particularly attracted to the prominent abbesses, often women of wealth and high social standing, who exercised independent rule of their monastery. Although not feminists in the strict sense of the word, these abbesses wrote for women (and men), thought about women, and saw the capabilities of women. Some of the most famous abbesses were Hildegard of Bingen (1098–1179), Heloise (1100–1163/4), and Bridget of Sweden (1303–1373). The abbess exercised her authority visibly in the daily common meeting of the nuns ("the chapter"), where she instructed them on their rule, oversaw decisions concerning the monastery, and assigned penances for violations of the rule.

Until the Renaissance most religious women lived a contemplative life much like that of the Benedictine nuns. (See also MEDIEVAL WOMEN, Varieties of Religious Life.)

References. Penny Schine Gold, *The Lady and the Virgin: Image, Attitude and Experience in Twelfth-Century France* (Chicago, 1985); John A Nichols and Lillian Thomas Shank (eds.), *Distant Echoes: Medieval Religious Women*, vol. 1 (Kalamazoo, Mich., 1984); Suzanne Fonay Wemple, *Women in Frankish Society: Marriage and the Cloister, 500 to 900* (Philadelphia, 1981).

SHARON K. ELKINS

MEDIEVAL WOMEN. Lives of Urban Women were constrained by lifecycle stage, ideologies of gender, and the socioeconomic position of the household to which they belonged; however, women had more high-status participation in market production and in recognized female domains than they were to have in succeeding centuries.

The power and freedom a medieval laywoman possessed were directly linked to the status of her household in town society. As the fundamental organizing unit of life in the preindustrial town, the household (which included spouses, children, apprentices, and servants) often bound its members more tightly than kinship relations.

The relatively small "Northern European family" was the norm in cities during the later Middle Ages. Men and women married in their late 20s after accumulating the assets to establish an independent household. For the male this meant a guild membership or ownership of a business; for the female, a dowry. (See DOWRY, In Western Societies.) Given the high level of infant mortality, most urban households raised only two children to adulthood, though the wealthy had larger families than poor, artisan, or middle-class couples. Since few children survived to inherit the family business and civic position, town dynasties rarely developed. Females had a shorter life expectancy than males, typically about 31 years. Those women who did outlive their husbands often enjoyed financial independence and social status by becoming guild members in their husband's place, running the family business, and exercising financial and social power in the community. A rich widow was considered a good wife for the ambitious businessman, who then could control her assets.

For dowerless women or poor widows, marriage was unlikely, and a permanent female underclass typified the late medieval town. Poor single women and widows worked for low wages in a variety of industries or as servants. In Flanders and the Rhineland, where urban populations of unmarriageable women were enormous, women known as Beguines formed lay communities to support themselves through work as teachers, spinners, weavers, and nurses. By remaining celibate and achieving economic self-sufficiency in a household unit that resembled that of the religious orders, they escaped the primary institutions of male control: family and Church. (See MEDIEVAL WOMEN, Varieties of Religious Life.)

Women were important members of the domestic production unit. The typical crafts- or tradesperson's home was a timber, post-and-beam, two-story building, with the business or workshop located on the ground floor and living quarters above. Such a household manufactured and sold its product at home, using the labor of family members in addition to that of one or two apprentices. Few women were employed outside this domestic economic setting, but within it they acted as business partners, practiced crafts, and on occasion achieved independent trading status. Under *law merchant* (commercial law) a married woman could operate as a *feme sole* (a single woman), and her husband would not be liable for her debts.

Most training that women received was informal, but some women were formally apprenticed beginning at age 12 (the age of adulthood; for men it was 14). Female apprentices tended to cluster in the food trades, textile industries, and precious metalwork, all traditionally sex-linked skills. Women dominated the ale-brewing industry, and in some cities there were all-female guilds such as gold spinners or silk makers. Women rarely participated in long-distance trade or in such occupations as money changing, butchery, drapery, or pharmaceuticals. They were active in borrowing and lending money and in real estate management, but typically on a local level rather than in international finance. In this, women's lives reflected the medieval urban context in which social and economic life for all but the very wealthy centered on the parish or neighborhood where the household was located.

Expectations about female conduct also depended on family rank. Late medieval society recognized a clear status hierarchy, expressed and enforced through such means as sumptuary laws, regulation of clothing cost and fashion, and codes of behavior for each class. Aristocratic women had less freedom than women of craft or artisanal backgrounds, who moved about the town without chaperones, attended church services and festivals, and pursued their trades in public.

On festive occasions the hierarchy was at its most fluid, with a mixing of all ranks at feasts and funerals, religious holidays, and civic or craft events. Popular culture also bound the classes. Oral traditions lived on longest in those contexts that were not controlled by elite, literate, or professional culture; they were therefore more likely to survive in the context of women's activities than in men's.

Aside from festival occasions, the public ceremonial life of the town excluded not only women but also the young, the poor, and many male householders. Only elite males who were members of civic organizations, craft guilds, and religious organizations marched in public processions and performed in the public dramatic productions. The events in which women participated tended to ritualize the separateness of male and female roles.

Women had virtually no political role in the medieval town: they could not sit on town councils, serve in the courts, bear arms, or hold guild office. Educational opportunities also differed for men and women; women could not be admitted to the university, which offered professional training for careers in the church, law, and medicine. Many urban women were literate in the vernacular, but Latin remained a male professional status marker.

Given the large proportion of unmarried people in late medieval urban society, as well as the high infant mortality rate, marriage and parenthood were far from universal experiences; nor had the family and child rearing achieved the ideological importance they would after the Renaissance. As a ritual, marriage was still somewhat ambiguous. For canon law until the Council of Trent (1545–1563), a valid marriage consisted of a vow between two consenting adults, which did not have to be exchanged publicly or formalized by approval of civil or ecclesiastical authorities. The greatest number of cases in medieval church courts were breach of contract suits, concerned with promises of marriage made in private.

The activities and rituals surrounding childbirth were conducted entirely by women. Labor and delivery were public occasions, presided over by female friends, relatives, and midwives. Midwives were older single women or widows, usually lower-class, who took on apprentices. Midwifery* was regulated by the town council. Midwives attended normal deliveries and occasionally performed surgery in cases of cesarean section or stillbirth. The baptism of the newborn was also a female affair, with the midwife carrying the child to the ceremony in order to register the birth in the parish; the only men in attendance were the father and godfather of the child.

From the fifteenth century on, urban women's lives became increasingly restricted through legal, political, economic, and ideological factors. As production moved out of the household or came under stricter control of government and guild regulation, women lost their economic roles. Widows practicing the family trade; female apprentices, masters, and journeymen; the wives of craftsmen—all of whom had worked with freedom in the medieval town—were excluded from the market.

With the loss of public economic functions, the woman's role within the middle-class family corresponded increasingly to the mandates of reproduction and private domestic management articulated in female conduct literature. The Reformation gave marriage a status it had never held within a medieval ideology that esteemed virginity but simultaneously narrowed a wife's marital role to serving her husband in private. Political centralization also reinforced patriarchy as an image within the family of the national ruler's power.

References. Barbara Hanawalt (ed.), *Women and Work in Preindustrial Europe* (Bloomington, Ind., 1986); David Herlihy, *Medieval Households* (Cambridge, 1985); Martha Howell, *Women, Production, and Patriarchy in Late Medieval Cities* (Chicago, 1986); Charles Phythian-Adams, "Ceremony and the Citizen: The Communal Year at Coventry, 1450–1550," in Peter Clark and Paul Slack (eds.), *Crisis and Order in English Towns, 1500–1700* (Toronto, 1979), 57–85.

KATHLEEN ASHLEY

MEDIEVAL WOMEN. Noble (Lay)Women (*nobilis mulier*) were, from the twelfth century, praised and venerated all over Europe in the courtly literature, which was composed almost exclusively by men. External beauty was considered a symbol of internal virtue. This concept served as a forceful model in opposition to the clerical image of woman as an agent for man's seduction in accordance with the account of Adam and Eve in the book of Genesis (clerical misogyny). The ideal of the Virgin Mary, however, posed the contrary concept. Thus, praise and criticism of women often overlapped. Thirteenth-century scholasticism tended to depict woman as an imperfect form of man (Thomas Aquinas, *Summa theologica*, I, Question 92, lag.2) and, as such, as a sinful human being lacking in basic moral and ethical strength ("naturaliter est minoris virtutis et dignitatis quam vir"), while the courtly poets strongly relied on the woman as a source for man's ethical education and as a prod to move him toward a virtuous and chivalric way of life.

As women were often considered weak by nature, they did not receive the same physical and technical training as men, who were prepared for warfare early on. In consequence, noble girls, who stayed home and learned to read and write and who studied the Bible and other religious material, received a much better intellectual education than the boys did. However, since by the thirteenth century they were seldom taught Latin, most religious literature intended for them was translated or written in the vernacular. Despite their being cut off from the language of scholarship and thus also from the universities, some high-ranking noblewomen acquired an outstanding education since they were expected to represent their husbands at the courts in an appropriate manner (e.g., Isold in Gottfried of Strassburg's *Tristan*).

When the girl of a noble family married, she lost her rights and was considered second in rank after her husband. Girls were married sometimes as early as the age of 7 and often by the age of 12. In order to be regarded with respect they needed a solid dowry, which their fathers normally took great pains to procure for them. (See DOWRY, In Western Societies.) In their married life noblewomen were mostly occupied with the supervision of the large households and the upbringing of the children. Only when the husbands died did they gain real power as rulers.

Christine de Pizan outlined in her *Le Livre des Trois Vertus* (c. 1406) what a woman of the higher or upper nobility living on an estate ought to be able to do. Although the supervision of estates was a heavy burden, the noblewoman normally proved fully capable in the management of the domestic economy and in the political administration of her husband's goods. The necessary skills included the handling of tenure and feudal law, management of the estate, supervision of the household, and control of the family budget. Other skills were needlework and sewing, cooking, baking, and other housekeeping tasks—the food preparation and housekeeping tasks not for themselves but in order to assess the work done in their own households, on the home farm, and, in particular, in the dairy.

A well-trained noblewoman also knew how to ride horseback, raise falcons and hunt with them, play chess, dance, sing, compose poems, play an instrument, and read romances and poetry.

Often a woman shared the position of ruler with her husband or ruled after his death. Although the courtly poets mostly painted female rulers as weak and lacking in men's political and military strength, the thirteenth century in particular witnessed many female rulers who often used their position to improve their countries' infrastructure, industry, and arts, thus wielding tremendous power and influence at least equal to those of their male counterparts (see Ulrich von Etzenbach, *Wilhelm von Wenden*). In the absence of their husbands, noblewomen were known to have efficiently defended their castles against military attack (see the *Chansons de geste*; Wolfram von Eschenbach's Willehaln). War, Crusades, and political activities often took husbands away from their wives, who then controlled the entire estate by themselves.

Whereas widows were common in noble families and rose to powerful positions, those spinsters who lived by themselves were practically unknown because most girls who did not find a husband ended up in a nunnery. A few women who did not receive a good dowry and thus could not marry or who did not inherit land and did not join a convent became educators and entertainers for other noble families.

Noblewomen also had, on the average, a longer life expectancy than men because of the high death toll from war, chivalric fights, and the like. Although statistical evidence is scarce and mostly concentrates on urban populations, women seem, on the average, to have outlived men by a margin of 100 to 95. Scholars such as Vincent of Beauvais (*Speculum Naturale*), theologians such as Albert the Great (*Opera Omnia*, vol. 12), or even Renaissance poets such as Baldesare Castiglione (*The Book of the Courtier* from 1516) expressed their firm belief in women's longevity over men and thus tend to confirm the statistical data. Although the figure of children per family differs according to geographical area, social status within the nobility, women's fertility, and the century, noblewomen usually had not more than four to six children, many of whom died before they reached the age of 5.

Only a few women managed to marry according to their own wishes because marriage represented too powerful an instrument in family politics to be left to the girls alone. A single marriage contract could easily change the whole political map of medieval Europe. In order to unite children of equal rank and/or bring together advantageous property settlements, many nobles married their relatives of the third or fourth degree. The church reacted only mildly and often received a payment to legalize the marriage contract. Newborn infants were commonly handed over to wet nurses, and the young children were soon sent off to other noble households to learn courtly manners. Thus, noblewomen had little to do with child raising and could dedicate all their energies to the supervision and control of the household itself. Yet they made many efforts to give their children, including the girls, a thorough education and to procure them stable marriage partners.

The noblewoman always remained in a subordinate position and was ruled by her husband despite all her representational duties at court. Marital disloyalty by the wife was harshly punished, but the husband could enjoy many more liberties. However, as regards private rights and duties, widows were on a par with men. They could hold land, even by military tenure; they could make wills or a contract; and they could sue or be sued.

Although many high-ranking noblewomen appeared as patrons of the fine arts and literature, they hardly stood out as poets. Nevertheless, we know of a handful of female troubadour poets (*trobairitz*) and women writers such as Marie de France and Christine de Pizan.

Andreas Capellanus reported in his *The Art of Courtly Love* (c. 1184–1186) that a woman could gain noble status by marriage, whereas men never changed their nobility by marriage (1:6), which is confirmed by Hartmann von Aue in his contemporary romance *Der arme Heinrich*.

References. Joachim Bumke, *Hofische Kultur, Literatur und Gesellschaft im hohen Mittelalter*, 2 vols., 2d. ed. (Munich, 1986); Georges Duby and Michel Perrot (eds.), *A History of Women in the West, Vol. II: Silence of the Middle Ages* (Cambridge, 1992); Joan M. Ferrante, *To the Glory of Her Sex: Women's Roles in the Composition of Medieval Texts* (Bloomington and Indianapolis, 1997); David Herlihy, *Women in Medieval Society* (Houston, Tex., 1971); Peter Ketsch, *Frauen in Mittelalter, Quellen und Materialien*, 2 vols. (Düsseldorf, 1983, 1984); Margaret Wade Labarge, *Women in Medieval Life: A Small Sound of the Trumpet* (London, 1986); Shulamith Shahar, *The Fourth Estate: A History of Women in the Middle Ages*, trans. Chaya Galai (London, 1983).

ALBRECHT CLASSEN

MEDIEVAL WOMEN. Peasant Women were the largest part of the female population. The majority of the general population also lived in the country (70 to 95 percent). In contrast to modern times, the medieval peasant woman's social status was relatively equal to that of her husband. Both worked together on their farm and shared the necessary labor. However, the peasant woman had her own extensive domain in the vegetable garden. She also performed the domestic tasks of weaving, spinning, cooking, doing the laundry, and child care.

A considerable number of country women were involved in the brewing, baking, and butchering businesses geared toward the village or town market. Whereas the woman mostly took care of the smaller animals on the farm like the geese, sheep, or goats, the man controlled the larger animals. With the profits of the sales of garden and home-manufactured goods in local markets, the peasant woman was a decisive help in procuring cash for the family's budget and thus had a high economic value as a partner in the farming business. Hence, peasant women were as much productive members of the rural world as their husbands and were not exclusively reproductive members, solely in charge of bearing children, raising them, and managing the household.

In the early and high Middle Ages, peasant women were, for the most part, in charge of the textile production, both for their lords and for their own families. Early textile manufacturing sites, called *Genitia*, which existed in the countryside, were exclusively in the hands of women. However, when the cities took over textile production in the later Middle Ages, these rural "factories" quickly disappeared. Although the peasant economy was essentially a family economy, the role of the individual and, in particular, the peasant woman was much stronger than previously has been thought.

In contrast to bourgeois and aristocratic women, the peasant woman had very little time available to take care of her children because she was too busy with her work on the farm. Consequently, many children died in their early years due to accidents while they were left alone at home by their parents. These were painful and noticeable losses because peasant families did not include more than three to four children, on the average, throughout the Middle Ages.

Pregnant women enjoyed a particular legal position. Thus, they were allowed to pick grapes in the vineyards of their lord, and their husbands had the right to catch fish and hunt animals on the nobleman's estates. The husbands did not even have to join the military force if it took them away from their wives for more than 24 hours. Widows enjoyed similar privileges. Although peasant women had little legal say in the rural community, they could represent their husbands at their lord's court.

A uniform image of peasant women's legal position, however, cannot be drawn because of vast differences reflected in the documents such as *Weistümer* (judicial sentence collections), wills, estate rolls, and so on. Nevertheless, they generally lacked full equality with the men. Thus, when the husband died, the widow had only limited rights to inherit his goods, and then only in default of male heirs. French sources from the area of Lyon of the fourteenth and fifteenth centuries show, however, that peasant widows were left the guardianship of the children as well as the administration and *usufruct* (profit) of the family property. Thus, they were often much better off than contemporary noblewomen.

On the average, the peasant woman married between the ages of 18 and 22, and only in the later Middle Ages did the marriage age drop remarkably. The decision to marry largely depended on availability of a dowry. (See DOWRY, In Western Societies.) There was an astonishingly high number of women who paid the dowry from their own income as salaried workers or as independent manufacturers of rural products. Particularly in England, many women used their own resources to pay the *merchet*, a fine payable by the unfree to their lord upon marriage. Generalizations are not possible, but we know at least that fathers were not always in charge of the *merchet*. Those women who paid their own *merchet* would consequently marry late in life. The ecclesiastical prohibition against marriage within four degrees of family relationship meant that many girls had to look for a husband outside their village boundaries and thus permitted them a higher degree of mobility than the young men.

Because the peasant's life was rarely based exclusively on an agricultural economy, the image of the submissive and downtrodden peasant woman is a myth of modern times. Most medieval rural communities were composed of a wide range of peasant social classes ranging from the independent rich landowner down to the poor agricultural laborer. Hence, the scale of peasant women extended from wealthy peasant wives or widows down to poor maids and farmworkers.

Although it is almost impossible to find direct sources dealing with medieval peasant women, much information can be gained from manuscript illustrations such as the *Livres d'heures* (Hour Books), frescoes of a similar kind, legal documents, statutes (*capitularies*, charters, marriage licenses, and codified law books such as the *Sachsenspiegel*), and literary texts not written by peasant authors but closely reflecting the life of the peasants, such as Wernher der Gartenaere's *Helmbrecht*, the anonymous *Holy Maidenhead*, Langland's *Vision of William concerning Piers the Plowman*, Chaucer's *Nun's Priest Tale*, or Wittenwiler's *Ring*. These fictional works depict the life of the peasant woman as a simple and frugal, although not uncomfortable, existence, or denigrate it as miserable and contemptible. Late-medieval German lyric poetry even describes the peasant life as luxurious and pleasant in contrast to the knights' poverty (*Neidhart*). Reality, however, lies somewhere in between these extremes, since peasant women experienced more freedom and public recognition than the women in the noble class.

References. Emilie Amt (ed.), *Women's Lives in Medieval Europe. A Sourcebook* (New York and London, 1993); J. M. Bennett, "Medieval Peasant Marriage: An Examination of Marriage License Fines in *Liber Gersumarum*," in J. A. Raftis (ed.), *Pathways to Medieval Peasants*, Papers in Medieval Studies 2 (Toronto, 1981), 193–246; Peter Ketsch, *Frauen im Mittelalter*, 2 vols., *Geschichtsdidaktik-Studien*, ed. Annette Kuhn, Materialien 14 and 19 (Düsseldorf, 1983 and 1984); Margaret Wade Labarge, *Women in Medieval Life, a Small Sound of the Trumpet* (London, 1986); Eileen Power, *Medieval Women*, ed. M. M. Postan (Cambridge, 1975; repr. 1976).

ALBRECHT CLASSEN

MEDIEVAL WOMEN. Varieties of Religious Life were greater than the image of medieval woman as either wife or nun would indicate. Nevertheless, the higher a woman's social standing, the greater her opportunities for religious self-expression. Successive Church reforms circumscribed all women's religious life, and the enforcement of clerical celibacy further undermined the already ambivalent image of women in medieval theology. For women to structure their own religious lives and service was seen as dangerous and conducive to heresy, and women religious were increasingly isolated from the mainstream of society and stringently regulated by Roman authority.

In the early Church the line between religious and secular women was vague. The office of deaconess offered women an official social ministry within the hierarchy that was soon suppressed except for vestigial privileges retained by some women called canonesses. Women were patrons of local churches, and consecrated widows and virgins lived in their own homes or in small groups while working in the world.

In the church as elsewhere women have the greatest freedom in revolutionary movements and frontier societies. As law and order increase, women's autonomy decreases; and as monastic life developed, the church forced consecrated women into convents. A few independent women appear among the "Desert Fathers," but more opted for cenobitism. (See ASCETICISM, Ascetics, Recluses, and Mystics.) In far-flung western outposts of Christianity like Ireland and Anglo-Saxon England, women religious wielded considerable power. Abbesses like Hilda and Brigid trained future bishops, advised kings, gave spiritual counsel, and occasionally acted as confessors. Reformers, whether of early ninth-century Carolingian or Gregorian (late eleventh- and twelfth-century) mode, decreased women's involvement in the world and lessened their self-determination within their cloisters. Dependence on male clergy for the administration of the Sacraments was a vulnerability the Church exploited to increase its control over women religious.

Practical deterrents kept women from becoming hermits: lack of physical safety and lack of financial and ecclesiastical backing. Christina of Markyate, an unusual woman, found herself, like many successful hermits, to be the inadvertent founder of a community. Women solitaries more typically became anchoresses immured in small houses adjacent to churches or monasteries. The anchoress might be said to be the medieval hierarchy's ideal woman religious. Rigorously scrutinized before her immurement, she then lived under the eye of nearby priests in the strictest possible enclosure.

Medieval convents were small and drew recruits from the upper ranks of society for basic economic reasons. Women of lower rank were excluded unless they followed their mistresses into the cloister as lay sisters or convent servants. Lay sisters said simple prayers rather than the Office, which they could not read, and were often less rigidly enclosed. Strict enclosure was the aim of much legislation about nuns, and even the orders that emerged from the motley and peripatetic reform preaching of the late eleventh and early twelfth centuries were forced into traditional patterns. Fontevrault, founded to house a motley collection of both sexes, quickly became an aristocratic community of enclosed nuns with a subordinate male support staff. The great power of the abbesses of Fontevrault and Las Huelgas came from royal connections rather than any positive shift in the church's attitude. In fact, the twelfth-century monastic reform generally tried to exclude women. Nuns who were attracted to the Cistercian constitutions followed them, in the main, without official approval. Orders of both men and women like Premontré abandoned or segregated the women, though the sisters of Premontré were thus ironically upgraded to canonesses with full choir privileges. The Gilbertines' enormous houses of nuns, priests, and lay brothers and sisters recruited daughters of the gentry rather than aristocrats, and their administrative structure shows signs of women's influence. They also provided an intermediate status for women too old or frail to learn Latin for the choir but unsuited to the rough work of the lay sisters.

The epitome of the church's policy of isolation and regulation was the monasticization of the female followers of St. Francis. Originally uncloistered like the men of the order, they were soon required to stay behind their convent walls like other nuns. The most innovative contribution of the mendicant orders was the Third Order concept, which gave queens and commoners alike a chance they would never otherwise have had to participate in the life of a religious order. Members of the Third Order (or tertiaries), while living in the world, followed a simple rule of prayer and fasting patterned on that of the parent order.

Even more than the tertiaries, the Beguines brought new opportunities for religious expression to ordinary women. Beginning in the late twelfth century, the Beguine movement creatively bridged the gap between the aristocratic cloister and the secular lives of women of modest means. Living with family and friends as early Christian widows and virgins had done, they wore no habit, took no vows, and followed no rule but the Gospels. Even after they began to gather in communities, the Beguines worked in the secular world and enjoyed considerable autonomy. Though they were eventually incorporated into parishes under priestly supervision, the church never pressed the Beguines into the claustral mold. For two centuries these independent women kept the ideal of the apostolic life available to women for whom the cloister was either undesirable or unavailable.

References. Derek Baker (ed.), *Medieval Women* (Oxford, England, 1978); John A. Nichols and Lillian Thomas Shank (eds.), *Distant Echoes: Medieval Religious Women*, vol. 1 (Kalamazoo, Mich., 1984).

ELLEN M. BARRETT

MENARCHE, the first menstrual bleeding, results from multiple and complex neuroendocrine processes that occur throughout puberty. Menarche usually occurs late in the four- to five-year span needed for observable pubertal changes, such as breast development, growth spurt, and pubic hair growth.

There are tremendous variations in the age of onset of menarche. Generally, the mean age of menarche in American girls is reported to be 12.5 to 13 years of age, with 95 percent of girls reaching menarche between 10.5 and 14.5 years. However, age of menarche is dependent on cultural and environmental differences as well as individual differences related to genetic characteristics. Thus, menarche can be reached anywhere between 9 and 16 years and, with few exceptions, still be considered within the normal range of development.

Over the past century, the mean age of menarche has gradually declined by two to four months with each passing decade. This decline, referred to as the secular trend in the age at menarche, is attributed to improved nutritional standards and an increased opportunity for health care. With health and nutrition at higher levels in American girls, it is generally concluded that the age of menarche has plateaued.

Menarche has both biological and psychological significance. Biologically, menarche signals one's "becoming" reproductively capable. Regular cyclicity of the hormonal patterns important for initiating and maintaining a pregnancy do not usually occur simultaneously with menarche. In addition, the majority of menstrual cycles remain anovulatory (i.e., without releasing an egg) throughout the early menarcheal years. Even though regularity in hormones and ovulation is not usually attained immediately at menarche, it is possible to become pregnant shortly after menarche or in rare instances even prior to menarche, if the very first egg is fertilized.

Psychologically, menarche may bring with it mixed feelings and emotions. Some girls may feel proud or grown up at the onset of menarche while simultaneously having negative feelings or anxiety. In general, however, girls today view menarche as less traumatic than was reported in the past. Parents may also experience ambivalent feelings when their adolescent reaches menarche; this is a sign of the daughter's impending adulthood and growing up and a sign of the parents' aging. Research on changes in parent–adolescent interactions suggests that around the midpoint of the pubertal process, adolescents begin to press for greater voice in family decision making, especially pertaining to themselves; parents may resist and cause greater conflict or suppress the adolescent's attempts, or they may accommodate a relationship with more autonomy and responsibility for the adolescent. The role that menarche plays in parent–adolescent relations continues to be explored.

References. D. Apter and R. Vihko, "Hormonal Patterns of the First Menstrual Cycles," in S. Venturolz, C. Flamigni, and J. R. Givens (eds.), *Adolescence* in *Females* (Chicago, 1985), 215–238; S. Golub (ed.), *Menarche* (Lexington, Mass., 1983).

LORAH DORN and ANNE C. PETERSEN

MENOPAUSE (PHYSIOLOGICAL) is the ending of menstruation, considered complete when a woman has not had a period for one year. Menopause can happen anytime from age 35 to 60 but most commonly occurs around the ages of 45 to 50.

During perimenopause (the transition years before menopause) the ovaries gradually decrease estrogen production, but postmenopausal women still have estrogens in their bodies primarily because androgens produced by the adrenal glands and ovaries are converted to estrogens. Estrone, the form of estrogen predominant in postmenopausal women, is biologically less active than estradiol, the major estrogen in premenopausal women. Factors that seem to cause greater production of estrone include higher body fat levels, increasing age, and exercise.

Symptoms associated with menopause are different from one culture to another. In our society, approximately 20 percent of women experience no menopausal symptoms, and about 15 percent suffer severe problems, while most women notice changes but manage to live with these fairly comfortably. Only two of the symptoms associated with menopause are known to be related to the drop in estrogen. These are hot flashes (caused by blood vessels dilating and constricting irregularly and unpredictably) and changes in the vagina (thinning of walls, loss of elasticity, less lubrication). Although estrogen replacement therapy (ERT = estrogen only) and hormone replacement therapy (HRT = estrogen plus a progestin) do relieve these symptoms, their use and the safest ways to take them are controversial. Safer, more enjoyable ways to minimize vaginal changes include arousing sexual activity and Kegel exercises (contracting pelvic floor muscles). The relationship of long-term lowered estrogen and osteoporosis,* heart disease, memory loss, Alzheimer's disease, and conditions associated with aging is being studied.

Many of the symptoms associated with menopause have more to do with social than biological changes. For example, menopause may coincide with the stage when children are leaving home, and for the woman who has never had children, menopause clarifies that now she never will. The average age of widowhood is 56, so many women face widowhood and menopause simultaneously, and this is also an age at which people commonly lose or have lost their parents.

Menopause can be a difficult time for a woman in a society that values women primarily for their youthful beauty or reproductive capacity. Menopause is easier for women in a society that values the experience and wisdom of the older woman and gives them a definite role in the community.

References. Sandra Coney, *The Menopause Industry—How the Medical Establishment Exploits Women* (Alameda, Calif., 1994); Susan M. Love and Karen Lindsey, *Dr. Susan Love's Hormone Book—Making Informed Choices about Menopause* (New York, 1997); *Taking Hormones and Women's Health: Choices, Risks and Benefits* and other information on menopause are available from the National Women's Health Network, 514 Tenth Street, NW, Suite 400, Washington, DC 20004.

NANCY WORCESTER

MENOPAUSE (PSYCHOLOGICAL). The physiological changes of menopause are universal: it has been suggested that it is the only maturational event in adulthood comparable to maturational changes in childhood. The psychological significance of menopause to the individual, however, may also derive from the cultural context as it shapes her psychosexual history and the social framework of reproduction—and thus, in turn, shapes her response to the termination of fertility.

Like most organic changes of middle and old age, climacterium (a gradual involution of the ovaries and concomitant biological processes) is a biological loss. Its most salient consequences, however, are the cessation of fertility and menstruation; these changes may function to protect the aging woman from biological demands she has become less able to meet. Thus, as a physiological change, menopause may have both positive and negative implications.

Organ systems mature and age at differing rates: the reproductive system is mature at adolescence and senescent at menopause, many years before a woman is "old." Thus, menopause may be viewed as the "premature" aging of the ovaries, though it should also be noted that only comparatively recently has life expectancy increased to the point where women outlived their reproductive capacities by a substantial period.

A duality of psychological meaning—the loss of, together with freedom from, the vital and demanding function of reproduction—may be inferred from the physiological changes at menopause. A parallel ambiguity is found in psychoanalytic discussions of the significance of menopause. Helene Deutsch viewed menopause as involution and loss and claimed that women perceive the cessation of fertility primarily as an omen of aging and death. Those women who have experienced gratification in earlier phases of psychosexual development, according to Deutsch, adapt to the losses of menopause with relative ease, while women who have been unfulfilled at earlier life stages will experience menopause as the final "closing of the gates" on a potentiality that will be forever unfulfilled.

Therese Benedek offered an opposing interpretation, stressing freedom rather than loss as the primary significance of menopause. She viewed menopause as a development phase in which psychic energy, previously bound up in the fluctuations of the menstrual cycle,* is now freed for new purposes. Moreover, the capacity for adaptation that evolved in response to the demands of female physiology now becomes available as a psychic resource. Thus, Benedek saw menopause as a time of potential psychic expansion.

Developmental psychologists offer a more complex picture. Robert Havighurst termed menopause a developmental task—that is, a crisis precipitated by the confluence of maturational and social events, for which there exists an optimal solution. The potential freedom created by the loss of fertility and departure of children from the home is optimally utilized for emotional and intellectual growth.

A refinement of this view was provided by B. L. Neugarten et al., who conducted the first study of attitudes toward menopause among 100 normal, nonclinical middle-class women. These women did not view the biological change as a crisis but as a comparatively trivial event within the larger and more important context of family life cycle changes.

The question thus arises, How do culture and biology interact? How is the loss of fertility viewed by women with different childbearing histories? It might be expected, as Else Frenkel-Brunswich has suggested, that the extent of separation between the biological and biographical becomes greater as biography becomes increasingly independent of vital functions, and this separation will increase with increasing age, as, generally, research in adult development and aging has shown that individual differences increase over the life span with the cumulative effect of varied experience.

However, a broad-scale, cross-cultural study of the responses of normal, middle-aged women from traditional, transitional, and modern cultures to the changes of menopause and middle age showed just the opposite to be the case. Women across five widely varying ethnic groups universally welcomed the loss of fertility at menopause, despite dramatic differences in childbearing history, ranging, at the traditional extreme, from women who had been pregnant, childbearing, and nursing almost without interruption since marriage* and who entered middle age with small children still at home, to the modern extreme, women who bore no more than one or two children and indeed often expressed regret that they had not had more— but did not now want to become pregnant.

It would seem, then, that menopause is indeed a universal developmental event that may have universal meaning and that the biological gains and losses, which translate into conflicting psychoanalytic interpretations, are experienced by normal women as a welcome end to an ambiguous stimulus: the promise implicit in the potentiality of biological fertility, together with the burden of childrearing.

References. Therese Benedek, *Psychosexual Functions in Women* (New York, 1952); N. Datan, A. Antonovsky, and B. Maoz, *A Time to Reap: The Middle Age of Women in Five Israeli Sub-Cultures* (Baltimore, 1981); Helene Deutsch, *Psychology of Women*, vol. 2 (London, 1945); Else Frenkel-Brunswich, "Adjustments and Reorientation in the Course of the Lifespan," in R. G. Kuhlen and G. G. Thompson (eds.), *Psychological Studies of Human Development* (New York, 1963); Robert Havighurst, *Human Development and Education* (New York, 1953); B. L. Neugarten, V. Wood, and R. J. Kraines, "Women's Attitudes toward the Menopause," *Vita Humana* 6 (1963): 140–151.

NANCY DATAN

MEN'S STUDIES. If women's studies are construed as the study of women, that is, a field that takes women as the object of its analysis in ways analogous to those by which other academic disciplines constitute or seize upon their objects of inquiry, then the study of men lies either outside, or very much at the margins or in the background of, women's studies. But if women's studies are understood on a more expansive and, indeed, more accurate model that understands its domain to be all of knowledge as reconsidered from the standpoints of women, then the study of men, as part of that knowledge domain, is an integral and necessary component of women's studies.

Considered, then, as emerging out of such women's studies perspectives, men's studies represent an expansion of feminist analysis, a transgressive trespass into the belly of the patriarchal beast launched from vantage points pioneered by women's studies. From this women's studies perspective, women's studies and women's perspectives remain the foundational and central aspects of the men's studies feminist enterprise.

To this it must be added that men's studies are inconceivable not only without women's studies but also without the groundbreaking challenges to our understandings of gender made by lesbian and gay studies, as well as other analyses that stem from the perspectives of oppressed or marginalized groups.

The practitioners of men's studies are predominantly, but not exclusively, male. While not claiming the *last word* on gender, in accordance with the preceding analysis, these male practitioners of men's studies demonstrate that it may well be methodologically useful for feminist analysis to make men's accounts of their experience a *first word* starting point for women's studies research. That is to say, men's locations in patriarchal structures at a minimum make them useful informants for women's studies, offering opportunities for them to become what might perhaps be considered "traitors to the masculine cause," as male supporters of women's suffrage were called in England, breaking ranks with patriarchy in using their keys to the executive washrooms to let women in on the secrets of the male mystique. In addition, feminist (or pro-feminist, as some prefer) men may also use their insider status to generate their own (pro-) feminist analyses of masculinity/masculinities* and patriarchy/patriarchies.

What differentiates the new men's studies from the usual patriarchal pursuits of academe is, then, not the *what* of its subject, for, as women's studies have consistently and correctly argued, we do not need to turn an even higher disproportion of our resources toward men. Rather, the distinctive mark of the new men's studies is *how* it studies men. Men's studies turn the tables on patriarchal knowledge claims and produce feminist knowledge by following women's studies in "norming" women, thereby "othering men," in the process also taking on board the fundamental feminist insight that "gender" marks not merely difference but also hierarchy. Gender is a system of power, not merely an attribute of individuals.

One way that the women's studies critique of traditional scholarship has been articulated has been to begin by noting that in our language and culture, as in so many others, the term "man" is ostensibly ambiguous, meaning either "male" or "human being." Having deconstructed the myth that the latter usage is "neutral," women's studies have gone on to demonstrate that the ambiguity of "man" functions to denigrate women through the process by which specifically male norms and perspectives thereby come to be seen as generically human, by which standards women consequently come to be seen as deficient, as less than fully human. To this foundational insight of women's studies men's studies add the additional claim or twist that in thus overgeneralizing from "man" as male to "man" as generic human, not only do we disappear women, but in seeing males as paradigmatic generic humans we also remove from sight whatever might be specific to men *as* men, rather than as generic humans. While our vision of women has been blurred by pushing them into an undistinguished background, our vision of men has been blurred by bringing them into an overly highlighted foreground.

By illuminating the inner sanctums of male privilege to make them visible and subject to feminist scrutiny, men's studies empower women in the way that knowledge of one's opponent is always empowering. It represents a promising development in the study of gender.

HARRY BROD

MENSTRUAL CYCLE. *Biology.* The menstrual cycle is governed by the hypothalamus, a part of the brain, and results from systematic fluctuations of the ovarian hormones—estrogens and progesterone. During the menstrual flow, estrogen and progesterone are at a low level. Estrogen peaks about midcycle, and progesterone reaches a peak a few days later as a result of ovulation (the releasing of the egg from the ovary). Menstrual bleeding results from the decline in estrogen level (which is also accompanied by a decline in progesterone). The normal duration from one menstruation to the next ranges from 20 to 40 days. The usual bleeding phase lasts about 4 to 5 days. Ovulation generally occurs about 12 to 13 days before menstruation, although there is a great deal of variability in its timing. Menstruation in the absence of ovulation is very common. Women differ with respect to the amount and patterning of hormonal production. Other hormones from the pituitary and thyroid glands also fluctuate with the menstrual cycle.

The average age of menarche* (first menstruation) is leveling off at about age 12.5. Evidence suggests that reaching a particular body weight (about 105 lbs.) is associated with its onset, and an extensive loss in body fat can suppress menstruation. Menopause* (cessation of menstrual periods) occurs around age 52. There does not seem to be any connection between age at menarche and age at menopause, but similarities in age of menarche and menopause between mothers and daughters suggest that genetic factors influence their timing. Nutrition also plays a role.

There is no currently known analogous cycle in males; the cycling center, located in the hypothalamus, is suppressed prior to birth. Testosterone in males fluctuates predictably from morning to evening hours. All animals, including humans, are subject to a variety of cycles, which may be 24 hours, monthly, seasonal, and so on. The menstrual cycle is one of the more obvious of these biological rhythms.

Behavior. A number of studies have been made concerning mood changes and task performance over the menstrual cycle. Some studies used self-reports on questionnaires, while others studied actual performance of women at different times in their cycle. There is no support for a premenstrual or menstrual decline in such skills as judgment, learning, thinking, and related mental activities. There may be some individual exceptions, but properly designed studies of random samples of women show no such effect. It is not uncommon for women to believe they are impaired, even when their actual performance doesn't show it. Changes in mood are more often reported, but the findings are not consistent. When there is a mood change across the cycle, negative moods are more likely to be reported before or during menstruation. While factors associated with the menstrual cycle may affect mood, they seem less influential than environmental ones.

Pathological States. There are two general forms of menstrual distress, *dysmenorrhea* and *premenstrual symptoms.* It is difficult to gauge the incidence of menstrual distress because the numbers depend on how questions are asked. "Do you ever experience discomfort with menstruation?" might produce an affirmative response rate of 90 percent. If the question is, "During your last period, did you experience discomfort?" the affirmative answers are likely to be less than 10 percent. Although there have been no large-scale surveys on the topic, at a rough estimate, fewer than one-fourth of menstruating women have symptoms severe enough to induce them to stay home from work or school, stay in bed, or see a physician.

Dysmenorrhea refers to pain and discomfort accompanying menstrual flow and usually occurs only on the first day or two. The most common symptoms are uterine cramps and nausea. The source of the symptoms is believed to be an excessive amount of prostaglandin (a hormonelike substance) in the uterus. The prostaglandin level is linked with ovulation. Thus, cycles in which ovulation does not occur may be symptom-free. Psychological factors as well as general health may play a role in symptoms. The interpretation of pain and discomfort of any sort is subject to learning. Some people ignore discomfort; others emphasize it. Symptoms also may carry a symbolic meaning. For example, dysmenorrhea may be a threat to feelings of control or considered a sign of weakness or inferiority.

Premenstrual symptoms refer to changes that occur in the days immediately preceding menstruation. Women do not automatically become depressed, irritable, hostile, or weepy before or during their periods. Some women do report consistent and predictable symptoms and mood changes. Many others do not. The more common complaints are water retention, breast tenderness, mood change, and general physical discomfort. The mood change tends to be negative. On the most positive side an increase in activity level is frequently reported, as is increased sexual arousal.

Premenstrual changes stem from biological, social, and psychological factors. There is a cultural expectation that menstruation produces negative mood and behavior. Both boys and girls of junior high age have learned stereotypic attitudes about women and menstruation. There are considerable cross-cultural differences in the reporting of menstrual cycle symptoms. Because discomfort and mood change are private and subjective experiences, it is virtually impossible to know whether individual and cultural differences are true differences in symptoms or whether they reflect differences in reporting.

While many women report mild to moderate premenstrual symptoms of one type or another, only a few show marked behavioral change or physical impairment. The term premenstrual syndrome (PMS) has been applied to those cases where symptoms are so severe as to interfere with normal functioning. The use of "syndrome" has been controversial because of the wide range of symptoms to which it applies. The medical and psychiatric communities have developed a more strict definition labeled premenstrual dysphoric disorder (PDD). The specific criteria are listed in the Appendix of *Diagnostic and Statistical Manual* (DSM-IV) of the American Psychiatric Association. Other terms that have been used are *premenstrual tension, premenstrual tension syndrome* (PMT), and *premenstrual molimina.*

In contrast with dysmenorrhea, which can be treated with antiprostaglandins, a variety of therapies have been used for premenstrual symptoms, including nutritional and fitness improvement, psychoanalysis, vitamin and mineral supplements, and hormone therapy. Each treatment has worked for some women; no one therapy has been consistently successful.

Other pathological states associated with the menstrual cycle are amenorrhea, oligomenorrhea, and menorrhagia. *Primary amenorrhea* refers to the absence of menstruation at puberty. *Secondary amenorrhea* refers to the cessation of menstruation after it has been established at puberty. A marked weight loss (or failure to gain weight around the age of puberty) will produce amenorrhea. Hypothalamic control of estrogen production by the ovaries is probably involved in its occurrence. It is a common symptom of anorexia nervosa* and in women who recently have stopped using oral contraceptives.

Menorrhagia refers to excessive menstrual bleeding, either heavier than usual or of longer duration. *Oligomenorrhea* refers to scanty or irregular menstrual periods. The psychological aspects of menorrhagia and oligomenorrhea have not been studied, and they tend to be treated as strictly medical disorders.

References. Judith H. Gold and Sally K. Severino, *Premenstrual Dysphorias: Myths and Realities* (Washington, D.C., 1994); Sharon Golub, *Periods: From Me-*

narche to Menopause (Newbury Park, Calif., 1992); John T. E. Richardson, *Cognition and the Menstrual Cycle* (New York, 1992).

BARBARA SOMMER

MENSTRUATION is the periodic discharge of the lining of the uterus, from the Latin *mensis*, or month. The average age in America for the first menstruation (the menarche) is 12.5, the approximate age for the termination of the menstrual flow (the menopause) is 52 years.

Throughout the centuries the menstrual process has been surrounded by fear and superstition. In many cultures the menarcheal girl is secluded from the community or "tabooed," a term that may derive from a Polynesian word for menstruation, *tupua*. The Kolosh Indians of Alaska isolated their menarcheal girls in a hut for one full year, while some Australian peoples buried them in sand to reduce their danger to others. However, anthropologist Marjorie Shostak found that among the Kung of Africa, where men and women share labor and decision making, the menarche is not an object of fear.

Comparably few rituals mark the end of menstruation. Her childbearing years over, the menopausal woman is more frequently ignored, considered unessential to the needs of the community. George Devereuy found Mohave women to be an exception: for them menopause is a sign of achievement, freedom, and wisdom.

Superstitions surrounding the menstruating woman in preliterate societies are also evident in Euro-American and Middle Eastern cultures. The Greek philosopher Aristotle (384–322 B.C.) thought menstrual blood to be a residue of useless nourishment and the single female contribution to reproduction. The Roman naturalist Pliny (A.D. c. 23–79) held wilder notions: menstrual blood would sour wine, dull steel, and drive dogs mad. In the 1920s, Bela Schick and David Macht, as if imitating Pliny, independently discovered certain substances emitted by menstruating women (menotoxins) that would kill plants and prevent beer from fermenting.

Theologians have long considered the menstruating woman to be toxic, polluted, or dangerous. In the Koran, the sacred text of the Islamic religion, it is written: "They are a pollution. Separate yourselves therefore from women and approach them not, until they are cleansed." A similar injunction appears in Judeo-Christian Scripture: "And if a woman have an issue, and her issue in her flesh be blood, she shall be put apart seven days: and whosoever toucheth her shall be unclean until the even." (See Lev. 15. 19–33.)

Tabooed and put apart from the men she threatens, the menstruating woman nevertheless emerges as a significant presence in literature and mythology. Some of the early flood myths may have been, in part, a response to the male fear of menstrual blood, which is associated with wounds, battle, and death. In the Babylonian myth of creation, Tiamat, the Mother of All, creates monsters whose blood is poison. Marduk, her son, drains Tiamet's blood, instructing the winds to carry it to hidden places. Marduk's violence can be interpreted as the suppression of the menstrual process.

Edna St. Vincent Millay touches on similar images in her poem "Menses" (1939). The poem, told from a male point of view, is a modern depiction of the unclean or venomous woman, whose menstrual blood is "poison." Other modern poets use the figure of the witch to evoke the awesome powers of the menstruating woman, for example Anne Sexton ("The Double Image," 1960) and Sylvia Plath ("Maudlin," 1960, British edition).

Novelist Stephen King swells the menarche to mythic proportions in *Carrie* (1974). Carrie is showering in the school gym when in horror she discovers her first blood. Her classmates deluge her with tampons and later, during the prom coronation, with pig's blood. Blood is everywhere, an emblem of King's awe of the menstrual process.

Additionally, in the field of psychoanalysis, where women doctors played a substantial role in defining women, menstruation was generally viewed as a negative function. Such notable analysts as Helene Deutsch, Marie Bonaparte, Karen Horney, and Melanie Klein, writing roughly between World War I and World War II, argued at times that menstruating women were hysterical, perverse, and masochistic, that menstrual blood represented internal dismemberment, or that menstruation was a sign of woman's "lack," of her castration.

Despite the overwhelmingly negative attitudes toward menstruation, a more encouraging outlook has recently emerged, attributable, in part, to the new feminism of the 1970s. There is a new freedom—in advertising, television, film, literature, and the arts—coupled with a desire by many women to discuss openly what once was hidden in the closet. This openness coincides with the accessibility of menstrual apparatuses. Not until 1933 did Kotex persuade the magazine *Good Housekeeping* to advertise sanitary napkins, and not until 1972 was the ban against advertising feminine hygiene products finally lifted from radio and television.

Parallel developments have occurred with television programming. In March 1973, *All in the Family* broke the menstrual taboo by mentioning Gloria's periods. The episode, to which many viewers objected, opened the doors for menstruation's scattered appearances on network television: *The Mary Tyler Moore Show* (September 1973), *Maude* (January 1974), and *Santa Barbara* (February 1985) are examples.

Cinema, less hindered than television by codes and regulations, claims numerous menstrual references among its credits. These mainly have to do with missed periods (*Saturday Night and Sunday Morning*, Karel Reis, 1961); or with menstrual cramps (*They Shoot Horses, Don't They?* Sydney Pollack, 1969); or with the taboo against intercourse during menstruation (*McCabe and Mrs. Miller*, Robert Altman, 1971). Some films, however, treat menstruation more prominently. In Ingmar Bergman's *Cries and*

Whispers (1972), Ingrid Thulin cuts her genitals, simulating menstruation, to avoid sexual relations with her husband. In Brian DePalma's adaptation of *Carrie* (1976), Sissy Spacek responds in terror upon discovering menstrual blood on her thighs. In *Purple Rain* (Albert Magnoli, 1984), a member of a rock band insults a woman songwriter by saying : "God's got Wendy's periods reversed. About every twenty-eight days she starts acting nice. Lasts about a weekend." Part of this remark becomes woven into the title song, a song written by Wendy that celebrates women's rhythms. But the most aggressive menstrual performance belongs to Whoopi Goldberg, who, in Robert Altman's 1992 film *The Player*, mimics male law enforcers when she twirls a tampon as if it were a nightstick.

Women, it seems, must celebrate their own processes. May Sarton does this in a poem written in 1937, "She Shall Be Called Woman." According to Sarton, women are like stars, "as unresistant, as completely rhythmical." Menstruation is "a surging miracle of blood." For Doris Lessing menstruation is a sign of heightened awareness. Anna Wulf, a character in Lessing's *The Golden Notebook* (1962), chooses on the first day of a period to record every feeling and thought, to be "conscious of everything." The notebook entry includes a variety of responses to menstruation, from the intuitive to the irrational, and offers perhaps the most complex treatment of the menses yet to have appeared in fiction. Erica Jong, the flag bearer of the menstrual tradition in literature, creates menstrual metaphors in both her poetry and her novels. In the poem "Inventing My Life" (1983) Jong compares menstruation to writing, while in *Fear of Flying* (1973) she uses menstrual motifs in an ironic reworking of the male quest myth: Isadora Wing's return from the underworld coincides with the arrival of her period. Not until *Parachutes and Kisses* (1984), however, does Jong violate the ultimate menstrual taboo with her incredible Bean Sproul III, tampon-taster.

Certain French theorists, writing in the 1970s and 1980s, celebrated women's blood and other fluids as aspects of female productivity, of female *difference*. Luce Irigaray, Hélène Cixous, Catherine Clément, and other French feminists, desiring to separate the masculine from the feminine, questioned the dominant phallocentrism of psychoanalysis and used images of bleeding to represent cycles, flexibility, rhythm, joy, and other woman-affirming concepts.

Women writers and artists have come to see menstruation as a source for creativity and as a universal female experience. Judy Chicago's initially shocking lithograph *Red Flag* (1971) shows a woman's hand removing a reddened tampon. In giving artistic form to so common but private a ritual, Chicago and other artists like her (such as Judith Jurasek, Mary Beth Edelson, and Faith Wilding) demystify menstruation; in so doing they help bring to consciousness a crucial female experience too long clouded by superstition. To admit to women's bleeding is to recognize the consequence of gender in its biological, societal, and psychological representations; it is also to affirm female productivity and renewal.

References. All facts and citations are from Janice Delany, Mary Jane Lupton, and Emily Toth, *The Curse: A Cultural History of Menstruation* (New York, 1976; 2d ed. enlarged, Urbana, Ill., 1988), and from Mary Jane Lupton, *Menstruation and Psychoanalysis* (Urbana, Ill., 1993). For general information on the psychology of women see FEMALE DEVELOPMENT.

MARY JANE LUPTON

MENSTRUATION COMPLEX is a disputable theory introduced by one of Sigmund Freud's colleagues, Claude Dagmar Daly (1884–1950). According to John Rickman, Daly was a lieutenant colonel with the British army in India; he was also a psychoanalyst, having studied with Freud sometime in 1924 and, four years later, with Sandor Ferenczi. Rickman, who misspelled Daly's first and second names in the obituary he published in 1950 in *International Journal of Psycho-Analysis* (32: 290–291), alleged that during World War II "Claud Dangar" Daly's correspondence with Freud on the menstruation complex was destroyed in a fire.

Daly wrote no book. His discussions of the menstruation complex were nonetheless preserved in a series of articles he published in the most influential European psychoanalytic journals. Freudian analysis, because it is so exclusively concentrated on the masculine, rarely examined the mother/ subject, while Daly, who viewed women's menstruation as the center of the Oedipus complex, was revolutionary in his emphasis on female functions and female aggressiveness. His gender bias unfortunately prevented him from taking his argument to a woman-centered conclusion.

The menstruating mother is, he argued, the boy's object of desire during early infancy (what is called the "positive Oedipus complex") but later the object of repulsion (the "negative Oedipus complex"). In Daly's modification of the oedipal mother, she is primarily a negative figure, the object of incestuous desire; through the vehicle of her menstrual blood, she is repulsed by the son as a defense against his desire for her.

Daly's first contribution to the theory of menstruation was "Hindu-Mythologie und Kastrationskomplex," published in 1927 in *Imago* (13: 145–198). Here Daly emphasized the powers of Kali, goddess of death and blood; she is the dreaded woman of our dreams, the mother who first kindles man's desire and then, through her menstrual blood, destroys it. It is the dark aspect of the Hindu goddess to which Daly responded; her attributes of mutilation and bleeding dramatize the psychoanalytic constructions of castration and the prohibition against incest embodied in the negative Oedipus complex. By attaching a strong, psychoanalytic function to women's repetitive bleeding, Daly was able to construct his model for the menstruation complex, with its forceful, but negative, associations of castration, sexuality, and death.

In India Daly had witnessed firsthand the fervor of Hindu beliefs surrounding the aggressive female goddess. In some statues Kali holds emblems of castration—a bloody sword, a severed head. Or she may be represented as a cannibal who devours humans and animals, drinking their blood. It is likely that the Hindu concepts of Kali and blood that Daly confronted during his residency colored his psychoanalytic vision of the aggressive mother, making him overlook the more beneficial aspects of the goddess, such as healing and fertility. Daly turned a closed eye toward Kali's other side—her potential for nurture and renewal.

In his 1935 essay, "The Menstruation Complex in Literature," published in *Psychoanalytic Quarterly* (4: 307–340), Daly analyzed the works of Charles Baudelaire and Edgar Allan Poe to prove what he had unearthed in Hindu mythology: the existence of the menstruation complex. By examining a handful of Baudelaire's poems, Daly hoped to substantiate his thesis that as a child Baudelaire, attracted yet repelled by his mother's menstruation, repressed his desires for her. These desires surface in the poetry, in images of smell, sickness, blood, and castration. For some reason Daly does not relate Baudelaire's famed title, *Fleurs du Mal*, with menstruation, although "mal" (evil) could surely be translated as sickness (menstruation).

In the longer section on Poe, Daly interprets a number of Poe's stories of death and confinement through formulating a series of menstrual symbols—the Black Cat, the bleeding eye, the Red Death, and other images—arguing for the existence of a menstruation complex, defined as a repressed desire for the mother's bleeding vagina. Yet as we examine Daly's reading of Poe's "The Fall of the House of Usher," we observe a retreat from the concept of menstruation, exemplified by his own resistance to Madeline, the diseased female figure in the story.

So, too, in his analysis of Poe's famous story "The Masque of the Red Death," Daly appears to have masked his reading of menstruation. Somewhat surprisingly, in "The Menstruation Complex in Literature" Daly identifies the Red Death in masculine terms, as the death-bearing father who desires to castrate the prince. One could more readily argue, given the theory of the menstruation complex, that the ghastly red figure of Poe's story is the destructive female or menstruating mother who, breaking through the barriers, removes the psychoanalytic repressions against incest. Both stories demand a more specific treatment of menstruation that would locate its awesome power in the woman's body rather than in the son's reaction to it.

While there are gaps and contradictions in Daly's essays, they are commendable in their attempts to place menstruation—and therefore women—within the psychoanalytic argument. Unfortunately, Claude Dagmar Daly was unable to convince his colleagues of the relevance of menstruation to female development. Nor was he apt to win supporters with his remark that the idea of the menstruation complex posed a threat to the masculine bias of psychoanalytic theory and to its historic repression of women. Entangled in the dilemma of positioning the menstruating mother within a hostile psychoanalytic structure, Daly ultimately resorted to a male perspective with few followers.

Despite Daly's failure to create a woman-focused theory of menstruation, he is significant to contemporary feminist and psychoanalytic theory, particularly in his insistence that woman's vitality, signaled by her menstruation, has been historically and culturally suppressed. In unveiling the menstruating woman, Daly contributed to an understanding that menstruation is not a periodic psychosis but a biological/psychological process that men, in their fear of female periodicity, have been compelled to deny.

References. Mary Jane Lupton, *Menstruation and Psychoanalysis* (Urbana, Ill., 1993); Mary Jane Lupton and Julia Reinhard Lupton, "Annotated Bibliography of Claude Dagmar Daly (1884–1950)," *American Imago* 47 (1990): 81–91.

MARY JANE LUPTON

MENTAL ILLNESS. Psychiatric classifications have historically derived from social constructions in which women figured prominently in the understanding of insanity; and qualities of madness, lunacy, melancholia, and mental illness have been attributed to women due to gender or social characteristics since the Middle Ages.

Characterizations of mad women became commonplace in literature and on the stage by the time of the Renaissance, and a broad range characterized many of the popularly held views of women's insanity. Shakespeare's Ophelia, for example, illustrates one element: driven insane by grief after her father's death, she embodies the melancholic gone mad. Morose and lonely women with darkened personalities were joined by another face of madness: those with gifted wit, insight, and creativity. This prototype for madness was first articulated by Aristotle. Efforts to "help" such women whose faculties (mostly reason) had somehow become deranged consisted of little more than physical restraint through the eighteenth century.

Reasons given for the causes of insanity have been drawn from a variety of explanations. They include the supernatural (distraction), biological (humoral, gynecological, or other anatomical irregularities), or environmental causes (socially promoted aggression or lack of conformity with gender expectations). By the nineteenth century, after almost 100 years of sifting theories, "insanity" assumed the status of a medical problem. By the 1970s and 1980s, psychiatrists had recognized that mental illness constitutes a family of disorders in which biological and genetic factors play a part.

Early "insane asylums" were undifferentiated from almshouses, and the seventeenth- and eighteenth-century hospitals, located in industrializing regions, were built for the correction of vagrants or paupers. Michel Foucault dates the middle of the seventeenth century as the period of "Great Confinement" throughout Western Europe and England, when idleness and poverty were called criminal, and poor laws and statutes threatened exile or confinement. By the next century in England, for example, it was permissible to detain persons with "disordered senses" (often the same as the unemployed or the socially dislocated), and a justice of the peace was empowered to lock up the lunatic/vagrant (1744 Vagrancy Act). By the nineteenth century, the physicians' power to detain persons arose from a prerogative resulting from the medicalization of mental illness.

Social dislocation caused by poverty affected women profoundly during industrialization. Charles Dickens, Harriet Martineau, and Charlotte Brontë all write of poor women who were thought to be particularly vulnerable to lunacy. Whether there is a differential rate of disease, diagnosis, and treatment of women and men for mental illness remains unclear. For example, women outnumbered men in the public asylums in England, and 63 percent of the patients of seventeenth-century English physician Richard Napier were women. A similar sex disparity was reported in a 1984 psychiatric journal: six-month prevalence rates from community surveys of psychiatric disorders in the United States found that major depression was two and a half times more frequent in women than men. However, records of psychiatric hospitalization in America between 1840 and 1980 reveal that fewer women than men were institutionalized.

Treatments to correct the deficiency or the imbalance that originally led to insanity followed from contemporary theories of causation. This explains the unique "cures" imposed on nineteenth-century women at a time when insanity was thought to be strongly associated with behavior that violated the gender code. The ranks of the psychiatrically unfit were found among women who were "too sexual" or otherwise bold, competitive, or deranged as a result of the malfunctioning of their complicated reproductive organs. Nineteenth-century women who ended up in asylums were treated under the new moral management that replaced shackles, and therapy included attention to the environment, which was supposed to be kind, firm, comfortable, religious, and moral. Therapy consisted of learning useful trades and skills within the domestic arts, such as sewing, cooking, or needlework. Other women, whose misfortune included being treated by a gynecologist, might encounter sexual surgery to remove the clitoris and "tame aggression."

The persistence of gender-defined explanations for mental illness reached its apotheosis under psychoanalytic theories advanced by Sigmund Freud and his followers. Introducing a new vocabulary, which included penis envy, Oedipus complex, castration complex, and processes such as the unconscious, displacement, sublimation, and repression, psychoanalytic theory fused biological and mental functioning into a new determinism that preserved the social order. By the turn of the century, psychoanalytic theory had defined and refined neurosis, and by the second half of the twentieth century, feminist theorists such as Juliet Mitchell had begun to question their applicability to understanding women's lives.

In the period after World War II and simultaneous to the height of psychoanalytic explanations, drug therapies became widespread for at least one of the major mental illnesses, depression, signaling a pursuit of biochemical causes. By the 1980s psychiatry began to more actively pursue biochemical or genetic explanations in other major illnesses as well, thus modifying social influences.

The cultural and environmental explanations that gathered strength from a scientific void still command professional attention. Whether women with mental illness suffer from unique conditions attributable to genetic, hormonal, and political or social repression continues to be discussed in both lay and professional circles. There is now an effort to locate specific genes that may be associated with greater frequencies of certain illnesses.

References. Michel Foucault, *Madness and Civilization* (New York, 1973); Juliet Mitchell, *Psychoanalysis and Feminism* (New York, 1974); Elaine Showalter, *The Female Malady: Women, Madness and Culture in England* (New York, 1985).

PHYLLIS VINE

MENTAL ILLNESS AND GENDER. The belief that women have a higher rate of mental illness than men is based on the way the label "mental illness" is used. Women have higher rates of neuroses and functional nonorganic psychoses; men have higher rates of "personality disorders," organic disorders, and chemical addiction. More men are admitted to mental hospitals and psychiatric wards than are women, but women tend to be hospitalized for longer periods. For instance, in 1980, 51.7 percent of admissions to state and county mental hospitals, private psychiatric hospitals, and nonfederal general hospitals were male; and 97 percent of admissions to Veterans Administration Mental Hospitals were male. The average stay in a psychiatric hospital or unit for women was longer than for men in every age category (Manderscheid and Barrett).

Schizophrenia, one of the most disabling illnesses, shows no gender preference. Depression,* which, like schizophrenia, is highly disabling, occurs about twice as often in women as in men. Other leading disorders more common to women than men are agoraphobia* and anorexia nervosa,* overwhelmingly (95 percent) a young woman's disorder.

The higher incidence of neuroses and nonorganic psychoses among women has been attributed to women's traditional role of dependence, which may produce frustrations and stress that lead to psychological problems. It has also been attributed to women's being more likely to admit to loss of control and to seek help. Damage caused by rape, violence, and child sexual abuse that may not surface in mental health problems until years later also needs to be given serious consideration.

Women and men seeking treatment from mental health professionals may receive differential treatment. Labeling of mental health and mental illness has been largely at the hands of male professionals, and their interpretations have been applied by male therapists, who necessarily bring their own cultural values with them into treatment. What is "mentally healthy" for a woman may be judged quite different from what is "mentally healthy" for a man. When treating women, a male therapist (or a female therapist who has been conditioned by male ideologies) may be less likely to listen to what a woman is actually saying and more likely to be guided by his own interpretation of the situation than by her feelings about it than would be the case were he dealing with a man. Therapists are also more likely to advise women to adjust to the situation that has caused the problem than they are to advise adjustment for men.

In 1972 Phyllis Chesler called the unequal psychiatrist–patient relationship into question. The dominant position of the male in the male psychiatrist, female patient relationship re-creates the same subordinate position for the patient that in many cases is a major source of her problem. Chesler also charged that psychiatrists frequently exploit their position by having sexual relationships with female patients. Professional associations, while, of course, denying that the practice was frequent, developed ethical codes for their membership.

Reform movements of the 1970s, including mental health care reform, the women's health movement,* the movement to reform health care delivery, and feminist criticism of psychiatry have all affected mental health care. There has been a growing diversity of theoretical approaches and alternative therapies. Feminist therapies building on consciousness-raising* techniques eschew power relations. Reforms and rethinking of basic concepts have brought some improvements, but much of the old thinking remains.

A major reform that had unexpected consequences was the deinstitutionalizing of mental health care. Those suffering from mental disorders are now hospitalized for as short a time as possible, then discharged to be taken care of by the local community. But few communities have adequate facilities to care for the mentally ill. It is estimated that in 1980 there were from 1.7 to 2.4 million chronically mentally ill, of whom 900,000 were in hospitals, 750,000 in nursing homes, and the rest in the local community: in their own homes, under community care, which may be adequate but is often a single room in an unsafe and unhealthy welfare hotel, or on the streets (Manderscheid and Barrett). Single women are especially likely to be among the homeless on the streets, where they are targets for violence. Those chronically ill who have homes to return to will usually be cared for by a female relative.

References. Phyllis Chesler, *Women and Madness* (Garden City, N.Y., 1972); R. W. Manderscheid and S. A. Barrett (eds.), *Mental Health, United States, 1987* (Washington, D.C., 1987).

MENTOR is an individual who acts as a career adviser or sponsor to a particular person, the latter sometimes referred to as a protégé or mentee. In the usual case, the mentor is older and more established than the protégé and is in a more powerful position from which to help the mentee by providing access to inside information and important people. Mentors also provide mentees assistance, support, advice, encouragement, and example. Though similar in some respects to "role models," mentors also have features that set them apart. A mentoring relationship is usually more intense, exclusive, and mutually recognized than one involving a role model. Even though both mentors and role models are transitional figures in an individual's personal and professional development, the termination of a mentoring relationship is also thought to be more emotional and conflictful.

"Mentor" is first heard of in Homer's *Odyssey* as the name adopted by the goddess Athena when she assumed the form of a man charged with converting a naive and meek boy (Telemachus) into a mature and accomplished adult. Despite the "feminine" origins of the term "mentor," the history of traditional mentoring has been more a history of relationships between men. In fact, mentoring first gained attention with the publication of Patrick M. Morley's *The Seasons of a Man's Life* in 1978. Numerous subsequent social science and business articles have testified to the importance of mentoring for career success and have ventured the debatable hypothesis that women's lack of advancement might be substantially attributed to the absence of mentoring in their lives.

Research does indicate that women are less involved in mentoring relationships than men. A number of factors are thought to account for this: (1) there are fewer women than men in top positions and hence few women available to be mentors; (2) male mentors are more likely to select male mentees; (3) informal organizational networks exclude women; (4) high-ranking women are under tremendous demands and hence have little time to devote to mentoring; (5) women are less positively disposed to the hierarchical influence typical of mentoring; and (6) mixed-sex mentoring relationships can be problematic in ways not characteristic of same-sex pairings, including issues of sexuality and expected patterns of male dominance–female submission.

Mentoring has been hailed as an important, but underused, resource for the advancement of women. While there are benefits to the recipients, there can also be drawbacks. Mentoring relationships can be exploitative and restrictive, may lead to peer rejection, can produce real or perceived dependency, or may disintegrate or disappear, leaving the

mentee without a base of support. Mentors can provide significant resources for women, but questions remain about the extent and exclusive-
ness of these benefits.

References. R. Hall and B. Sandler, *Academic Mentoring for Women Students
and Faculty: A New Look at an Old Way to Get Ahead* (Washington, D.C., 1983);
M. P. Rowe, "Building Mentorship Frameworks as Part of an Effective Equal Op-
portunity Ecology," in J. Farley (ed.), *Sex Discrimination in Higher Education
Strategies for Equality* (Ithaca, N.Y., 1981); J. Speizer, "Role Models, Mentors and
Sponsors: The Elusive Concepts," *Signs* 12 (1981): 692–712.

                                                                                        MARIANNE LAFRANCE

MEXICAN REVOLUTION. Though their exploits are less well chronicled
than those of their male counterparts, women participated in every phase
of the Mexican Revolution, the dramatic upheaval that dislodged the 35-
year dictatorship of Porfirio Díaz in 1911 and moved the nation spasmod-
ically to a stable constitutional system by 1940.

Most conspicuous among the female revolutionaries were the *soldaderas*,
who were celebrated in contemporary songs, photographs, articles, and
murals. Foreign correspondents waxed sympathetic over the typically poor
Indian or *mestiza* (woman of mixed ancestry) who escorted her man, often
with children, to battle in support of Francisco Madero, Emiliano Zapata,
Pancho Villa, Venustiano Carranza, or transient revolutionary leaders.
They performed domestic duties under wartime conditions but also donned
cartridge belts, pistols, and carbines as the occasion arose. Revolutionary
women organized battalions; acted as nurses, purchasing agents, and spies;
and won the hearts of male combatants, who sang the praises of "Adelita"
and "La Valentina," an underaged girl disguised as a boy who enlisted in
military service. However, the *soldaderas* walked when the men rode, suffered sexual exploitation, and failed to receive recognition.

Women displayed a presence in the Mexican Revolution beyond a narrow military role, but frustration largely accompanied those efforts as well.
Activist Juana Gutiérrez de Mendoza fashioned a career as organizer and
journalist that circumscribed the entire period. Imprisoned four times, the
modestly educated daughter of a Durango laborer founded an anti-Díaz
newspaper in 1901, joined the insurgent Flores Magón movement, and
attained the rank of colonel in Zapata's army. In later years she published
newspapers in Mexico City, created worker and feminist groups, and
served as president of the National Council of Women. For her activities
on behalf of the revolution, Juana Gutiérrez ended her days with only a
meager government pension separating her from poverty.

Not only the lower economic classes of women sought advantage from
the Mexican Revolution. While the humblest—peasants, domestics, prostitutes, and unskilled laborers—stood to gain the most from social change,
Porfirian Mexico restricted the feminine sex generally. Steeped in Hispanic

tradition despite the scientific rhetoric of the Díaz regime, prerevolutionary Mexico disallowed divorce, scorned the unmarried woman, and discouraged economic enterprise among women. However, these victims of discrimination shared a collective experience of selective decision making, particularly in home management, administration of property by widows, and direction of social and benevolent organizations. Unsurprisingly, the least manacled segments of the population, notably teachers and writers, launched the first wave of criticism. At the other end of the spectrum, *obreras* (female workers) enthusiastically participated in strikes at Cananea and Rio Blanco, confrontations that weakened the faltering dictatorship.

Just as men embraced the revolution for a variety of reasons, women also acted from disparate motivations. Devout Catholics sought reform as a means of enhancing the roles of wives and mothers, Marxists aspired to the creation of a new social order, and moderates occupied a number of intermediate positions. After the death of Madero (1913) and the increasingly anticlerical tactics of his proclaimed disciples, the church set itself against revolutionary administrations, and many Catholic women mobilized against the regimes of Carranza, Alvare Obregón, and Plutarcho Calles. They risked government reprisals by staging public religious demonstrations and supporting the clergy in the Cristero Rebellion (1926). The assassination of President Obregón (1928), allegedly by a religious fanatic under the influence of a zealous nun, sharply divided women and reinforced the opposition of many revolutionaries to women's suffrage.

The agriculturally prosperous state of Yucatán showcased the women's rights campaign between 1915 and 1924. Governors Salvador Alvarado and Felipe Carrillo Puerto, sometimes allied with feminist leaders Elena Torres and Elvia Carrillo Puerto, enacted equal pay legislation, antiprostitution laws, and divorce enabling acts and convened the first two women's conferences of the period. But controversies regarding divorce, birth control, and political rights splintered the movement even before the assassination of Governor Carrillo Puerto. The focus of the campaign then shifted to the Federal District.

Nationally, the stabilization of the revolution under Carranza Obregón (in the period 1915–1924) brought feminists only mixed results. Carranza issued early decrees legalizing divorce, alimony, and the right of women to own and manage property. The federal Constitution of 1917 included women in its largely unenforceable protections to laborers but carried no equal employment provision and failed to clarify a right of suffrage. Accordingly, only a few states allowed women the vote, and then only in municipal elections. Elvia Carrillo Puerto, sister of the martyred governor, narrowly escaped assassination while winning a seat in the federal Congress from San Luis Potosí in 1925. However, the victory was short-lived as the national legislature subsequently judged her unqualified because of her sex.

Undaunted, Mexican women continued to organize during the 1920s and

1930s on behalf of social, economic, and political goals. María del Refugio Garza, who as a child had defied Díaz and later criticized a series of chief executives for insensitivity to women, organized the most formidable association, the United Front for Women's Rights, in 1935. As the United Front strove to coordinate the work of hundreds of existing groups in equalizing legal, political, economic, and educational opportunities, it found a more sympathetic administration in the presidency of Lázaro Cárdenas (1934–1940).

Nevertheless, even this receptive regime produced incomplete success. A modus vivendi with the Catholic Church and a strengthening of the official political party eased the path toward women's suffrage. Women gained the right to vote in primaries but a fully enfranchising amendment, despite initial approval by Congress and the states, lacked legislative enactment and awaited implementation until 1953.

Years after the ebbing of the Mexican Revolution, complete constitutional equality still eluded more than half the population. Promise often outpaced accomplishment, and male-oriented tradition maintained a firm, if yielding, grasp on mores. Nonetheless, women had contributed significantly toward shaping a system more amenable to expanding opportunities. By midcentury they had penetrated virtually every male-dominated echelon and excelled in medicine, law, social and behavioral sciences, and other fields.

Toward these ends, history rightly credits, among others, textile worker María del Carmen, journalist Emilia Enríquez de Rivera, teacher Consuelo Zavala, and nurse Ana María Ruiz Reyes of the formative period. But acknowledgment must also extend to the numerous heroines of the revolution who reside only marginally in memory.

References. Asunción Lavrin (ed.), *Latin American Women: Historical Perspectives* (Westport, Conn., 1978); Shirlene Ann Soto, *The Mexican Woman: A Study of Her Participation in the Revolution, 1910–1940* (Palo Alto, Calif., 1979).

GARNA L. CHRISTIAN

MIDWIFERY in the past encompassed a female community's knowledge, beliefs, and techniques for the care of women and newborns. Female traditions and cultural restrictions reinforced the midwife's important and diverse roles. In time the expansion of medical knowledge and women's search for a safe and less painful birth experience challenged the traditional role and authority of the midwife. Men had entered the birthing chamber for routine deliveries of ordinary women by the eighteenth century. The professionalization of medicine, the emergence of obstetrics as a medical specialty and other social and cultural changes further altered the practice of midwifery abroad and brought about its almost complete disappearance in the United States.

In medieval and early modern Europe, many midwives had no formal training. Whenever possible, a woman apprenticed herself to an experienced midwife. Although custom ordained that a midwife be a married or widowed woman at least 45 years of age who had children of her own, sometimes mothers taught their unmarried daughters the required skills. There are indications that a midwife was usually of the artisanal, trade, or farming classes. While many worked as a midwife part-time within a tradition of "neighborly support," others worked continuously throughout their lives. Their economic contribution to their families was usually welcome, if not always essential.

A midwife might advise a pregnant woman on health matters before the birth of a child. After birth she brought the newborn to church for its baptism or, for a dying newborn, performed an emergency baptism and, after the baby died, prepared the body for burial. Midwives also sometimes functioned as lay healers.

Birth was a lesson in patience. Many midwives believed in letting nature take its course. Along the way, they would offer the mother psychological support. On the other hand, birth manuals suggest that to ease delivery and fortify the mother, midwives oiled the stomach and prepared special drinks, herbal remedies, and food. Often midwives stayed to help the mother after the birth as well, cooking, cleaning, and caring for mother and newborn. The fee was nominal and usually in kind.

Sometime during the Middle Ages, the Catholic Church required that midwives be recognized officially by a group of their peers and the local bishop. The basis for a midwife's acceptance was her respectability and religiosity, not her medical expertise. The church's main concern was to ensure that a midwife would not perform an abortion, assist a mother in committing infanticide, or conceal the name of an unknown father, if the mother revealed it during labor. A midwife was also required to know the correct prayers to use in emergency baptism.

Midwives also played a medicolegal role in their communities, which suggests that they enjoyed a high level of public recognition. City governments assigned to midwives the task of examining women in cases of alleged rape, claimed virginity, or pregnancy. In sixteenth-century France, male practitioners began to supervise midwives who performed this function and eventually took over this role completely.

The midwife's close association with birth and death as well as her knowledge of abortifacients and other medicaments have led some historians to claim that the early modern midwife was vulnerable to witchcraft accusations. The extent of the midwife's involvement in witchcraft is difficult to document. There has been no comprehensive study to determine how many midwives were accused of witchcraft or whether a midwife who was accused of witchcraft was held in suspicion because of her occupation or for other unrelated reasons.

The first written regulations for midwives were those of Regensburg (Bavaria) in 1452. Candidates were required to be examined publicly by "honorable, sworn women." Unlike other artisans, most urban midwives did not enjoy the benefits of being members of an independent guild structure. Some urban regulations put them under the tutelage of "honorable women," as in Regensburg, but more commonly midwives were supervised by a group of physicians, surgeons, and sworn midwives. These urban regulations marked the official beginning of secular control over a domain that was perceived as "natural" to women. As a result male practitioners became increasingly interested in this traditionally female domain, while the midwives became more conscious of their own work identity.

During the sixteenth and seventeenth centuries the development of anatomical science and new obstetrical knowledge challenged the traditional lore and practice of midwives. Barber-surgeons in France and England used the new knowledge to advance themselves professionally. The French reintroduced the ancient technique of version, a method of grasping a child lying sideways in the uterus so that it could be delivered feet first. The invention of the forceps eventually brought men ever more frequently into the birthing chamber. Although invented in England in the seventeenth century, this instrument had been kept a proprietary secret by the Chamberlain family until 1728.

By the mid-eighteenth century in England, men had established a firm niche in what had once been almost exclusively women's territory. The English Dr. William Smellie's innovative techniques allowed forceps deliveries without mutilation of the newborns. The appearance of private clinics and maternity hospitals for poor women allowed more practitioners to observe and learn about the birthing process firsthand. Not having equal access to educational institutions and hospitals, English midwives did not benefit from the growth of the new knowledge to the same degree as men. Men were also reluctant to allow women to use the forceps, and custom made many midwives, though not all, reluctant to use them.

During the seventeenth and eighteenth centuries town authorities and some medical groups across Europe began to found schools for midwives. The presence of midwifery schools created divisions between the majority of midwives who were apprentice-trained and those who were trained in schools. In Italy such divisions polarized traditional, empirically trained midwives and the Church against school-trained midwives and the state. In the nineteenth century, pro-natalist governments in Denmark, Russia, France, and other European countries continued to raise the standards of midwife practice and improved midwife services to the poor. These state-initiated and -subsidized improvements in midwifery education contrast with the situation in England, where the state did not attempt to regulate midwives or provide for their education until 1902.

In spite of the introduction of formal training for midwives on the continent, royal, noble, and wealthy women sought the services of male midwives or "accoucheurs" just as their English counterparts did. The promise of safer and more comfortable deliveries as well as fashion seem to have been the motivating factors. Midwives, however, continued to deliver the majority of babies.

Midwifery in the American colonies closely resembled midwifery in England. The colonial midwife played a key role in the birthing chamber. She also healed a variety of ailments and acted as an expert witness in the courtroom in cases pertaining to sexual misconduct, abortions, and the like. The late eighteenth-century diary of midwife Martha Ballard documents these aspects of the midwife's practice and also reveals deep attachment to her vocation.

The few professional and legal regulations that existed in colonial America functioned to ensure that the midwife was of good moral standing in her community. Her medical expertise was not evaluated. Some colonies, such as New York, appointed official midwives. In southern colonies many plantations had their own midwife, often a slave.

As in England, few American women were able to learn the new midwifery techniques developed by Smellie and others. The lack of government support explains, in part, why few American women acquired formal training and were unable to compete on equal terms with men. American-born midwives continued to learn from each other informally, while immigrant women who practiced midwifery were highly competent. They often had learned their craft in formal settings in Europe.

At the turn of the century, midwives presided over approximately 50 percent of all recorded births in the United States. In these same early decades of the twentieth century, infant and maternal mortality rates in this country soared above those of European countries. These statistics compelled physicians and other health officials to look for causes and solutions. This led to the "midwife debate" of the period 1910–1930.

While the findings of government-sponsored commissions ascertained that physicians were as much or more to blame for high maternal mortality rates as midwives, newspapers and publicists ignored these facts in order to present the more popular view that midwives were the main culprits. Physicians and journalists further maligned midwives by accusing them of engaging in illegal and dangerous abortions, while physicians who engaged in the same activities were ignored. Various solutions were offered. Individuals representing the newly emerging specialty of obstetrics wished to see the complete elimination of all midwives. Included in this group were female specialists in obstetrics who saw midwives as their rivals. Nurses saw midwives as competition as well. Others, including health officials and Progressive Era reformers, wished to improve and regularize midwifery training and licensing. Still others saw the midwife as a "necessary evil" to be eliminated gradually.

This debate helped to polarize opinion concerning the role of the midwife. Other factors must also be considered when explaining her gradual demise. American women searching for a safe and painless birth influenced trends. Demographics also played a role. As birthrates declined, birth itself became a "special event" requiring the attendance of a male physician. The newly emerging professional model of the birth attendant clashed with the traditional model by which most midwives shaped their identity and developed their skills. The latter model projected the married, mature woman as the ideal midwife, while the former model projected the image of a young male physician trained in the latest scientific techniques. This new ideal prevented midwifery from becoming a respected profession in the United States. Immigrant midwives who had enjoyed power and prestige in their own rural and urban communities gradually found themselves in disfavor as the scientific knowledge of the physician became more valued than the midwives' artisanal skills.

Between 1921 and 1929 American midwives enjoyed a brief period of government support under the Sheppard-Towner Maternity and Infant Protection Act in the midst of what was otherwise a period of decline. Midwife training and maternal education programs that improved childbirth practices and maternal health in rural America were launched. These programs suffered from inadequate funding and were discontinued due to opposition of the American Medical Association. The number of midwives also greatly decreased. By 1930 midwives attended only 15 percent of all recorded births in the United States, although in 1950 lay midwives delivered nearly half of babies born to black women in southern states.

As traditional midwifery declined, the needs of the urban and rural poor helped to bring about the foundation of the Kentucky Frontier Nursing Service by Mary Breckinridge in 1925, the Maternity Center Association in New York in 1918, and a center for midwifery training and regulation in Newark, New Jersey, by Dr. Julius Levy in the 1920s. These institutions trained nurses to become midwives for the indigent. Thus, the concept and reality of the "nurse-midwife" were born, restricted, however, to the care of the poor. Statistics suggest that the trained midwife was as safe or safer than the physician.

In 1955 the American College of Nurse-Midwives (ACNM) organized nurse-midwives on a national level. By 1984 certified nurse-midwives had established a legal basis for practice in all but two jurisdictions in the United States. Today, nurse-midwives are registered nurses with a postgraduate education in midwifery. However, their legitimacy has been won at the price of losing much of their distinctiveness and autonomy.

At the present time, nurse-midwives are underutilized. In 1980 they attended 1.7 percent of the nation's births; and in 1992, 4.9 percent. These numbers suggest that midwives represent about 15 percent of the obstetric workforce. Various studies have shown that midwife care is the safest, least expensive approach to all low-risk births. With the growth of health maintenance organizations in the last 10 years, midwives may become the preferred option for the majority of women.

In contrast, the traditional midwife's future is much more problematic. While the lay midwife and home-birth movement of the 1970s reflected discontent with the psychological and financial costs of medicalized, hospitalized birth, the lay or traditional midwife's legal status has always hindered the development and growth of traditional midwifery. Even in states where laws allow for licensing, licenses are often difficult or impossible to acquire.

The advent of anatomical science, of modern obstetrics as a specialized profession, and of women's search for a safe, painless childbirth gradually undermined the traditional roles of female midwives. A variety of transitions in beliefs and practices has been observed. None has completely disappeared. Myths, religious sanctions, power struggles, economics, and political and legal interventions and interdictions still operate. In contemporary American society, the emergence of health maintenance organizations could increase and enhance the role American midwives play. In Europe, on the other hand, where midwives have been trained by the state since the eighteenth and nineteenth centuries, they have continued to maintain an important, though subordinate, position in the health system.

References. C. Borst, *Catching Babies: The Professionalization of Childbirth, 1870–1920* (Cambridge, 1995); R. G. DeVries, *Making Midwives Legal. Childbirth, Medicine, and the Law,* 2d ed. (Columbus, Ohio, 1996); J. W. Leavitt, *Brought to Bed* (New York, 1986); J. B. Litoff, *American Midwives: 1860 to the Present* (Westport, Conn., 1978); Hilary Marland (ed.), *The Art of Midwifery: Early Modern Midwives in Europe* (London, 1993); Laura Thatcher Ulrich, *A Midwife's Tale: The Life of Martha Ballard Based on Her Diary, 1785–1812* (New York, 1991).

ALISON KLAIRMONT-LINGO

MILITARY SERVICE. Throughout history women have been a part, in one way or another, of the military establishment. As camp followers (wives, daughters, widows, prostitutes) they served as a support service, doing cooking, sewing, nursing, laundry, sexual servicing, acting as sutlers and "molly pitchers" (women who cooled off cannon between firings); as rulers and charismatic leaders they took troops into battle; and they fought, mostly by enlisting disguised as men but occasionally in female units. Not, however, until the late nineteenth and early twentieth centuries did Western countries form permanent, legally recognized women's auxiliary units and not until World War II did they become a permanent part of the regular professional military service.

The first women's unit in the U.S. military was the Army Nurse Corps, founded in 1901 as an auxiliary service. The women held no rank and did not receive equal pay or benefits. The Navy Nurse Corps was established in 1908 along the same lines. In 1920 nurses were given officer status and "relative rank" (up to major) but not relative pay or benefits. Not until 1944 did the nursing corps attain full military status, and in 1947 they became permanent staff corps.

Women served briefly as enlisted reserves in the navy during World War I when the secretary of the navy used a loophole (the absence of the word "male") in the navy's authorization to enlist in order to recruit women to do clerical work. As soon as the war ended, women sailors (and marines, enlisted in 1918) were demobilized, and in 1925 the word "male" was added to the naval authorization to enlist civilians.

All the services enlisted women in World War II. The army moved first, reluctantly establishing the Women's Army Auxiliary Corps (WAAC) in 1941, but its auxiliary status, unequal pay, and lack of benefits hurt recruiting and morale, especially after the other services gave women reserve status. In 1943 the army changed the WAAC to the Women's Army Corps (WAC). In addition to the other military programs the WASPS, 1,000 women pilots, served for three years under civil service status. Congress granted veteran status to survivors in 1977.

Servicewomen were employed in "suitable jobs"—any job that might suggest a form of control over men was not "suitable." There were problems. The services paid little attention to the real needs of their women (e.g., the clothing issued to women was often unsuited to the conditions they were sent into), and condescension and sexual harassment* were rife. Women had to constantly prove themselves and faced resentment because they were women in "this man's army" or because the men resented being replaced from safe jobs to go into combat. Slanderous attacks were a particularly ugly problem. A widespread and vicious slander campaign against the WACs in 1943 damaged the reputation of all servicewomen with the public and hurt recruiting. Nevertheless, morale and performance remained generally high.

The women's programs outside the health services, originally meant to be "for the duration" only, proved so valuable that they were made permanent by the Women's Armed Services Integration Act of 1948. The number of women in the services was to be kept under 2 percent, a small nucleus that would be used as a base for mobilization in case of need. From the end of the Korean War until the late 1960s, however, the number did not even approach 2 percent. The peacetime service was not a great career for women.

Dissatisfaction and turnover were high. More and more jobs were classified as "unsuitable" for women (90 percent did clerical work), and discrimination* permeated the services. Officer promotions were limited. The highest rank was colonel (navy captain), and each service had only one, who was limited to a four-year term. Some of the few who reached that rank had to take a demotion after their four-year term in order to stay in the service long enough to earn retirement. Promotions to the next highest rank, lieutenant colonel (or commander), were limited to 10 percent. Mandatory retirement was earlier for female than for male officers.

There was a double standard for enlistment. Women's age and intelligence requirements were higher, and women with children were not accepted. Most resented was the "special rule": the secretary of defense could dismiss any woman at any time "under circumstances and in accordance with regulations prescribed by the President." The rule existed to dismiss any women who became pregnant, adopted a child, or acquired a child by marriage. Dependency rules differed. A woman who had a dependent child living with her for more than 30 days was dismissed from service. She could claim her husband only if she could prove that he depended on her for over half his support. Service couples could not claim each other but were classed as single, not eligible for base housing or housing allowances. Marriage between officer and enlisted ended the careers of both.

In the early 1960s with the draft, the services had more men than they needed and enlisted very few women. For those few, femininity and physical appearance took on major importance. The marines were looking for "a few good-looking women." Physical appearance was a leading criterion for air force recruits.

Then in the late 1960s and the 1970s enormous changes in the position of women in the military, unthinkable 10 years before, were brought about by the confluence of different movements: the rising draft resistance, the Vietnam War, the civil rights and feminist movements, congressional passage of the Equal Rights Amendment (ERA), the end of the draft, and the all-volunteer force (AVF). Change began modestly in 1967, then gained momentum, with the greatest changes occurring from 1973 to 1977 as the draft ended and the services adjusted to the AVF. By the 1980s most of the institutional discrimination had been eliminated, and the U.S. military forces had the largest number and largest percentage of women of any army in the world.

The major changes were the result of the ERA, the AVF, and the rising determination of women in the services to fight the institutional discrimination that surrounded them. The Defense Department, having to concern itself with the effect of the ERA on its personnel policies with respect to women and with the effects of the discontinuation of the draft, realized that to maintain a large AVF would require increased use of women and that to attract more women, institutional discrimination would have to be eliminated.

In 1972 women made up 1.6 percent of the military; by 1982 they were 7 percent of all service personnel. Job classifications were studied, and, by 1982, 805 occupations had been opened to women.

The Carter administration moved to integrate women into every facet of the military. Enlistment criteria were equalized, and most procurement and training programs for males and females were combined. Women were assigned to most noncombat units and to some combat units on an interchangeable basis. The remains of the women's support systems in the services were abolished.

Family policy was slowly reversed, much of it from the pressure of class action suits working their way through the courts during this period. Although many of the early suits were unsuccessful, the litigation helped spur the services to make changes. They had accepted married women in 1964; in the 1970s those with minor children were granted exemptions by individual waivers that became automatic, but dependency allowances were fought all the way to the Supreme Court. The major battle was over dismissal for pregnancy. Faced with litigation, the navy finally gave in, but the army held out until the Supreme Court declared the practice a violation of woman's rights in 1975.

Integration of officer training began in the late 1960s on a small scale and proceeded quietly during the 1970s before public attention was drawn to the integration of the service academies, which began in 1976. The attrition rate of women in the first class, of 1980, was 34 percent, not very different from the 30 percent rate of men students.

Some integration was not as successful, and the services had to pull back. For instance, affirmative action quotas were used to bring more women into nontraditional occupations, but in some cases they were placed in occupations beyond their physical ability, and there was some movement out of nontraditional occupations back toward clerical work, preferred by many of the women recruits.

The 1948 Women's Armed Forces Integration Act restricted women from combat and from service on some kinds of ships and aircraft, but it did not restrict them from serving in combat positions. Gradually, they began to be trained as pilots for aircraft and helicopters; in 1978 they began serving on ships; and in the 1980s they were assigned to combat arms branches such as the field artillery, combat engineers, and missile-launching crews.

By the mid-1980s, there were almost 223,000 women in the armed forces, 10 percent of the entire service. Basic training was integrated in all services except the marines, and women were in all officer grades up to brigadier general (rear admiral). They were in the armed forces that invaded Grenada in 1983, on planes that raided Libya in 1986, and on the destroyer tender sent to repair the *Stark*, damaged by a missile in the Persian Gulf in 1987, and in 1991 they took part in "Desert Storm," one woman being captured by the Iraqis. In 1993 they were authorized to serve on warships and to fly combat aircraft. Most institutional discrimination against heterosexual women had been eliminated, but attitudes are harder to change. Sexist behaviors and sexual harassment remain serious problems.

In 1997 women made up 13 percent of the military, but they were 20 percent of recruits. Sexism in various forms helps account for the high turnover. In 1988, 64 percent of women surveyed said they had experienced some form of sexual harassment within the previous 12 months. In 1991 the navy was wracked by the charges that drunken officers had assaulted women, military and civilian, in a Las Vegas hotel during an aviators' conference (Tailhook). This and charges of sexual harassment at the Naval Academy led to some action to correct abuses. In the 1995 survey, which found 55 percent of military women claiming some form of harassment, the rate for the navy dropped 13 percent. But the army rate dropped only 7 percent, and the next year it was hit with more serious charges of rape and harassment by drill instructors at Aberdeen Proving Ground Ordinance Center. A "hot line" for reporting abuses took thousands of calls from women throughout the army.

The armed services are now so integrated that the presence of women is vital to the combat effectiveness of the military. During the late 1960s and the 1970s the services ended institutional discrimination. The continued recruitment and retention of women will be affected by their ability to end the toleration of sexual discrimination and abuse by individuals within the services.

MISOGYNY means woman-hating. The use of the terms "misogyny" or "misogynist" dates back to the seventeenth century in literature. The word "misogynist" can be used to refer to an individual who is a woman-hater, but more recently the concept has been broadened to include certain social traditions (e.g., sexism*) thought to both underlie and perpetuate woman-hating. Contemporary usage has so broadened the term that it is now often used synonymously with the terms "sexism," "sex discrimination,"* "patriarchy,"* or "male dominance."

The first recorded instance of the use of the word "misogynist" was in 1620, in the treatise *Swetnam Arraigned*, referring to the misogynist character who was its subject. However, the history of literature is so replete with misogyny as to be the topic of an entire book, (Rogers). According to Rogers, there are strong misogynous themes in ancient, medieval, and Renaissance literature in the West. Misogyny is also evident in Eastern literature, most notably, in the writings of Confucius.

Misogynist literature, according to Kate Millett, is a primary repository of male hostility and is a major instrument of patriarchal propaganda. Its goal is to reinforce the unequal statuses of the sexes. In this way, misogynist literature is related to the so-called battle of the sexes, acting in some sense as ammunition for the imposition of male authority.

Scholarly discourse of a misogynous nature is not, however, limited to literary fields. For example, many feminist writers cite the psychological theories of Sigmund Freud as among the most misogynous. His theory of female sexuality, especially, is based on the male-as-norm assumption that females are incomplete or imperfect males. Freud's ideas about the female "castration complex" revolve around the assumption that females develop penis envy as a result of having discovered their own castration (as evidenced by the missing penis). The "inferior" female organs and the desire to have a penis have lasting affects on female psychology, according to Freud.

Contemporary feminist theorists note the connection between misogyny and gender-role socialization, male dominance, and sexism. Gender-role socialization is thought by some feminist theorists to instill misogynist attitudes early in little boys. The making of a man requires the repudiation of all things feminine, both in himself and in others. The rejection of girlish or "sissy" behaviors is the first expression of the misogynist attitudes soon to be fairly embedded in his adult male gender role.

Misogyny is related to male dominance, according to Judith Long Laws. In our society males are the dominant class, and women are the deviant class. Males and maleness are the norm, while females and femaleness are a deviation from that norm. Thus, woman's experience has been described and interpreted for her through a male filter. Rarely has she been allowed to express her experience, as the means to such expression in media, literature, and scientific publication are male-controlled.

The concept of misogyny is also important to feminist theory* because of its close association with sexism (see Andrea Dworkin). The general misogynist character of our society, according to feminist theorists, is evidenced by the prevalence of pornographic images of women; the implicit acceptability of rape* and other forms of violence against women; the stigma and secrecy surrounding the natural functions of the female body, such as menstruation, pregnancy, and lactation; the devaluation of women's work, whether paid or unpaid; the inherent sexism within our social institutions (e.g., marriage,* medicine, law enforcement, religion, education); and so on.

In summary, most feminist theorists would agree with Jessie Bernard that while individual men may deeply love individual women, the male world as a whole does not. The term "misogyny" has come to represent the broader implications of hatred and hostility toward women as a class by men as a class. Among feminist theorists, misogyny has become a catchall term used to describe the fundamental relationship of gender and power in contemporary society.

References. Jessie Bernard, *The Female World* (New York, 1981); Andrea Dworkin, *Woman Hating* (New York, 1974); Judith Long Laws; *The Second X* (New York, 1979); Kate Millett, *Sexual Politics* (Garden City, N.Y., 1970); Katherine M. Rogers, *The Troublesome Helpmate: A History of Misogyny* (Seattle, 1966).

PATRICIA D. ROZEE

MODE OF PRODUCTION, in Marxist economics, includes the material forces and the social relations of production. Material forces include not only factories, equipment, and tools but education, skills, techniques, and labor power necessary for production. The social relations of production arise from the acquisition, ownership, and control of the material forces of production. The most important social relation is the one between the classes that is formed on the basis of ownership and control of the forces of production. Housework* contributes to the reproduction of labor power* but not directly to production, so that women's labor power in caring for the home and its members is not included in the material forces of production.

MONASTICISM, CHRISTIAN, was a religious vocation for Christian women and men dedicated to serving God in a life of prayer within a monastery, giving up the secular world, and taking on a simple, chaste, communal existence following a religious rule. The word "monasticism" derives from the Greek *monos* (alone or solitary), for the female and male hermits who were seen as founders of the new way of life. Scholars have credited the impetus for the monastic life to Anthony (251–356), who withdrew into the Egyptian desert in A.D. 271 to live a hermit's life of severe asceticism and prayer. However, according to his contemporary biographer Athanasius, before beginning this solitary existence, Anthony placed his sister in a Parthenon, or primitive convent, of nuns in Alexandria. If so, Anthony's attribution as founder of monasticism is incorrect, since communities of religious women predated his self-exile in the desert. Anthony's reputation attracted men and women who gathered near him to imitate his eremitical existence; enthusiasm for a rigorous spiritual life grew, and the first true monastic community was established in the next century by Pachomius (286–346) in southern Egypt. Here Pachomius founded a cluster of monastic dwellings in which men and women lived in communal, but separate, houses under the simple rules he composed that set forth the three conditions of monastic life, which still hold today: poverty, chastity, and obedience.

From such early, unprepossessing beginnings, the monastic ideal for women and men spread rapidly into both the Eastern Empire and Western Europe, carrying with it from its early austere and penitential beginnings an abhorrence for the flesh. Surviving monastic writing from this early period is all by men and often expresses an exaggerated fear of women, who could lure monks from their chosen virginal path. Part of the negative legacy of monasticism for women stems from this identification of women as threatening to the monk's vow of celibacy, which fueled the underlying distrust of women that had first entered Christianity in Paul's writing.

As well as perpetuating destructive attitudes about women, monasticism served as a positive, equalizing force. For instance, women were close to, and influenced, many of the key men who are usually designated as shapers of this new institution; pious women like Macrina, sister of Basil the Great (c.329–379); Perpetua, sister of Augustine of Hippo (354–430); and Scholastica, sister of Benedict of Nursia (c.480–c.547), were all nuns who probably contributed to the formative era of monasticism but have been overlooked by later writers operating under an antifemale bias. Benedict, drawing heavily on available sources, constructed his highly influential rule in the mid-sixth century. At the same time in southern France, the first nuns' rule was written by Cesarius of Arles for his sister, Cesaria, but this and other attempts to legislate specifically for women failed to gain lasting acceptance. Rather, the Benedictine Rule became for women, as for men, the organizing principle for monastic life in the West, while Basil's rules served as the norm for monastics of both sexes in the East. Thus, spiritual commonality rather than gender differentiation was originally inherent in the shared rules that form the backbone of monasticism.

Monasticism flourished particularly from 550 to 1150, when it was the paramount institution in Europe. It appealed to women, at least in part, because, until the late nineteenth century, it offered them their only real option to marriage, and their presence was felt in all medieval monastic orders. Although convents could be used by families as dumping grounds for unwanted daughters, nunneries were also entered freely by many women who chose a positive life of spirituality, community, and learning and/or an escape from marriage, a husband's control, and the dangers of childbirth. During the early and central Middle Ages, female monasteries often enjoyed a high level of scholarship, while the abbesses of rich houses exercised great power and enjoyed independence and prestige that could equal those of male prelates. Huge numbers of women turned to monasticism in the twelfth century, creating a golden age of women's convent life.

An adaptation of monasticism that has received a good deal of scholarly interest is the "double monastery"—a composite house of nuns and monks under the direction of an abbess—which was common in Europe in the early Middle Ages, particularly in Anglo-Saxon England. This practice is usually seen as having ended in the early twelfth century. A feminist reassessment of the history leads to the conclusion that designating some nunneries as "double" is actually misleading, since all convents had some monks or canons. Medieval writers did not consider it particularly noteworthy that religious men followed the direction of an abbess; rather, modern scholars have felt obliged to explain this phenomenon and dilute the abbess' authority with the designation of "double" instead of acknowledging that sometimes women ran huge and famous abbeys with significant numbers of men under their direction.

Convents of women, just as with houses of men, served society in a myriad of ways. Monasteries offered spiritual comfort and support by the prayers of their members; they accepted as nuns both those with a vocation and those who were in some way unfit for the secular life; they took in the elderly, the sick, and travelers; they educated the young and transmitted ideas and learning within their own ranks; they served as peacemakers and as foci for agrarian and mercantile growth; and they buried the dead and prayed for their souls. Not all houses of women or of men operated at their best all the time, yet overall, the record of nuns' and monks' contributions to their environment is a positive one. Despite their extensive spiritual and social contributions, monastics were often criticized, sometimes with reason, for laxness and easy living, but the most biting attacks were reserved for the sexual misconduct of nuns.

Although the stereotype of nuns as immoral and decadent, which was penned by hostile male writers, persists into modern times, current scholarship suggests that medieval nuns generally lived by their rule and were no more apt to break their vows than were monks. Further, nuns shared a high degree of equality with monks, reflected by their receiving equal amounts of support and respect from their surrounding society. Two serious differences existed between the lives of female and male monastics. Nuns were subject to the theory that they should be more tightly cloistered than the monks due to the "weakness of their sex" and were never to leave their abbeys, even in death. Practices were much looser than theory in most of the medieval period, but harsh cloistering was enforced in parts of Europe, particularly during times of church reform. In addition, since women were forbidden ordination to the priesthood, male priests were needed to celebrate the Sacraments, making nuns permanently dependent on male celebrants and confessors.

Ironically, at the height of female monastic enthusiasm (c. 1150) the tide began to turn against religious women. Virulent misogyny grew both in response to a demographic imbalance in which women dramatically outnumbered men and because of a generalized reactionary backlash that followed the failed Crusades. Male orders began to divest themselves of dependent nunneries, legislation was passed to limit or decrease the number of nuns, and the monastic opportunities for women dwindled rapidly during the late Middle Ages. The superior position of monks was enhanced as they increasingly sought ordination, further eroding the gender equality of earlier monasticism. From the thirteenth through the fifteenth centuries, some women channeled their religious enthusiasm outside the nunnery into mysticism, heretical movements, and the life of the Beguines. Following the Reformation of the sixteenth century, Protestant countries banned the celibate monastic life; it continued in Catholic countries, becoming an increasingly feminized profession as the numbers of men entering orders dwindled, and many specifically female orders, usually tightly cloistered and under the close control of the church hierarchy, were founded. In the nineteenth century, cloistering was somewhat relaxed, as female orders, providing professional opportunities not always available to secular women, began to send out nuns as teachers and nurses into newly opened frontiers.

The Second Vatican Council (1962–1965) directed all religious orders to reform and renew themselves. Although changes have been less dramatic for European, Asian, and African nuns and monks, most American orders modernized significantly, removing the last vestiges of cloistering, the wearing of habits, and vocational constraints. Today, despite substantial loosening of restrictions, fewer and fewer women are entering monastic orders, because they are repelled by a life dictated by a patriarchal Church that denies them sacerdotal functions and are attracted by the opportunities available outside the cloister. Although their numbers have shrunk drastically everywhere, nuns today can often be found in the forefront of social and feminist activism—particularly in the Third World—attesting despite all its problems to the surviving strength of the monastic ideal based on a community of women sharing spiritual goals. (See also MEDIEVAL WOMEN, Daily Life of Religious; MEDIEVAL WOMEN, Varieties of Religious Life.)

References. Brenda M. Bolton, "Mulieres Sanctae," in Susan M. Stuard (ed.), *Women in Medieval Society* (Philadelphia, 1976), 141–158; Lina Eckenstein, *Women under Monasticism* (New York, repr. 1963); John A. Nichols and Lillian T. Shank (eds.), *Distant Echoes*, Vol. 1, *Medieval Religious Women* (Kalamazoo, Mich., 1984).

PENELOPE D. JOHNSON

MORMONS is the popular term for members of the Church of Jesus Christ of Latter-day Saints, founded by Joseph Smith in 1830. Migrating from New York to Ohio, Missouri, and then Illinois, the early church was marked by conflicts with non-Mormon neighbors that ended with the murder of Joseph Smith. Brigham Young assumed leadership of the group, leading it on a heroic trek into the intermountain West, founding Salt Lake City and establishing the State of Deseret (Territory of Utah).

In 1852 the Latter-day Saints published the revelation on plural (celestial) marriage received by Joseph Smith in 1843, thereby making public their secret practice of polygamy. Mormons sometimes referred to the practice as "patriarchal marriage," linking it to the marriages of biblical, Old Testament patriarchs. The Mormon priesthood, ultimate basis for all religious and social authority within the church, could be held only by men. Women shared in this priesthood only indirectly by marriage. Since marriage continued into eternity, the wife of a worthy man could be assured of salvation.

The practice of polygamy scandalized the non-Mormon (Gentile) world and increased hostility to the Mormons, which delayed the granting of Utah statehood. After the Civil War, opponents of the Mormons suggested that Mormon women be enfranchised to enable them to throw off the bonds of polygamy. The Mormon men responded by granting Utah's women the vote, and the territory became the second in the United States with female suffrage. Although there was no feminist agitation leading to Utah woman suffrage, Utah women were not passive in the process and soon emerged to identify themselves with the contemporary suffrage movement. By 1873 the Mormon women began publication of a woman-managed and supported periodical, *Woman's Exponent*, which established contact with leading woman's rights activists. Mormon women held office in the National Woman Suffrage Association (NWSA) as early as 1872.

With the rise of the "social purity" reformers and the home mission movement in the second half of the nineteenth century a national antipolygamy campaign developed. (See SOCIAL PURITY MOVEMENT.) This crusade rose to a peak in the 1880s, resulting in federal legislation that criminalized polygamy, disfranchised the women of Utah, and seized church property. Capitulating to the federal crusade, the president of the church issued the Woodruff Manifesto (1890), declaring that polygamous marriage would no longer be sanctioned. Following this, Utah was awarded statehood in 1895 and, due to the exceptional effort of the Utah Woman Suffrage Association, entered with a Constitution that restored woman suffrage.

The antipolygamy crusade was carried on in the name of woman's rights, and the Mormon women defended plural marriage on the same grounds, arguing in eugenic and utopian terms. Polygamy ensured all women their right to marry a worthy man, offered an alternative to uncontrolled male sexuality, and institutionalized the double sexual standard. Despite these justifications, the majority of Mormons were obviously reluctant to accept the practice and, even with strong theological pressure, remained monogamous. Plural marriage, however, was practiced by the church elite, and having more than one wife was advantageous to advancement in the church hierarchy.

Mormon polygamy involved ironies and contradictions. Offered as a millennial reform and argued within the context of woman's rights, it closely adhered to the most conservative Victorian ideals of family, motherhood, and child rearing. Mormon women leaders, who were members of the NWSA and the National Council of Women, were often attacked in these groups by social purity reformers with whom they shared the ideal of a purified larger society. In actual practice, plural marriage may have undermined Victorian and patriarchal ideals: the divorce rate in Utah was high; many plural wives, through maintenance of separate residences or the absence of the husband, acted independently as head of the household; the detachment and emotional self-protection necessary for sharing affection and avoiding jealousy operated against romantic love and fostered increased independence. Polygamy, moreover, could offer, through cooperation and shared duties, increased freedom for women.

Although the primary role for woman in Mormon society was that of wife and mother, the women of the territory, encouraged by Brigham Young to play a more active role in the frontier society, engaged in an unusually wide range of activities. Women dominated the medical profession and participated in numerous economic and social support activities. From the earliest days of the church Mormon women participated in religious rites and were active through the Relief Society, which had been founded with the blessing of Joseph Smith.

The abandonment of plural marriage with the Woodruff Manifesto did not immediately end the practice. In 1898, the antipolygamy movement was reactivated by the election of Utah polygamist B. H. Roberts to the House of Representatives. Marshaling the opposition of many women's groups, antipolygamy forces prevented the seating of Roberts and began a campaign to pass an antipolygamy amendment to the Constitution. The same groups were unsuccessful in their attempt to unseat Utah Senator Reed Smoot in the period 1903–1907. In this last major battle, the Mormons restated their antipolygamy position (second manifesto), and gradually the hostility of mainstream Americans began to diminish. In shedding polygamy, the Church of Jesus Christ of Latter-Day Saints (LDS) has been transformed into a highly respectable, indeed, conservative contemporary institution. The years of increasing respectability also brought a less autonomous role for the Mormon women's Relief Society.

The leadership of the LDS called on its members to help defeat the federal Equal Rights Amendment. Utilizing the structure of the women's Relief Society, the Mormons were able to mount an offensive against ERA during the International Woman's Year Conference in Salt Lake City (June 1977). Dissidents from this position formed "Mormons for ERA," and the resultant controversy led to the excommunication of the Mormon feminist Sonia Johnson. More recently, in September 1993, the church disciplined six Mormon scholars, including feminists who had written about women and the priesthood, a female deity (Mother in Heaven), and other feminist issues.

References. Maureen Ursenbach Beecher and Lavinia Fielding Anderson (eds.), *Sisters in Spirit* (Urbana, Ill., 1987); Maxine Hanks (ed.), *Women and Authority. Re-emerging Mormon Feminism* (Salt Lake City, 1992); Joan Iversen and Julie Dunfey, with intro. by Mary Ryan, "Proto-Feminism or Victims of Patriarchy: Two Interpretations of Mormon Polygamy," *Feminist Studies* 10 (1984): 504–537; Lola Van Wagenen, "Sister-Wives and Suffragists: Polygamy and the Politics of Woman Suffrage, 1870–1896," Ph.D. diss. New York University, 1994.

JOAN IVERSEN

MOTHERHOOD, SCIENTIFIC, an ideology that developed in the nineteenth century, gives mothers the central role in child rearing while promoting scientific and medical expertise as the chief guides in fulfilling women's familial responsibility. In the nineteenth century, science promised to solve all society's problems; so mothers, concerned over high rates of infant mortality, turned to scientific experts for advice.

Rapidly expanding print media, emerging governmental health agencies, the developing medical specialty of pediatrics, and the increasing institutionalization of childbirth all spread the new ideology. The best-known example of scientific motherhood literature was *Infant Care*, first published in 1914 by the U.S. Children's Bureau, which distributed 59 million copies by the 1970s. The original author, Mrs. Max West, a mother of five and graduate of the University of Minnesota, complemented the works of leading physicians with her experience. Advertisements for child care products also promoted scientific motherhood with testimonials from physicians acclaiming their medical validity.

These sources grew in importance as old information systems broke down or became less feasible or less attractive. In an increasingly mobile society, women who found themselves without supportive relatives and friends to answer questions and give suggestions instead utilized available resources, often publications and physicians. Immigrants and their daughters, partly influenced by public health personnel and educators, wanted to raise their children the "American way." This Americanization process discouraged reliance on family and tradition, replacing them with professional expertise.

Physicians concerned with high infant mortality rates echoed sentiments of lay authors: mother-craft education could prevent many infant deaths. Some doctors also recognized the economic potential of the emerging specialty of pediatrics. Moreover, physicians expected that educated mothers would better appreciate the physician's advice in child care. But women received advice from other sources, which, in essence, supplanted the physician's authority. Believing mothers should look to medical experts for direction, professional medical organizations attempted to limit information available from nonmedical sources and to encourage mothers to visit physicians. For example, in the late 1910s, an Advisory Committee, composed of representatives from the leading medical and pediatric societies, proposed that it review all Children's Bureau publications dealing with child care techniques. By the late 1920s the compilers of *Infant Care* were physicians.

In time, more and more women birthed in hospitals, accelerating the medicalization of motherhood, the modern form of scientific motherhood. In 1920 under 20 percent of American women delivered their babies in hospitals; by 1950 the number had grown to over 80 percent. The hospital, cloaked in the aura of medical authority, provided a fertile ground for scientific motherhood training. New mothers were taught child care practices in hospital classrooms; they also learned from hospital routines that suggested mothers needed the expertise of medical personnel in handling their infants.

Scientific motherhood was a broad-based, socially sanctioned ideology prescribing women's relationship to medical expertise and experts. Its development was not limited to the United States. It appeared in various forms in many parts of the globe, especially Europe, other parts of North America, and the Antipodes.

Nineteenth-century scientific motherhood stressed self-education: mothers were responsible for child rearing and for using science to shape their mothering practices. Dr. Benjamin Spock's "Trust your own instincts, and follow the directions that your doctor gives you" exemplifies the mid-twentieth-century version. Ultimately, women believed that the most successful child rearing was done under scientifically informed medical supervision. Not that all women everywhere and at all times slavishly followed the dictates of scientific and medical experts in raising their children. They could and did temper their faith in scientific expertise with greater and lesser doses of common sense and self-confidence in their own abilities. Scientific motherhood is not a static construct, and today a new model is evolving, the goal of which is a partnership between mothers and physicians. Women do not deny the benefits of scientific and medical advice, but they seek to once again be actively involved in decision making about their family's health.

References. Rima D. Apple, "Constructing Mothers: Scientific Motherhood in the Nineteenth and Twentieth Centuries," *Social History of Medicine* 8 (1995): 161–178; Rima D. Apple, *Mothers and Medicine: A Social History of Infant Feeding, 1890–1950* (Madison, Wisc., 1987); Katherine Arnup, *Education for Motherhood: Advice for Mothers in Twentieth-Century Canada* (Toronto, 1994); Phillippa Mein Smith, "Mothers, Babies, and the Mothers and Babies Movement: Australia through Depression and War," *Social History of Medicine* 6 (1993): 51–83; Erik Olssen, "Truby King and the Plunket Society: Analysis of a Prescriptive Ideology," *New Zealand Journal of History* 15 (1981): 3–23; Kerreen M. Reiger, *The Disenchantment of the Home: Modernizing the Australian Family, 1880–1940* (Melbourne, 1985); Benjamin Spock, *The Common Sense Book of Baby and Child Care* (New York, 1945); Nancy Pottisham Weiss, "Mother, the Invention of Necessity: Dr. Benjamin Spock's *Baby and Child Care*," *American Quarterly* 29 (1977): 519–546.

RIMA D. APPLE

MS. AS A TITLE OF ADDRESS. American and Canadian women have recently been able to choose a "traditional" title of address indicating their marital status (i.e., "Miss" or "Mrs.") or a nontraditional one. Does it matter which title a woman chooses or prefers to have others use in addressing her? Social psychologists have long known that perceivers rely on stereotypes (i.e., perceptions and expectations about someone's expected traits or behaviors) to form impressions of others based on personal features such as ethnicity, race, sex, physical attractiveness, height, weight, or even first name. Likewise, a woman's title of address could affect others' impressions.

Madeline E. Heilman (516–517) was apparently first to explore the effects of titles of address on others' impressions, by conducting two studies in which male college and college-bound students evaluated a prospective technical or nontechnical university course to be taught by an instructor named "J. R. Erwin," who was also identified with the title of either Ms., Miss, Mrs., Mr., or no title. While the instructor's title did not influence evaluation of the technical course, it did affect evaluation of the nontechnical one. The nontechnical course was rated as less enjoyable and intellectually stimulating if taught by a traditionally titled woman compared to the alternatives. By contrast, a nontechnical course with a Ms.-titled female instructor was rated as positively as one offered by an instructor with the title of Mr. or no title at all.

Kenneth L. Dion hypothesized that findings like Heilman's implied that the title "Ms." is a stereotypic cue eliciting specific expectations in "the eye of the beholder." He proposed that the title "Ms." evoked perceptions of greater competence and leadership in a woman than the titles "Miss" or "Mrs." The Ms. stereotype was also hypothesized to overlap more with the traditional gender stereotype of males, emphasizing competence, leadership, and other "agentic" qualities, as opposed to the traditional gender stereotype of females stressing warmth, expressiveness, and similar traits suggestive of "communion."

The Ms. stereotype hypothesis was initially tested by two experiments in which Canadian university students of both sexes received a brief description of a stimulus person whose age and employment status were kept constant but whose title of address was systematically varied (i.e., Ms., Mrs., Miss, or Mr.) and asked to evaluate the stimulus person on personality dimensions. A woman who prefers the title Ms. was perceived as being more achievement-oriented, and more socially assertive and dynamic but less interpersonally warm, relative to her female counterparts with traditional titles of address or a male counterpart, thus supporting the "Ms. stereotype" hypothesis.

Subsequent studies with similar methods (Dion and Schuller, "The Ms. Stereotype") explored the generality of the Ms. stereotype among adults visiting the Ontario Science Centre who were primarily nonstudents and represented a range of age and occupation and both sexes, as well as Canadian and American nationalities. The Ms.-titled woman was once again seen as higher in achievement motivation and stereotypical masculinity but

lower in likability than a traditionally titled woman—similar to the afore-
mentioned findings with university students. Thus, a woman's preference
for title of address is a stereotypic cue for adult perceivers, both students
and nonstudents alike.

The preceding experiments (see also Dion and Schuller, "Ms. and the
Manager") also investigated the relation of the Ms. stereotype to the marital status stereotype and the "successful manager" stereotype, respectively.
University students have been known to stereotype a woman on the basis
of marital status, with a married woman generally seen as having more
positive personality traits than her unmarried female counterparts. To explore the potential impact of marital status, Dion and Schuller's experiments described the stimulus person as "married" or "unmarried,"
independently of varying title of address. The stimulus person's purported
marital status neither influenced the Ms. stereotype nor had any effects of
its own on the adult perceivers, who (unlike most students) generally were
presently or previously married themselves.

However, a close link emerged between the Ms. stereotype and the stereotype of the "successful manager." In the 1970s, Virginia E. Schein
showed that male and female businesspersons perceived a successful middle
manager (no sex specified) as having personality characteristics more commonly ascribed to men than to women. Likewise, in the Dion and Schuller
experiments, a close resemblance was observed between respondents' trait
ratings of a woman who prefers Ms. as her title of address and those of a
successful middle manager. However, no resemblance was found between
a successful middle manager and a woman who prefers a traditional title
of address for herself.

The preceding studies by Dion and his associates always indicated the
female stimulus person preferred her title of address, suggesting the choice
reflected something about her personality. Merely appending a title of address to a woman without information that it is her personal preference
is unlikely to evoke the Ms. stereotype. Indeed, Dion and Cota showed
the Ms. stereotype occurs *only* when the perceiver is explicitly told the
female stimulus person prefers the traditional or nontraditional (i.e., Ms.)
title.

A woman has an advantage over a man in being able to choose the title
of address that accentuates the type of image (i.e., feminine or masculine)
she may wish to convey in one or more situations. A woman's preference
for the title Ms. seems to blunt the traditional female stereotype in the "eye
of the beholder" and leads her to be perceived like a man in personality
and managerial characteristics.

References. Kenneth L. Dion, "What's in a Title? The Ms. Stereotype and Images
of Women's Titles of Address," *Psychology of Women Quarterly* 11 (1987): 21–
36; Kenneth L. Dion and Albert A. Cota, "The Ms. Stereotype: Its Domain and
the Role of Explicitness in Title Preference," *Psychology of Women Quarterly* 15

(1991): 403–410; Kenneth L. Dion and Regina A. Schuller, "Ms. and the Manager: A Tale of Two Stereotypes," *Sex Roles* 22 (1990): 569–577; Kenneth L. Dion and Regina A. Schuller, "The Ms. Stereotype: Its Generality and Its Relation to Managerial and Marital Status Stereotypes," *Canadian Journal of Behavioural Science* 23 (1991): 25–40; Madeline E. Heilman "Miss, Mrs., Ms. or None of the Above," *American Psychologist* 30 (1975); Virginia E. Schein, "The Relationship between Sex Role Stereotypes and Requisite Management Characteristics," *Journal of Applied Psychology* 57 (1973): 95–100.

KENNETH L. DION

MULTIPLE REGRESSION ANALYSIS is a statistical method for predicting the value of a dependent variable from the known values of independent variables. It is one of the most successful methods for investigating salaries within an organization or unit of an organization for evidence of discrimination.* When salaries of women and/or minorities as a group fall below their predicted values, there is thus prima facie evidence of discrimination.

MUSIC BUSINESS (CLASSIC). Traditionally, those who have succeeded in music recognize their field as both an art form and a business. Musicians, composers, and conductors must be their own bosses and manage their own careers at a stage critical to their professional growth: the beginning. Those who lack the initiative to do so rely on talent alone to attract the attention of managers and patrons who will run their affairs, and inevitably the artists lose control. They are less prepared to take advantage of opportunities as they arise, and their instincts with regard to professional growth are untested and underdeveloped.

This entrepreneurial spirit is characteristic of women who have had a significant impact on the music business as we know it today. Most music histories ignore the contribution of women because musicologists focus on the development of style rather than the sociology of music. Women were not leaders in style changes because they were excluded, for the most part, from professional positions. Their music was fostered and appreciated only in domestic circles. Playing was considered one of the social graces, and teaching was respectable and appropriate for women who chose to work, but it was also deemed a profession of low status; in 1870, 60 percent of music teachers were women (see Ammer).

After the Nineteenth Amendment granted suffrage to women in 1920, American women became increasingly vocal about their status and contributions as musicians. The country's economic boom during the 1920s made way for a surge in the growth of American music. More concert halls were built, performance seasons were expanded, and orchestras increased in number. Women were still excluded from symphony jobs, though, so some 30 women's orchestras were founded to provide a vehicle for artistic expression and growth. Female players and conductors sought recognition and professional status in hopes of creating a "mixed" orchestra. They did not want to make music alone; they wanted to play with their male counterparts. In the early 1920s women constituted the majority of U.S. music students but were barred from the professional mainstream, with the exception of a select few who achieved in opera, solo concert, and choral work. Yet women continued to play a critical role in the management of musical organizations like Symphonic Ladies. These patrons and support groups assumed responsibility for fund-raising, public relations, and ticket sales, which were critical to the survival of orchestras, opera companies, and other organizations. Women, in essence, defined the role of our first music managers. Then, shortly after the United States entered World War II, the work of these women was formalized with the creation of the American Symphony Orchestra League—a service organization that continues a strong presence today.

Discrimination against women players remained prevalent through World War II. With the depression, many resorts and restaurants were forced to dispense with their orchestras, and theater orchestras became obsolete with the introduction of talkies. Women's orchestras continued to emerge, however, in response to the number of fine female players and conductors. In the 1940s many of the women's orchestras disbanded as World War II enabled women players to get jobs in traditional male settings because of a shortage of civilian men.

Women conductors and composers also suffered from a lack of opportunity. In order to be heard, many of them formed their own ensembles and composers groups. For example, in 1926 Margaret Dessoff (1874–1944) was the first woman to conduct a major New York choral concert; she also founded a women's chorus and mixed chorus in New York to provide some consistency for her work and her career. A decade earlier, Mrs. Davenport Engberg was cited by *Etude* as the "only lady conductor of a symphony orchestra in the world" (quoted in Ammer, 211). She was also the founder of a symphony in Bellingham, Washington.

As managers and especially teachers, women musicians have been more visible—to a point. Orchestras have hired women managers since the late nineteenth century, though as the urban musical organizations grew in influence, men assumed the decision-making posts. In 1969, Helen Thompson became the first woman to manage a major orchestra, the New York Philharmonic. Already a leader in her field, she was one of the founders of the American Symphony Orchestra League.

In music education women were allowed to shine, partly because male performers found education beneath them. Women taught privately in the early nineteenth century and taught in the full-scale conservatories when they were being established in midcentury. But once recognized by society at large, these institutions began hiring more men than women. As late as the 1970s, although women students still outnumbered men in conservatories, faculties were predominantly male. Ammer (233) cites the ratio of men to women hired for teaching positions in the 1970s at 4 to 1, while the ratio of those with full professorships was 9 to 1.

Today the struggle of women in music continues toward equality in the workplace. Statistically, the percentage of women in professional jobs is increasing, but the numbers are still disproportionate to the working population. In the decade ending with 1975, female players in 27 U.S. orchestras increased by 36 percent (*Boston Globe*, June 16, 1976). Although more than half of all music students are female, and some 45 percent of all American women are in the workforce, only 10 to 15 percent are in the top echelons of professional music (Ammer, 223). Furthermore, full-time, male music administrators with comparable responsibilities, education, and years in the field are earning salaries averaging 20 percent higher than those of their female peers. As in other fields, some women have attempted lawsuits to rectify these inequalities, but discrimination has been very difficult to prove. The assessment or evaluation of one's musical abilities and talent is most often viewed as a subjective matter. In the 1970s, when all major orchestras began conducting blind auditions aided by the use of a screen, the percentage of women hired increased substantially.

The search for recognition of women in music is reflective of a struggle for woman's rights in general, and there are indications that the situation is changing. For example, the salary discrepancies between men and women in music administration are decreasing among those entering the field. Of particular note, however, has been the tendency of women to take the initiative to forge their own careers where more traditional opportunities may not have existed. This tendency was true in the 1920s and 1930s with the cultivation of women's orchestras, and it is true today with the prevalence of women's ensembles, festivals, and composers groups. Those women in music who take control of their careers by creating new opportunities will have a better chance of being fulfilled artistically and professionally. Music, as an art form, is reflective of the world in which we live, and its ambassadors—male and female—must always find new ways of being heard and appreciated.

References. Christine Ammer, *Unsung: A History of Women in American Music* (Westport, Conn., 1980); *Association of College, University and Community Arts Administrators Bulletin* 3, 7 (July/August 1987); *Boston Globe*, June 16 (1976); Jane Bowers and Judith Tick (eds.), *Women Making Music: The Western Art Tradition 1150–1950* (Urbana, Ill., 1986).

ROBIN WHEELER

MUSICIANS (PRE–TWENTIETH-CENTURY). Although Sophie Drinker's conjectures that the art of music may have begun in the singing of magic by women and that women were the first musicians cannot be substantiated, cave paintings illustrate prehistoric women musicians. Among the oldest records of organized and systematized music, Sumerian texts from the third millennium B.C. speak of several classes of ecclesiastical singers and players, both male and female. Sumerian art also depicted female singers, and in certain royal tombs both male and female musicians were buried with their master.

From ancient Egypt we have pictures of women dancing, singing, and taking part in religious services as priestesses. A 5th-dynasty (2563–2423 B.C.) tomb at Saqqarah depicts Iti, a prominent woman singer, accompanied by Hekenu, the first woman harpist to be known by name. Members of sacred women's choirs were led by a highly placed person such as the wife of the high priest, and at the beginning of the 18th dynasty (1575–1352 B.C.) Queen Ahmes-Nefretere was leader of the singers of Amen, the protecting god of Thebes. Sacred female musicians are frequently depicted singing, hand clapping, and playing the sistrum, the instrument of sacerdotal potency. During the 18th dynasty female musicians were brought in large numbers from Semitic lands and placed in harems at court and in the palaces of the nobility.

In ancient Greece women took part in religious rites as priestesses and members of religious societies, dancing and singing hymns. They also ritually lamented the death of a family member (or sometimes female musicians were hired for this responsibility), a tradition still maintained in parts of Greece today. Out of the rich musical life of Greece came a number of female poet-musicians, most famous of whom is Sappho of Lesbos (b. c. 612 B.C.). Little but legend is preserved of her life, yet she is credited with being the first to use the pectis, a plucked string instrument, and with inventing the Mixolydian mode and Sapphic stanza. Later women known for music making were the hetaerae, courtesans who by the fourth century B.C. were devoting themselves to philosophy, literature, and the arts, including the playing of musical instruments and dancing. Manumission records from fourth-century Athens give the occupations of three freedwomen as harpist and aulos players.

In pre-Islamic Arabia, music was practiced mainly by women, especially by singing girls (*gaināt*) attached to upper-class households or employed at places of entertainment. With the rise of Islam, the male musician came to the fore, yet Jamila (d. c. 720), a famous singer who gained her freedom, led her orchestra of 50 singing women with lutes on pilgrimage to Mecca in splendid litters, one of the great musical events of the Umayyad period (A.D. 661–750). During the following Abbasid period (A.D. 750–1258), the caliph, princes, and wealthy Arabs in Baghdad maintained harems of highly skilled women slaves (*al-Jawari*) who sang and played instruments such as the ud (lute).

In some places, the harem musician had a religious counterpart. In India, from around the third century A.D., *devadasis* (maidservants of God) were trained in music and dance and dedicated to Hindu temples. With the destruction of the great temples by Muslim invaders, the institution of *devadasis* began to decline in north India. But in south India, it flourished into the nineteenth century and was outlawed only in 1947.

In ancient China the aristocracy kept scores, even hundreds, of private "sing-song" girls, who danced, sang, and played musical instruments. During the Tang dynasty (A.D. 618–907), sing-song girls conversant with arts and letters moved among poets, artists, scholars, and officials, entertaining them in the capacity of hostesses. Paintings from both the Tang and Song (A.D. 960–1279) dynasties depict entire female orchestras. Under Emperor Ming Huang (713–756), an institution for the performance of music and dance by female court musicians, the *chiao-fang*, was established; during this period, it had more than 3,000 female musicians. As late as 1900, sing-song girls still performed in places of public entertainment, but soon after that their activities were restricted. As with the *devadasis* in India, their status declined considerably; toward the end they were classed with prostitutes of the lower ranks. In Korea, the *kisaeng*, professional female entertainers active at court over many centuries, formed a counterpart to the Chinese sing-song girl, as did the geisha in Japan.

In the West after ancient times there was virtually no comparable development of female musical ensembles or courtesan musicians. Still, during the early centuries of the Christian church, women were active in sacred music and in singing at divine worship. But as the church grew, so did opposition to women's participation; the performance of church music increasingly became the province of trained male singers and priests. For more than a millennium, women were excluded from music making in the church. In convents, however, women sang, and the first extant works by a woman composer are liturgical compositions and a few other works by the ninth-century Byzantine nun Kassia; the second, the liturgical plainsong compositions and a liturgical morality play by the twelfth-century abbess Hildegard of Bingen. While women of other classes occasionally made their living as itinerant performers and household musicians, aristocratic women frequently sang and played for their own pleasure. A handful of them (the *trobairitz* and female *trouvères*) also wrote and set courtly poems to music. (See TROUBADOUR LITERATURE.) For the Middle Ages as a whole, nevertheless, women were excluded from advanced musical training and musical positions of high status.

During most of the Renaissance, a similar situation obtained. Women of the classes from which most male musicians emerged, unless born into musical families, had virtually no chance of acquiring a thorough music education. Likewise, the principal music professions were closed to them. Nevertheless, a few women, primarily singers, made their living in low-status jobs, and girls born into noble or wealthy families were frequently provided with private music teachers and as adults continued to perform within their private social circles.

Toward the end of the sixteenth century the participation of women in professional singing began to increase radically as the result of the establishment of small ensembles of women musicians at northern Italian courts. During the next century, the rapid growth of opera and musical establishments in upper-class households provided work for a substantial number of women singers, some of whom reached the very apex of the profession. During the same period, women composers began to emerge from obscurity. The first published compositions by a woman—madrigals of Madalena Casulana—appeared in Venice in 1566, and throughout the rest of that century and the next, numerous other works by Italian women followed. The emergence of women composers at this time seems closely linked to four principal factors: (1) the development of careers for women singers; (2) the increased cultivation of polyphonic music in convents; (3) the growth of private music instruction; and (4) the growth of music printing. Some women, such as Francesca Caccini, Barbara Strozzi, and Isabella Leonarda, composed seriously over a long period of time. Still, women did not benefit from many of the advances in music making during this period, and their achievements in composition remained considerably slighter than those of men.

The burgeoning of public and private concerts in the late seventeenth and eighteenth centuries brought about the next significant increase of professional women musicians. This took place first in Paris, where, at the Concert Spirituel (est. 1725), before the century was out, women sang and performed on the harpsichord, organ, fortepiano, flute, violin, harp, and horn, sometimes playing their own compositions. As increasing numbers of aristocrats and bourgeoisie took up singing and playing, Frenchwomen also moved into private music teaching and, as demand for printed music increased, into music engraving and publishing. But they did not benefit from many of the routine employment opportunities open to men; for example, they were not hired to play in the orchestras that accompanied soloists at public concerts, even though these soloists were women.

Elsewhere during the eighteenth century, women joined the expanding ranks of touring virtuosos. Some, late in the century, were occasionally appointed church organists; finally, the barriers to women's performing in church were beginning to break down, although it would be some time before mixed choirs became common. As women entered music professions in increasing numbers, more began to emerge as composers. In France this trend was under way by 1700; in countries such as England, Germany, and Austria, it began primarily after 1750. It was principally the smaller instrumental genres and solo songs—mainly intended for domestic consumption by amateur musicians, many of whom were also women—that women cultivated, few symphonies or concertos coming from their pens. The exceptional Elisabeth-Claude Jacquet de la Guerre, however, composed over a wide range of genres and styles and was the first woman to compose a complete opera (1694).

During the nineteenth century, a crucial change was the establishment of public music conservatories, a number of which were open to women. As women increasingly gained advanced instruction in music, composers set their sights higher than domestic music. In France, for example, Louise Bertin, Louise Farrenc, and Augusta Holmès tackled some of the largest genres of their day—grand opera, symphonies, symphonic poems, and dramatic odes. In the last decade of the century, Amy Beach in the United States and Ethel Smyth in England began to astonish audiences and critics with powerful orchestral and choral works, which in no sense exhibited the limitations normally associated with women's work.

Women made great strides as performers as well. Although singing, both in opera and on the concert stage, remained the major outlet, more women became prominent instrumental virtuosos, first as pianists and later as performers on other instruments, such as violin. Some reached the very peak of their profession—among them, Clara Schumann, indisputably one of the greatest pianists of the century. Women also began to be appointed as teachers, like Farrenc and Schumann, at major conservatories of music and even, like Caroline B. Nichols, entered the conducting field. But while opportunities for professional musical employment increased, they did not keep pace with the new kinds of training women were receiving as musicians. One response to the sense of frustration women felt under these circumstances was to form women's orchestras and chamber music groups. But, women did not achieve their goal of joining established groups of male musicians until after the beginning of the twentieth century.

Women's advances also brought about a sort of backlash. Ideas about musical creativity solidified into a rock of masculine prerogative. Music was a "masculine idea," and music criticism of women's works used gender for leverage: "One will scarcely encounter a bold turn or startling episode with this woman, and should she nevertheless once fall into a distant modulation, so genuinely female, she ponders immediately how she can most quickly find her way home again" (Eduard Hanslick on Luise Adolpha Le Beau).

By 1900, while the idea of music as an "accomplishment" for women still lingered on in part, it was no longer the principal manner in which women could choose to relate to music. This change was signaled in 1904 by James Huneker, an American critic, who wrote:

Passed away is the girl who played the piano in the stiff Victorian drawing rooms of our mother. . . . The new girl is too busy to play the piano unless she has the gift; then she plays with consuming earnestness. We listen to her, for we know that this is an age of specialization, an age when woman is coming into her own, be it nursing, electoral suffrage, or the writing of plays; so our poets no longer make sonnets to our Ladies of Ivories, nor are budding girls chained to the keyboard.

References. Jane Bowers and Judith Tick (eds.), *Women Making Music: The Western Art Tradition, 1150–1950* (Urbana, Ill., 1986); Aaron I. Cohen, *Interna-*

tional Encyclopedia of Women Composers (New York, 1981); Sophie Drinker, *Music and Women: The Story of Women in Their Relation to Music* (1948; rep. ed., Washington, D.C., 1977) (should be used with caution) Eduard Hanslick, *The Beautiful in Music* (London, 1891); James Huneker, *Overtones, a Book of Temperaments* (New York, 1904).

JANE BOWERS

MUSICIANS (TWENTIETH-CENTURY). See COMPOSERS; CONCERT ARTISTS; CONDUCTORS; MUSIC BUSINESS (CLASSIC)

MYSTICISM, CHRISTIAN (TWELFTH TO TWENTIETH CENTURIES). Mysticism belongs to the core of most religions insofar as the mystics believe in a transcending reality and in divine ways to reach God in the utmost immediacy (Thomas Aquinas: *cognitio Dei experimentalis,* Summ. Theol. II-II, 97, a.2) and to achieve union with him (*uniri cum Deo*).

The mystics' totally absorbing self-reflections and their move toward the Godhead with the help of a tripartite gradation toward God (*via purgativa, via illuminativa,* and *via unitiva*) never assumed the dimension of a mass movement; instead, it was a very private and individual form of religious experience. Nevertheless, a disproportionate number of thirteenth- through fifteenth-century women turned to mysticism and thus contributed in relatively large numbers to the literature of their time.

Mystic women searched for unmediated contact or even physical union with God (*unio mystica*) and often expressed their experiences (revelations and visions) in images of God as their bridegroom or in motherhood images.

Practically all mystics were reluctant to record their experiences because of the inadequacy of language. Yet, all were eventually encouraged by their divine source to write or dictate an account of their visions. Women mystics almost always stood under the guidance of male advisers who helped them formulate their experiences in literary terms, because they often lacked advanced school training. Since they mostly did not know Latin, they resorted to the vernacular for their mystical writings. In most cases women mystics felt a need to emphasize that their works were, in fact, written by God and that they themselves were only his unworthy instruments. Overall, their writings are far more imaginative and sensuous than those of male mystics.

In general, however, there are no clear distinctions between male and female mysticism. Whereas male authors rather stressed theoretical and abstract aspects of mysticism primarily and rarely related any ecstatic experiences, women favored images of a visionary and extremely emotional nature. This can be explained with the different levels of intellectual education and with the fact that women were denied access to the universities. However, women's mystical writings gave them the first and decisive mode of literary expression in the Middle Ages and hence a form of compensation for the denial of female priesthood. Thus, female mysticism was the clearest opposition to dominant male misogyny.

As early as the twelfth century, mystically inspired women such as Hildegard of Bingen (1098–1179), Elizabeth of Schönau (1129–1164), and Mechthild of Magdeburg (c. 1212–1282/1283) in Germany, as well as the *mulieres sanctae* (holy women) of the Low Countries witnessed mystical visions and related them to their fellow sisters and confessors. All these mystical women either wrote their revelations down themselves or dictated them for others to record.

One of the major centers of European female mysticism was the Cistercian/Benedictine convent of Helfta in Low Germany, where Mechthild von Magdeburg, Mechthild of Hackeborn (1241–1299), and Gertrude the Great (1256–1301/1302) lived. The best-known Dutch mystics were Beatrice of Nazareth (c. 1200–1268) and Hadewijch (c. 1230–1260). The latter strove to imitate Christ's life in a highly individualized manner and intended her writings only for a selective and exclusive audience of women friends. In contrast to other mystics, she refrained from any criticism against the established church. Instead, she isolated herself in her private spiritual world of visions and hoped only to demonstrate to her fellow sisters how they also could achieve a mystical union with God here on earth.

The thirteenth and fourteenth centuries witnessed an extraordinary flowering of mysticism on the European mainland, in England, above all. Meister Eckhart (1260–1327), Johann Tauler (1300–1361), and Heinrich Seusa (1300–1366) were founders of a mystical movement in Germany. Particularly, Eckhart succeeded in synthesizing the Greek and Augustinian theories of mysticism with a daring negative theology into one unifying system. Soon Eckhart's doctrine found an enormous reception, particularly among those women who were members of the newly established Dominican and Franciscan orders.

In southern Germany and Switzerland, mystics such as Elsbeth Stagel (d. c. 1360) in Töss, Margaret Ebner (c. 1291–1351) in Maria-Medingen, Christine Ebner (1277–1356) and Adelhaid Langmann (c. 1312–1375) in Engeltal composed *Sisterbooks*, which consisted of the *Vitae* of their mystic sisters and diaries, letters, and other revelation literature.

The French mystic Beguine Margaret Porete (d. 1310) wrote a manual on the progressive spiritual life (*The Mirror of Simple Souls*). Angela of Foligno (1248–1309), like many others, was the author of a spiritual autobiography (*Memoriale de fra Arnaldo*). One of the most important fourteenth-century women mystics was Catherine of Siena (1347–1380), who expressed her political and religious concerns in more than 380 letters to personalities all over Europe and successfully strove to convince the pope to return the Holy See from its "Babylonian Captivity" in Avignon, France, to Rome. Similarly important was Birgitta of Sweden (c. 1303–1373), who combined her mystical experiences with political concerns about the welfare of the church. She founded the most influential religious order for women in Scandinavia, the Order of the Most Holy Savior, which subsequently flourished throughout Europe. Catherine of Genoa (1447–1510) continued the mystical tradition far into the late Middle Ages.

In England, Dame Julian of Norwich (1342–1416/1423) left, as her spiritual legacy, the *Revelations of Divine Love*; whereas Margery Kempe of Lynn (c. 1373–after 1438) composed an autobiography in which she described her life in mystical terms.

Mysticism did not come to an end with the age of Reformation, although its center of gravity, after a final bloom with the *Devotion moderna*, revived religious spirituality, which emerged in the Low Countries and shifted to France and Spain in particular. Teresa of Ávila (1515–1582) is considered to be one of the most influential mystics of Southwest Europe. Her "conversations" with God instigated her to impose stricter laws on the life of the Carmelite Order. In her autobiographical writings (*Libro de su vida*) she described her struggles to reach spiritual perfection and how human life could become a vision of God. Teresa was famous particularly for her mystical concept of praying. In her masterwork *Las Moradas* she advocated a system of prayers that was finally to lead the mystic's soul through seven "mansions" (*moradas*) to an unmediated contact with God. She also wrote more than 400 letters.

Jeanne F. F. de Chantal (1572–1641) soon followed a similar path in France, where she founded, together with François de Sales, the Order of the Visitation. At the same time, Marie of the Incarnation (1599–1671) developed the "apostolic orientation of mysticism," in which she sought spiritual marriage with Jesus Christ. She is better known, however, for her voyage to Canada, where she established a mission in Quebec for the conversion of North American Indians to Christianity. Similar to her predecessors, Marie strove for increasing intimacies with Christ.

Jeanne Marie de la Mothe-Guyon (1648–1717) adhered to a form of mysticism that was dominated by images of spiritual motherhood and marriage with Christ. She related her contemplations and visions in a number of texts, such as *Moyen court est très facile pour l'oraison* (1685). Both Chantal and Guyon were closely related with quietism, which soon was disseminated into Germany, where it found a new spiritual leader in the Pietist Countess Hedwig-Sophia of Sayn Wittengenstein (1669–1738). Elisabeth of the Palatinate (1618–1680), abbess of the Herford convent, became the core of German Pietism and had close contacts with Gottfried Leibnitz and Nicolas de Malebranche. Often, however, mystic women of the eighteenth century did not follow this school of thought and remained outside of the Pietists' organization; for instance, Susanna Katharina of Klettenberg (1723–1774), who is mostly known through Johann Goethe's description of her as "Die schöne Seele" (the beautiful soul).

Among modern mystic women are Theresa of Lisieux (1873–1897), who perceived herself as Jesus' doll, and Elisabeth of the Holy Trinity (1880–1960). Both were members of the Carmelite order. The British nurse Florence Nightingale (1820–1910) has also been characterized as a mystically inspired person. The Frenchwoman Simone Weil (1903–1943) represents a remarkable example of socially inspired mysticism. A Jew who never converted to Catholicism, she had visions of Christ and other revelations that induced her to follow a life of social asceticism, from which, however, she suffered an early death. As an intellectual she searched for the lowest point of existence among the poorest of society and thus found her sanctity both in practical activities and in spiritual transcendentalism.

An amazing and inexplicable example of a mystic woman was Theresa Neumann (1898–1962) from Regensburg, West Germany, who, despite a life of total fasting, never lost weight. Close surveillance was never able to detect any source of nourishment. She experienced regular visions. An American mystic Margaret Prescot Montague (1878–1955) described her spiritual visions in a book called *Twenty Minutes of Reality* (1917).

References. Peter Dinzelbacher (ed.), *Wörterbuch der Mystic* (Stuttgart, 1989); Peter Dinzelbacher and Dieter R. Bauer (eds.), *Frauenmystik in Mittelalter* (Ostfildern bei Stuttgart, 1985); John Fergusson, *An Illustrated Encyclopedia of Mysticism and the Mystery Religions* (London, 1976); Valerie M. Lagorio, "Mysticism, Christian: Continental (Women)," in Joseph R. Strayer (ed.), *Dictionary of the Middle Ages*, vol. 9 (New York, 1987), 8–17.

ALBRECHT CLASSEN

MYTH, REVISION OF. The publication of two critical texts has signaled a new focus on mythology as a source of feminist energy: Charlene Spretnak, *Lost Goddesses of Early Greece: A Collection of Pre-Hellenic Myths* (Berkeley, Calif., 1978) and Diane Wolkstein and Samuel Noah Kramer (eds.), *Inanna, Queen of Heaven and Earth* (New York, 1983). The Spretnak text brings together, in clear and straightforward versions, images of the Greek goddesses that long anticipate the patriarchal distortions firmly entrenched by Hellenic times and perpetuated through much of British and American literature and classics study. Wolkstein and Kramer's text brings to nonspecialists the first full translation and interpretation of the cycle of stories and hymns devoted to the Sumerian goddess Inanna, whose tarnished image previously came to us in the forms of Ishtar and Aphrodite, goddesses of war and of love. Current feminist theory, especially that of Marilyn French and Gerda Lerner, asserts that a key series of events in the transformation of culture from matrifocal to patriarchal must have been the shift from worship of powerful goddesses to dominant male gods.

Much feminist thought and research are now devoted to study of the cultural transformation, rather than solely to the recovered images, of the ancient goddesses. In 1985, Heide Gottner-Abendroth acknowledged the early research and reconstruction of goddesses by such scholars as J. J. Bachoven and Robert Graves, while going on to chart the regular and predictable transformation of goddess worship into god worship; her article not only serves as an expression of what is now known about the transformation of worship but identifies as well a new interest in the rediscovery of goddess worship for contemporary feminists. A consistent pattern has been identified by many scholars. It consists of worship of a female principle of creation, followed by a battle for control between male and female creation principles and succeeded by joint rule or male dominance. The creation mythology of many cultures has been demonstrated to follow such a pattern, testifying to invasions by successful, usually warlike patriarchal cultures such as the early Greek.

The revision of mythology owes much to the integration of several disciplines, including art history, political theory, and classics. So urgent does reconsideration of myth appear to contemporary feminists eager to make sense of their current status within a patriarchal culture that specialists within disciplines have taken risks to study the new information about early goddess worship across disciplines. The importance of myth in the development of culture has long been clear. However, the proliferation of studies within the past 10 years, including the reissuing of Philip E. Slater's much disputed *The Glory of Hera: Greek Mythology and the Greek Family* (Boston, 1968), demonstrates the growing awareness that proper understanding of myth is a precondition for full awareness of the sources for gender images over time and for contemporary religious practices.

Mesopotamia, long identified as the cradle of Judeo-Christian civilization, and Hellenic Greece, regularly claimed as the source of Anglo-American political structure, are of crucial importance in the current attempts to uncover and reinterpret long-suppressed information about goddesses and goddess worship. Disagreement among scholars persists about the meaning of the prevalence of powerful goddesses such as Inanna and Hera; some scholars believe that religious myth and imagery attest to female power in the social and political world, while others insist on a distinction between myth and history. As scholars, especially feminists, uncover more information about the earliest goddesses, classical texts long understood in patriarchal context take on new meaning. Goddesses such as Athena and Artemis, important throughout classical literature, acquire new forms of identity and power, new archetypal implications, when studied in the light of recent feminist inquiry. It seems certain that such disciplines as psychology and literary criticism must be affected by the current determination to investigate and uncover the earliest forms of myth as well as the meaning of the supplanting of goddess worship by the worship of male gods.

References. Marilyn French, *Beyond Power: On Women, Men, and Morals* (New York, 1985); Heide Gottner-Abendroth, "Thou Gaia Art I: Matriarchal Mythology in Former Times and Today," *Trivia, a Journal of Ideas* 7 (Summer 1985); Gerda Lerner, *The Creation of Patriarchy* (New York, 1986); Barbara G. Walker, *Woman's Encyclopedia of Myths and Secrets* (San Francisco, 1983).

RUTH NADELHAFT

MYTHOLOGY is both the study of sacred symbols, narratives, and rites and their dynamic expression in human psyches and societies and also the collective term for myths from a specific group or about a certain entity. As generally understood and undertaken, mythology is based primarily on extant documents, field data, and interpretations by male scribes, scholars, artists, and "informants" and thus concerns men's myths and rituals. Far more is known about women *in* mythology, about the female figures who people male narratives, enactments, philosophies, theologies, and analyses, than about women *and* mythology or women's mythologies—the stories they recount among themselves and in the company of children, the rituals they perform, and the elaboration, exegesis, and evaluation of their own and men's profoundly moving and significant symbolic expressions.

Creation myths, particularly cosmogonic accounts, are accorded high status by mythologists. Female creator deities are rare. In ordinary, contemporary English usage the verb "to create" means *creatio ex nihilo* (creation from nothing) by thought, dream, spirit, laughter, or speech or the crafting of the world and its inhabitants by an artisan or architect. "To create," then, is not the same as "to give birth to" or "to mother," so (symbolic or spiritual) creation is not equivalent to (natural or biological) procreation. Thus, emergence myths that tell how in the beginning people, animals, plants, and so on ascend through, and emerge from, the womb or wombs of the earth mother are seldom considered as significant as myths telling of creation by the word and by a *deus faber* or craftsman god, for example, in Genesis 1 and 2. Most such deities are portrayed as male or bisexual/androgynous, in which case the male aspect tends to predominate linguistically and/or mythologically. Whether worship of goddesses or gods is prior and primary historically or developmentally continues to be debated. In any case, worship of strong goddesses does not necessarily mean women enjoy social power.

Culture heroes bring or bring about valuable objects, teachings, and natural changes that make possible human survival and society. Fire, weather, agriculture, hunting techniques, rituals, and the healing arts are important among such benefactions. The feminine forms of *culture hero* and *creator, culture heroine* and *creatrix* are awkward, marked terms, reflecting the relatively weaker roles women play in creation, transformation, and origin myths—when they appear at all in such accounts of ordering the world. Despite their natural procreative ability, goddesses, human women, and female animals are much more likely to be depicted in myth as destructive or static monsters than as creative benefactors.

In the beginning is also the end, that is, the *telos* or destiny. Origin myths—whether of the cosmos, humans, animals, plants, or customs—are used to validate and charter contemporary social and natural order, a theory attributed to British anthropologist Bronislaw Malinowski. Women's position in society is thought to derive from how they originated and their behavior in mythic times, as in the well-known Western myths of Lilith, Eve, and Pandora. According to this view, myths of matriarchy and Amazons would be used to justify present patriarchy by portraying women as losers in the crucial mythic power struggles and thus as unfit for present social status. Viewed from a feminist perspective, such myths present compelling, imaginative explorations of alternate lifeways.

Rites of passage, especially those associated with birth, puberty, marriage, death, and initiation into mysteries, are important in mythology. The lunar (and in women, menstrual) cycle serves as a ready measure for months and human lives and is almost paradigmatic for a woman's life, even though she may menstruate for only part of that time. The related measures of moons, months, and menses have more usually been viewed as dark and dangerous to the diurnal solar, which is generally equated with the masculine, than as sources of fructifying power for either women or men. On the whole, in Western tradition the lunar has come to be associated with the feminine and the unconscious, the solar with the masculine and the conscious and thus the more valuable domains.

Death is a passage requiring gnosis, or spiritual knowledge, and heroism. Death is sometimes depicted as a female figure like Ereshkigal, Sumerian goddess of the underworld, or Doña Sebastiana, the skeletal *memento mori* in Hispanic New Mexican folk tradition. Although the central experience of Demeter's Eleusinian Mysteries has remained secret, like many other mysteries, it apparently involved revelations about dying and the afterlife.

Heroic journeys often entail a confrontation with death. Western notions of heroism are basically masculine, influenced by the Homeric epics and feudal ideas of kingship and military prowess. Joseph Campbell almost exclusively uses male exemplars of the "monomyth" (departure, initiation, and return) of "the adventure of the hero," a "man or woman who has been able to battle past his [*sic*] personal and historical limitations to the generally valid, normally human forms." These normative biographical patterns usually say little about women's life stories, and in collections and analyses of myths women more often appear as passive and auxiliary like Odysseus' wife, Penelope, than as agents of their own and others' destiny like Psyche.

Much of the difficulty in discussing women and mythology comes from the differential evaluation of *mythos*, derived from Greek words relating to the mouth, speech, and oral story-telling, and *mundus*, this world, the mundane. Mythology as presently defined deals with time beyond time, the otherworldly, the extraordinary, but not with the present, flux, the everyday, the commonplace and ordinary. *Mundus* has been devalued, and *mythos* exalted as the cherished expression and object of study.

In many societies, women have been silenced altogether, or their speech, especially that dismissed as mere gossip or old wives' tales has been disregarded. (See GOSSIP; OLD WIVES' TALES.) When more is known of women's speech, narration, song, and ceremony with one another, it may be that gossip in its best sense will be seen as the mundane equivalent of supernatural myth narration. Mythology as heretofore defined and studied—as a public, collective, male-dominated means of communication pertaining to cyclic time and metaphysical, numinous being—will then be seen as but one aspect of all powerful human expressions of inter- and intrapersonal realities.

References. Joseph Campbell, *The Hero with a Thousand Faces* (New York, 1949, 1968); Carolyne Larrington (ed.), *The Feminist Companion to Mythology* (London, 1992); Barbara G. Walker, *The Woman's Encyclopedia of Myths and Secrets* (San Francisco, 1983); Marta Weigle, *Creation and Procreation: Feminist Reflections on Mythologies of Cosmogony and Parturition* (Philadelphia, 1989); Marta Weigle, *Spiders and Spinsters: Women and Mythology* (Albuquerque, 1982).

MARTA WEIGLE

N

NATIONAL ASSOCIATION OF COLORED WOMEN (NACW) was organized on July 21, 1896, in the 19th Street Baptist Church in Washington, D.C. It was formed from the union of the National Federation of Afro-American Women of Boston and the Colored Women's League of Washington, D.C. The event that catalyzed its formation was the disclosure of a scurrilous letter written in 1895 by James W. Jack, president of the Missouri Press Association, which attacked the morality of African American women. In this letter to Florence Belgarnie of England, secretary of the Anti-Slavery Society, Jack stated that "the Negroes of this country are wholly devoid of morality, the women are prostitutes and are natural thieves and liars" (James W. Jack letter, Mary Church Terrell Papers, Box 102–5, folder 60, Moorland Spingain Collection, Washington, D.C.). Copies of the letter were disseminated to leading blacks, men and women, to gauge their opinions. In July 1895, African American women convened the first national conference of African American women to denounce these charges. Soon afterward this same group evolved into the NACW.

The membership of the NACW consisted of a heterogeneous group of elite, middle-class women—educators, businesswomen, doctors, and women of social status. Their motto, "Lifting As We Climb," reflected their belief that their fate was bound with that of the masses and that altering the environment would provide opportunities for a better life for their "lowly sisters." Imbued with this self-help ideology, the NACW created kindergartens, nurseries, mothers' clubs, and homes for girls, the aged, and the infirm. In 1917, it financially rescued the home of the late Frederick Douglass. The house, located in Anacostia, a suburb of Washington, D.C., is today a museum and historical center that houses his memorabilia. The NACW makes annual contributions to the United Negro College Fund, the Career Emergency Fund, and the Hallie U. Brown Fund, which provide scholarships to young people in higher education. Throughout its history, the NACW has been politically active on issues pertaining to suffrage, voting rights, and discrimination. In 1990, its membership was 45,000 women in 1,000 chapters.

The office of president has been held by women such as Mary Church Terrell, one of the wealthiest and best-educated black women of the late nineteenth and early twentieth centuries; Margaret Murray Washington, the wife of Booker T. Washington and a noted educator; and Mary McLeod Bethune, founder of Bethune-Cookman College and director of the National Youth Administration under President Franklin D. Roosevelt.

BEVERLY W. JONES

NATIONAL CONSUMERS LEAGUE (NCL) is a social feminist organization founded in 1891 by Josephine Shaw Lowell with other upper-class New York women to better the conditions of working-class women. It was most effective in the period before World War I, in large part, through the support it could draw from the wealthy and prominent friends and connections of its volunteer members.

The NCL investigated and publicized abuses, made direct contact with employers to try to effect changes, and worked for the enactment of protective legislation. Its first concern was with women in retail stores, and it used consumer pressure, establishing a "white list" of business concerns that consumers should patronize exclusively. At the turn of the century it promoted a "white label" campaign—clothing manufacturers whose labor policies met NCL approval were authorized to use the label. By 1914, around 70 companies were doing so. After 1907 the NCL turned its efforts to the passage of maximum hour and minimum wage laws for women.

The socially prominent membership of the NCL was backed by an excellent group of young professional women, including Frances Perkins and Josephine Goldmark. In 1899 Florence Kelley became general secretary, and within a few years she had organized leagues in major cities across the United States and two international conferences.

After World War I the league continued to do valuable work, but, as the socially prominent volunteers of the founding period were not replaced in the next generation, its influence was never as great as it had been during the Progressive Era.

NATIONAL COUNCIL OF NEGRO WOMEN (NCNW) was founded by Mary McLeod Bethune, a native of Mayesville, South Carolina, and 15th child in a family of 17, on December 5, 1935, at the 137th Street branch of the Young Men's Christian Association (YMCA) in Harlem (New York). As the founder of the Daytona School for Girls (1904), later known as Bethune-Cookman College, and a former president of the National Association of Colored Women (NACW) (1924–1928), Bethune was a visionary who established the NCNW as a response to the changing social conditions of African American life in the 1930s. She was one of the first to realize that the NACW, faced with the financial woes of the depression, had become anachronistic by 1930. It had reduced its 38 departments to 2 and focused primarily on the home as the panacea for black problems. By 1930, many of its programs were discontinued because other organizations, which had more money, were doing a better job.

Bethune viewed the diminution of the scope and function of the NACW as an indicator that a new women's organization was needed to coordinate the special interests of a particular group with broader issues of race, education, and young people. The NCNW, thus, became the coordinator of the activities of all women's groups in order to make an impact on the public policies of the nation.

This goal is reflected in the objectives of the organization:

1. To unite national organizations into a National Council of Negro Women;
2. To educate, encourage and effect the participation of Negro women in civic, economic and educational activities and institutions;
3. To serve as a clearinghouse for the dissemination of activities concerning women;
4. To plan, initiate and carry out projects which develop, benefit and integrate the Negro and the nation. [Minutes, National Council of Negro Women Meeting, December 5, 1935. National Archives for Black Women's History, Mary McLeod Bethune Memorial Museum, Washington, D.C.]

The National Council of Negro Women has continued to pursue these goals. Today it is a coalition of 27 African American and other minority women's groups that focuses on the social, economic, and political aspects of American life in order to ensure the participation of all groups and improve the quality of life for all individuals. The programs of the council have expanded to include juvenile justice, public health, career counseling and development, and women's history.

BEVERLY W. JONES

NATIONAL WOMEN'S TRADE UNION LEAGUE (NWTUL), organized in 1903 by William English Walling, a New York settlement house worker, and Mary Kenney O'Sullivan, a labor organizer and factory inspector, was modeled after Mrs. Emma Patterson's Women's Protective and Provident League in England (1873; in 1890 renamed the Women's Trade Union League). For three decades the NWTUL worked to further trade unionization among women workers and promote the passage of protective legislation. Its membership included trade unionists and their allies, professional women from the settlement house movement, and women of means, but union members had to be in a majority on the executive board.

Organizing women proved difficult. Its greatest success was among Jewish workingwomen, with whom socialism was a major force, but most women workers were unskilled and uncommitted to the union movement. It tried to get the American Federation of Labor (AFL) to mount organizing campaigns among women workers, but neither the national executive council nor individual unions were committed to unionizing women workers, and some were definitely hostile. The AFL used the league's feminism and upper-class membership to keep it at a distance while benefiting from its efforts on behalf of workers.

The feminist and labor agendas of the NWTUL were not always compatible, and the contradictions between them remained unresolved, but, in addition to its direct efforts on behalf of workingwomen (organizing, picketing, working for protective legislation, etc.) the NWTUL was important for bringing some wealthy women into contact with the labor movement and for developing an outstanding group of working-class women who eventually dominated the league: Rose Schneiderman, Leonora O'Reilly, Helen Morot, and Pauline Newman.

NATIVE AMERICAN WRITERS, after the establishment of reservations in 1851, attended reservation schools where they learned English as one of their first written languages (most Native languages were not written). Many were sent to schools off the reservation such as the one founded in Carlisle, Pennsylvania, in 1879. Even before the turn of the century, a number of Native women were highly educated, and some had college degrees. These writers took elements of the oral storytelling tradition that had always been an integral part of their culture and incorporated them into the genres of novels, short stories, essays, and poetry. In the traditional cultures, the stories both preserved values of the culture, ensuring solidarity, and also entertained. In most tribes, the art of storytelling was practiced by both men and women, and in some, particularly in the Southwest, the grandmother carried on the storytelling tradition. Native writers extended such elements into their writings as the sacredness of language, attention to place and landscape, and concern for tribal welfare as opposed to concern for the individual. Storytelling is a participatory event, and a good storyteller draws the story from the audience. A novel by a Native American writer is not so much fiction as witnessing significant events through time.

Sophia Alice Callahan, a highly educated Creek, is thought to be the first Native woman to write a novel. *Wynema* (1891) was intended by the author "to open the eyes and heart of the world to our afflictions, and thus speedily issue into existence an era of good feeling and just dealing toward us." Although *Wynema* has a romantic plot, the novel is quite political, criticizing the slaughter of women and children at Wounded Knee, and even has a passage supporting suffrage.

Other Native women wrote articles, stories, and poetry for the many

Native journals and newspapers of the time period. For example, at age 20, Ora V. Eddleman Reed, a Cherokee, was the editor and a contributor to *Twin Territories: The Indian Magazine* (Washington, D.C.) beginning in 1916. Zitkala-Sa also wrote a collection of stories for children, *Old Indian Legends* (1901), and in 1921 published *American Indian Stories*, which are mostly autobiographical.

Sarah Winnemucca Hopkins, a Piute, wrote one of the first personal narratives by a Native American woman, *Life among the Piutes* (1883). Like other writers of the time, she hoped to generate sympathy among her readers for the conditions in which her people lived. Other narratives of Native women such as the 1936 *Autobiography of a Papago Woman* by Ruth Underhill were told to, and recorded by, anthopologists in response to questions. A more recent example is the 1981 *Mountain Wolf Woman* by Ojibway storyteller Ignatia Broker, who relates the story of one of the grandmothers of her parents.

Emily Pauline Johnson, Mohawk, was a prolific writer of short fiction, essays, and poetry at the turn of the century. Some of her works include *Canadian Born* (1903), *Flint and Feather* (1914; poetry), *Legends of Vancouver* (1911), and *The Moccasin Maker* (1913).

Another important writer, Humishuma (Mourning Dove), an Okanogan, used her tribal traditions to create a novel examining the contemporary problem of being a mixed-breed person. To make up for her lack of education, she collaborated with Lucullus V. McWhorter, a student of Indian history and lore, in writing *Cogewea, The Half Blood* in 1927.

In recent years, critics have noted that Native American literature has had a renaissance. As part of this revival, Native women have created an entire body of literature—novels, poetry, short stories, and the attendant critical essays. Leslie Marmon Silko, Laguna Pueblo, has volumes of poetry, and her *Storyteller* (1981) is a collection of poetry, family history, and stories. In her widely acclaimed novel *Ceremony* (1977), Silko has woven the traditional mythology of the Laguna into a modern story that shows how the values of the past can be pertinent to the present. Silko's novel has more than a little suggestion of the healing power of words, coming from the Native tradition of the sacredness of words. Her most controversial novel, *Almanac of the Dead* (1991) documents 500 years of European abuse and oppression of Native Americans and the land. Although a graphic and disturbing novel, *Almanac* is a testimony to her belief in the power of words to sustain and preserve a culture.

Paula Gunn Allen, Laguna Pueblo/Sioux, has written one of the first novels since *Cogewea* to have a Native woman as its central character. Her *The Woman Who Owned the Shadows* (1983), which explores the role of a Native woman in contemporary culture and the influence of the past, has a lesbian-feminist theme. In addition to being a prolific writer of poetry (see, for instance, *Shadow Country* [1982]) and fiction, Allen is also a noted scholar and critic. Her *Studies in American Indian Literature* (1983), *The Sacred Hoop* (1986), *Spider Woman's Granddaughters: Traditional Tales and Contemporary Writings by Native American Women* (1990), and *Grandmother of the Light: A Medicine Woman's Sourcebook* (1991) are invaluable for the feminist scholar. In her work, Allen points out the inherent feminism in many Native cultures.

The resurgence of Native writers includes many other excellent women writers. Louise Erdrich, Turtle Mountain Chippewa, has received national recognition for her poetry, *Jacklight* (1984) and *Baptism of Desire* (1989), and her novels, *Love Medicine* (1984), *The Beet Queen* (1986), *Tracks* (1988), *Bingo Palace* (1994), and *Tales of Burning Love* (1996). The novels trace the lives of characters from the Turtle Mountain reservation and the surrounding North Dakota area from 1912 to the present. They are told through the eyes of various characters as if readers are listening to community gossip so that readers must decide for themselves what really happens. Erdrich is also known for her writing collaboration with her husband, Michael Dorris (Modoc) before his death in 1997, and together they wrote *Crown of Columbus* (1991). Linda Hogan, Chickasaw, writes short stories and has a novel, *Mean Streets* (1990). Her numerous volumes of poetry include *Eclipse* (1983), *Daughters, I Love You* (1981), and *Calling Myself Home* (1979). Janet Campbell Hale, Sioux, has a volume of poetry, *Custer Lives in Humbolt County* (1978); a youth novel, *The Owl's Song* (1974); another novel, *The Jailing of Cecilia Capture* (1985); and a book of autobiographical essays, *Bloodlines, Odyssey of a Native Daughter* (1993). Maria Campbell, Metis, writes of her personal experience of the pain of growing up a mixed breed in *Halfbreed* (1973). Anna Lee Walters, Pawnee/Otoe, has a collection of short stories, *The Sun Is Not Merciful* (1985); a novel, *Ghost Singer* (1988); and a collection of personal essays, *Talking Indian* (1992). Shirley Hill Witt, Akwesansne Mohawk, writes of the intersection of Native culture and Hispanic culture in her stories and poems anthologized in Rayna Green's *That's What She Said: Contemporary Poetry and Fiction by Native American Women* (1984). This volume by Green, who is a Cherokee poet, scholar, and editor, is one of the best collections to date of Native women writers and contains a good bibliography.

Beth Brant, Mohawk, edited the groundbreaking collection of fiction, poetry, and narratives, including work of Native lesbians, *A Gathering of Spirit* (1984), and has a book of personal narrative and poetry, *Mohawk Trail* (1985), and short stories, *Food and Spirits* (1991). Writing of Native lesbians is also anthologized in *This Bridge Called My Back* (1981), edited by Cherrie Moraga and Gloria Anzaldua.

Poetry seems to be the dominant genre for a number of Native writers. Joy Harjo, Creek, is the author of *She Had Some Horses* (1982), *What Moon Drove Me to This* (1978), and *The Woman Who Fell from the Sky*

(1994). Wendy Rose, Hopi/Miwok, has written *Academic Squaw* (1977) and *What Happened When That Hopi Hit New York* (1983), among others. Other poets of note and their works are Mary Tall Mountain, Athabaskan, *There Is No Word for Goodbye* (1982); Roberta Hill Whiteman, Oneida, *Star Quilt* (1984); Anita Endrizze-Danielson, Yaqui, *Claiming Lives* (1983); Diane Burns, Anishinabe/Chemehuevi, *Riding the One-Eyed Ford* (1981); and Elizabeth Cook-Lynn, Sioux, *Then the Badger Said This* (1977) and *Seek the House of Relatives* (1984). Carol Lee Sanchez, Laguna Pueblo/Sioux, has several books of poetry, among them *Coyote's Journal* (1981), *Message Bringer Woman* (1977), and *Morning Prayer* (1977).

References. Gretchen Bataille, *Native American Women: A Biographical Dictionary* (Hamden, Conn., 1992); Gretchen Bataille and Kathleen Sands, *American Indian Women, Telling Their Lives* (Lincoln, Nebr., 1984); Rayna Green, *Native American Women: A Contextual Bibliography* (Bloomington, Ind., 1983).

ANNETTE VAN DYKE

NAZI PROPAGANDA ran the gamut from implicit misogyny to conservative feminism in its portrayal of women. Pro-natalism based on racist eugenics was the backbone of the Nazi concept of womanhood. As a result, all national socialist ideologues were rabidly anti-abortion for the so-called Aryan race and pro-sterilization when it involved Jews, gypsies, or Aryans with supposedly defective genes. Maintaining the superiority of the "Nordic" or Aryan race was a common goal of Nazi propaganda; the suggested means varied widely among national socialists.

Regarding "woman's place," three major ideological groupings can be identified: the male leadership, which wrote little about this topic but whose sexist views determined policy decisions concerning women more than any other faction; mainstream propagandists or traditionalists, who did not consider themselves a group but whose opinions place them in the center of the national socialist spectrum; and the Nazi militants, several dozen Nazi women who were allowed to publish their feminist views until 1937.

The major figures in the Nazi leadership, including Adolf Hitler and his propaganda chiefs Joseph Goebbels and Alfred Rosenberg, while employing exalted language to laud German women, displayed an attitude of implicit distrust of, and superiority toward, their female counterparts. Often this opinion led to parallel views of Jews and women, since both were seen as capable of "ruining the Aryan race" with their calls for "erotic freedom" (Rosenberg). Such demands ran counter to the Nazi leadership's conception of women's "holy mission" as "mother of the German *Volk*" (Goebbels). These ideologues viewed motherhood in purely biological terms, as bearing sons for the fatherland. Giving birth was likened to the heroic combat of the German soldier, a formulation that implied the imperialistic aims of Nazi population policy. Moreover, the male leadership suggested that women should be restricted to the home. Not only would this eliminate (male) unemployment, but it would also re-create politics as a "male enclave" (Rosenberg) and "restore women to their essential honor" (Goebbels).

In contrast, Nazi traditionalists, including Gertrud Scholtz-Klink, women's leader of the Reich, reflected views prevalent among German women. Largely unqualified to successfully compete with men, they had no desire to change attitudes toward women in the professions but instead wanted society to bestow greater status on women's traditional responsibilities. Consequently, mainstream propagandists urged that housework be professionalized and that motherhood, which they regarded as granting women's "eternal worth," be more highly rewarded. Both they and the Nazi leadership posited a polarity of male and female characteristics. Unlike the leadership, however, traditionalists did not see "feminine" qualities as the basis for women's inferiority but as complementary human aspects of equal or higher value. The term "spiritual motherhood" combined several of these female traits to designate an innate quality that suited women for certain types of employment. By thus broadening the definition of women's customary societal function, traditionalists sidestepped the controversy of women's expanding role in the economy.

Nazi militants, a group associated with the publication *Die deutsche Kämpferin* (The German Woman Warrior), which was edited by Sophie Rogge-Börner, saw their mission as furthering women's participation in the new Nazi state. By restoring women to the equality they had once enjoyed within the Nordic race, these German women warriors believed a true "natural aristocracy" could be reestablished with achievement, not gender, as its criterion. As a result, Nazi militants criticized the party leadership for their attacks on women in higher education and in the professions, for the double earners' campaign (which laid off women whose husbands were employed), and for excluding women from law, politics, and the army. They also assailed sexist German laws (concerning, e.g., marital property and rape), as well as sexist German practices (e.g., sexual objectification, sexist socialization and education, prostitution, and woman battering). According to them, women's difficulties in Germany could be attributed to the "degeneration of Germanic instincts" due to the "bastardization of the Nordic race," including the reputed importation of gallant customs from the south and west, the supposedly Slavic conception of woman as man's beast of burden, and the "Oriental" (i.e., Jewish) "denigration of women as sexual prey and breeders" (Rogge-Börner).

Reference. Nancy Vedder-Shults, "Motherhood for the Fatherland: The Portrayal of Women in Nazi Propaganda," Ph.D. diss., University of Wisconsin–Madison, 1982.

NANCY VEDDER-SHULTS

NEOLITHIC is an archaeological stage of human development usually implying the presence of either food production or pottery. The term was coined with reference to prehistoric sites containing stone tools finished by grinding and polishing (Neolithic = new stone). In the preceding Paleolithic and Mesolithic periods stone tools were made by flaking, while the Neolithic was followed by the use of metals for tools. An interesting feature of many Neolithic sites is an abundance of female figurines.

The term "Neolithic" is somewhat out of currency in archaeology and prehistory, but no acceptable general term has arisen to take its place. In Europe and Southwest Asia "Neolithic" minimally implies food production, while in South and East Asia the term usually is applied to sites with pottery but without metals, having no necessary implication of plant or animal domestication. In the Americas an equivalent stage is called Formative.

The minimal meaning of "Neolithic" is often expanded to refer to a complex of traits, including permanent villages, pottery containers, weaving, and domesticated plants and animals. These attributes of the extended definition of Neolithic were at one time believed to have appeared more or less simultaneously as a decisive step in human cultural evolution. This event was dubbed the Neolithic Revolution (Childe, 59–86). However, subsequent research, especially the application of radiocarbon dating, has unraveled this concept, for the traits are first found singly and in widely separate locations. For example, the earliest pottery containers have been found in Japan dated around 10,000 B.C., unaccompanied by evidence of plant or animal domestication for several thousand years; the earliest settled villages appear in the Upper Paleolithic; advanced weaving is found on the coast of Peru long before the advent of pottery, domestication, or settled villages; and even ground and polished stone appears in the Hoabinhian (early postglacial) tradition of Southeast Asia without being accompanied by any other Neolithic traits. One can only conclude that from a worldwide perspective there was no Neolithic Revolution.

Although the term "Neolithic" is one coined by archaeologists, it is sometimes extended to apply to ethnographic groups that do not produce metal tools but do practice horticulture. In this sense, the Neolithic began independently in many places as the glaciers of the last Ice Age melted, and it continues in a few places into the present or recent past.

It is interesting to note that all of the Neolithic accomplishments, with the exception of polished stone tools, are designated more often as women's work than men's work in cultures around the world. Women are more frequently potters, weavers, gardeners, and even house builders. This does not mean women have necessarily been given credit for these inventions, nor that scholars have accorded them respect for these purported accomplishments. For example, Childe speculated, "Probably at first cultivation was an incidental activity of the women while their lords were engaged in the really serious business of the chase" (71). Partly because of the association of women with early domestication, one school of nineteenth-century thinkers postulated a matriarchal stage in human evolution. The work of Lewis Henry Morgan also assumed an early stage of matrilineality based on kinship terminology, which he called "barbarian." Appropriated by Friedrich Engels, Morgan's stages became part of Marxist doctrine, accounting for the almost universal assertion of a matriarchal society for Neolithic sites in the USSR and the People's Republic of China.

Another proposed trait of the Neolithic is the worship of the Goddess, based on the existence of female figurines, which are common but not ubiquitous in the Neolithic. They are not the earliest portrayals of the human body, for about 200 statuettes of women have been found on the Eurasian continent dating from the Upper Paleolithic, and Mesolithic rock art depicts the activities of both women and men. Interpretations of the uses of Neolithic figurines and the meanings of the cultures in which they are found tend to focus on fertility rites for agriculture, although it seems unlikely that one explanation will suffice for the function of all Neolithic figurines. There are marked differences in the contexts of the finds, as well as in the figurines themselves. Some examples that illustrate these contrasts are from Japan, Mesoamerica, Eastern Europe, and Turkey.

The first figurines of Japan belong to the stage known as Earliest Jomon. These are rare, very crude, and little is known of their context. However, by Middle Jomon (3600–2500 B.C.) the figurines are found in large numbers, with sometimes more than 100 at a single site. Although clearly human in their stance and clearly female with breasts well delineated, these figurines were not intended to depict real people. They are highly ornamented and often grotesque. Even when broken, the figurines were sometimes given deliberate burial, encircled by stones and covered by stone slabs. More often they are found in pits, jars, and house floors, or simply in the trash. J. E. Kidder argued for the presence of food production in the Middle Jomon on the basis of these figurines, which he believed to represent a cult with "a direct bearing on the fertility of the land." To him this "would represent the material form of cults surrounding an embryonic form of cultivation . . . from the Middle Jomon period onward" (5). In recent years more direct evidence of plant cultivation in these sites has been accumulating, adding considerable weight to this suggestion. M. Nagamine, while asserting that subsistence was still based on foraging, proposes that "women may have been raising very young wild animals for ritualistic sacrifice" (261).

More realistic female figurines are found in Mesoamerican Formative sites (1500–1000 B.C.), especially in the valleys of Mexico, Oaxaca, and Tehuacan. Depicted with wasp waists and large thighs, they wear a variety of headdresses and jewelry and appear in many poses. Although some figurines are male, the bulk are female, sometimes thousands of them in a single site. Most often they are found fragmented in the trash deposits— along with potsherds, in a ratio of about 4:1000 in one site where they are quantified. Therefore, it is assumed that all households participated in whatever ritual event involved the figurines and that it occurred with some frequency. One group of four figurines found buried together included three women standing with folded arms and one sitting with crossed legs. There is no question that these sites were inhabited by food producers who lived in sedentary villages (Drennan).

Figurines from the Neolithic of Eastern Europe (7000–5000 B.C.) are more realistic than those of Japan but more stylized than the "pretty ladies" of the Valley of Mexico. They are often shown sitting, and the poses are naturalistic. Again, male representations exist, but the figurines are preponderantly female. Often they were found in oversized buildings or in conjunction with shrines, implying villagewide rather than household use. Marija Gimbutas interprets these sites as "characterized by a dominance of woman in society and worship of a Goddess incarnating the creative principle as Source and Giver of All" (9).

Çatal Hüyük in Turkey has produced not only a profusion of female figurines but solid evidence for the centrality of women's place in that society. Many figurines are of corpulent women, often associated with wild animals. They are usually found in shrines with other evidence of goddess worship, including wall paintings. Human remains indicate differential treatment of women and men at death. Graves more commonly contain women than men. All the burials with obsidian mirrors are female, as are all those that were sprinkled with red ocher. The excavator of the site concluded, "The position of women was obviously an important one in an agricultural society with a fertility cult in which a goddess was the principal deity" (Mellaart, 181). It appears that an interpretation of the Neolithic as a period when women were at least not unequal is a valid one.

References. V. G. Childe, *Man Makes Himself* (New York, 1951); C. W. Cowan and Patty Jo Watson (eds.), *The Origins of Agriculture, an International Perspective* (Washington, D.C., 1992); R. Drennan, "Religion and Social Evolution in Formative Mesoamerica," in K. V. Flannery (ed.), *The Early Mesoamerican Village* (Orlando, Fla., 1976), 345–368; Friedrich Engels, *The Origin of the Family, Private Property, and the State* (London, 1884; Anne Brigitte Gebauer and T. Douglas Price (eds.), *Transitions to Agriculture in Prehistory*, Monographs in World Archaeology No. 4 (Madison, Wisc., 1992); Marija Gimbutas, *The Civilizations of the Goddess: The World of Old Europe* (San Francisco, 1991); Marija Gimbutas, *The Goddesses and Gods of Old Europe* (London, 1982); J. E. Kidder, *The Birth of Japanese Art* (London, 1965); James Mellaart, *Çatal Hüyük, a Neolithic Town in Anatolia* (New York, 1967); Lewis Henry Morgan, *Ancient Society* (Cambridge, Mass., 1881); M. Nagamine, "Clay Figurines and Jomon Society," in J. R. Pearson (ed.), *Windows on the Japanese Past: Studies in Archaeology and Prehistory* (Ann Arbor, 1986), 255–266.

SARAH M. NELSON

NETHERLANDISH ARTISTS (1600–1800). Nearly 250 women artists, amateur and professional, were recorded in the Low Countries (present-day Holland and Belgium) between the mid-sixteenth and the late eighteenth centuries. A small number were well known in their native Holland or Flanders, although they never enjoyed international distinction. These artists include such figures as genre/portrait painter Judith Leyster and watercolorist Margaretha de Heer. An even smaller group, including still-life specialists Maria van Oosterwyck and Rachel Ruysch, won international artistic recognition. Their accomplishments were discussed in the major biographies of Netherlandish painters by Arnold Houbraken and Johan van Gool, and their work attracted the patronage of European nobility.

Unlike Italy, France, and Spain, where artwork was almost exclusively made-to-order for the very wealthy, in seventeenth-century Holland, art became a portable commodity affordable to the middle class. This development encouraged a diversity of subjects and techniques, and consequently Dutch painters were the first Europeans to develop fully the genres of still life, seascape, townscape, landscape, and scenes from everyday life.

Women artists, however, tended to avoid certain subjects. Unable to study anatomy from the nude, most could not acquire enough proficiency to compose groups of human figures in action, as was necessary for painting successful historical or religious subjects. Seascapes or town views were seldom popular subjects, perhaps because women needed chaperones to study them. With the exception of wax modeling and silhouette cutting, few women produced much sculpture.

Beginning in the late seventeenth century many women took up printmaking. Most made reproductive prints of works by old masters and by their male relatives. Geertruyt Roghman (d. after 1658), however, made original engravings depicting women's chores and occupations—a subject characteristic of contemporary women's genre painting as well. A few artists, such as Antonyna Houbraken (1686–1736; daughter of the famous artistic biographer), Rachel Ruysch, Michaelina Wautieres, and Henriette Wolters had their works engraved by men.

Although there were exceptions, the majority of Netherlandish women painters practiced still life and/or portraiture. For women artists of the north, the portrait tradition seems to have peaked not in the golden age of painting but in the century preceding it with Levina Teerlinc (Bruges, c. 1520–1576) and Caterina van Hemessen (1528–after 1587, Antwerp).

According to Houbraken, Anna Françoise de Bruyns (1605–after 1629) of Brussels was the best woman painter of her time. Her uncle and teacher, Jacques Francquart, presented her to the Infanta Isabella of Spain, for whom she painted religious scenes. Although she is recorded to have produced 245 portraits, de Bruyns' work is known only by engravings made after her paintings.

The few known portraits by Michaelina Wautiers (b. Mons, before 1627); Gertrude van Veen of Antwerp (1602–1643), daughter of Rubens' teacher, Otton van Veen; Catherina Pepijn of Antwerp (1619–1688), daughter of Rubens' rival, Martin Pepijn; Aleijda Wolfsen of Zwolle (1648–after 1690); and Margareta van Huyssen (fl. 1688–1706) show a high degree of competence. On the basis of such a small number of works, however, it is difficult to determine the precise nature of each painter's achievements.

Judith Leyster (1609–1660), one of the outstanding artists of her time, created portraits and genre scenes that sparkle with the spirited brushwork characteristic of the work of fellow Haarlemmer Frans Hals. Her subject matter, however, adopts a woman's viewpoint. She excelled in renderings of children with their pets and musical instruments, and perhaps her most notable painting, *The Proposition* (1631; Mauritshuis, The Hague), is a sympathetic portrayal of a harassed woman repulsing the advances of a drunk. The psychological poignancy of this work is enhanced by the sophisticated color harmonies and the use of candlelight to reveal the woman's expression of annoyance. Leyster was elected member of the Haarlem painters' guild in 1633 and married the genre painter Jan Miense Molenaer in 1636. Her productivity declined after her marriage.

Henrietta Wolters (1692–1741) of Amsterdam, daughter of painter Theodor van Pee, was an extremely popular portrait miniaturist. Despite exceptional offers from Peter the Great and the king of Prussia to work at St. Petersburg and Berlin, Wolters chose to remain in her birthplace.

While only a few excelled in portraiture, Netherlandish women produced many of the most spectacular examples of still life in all of Europe. They generally preferred fruit, flower, and banquet pieces. At the beginning of the eighteenth century, when the flower piece reached the height of its popularity, flower painters of both sexes were paid astronomical sums for their richly detailed bouquets.

Clara Peeters (Antwerp, 1594–n.d.) was a major innovator of still-life painting in the north. We know nothing of her training, but the technical virtuosity of her early work (1608–1612) makes it most unlikely that she was self-taught. Her paintings belong to two categories of still life that were virtually undeveloped at the time she began to paint—"banquet pieces" and "breakfast pieces." Her early works are of the banquet type and include a great variety of expensive objects: Venetian glasses, rare shells, artichokes, knives with ornate handles, and vases of flowers. After about 1620, Peeters painted in a much plainer style, employing the monochromatic schemes then favored by Haarlem painters Pieter Claesz and Willem Claesz Heda. These later works depict simple meals featuring stacks of cheese, pretzels, and stoneware jugs. Four of her magnificent banquet pieces are in the Prado Museum, Madrid.

Maria van Oosterwyck (1630–1693), a painter of floral still lifes and vanity pieces, was born in Nootdorp near Delft, six years before Delft painter Johannes Vermeer. She studied still-life painting with Jan Davidsz de Heem, who brought about an exchange of still-life trends between the northern and southern Netherlands in the mid-seventeenth century. Van Oosterwyck's paintings possess the sumptuousness of De Heem's work plus a sharp, almost porcelain finish characteristic of the work of Delft-born flower painter Willem van Aelst, with whom she may also have studied. Houbraken reported that Van Aelst courted her, but this report cannot be verified; it is known that she never married. She was an extremely devout woman. She used some of her money to buy freedom for Dutch sailors captured by Barbary pirates and enslaved in Algiers.

The royalty of several countries, including Louis XIV of France, William and Mary of England, Emperor Leopold I, and the king of Poland, paid high prices for Van Oosterwyck's paintings.

Rachel Ruysch (1664–1750), whose exquisite fruit and flower extravaganzas sold for more than Rembrandt's work, served as court painter to the elector palatine in Düsseldorf from 1708 to 1716. Her fame spread to Italy when the elector sent two of her pendant still lifes to the grand duke of Tuscany. In 1723, Ruysch, her husband, and their son Georgio split a lottery jackpot of 60,000 guilders—equivalent to about a million dollars today. She continued to paint until the age of 83, two years before her death.

Ruysch's floral compositions possess a graceful, sweeping S-curve; a knot of brightly illuminated roses at the heart of the design; a plethora of butterflies, inchworms, and beetles among the flowers; and a snail on the ledge. Her bouquets frequently include exotic horticultural specimens that she would have seen in Amsterdam's botanical garden, where her father was supervisor for 46 years.

Maria Sibylla Merian (1647–1717) was born in Frankfurt am Main. When she was a very young girl, her father, Matthaeus Merian, produced magnificent engravings for one of the earliest catalogs of different flower species. Perhaps this early experience sparked Maria Merian's interest in recording the natural world. After her father died in 1650, she took her first lessons in flower painting with her stepfather, Jacob Marrel, and subsequently with one of his most talented students, Abraham Mignon. Although Merian painted a few competent flower pieces, her work as a naturalist and scientific illustrator is her most distinguished contribution. She studied entomological, zoological, and botanical species in Europe and the Dutch South American province of Surinam and published the results of her research in magnificently illustrated books. Her three-volume work, *Der Raupen wunderbare Verwandlung und sonderbare Blumennahrung* (The Wonderful Transformation of Caterpillars and [Their] Singular Plant Nourishment) (1679, 1683, 1717), presented her revolutionary discovery that caterpillars and adult butterflies were the same species of insect at different stages of development. Previously, the life cycles of insects were so mysterious that people believed the creatures to have sprung fully formed from dirt and mud. Merian died in Amsterdam.

A number of women, including several with enormous reputations in their lifetimes, experimented with a variety of pursuits. They achieved notice not simply through the excellence of their work but through its range and variety.

Johanna Koerten was a multitalented artist from Amsterdam (1650–1715), contemporary with Rachel Ruysch. She not only painted and drew but also was a silhouette cutter, embroiderer, etcher on glass, and wax modeler. She gained wide international fame and many honors, particularly for her silhouettes. Peter the Great, the queen of England, the empress of Germany, and other royalty paid high prices for the landscapes, seascapes, animals, flowers, religious subjects, and portraits she cut from white paper and mounted on black. Unfortunately, few of her works are known today.

Anna Maria von Schurman (b. Cologne, 1607; d. 1678, near Leeuwarden, Friesland) was perhaps the greatest Renaissance woman living in the Low Countries during the golden age. Her artistic pursuits included oil painting, wood and ivory carving, wax modeling, silhouette and paper cutting, and engraving and etching on copper and glass. Patronized by Queen Christina of Sweden, von Schurman was the first artist in Holland to work in pastel. Von Schurman was also a musician, celebrated linguist, scholar, and poet, and she agitated for improved educational opportunities for women; she never married.

Elisabeth Ryberg (Rotterdam, fl. 1710) was a cut paper artist whose exquisite flowers, landscapes, architectural subjects, and seascapes attracted the attention of Johann Wilheim of Düsseldorf, Rachel Ruysch's great patron. He bought a number of Ryberg's cut paper pieces for his enormous art gallery, which included paintings by Rembrandt and Rubens.

Before 1800, most women artists were born into artistic families and learned their craft from male masters who were relatives, usually fathers or brothers. Unfortunately, the work of these well-trained women has often been credited to their teachers or to the most famous men of the familial artistic dynasty because of the work's general stylistic similarity.

The problem of misattribution of works affected even the most celebrated women artists. Until recently, Leyster's genre scenes were credited to Frans Hals. In 1723, one year after her election to the French Royal Academy of Art, flower painter Margaretha Haverman (1693–after 1750) was expelled; the academicians (all men) ruled that her *morceau de réception* was the work of her teacher, Jan van Huysum. Contemporary scholars agree, however, that the painting was from her hand.

It was common for women artists to marry artists. Most married women from the Netherlands signed their work with their maiden names—a bride was not required to forfeit her maiden name and assume her husband's. Although pastel portraitist Anna Charlotte van der Haer (1748–1802) and Judith Leyster produced little art after their marriages, many other Netherlandish women were able to sustain a steady artistic production throughout their lives. One extraordinary case is that of Rachel Ruysch. Ruysch painted for some 65 years and bore 10 children to her husband, portraitist Juriaen Pool II, who in midlife apparently gave up his painting career to support and promote his wife's much more brilliant one. Ruysch painted her finest pictures during her childbearing years.

By the beginning of the eighteenth century, it was no longer unusual in the Low Countries for a woman to practice art as a living. Painters' guilds had numerous women members, particularly the Confrerie [Brotherhood] Pictura in The Hague.

References. Germaine Greer, *The Obstacle Race* (New York, 1979); Arnold Houbraken, *De Groote Schouburgh der Nederlantsche Konstschilders en Schilderessen*, 3 vols. (1718, 1719, 1721); facsimile ed., Amsterdam, 1976); Chris Petteys, *Dictionary of Women Artists: An International Dictionary of Women Artists Born before 1900* (Boston, 1985); Ann Sutherland and Linda Nochlin, *Women Artists: 1550–1950* (Cat. for exhibition, Los Angeles, 1977); U. Thieme and F. Becker, *Allgemeines Lexikon der bildenden Künstler*, 37 vols. (Leipzig, 1907–1950); Johan van Gool (*De Nieuwe Schouburgh der Nederlantsche Kunstschilders en Schilderessen*, 2 vols. (1750–1751; facsimile ed., Soest, 1971).

MARIANNE BERARDI

NEW DEAL (1933–1941). During the New Deal, a women's network of political allies and personal friends, centered around Eleanor Roosevelt (ER), acted as a pressure group vis-à-vis the Democratic Party and the federal government, demanding that women's issues be given attention and that women be given prominent roles in government. Roosevelt and her cohorts' quest for women's political participation was part of a larger reform effort. Like female reformers of the Progressive Era and the 1920s, the New Deal women were dedicated to female and child labor reform, education, public health, and eradicating the problems of unemployment. They believed women, because of their experience and, to some extent, their nature, were particularly committed to, and capable of dealing with, these issues; they were determined to enlarge women's participation in the civic community. Furthermore, the reformers believed such issues could no longer be dealt with through traditional voluntarism: they were political and governmental concerns requiring trained professionals. New Deal women thus fought for their right to participate in politics and government along with men.

From the beginning of Franklin Delano Roosevelt's (FDR) presidency, women played greater roles in the federal government than ever before. ER and friend Molly Dewson, onetime social worker and activist in the National Consumers League (NCL) and now head of the Women's Division of the Democratic Party, pressured FDR aide Postmaster General James Farley to grant women high-level positions in the New Deal. In part, they wanted to place talented women committed to reform, but they also believed women who were active in the 1932 Democratic campaign should receive patronage, as did the men. ER and Dewson's most important achievement was the appointment of Frances Perkins as secretary of labor, the first female cabinet officer in U.S. history. Also a former social worker, Perkins had been active in New York progressive reform circles and was New York industrial commissioner under then-governor Roosevelt.

Most New Deal appointments for women were in areas focusing on the conditions of women and children. Mary Anderson continued her post in the Women's Bureau and Grace Abbot in the Children's Bureau; both were under Perkins' Department of Labor. Ellen Woodward headed up the women's projects in the Federal Emergency Relief Agency (FERA) and the Civil Works Administration (CWA). Women also tended to cluster in the temporary advising boards, for example, Emily Newell Blair of the National Recovery Administration (NRA) consumer advisory board or Rose Schneiderman of the NRA's labor advisory board. All were known to ER and Dewson through their activities in the Women's Trade Union League, the NCL, the League of Women Voters, social welfare work, or the Women's Division of the Democratic Party. Personal friendship was also an important aspect of their ties. Mary McLeod Bethune, founder and president of Bethune-Cookman College, headed the Office of Minority Affairs for the National Youth Administration. She led FDR's "black cabinet," which pushed for black rights, and she was closely connected with ER, but as an African American, she remained outside the personal network of Mrs. Roosevelt's political allies, and she viewed herself as representing the interests of blacks rather than women.

While positions for women concentrated in traditionally "female" areas, ER and her cohorts were also interested in widening opportunities for women in other areas. When the First Lady instituted her weekly press conferences in 1933, she opened them only to female reporters because she was concerned that unless more work for them was generated, newspaperwomen would soon face unemployment. Along with the National Woman's Party (NWP) the New Dealers fought for the repeal of legislation that, from 1932 to 1937, prohibited federal employment for anyone whose spouse was also a federal employee.

For New Deal women, however, questions of economic and Social Security for poor women were higher priorities than the extension of political and social rights of women per se. Their early opposition to the Equal Rights Amendment stemmed from their rightful fear that the amendment would eliminate protective labor legislation for working-class women. By the same token, in 1933, when codes to improve working conditions and wages were being written for industries participating in the NRA, the women pushed hard to have jobs that were heavily dominated by women included in the regulations; they also fought, although not always successfully, for equal pay for equal work.

Concern for poor women motivated New Deal activists to focus attention on the lack of relief for unemployed females. The federal relief programs of the New Deal were originally oriented toward men. In November
1933, ER organized a White House Conference on the Emergency Needs
of Women to focus attention on unemployed women's needs. By the end
of 1933, some 100,000 jobs (out of 2 million) had been allocated to women
under the FERA and the CWA, both under the direction of Ellen Woodward. At the urging of Secretary Perkins and Eleanor Roosevelt, female
counterparts to the Civil Conservation Corps camps were set up under the
FERA; by 1935, 28 camps for girls were in operation under the direction
of Hilda Smith, former director of the Bryn Mawr College summer school
for women workers.

Reformers' efforts to provide adequate relief for women met with little
success. Most women participating in relief projects were confined to menial, poorly paid jobs that provided little training for future decent employment. Only a small minority found jobs as a result of vocational
training and placement guidance at the youth camps. While the New Deal
women often expressed frustration about the problems, they failed to confront the reality that as long as the larger job market remained so sex-
segregated, there were constraints in providing women with decent job
training or opportunities in relief agencies. The CWA, for example,
achieved its greatest success for women in providing clerical work, one of
the few areas of expanding opportunity in the general occupational structure. The New Deal activists did not focus attention on the lack of opportunities for women in the larger job market, partly because while they
believed that some, particularly single, women would enter professions as
ongoing careers, they assumed most wanted, and ought to concentrate on,
homemaking and child rearing.

If the New Deal failed to adequately address women's needs, the female
activists did see implementation of crucial elements of the welfare state for
which they had crusaded over decades. Frances Perkins was a key figure in
the passage of legislation regulating working conditions, old age insurance,
and unemployment compensation. The Fair Labor Standards Act (FLSA)
of 1937 set a federal minimum wage that covered both men and women
(although a number of occupations, heavily dominated by women, were
first exempt, the FLSA has been extended since); it also set maximum hours
for men and women and prohibited child labor in most occupations. In
addition to instituting old age insurance and a permanent system of unemployment compensation, the Social Security Act of 1935 provided aid
to dependent children, some public health services, and maternal and infant
care. For women who had worked so hard for mother's pension programs
on the state level, and for the short-lived federal Shepherd–Towner Act
(1921–1929) providing for maternal and infant care, the provisions of the
Social Security Act aimed at poor children and mothers must have been

particularly satisfying triumphs. In an earlier age, even during the Progressive years, such causes and the women who championed them may have been marginal in terms of power politics; however, with the crisis of the depression, the welfare state became a reality, and female welfare reformers moved closer to center stage to help implement and enforce the new laws of the land.

References. Joan Hoff-Wilson and Marjorie Lightman (eds.), *Without Precedent, the Life and Career of ER* (Bloomington, Ind., 1984); Bonnie Fox Schwartz, "A New Deal for Women? The Civil Works Experience, 1933–34" (paper presented at Vassar College Centennial Conference on "The Vision of Eleanor Roosevelt, Past, Present and Future," October 1984, Poughkeepsie, N.Y.); Susan Ware, *Beyond Suffrage: Women in the New Deal* (Cambridge, Mass., 1981); Nancy Woloch, *Women and the American Experience* (New York, 1984), chs. 17 and 18.

MIRIAM COHEN

"NEW WOMAN" IN VICTORIAN LITERATURE. During the 1890s a group of popular English writers focused on women's issues, including careers, education, alternatives to marriage and motherhood, and freedom for women to express their sexuality. Their works feature women who take advantage of the changes during the nineteenth century and adopt nontraditional roles—new women. The emphasis on all aspects of women's psychology and sexual behavior opened areas that had been taboo and had a profound impact upon modern English fiction.

Favorite subjects of these writers are the ways the feminine role (including innocence about sexuality, marriage, and motherhood and subordination to men) oppressed women. Thus, works by new woman writers show women trapped in unhappy marriages and innocent women and children ravaged by venereal disease as well as more sensational subjects, including adultery, free love, and prostitution.

While contemporary readers and reviewers consistently label certain authors new woman writers, the authors do not set out to establish a school, and their works do not present a consistent view. Some, working from a feminist perspective, suggest that human relationships would improve when more people adopt the ideals of their heroines while others demonstrate that the new woman is a threat. Furthermore, while all new woman writers are frank about sexual matters, some want women to be better informed while others want them to be experienced, too.

As a result, H.E.M. Stutfield divided new woman writers into two groups The "purity school" consisted of Sarah Grand (pseud. for Frances McFall), Iota (pseud. for Kathleen Caffyn), and Grant Allen, while the "neurotic school" included George Egerton (pseud. for Mary Chavelita Dunn), Emma Frances Brooke, Mona Caird, and Menie Muriel Dowie (pseud. for Mrs. Henry Norman).

In addition, Olive Schreiner, Thomas Hardy, George Meredith, and

George Gissing are sometimes classified as new woman writers because they treat the same subjects and focus on the same kind of heroine. The heroine of Schreiner's *The Story of an African Farm* (1883) proposes marriage to one man when she is pregnant by another. Sue Bridehead in *Jude the Obscure* (1896) argues for free love and has four illegitimate children. Gissing's *The Odd Woman* (1893), *In the Year of the Jubilee* (1894), and *The Whirlpool* (1897) and Meredith's *Lord Ormont and His Aminta* (1894) and *The Amazing Marriage* (1895) have characteristics usually associated with the new woman.

The "purity school" seeks to establish an ideal of feminine purity that is derived not from innocence of the world but from knowledge and even experience of it. Grand's *The Heavenly Twins* (1893), usually considered the first new woman novel, focuses on three women. The innocent, Edith Beales, dies after contracting syphilis from her husband; Evadne, learning of her husband's former mistress, refuses to consummate her marriage; and Angelica proposes to her future husband and dresses in masculine clothing to learn more of the world. Other works of the purity school are Iota's *A Yellow Aster* (1894) and Allen's *The Woman Who Did* (1895), *The British Barbarians* (1895), *A Splendid Sin* (1896), and *Miss Cayley's Adventures* (1899). *The Woman Who Did*, the most sensational of new woman novels, features a heroine, Herminia Barton, who not only advocates free love but practices it as well.

Works of the "neurotic school" are more diverse, but a common theme is that women suffer because they struggle alone against a corrupt society, and heroines of these works often succumb to suicidal depression or madness or give up the struggle to achieve anything genuinely new. *Keynotes* (1893) by Egerton, the first of this school, features openly sensual women as well as those who rebel against conventional roles. The publisher, John Lane, was so impressed that he made it the first of a series and commissioned Beardsley to design a cover. *Keynotes* was followed by *Discords* (1894), *Symphonies* (1897) and *Fantasies* (1898), but the latter two volumes were less popular. Other works of this school are Brooke's *A Superfluous Woman* (1894); Caird's *The Daughters of Danaus* (1894), *The Morality of Marriage* (1897), and *The Pathway of the Gods* (1898); and Dowie's *Gallia* (1895) and *The Crook of the Bough* (1898).

Despite obvious differences, all these works feature women who feel free to initiate sexual relationships, to explore alternatives to marriage and motherhood, to adopt careers in nontraditional professions—medicine, science, and business—and to discuss sexual matters. New woman heroines rarely achieve lasting happiness and almost never achieve lasting change, but the emphasis on these subjects and characters helped to destroy the idealized feminine character of earlier Victorian fiction and, therefore, had a liberating effect on twentieth-century English literature.

References. Gail Cunningham, *The New Woman and the Victorian Novel* (New York, 1978); Lloyd Fernando, *"New Women" in the Late Victorian Novel* (University Park, Pa., 1977); Elaine Showalter, *A Literature of Their Own: British Women Novelists from Brontë to Lessing* (Princeton, 1977); H.E.M. Stutfield, "The Psychology of Feminism," *Blackwood's Magazine* (January 1897).

CAROL A. SENF

NEW ZEALAND. Women are 50.5 percent of a population of 3.25 million. Most are of British (Pakeha) descent, with a sizable minority (12.3 percent) of Maori women. British women came to the colony of New Zealand starting in the middle of the nineteenth century, either with their families or as single assisted migrants, destined for domestic labor before and after marriage. In a remote frontier environment where women were essential to the family economy, their role in the family was lauded above all else, an attitude widely prevalent even now, when 85 percent of women live in urban areas. Most New Zealand women are married (54 percent) despite a trend to less formal partnerships, but motherhood is no longer a lifelong occupation now that the average family has only two to three children. Married women make up more than half the female workforce.

Opportunities for Pakeha women in the public sphere came early. Education was seen as the key to advancement for both sexes; the first state high school for girls in the Southern Hemisphere was opened in New Zealand in 1871, and in the same decade the new university was opened to women, many of whom became teachers. By the 1890s women were graduating in medicine and law as well. However, the momentum was not maintained. Women are still less highly educated than men: only half as many hold university degrees. In teaching, although the majority of primary teachers are women, few are heads of schools; in secondary, and even more in tertiary, education, few women achieve top posts. There are signs of a change in attitude and positive moves toward equal opportunity policies, notably in the state sector, but economic constraints tend to delay change. The universities, including the medical and law schools, have just reached parity between the sexes in their intake. Women in the professions face systemic discrimination, such as the need to choose between postgraduate study and children or the difficulty of buying into legal partnerships. At a less specialized level of employment, most women are employed in clerical, sales, and related work. In spite of equal pay legislation in place since 1972, the average female wage is only three-quarters of the male wage. Maori women are most disadvantaged in employment as well as in educational opportunities.

The national passion for sports has not traditionally extended to much support for women's sports, although individual achievers have been greatly admired. The world success of the 1987 women's netball team set a new level in media coverage and popular support.

In the arts, writers Katherine Mansfield (1888–1923) and Janet Frame (b. 1924), painter Frances Hodkins (1869–1947), and singer Kiri Te Kanawa (b. 1944) are outstanding. The current of female talent in the arts is running strongly.

The women's movement in New Zealand has followed a pattern of early strength, decline, and revival. Women organized through the Women's Christian Temperance Movement to claim the vote by 1893 and set up a forward-thinking National Council of Women three years later, but the impetus was lost early in this century, and the opportunities opened to women during the two world wars proved only temporary. The interwar years saw a proliferation of women's organizations, typically moderate and rather elitist. With the new wave of feminism of the 1970s came a new energy and a new radicalism for both Pakeha and Maori women. The role and status of women in New Zealand are being studied by such groups as the Society for Research on Women, the Women's Studies Association, and the Maori Women's Welfare League, all of which publish their findings. Women are demanding full equality in employment, including the quality child care that must underpin it, and the right to take fuller responsibility for their own health and fertility control. Maori women, while sharing the concern for health issues especially, are also assuming a higher profile, alongside Maori men, in reclaiming rights over land used by the European settlers since last century.

In public life, early advance was followed by a period of stagnation, which is now ended. Only in 1933, 40 years after female franchise was introduced, did the first woman cabinet minister take office. The present Parliament, with 14 women, including three ministers, out of 97 members, has much the highest proportion of women to date. A most significant development has been the establishment of a Ministry of Women's Affairs (1985) to scrutinize legislation as it affects women and to make known to government the concerns of women in the community. In local government there has been a dramatic increase in the number of women elected in the 1980s.

References. Statistics are from the 1986 census, and the New Zealand Department of Statistics, *Profile of Women* (Wellington, 1985). See also Barbara Brookes, Charlotte Macdonald, and Margaret Tennant (eds.), *Women in History* (Wellington, 1986), which has an extensive bibliography, and Shelagh Cox (ed.), *Public and Private Worlds* (Wellington, 1987). (See also AUSTRALIAN AND NEW ZEALAND WRITERS.)

DOROTHY PAGE

NO-FAULT DIVORCE is the term used for divorce* granted on the basis of "irreconcilable differences" without consideration of fault. California in 1969 instituted the first nonadversarial divorce procedure as a reform to eliminate the hostility and fraud prevalent in adversarial divorce proceedings. The reform quickly swept the country. By 1988 all states had some form of no-fault divorce, but less than half of those adopted California's system, in which either party can unilaterally decide to end the marriage, and only a few followed California in requiring equal division of property. Twenty-two states added no-fault but kept fault-based divorce as well. Retaining both systems allows for economic negotiations between the parties, with resort to the adversarial system as a threat. Several states have simplified divorce proceedings for childless couples to the point that "mail order" divorce, without a court appearance, is permitted.

In the days when proof of adultery or cruelty was needed before a divorce could be granted, there would be bargaining between husband and wife: she would agree to testify to cruel treatment if he would give her sole custody of the children. Under no-fault systems, when her testimony was no longer needed, custody became the battleground and the trade-off often became the granting of custody to the mother in exchange for reduced child support payments. The children were the ultimate victims of the change. Women and children suffer an average drop of 30 percent in living standards, while the income of most men increases considerably.

Groups working to modify or eliminate no-fault divorce charge that it victimizes women and children, citing its effects on displaced middle-aged and elderly homemakers and statistics indicating that one-quarter of all children live in single-parent homes. Advocates for battered women, on the other hand, contend that ending no-fault divorce will make it harder for women to leave abusive relationships and that fear of retaliation will keep them from testifying to the abuse in court. Those opposed to ending no-fault divorce also contend that doing so would do little to reduce the number of divorces; it would bring a return to the acrimony and hostility that accompany fault-based divorce.

For these reasons, a two-tiered divorce system is being considered in Michigan and Iowa. Divorce would be simple if both parties agreed to it or if there were no children; otherwise, waiting periods would increase and the process would be made more difficult. Illinois, Virginia, Washington, and Georgia have expressed interest in similar legislation to protect children and families.

A most controversial revision to no-fault divorce has been enacted into law in Louisiana. Rather than simply revising divorce law, Louisiana has radically changed the law defining marriage. Couples may choose a "contract marriage," the easily dissolved marriage that has existed since the no-fault revolution, or a "covenant marriage," dissolvable only by two years of separation or proof of fault.

References. Los Angeles Times Sunday edition, April 12, 1998; "The Limits of Limits on Divorce," Yale Law Journal 107, 5 (1998): 1435–1465.

NONVERBAL COMMUNICATION is an area of social psychology examining behaviors that allow both the sending and receiving of information that may be redundant to spoken language but often provides information additional to it. Nonverbal behaviors serve a number of functions. They may either supplement or negate verbal messages and also provide insight into the emotional states of, and/or relationships between, interactants. Nonverbal behaviors are sufficiently subtle and occur in ways that may be out of the awareness of either the encoder, who sends the message, or the decoder, who receives it. Researchers have concentrated on five major channels of nonverbal behaviors: *paralanguage, kinesics, proxemics, facial expression*, and *visual behavior*.

Paralanguage includes vocal nonverbal aspects of speech and vocal sounds: nonlanguage sounds (yawns, sighs, etc.), nonwords ("er," "humm," etc.) and spoken variables such as intensity, pitch, tempo, regional accents, and speech disturbances, all the information that is conveyed by a spoken message less the semantic meaning of the words. The 1974 U.S. Supreme Court decision that the transcripts of President Nixon's Watergate-related conversations were less informative than the audiotapes pointed out the importance of paralanguage. How something is said may be more meaningful than simply what is said.

Kinesics refers to all discernible bodily movements except facial expressions and eye movements. A distinction is often made between two classes of gestures. *Emphasis gestures*, which supplement verbal messages, are usually directed away from the body. They may be emblematic, may be directly translatable into words such as a wave good-bye, or may illustrate and/or regulate the flow of an ongoing conversation. *Comfort gestures*, directed toward one's body, are, on the other hand, usually indicative of the behaver's emotional state. Scratching, rubbing, or twirling one's hair are examples. Kinesics also includes posture, postural adjustments, and movements through space. Consider the very real difference between the graceful leap of the dancer and the clumsy stagger of the drunk.

Proxemics refers to how people structure, use, and are affected by space and spatial considerations in their interaction with others. The amount of space around and between bodies is an important variable; different social functions are served by various interactional distances. Generally, the space directly around our bodies is reserved for others who by invitation or relationship are allowed intimate proximity. Occasionally, we may have little or no control over this variable, as in a crowded subway or elevator. When this happens, we avoid eye contact, position objects, and decrease communication in an attempt to minimize the impact of the invasion of our personal space. In other settings, the use of furniture and seating arrangements may also mediate spatial usage. Evidence indicates that different amounts of space are culturally appropriate for different types of interaction, based on relationships and the task at hand. Studies of personal space protection and invasion have documented the use of defenses and retreats. How people use and are affected by space varies by culture as well as by sex, age, and personality differences. There is strong evidence that men tend to spread their bodies out and take up more space than do women, even after relative body size is controlled for. Included in proxemics is research of the most proximal of behaviors: touching. Touching signals and demands involvement such as aggression, affiliation, or sexual interest. Research into female–male differences indicates that women and men evaluate and respond to the touch of another person in different ways. North American women not only touch same-sex others more often than men do but evaluate the touch of others based on their relationship with the toucher and the situation in which touch occurs. Men seem predisposed to evaluate the touch of a woman as sexual in nature. Men also touch women more than women touch men; one might speculate that this is a masculine power ploy since touching, as opposed to being touched, signals power and status in same-sex interactions such as between employer and employee.

Facial expressions may be the most important channel for nonverbal communication. It is the face more than any other bodily part to which others attend. Historically, research on facial expression has addressed the universality and classification of various displays and the use of facial display in the sending and attribution of emotion or mood. The intricate muscles of the human face allow for a variety of expressions, which researchers have examined in cross-cultural and even cross-species contexts.

Arising out of the facial display literature, *visual behavior* has become a separate area of research. Based on the fundamental significance that interpersonal gaze plays in human interaction, this is not surprising. Visual interaction signals involvement with another. It is also an important moderator in the giving and taking of the floor inherent in normal conversation. The eyes are used to signal attention, understanding, and puzzlement and provide feedback. Visual behavior has been shown to be an important variable in social encounters such as aggression, attraction, and self-defense and in situations involving power and dominance. The stare may be interpreted as a threat or flirtation depending on the situation and the relationship between interactants. Higher ratios of looking while speaking to, looking while listening (*visual dominance behavior*) have been shown to affect both the encoding and decoding of power in an interpersonal context. Research has shown that when women and men interact in a setting of equal power, men visually behave as if they are in high power position, while women show normal visual behavior. When men interact with men in similar settings, they do not exhibit such visual dominance behavior. Other important areas of gaze research have focused on sex, cultural, and personality differences. Lastly, there is also speculative research into the role of pupillary dilation as an unconscious indicator of interest in what is being viewed.

Probably the most important factor with regard to all nonverbal behaviors and their meaning, singly and in combination, is the social context in which they occur. Behaviors "mean" different things in different situations.

In some settings, touching, staring, being close, whispering, and smiling are likely to be signs of intimacy, maybe even part of courtship. In another setting, they may indicate a fight is imminent. On a broader level, there is good evidence that nonverbal behaviors are, for the most part, learned behaviors that differ from culture to culture. Interacting with someone of a different culture may lead to "language problems" of a nonverbal nature.

Many differences between women and men in their use of, and response to, nonverbal behaviors parallel differences associated with interpersonal power and status. It is unclear whether these are diffuse status characteristics, merely reflecting existing power inequity, or are evidence of a strategy of dominance covertly employed by males to perpetuate such differences. One conclusion from the literature argues that women are more sensitive to nonverbal behaviors than are men, perhaps because that information and its monitoring are more important to those who have traditionally been subjected to socially disadvantaged positions, or it may also be based on the traditional feminine gender role of intuitiveness, self-disclosure, and social sensitivity.

Lastly, nonverbal behavior has been cited as having potential for those seeking to explore more unbiased or comfortable personal styles (i.e., nonsexist and/or assertive). Because nonverbal behaviors are "low in profile," and one is generally held less accountable for their display, they may be a fruitful "testing ground" for someone attempting to effect personal change. However, there is a potential disadvantage, from a feminist perspective, in that men may misinterpret such behavior. The possibility for perpetuation of sexual inequality (predominantly, but not exclusively, by males) through subtle and not so subtle means may be both a strategy and a result of the use of nonverbal behaviors.

References. S. L. Ellyson and J. F. Dovidio, *Power, Dominance, and Nonverbal Behavior* (New York, 1985); N. M. Henley, *Body Politics* (Englewood Cliffs, N.J., 1977).

STEVE L. ELLYSON

NORWAY. Modern Norwegian women's history and politics are located at the intersection of women's tripartite roles as earners, mothers, and citizens. For example, various late nineteenth- and early twentieth-century women's movements championed women's right to education and employment, "voluntary motherhood," and suffrage. The labor movement in the first half of the twentieth century focused on the promotion of a family wage and the development of welfare state employment-related services, for example, unemployment insurance and pensions. After World War II the welfare state vastly expanded its reproductive services, such as child care, family allowances, and maternity leaves. From the 1970s, the new women's movement framed issues in more explicitly feminist terms, taking up such issues as abortion rights and women's political representation.

Presently, Norwegian women's studies scholars are debating the extent to which the Scandinavian welfare state is gendered. They are also examining the organization and quality of social care work in light of new threats to the funding of welfare state programs.

Current Conditions. *Demography.* The low infant mortality rate of 5.0 (per 1,000 live births in 1993) is similar to that of other Scandinavian countries and consistent with the priority Norway places on universally accessible, high-quality health care for pregnant women and their infants. Perhaps responding to pro-natalist national policies, more women than ever are becoming mothers, but fewer of them are having more than one or two children. The total fertility rate per woman declined from 2.9 in 1960 to 1.9 in 1993. The average household of 2.18 persons (1989) masks the fact the 47.9 percent of Norwegian households consists of a single adult (in 1993). Add to this the 4.4 percent of households consisting of a single parent and children (in 1993), and the majority of Norwegian households have only one adult member. Household size is related to the relatively low marriage rate of 4.5 (per 1,000 persons in 1993), a divorce rate of 2.54 (per 1,000 people in 1993), the 36.0 percent (1990) of births out of wedlock, and the longer life expectancy of women (80.3) relative to men (74.2) in 1993.

Welfare State Benefits. The number of single adult households might also be attributed to the post–World War II expansion of welfare state reproductive services that lessened the economic dependence of individual women and their children on individual men. In 1992 these services included 2 weeks of full paid leave prior to the birth and 33 weeks of parental leave at full pay after birth (or 42 weeks at 80 percent pay), a maternity grant for mothers who are not earners, 10 days a year leave to care for sick children, and family allowances for all children up to age 16. Services are expanded for single parents, with an extra 10 days of child sick leave and one extra family allowance above the number of children. Medical services of birthing, as well as pre- and postnatal care, are provided free by the public health care system.

Although the state and municipalities supported 81.4 percent of the costs of paid infant and child day care in 1987, unconditional access to public day care is not defined as a parental right by the Norwegian welfare state. In 1989 almost 70 percent of mothers with children under the age of 3 were in the workforce, but only 10 percent of the children had access to public child care. In 1992, of all children age 0–6, only 40 percent were in child care centers. Shortages are, however, perceived as a problem within the welfare state goal of universal, publicly supported, high-quality early childhood education.

The reproductive rights of women include the right to state-funded abortion on demand up to the 12th week of pregnancy and, after that, subject to the approval of two doctors, and to free contraceptive counseling.

Economic and Political Status. In 1994 women represented 45.8 percent of the labor force, up from 23 percent in 1960. Their labor force partici- pation rate rose from 50.6 percent in 1973 to 72.8 percent in 1988. The rise in women's labor force participation rate is concentrated in service sector jobs, especially in the public sector, where 70 percent of the em- ployees are women and in part-time employment. In 1989, 48 percent of employed women were working part-time. Women make up 30 percent of the 75,000 members of the Norwegian Federation of Trade Unions. In 1951 Norway ratified the International Labor Organization convention on equal pay for equal work. In 1993 women's wages as a percentage of men's were 87 percent in industry and 76 percent in clerical work. The continuing difference in wages is largely attributable to the fact that Norway has the most sex-segregated labor force of the Nordic countries, with 85 percent of women in female-dominated jobs.

Since the 1970s, Norway has been noted for the number of women in politics, including Gro Harlem Brundtland, the prime minister, and 40–50 percent of the other ministries. Women comprise about one-third of the members of Parliament and of the county and municipal councils. The increase in women's political representation is attributed to the women's movement's promotion of gender consciousness in the candidates list and in voting, including advocating the use of 40 percent sex quotas.

The Equal Status Council (Likestillingsrådet) was established by Parlia- ment in 1972 to "work for equal status in all sectors of society, family life, working life, education and the community in general."

History. The end of the nineteenth century saw a push for women's rights, including suffrage. Among the organizations supporting equal rights was the Norwegian Association for the Rights of Women, established in 1882, which promoted educational, economic, and legal rights. Suffrage organizations included the Association for Women's Suffrage, founded in 1885, and the more militant National Association for Women's Suffrage, formed in 1898. After suffrage was achieved in 1913, women continued to promote women's interests through various types of organizations, includ- ing women's sections of trade unions and political parties, as well as the Norwegian National Council of Women (NKN), an umbrella organization founded in 1904.

An issue related to women's economic and political rights was the pro- motion of women's reproductive rights in the form of "voluntary moth- erhood," led by Katti Anker Møller of the women's movement within the Labor Party. The voluntary motherhood movement, promoting women's right to contraceptives and abortion, questioned the equivalence of interests of women with those of family and children at a time when most women did not question it.

The voluntary motherhood movement also articulated the ideal that motherhood was a profession; this conception of motherhood supported Labor Party's proposals for a mother's wage. These ideals came to fruition in 1946 in the form of the more gender-neutral "family allowance" and in 1966 in the National Insurance Act benefits for single parents.

A new women's movement arose in Norway in the early 1970s, the main branches of which were the New Feminists and the Women's Front. The difference between them was largely defined by whether they placed the stress on gender or class, respectively. The Lesbian Movement arose in 1975 from the new women's movement. As a whole, the new women's movement arose to confront the gap between the vaunted ideal of equality and the actual position of women. It differed from previous women's movements in the degree to which it constructed a distinctly gendered consciousness. It raised issues, such as abortion on demand, choice of sexuality, pornography as offensive to women, and opposition to domestic abuse, all of which politicized what had usually been seen as questions of personal life. Their opposition to Norway's membership in the European Economic Community (now the European Union) was also a distinctly gendered opposition. They feared that Norwegian women would have less access to a distant European bureaucracy than they had to their own political institutions and that they would face threats to the reproductive services of the welfare state. The organizational structure of new women's movement organizations was nonhierarchical and radical and therefore in conflict with mainstream political channels. The crisis centers, which they established, were initially run with nonhierarchical structures, but with their institutionalization and concomitant government funding came more highly structured and regulated decision making.

They met with early support from the political parties of the Left and older, women's rights organizations in their campaign for abortion on demand. Active opposition from the officials of state church and other Christians and a split in the Venstre Socialister between the Christian socialists and others delayed passage of legislation permitting abortion on demand in the first 12 weeks of pregnancy until 1978. The closeness of the vote portended the continuing anti-abortion activism of today.

The campaign to increase the percentage of women in government and politics had two basic strategies; one was legislative—the Equal Status Act—and the other was consciousness raising* and organizing to promote women's voting for women candidates. Using the possibility in the voting law, women voters moved female candidates up on the list or replaced a male candidate's name with a woman's and succeeded in raising the number of women elected by 5–15 percent in the 1967 and 1971 elections. They were also successful in getting the socialist Left and Liberal parties to institute 40 percent sex quotas on their candidates list. Article 21 of the Equal Status Act of 1978 requires all national and local appointed committees to nominate at least 40 percent of both sexes. In general, the act advocates equal rights for women and men in employment, politics, and education.

Current Debates. Women's studies scholars and "state feminists" in Norway debate whether the Norwegian welfare state is woman-friendly, as evidenced by state-supported child care and parental leaves, or whether it is a form of public patriarchy, as evidenced by the fact that women take parental leave, by the shortage of public child care, and by the sex-segregated labor force. All agree, however, that what Kari Waerness calls "carework" is still very much women's work, both in the private and in the public spheres. She argues that recent criticisms of public carework as insufficiently caring and new demands for more community-based care are not reasons to privatize caring any more than it already is. Rather, these criticisms and demands should be seen as public support for a new form of rationality—"rationality of caring." Such a rationality would bring aspects of women's work as private carers, that it is both work and caring, into the public sphere. Arnlaug Leira argues that until equal status policies take gender relations in the private sphere seriously, efforts to achieve real gender equality will fail. She predicts increasing political conflicts over the welfare state but sees hopeful signs in the numbers of women in government and politics and in the fact that women are more likely to support the continuing and expansion of welfare state provisions than men are.

References. Arnlaug Leira, *Welfare States and Working Mothers: The Scandinavian Experience* (Cambridge, 1992); Kari Waerness, "On the Rationality of Caring," in Anne Showstack Sassoon (ed.), *Women and the State* (London, 1992).

LYNN WALTER

NORWAY. Norwegian Writers trace their roots back to Dorothe Engelbretsdatter (1634–1716), the first woman both to publish and to make writing her career. She wrote in the popular genres of the seventeenth century, that is, poetry, psalms, and songs, and was, in turn, one of her time's most popular poets. Two hundred years later Camilla Collett (1813–1895) established the popular genre of her century with the publication of *Amtmandens døttre* (1854–1855; The District Governor's Daughters), the first modern novel of Norway. Prose became the medium par excellence for writers of the nineteenth and twentieth centuries, though they experimented with the drama and developed the poetic tradition of Engelbretsdatter.

Amtmandens døttre is a sociopolitical portrayal of the inhibiting influences of society, the family, and marriage on the growth of young women. Collett's Sophie yearns to discover herself. But external and internal pressures to become the dutiful wife of a superior man defeat her, and, relinquishing herself, she retreats into a traditional marriage. Criticized for painting an uncomplimentary picture of the family, Collett replied that people were not yet ready for the truth. *Amtmandens døttre* became the prototype for the novel of women's "education" for the next 100 years.

Amalie Skram (1846–1905) was one of the great prose writers of the nineteenth century, if the public was even less ready for her truth. Collett had defined the novel. Skram defined the naturalistic novel, depicting bourgeois society as not only inhibiting but deadly to women's growth. Her debut novel was *Constancè Ring* (1885), a scathing portrayal of marriage and the patriarchal family and an open examination of female sexuality within their confines. Skram's focus was Constance, who takes her own life after a series of painful confrontations with men and, through them, her repressed sexual longings. Skram wrote three other marriage novels, all of them brilliant, if disillusioned, psychological studies of women whose natures are fatally corrupted by traditional norms. In her two romans à clef, *Professor Hieronimus* (1895) and *På Sct. Jørgen* (1895; At St. Jørgen's) Skram exposed the misuse of modern medical science by men of power to control the minds of women. In Skram's hands the novel became a sophisticated instrument through which she probed the pathology of both society and female psychology.

Twentieth-century writers have built on the strong prose tradition of Collett and Skram. Representative among them are, first of all, Sigrid Undset (1882–1949), one of five women to win the Nobel Prize. She debuted in 1907 but first roused public attention and ire with her novel *Jenny* (1913), about a young Norwegian painter in Rome, longing to find fulfillment as a woman and an artist. Ending with Jenny's suicide, the novel is a Freudian exploration of a woman's crippling ambivalence toward her own creativity and sexuality. Undset is best known for the epic trilogy *Kristian Lavransdatter* (1920–1922), in which she richly re-created medieval Norway, torn between pagan and Christian traditions. But once again she took up the question of a (modern) woman's creative/procreative/erotic nature in the more robust character of Kristin, torn like her country between her duty to herself as lover (the pagan) and her duty to others as wife and mother (the Christian). Undset remained ambivalent throughout her own life as to which role provided a woman her greatest fulfillment. Publicly she disassociated herself from the feminist movement. At the same time she was one of the most prolific writers of the first half of the century, writing contemporary and medieval novels, short stories, plays, essays, and cultural history.

Cora Sandel (Sara Fabricius, 1880–1974), like Undset, worked in several different genres. She debuted with her trilogy *Alberte og Jakob* (1926; *Alberta and Jacob*, 1962), *Alberte og friheten* (1931; *Alberta and Freedom*, 1963), and *Bare Alberte* (1939; *Alberta Alone*, 1965). An immediate, extraordinary success, the Alberte books are a feminist "novel of education." With psychological and sociological insight equal to Skram's, if not so disillusioned, Sandel traces Alberte's journey: struggling to express herself as she comes of age in northern Norway, traveling to Paris, where she confronts herself as an artist and a sexual woman, and returning to Norway, where she leaves her husband and child to write on her own, rather than risk losing herself to others. In 1927 Sandel published *En blå sofa* (A Blue Sofa), the first of five short story collections, generally dealing with women but also with men of little power in confrontation with a conventional, discriminating society. In 1945 she published the magnificent *Kranes konditori (Krane's Cafe*, subtitled "Interior with Figures"; Eng. publ. 1968). Stylistically her most radical work, it is a study of the narrow-minded, middle-class milieu at its worst. One day a timid seamstress sits down in Krane's Cafe and refuses to sew any more dresses for the rich ladies of the town. In this nice café for nice people, her revolt is a scandal. Sandel's brand of realism, sharp but understated, sympathetic but unsentimental, is unrivaled in Norway.

Torborg Nedreaas (1906–1987), like Sandel, was a master both of the novel and of the short story. She debuted in 1945 with a collection of short stories, *Bak skapet står øksen* (The Ax Is behind the Cupboard), dealing with the daily life of occupied Norway, most poignantly with the *tysketøser* (the Norwegian girlfriends of German soldiers) who fall victim to the brutality of the occupiers. Nedreaas' first novel, *Av måneskinn gror det ingenting* (1947; *Nothing Grows by Moonlight*, 1987), again about a woman as victim but also about men and patriarchal society in general, is a cry against sexual oppression. In 1950 Nedreaas published *Trylleglasset* (The Magic Prism), one of the finest short story collections of the decade. In it she introduced her character, Herdis, an artistic child, torn between her aesthetic calling and societal demands and responsibilities. Nedreaas followed Herdis' development in the later novels *Musikk fra en blå brønn* (1960; Music from a Blue Well) and *Ved neste nymåne* (1971; By the Next New Moon). The Herdis books are as central to the postwar years as Sandel's Alberte books are to the years between the wars.

In the 1960s Bjørg Vik (b. 1935) was one of the major writers to emerge with three collections of short stories, followed by a novel, *Gråt elskede mann* (Weep Dear Man), in 1970. Writing from an increasingly feminist perspective, Vik for the most part portrays girls and women and their yearning for love in relation to the alienating society that has created and rejected them. The prose tradition has continued to flourish in the 1970s and 1980s. Liv Køltzow (b. 1945), working, like Vik, with both the novel and the short story, published the classic, modern feminist "novel of recognition," *Historien om Eli* (The Story of Eli), in 1975. In a clipped, flat prose style, Køltzow relentlessly depicts the conditions that hinder women's liberation. Herbjørg Wassmo (b. 1942), preoccupied, too, with the oppression of women, but also their capacity for hope and survival, published the first volume of her Tora trilogy in 1981, *Huset med den blinde glass-*

veranda (The House with the Blind Glass Veranda, 1987), exploring the growth of Tora, a sexually abused child who survives, for a time, on her fantasies. Cecilie Løveid (b. 1951) is one of the most experimental and vital writers of the 1970s and 1980s, working with a unique prose/poetry, as in *Sug* (1982; Suck). The title suggests her obsession with the human capacity—constructive and destructive—for longing and love.

The dramatic tradition is slight by comparison to the prose tradition, though women of the late nineteenth century did write plays, generally about women's precarious position in a man's society. Prominent among them were Laura Kieler (1849–1932), Ibsen's model for Nora in *A Doll's House*; Alvilde Prydz (1846–1922); Hulda Garborg (1862–1934); and A. Skram, whose *Agnete* (1893) is the most crafted drama of the period. It is a deeply pessimistic play about the inexorable differences between women's and men's value systems. Twentieth-century writers who have experimented with the drama form are, among others, the prose writers S. Undset and B. Vik, whose *To akter for fem kvinner* (1974; *Two Acts for Five Women*) has been performed in Europe and off-Broadway. C. Løvied is again the most experimental with her acclaimed radio and stage plays such as *Måkespisere* (1983; Seagull Eaters), providing a model for women in the theater arena of the future.

Poetry has been a more expressive medium than the drama. Magdalene Thoresen (1819–1903) published *Digte av en dame* (Poems by a Woman) in 1860. To poetry what Collett was to prose, Thoresen explored the theme of female eros with radical honesty. Twentieth-century poets have elaborated in individual ways upon the themes of love and eros, from the earlier Aslaug Vaa (1889–1965), Inger Hagerup (1905–1984), and Halldis Moren Vesaas (b. 1907) to the later Marie Takvam (b. 1926) and Sidsel Mørck (b. 1937). Woman's longing to merge juxtaposed to the reality of being alone is a pervasive paradox. Poetry has also been a source of humor, for adults and children, as in the hands of Hagerup; or a political weapon, registering the loneliness of the emigrants, as in the hands of Ingeborg Refling Hagen (b. 1895); or our "thing" society, as in Mørck's; or discrimination, as in Takvam's. In their styles these writers have been as varied as the women themselves, from the modernist Kate Næss (b. 1938) to the antimodernist Tove Lie (b. 1942). They share, however, their deep conviction about the preciousness of life. Nature mysticism, common to the Norwegian spirit, strongly informs Norway's women poets.

References. Englestad et al. (eds.), *Norsk kvinnelitteratur historie* (Oslo, 1988); Janet Garton, *Norwegian Women's Writing: 1850–1990* (London, 1993); Faith Ingwersen, "Norwegian Women Writers," in Harald S. Naess (ed.), *A History of Norwegian Literature*, vol. 2 of *A History of Scandinavian Literatures*, ed. by Sven H. Rossel (Lincoln, Nebr., 1993); Elisabeth Møller Jensen et al. (eds.), *Nordisk kvindelitteraturhistorie* (Copenhagen, 1993–1995); Mary Kay Norseng, "A Child's Liberation of Space: H. Wassmo's Huset med den blinde glassveranda," *Scandi-*

navian Studies 58, 1 (1986); Virpi Zuck, "Cora Sandel, a Norwegian Feminist," *Edda* 1 (1981).

MARY KAY NORSENG

NOVELISTS, BRITISH (EIGHTEENTH-CENTURY). Feminine novelists articulated the concerns important to women's lives and fates, 1715–1798. The majority of these novelists present us with a femiocentric story, a text that codes female sexual vulnerability as the controlling motive in female and male behavior; they do so, however, in categorically different modes. Penelope Aubin and Elizabeth Rowe, for example, code this vulnerability in the pious polemic, and Delariviere Manley and Eliza Haywood (in her satiric pieces like *The Court of Caramania*) do so in the *chronique scandeleuse*; Mary Collyer explores female passivity through epistolary fiction. The majority of the writers, however, turn to the romance, the novella, and later the three-volume romance-novel for their metaphoric investigation of the femiocentric state. In the years before 1740 (Richardson's *Pamela; or, Virtue Rewarded* serves as a watershed even for this feminine fiction), all of these modes were used; the years after 1740 witnessed a movement away from these earlier, pure forms, first to parodies and satires of them, then to more serious reproductions of the forms combined with the educational novel and political fiction. By the last decade of the century, the novel of manners had become the prime feminine mode.

In the earlier years, the novelists were concerned with confronting and combating the two controlling feminine ideologies of the age: that of romantic love, based on the assumption that female life gains value only through romantically conceived marriage, and that of female powerlessness, a vision of female life that presents the reader with a very low ceiling of female expectations and aspirations. Romantic love was the reason, it was argued, that women were powerless.

The ideologies were founded on tenets that defined woman as subordinate, submissive, passive. In the opinion of the majority of the feminine writers of the period such acquiescence was no longer viable (if it ever was), either for themselves, for their heroines, or for their readers. They combat these ideologies and assert themselves and their fictions in several ways, most importantly in the presentation of heroines who are split into two selves: virgin and virago. The virgins profess the controlling ideology: they are submissive and acquiescent. The viragos, though minor figures in the early fiction who grow into larger, more complex roles in the later works, express their author's frustration and the antithetical ideology as they display aggressive, independent, even feisty natures. Predictably, however, such characters are not allowed to predominate and survive; the end of their fictions finds them denied any positive state. Yet even the virgins, in the majority of cases, are not permitted a pleasant, happily-ever-after conclusion; instead, their lives, too, end in exile, despair, madness, or death.

Through seemingly inane, yet actually highly sophisticated, femiocentric texts, these eighteenth-century feminine novelists detail the state of the divided female in an effort to present an accurate picture of the feminine eighteenth-century world.

A second way these writers combat female trivialization is through their use of the masquerade set piece. (The masquerade, introduced by Count Heidegger in the very early years of the century, was an established and ubiquitous feature of English life by the 1720s.) The very raison d'être of the masquerade defines its efficacy for these novelists: a disguise, by its very nature, allows one to be an "other," to participate and be someone other than one's real self. Thus, the docile heroine could hide behind the aggressive mask of the gypsy, the submissive shepherdess could become a tyrannical amazon, the quasi-conforming novelist could actually speak her mind. The disguise displays a spirit of liberty, and though an "illusion," the mask is really the true face of the female. The use of the virgin-virago duality, together with the masquerade set piece, allows these novelists to adopt what Nancy K. Miller has labeled a "posture of imposture," a stance that permits them the "cover" of the romance story for their more aggressive, femiocentric texts. They tell a romance story that contradicts the usual expectations. They engage in a process of double writing. Not content merely to adopt a masquerade technique in terms of their female protagonists, these novelists use the cover story of their romance plots to mask their feminist, aggressive intentions and to unmask the facile and fatuous fictions they are supposed to be writing as members of the weaker sex.

Penelope Aubin's (1685–1731) women, for example, are besieged, abducted, seduced, trappaned, raped—there seems to be no crime of which they are not victims; disguise becomes a necessity for existence, and this pervasiveness of the evil is startling even by twentieth-century tastes. Jane Barker (1688–1718) and Mary Davys (1674–1732) exceed all expectations of the genre with, for example, Barker's *Love Intrigues* (1713) when the heroine, Galesia, actually chooses to leave the hero and pursue her own course of study. Mary Davys' *Familiar Letters* (1713) is equally outspoken. Berina clearly and forthrightly speaks of her love for Artander long before he does; the male is left weak and emasculated by such a woman. By far the ringleader is Eliza Haywood (1693–1756), the most popular and prolific of these writers, with about 60 novels and romances to her credit. (She was also the editor of the first magazine written by and for women.) Though she couches her revolutionary tales well within romance confines, she was able to impose her own feminine rhetoric on the forms. Thus it was that the very popular *Philidore and Placentia; or, L'Amour trop Delicat* (1727) was able to have a happy ending; yet Placentia, the heroine, was extraordinarily aggressive, virtually seducing the shy, reserved Philidore. The majority of Haywood's novels, however, do not end happily; *Idalia; or, The Unfortunate Mistress* (1723) is the best example of this tale of horror for the female. Seduced and raped by Floreo, Don Ferdinand, Henriquez, and Don Myrtano, Idalia has no self but functions only as the female mask these men have forced her to adopt. Similarly, tales like *The Perplex'd Dutchess* (1725) or *The Injur'd Husband* (1728) that feature the aggressive, domineering Gigantilla and the Baroness de Tortileé explore the nightmare world of the aggressive female. Yet the conclusions revert back to conventional attitudes, and so Gigantilla and the Baroness are "punished" for their self-assertion. Such outspokenness continued with Sarah Fielding (1710–1768). Her concern with women's position and rights was so strong that she threw caution to the winds, as did her contemporary Charlotte Smith (1749–1806), by disregarding the forms and telling a story very much not of the romance convention. Fielding actually anatomizes the romance genre in *The Cry: A New Dramatic Fable* (1754). In *The History of the Countess of Dellwyn* (1759) she explores the "Circaen Transformation" of the docile Miss Lucum into the Amazonian Countess and clearly uncovers more than one cares to see. Smith even goes so far as to unmask her very own self in her novels, thus totally uncovering the feminine fiction. During both mid- and late century, then, the romance form was meeting great opposition. The women writers with their aggressive texts were accepted enough that Charlotte Lennox (1720–1804) was able to write *The Female Quixote* (1752) and parody the popular romance form while investigating the entire issue of female power. Late in the century, Elizabeth Inchbald's (1753–1821) *A Simple Story* (1791) continues this analysis of the romance form and rings the death knell on the aggressive text. With Jane West (1758–1852) the eighteenth-century feminine writers had mellowed. Late in the century there was less assertiveness in the telling of their stories, together with less aggressive use of the romance form. The way was paved for Jane Austen and her nonthreatening novel of manners. (See MANNERS, NOVEL OF.)

Reference. "Emphasis Added: Plots and Plausibilities in Women's Fiction," *PMLA* 96 (1981): 36–48.

MARY ANNE SCHOFIELD

NOVELISTS, BRITISH (NINETEENTH-CENTURY VICTORIANS), were generally middle-class women who found writing a form of self-expression and a means of financial support. In spite of the impression that women were flooding the market with books, female novelists made up only about 20 percent of the literary profession. This incidence remained true until well into the twentieth century, when opportunities for women's education expanded. It also was held that women took up writing merely for amusement; in fact, many supported themselves and their families with their work. Most managed to balance their domestic and professional duties, since writing could be done at home. To ensure that their fiction would be treated with the same critical objectivity as that of their male counterparts—and to allow a wider range of expression—Victorian women novelists sometimes adopted male pseudonyms.

Of the women who published novels in the Victorian period, four are generally ranked with the major novelists of the day. Charlotte (1816–1855) and Emily (1818–1848) Brontë, Elizabeth Cleghorn Gaskell (1810–1865), and George Eliot (Mary Ann Evans, 1819–1880) are given the same critical attention as Dickens, Thackeray, and Trollope.

The daughters of a Yorkshire clergyman, the Brontës drew much of their imaginative energy from the Yorkshire moors. This atmosphere permeates Emily Brontë's only novel, *Wuthering Heights* (1847). Although not a popular success, its mystical vision of transcendent passion established it as a masterpiece that goes beyond the gothic romances it superficially resembles. Emily Brontë's reputation as a novelist rests on this single work of genius.

Charlotte Brontë's novels are more realistic, but they, too, are unconventional in their handling of passionate love and female self-definition. *Jane Eyre* (1847) was an enormous popular and critical success, although one contemporary critic, Elizabeth Rigby, condemned it as un-Christian and refused to believe that any decent woman could have written it. *Shirley* (1849), Brontë's one attempt at an industrial novel, was based on an 1807–1812 conflict with Yorkshire mill owners. The least successful of her novels, *Shirley* is of interest because of its strong-willed protagonist, Shirley Keeldar. *Villette* (1853) and Brontë's first novel, *The Professor* (published posthumously, 1857), are seen as versions of Charlotte's unrequited love for her Brussels professor, M. Heger, a married man. In 1854 Brontë married her father's curate, Arthur Bell Nichols; she died a year later.

Elizabeth Cleghorn Gaskell was the wife of a Unitarian minister and the mother of four daughters. She was encouraged to write fiction after the death of her infant son, William. Her first novel, *Mary Barton* (1848), draws on her work in the slums of Manchester and empathizes with weavers in their conflict with mill owners. Later in *North and South* (1854–1855) she provides a more sympathetic picture of the manufacturers. A third social-problem novel, *Ruth* (1853), centers on an unmarried mother and argues for a single standard of sexual morality.

Mrs. Gaskell's *Cranford* (1851–1853) was published serially in Dickens' *Household Words*. It began as a series of sketches about a group of elderly widows and spinsters living in genteel poverty in a provincial town. Frequently viewed as a nostalgic look at a dying way of life, *Cranford* suggests the tensions of the emerging industrial age; its domestic realism foreshadows *Wives and Daughters* (1864–1866), which examines family relationships and generational and class conflicts. Mrs. Gaskell's fiction also includes *Sylvia's Lovers* (1863) and *Cousin Phyllis* (1863–1864). A friend of Charlotte Brontë, Gaskell wrote her *Life* in 1857.

Too intellectual to achieve wide popularity, George Eliot used the novel as a vehicle for serious ideas. In spite of her strongly Evangelical education,

Eliot became an agnostic and developed a positivistic, humanistic philosophy that her novels reflect. She lived out of wedlock for nearly 25 years with George Henry Lewes; after Lewes' death she married J. W. Cross (1880).

Most of Eliot's early fiction centers on the ordinary people from her Warwickshire background. *Scenes of Clerical Life* (1857), a collection of three stories, was followed by *Adam Bede* (1859), set in rural preindustrial England. *The Mill on the Floss* (1860) presents the psychological development of Maggie Tulliver; it often is seen as semiautobiographical, reflecting Eliot's own spiritual and emotional struggles as a young woman. *Silas Marner* (1861), also set in rural England, develops Eliot's humanistic morality in a simple, almost Wordsworthian, manner.

Romola (1862–1863), Eliot's only historical romance, is set in fifteenth-century Florence. *Felix Holt, the Radical* (1866) moves back to modern England and the politics of the Reform Bill. Eliot's masterpiece, *Middlemarch* (1871–1872), illustrates her theories of character development and personal responsibility through a focus on several groups of characters rather than a single individual. It also addresses the issue of women in the nineteenth century. Her last novel, *Daniel Deronda* (1876), applies her theories to society life; its overt didacticism is a characteristic weakness. All of Eliot's novels show characters confronted with significant moral choices; her primary concern is with their complex inner lives.

Many female novelists of the period were both more prolific and more popular than the Brontës, Gaskell, and Eliot. Writers of sensational fiction Mary Elizabeth Braddon (1835–1915) and Mrs. Henry Wood (Ellen Price, 1814–1887) produced enormous quantities of work. Braddon, whose *Lady Audley's Secret* (1862) sold nearly a million copies, wrote over 80 novels during her career; in addition to sensational novels, she wrote historical fiction and novels of manners. Mrs. Henry Wood wrote over 50 novels; her sensational *East Lynne* (1861) was a best-seller. Both Braddon and Wood were known for their unusual combination of domestic conventions and sensational matter.

Writers of romantic fiction included Ouida (Marie Louise Ramee, 1839–1908) and Marie Corelli (Mary Mackay, 1855–1924). Ouida's most popular romances were *Under Two Flags* (1867) and *Moths* (1880). Corelli, one of the best-selling novelists of the late nineteenth century, was best known for *The Sorrows of Satan* (1895), which sold more copies than any previous novel in English.

Female novelists often used the novel for moral purposes and for encouragement of social reform. Harriet Martineau (1802–1876) expressed her interest in Utilitarian political philosophy in didactic stories and somewhat more tempered novels, including *Deerbrook* (1839) and *The Hour of Man* (1841), a historical novel. Dinah Maria Mulock Craik (1826–1887) wrote a best-seller, *John Halifax, Gentleman* (1856), which chronicled the rags-to-riches story of a morally superior young man. Charlotte Mary Yonge (1832–1901), strongly influenced by the Tractarian movement, published nearly 75 novels and donated the profits to charity; *The Heir of Redclyffe* (1853) was a best-seller.

In addition to her travel books and other writings, Frances Trollope (1780–1863) supported her family with her novels. Mrs. Humphry Ward (Mary Augusta, 1851–1920) was active in the literary world and saw herself as a successor to George Eliot; *Robert Elsmere* (1888) was a best-seller, and she produced numerous other novels in the last part of the century. One of the most prolific writers of the period, Margaret Oliphant (1828–1897) was another example of a woman who supported her family (and her brother's) with her writing. She wrote novels of Scottish life—*Katie Stewart* (1853) and *Kirsteen* (1890)—and an acclaimed series of novels, *The Chronicles of Carlingford* (1863–1876). Scores of other female novelists wrote for a combination of pleasure, purpose, and profit in the Victorian period.

References. Sandra M. Gilbert and Susan Gubar, *The Madwoman in the Attic* (New Haven, Conn., 1979); Ellen Moers, *Literary Women* (New York, 1977); Elaine Showalter, *A Literature of Their Own* (Princeton, 1977); Michael Wheeler, *English Fiction of the Victorian Period* (New York, 1985).

SHARON LOCY

NOVELISTS, BRITISH (TWENTIETH-CENTURY). The most important British woman novelist of the century is, without doubt, Virginia Woolf (1882–1941). She is best known for her special adaptations of stream of consciousness to a form of interior monologue that grows increasingly experimental from *Mrs. Dalloway* to *The Waves*. Using what she called her tunneling method, she gives temporal dimension to characters depicted in the immediacy of their present existence by providing them with a rich consciousness of their own past. Since the 1970s the political concerns of her novels that were once ignored have been recognized, especially by American feminists who reevaluated her less acclaimed novels *The Voyage Out* (1915), *Night and Day*, (1919), *The Years* (1937), and *Between the Acts* (1941). The same preoccupations with the economic oppression of women and the relation between social institutions and war that are clearly articulated in her book-length essays *A Room of One's Own* and *Three Guineas* have now been recognized as informing elements in all her novels. Nevertheless, her greatest achievement as a novelist is the creation of her characters' sensuous apprehension of reality. Woolf uses language to get closer and closer to the experience of felt life: sailing off the coast of England, walking out into Bond Street on a June morning, watching the stroke of light from a lighthouse on a floor, looking into the heart of a crocus. In some of the most arresting moments of her most successful novels, *Mrs. Dalloway* (1925), *To the Lighthouse* (1927), and *The Waves* (1931), she has almost obliterated the distinction between poetry and prose.

Actually, Dorothy Richardson (1873–1957) preceded Woolf in her experimentation, publishing in 1915 the first novel in a series that eventually grew into 13 volumes of fictionalized autobiography called *Pilgrimage*. (After the publication of Richardson's first 3 books, May Sinclair applied the term "stream of consciousness" to them, using William James' phrase for the first time in literary criticism.) In 1938, when 12 of the books were published together for the first time in a four-volume edition, the heroine Miriam Henderson's adventures extended from *Pointed Roof* to *Dimple Hill*, from her experiences as a teacher at Fraülein Pfaff's school in Hanover to her life with a Quaker family in Sussex. The most engrossing and sustained excursion into stream of consciousness is Miriam's long walk in *Revolving Lights*. In 1967 a new edition of *Pilgrimage* came out, including for the first time a final book, *March Moonlight*, which rounds off Miriam's experiences through her encounter with Mr. Noble, the man who will become her husband.

May Sinclair (1865–1946) and Rose Macaulay (1881–1958) were both popular novelists of the same period. At great length in *Mary Olivier* (1919) and in small compass in *Life and Death of Harriet Frean* (1922), May Sinclair writes about unmarried daughters' relations with their tyrannical parents. Rose Macaulay treats similar situations more satirically. Her essay-novels (such as *Told by an Idiot* [1923]) are full of speculations as well as very articulate and comic characters. Perhaps her best novel is a much later one, *The Towers of Trebizond* (1956), which combines fiction and the travelogue.

One of the most promising novelists of the 1920s and 1930s, Winifred Holtby (1898–1935), died young. Her posthumously published novel *South Riding* (1936) has been an "underground classic" for generations. The novel documents the functioning of county government in Yorkshire, but it also embodies a conflict between passion and a lack of shared values, the struggle between a thinking woman like Sarah Burton and a traditional man like the fox-hunting Carne, whom she loves. *The Crooked Street* (1924), another Yorkshire novel, depicts the same kind of conflict between Muriel Hammond and Godfrey Neale. In both novels women's relations with each other as fellow workers occupy a large place.

Ivy Compton-Burnett (1884–1969) has created one of the most distinctive styles of the century. From the 1920s through the 1960s, she produced approximately four novels each decade. Among the most important are *Pastors and Masters* (1925), *A Family and a Fortune* (1939), *Parents and Children* (1941), and *Mother and Son* (1955). All of her novels are family-centered and take place in late Victorian or Edwardian England. They are composed almost entirely of highly stylized dialogue and culminate in scenes of revelation and discovery. Letters and photographs contribute to almost Wildean moments of hilarious exposure of human foibles; meals create the ebb and flow of action and talk in which money uncovers hidden hypocrisies. Fairy-tale qualities combine with dry, psychological analysis to undermine any sense of human control of events, and people become wooden pieces in the chesslike movements of her elaborately structured plots.

Although the Anglo-Irish novelist Elizabeth Bowen (1899–1973) has received less critical attention than she deserves, at least two of her novels have become widely known: *The Death of the Heart* (1939), a funny and touching novel about an adolescent girl who goes to live with her married brother after the death of her mother, and *The Heat of the Day* (1949), one of the finest depictions of life in London during the blitz of World War II. Both works dramatize the painful encounter of the inner demands for the ceremonies of love and loyalty with a dessicating and unresponsive world. Betrayal and the wreckage wrought by innocence are always linked up in Bowen with the places in which they occur, for example, the burning of a great manor house in Ireland in *The Last September* (1929) and the suspension of two children's fate in a house that reverberates with the past out of which they were created in *The House in Paris* (1935).

The four most important novelists to have emerged since World War II are Muriel Spark, Doris Lessing, Iris Murdoch, and Margaret Drabble.

Muriel Spark (b. 1918) specializes in the short novel with rapidly sketched-in characters who plunge into parable situations that test their moral fiber. As a Catholic, she is a religious humorist who explores some of the most perplexing social problems of the day. In her two best-known novels, *Memento Mori* (1958) and *The Prime of Miss Jean Brodie* (1961), neither old ladies nor children are sentimentalized; they are people always in their prime if "prime" means the moment we are made for, the moment of crisis and choice. Her theological perspective on old age and dying, on sex and war permits her to treat tragedy as comedy.

Doris Lessing (b. 1919), an author who achieved literary fame in the 1950s and 1960s, continues to explore new possibilities of fiction. Her most recent novels of fantasy, the Canopus series, combine mythology and science fiction in a vision of the future that transforms the present into a past. But her two most substantial achievements so far are her five-volumed *Children of Violence* (1952–1969) and *The Golden Notebook* (1962). Like Richardson's *Pilgrimage*, Lessing's *Children of Violence* is fictionalized autobiography. Martha Quest, the heroine who grows up as the author did in Southern Rhodesia (now Zimbabwe), leaves for England after breaking away from marriages and love affairs. There, again like the author, she becomes disillusioned with communism after the Hungarian uprising. Throughout the series, violence pervades private and public life. In *The Golden Notebook* madness replaces violence as a metaphor for contemporary society: here Anne Wulf experiences her own personal madness as a counterpart of the splitting off of one area of life from another that characterizes the world she lives in. She keeps a series of notebooks (black, red, yellow, and blue) that underscore the compartmentalization that afflicts both the individual and society. Lessing's novels are always richly textured, full of the data of racial and sexual relations, political events, fads in the arts, social changes in food, clothing, modes of travel. Out of the chaos of that experience *The Golden Notebook* attempts to shape wholeness rather than flounder in fragments.

Iris Murdoch (b. 1919) is rather an oddity in English fiction, a philosophical novelist. The influence of Sartre and of existentialism in general is felt in all her novels (e.g., *Under the Net* [1954], *The Severed Head* [1961], *Bruno's Dream* [1969], *A Fairly Honorable Defeat* [1970]), where life is solitary, although always "in company" of others.

Margaret Drabble (b. 1939) raises the ordinary and the commonplace to the level of poetry through her emphasis on the human capacity to rescue beauty from dehumanizing circumstances. Her morality is rooted not in any religious tradition but in respect for human affection and responsibility. Her most successful novel to date, *The Needle's Eye* (1972), endorses a kind of moral resilience that allows each individual to turn chance into choice. Drabble lacks the thickly textured, political analysis of Lessing, the theological assurance of Spark, the philosophical sophistication of Murdoch. Her emotional immersion in the gritty facticity of life aligns her with earlier twentieth-century writers such as Winifred Holtby and Arnold Bennett.

References. Diva Daims and Janet Grimes, with ed. assist. from Doris Robinson, *Toward a Feminist Tradition: An Annotated Bibliography of Novels in English by Women, 1891–1920* (New York, 1982); Sydney Janet Kaplan, *Feminine Consciousness in the Modern British Novel* (Urbana, Ill., 1975).

JO O'BRIEN SCHAEFER

NOVELISTS, U.S. (TO WORLD WAR I). The earliest American women novelists, publishing in the 1790s, wrote primarily the seduction novel, modeled upon British examples but having a North American setting, or the frontier romance, a new genre detailing European settlers' experiences of abduction by Indian natives. Continuing to appear until the Civil War, these two genres merged afterward into literary realism.

During the seventeenth century, authors of captivity narratives, in recording their experiences, had initiated the tradition of writing about the frontier wilderness. In 1779 Ann Eliza Bleecker wrote *The History of Maria Kittle* (1791), the earliest-known frontier romance, an innovative blend of epistolary novel and fictionalized captivity narrative with its obligatory Indian abductors. Lydia Maria Child's *Hobomok* of 1825 was followed two years later by Catharine Sedgwick's *Hope Leslie.* Whereas Bleecker de-

picted Indians as wild savages, Child and Sedgwick both explored misce-
genation, and Sedgwick's white character even preferred Indian to European ways. By 1839, Caroline Kirkland in *A New Home—Who'll Follow?*
replaced an idealized, romantic view with an experiential, realistic view of
frontier living as she revealed the deprivations women endured as they
followed male relatives westward—often as nearly captive as any earlier
heroines were of Indian abductors, or as African slaves were of their owners. The first known novel by a black woman, *Our Nig* (1859) by Harriet
E. Wilson, derived from the slave narrative, as the frontier romance had
from the autobiographical captivity narrative. Helen Hunt Jackson's *Ra-
mona* (1884), a sympathetic, idealized romance between Spaniard and Indian, is laced with harshly realistic depictions of European treatment of
Native American Indians. Later expressions of frontier romance and realism appear in utopian writings. (See UTOPIAS, U.S.) By the end of the
century what had begun as frontier writing became local color or regional
realism, while social or psychological realism had its roots in the novel of
seduction.

Also appearing during the 1790s, seduction novels, too, revealed
women's subordinate role. The first North American best-seller, *Charlotte,
a Tale of Truth* (1794) by Susanna Rowson, combined the titillation of a
seduction with the didactic intent of warning naive female readers. Three
years later Hannah Foster published an epistolary novel, *The Coquette.*
Both Rowson and Foster warn readers in accounts of heroines' being punished in deaths associated with childbirth, but Foster depicts manners more
realistically.

Humorous, satiric treatment occurs in *Female Quixotism* (1801, by Ta-
bitha Gilman Tenney [1762–1837]) and *Kelroy* (1812, by Rebecca Rush
[b. 1779]).

Both novels contained seeds of the "woman's novel," which reigned between 1820 and 1870. Plots of the woman's novel concern the trials the
heroine, orphan, or heiress must overcome as she develops her capacities
so as to triumph over inner and outer obstacles, rather than succumb as in
the seduction novel (Baym). As the first American novel to sell 1 million
copies, *The Wide, Wide World* (1850) by Susan Warner (pseud. Elizabeth
Wetherell) indicates the popularity of this genre. It depicts the education
of a strong-willed heroine to submit to patriarchal authority and to know
good from evil. In a variation of the genre, *Ruth Hall* (1855) by Sara Parton
(pseud. Fanny Fern), a writer not only triumphs over cruel relatives but
also rises above dependence on marriage and family. *The Hidden Hand*
(1859), by the widely read E.D.E.N. Southworth, sports a lively heroine,
Capitola, who defies authority, assumes male prerogatives, and earns rewards for such behavior. The novel's melodramatic plot suggests British
gothic thrillers. Woman's fiction after the Civil War continued to be written
for a juvenile audience or by black women. Louisa May Alcott's *Little*

Women (1868) is the outstanding example of the former, while in works by black women, heroines surmount the trials of women living in a racist society and triumph as advocates of their race. Frances E. W. Harper in *Iola Leroy* (1892) and Pauline E. Hopkins in *Contending Forces* (1900) follow this pattern.

Works by the outstanding U.S. novelist before the Civil War, Harriet Beecher Stowe, partake of woman's fiction features and anticipate literary realism. *Uncle Tom's Cabin* (1852) argues that maternal values should supplant masculinist views prevalent in society, thereby eradicating slavery and permitting black families to exist intact. *The Pearl of Orr's Island* (1862) describes gender stereotyping in the education of youth while minutely delineating a regional environment. Her most carefully wrought novel, *Oldtown Folks* (1869), provides a fictional portrait of New England village life at the turn of the last century. Stowe's fictional designs reveal both her wish to change radically the arrangements between the races and between the sexes and her awareness of the impact of specific geographical regions upon human lives.

The next generation of writers completes the transition from amateur to professional. The domestic priority of the previous generation disappeared as plots and heroines more frequently extended beyond the home. Stowe's immediate literary descendants include Elizabeth Stuart Phelps, Sarah Orne Jewett, and Mary E. Wilkins Freeman. All three produced works of regional, social, and psychological realism. Jewett's *The Country of the Pointed Firs* (1896), the most centrally regional of their works, eulogizes a lost world of maternal values. Phelps' *The Silent Partner* (1871) and Freeman's *The Portion of Labor* (1901) critique masculinist, urban industrialization within New England. New roles for women appear in the same setting: Phelps' *Doctor Zay* (1882) and Jewett's *A Country Doctor* (1886). Tragic psychological realism informs Freeman's *Pembroke* (1894).

As the maternal and domestic focus in women's fiction decreased, artistic and literary purpose increased. Phelps' *kunstlerroman* (artist novel) *The Story of Avis* (1877) portrays one woman's inner strife between domestic and artistic vocation. St. Louis author Kate Chopin in *The Awakening* (1899) pushes this strife to a tragic outcome in Edna Pontellier's renunciation of life rather than loss of self. Californian Mary Austin in *A Woman of Genius* (1912) and midwesterner Willa Cather in *Song of the Lark* (1915) created heroines who find artistic success by choosing to avoid domestic commitment.

The literary generation arising at the turn of the century extended well beyond New England. Cather, following the regional example of Jewett, wrote of immigrant survivors on her own midwestern plains in *O Pioneers!* (1913) and *My Antonia* (1918). Ellen Glasgow began in *The Battleground* (1902) an exploration of Virginia history and society. Edith Wharton in *House of Mirth* (1905) and *Custom of the Country* (1913) revealed how upper-class, New York society ravaged its women. From Paris Gertrude Stein looked homeward to create in *Three Lives* (1909) stylistically experimental and ethnically diverse psychological portraits of women. By the turn of the century women had come of age as literary artists. Abandoning the prescriptive mode of the previous century—idealistic, romantic, or moralistic—they adopted realism, a descriptive mode that set characters within a regional setting and sought to reveal their inner psychological and outer social development.

References. Elizabeth Ammons, *Conflicting Stories: American Women Writers at the Turn into the Twentieth Century* (Oxford, 1991); Nina Baym, *Woman's Fiction* (Urbana, Ill., 1993); Susan K. Harris, *19th-Century American Women's Novels: Interpretive Strategies* (Cambridge, 1990); Mary Kelley, *Private Women, Public Stage: Literary Domesticity in Nineteenth-Century America* (New York, 1984); Annette Kolodny, *The Land before Her: Fantasy and Experience of the American Frontiers, 1630–1860* (Chapel Hill, N.C., 1984); Joyce W. Warren (ed.), *The (Other) American Traditions: Nineteenth-Century Women Writers* (New Brunswick, N.J., 1993); *Legacy: A Journal of American Women Writers*, 1–(1984–).

CAROL FARLEY KESSLER

NOVELISTS, U.S. (AFTER WORLD WAR I). The twentieth century has been marked by revolution, chaos, and despair. Ours is a century of firsts: the first world wars; the first atomic explosion; the first technologically produced Holocaust; the first humans in space; the first babies in test tubes. We are the first century to attempt life without God and to substitute science, psychoanalysis, and politics in his or her place. To some extent, the artistic response to these historical and cultural occurrences enacts itself through two major literary movements in the century, modernism and postmodernism, the former dating roughly from the opening years of the century through the 1920s and the latter from the 1960s through the 1980s. While women writers have participated in these movements, they have worked predominantly in the realistic tradition through fiction dramatizing aspects of quotidian reality: emotional connection, child rearing, housekeeping.

Three writers at work in the early decades of the century establish themselves as major literary figures by the 1920s: Edith Wharton (1862–1937), Gertrude Stein (1874–1946), and Willa Cather (1873–1947). Wharton, best known for her incisive, realistic portraits of upper-class society and the demands its superficiality and materialism make upon women, represents this world most brutally in *The House of Mirth* (1905). Other well-known novels include *Ethan Frome* (1911) and *The Age of Innocence* (1920), considered to be her greatest. If Wharton is the consummate novelist of manners, then Gertrude Stein is the consummate innovator, the most radical of the modernists, whose best-known work, *Three Lives* (1909), remains her most accessible. Unlike Stein's reputation, Cather's has been based, until fairly recently, upon an ostensible "regionalism," presumably because of the midwest setting in such novels as *O Pioneers!* (1913), *Song of the Lark* (1915), and *The Professor's House* (1925), including her greatest, *My Antonia* (1918), set in Nebraska. As critics now acknowledge, her texts are by no means limited to a "regional focus," for she explores themes and issues vital to the modernist enterprise: the conflict over traditional values and modern technocracy; the disconnection between the natural/mythic worlds of the past and the alienating effects of the modern; the role of the artist and her relationship to society.

Two additional writers, whose fiction evolves from 1913 to 1919 and in the 1920s, deserve mention. Mary Austin (1868–1934) publishes *A Woman of Genius* in 1912, an early portrayal of the woman artist and an influence on Cather's characterization of Thea Kronberg in *Song of the Lark*. Evelyn Scott (1893–1963) deserves greater notice for attempting to meld an extreme realism with her own version of stream of consciousness in *The Narrow House* (1921).

By the 1930s, modernist experimentation is established as a literary option. Along with Stein, Djuna Barnes (1892–1982) writes highly elusive, yet suggestive, fiction and her novel, *Nightwood* (1937), remains enigmatic and difficult. Zora Neale Hurston (1901?–1960) also employs modernist techniques yet contributes her own African American perspective and background training in folklore and anthropology. With the publication of *Their Eyes Were Watching God* (1937), Hurston achieves literary maturity and prominence. Hurston's emphasis upon a particular community is echoed in other women writers who turn to radical politics and the writing of committed literature as a way out of the global misery created by the Great Depression and the rise of fascism. In fact, Agnes Smedley's *Daughter of Earth* (1929) probably inaugurates proletarian fiction, which may be defined as a simplified realism emphasizing working-class characters, social themes, and, all too often, a melodramatic tone. Josephine Herbst (1892–1969)—*Rope of Gold* (1939)—and Meridel LeSueur (b. 1900)—*The Girl* (written 1939, published 1978)—are two of the more effective writers in this tradition.

The post–World War II period may be looked at in two phases. The first ends in 1964, the year of Flannery O'Connor's death and the beginning of America's active involvement in Vietnam, and may be viewed as a time of consolidation. The second phase may be more accurately viewed as a time of innovation with "postmodernism" its most dominant feature.

Carson McCullers (1917–1967), Eudora Welty (b. 1909), and Flannery O'Connor (1925–1964) constitute an influential triad of writers, who also happen to be southern, in the 1940s, 1950s, and early 1960s. They enlarge the realistic tradition, with McCullers emphasizing the irremedial losses of childhood in *The Heart Is a Lonely Hunter* (1940); Welty emphasizing the endurance of human character in *Delta Wedding* (1946), *The Ponder Heart* (1954), and *The Optimist's Daughter* (1972); and O'Connor, the most gifted woman writer in the period, emphasizing the mysterious relationship between action, spirit, and grace in *Wise Blood* (1952) and *The Violent Bear It Away* (1960).

If the term "postmodern" resonates with any significance at all, it may be in its designation of an aftermath, the postmodern "sensibility" defined by an extreme self-reflexivity that is always aware of its own belatedness. Literarily, postmodernism most often defines itself through a rejection of modernist aesthetics and values while attempting to promote its own kinds of experimentation with literary tradition, genre, and structure. In revising the literary past, writers may utilize parody, pastiche, and plagiarism. Kathy Acker's (1944–1997) fondness for plagiarism is particularly evident in titles such as *Great Expectations* (1983) and *Don Quixote* (1986), while her compositional use of pastiche, evident throughout her novels, is most effective in *Blood and Guts in High School* (1977) and *Empire of the Senseless* (1988). Far less radically, Joyce Carol Oates (b. 1938) playfully revises the Gothic romance tradition in *Bellefleur* (1980) and *A Bloodsmoor Romance* (1982), while Marilynne Robinson (b. 1944) seriously produces a neo-Romantic novel in *Housekeeping* (1981). Both Joanna Russ (b. 1937) and Amanda Cross (b. 1926) extend the possibilities of their respective generic options, the former in science fiction (*The Female Man*, 1975; *The Two of Them*, 1978) and the latter in detective fiction (*Death in a Tenured Position*, 1981; *No Word from Winifred*, 1986).

In the 1960s, competing impulses dramatize writers' differences from one another as well as from postmodernism. Certain writers, susceptible to the burdens of history, present overtly political responses, for example, Marge Piercy (b. 1936) in *Woman on the Edge of Time* (1976), *Vida* (1979), and *Braided Lives* (1982). Ann Tyler (b. 1941), on the other hand, portrays the traditional "story" of family dynamics in an eccentric and contemporary way most successfully in *Dinner at the Homesick Restaurant* (1982). Perhaps the strongest impulse countering postmodernism is the "multicultural." Ethnic, racial, and cultural identifications serve as the necessary vehicle to dramatize social/historical/personal connectedness. Thus, Maxine Hong Kingston (b. 1940) presents Asian American experience in *The Woman Warrior* (1976); Leslie Silko (b. 1948), that of Native Americans in *Ceremony* (1977) and *The Almanac of the Dead* (1991); and Cynthia Ozick (b. 1928), that of Jewish Americans in *Trust* (1966). The number of African American writers achieving critical and popular success continues to grow. From this group emerges, arguably, the most important American writer in the last decades of the century, Toni Morrison (b. 1931), winner of the 1993 Nobel Prize in literature and author of a number of works including *Song of Solomon* (1977), *Beloved* (1987), *Jazz* (1992), and *Par-*

adise (1998). In *Beloved* she has written America's first great novel about slavery, and it is a tribute to her particular genius that what the reader gains from the text is a sense of triumph, great compassion, and love.

SUSAN E. HAWKINS

NURSING. See HEALTH CARE PROVIDERS

NURSING REFORM (U.S.) created institutions to train women to nurse. Under these reforms, nursing was "feminized" by changing the class-defined behavior, rather than the gender, of the workforce. However, the cultural assumptions that women were "born to nurse" and that the work was merely the carrying out of physicians' orders hampered sustained efforts to professionalize and upgrade nursing training and practice.

Until the second and third decades of the twentieth century, most Americans received their health care at home. Female relatives or neighbors became a family's nurses. If neither were available, an older woman, usually a former domestic servant or widow, who "professed" to having nursing skills, might be hired.

Some nursing was also provided in the relatively few hospitals (178 in the entire country at the first national census in 1873) that served primarily poor, urban populations. Some of the "nurses" in these institutions spent their lives perfecting a modicum of skill in caring and observing, but others carried out life-threatening procedures and haphazardly handed out food while pillaging the alcohol supplies as they moved between lives in the hospitals and almshouses or streets. Despite the diversity, hospital nursing was culturally labeled as loathsome work, and hospital nurses were perceived as besotten, immoral lowlifes.

The Civil War years created the necessity for change and educated a critical group of philanthropic women in ways to make it possible. Under the umbrella of the U.S. Sanitary Commission, a civil organization created to provide funds, medical supplies, and care for the Union army, thousands of middle- and upper-class women learned or deepened their skills at organizing caregiving, or participated for the first time in the actual provision of such care. Despite physician objections to what was labeled "womanly meddling," critical improvements were made in the military medical system, and the public was slowly educated on the importance of nursing care ministered by "respectable" women.

Florence Nightingale had similar experiences trying to reorganize the British military medical care during the Crimean War in the mid-1850s. Upon her triumphant return to London and with funds donated by the British public for her heroic work, she established a training school at St. Thomas' Hospital. Nightingale thought women's special nature and virtue could be honed through a disciplined process to create trained nurses. Under her model, training was to take place on a hospital's wards under the strict and watchful eye of the nursing superintendent and senior nurses. Lectures were to be provided by physicians after students finished eight to ten hours of ward work. Nightingale stressed character development, laws of health that emphasized fresh air and cleanliness, and a strict adherence to orders passed through a female hierarchy. Her efforts were given much coverage in the American press, and her work was well known and praised.

Thus, when many philanthropic women returned to their northern cities after the Civil War to find "unspeakable conditions" (as one reformer put it) in urban hospitals, they had considerable experience in institutional reform and a model of what might make improvements possible. Since many already served on hospital visiting committees or were related by marriage or blood to upper-class male trustees, they also had the connections and the political experience to begin the enormous effort at change. Finally, the human devastation of the war and the subsequent major economic depression of the early 1870s had deeply affected the economic status and marriage prospects of "respectable" young women. As such women entered the cities in search of work, nursing promised them a living and a halo. By 1872, the New England Hospital for Women and Children in Boston admitted five probationers into the first American training program. A year later, in 1873, committees in New Haven, New York, and Boston formally began training schools based on the Nightingale model and connected, respectively, to the State Hospital of New Haven, Bellevue Hospital, and Massachusetts General Hospital.

In the context of hospital expansion and the cultural emphasis on female duty, however, nursing reform was soon engulfed in a series of dilemmas. Hospital trustees and administrators quickly realized that the opening of something labeled a "nursing school" provided them with a young, disciplined, and cheap labor force with which to staff their wards. Students came to be educated, but primarily what they did was work. Altruism, sacrifice, and submission to rigid rules were expected, encouraged, and demanded. Nursing became an overcrowded arena of work, with ill-defined standards and very unevenly trained workers. Thus, between 1890 and 1920, the number of nursing schools jumped from 35 to 1,775, and the number of trained nurses rose from 16 per 100,000 in the population to 141 per 100,000.

By the mid-1880s, nurses began to call for some kind of national organization to improve this situation. In 1893, after a meeting convened by the Johns Hopkins Hospital nursing superintendent Isabel Hampton, the precursors to the two major professional organizations, the National League for Nursing and the American Nurses Association, were created. Through these organizations, nursing leaders sought to raise both educational standards in the schools and the criterion for entry into nursing practice, to use the power of the state to register nurses once they completed training, and to gain acceptance for the knowledge base and increasingly complex skills of the nurse. They established journals and began to write texts and to urge higher standards for nursing.

However, the continued cultural assumption that a nurse should merely take a doctor's orders, the difficulty of demanding any kind of legislative reform when women still did not have the vote, physician and hospital resistance to the upgrading of nurses' training, and the increasing division within the nursing ranks between educators and those doing the work thwarted many of these efforts. Despite many gains in the twentieth century, nurses still face the continued difficulty of having their work properly valued and understood, as the cultural expectation persists that the duty to care is somehow a naturally female, subordinate, and unimportant task.

References. Philip and Beatrice Kalisch, *The Advance of American Nursing* (Boston, 1978); Barbara Melosh, *"The Physician's Hand": Work, Culture and Conflict in American Nursing* (Philadelphia, 1982); Susan Reverby, *Ordered to Care: The Dilemma of American Nursing* (New York, 1987).

SUSAN REVERBY

O

OBSTETRICS. See GYNECOLOGY/OBSTETRICS (OB/GYN)

OCCUPATIONAL SEGREGATION refers to the pronounced tendency of women and men in the labor market to work in different occupations. For example, in 1989, women constituted over 90 percent of child care workers, registered nurses, secretaries, kindergarten teachers, and bank tellers, while over 90 percent of engineers, dentists, mechanics and repairers, airplane pilots and navigators, and truck drivers were men.

The extent of occupational segregation may be measured using an index of segregation that gives the proportion of women (or men) in the workforce who would have to change jobs in order for the occupational distribution of the two groups to be the same. In 1990, the index was 53 percent. While the extent of occupational segregation by sex is substantial, there was some modest progress in reducing segregation. The pace of change accelerated during the 1970s, when the index fell by nearly 8 percentage points. The decline continued into the 1980s. Overall, the index fell by nearly 15 percentage points between 1970 and 1990. The gains have been concentrated in white collar and service jobs, where there have been remarkable increases in the representation of women in some traditionally male occupations. However, little progress has been made in integrating male blue-collar jobs.

Explanations for occupational segregation tend to emphasize either differences in the choices that women and men themselves make (supply-side factors) or differences in employer treatment of women and men (demand-side factors). Both sets of factors most likely play a role in producing the observed gender differences in occupational distribution.

On the supply side, the human capital explanation has received the most attention. (See HUMAN CAPITAL THEORY.) Human capital theorists argue that women who adhere to traditional roles in the family will anticipate a shorter and more discontinuous pattern of labor market experience than men. They will have fewer incentives to invest in work-related education and on-the-job training* and will thus select occupations where such human capital investments are less important. In this view, female jobs pay less than male jobs because of their lower skills.

The human capital model emphasizes the impact of rational decision making and the voluntary choices of men and women. However, women's decisions about the role of work in their lives and about what occupations to pursue may also be a response to societal discrimination.* This refers to the situation in which the influences of family, friends, school, and the media adversely affect women's choices.

On the demand side, labor market discrimination may also constrain the occupational opportunities of women. This occurs when employers discriminate against equally qualified women in hiring, placement, access to training programs, and promotion for traditionally male jobs. Employers may be motivated to discriminate against women by their own prejudices or because the prejudices of their male employees or customers make it less profitable for them to hire women than men. They may also believe, perhaps incorrectly, that on average, women would be less desirable employees—for example, because they would be more likely to quit their jobs. It is also the case that the anticipation of such labor market discrimination may lower women's incentives to aspire to, or train for, what are perceived to be "male" jobs.

One reason that occupational segregation is a cause for concern is that many economists believe it lowers the earnings of women relative to men. It has, indeed, been found that women and men workers in predominantly female jobs earn less than equally qualified workers in predominantly male jobs. This is believed to occur because of "crowding." That is, due to the concentration of women in such female occupations, the supply of labor in those jobs tends to be large relative to the demand, depressing wages in the female sector.

References. Francine D. Blau, Marianne A. Ferber, and Anne E. Winkler, *The Economics of Women, Men, and Work*, 3d ed. (Englewood Cliffs, N.J., 1998); Francine D. Blau, Patricia Simpson, and Deborah Anderson, "Continuing Progress? Trends in Occupational Segregation over the 1970s and 1980s," in *Feminist Economics* (forthcoming); B. F. Reskin and H. I. Hartmann (eds.), *Women's Work, Men's Work: Sex Segregation on the Job* (Washington, D.C., 1986).

FRANCINE D. BLAU

OFFENDER. The definition, presence, characteristics, and disposition of the woman offender can be viewed as representing in microcosm women's political and legal status crosscut by realities of class and race. The very definition of a woman offender is complex. It may include any woman who has violated a range of federal and state criminal statutes (some of which are themselves gender-specific), a population unknown and, with the exception of self-report data, unknowable. Or the image of the offender may be limited to women who have been arrested and are identifiable as a group by offense, race, and age statistics. Finally, our perception of the woman offender may be shaped by our knowledge of the backgrounds and characteristics of women visible in our jails and prisons.

Most self-report data involve juveniles. Young males consistently report more serious and repeated illegal activities than young women, but young women appear in all offense categories. Almost equal percentages report drug, alcohol, and petty theft violations, but significantly lower numbers of young women engage in acts of violence or vandalism. Differences of race and class are less evident when we examine self-report data.

Despite the media coverage of Freda Adler's description of an increasingly violent and aggressive "new female criminal," attributed in the 1970s to the women's movement, later research found no significant change in arrest rates for women in male-dominated violent crimes. In 1996, according to U.S. Department of Justice figures, men accounted for approximately 89 percent of all murder, robbery, and burglary arrests. Sixteen percent of all women's arrests in 1996 were for larceny-theft, as opposed to 8.2 percent of male arrests. The increasing number of women arrested for property offenses appears more reflective of a "feminization of poverty"* than of women's liberation. Of 11 million arrests in 1996, 21 percent were women, but they accounted for 34 percent of the larceny-theft, 42 percent of fraud and embezzlement, and 64 percent of prostitution arrests. However, prostitution, often associated with the woman offender, accounted for only 2 percent of their arrests.

Explanations for these differential arrest figures have remained remarkably stable through time. Francis Lieber's exposition, (de Beaumont and de Tocqueville) of why only 9 percent of the prisoners were women in 1833 is similar to Merlo and Pollock's summary of the nature of female criminality 162 years later. Both attribute the levels and patterns of women's offenses to their position in "civil society," resulting in differing role expectations and socialization, differential social control and opportunity to commit offenses, and the statutory gender specification of some offenses.

The "chivalry factor" in arrest and disposition of women offenders remains a disputed question, but there is evidence of differential sentencing and sentence length linked to paternalism, assumptions regarding the degree of women's naïveté, victimization, and dangerousness, as well as their responsibility for children (Daly). However, these differentials become less evident when class, race, and changes in sentencing guidelines are explored.

While in 1997 women made up 6.4 percent of the prison population rather than the 9 percent of 1833, in 1973 they were only 3 percent. On any given day in 1980 a man was 25 times more likely to be in prison than a woman, but by 1997 that ratio had dropped to 16. In turn, 1993 statistics indicated that a black woman was seven times more likely to be in prison than a white woman (Bureau of Justice Statistics, Table 11).

The change for women has been attributed to one major factor, reflected in a report's title: "Women in California Prisons: Hidden Victims of the War on Drugs" (Bloom, Chesney-Lind, and Owen). While the percentage change in incarceration for men rose 214 percent from 1980 to 1994, women's rose 386 percent! In 1980 approximately 1 in 10 women in state and federal prisons was there for drug offenses; by 1991, one out of three; and by 1993, two-thirds of the Federal Bureau of Prison's women inmates were committed for drug or alcohol offenses. Gender-blind, "get-tough" sentencing guidelines and long mandatory prison terms for drug offenses envisioned for "violent males" and drug "kingpins" have disproportion-ately resulted in sending more women to prison.

When we examine the characteristics of women offenders who are in prison, the dynamics of the criminal justice system and the status of women are more clearly revealed. The 1993 California study found 72 percent of the women serving sentences for property and drug offenses. Nearly 40 percent had not completed high school, 80 percent reported some form of abuse, and over half had been runaways. A majority had never been em-ployed, while almost half of those with "legitimate" jobs supplemented their wages by dealing drugs. Almost 80 percent were mothers with de-pendent children. The report concludes that the women filling the Califor-nia prisons were "the most vulnerable: women of color, the economically marginalized, and the victims of physical and sexual abuse." Women of-fenders in prison are disadvantaged losers in a competitive and increasingly punitive society.

References. Freda Adler, *Sisters in Crime* (New York, 1975); Barbara Bloom, Meda Chesney-Lind, and Barbara Owen, "Women in California Prisons," *Report from the Center on Juvenile and Criminal Justice* (San Francisco, May 1994); Bu-reau of Justice Statistics, "Prisoners in 1994" (Washington, D.C., August 1995); Kathleen Daly, *Gender, Crime and Punishment* (New Haven, Conn., 1994); Clarice Feinman, *Women in the Criminal Justice System*, 3d ed. (Westport, Conn., 1994); Francis Lieber, "Introduction," in Gustave de Beaumont and Alexis de Tocqueville, *On the Penitentiary System in the United States* (Philadelphia, 1833); Alida V. Merlo and Joycylyn M. Pollock, *Women, Law, and Social Control* (Boston, 1995); Barbara Owen, *In the Mix: Struggle and Survival in a Women's Prison* (Albany, N.Y., 1998).

ESTHER HEFFERNAN

OLD WIVES' TALES are the sayings, popular beliefs, precepts, and nar-ratives once valued as the wisdom and wit of experienced, older women but now applied metaphorically to discredit forms of women's and men's speech as idle untruths. Both the *Oxford English Dictionary* definition, "a trivial story such as is told by garrulous old women," and that in *Webster's*

New World Dictionary, "a silly story or superstitious belief such as might be passed around by gossipy old women," promulgate the common, sexist usage. There is no equally derogatory literal or metaphoric term commonly associated with old men's/husbands' verbal arts and lore. (See GOSSIP.)

Social recognition of older or otherwise knowledgeable women as persons of substance, spirit, wisdom, and valued verbal/nonverbal performance skills varies historically and cross-culturally. In many societies, postmenopausal women are freed from social restraints over those capable of childbearing and may participate fully in public ritual, politics, licentiousness, and entertainment. Often, older and younger women who practice healing, divination, midwifery,* and other skills based on physical/ social observation and analysis are considered valuable members of society by both women and men. This opinion is not the case either in Western scientific tradition, which generally has denounced women's traditional lore as irrational "old wives' tales," or in official Christian tradition, as reflected, for example, in Paul's injunction (1 Tim. 4:7, Tindale, 1526): "Cast away vngostly and olde wyves' fables," later translated as "Have nothing to do with godless and silly myths" (Revised Standard Version, 1971). (See MYTHOLOGY.)

Women verbal artists generally do not enjoy wide acclaim. Folklorists and anthropologists, for the most part, have assumed that women possess speaking and narrating competence informally with children but have ignored skills displayed with each other or in mixed adult audiences. However, there is historical evidence for the latter, like George Peele's 1595 play, *The Old Wives Tale*, framed as "a merry winter's tale [that] would drive away the time trimly" for three male pages spending the night with the blacksmith Clunch and his old wife Madge, who narrates the story within the drama until "cock's-crow." Among the Xhosa of South Africa, women are considered the best performers of valued dramatic narratives called *ntsomi* (Scheub). Nevertheless, women's enlightenment and entertainment of each other, their skillful, artistic use of old wives' tales to educate, constrain, and/or enable other women are matters still in need of study.

References. Mary Chamberlain, *Old Wives' Tales: Their History, Remedies and Spells* (London, 1981); Harold Scheub, "The Art of [Mrs.] Nongenile Mazithathu Zenani, a Gcaleka Ntsomi Performer," in Richard M. Dorson (ed.), *African Folklore* (Bloomington, Ind., 1972), 115–142; Barbara G. Walker, *The Crone: Women of Age, Wisdom, and Power* (San Francisco, 1985).

MARTA WEIGLE

ONEIDA is the most prominent of the utopian communities. Founded by John Humphrey Noyes (1811–1886) in 1848 near Kenwood, New York, Oneida practiced free sexual association, birth control, and eugenics while advocating abolition of the traditional family and private property. It lasted in this experimental form, under the charismatic domination of Noyes, from 1848 to 1879, when it was disbanded and reorganized into its present format of a joint stock company.

Noyes, influenced by Fourier and the Shakers, developed his ideas from Christian perfectionism. (See UTOPIAN SOCIALIST MOVEMENTS; SHAKERS.) Noyes' theology held that the kingdom of God had arrived, and traditional marriage was no longer valid. Monogamy was seen as selfish and exclusive, to be replaced by "complex marriage" in which each member of the community would be married to all other members (pantagamy). Fundamental to the practice of "complex marriage" was Noyes' invention of "male continence," a method of birth control that required that males engage in sexual activity without achieving orgasm (*coitus reservatus*). Noyes advocated male continence to avoid involuntary procreation but also, in his words, to stop "the drain of life on the part of man." Sex was purified and glorified in Oneida. Women's sexuality was acknowledged, as was their right to sexual satisfaction. However, sexual intercourse was intended to transcend lust, and, therefore, male continence, which required transcendental control, was more noble and unselfish.

In practice, sexual relations were regulated by the community. Younger men, not yet adept at male continence, were not allowed sex with any but postmenopausal women. Noyes generally preempted the task of initiating virgins himself. While sexual activity might begin as young as 14 for a girl, she might not have a sexual partner her own age for 10 years. Males initiated all requests for sexual meetings through an intermediary, and women, theoretically, had the right to decline, although this right was subject to communal pressures. Vigilance was exercised to prevent exclusive affections. One discontented Oneida woman stated, "It was a man's plan, not a woman's."

The community embarked on an experiment in eugenics, termed "stirpiculture," during which 58 children were born. Noyes and a committee of elders approved couples for potential parenthood. Males were chosen on the basis of religious qualifications, and women under 20 years of age were excluded. In keeping with the community's attempts to enlarge the family unit, children were to be raised communally. After 15 months of age, the child was placed in a common nursery during the day. At age 4, the child moved to a separate children's quarters. Exclusive maternal love was condemned, as Oneidans regarded it as a deficiency in spiritual development, an example of the selfish and exclusive affections found in the larger society. In a ritual attempt to control the maternal instinct, the commune once held a ceremony in which the Oneida women and girls destroyed all their dolls in a fire.

Oneida endorsed the rhetoric of woman's rights, openly espousing the cause in its publications and adopting dress reform based on the bloomer costume, but it did not believe in the innate equality of the sexes. Generally, spirituality was the basis for authority at Oneida, and the more advanced members were accorded the status of "ascending fellowship." While women could hold this status, Noyes believed males to be superior. However, attempts were made to widen the occupational roles of women, and contemporaries were struck by the roles women held in the Oneida businesses. Visitors also remarked on seeing an occasional Oneida man knitting. Generally, though, work was sexually stereotyped, and women were assigned to the tasks of housecleaning and cooking.

The end of the community came with the weakening of the elderly Noyes' authority. The stirpiculture experiment had left a legacy of patterns of familial affection, and younger members of Oneida wished greater control over sexual choices and a return to monogamy. Factions arose within the commune as attacks from the outside accelerated due to the increasing strength of the purity crusade. (See SOCIAL PURITY MOVEMENT.) Noyes suggested the process whereby Oneida ended the practice of complex marriage in August 1879. Within a year, remaining members abandoned communal property as well.

References. Robert S. Fogarty (ed.), *Special Love/ Special Sex: An Oneida Community Diary* (Syracuse, N.Y., 1994); Lawrence Foster, *Women, Family, and Utopia, Communal Experiments of the Shakers, the Oneida Community, and the Mormons* (Syracuse, N.Y., 1991); Louis J. Kern, *An Ordered Love: Sex Roles and Sexuality in Victorian Utopias* (Chapel Hill, N.C., 1981); Constance Noyes Robertson, *Oneida Community: The Breakup, 1876–1881* (Syracuse, N.Y., 1972).

JOAN IVERSEN

ORGASM is a psychophysiological experience, and recently it has become a symbol of sexual equality and female sexual entitlement. Although, as Margaret Mead pointed out, female orgasm is unknown and apparently unmissed in many societies, it is presented in most contemporary Western texts as an important, innate, universally pleasurable biofunction, a simple somatic response consisting of involuntary pelvic muscle contractions that occur in reaction to a neurovascular buildup of tension in the genitalia. The immense societal attention paid in the West to this little physical event, however, and its absence from sexual practice in some cultures indicate that whatever the physical value of orgasm as pleasurable reliever of vascular congestion, its symbolic value has varied and continues to vary and require study.

Until the writings of feminists and sexologists in the late 1960s and 1970s, orgasm was said to occur during vaginal intercourse if a woman was well adjusted and could just let herself go ("surrender") in a sexual encounter. Any woman not so capable was considered to have a problem that required professional treatment. At that point, however, feminists began to criticize those norms and the ways that Freudian theory, traditional heterosexual technique, and gender socialization all prevented women from experiencing orgasm. Sexologists stressed that women's anatomy made orgasm during vaginal intercourse far less likely than with an act that stimulated the sensitive clitoris directly and that with "proper" stimulation and sexual assertiveness women were actually more orgasmically capable than men, even having "multiple" orgasms. Sexual liberation for women became, for a while, focused on asserting a political right to orgasm justified by the biological equality of male and female sexual response presumably demonstrated by the scientific research of Alfred Kinsey and, later, of William Masters and Virginia Johnson. Women in consciousness-raising* and other groups recommended masturbation and the use of vibrators to learn orgasm.

As a result of the writings of this period and the social changes they fostered, orgasm was said to occur during any sexual act if a woman was well adjusted and had knowledge of her own body and the ability and opportunity for communication and assertion. Ironically, the importance given to orgasm as a symbol for female sexual equality has resulted, for some, in a technical, goal-oriented focus for sexual relations that may or may not have improved women's overall sexual satisfaction, sexual freedom, or sexual self-knowledge. Orgasm is still considered, by most, the centerpiece and goal of a sexual encounter, and women not having that experience are still considered to have a problem that requires professional treatment. It will take, it seems, further research and further revolution before women achieve true sexual self-determination.

References. B. Ehrenreich, E. Hess, and G. Jacobs, *Remaking Love: The Feminization of Sex* (Garden City, N.Y., 1986); A. C. Kinsey, W. B. Pomeroy, C. E. Martin, and P. H. Gebhard, *Sexual Behavior in the Human Female* (Philadelphia, 1953); William Masters and Virginia Johnson, *Human Sexual Response* (Boston, 1966); Margaret Mead, *Male and Female: A Study of the Sexes in a Changing World* (New York, 1955; orig. pub. 1949); L. Tiefer, *Sex Is Not a Natural Act, and Other Essays* (Boulder, Colo., 1995).

LEONORE TIEFER

ORIGIN OF THE FAMILY, PRIVATE PROPERTY, AND THE STATE, by Friedrich Engels, since its first appearance in 1884, was considered the classic Marxist statement on women and the family that accurately reflects Marx's views. By 1891, it had gone through four editions and been translated into four languages.

Engels had just completed *The Condition of the Working Class in England in 1844,* in which he deals with the actual experiences of working-class women, when he turned to writing the *Origin.* The hasty composition of this theoretical study was apparently in response to the appearance in 1883 of the second edition of August Bebel's very popular *Women in the Past, Present and Future* (orig. pub. 1879). To counter the utopian socialist influence evident in *Women,* Engels in *Origin* laid down a theoretical foundation, in strict accord with Marx's ideas, for socialist thought on the woman question. That only the first part of the work is on women and the family is indicative of its limited purpose to fix the theoretical context of the woman question in a historical basis.

In developing his ideas Engels drew heavily on the work of nineteenth-century anthropologists who disputed the idea that society had always been patriarchal. Rather, they believed there had been previous stages of promiscuity and "mother right" or some form of matriarchal organization. Engels' materialist theory of the evolution of society follows Lewis Henry Morgan's (*Ancient Society*, 1877) stages of development, which Engels called "savagery," "barbarism," and "civilization." According to *Origin* a prehistoric, communal society based on the matrilineal gens (clan) was overturned or superseded by patriarchy, an intermediate stage, at the end of the period of savagery. Then, toward the upper end of the period of barbarism, the monogamous family was developed, a sign of the beginning of civilization.

Before the change to patriarchy there was sexual division of labor, based on natural sexual functions, but within their respective spheres, each sex held equal power. The equality of the mother stemmed from the fact that society was based on the woman-controlled gens and the collective household. The transition to patriarchy and the subordination of women accompanied and were the result of the appearance of private property and the exchange of goods for profit, both controlled by men. With patriarchy women no longer took part in social production but were confined to production and reproduction within the now privatized household. The wife was the first domestic servant.

Monogamy arose with the concentration of wealth in the hands of man. To assure that this wealth passed only to his own children, he had to assure their unquestioned paternity. Engels called the development of monogamy the "world historical defeat of the female sex" and "the first class opposition that appears in history."

Although Engels posits gender oppression as the first class oppression, he still considers women's oppression as secondary to class oppression. Ending class oppression will liberate women—the central tenet of the Marxist socialist program for women. To further the process of change he advocates that women enter the full-time waged labor force, thus eliminating the monogamous family as the economic unit of society, upon which the capitalist exploitation of labor rests. The monogamous family will not disappear but will remain as an affective unit, a sexual union based on love, not property.

Feminist criticism of *Origin* crosses the spectrum, from condemnation as patriarchal to appreciation as the necessary starting point for any materialist analysis of gender relations. Perhaps its greatest contribution is its recognition that present forms of marriage, family life, and sexual and gender relations are not preordained by nature but subject to change over time and among different classes within the same time period. Although Engels, as a man of the nineteenth century, considered the sexual division of labor as natural, he could not conceive of a sexual hierarchy within that division of labor before the rise of private property led to class divisions.

Origin, the theoretical base of the late nineteenth-century Marxist stance on the woman question, was taken as a starting point by second-wave feminist theorists and remains an important root of much contemporary socialist and radical feminist theory.

But feminist theorists have also taken issue with Engels' and subsequent Marxist analysis that places women's oppression as secondary to class oppression. They have been critical of Engels' treating the sexual division of labor as natural and of his broad generalizations from a limited nineteenth-century bourgeois form of family life and sexual ideology. They point out that Engels' call for women's entry into the waged labor force, rather than bringing more freedom, has increased women's burden, adding public labor without reducing their unpaid domestic labor. Feminist theorists argue that to assume gender oppression will disappear with the destruction of capitalism too easily assumes gender's secondary importance and completely ignores obvious symbols of male dominance in precapitalist societies (e.g., foot-binding,* clitoridectomy).

References. Josephine Donovan, *Feminist Theory: The Intellectual Traditions of American Feminism*, ch. 3 (New York, 1985); Friedrich Engels, *Origin of the Family, Private Property, and the State* (New York, 1972); Janet Sayers, Mary Evans, Nanneke Redclift (eds.), *Engels Revisited* (London, 1987); Lise Vogel, *Marxism and the Oppression of Women: Toward a Unitary Theory* (New Brunswick, N.J., 1983).

OSTEOPOROSIS is a condition of increased porosity of the bones that results in their increased fragility. It is more common in women than men and is most common in postmenopausal women.

It is a biological condition with immense social ramifications, too often turning a lively, independent woman into a dependent "little old lady." Women may lose as much as eight inches in height, as one or more vertebrae collapse. Fractures from falls (falls may actually be the result of weakened bones) often have serious complications. More than half of women with hip fractures never regain normal functioning; nearly one-third die within a year of the fracture.

Bone remodeling (constant process of breaking down and reforming) is a complex interaction of hormonal, dietary, and physical activity factors. Estrogen and hormone replacement therapy seem to slow the rate of bone loss in the years immediately around menopause* (the time of most rapid bone loss). However, ERT (estrogen only) or HRT (estrogen plus a progestin) is effective only as long as it is taken. As the safety of these products is questionable, emphasis should be placed on other preventive measures. Regular weight-bearing exercise (such as walking) is an excellent preventive measure. Calcium intake, in the diet or as supplements, also needs to be stressed as a prophylactic measure because while women's calcium requirements increase with age, calcium absorption decreases with age, and many women do not take in sufficient calcium. (Recommendation: 800–1,000 mg. calcium per day before menopause, 1,200–1,400 mg. calcium during and after menopause.) Vitamin D and fluoride are also important. Factors known to have an adverse effect on bone restructuring include high intakes of alcohol, caffeine, phosphorus, protein, and salt.

Although osteoporosis is probably preventable in most women, some women have more natural protection than others. Black women, for example, are less likely to develop osteoporosis than light-skinned women. Fat women are less prone to the condition than thin women. Osteoporosis is a prime example of why a life cycle approach to women's health promotion needs to be emphasized. Early and continued good nutrition and weight-bearing exercise help prevent osteoporosis by building strong bones and minimizing bone loss. The most rapid loss of bone takes place during menopause, but the consequences of bone loss are most apparent later in life. There is increasing evidence that "it is never too late" to adapt bone-strengthening measures.

As the preceding statements indicate, osteoporosis is certainly a serious issue. However, in order to create markets for their products, drug and nutrient supplement companies and makers of osteoporosis screening equipment have very deliberately used the media to scare people about this condition. In fact, osteoporosis and how it affects people are much more complicated and unpredictable than product-promoting information suggests. Osteoporosis is not an "all or nothing" condition—a person does not simply "have it" or "not have it." The very definition of osteoporosis, which compares the density of bones of older people to young adults, must be questioned.

Medical facilities are increasingly responding to women's fears of osteoporosis by marketing a range of bone density measurement services. Some points must be clarified for potential consumers. Bone density measurements cannot predict whether or not a person will develop osteoporosis; measurements can only detect signs of osteoporosis as they occur. Bone measurements at one site do not necessarily predict the presence or absence of osteoporosis at another site.

Low bone density does not predict for fractures; some women with good bone density experience fractures, while others with severe bone thinning never suffer a fracture. Regarding the most frightening issue of the relationship of osteoporosis to life-threatening hip fractures, there is evidence that "hip fracture may often be a marker and not the cause of declining health and impending death" ("Osteoporosis").

Reference. "Osteoporosis: Common Test Can't Predict Hip Fractures," *Health Facts* 21, 206 (July 1996): 1, 4–5.

NANCY WORCESTER

P

PAINTERS (TWENTIETH-CENTURY). Although there had been internationally successful women painters since the 1500s, our own century has seen a tremendous increase in the number of European and American women supporting their families and making important cultural contributions through their art.

During the first decades of the twentieth century educational and societal barriers confronting female art students began to fall. At the same time, an explosion of scientific and technological discoveries, along with the traumas of World War I, led to an unprecedented questioning of traditional values and beliefs about all aspects of the world. Women painters played important roles in the radical "isms" that followed one another in rapid succession, including that most remarkable break with the art of the past: abstraction.

Fauvism and expressionism—which originated c. 1905 in France and Germany, respectively—were the first two revolutionary movements in twentieth-century art. Both of these influential styles evolved from the post-impressionist paintings of Cézanne, Seurat, Van Gogh, and Gauguin, and both feature images taken from the real world but stylized through the use of heavy outlines, intense colors, thick pigment, and flattened space. In general, fauve art stresses joyous sensuality, while expressionism evokes a darker mood. The fauve-inspired art of Suzanne Valadon (1865–1938) celebrates the human body, often unashamedly nude and made up of solid, powerfully modeled forms and shocking juxtapositions of violent hues. Fauvism was a significant influence on the late northwestern landscapes of Canadian painter Emily Carr (1871–1945) and on the American Lois Mailou Jones (b. 1905), whose work also reflects her interest in Haitian and African tribal art.

Among the most important German Expressionist artists was Gabriela

Münter (1877–1962). Barred from the official art academies in Munich and Düsseldorf, Münter studied at the coeducational Phalanx School, established by Kandinsky. Münter's highly colored still lifes, landscapes, and figure studies were denounced by the Nazis as "degenerate," along with the art of her countrywoman Käthe Kollwitz (1867–1945).

Probably the most influential modernist style to develop during the first decade of the twentieth century was cubism. Coinvented by Picasso and Braque, cubism, with its distorted spaces and often illegible subject matter, challenged many of the basic tenets of Western art and spawned numerous offshoots, from England's vorticism to Italian futurism. A French variation known as orphism was developed around 1911 by Sonia Terk Delaunay (1885–1979) and her husband, Robert Delaunay. Russian-born and German-trained, Delaunay was strongly affected by the avant-garde artists she encountered on moving to Paris; her mature paintings feature complex arrangements of brightly colored, interlacing arcs. A number of modern art pioneers came from prerevolutionary Russia. One of these was Natalya Goncharova (1881–1962), who, along with Mikhail Larionov, developed a cubist offshoot called rayonism, in which highly stylized forms are crisscrossed by a series of diagonal lines, or "rays."

The work of the American painter Georgia O'Keeffe (1887–1986) is related to, but not directly influenced by, early twentieth-century European experimental art. Best known for her compelling images of flowers and sun-bleached bones, O'Keeffe is significant in art history primarily because of the spare, elegant watercolor abstractions she produced as early as 1915.

During the late 1920s and 1930s, surrealism became a powerful force in avantgarde literature and visual and performing arts. Like their male counterparts, American painters Kay Sage (1898–1963) and Dorothea Tanning (b. 1910), Spaniard Remedios Varo (1913–1963), British artist Leonora Carrington (b. 1917), and the Argentine Léonor Fini (b. 1908) created irrational, often erotic and/or violent compositions juxtaposing unrelated objects derived from their subconscious minds. The art of Frida Kahlo (1910–1954) is also surreal, combining Christian symbols with references to the folk art of her native Mexico.

In the United States the 1930s and early 1940s were dominated by American scene painting—realistic representations of identifiably American subjects. In painting the landscape of New York City, Isabel Bishop (1902–1988) lovingly describes such ordinary moments as two office workers on their lunch break or a man getting a shoeshine.

At midcentury American art underwent an unprecedented change. The international art world shifted its center from Europe to the United States, specifically, New York, with the development of abstract expressionism: a radically new kind of abstraction—less cerebral than cubism, visceral, highly personal, and more appropriate to the post–World War II environment. While traditionally regarded as a male phenomenon—exemplified by the hard-drinking, chain-smoking, aggressively macho figure of Jackson Pollock—there were many important female abstract expressionists. Chief among these was Lee Krasner (1908–1984), whose "Little Image" paintings of the late 1940s were quintessential examples of this style. Other important abstract expressionist painters include Elaine Fried De Kooning (b. 1920), Grace Hartigan (b. 1922), Joan Mitchell (b. 1926), and Helen Frankenthaler (b. 1928).

The generation of painters who matured during the 1960s tended to react against what they perceived as the emotional excesses of abstract expressionism by moving either toward a form of realism that stressed the brand-name, throwaway nature of American culture (pop art) or toward an exploration of emotionally neutral abstraction—using simple forms, unmodulated colors, and smooth surfaces (postpainterly abstraction). Prominent among the latter group is the English artist Bridget Riley (b. 1931), who made her reputation with a series of sophisticated canvases in which repeating black, white, and gray shapes curve in and out through illusionistic space.

The tremendous growth of the women's movement during the 1960s was reflected in the new prominence of openly feminist artists such as Toronto-born Miriam Schapiro (b. 1923). Trained as an abstract expressionist, Schapiro developed what she calls "femmage"—a technique combining colorful, commonplace materials traditionally associated with women, such as scraps of lace, sequins, and tea towels—into elaborate compositions. Along with Judy Chicago (b. 1939), Schapiro organized the first feminist art program in the United States at the California Institute of Arts.

A popular phenomenon of the early 1970s was photorealism—extraordinarily detailed paintings that painstakingly reproduce the optical effects (including out-of-focus areas) seen in actual photos. Audrey Flack (b. 1931) is a New York painter known for her large-scale, photorealistic still lifes, which include a remarkable amount of iconographic content.

The many and varied approaches that have characterized avant-garde painting in the 1980s—including neo-expressionism, serial repetition, image appropriation, and the incorporation of three-dimensional objects into canvases—have all been explored by important women artists, notably Susan Rothenberg (b. 1945), Jennifer Bartlett (b. 1941), Sherrie Levine (b. 1947), and Elizabeth Murray (b. 1940).

References. Ann Sutherland Harris and Linda Nochlin, *Women Artists: 1550–1950* (Los Angeles, 1976); Randy Rosen and Catherine C. Brawer et al., *Making Their Mark: Women Artists Move into the Mainstream, 1970–1985* (New York, 1989).

NANCY G. HELLER

PAINTERS, U.S. (BEFORE WORLD WAR I). Women painters, often self-taught, were active participants in the arts of the new American republic as folk artists, miniaturists, and, later, landscape, history, and genre painters.

The work of self-taught women helped meet the need for wall decorations. One of the most original painters was Eunice Griswold Pinney (1770–1849) of New York State. In strong, two-dimensional watercolors, such as *Two Women* (c. 1815), the flattened perspective and careful arrangement of objects contribute to the design. Among numerous other folk painters are Mary Ann Willson (fl. 1810–1825) of Green County, New York, who used crude, homemade paints in brightly colored scenes from the Bible, history, and literature; Ruth Miles Bascom (1772–1848), who did profile-portraits of friends and neighbors in rural Massachusetts; and anonymous Shaker women, whose "spirit drawings" were inspired by the spirit of their deceased leader Ann Lee.

Although art academies opened at the beginning of the nineteenth century, women were not admitted as students for several decades but had to rely for training on private lessons, usually with a family member. Nonetheless, the American academies were more open to women than were their European counterparts. The Pennsylvania Academy of Fine Arts in Philadelphia (opened 1805) included women in its first exhibit in 1811. Approximately 6 percent of the artists who exhibited between 1826 and 1860 at the National Academy of Design (founded in New York, 1825) were women, and 11 associate, 4 honorary, and 1 full membership were held by women. The New York academy accepted women on a regular basis from 1846. Anna and Sarah Peale were elected to the Pennsylvania Academy in 1824, and Jane Sully in 1831; the first evidence that women were regular students comes in 1844.

Admission as students did not include attendance at life classes with nude models. Beginning in 1844 the Pennsylvania Academy closed its antique sculpture gallery for three hours a week so women could study the figures. In 1856 gallery attendance was desegregated, but close-fitting fig leaves had been added to male figures as necessary. Live female models were introduced into women's segregated life classes in 1860; male models in 1877. The National Academy allowed women in life classes in 1871.

Miniatures were considered most suitable for women painters in the early nineteenth century, as they had been in the eighteenth, when Henrietta Johnston (d. 1728–1729) became the first American woman professional artist. Sarah Goodrich (1788–1853) of rural Massachusetts did miniatures on ivory of portraitist Gilbert Stuart, leading members of Boston society, and government leaders in Washington. Gilbert Stuart taught students, including Goodrich, but not members of his own family. Jane Stuart (1812–1888), his youngest, was able to pick up information from his instruction of others while filling in his backgrounds and grinding paints. After his death in 1828, she supported her mother and three sisters by making copies of his work, especially his *Athenaeum Head of George Washington*, and by her original portraits. She also did biblical and literary scenes.

Ann Hall (1792–1863), miniaturist from Connecticut, was the first woman to be a full member of the National Academy of Design (1833). Her group portraits of upper-class women and children had a delicacy and flattering "sweetness" highly admired at the time.

The "Painting Peales" of Philadelphia were the most famous family of painters in early America. Several daughters of James Peale became professional artists. Anna Claypoole Peale (1791–1878), who learned painting on ivory from her father, shared a studio in Washington, D.C., with the most famous Peale, her uncle Charles Willson Peale, and painted such worthies as General Jackson and President Monroe. She retired during her second marriage, then continued her career in Philadelphia when widowed.

Sarah Miriam Peale (1800–1885), the most successful of the Peale women, did full-size portraits during a long career. In Baltimore she competed successfully with some of the leading male portraitists of the day. After 22 years in Baltimore she went to St. Louis for a rest and stayed over 30 years. In her late 70s she returned to Philadelphia and continued painting, principally still lifes. Her portraits show people in their best light, dignified but not idealized.

Other female "Painting Peales" include still-life artist Margarette Angelicia Peale (1795–1882), another daughter of James, and, in the next generation, Mary Jane Simes (1807–1852), granddaughter of James, miniaturist, and Mary Jane Peale (1827–1902), granddaughter of Charles Willson, portrait painter.

By midcentury the increasingly affluent middle class provided a new group of art patrons looking for paintings that satisfied their taste for the romantic and the sentimental and reinforced their moral values. Women painters turned increasingly to genre, history, and allegory.

Herminia Borchard Dassel (d. 1858), born in Germany, studied in Düsseldorf and Italy, leaving Italy for America when revolution broke out in 1848. In the United States, she turned to the American scene for her genre paintings, including romantic paintings of American Indians.

Lilly Martin Spencer (1822–1902) from Ohio was a leading American genre painter of midcentury. In 1848 she moved to New York, where she supported her husband and large family by her painting (Benjamin Spencer assisted his wife and did much of the running of the household). Mrs. Spencer was interested in allegorical and literary subjects and used the portrait as a vehicle for allegory (*We Both Must Fade* [1869]), but her reputation rested on her genre paintings. She met the public taste for sentiment by domestic scenes, often with a vein of humor (*Peeling Onions* [c. 1852]). Prints from engravings and lithographs of her work entered homes all over America and sometimes abroad, but she had difficulty keeping her family afloat financially—she was paid only for the original painting. After the Civil War, as buyers of art preferred European paintings, her financial plight grew even worse; she sometimes had to barter her paintings for food.

Representative of the many women painters active in the second and third quarter of the nineteenth century and of the subjects women painted are the following. Charlotte Buell Coman (1833–1924) of New York was a "tonalist" landscape artist whose quiet, misty scenes were designed to create a mood in the viewer. Typical are her *Early Summer* (1907) and *Clearing Off* (1912). Fidelia Bridges (1834–1932) of Massachusetts, nature artist, did close-up studies of grasses, ferns, flowers, birds, as in *Daises and Clover* (1871) and *Thrush in Wild Flower* (1874). Anna Elizabeth Hardy (1839–1934) of Bangor, Maine, was a still-life artist whose best works are the well-defined fruit and flower studies of her early career. Susan Moore Waters (1823–1900) of Binghamton, New York, was an animal painter especially noted for her pictures of sheep.

During the "Gilded Age" (1876–1900) affluent Americans looked to Europe for culture and found things American inferior. Art students traveled to Europe, especially to Paris, international mecca of the arts. In the art academies open to women (the École des Beaux Arts and the Royal Academy in London did not open until the last decade of the century), women's life classes were segregated, cost more, and had inferior models and lower standards, but women flocked to them nonetheless. Most women went to Europe for a few years; a few remained for the rest of their lives, returning to America only for visits.

The expatriates include one of the century's greatest artists, Mary Cassatt. (See FRENCH IMPRESSIONIST PAINTERS.) Another expatriate was Elizabeth Gardener (Bouguereau) (1833–1922), the first American woman to receive a gold medal at the Paris Salon. Living in Paris, she painted sentimental genre and allegory and finally married William Bouguereau after his mother, who opposed the marriage, died (he was 71; she 58). Among other expatriate women artists were Ann Lea Merrit (1844–1930) and Sarah Paxton Dodson (1847–1906), academic painters who settled in England, Cecile Smith de Wentworth (1853?–1933), best known for her portrait of Leo XIII, and Elizabeth Nouse (1859–1938), noted for her outstanding studies of European peasant women, who settled in France.

Growing dissatisfaction with American art schools not only gave impetus to the flight to Paris but led to the formation of the progressive Art Students League in 1875 and in 1877 the Society of American Artists, one of whose aims was to encourage women artists. (See ART STUDENTS LEAGUE.) As the number of women artists continued to increase, a sign of the art schools' growing dependence on women students was the Pennsylvania Academy of Fine Arts' hiring of Catherine Drinker (Janvier) (1841–1922) in 1878 as part-time lecturer and Cecilia Beaux as the first full-time woman instructor in 1895.

Susan Macdowell Eakins (1851–1938) of Philadelphia, realist painter and first recipient of the Pennsylvania Academy's Mary Smith Award (1879), married her teacher Thomas Eakins in 1884. During their marriage she placed his career first, greatly reducing her own production, but after his death in 1916 she immersed herself in painting again. Her work (*Two Sisters* [1879] and *Portrait of a Lady* [1880] are among her best) is marked by strong characterization and lack of sentimentality.

Cecilia Beaux (1855–1942) was a leading portraitist of the late nineteenth century. She achieved success with her first major work, *Les Derniers Jours d'Enfance* (1883–1885), which won the Mary Smith Award and was accepted at the Paris Salon in 1887. Another of her finest paintings, *Fanny Travis Cochran* (1887), dates from her early period. After study in Europe she established a New York studio and joined the world of the New York social and intellectual elite. There in the 1890s she did a series of double portraits, including *Mother and Daughter* (1898), her most highly acclaimed and honored work. A major triumph of the early twentieth century is *After the Meeting* (1914).

Anna Elizabeth Klumpke (1856–1942) was born in San Francisco but received her education in Europe. She won honorable mention in Paris salons in 1885 and 1887, the latter for her portrait of Elizabeth Cady Stanton, then 71. She was teaching and painting in Boston when she wrote Rosa Bonheur asking to do her portrait (See FRENCH ACADEMIC ARTISTS.) In 1898 she went to By, Bonheur's estate at Fontainebleau, where a deep friendship developed, and Bonheur asked her to remain and to write her biography. The portrait of Bonheur in 1898 is Klumpke's finest work. The biography was published in 1908. Klumpke's last years were spent between San Francisco, Boston, and By.

A few of the many other American women artists of note during the last quarter of the nineteenth century include Mary Lizzie Macomber (1861–1916), Pre-Raphaelite painter; Lucia Fairchild Fuller (1870–1924), one of the few miniaturists of the period; Anna Richards Brewster (1870–1952), landscape artist; Lilla Cabot Perry (1848–1933), impressionist; Mary Oakey Dewing (1845–1927) and Claude Raguet Hirst (1855–1942), still-life painters; Jennie Augusta Brownscombe (1850–1936), commercial artist and American history painter; Alice Baker Stephenson (1858–1932), one of the best-known illustrators in America at the time; and Grace Carpenter Hudson, painter of American Indians.

Both the Philadelphia Centennial Exposition in 1876 and the World's Columbian Exposition in Chicago in 1893 provided a showcase for women's accomplishments in the arts. In both, a separate building housed exhibitions of women's accomplishments, in the arts as well as in other areas, and in both, women's artworks were not limited to the women's building. The works on display demonstrated the rich variety and the quality of nineteenth-century art by women.

Reference. Charlotte Streifer Rubinstein, *American Women Artists: From Early Indian Times to the Present* (Boston, 1982).

PAKISTAN, created in 1947 at the partition of British India into predominantly Hindu India and Muslim Pakistan, consists of four provinces, Sind, Baluchistan, Punjab, the North-West Frontier (NWFP), and the federally administered tribal areas. Economic and health statistics are typical of a poor, densely populated country. The U.S. Central Intelligence Agency supplies estimated 1996 statistics for the country: 42 percent of the population of 129,275,660 is between the ages of 0 and 14 years; thus, a very high percentage of the population is dependent and too young to be productive. The infant mortality rate is 96.8/1,000 live births. The total fertility rate is 5.25 children per woman. The population growth rate is 2.24 percent. Life expectancy at birth is 57.7 years for males, 59.25 years for females. The literacy rate (people over the age of 15 who can read and write) is 50 percent of males, 24.4 percent of females. The inflation rate in 1995 was 13 percent.

The position of women varies from province to province, but a general construction of the proper behavior of women maintains throughout the country. Culturally, a woman's sphere of activity is seen to be in the home. Pakistan is officially an Islamic state, and 97 percent of its citizens are Muslim. Women are expected to avoid the company of unrelated males and to cover hair and face in public. Observance of purdah* (the isolation of women in the home, away from the gaze of unrelated males) is seen as an ideal. (Purdah has always been an ideal, rather than a common, practice: women in rural areas work in the fields with their male relatives; in towns, poor women work as servants and street cleaners and in factories. Purdah demonstrates economic standing as well as piety.) There is to be no suggestion, particularly, of sexual activity outside marriage. Such activity lowers the honor of the family, and the male relatives of a transgressing female are expected to kill her. The Human Rights Commission of Pakistan reported that in 1996 over 300 women were killed to avenge an insult or protect the honor of the family. The commission also reported that, on average, a female was raped every three hours in 1996, and half of those raped were children.

Since independence, the country has alternated between elected governments and martial law imposed by the military or bureaucracy. Political instability has given a considerable amount of influence to well-organized groups such as the Islamic political parties. While the Islamic parties have done badly in elections, they have been influential in bringing about legislation to correspond more closely with Islamic law as interpreted by conservative religious leaders.

Islam is not a monolithic religious belief system; there are conflicting interpretations of Islam within the Islamic world. The modernist position argues that some parts of the Koran and teachings of the Prophet apply to the time of Muhammad and that one of the Koranic bases of legislation, *ijtihad*, interpretation, is to be applied to modern problems to find modern solutions. The traditionalists, on the contrary, argue that the Koran and teachings of the Prophet are to be interpreted literally.

General Zia-ul-Haq, in a bloodless coup in 1977, seized power from Prime Minister Zulfikar Ali Bhutto. Bhutto was tried and hanged for arranging the murder of a political opponent in 1979. Zia announced that he would retain power until the country was "Islamized." He adopted the most traditional of viewpoints, and his "Islamization" attacked the weakest parts of the society, women and minority religious groups.

In 1979, Zia introduced the Hudood Ordinance, which covers theft, drunkenness, adultery, rape, and bearing false witness. The maximum penalty for fornication by a married person is stoning to death; by an unmarried person, 100 lashes. Conviction of rape requires the testimony of four male witnesses of good repute. A woman who registers a complaint of rape can have her testimony used against her in a prosecution for fornication while her rapist goes free, as happened in the Safia Bibi case.

Safia Bibi, a young blind girl, was raped by her employer and his son. Under the Hudood Ordinance, the case was dismissed for lack of evidence, and the young woman's evidence was used to charge her with fornication. She was sentenced to public lashing (15 lashes), three years' imprisonment, and a fine of Rs. 1,000. Women's groups took up her case, which was widely publicized both within Pakistan and outside the country.

Arguments concerning such cases (and the legislation that makes them possible) have been conducted in Pakistan within an Islamic perspective: rather than arguing for the rights of women (tainted by association of women's rights with colonialism and the perceived immorality of the West), women and male supporters have argued from an Islamic position. The Women's Action Forum, in conjunction with other women's groups, took up the case and prepared an appeal. The Federal Shariat [religious] Court overturned the lower court's ruling, and Safia Bibi was declared innocent. In addition, the judge criticized the Hudood Ordinance from an Islamic legal perspective.

A series of laws inimical to the rights of women were passed, culminating in the Shariat Bill in 1986. This states that the Koran and Sunnah (life of the Prophet Muhammad) are to be the source of law, and, further, the bill establishes that judges are to be appointed from only one of the four major schools of Islamic jurisprudence, the conservative Hannafi legal school of

Sunni Islam. The bill has not been implemented. It was opposed by all major political parties, non-Sunni Muslim groups, and minority religious groups.

Zia-ul-Haq controlled Pakistan until his death in an unexplained air crash in August 1988. He left a corrupt, bankrupt, and violent society, awash in arms and drugs and the money that comes from dealing in illicit arms and drugs.

Benazir Bhutto, daughter of the hanged prime minister Zulifikar Ali Bhutto, had led political opposition to Zia during his life. After his death, she was elected prime minister of the country. Great optimism greeted the restoration of democracy in 1988. Benazir Bhutto, like her father, ran on a populist platform promising economic and social reform, including the repeal of legislation detrimental to women. Her party, the PPP (the People's Party of Pakistan, founded by Zulifikar), lacked a clear parliamentary majority after the 1988 election. The PPP received only 2 percent more popular votes than its closest rivals, a coalition of conservative and religious parties. This very slim parliamentary majority considerably constrained what Prime Minister Bhutto could do. Even with a large majority, Benazir Bhutto could not have satisfied the expectations of her supporters.

Reform would involve curtailing the power of the most powerful sections of Pakistani society, including the military, and no elected politician could win such a confrontation. Benazir Bhutto attempted to compromise with the military and landlord elite, as her father had done, and her own populist program was jettisoned.

Benazir Bhutto was the first woman elected head of an Islamic state. Religious leaders attempted (unsuccessfully) to pass a constitutional amendment banning a woman from heading the government. Attacks based on her sex were a minor problem compared with other problems. Sind, particularly Karachi, became a battleground. Ethnic rivalries, communal rivalries, and competing drug and arms gang rivalries were resolved in open warfare. The prime minister and her government were seen as incompetent, weak, and, in addition, corrupt. Prime Minister Bhutto's husband was charged with taking bribes to influence awarding government contracts. He was popularly known as "Mr. 20%," the percentage he was alleged to have charged for arranging contracts.

In 1990, her government was dismissed by the president, who cited civil disorder in Sind and corruption as the cause for calling new elections. Mien Nawaz Sharif, a Lahori businessman, became prime minister. In 1993, his government was dismissed on charges of corruption, and new elections were held. Benazir Bhutto again became prime minister, and in 1996 her government was dissolved by the president on charges of corruption, again largely related to the behavior of her husband. New elections were held, and Nawaz Sharif again became prime minister.

The social and legal disabilities women face are serious. Active women's groups in the country, with the support of many men, are challenging these disabilities with some success. Economic, social, and human rights problems faced by both women and men seem far less susceptible to solution.

References. Hamza Alavi, "Pakistan and Islam: Ethnicity and Ideology," in Fred Halliday and Hamza Alavi (eds.), *State and Ideology in the Middle East and Pakistan* (New York, 1988); Jalal Ayesha, *Democracy and Authoritarianism in South Asia* (Cambridge, U.K., 1995); Khawar Mumtaz and Ferida Shaheed, *Women of Pakistan: Two Steps Forward, One Step Back?* (Lahore, 1987). The Internet is a good source of current information on Pakistan. All of the major Pakistan English-language newspapers are available on-line: *The Nation*: http://brain.brain.net.pk/nation and http//www.syberwurx.com/nation/, *The News*: http://www.jang-group.com/thenews/; *Pakistan Today*: http://www.10mb.com/paktoday/; *Dawn*: http://xiber.com/dawn. Statistical information came from "Pakistan" in the Central Intelligence Agency 1995 World Factbook http://www.odci.gov/cia/publications/nsolo/factbook/pk/htm. Other addresses: Khanum Gauhar, "Career Women in Pakistan Chances and Scopes in Professional Life in an Islamic Society" at http://berlin.snafu.de/ ˜dgfk /PAKWomen.html; Wenonah Lyon, "Three Women: Getting By in Lahore," at http://lucy.ukc.ac.uk/CSACSIA/Vol11/Papers/lyon/3Women/3Women.html.

WENONAH L. LYON

PAP SMEAR is a method developed by the American scientist Dr. George Papanicolaou for detecting changes in cells. Its principal use is in detecting cancerous and precancerous cells in the cervix. It can also detect inflammatory cell changes and the presence of viruses (e.g., herpes) and can be used to test cell changes in areas other than the cervix. Cells are collected from the surface of the cervix (or other area) and spread thinly on a slide. The slide is sent to a laboratory where it is stained and examined microscopically.

The Pap smear is not completely accurate. Mistakes in collecting cells and handling the slide are sometimes made. It is also possible, without anyone's being at fault, that the test may not detect cancer when it is present or may suggest the presence of malignancy when none is present. The most common inaccuracy lies in the pathologist's classification of the degree of abnormality, if abnormality is detected. Any finding of abnormality needs to be followed up by a biopsy.* All women over 20, or younger if they are hetrosexually active, should have periodic Pap smears.

PARTURITION is the process of giving birth. The first of the three stages of parturition, or childbirth,* begins with labor, involuntary rhythmic contractions that strengthen in intensity and discomfort as they continue. The contractions shorten and dilate (open) the cervix and break the fetal membrane. When the cervix is fully dilated, it is large enough for the baby to pass through.

In the second stage, after the dilation of the cervix, labor contractions begin to push the baby through the birth canal. In 95 percent of the cases, the baby is in the optimal position, with the top of the head presented first. Following the appearance of the head, there is usually a quarter turn, then the shoulders come out one at a time, followed by the body. In other cases the head may appear first, but with the face or brow presented. In breech births, the buttocks or the feet appear first; in a transverse birth, one of the shoulders comes first.

The baby may nurse right away or may not. Suckling helps to bring about the third and final stage, which should follow within a half hour of delivery. There is a return of uterine contractions, which expel the after-birth (the placenta and fetal membrane).

PASTORAL SOCIETIES. In pastoral societies women occupy a pivotal position in the organization of production. Among the nomadic groups that specialize in raising sheep and goats in the mountainous regions of the Middle East, a woman's labor and decision-making input are prodigious. (1) She performs nearly all daily chores, including milking and processing of the milk into yogurt, cheese curds, butter, or ghee (clarified butter) for domestic consumption and exchange. (2) She bears enormous, though not exclusive, responsibility for the maintenance of the flock and the newborns while in the camp. (3) She has a prominent role in hiring shepherds and dairymaids who are recruited from kinsmen with surplus labor. (4) Although men do assist in shearing the animals, she alone does the carding and spinning of wool and goat hair. Woven pile rugs, blankets, kilims (flat-woven rugs), tent cloth, saddlebags, horse covers, grain sacks, and ropes are among a large number of utilitarian and ornamental objects crafted by women. These items constitute the savings of a family and can be readily converted into cash to meet economic and social obligations. (5) She takes an active part in the allocation of all products for market, local barter, and ceremonial occasions. In this respect men and women share similar power. (6) Her intimate knowledge of the flock and concern for its continual growth perforce give her a strong voice in decisions with respect to the sale of animals to raise cash or to repay debts to urban creditors. (7) Her routine managerial duties become even more onerous during the annual migrations between the summer and winter pastures. In this labor-intensive period she carries out such seemingly masculine activities as loading and unloading baggage animals. These demanding tasks, however, free the men to devote full attention to the security of the herd while en route. As an adult member of the camping community (comprising several tent households of close kinsmen), she participates in deliberations about departure time, the distance of daily moves, and the relative advantage of the various stops along the migration route.

Typically, the tent households that make up a camping unit share a corporate interest in all aspects of herding. Matters regarding pasture, water, seasonal migration and movements, selection of camping sites, and the safety of the migration routes all require collective decision making that transcends the private sphere. Put differently, concern for the well-being, care, and growth of the family herd bridges the private and public domains.

Although the majority of pastoral nomads engage in some subsidiary farming, the optimal herd of about 30 head forms the economic underpinning of the family. To illustrate, pastoral products are of crucial importance for obtaining credit from the urban trade partners. Meat, though conspicuously absent from the daily diet, is consumed ceremonially as an integral part of the collective observance of all life crises. The generational continuity of the nomadic lifestyle itself is dependent on the herd; the son's bride-price as well as the nucleus of his productive capital (considered his patrimony) after marriage are allocated from the main herd. The daughter, however, does not receive an analogous anticipatory inheritance upon marriage, even though Islam prescribes a share equal to one-half of the male's.

Similarly, in these intensely patrilineal societies women do not inherit political office and play no part in the formal leadership structure. Nevertheless, they wield considerable influence in the public arena. Women among the ruling elite, in particular, have historically achieved a legendary reputation for their ability to exercise informal power in favor of male relatives.

The foregoing discussion may permit at least two generalizations: first, among the transhumant groups women enjoy an extraordinary decision-making power by virtue of their dominant role in the economy. Second, the community's overarching interests seem to preclude a clear-cut division between the private and public spheres; the two dimensions of power are interdependent and inseparable, and the public emanates from the private as a necessary and logical extension.

In the past few decades nomadic pastoral societies in nearly every country in the Middle East have increasingly been undergoing change in response to both internal and external pressures. While the causes are manifold and vary from one country to another, a confluence of demographic and ecological factors has had significant effects. Modern medicine, for instance, has been responsible for an unprecedented rate of human population growth and a parallel rise in animal population. The result is often widespread overgrazing and severe animal epidemics occurring with an alarming frequency.

Setbacks in the pastoral economy, on the other hand, are almost predictably accompanied by a shift to full-time subsistence farming and an attendant reduction in female-dominated economic activities. Though women customarily assist with the harvesting of crops, the main agricultural tasks are performed by the men. One important corollary of a male-dominated production is generally an increase in the men's control over the recruitment and deployment of labor and the allocation of resources.

In sum, to the extent that nomadic herding is replaced by settled farming, women will experience a decline in their economic role and social status.

REZA FAZEL

PATRIARCHY is the system of male dominance by which men as a group acquire and maintain power over women as a group.

Literally, patriarchy means "rule of the father." Prior to its use by radical feminists, it was employed primarily by students of anthropology and history to designate the structure of pastoral and nomadic societies. The early seventeenth-century English writer Robert Filmer used the model of the patriarchal family as the basis of his vision of government, in which rulers act toward their subjects as men act toward their wives and children. Responding to Filmer, political theorist John Locke rejected the parallel between family and state without rejecting the legitimacy of father rule within families. Late nineteenth-century writers such as Lewis Morgan (*Systems of Consanguinity and Affinity of the Human Family* [1871]) and Johann J. Bachofen (*Mother Right* [1861]) used the term to debate whether the earliest human societies were male- or female-dominated.

Contemporary feminists have inherited some of these debates and have also tried to go beyond them. Disputes among feminists about the origins of patriarchy, the historical status of matriarchy,* and the wisdom of using the term "patriarchy" at all make generalizations difficult. Feminists such as Michele Rosaldo and Allison Jaggar have objected to such a blanket term because it implies a lack of attention to the historical particularities of different systems of male dominance, while others, such as Mary Daly, have insisted on the importance of naming the common patterns of women's subordination and men's power across historical circumstances. While many radical feminists speak of patriarchy as universal, feminist anthropologist Peggy Sanday argues that many early societies had substantially egalitarian relations between the sexes and that patriarchy develops out of particular environmental and social circumstances. In some ways patriarchy is most important to feminism* not for what it *is* but for what it *is not*: it signifies the systemic conditions of female subordination that feminism opposes. It also makes possible the conditions through which feminism arises as a movement for social change.

Patriarchy refers both to institutions and to discursive accounts of the world within which institutions are embedded. On the institutional level feminists have pointed to male dominance within family, state, religion, capitalism, education, and other social structures and have analyzed the practices by which male dominance is established and maintained. Further, feminist analyses of conventional relations between women and men show how male power insinuates itself into the psyches of women, teaching them to collaborate in defining themselves as subordinate to, and dependent on, men. Yet the experiences women have within patriarchy, especially those binding them to other women in recognition of their common plight, can be the source of feminist resistance.

On the level of discourse, feminists have condemned patriarchy for creating and reflecting an exclusively masculine view of the world and for rendering women's experiences and women's perspectives invisible. Patriarchal thought is characterized by the imposition of dualisms and oppositions onto the disparate flow of experience: reason versus emotions; mind versus body; subject versus object. Patriarchy then favors one side of each pair over the other, establishing a hierarchy of classifications in which what is associated with the male is given priority to what represents the female. Thus patriarchy establishes male dominance in its basic accounts of the world and its standards of knowledge and judgment, as well as in its concrete institutions and practices. But once again women's experiences as marginalized within patriarchy can spur a more determined articulation of their points of view, thus evoking a set of feminist discourses that arise to challenge the dominant patriarchal view.

Despite differences over proper usage of the term, most feminists would agree that patriarchy entails efforts by men to control women's bodies. Patriarchal discourse defines women as uniquely, sometimes solely, suited for bearing and raising children. Through patriarchal institutions men in power attempt to control women's fertility by restricting or imposing contraception and abortion. Through direct violence against women, through rape* and the threat of rape, men exercise control over the activities and choices of women. Through the reduction of women to objects of male sexual desire, men turn women's bodies into possessions and reward women for successful competition with one another for the attention, approval, and protection of men. Yet once again patriarchy can be turned on itself, and the controls imposed on women's bodies can be transformed into vehicles for their liberation; thus, some feminists have embraced the values and practices of mothering as the source of alternatives to patriarchal institutions, and others have looked to knowledge residing in the body to confront patriarchal discourse.

Different conceptualizations of patriarchy imply distinct strategies of analysis. Feminists who emphasize the universal or nearly universal character of male dominance tend to see patriarchy as a single thing and to stress the search for its origins. Feminists who take a more historically specific approach tend to advocate the investigation of particular institutions and processes within concrete settings.

Differing conceptualizations of patriarchy also lead to different strategies of resistance and change. Those who conceive of it as a nearly universal web of male dominance tend to embrace a strategy of cultural change, whereby women are encouraged to establish a separate women's culture with a woman-centered set of rituals, symbols, and languages. Those who emphasize the historical particularity of male power tend to look to its operation within particular institutions and practices and to stress resistance to these structures. Some emphasize marriage as the crucial institution to be resisted, while others point to compulsory heterosexuality* or to the control of women's productive and reproductive labor by men.

In recent years controversies in feminism surrounding the term "patriarchy" have diminished. Now feminists tend to take patriarchy as a general descriptor of male dominance. Perhaps the linguistic turn in recent feminist theory has given more significance to specifically discursive terms, such as phallocentrism, while feminist suspicions about the dangers of overly broad categories make sweeping generalizations about men suspect.

References. Diana H. Coole, *Women in Political Theory* (Boulder, Colo., 1988); Mary Daly, *Gyn/Ecology: The Metaethics of Radical Feminism* (Boston, 1978); Allison Jaggar, *Feminist Politics and Human Nature* (Totowa, N.J., 1983); Gerda Lerner, *The Creation of Patriarchy* (New York, 1986); L. Nicholson, *Gender and History: The Limits of Social Theory in the Age of the Family* (New York, 1986); Michele Rosaldo, "The Use and Abuse of Anthropology: Reflections on Feminism and Cross-Cultural Understanding," *Signs* 5 (1980): 389–417; Peggy Sanday, *Female Power and Male Dominance* (New York, 1981); Mary L. Shanley and Carole Pateman (eds.), *Feminist Interpretations and Political Theory* (University Park, Pa., 1991).

KATHY E. FERGUSON

PATRILINY, descent through the male line, is the lineage system that has prevailed in Western society. Descent cannot be passed through a woman, although women are accounted as patrilineal kin. The need of men to be assured of the continuation of their lineage, for the performance of rites and the inheritance of property, has been cited as a primary factor in the subjection of women.

PATRONS AND COLLECTORS, U.S., have yet to undergo serious study. At this time only a random sample of women's contributions, through patronage, to U.S. cultural life is possible.

In Europe women of royal and aristocratic families, as part of their social and political roles, served as patrons of arts and letters. Since the French Revolution, as monarchies were eliminated, their art collections were opened to the public (e.g., the Louvre in Paris, the Hermitage in Leningrad), and the new republican governments took over the function of promoting and supporting the arts. Where monarchy persists, although royal influence can be important in promoting cultural forms, as the powers of the monarch were transferred to elective governments, so, too, was the support of the cultural life of the community.

In the United States, where republican government was established under Enlightenment ideals that restricted the government's role to the protection of life, liberty, and property and where there was no royalty or titled aristocracy with a tradition of patronage, promotion of the arts was slow to develop and fell to private individuals and groups. State and local governments became involved, beyond granting tax exemptions to cultural organizations, only from the latter nineteenth century, when they began to include art and music in school curricula and sometimes helped to support concert halls, museums, and libraries originally established by private means. Not until the mid-twentieth century did the federal government become involved, indirectly through the Works Progress Administration during the depression and, since the 1960s, through the National Endowments for the Arts and Humanities.

Patronage of the arts in the United States, then, has been, and continues to be, primarily private, often by the combined efforts of people of relatively moderate wealth. Women's clubs, since the latter half of the nineteenth century organized by women for personal and social betterment, have been responsible for much of the promotion of the performing arts.

Mutual interest in music led to the formation of women's music clubs; the oldest was the Rossini Club of Portland, Maine, founded in 1868 by five women for the advancement of music in their community. These women's clubs gave concerts by their own members and by professional artists. The clubs booked the artists, rented the hall, promoted the event, sold tickets, and sometimes did the janitor work as well. The Mozart Society of New York City in the 1920s sponsored monthly Saturday musicals, evening concerts, a women's chorus, and social events. The women's music club in Oklahoma City organized a string orchestra and engaged a conductor. By 1927 the Oklahoma City Symphony Orchestra had 68 players. Women's clubs, by combining, could arrange a tour that brought great artists to smaller cities. For example, in the early twentieth century the Peoria music club, under Emily Roderick (Mrs. William Fisher), a public school music teacher, brought in the best talent of the day, including orchestras such as the Boston Symphony. The clubs also showed interest in making good music affordable to the poor in their cities and in music education for children. At the turn of the century, the Women's Philharmonic Society of New York sponsored concerts at low prices in tenement districts, music classes for children, and a children's orchestra.

The financial support given by women's committees and associations has been vital to symphonies since 1898, when women in New York founded a committee to support the New York Symphony Orchestra. By the mid-1970s there were over 75 women's symphony orchestra associations in the United States. In 1983 Constance Hoguet, first woman president of the New York Philharmonic Symphony Society, founded and cochaired the Friends of the Philharmonic, which raised $2.675 million for the symphony in 1983. To raise funds and to "democratize" opera, in 1935 Eleanor Elise

Robson Belmont founded the Metropolitan Opera Guild. Scaled membership in the guild helped raise funds and also gave members a sense of ownership and a share in its privileges.

Many of the major cultural institutions in the United States owe their foundation to men and women of great wealth who established museums, conservatories, art institutes, concert halls, festivals, and so on. They and others of lesser means have also supported the arts by establishing scholarships and competitions, acting as sponsors of young artists and musicians, becoming collectors—often later giving some or all of their collections to museums or founding museums to house them—and in other ways.

Only a few women patrons and collectors can be mentioned here, but they represent the many women whose support has helped to enrich life in the United States.

Irene Lewisohn, with her sister Alice, established one of the earliest "little theatres" in the United States, the Neighborhood Playhouse in New York, a major center of experimental theatre from 1915 to 1927. In 1928 she became cofounder and codirector of the Neighborhood Playhouse School and in 1937 founded the Costume Institute, now part of the Metropolitan Museum of Art.

Marie Leontine Graves Bullock in 1934 founded the Academy of American Poets to increase the appreciation of poetry, reward excellent poetry, and encourage new poets. The academy awards scholarships, prizes, and book awards. Elizabeth Kray, executive director of the academy from 1963 to 1981, founded with poet Stanley Kunitz the Poets House as a meeting place for poets.

Mary Curtis Bok Zimbalist founded the Curtis Institute in Philadelphia in 1924. Elizabeth Sprague Collidge devoted her energies and her fortune to the promotion of chamber music. From 1918 to 1925 she put on seven Berkshire festivals of chamber music and from 1923 also arranged festivals in European cities. In 1925 she set up the Elizabeth Sprague Coolidge Foundation at the Library of Congress and donated an auditorium to the library for chamber music concerts. The foundation then became her principal philanthropy, but she continued to encourage chamber music through other avenues as well.

Martha Baird Rockefeller, a former pianist, set up a fund for young musicians and was a major supporter of music institutions in New York and New England. Betty Freeman, a patron of new music, subsidized about 30 composers, including John Cage and Daniel Lentz. She helped finance concerts of new and minimalist music and in 1981 began monthly musicales in her home. A patron of jazz who moved to the United States in the 1950s, Baroness Pannonica de Keonigswarter befriended Charlie Parker and Thelonious Monk and helped finance Barry Harris' Jazz Cultural Theater.

Through the advice of painter Mary Cassatt to wealthy friends, many of Europe's most outstanding paintings made their way to America and, eventually, into its museums. One of these wealthy friends was Bertha Honoré Palmer, social arbiter of Chicago and one of the first to introduce French impressionists to America. On her death in 1918 she left $100,000 in objets d'art to the Chicago Art Institute. Louisine Waldron Elder Havemeyer was introduced to French impressionist art by Cassatt when she was a young girl. She and her husband assembled a remarkable collection of moderns and Spanish paintings. When they left 142 art objects to the Metropolitan Museum of Art, that museum, which had refused to buy moderns, suddenly became one of the world's greatest holders in this area.

To the Havemeyers' dismay, their daughter Electra Havemeyer Webb began quite early to collect what they considered "junk." The result is the Shelburne Museum in Vermont, founded in 1947. It is a 45-acre, open-air museum containing American art, artifacts, and regional architecture: c. 27,000 pieces in 37 buildings, a steam engine, private railway car, and the SS *Ticonderoga*.

Many collections of art were built by husband-and-wife teams; others have been built entirely by women. Jane Stanford collected art objects from around the world to honor the memory of her son Leland, Jr., then, with her husband, built a museum to house them in Palo Alto, California, in 1885. Etta and Clara Cone's collection of twentieth-century art is in the Baltimore Museum of Art; Ola Hirshhorn's is in the Hirshhorn Museum and Sculpture Garden, now part of the Smithsonian. Abby Aldrich Rockefeller, one of three women instrumental in founding the Museum of Modern Art in New York, gave it a large collection (over 2,000 objects) and an unrestricted fund for future purchases. The Abby Aldrich Rockefeller Folk Art Center at Williamsburg attests to her interest in utilitarian arts. Eleanor Biddle Lloyd was a founder of the Washington Gallery of Modern Art in 1950 and Institute of Contemporary Art at the University of Pennsylvania. Gertrude Vanderbilt Whitney, sculptor and patron of artists, with Juliana Force in an association that lasted from about 1907 to Whitney's death in 1942, promoted American art and living American artists, culminating in the Whitney Museum of American Art.

Progeny of philanthropists often continue the family interest in a foundation and may add to it or found new institutions in the same or related fields. Helen Clay Frick served as trustee of the Frick Art Museum (Pittsburgh), founded by her father. She also founded the Frick Art Reference Library in 1924 in New York City and in 1927 financed the Henry Clay Frick Fine Arts Department of the University of Pittsburgh. Flora Whitney Miller, daughter of Gertrude Vanderbilt Whitney, served as chairperson and president of Whitney Museum. Under her leadership the museum and its activities gained national stature.

One of the most avid collectors was Peggy Guggenheim. Her interest peaked to a frenzy of buying in the summer of 1941, when she went through Europe averaging a painting a day, despite the war raging at the time. After her return to America in late 1941 she established a gallery, Art of This Century, which quickly became the center of avant-garde art in New York. She gave generously to many museums in the United States, then in 1947 settled in Venice, where the Peggy Guggenheim Museum is today located.

Collectors of the latter twentieth century include Alice Dresel Beal Van Santvoord of Newburgh, New York, benefactor for artists Childe Hassam, Walt Kuhn, and Timothy Cole. Florence Lacaze Gould and her husband, Frank Jay Gould, were literary patrons and collectors of art of all periods. Later in her life Mrs. Gould became interested in impressionist and post-impressionist painters. Edith and Robert Scull (divorced in 1974) were among the most important collectors of the late 1950s and 1960s. They collected pop art.

There have also been women who collected women's art. Henrietta Louisa Koenen specialized in collecting engravings, etchings, and lithographs by women from 1848 to her death in 1861. In the early 1960s Louise Noun began to collect art by women, and Wilhelmina Cole Holladay, with her husband, Wallace, began specializing in women's art in the late 1960s. Chris Petteys began her collection in the early 1970s. Marge Greenbaum specializes in art by nineteenth- and twentieth-century American women artists. "Billie" Holladay's collection became the core of the National Museum of Women in the Arts, which opened in April 1987, with Holladay as first president.

HELEN TIERNEY with MELISSA HENSLEY

PATRONS OF THE ARTS (MIDDLE AGES AND RENAISSANCE). Although Herbert Grundmann (*Archiv für Kulturgeschichte*) convincingly argued as early as 1936 that the development of vernacular literature in the Middle Ages can be credited to the patronage of women and to their need to have Latin works translated into the vernacular, little attention has heretofore been given to the role of women patrons for medieval literature. Recent studies, however, have unearthed a wealth of new information about female patronage in the early and high Middle Ages. A comprehensive picture is nevertheless still missing.

Judith (d. 843), empress and wife of Louis the Pious, was highly acclaimed for her literary interests. Hrabanus Maurus, Bishop Prudentius of Troyes, and Walahfrid Strabo dedicated their works to this woman. Matilde (d. 968), mother of Emperor Otto I; Empress Adelheid (d. 999), Otto I's second wife; and her two daughters, Mathilde (d. 999) and Gerberg (d. 1011), continued this tradition of patronizing poetry and the arts. Widukind of Corvey and Hrotsvit of Gandersheim dedicated their poems to the Empress Mathilde.

Throughout the Middle Ages needlework provided women with vast opportunities in the visual arts. Women's activity as embroiderers, weavers, and makers of tapestry is well documented, for instance, in the highly acclaimed Bayeux Tapestry (1066), commissioned by Mathilda, wife of William the Conqueror, and the opus Anglicanum, embroidery work from England in the twelfth and thirteenth centuries. Queen Margaret of Scotland (eleventh century) was at the center of a highly productive workshop of textiles and their ornamentation. Particularly, abbesses of many convents gained a high reputation for their support of these skills. Book production and illustration were almost exclusively in the hands of monasteries and convents. Gisela, Charlemagne's sister, directed the first Carolingian convent scriptorium at Chelles. *The Gerona Apocalypse* from 975 was produced and signed by a woman painter.

In the twelfth century, Maud of Scotland (d. 1118) and Adeliza of Brabant, both wives of the English king Henry I (d. 1135), established an important cultural circle at their courts. Adeliza, in particular, is famous for being the patron of the first vernacular English poems, whereas Maud commissioned *The Voyage of Saint Brendan* in Latin and later in Anglo-Norman translation.

Best known as a patron of the arts was, however, Eleanor of Aquitaine (d. 1204), wife of both King Louis VII of France and King Henry II of England, because she was particularly responsible for the development and promotion of the Arthurian romances in England and France. Her two daughters Marie and Alice followed in her path. Marie, countess of the Champagne since 1164, supported Chrétien de Troyes; and Alice, countess of Blois, supported Gautier d'Arras. Modern research has, however, dismissed the theory that Andreas Capellanus composed his famous treatise *De amore* at Marie's court. At the suggestion of another of Eleanor's daughters, Mathilde, the duchess of Saxonia since 1168, the French *Chanson de Roland* was translated into German by the cleric Konrad. She was probably also responsible for having arranged the translation of the *Roman de Tristan* by Eilhart of Oberg.

The court of Margarete of Cleve in northwest Germany made possible the first major translation of the French *Roman d'Eneas* into Middle High German through Heinrich von Veldeke. The philosopher and theologian Vincent of Beauvais wrote his treatise *De eruditione filiorum nobilium* (c. 1247–1248) at the request of Queen Margaret of Provence. In 1328 she commissioned John de Vignai to translate Vincent's famous *Speculum historiale*. When, in 1382, Anne of Bohemia arrived in England to marry King Richard II, she brought with her, along with a large library, a host of book illustrators. Very soon afterward she ordered an English translation of the Gospel. Critical of Chaucer's antifeminist *Troilus and Criseyde*, she also inspired the poet to compose his *The Legend of Good Women*. Most didactic and instructional reading materials (primers, psalters, gospels, etc.)

were ordered by women who were in charge of their children's education. Moreover, the vast body of "books of hours," medieval religious pocket books, was strongly influenced by female patronage as early as the thirteenth century.

From the thirteenth century, legendary literature became the favorite object of female patrons, such as Guta (d. 1297), wife of King Wenceslaus II of Bohemia. She was glorified by Ulrich von Etzenbach in his romance *Wilhelm von Wenden*. Other texts particularly popular among women and thus often commissioned by female heads of royal households were *Books of Hours*.

Elizabeth (d. 1231), wife of Duke Louis of Thuringia, deeply influenced Wolfram von Eschenbach's composition of his *Willehalm* and his *Titurel* fragment around 1220. Possibly, Duchess Agnes, wife of Duke Otto I of Wittelsbach, was the patron of the heroic epic *Kudrun* (c. 1250). Well known as a patron of poetry was Mahaut, countess of Artois, who commissioned and collected a large library between 1300 and 1330. Especially important for our understanding of late medieval French literature is the patronage Queen Bonne extended to Guillaume de Machaut after her marriage to the future king Jean le Bon in 1332.

Late medieval women patrons can be detected at the various courts all over Europe and need not be listed all by name. However, Duchess Mechthild of Austria (d. 1482), a leading personality for the development of German literature in Swabia, deserves mention here. While she lived in her widowhood residence in Rottenburg near Stuttgart, her dedication to poetry opened the door for the first major German adaptations and translations of Italian poetry. Her sister-in-law Margarete of Savoy can be credited with stimulating her interest in literature, because she also gained a high reputation for her patronizing poetry and the arts.

Countess Elisabeth of Nassau-Saarbrücken (d. 1456) was active both as author and as patron. Her close family connections with the royal court in Paris helped to introduce a large body of prose romances into Germany. Equally important was Eleonore of Austria (d. 1480), daughter of the Scottish King James I, who imbued the court of her husband Siegmund of Tyrol with a new literary spirit. Eleonore, mother of the Emperor Maximilian I, entertained lively contacts with scholarly writers such as the astronomer Johannes Regiomantibus. Margaret of York, while duchess of Burgundy, encouraged William Caxton to translate from French and to print *The History of Troyes* in 1476. From 1473 when Eleanor of Aragon married Ercole I d'Este of Ferrara, she established another important Renaissance court with strong cultural interests. Her highly educated daughter Isabella d'Este, countess of Gonzaga (1474–1539), also became a leading patron of literature and art. Her patronage, which reveals the guidance of humanist advisors, earned her general and high praise and made her court at Mantua one of the most famous cultural centers of the Italian Renaissance.

References. Susan Groag Bell, "Medieval Women Book Owners: Arbiters of Lay Piety and Ambassadors of Culture," in Mary Erler and Maryanne Kowalski (eds.), *Women and Power in the Middle Ages* (Athens, Ga., 1988), 149–187; Joachim Bumke, *Mäzene in Mittelaltèr* (Munich, 1979); William C. McDonald, with Ulrich Goebel, *German Medieval Literary Patronage from Charlemagne to Maximilian I* (Amsterdam, 1973); David Wilkins, "Women as Artists and Patrons in the Middle Ages and the Renaissance," in Douglas Radcliffe-Umstead (ed.), *The Roles and Images of Women in the Middle Ages and the Renaissance* (Pittsburgh, 1975), 107–125; June Hall McCash, ed., *The Cultural Patronage of Medieval Women* (Athens, Ga., and London, 1996).

ALBRECHT CLASSEN

PATTERN AND PRACTICE APPROACH TO DISCRIMINATION is the approach used when plantwide evidence that women and/or minorities are concentrated in low-paying jobs is used to argue that discriminatory policies (even though not necessarily discriminatory intent) are in operation. It is to be contrasted to an approach where complaints by individuals are dealt with on a case-by-case basis or with "small" class action suits where each member of the affected class is specifically named.

SUSAN B. CARTER

PAUL (SAINT) AND WOMEN is a subject around which a great deal of misinformation abounds. Involved in the discussion is the question of which of the 13 letters in the Pauline corpus were actually written by Paul. There is widespread agreement among historical scholars that the Pastoral Epistles (I and II Timothy and Titus) are not from Paul's hand but were written a generation after Paul; and an increasing number of scholars doubt the Pauline authorship of Colossians or Ephesians. These letters seem to illuminate post-Pauline theology and life.

Paul's own view of the way in which women are to function in the church and live out their lives in Christ is asserted in his unequivocal statement—remarkable in our time, and unthinkable in Paul's—those who are baptized into Christ Jesus have put on Christ; and among them "there is no longer Jew or Greek, there is no longer enslaved or free, there is no longer male and female for you are all one in Christ Jesus" (Gal. 3:28). Consequently, for Paul, the three major ways in which humanity divided itself were overcome and denied in the Church. Not only are Jews and Greeks, and masters and slaves equal in every respect in the Church, but so also are men and women, who in the world represent the human and the aberration of humanity—both are to be considered fully equal.

For Paul, neither natural status nor moral achievement has a bearing on salvation or on life in the community in which Christ is sovereign. Rather, grace meets one where one is; and in a community where everyone receives and lives out of grace, where everyone understands life to be a gift, where all are "dressed in the same clothes" (have "put on" Christ)—in such a community there cannot be the superior and the inferior, the greater and the lesser, the human and the subhuman. Not in Jesus Christ!

Moreover, we learn from Paul's letters that he regularly lived out in the church the mutuality and equality expressed in Gal. 3:28. Women participated in the Church in the same ways and to the same degree that men did. Phoebe, for example, was a deacon in the church (Rom. 16:1–2), just as Paul himself was a deacon. Paul also calls Phoebe a "guardian" or "defender" (New Revised Standard Edition "benefactor") of many—a word used in a slightly later writing to refer to Christ. Another woman, Junia (Revised Standard Edition "Junias," misinterpreting the name to be masculine), was an apostle—Paul's primary word to describe his own special calling in Christ; and in fact, Junia, along with Andronicus (probably her husband), was said by Paul to be "outstanding among the apostles" (Rom. 16:7).

Another woman, Prisca, with her husband Aquila, was an instructor of the well-known Christian missionary Apollos (Acts 18:26) and was also one of Paul's "coworkers" in Christ Jesus (Rom. 16:3). The church in Corinth met in her home (1 Cor. 16:19).

In Romans 16:1–16, Paul sends greetings to a number of Christians—to 17 men and 10 women and to Christians, certainly including women, in the households of two other men. It is very striking that among those remembered by Paul, so many were women. Moreover, Paul refers to 4 of these women as "hard workers in the Sovereign" (Rom. 16:12), a phrase that probably characterizes their missionary endeavors.

In Phil. 4:2 Paul begs two women, Euodia and Syntyche, to "agree in the Sovereign," for they had labored "side by side" with Paul in promoting the gospel. They were evangelists whose disagreement was apparently over theological or ecclesiastical matters, or Paul would hardly have mentioned it in a letter to the whole Church. We may therefore assume that these women were highly significant members of the church at Philippi.

We come now to two passages in another letter undoubtedly written by Paul—1 Cor. 11:2–16 and 14:33b–36. In the first passage the issue has nothing to do with the equality of men and women in the life and worship of the Church. The passage explicitly affirms that women function in the church in exactly the same ways in which men do—they both "pray and prophesy" (1 Cor. 11:4–5). The issue in Corinth was rather the narrow question of whether women should follow the general custom of wearing long hair and veils at services of worship, which were public meetings. Why was Paul so exercised about this question? It may be because some charismatic women in the Corinthian church were pressing for an androgynous, spiritual appearance, different from the secular custom, and Paul argues that women who are Christians should not dress differently in public from women who are not. There is to be no holy attire.

However, Paul's assumption of equality in the body of Christ gave way soon after his death to the prejudice and practice of the culture. The general rules governing households, rules whereby wives were subject to their husbands, were incorporated in the Church. Colossians and Ephesians represent this shift. Still later, women were told that they were not to speak in worship and that they were to be subordinate to their husbands (see 1 Tim. 2:11–15). By the end of the first century C.E., Paul's vision of equality among all the children of God was rejected by the Church in its capitulation to the world.

Finally, a comment about 1 Cor. 14:33b–36: as this short paragraph breaks into Paul's discussion of prophecy, it seems clear that it is out of place, and it is doubtful that Paul wrote the words at all. Their point is clear: women are not to say anything at all in the church; it is disgraceful for them to do so. These words flatly contradict 1 Cor. 11:5, which speaks of women praying and prophesying—a difficult feat if one is to remain silent. In light of all the activity in which many women in Paul's churches were engaged, it seems to be the case that 1 Corinthians 14:33b–36 was written by someone holding the view expressed in 1 Timothy 2:11–12 and that these words got into the collection of fragments of letters put together to form our 1 and 2 Corinthians.

References. Elaine Pagels, "Paul and Women: A Response to Recent Discussion," *Journal of the American Academy of Religion* 42 (1979): 538–549; Robin Scroggs, "Paul and the Eschatological Woman: Revisited," *Journal of the American Academy of Religion* 42 (1979): 532–537.

BURTON H. THROCKMORTON, JR.

PAY EQUITY. See COMPARABLE WORTH

PEACE MOVEMENTS (U.S.). Acting as concerned citizens and as the "mother half of humanity," American women have played a significant role in movements against militarism and for peace since the early nineteenth century. Motivated by a variety of religious, political, humanitarian, and gender concerns, they have petitioned, lobbied, and demonstrated their opposition to America's major wars and military interventions from the Mexican-American War of 1846 to the Spanish-American War of 1898; from the sending of U.S. marines to Haiti in 1914 and Nicaragua in 1926 to World War I, World War II, and the U.S. intervention in Vietnam. Confined to the role of foreign policy outsiders, American women have, nevertheless, been the most active supporters and lobbyists for national legislation and international treaties to outlaw war and ban nuclear weapons.

The first autonomous woman's peace action was organized by Julia

Ward Howe in 1873. The noted author of the "Battle Hymn of the Republic," regretting her role in sending thousands of men into the bloody battles of the Civil War, organized a Mother's Peace Day, which was celebrated in 18 American cities in June 1873 and in one or two communities for a few years thereafter. By the end of the nineteenth century, a network of internationalist female peace activists developed through women's club and suffrage movements. Linking war to male control of government and the hope for peace to the enfranchisement of women, feminist pacifists and anti-imperialists called for arbitration of the Venezuelan border conflict with England in 1895, pressured President William McKinley to avoid war with Spain in 1898, opposed the annexation of the Philippines, and supported the 1899 Hague Conference on international disarmament and arbitration.

In the decade before World War I, such mass organizations of women as the General Federation of Women's Clubs, with 800,000 members; the Council of Mothers, with 100,000; the Women's Relief Corps, with 161,000; the Women's Christian Temperance Union, with 325,000; and the National Council of Women, comprising approximately 15 national organizations with hundreds of thousands of members, all included a peace plank in their agendas for a new world order. Outraged by the outbreak of World War I and disappointed by the passivity and silence of male peace leaders, a group of women reformers, including Jane Addams and Carrie Chapman Catt, organized the Women's Peace Party (WPP) in 1915. The WPP demanded immediate negotiations for an end to the war in Europe, the limitation of armaments, and the nationalization of the arms industry. In 1915 representatives of the WPP joined women from the belligerent nations of Europe in a historical International Congress of Women at The Hague. The congress endorsed a plan for continuous arbitration to end the European conflict and insisted on the right of the then-unenfranchised women in all nations to be consulted on issues of war and peace. When the United States entered World War I, Jeannette Rankin, the first woman in Congress, voted against the declaration of war. She was also the only member of Congress to vote against U.S. entry into World War II.

After the conclusion of World War I and the achievement of female suffrage, a number of women leaders in the settlement house and woman's rights movements turned their attention to the peace issue, establishing four women's peace groups. The Women's International League for Peace and Freedom, founded by Jane Addams and Emily Balch and still in existence today, was organized in 1919 to promote international cooperation among women for world peace based on social justice. The Women's Peace Society led by Fanny Garrison Villard, also founded in 1919, stressed total nonresistance and spiritual pacifism; and the Women's Peace Union, created by Caroline Lexow Babcock and Elinor Byrns in 1921, worked steadily throughout the 1920s and 1930s for a constitutional amendment to declare war illegal. In 1924 Carrie Chapman Catt, former president of the National American Women's Suffrage Association, organized the National Committee on the Causes and Cure of War (NCCCW). NCCCW was a coalition and clearinghouse of 12 mass organizations representing millions of women. It engaged tens of thousands of individuals in peace education and campaigns for U.S. membership in the World Court and for the ratification of the Kellog-Briand Pact.

Since the end of World War II American women have exerted political pressure for nuclear disarmament and for peaceful cooperation across national and ideological barriers. The Congress of American Women (CAW) was organized in 1948 to support international cooperation in the postwar world, particularly with the USSR, and to promote economic and sexual equality at home. In the Cold War political atmosphere of 1950, CAW was listed as subversive by the attorney general and was forced to disband. Women Strike for Peace, founded in 1961, brought tens of thousands of women into the campaign for the nuclear test ban treaty of 1963 and the movement against the Vietnam War. Another Mother for Peace, a brilliant, but small, group of female peace publicists, created the most memorable peace slogan of the Vietnam era: "War Is Not Healthy for Children and Other Living Things." In 1980–1981 the Women's Pentagon Action combined the issues of peace, social justice, and ecology, stressing the connection between racism, sexism, domestic violence, and war in dramatic guerrilla theater and passive resistance at the doors of the Pentagon. Helen Caldicott's Women's Action for Nuclear Disarmament mobilized additional thousands of women in maternalist opposition to the proliferation of nuclear weapons. In the 1980s, grassroots women's peace groups across the country developed new forms of protest such as peace camps adjacent to military bases. The Seneca Peace Encampment and the Puget Sound Encampment experimented with new formats for self-empowerment in the interest of class, race, and gender equality, which the participants view as the essential requisite for human survival in the nuclear age.

In the post–Cold War years, women's peace and environmental organizations in the United States and abroad began to perceive that only cooperative international approaches to peace and security along with widespread education on conflict resolution could put an end to worldwide instability, hot spots, and military violence. U.S. women's peace groups began, in the second half of the 1990s, to emphasize global campaigns, the national focus that had characterized the abandoning anti-Vietnam War movement and the antimissile campaigns of the 1980s, which had had only one goal—to change U.S. military policies.

In the last half of the 1990s U.S. women's peace groups, along with other members of the Non-Governmental Organizations of the United Nations, participating in the peace caucus for the Fourth World Congress on Women, held in Beijing, China, in August/September 1995, raised the demand that the nuclear powers put an end to the development, production, testing, storage, and deployment of nuclear, chemical, and biological weapons and that the production, sale, and use of land mines and laser weapons be banned. The women's peace caucus also called for the reduction of military budgets by half, the elimination of the arms trade, and the institution of training courses in the skills of nonviolent conflict resolution at all levels of education, particularly in military and police academies. Former U.S. congresswoman Bella Abzug reflected the conviction of the women peace activists who met in Beijing when she declared, "The time has come to challenge the male military mystique, and only a worldwide effort of women can do the job."

References. Harriet Hyman Alonso, *Peace as a Woman's Issue: A History of the U.S. Movement for World Peace and Women's Rights* (Syracuse, N.Y., 1993); Carrie Foster, *The Women and the Warriors: The U.S. Section of the Women's International League for Peace and Freedom 1915–1946* (Syracuse, N.Y., 1995); Amy Swerdlow, *Women Strike for Peace: Traditional Motherhood and Radical Politics in the 1960s* (Chicago, 1993).

AMY SWERDLOW

PEASANT SOCIETIES are primary producers who convert the natural resources of their environment into subsistence goods, typically through agricultural and home craft production within complex societies. The basic production and consumption unit is the household, usually composed of family members only but, in some cases, of servants as well. While the products of peasant labor are primarily for their own consumption, a portion (either in kind or cash) is directed to market exchange and to ceremonial exchange within the local community. Also, some of the peasant's product is siphoned out of the peasant household and community through taxes and rent to support state-level functions and functionaries (e.g., armies, bureaucrats, the aristocracy, the church). In addition to its products, peasant labor may be directly extracted in imperative labor services to the landlord, the state, the church, and the local community. As an ideal type, peasants are distinguished from primitive, village-level horticulturists by being economically and politically bound to towns and state and a subordinate rural class within a stratified society. Peasants differ from capitalist farmers in that peasant production is primarily for subsistence rather than for the market and profit, and from landless agricultural laborers in that peasants control the means of production (especially land) and, typically, do not view labor as a commodity to be bought and sold. For a more comprehensive analysis of the peasantry from an anthropological perspective, see Eric Wolf's definitive study.

Peasant, as an ideal type, encompasses enormous cross-cultural variety, from the villages of feudal Europe to the present Mexican campesino and the worker in a Chinese communist agricultural commune. Given the depth and breadth of variation between peasantries, few generalizations can be made about the position of women in peasant society. However, a significant one derives from Michelle Rosaldo's distinction between the domestic and public spheres of life. In social evolutionary terms, the distinction between domestic and public life is more significant in peasant societies than it is in simpler (and earlier) societies where kinship organizes economics and politics. In every society in which the peasantry are an important sector of the population, power is more centralized and more public and the centers of power more remote from the local community. Therefore, women's close association with domestic life (especially child rearing) places an additional handicap on their participation in public decision making and public power. Second, peasants, as opposed to primitives, live in class-stratified societies. Since stratification is a central organizing principle, patriarchy may be reinforced and reinforcing, as, for example, in ancient Chinese and Indian empires.

In general, then, the development of peasant societies with status and class stratification meant less involvement by women in public life and less public power. However, at the level of the local community, where public power is less significant, women's position within the peasantry varies considerably. It varies with inheritance patterns, the gender-based division of labor, and the weakness or strength of the patrilineal descent principle. Peasant women's status relative to men's is highest when women inherit productive resources equally with men, where women and men contribute equally to agricultural labor, and where patrilineal descent systems are either absent or weak. An example of this is the Otavalo Indian women of highland Ecuador, who enjoy relative equality of power with their men within the local village and ethnic group. An example of the opposite— where only men inherit land and perform the agricultural labor and where the patrilineal descent system is strong—is rural, upper-caste women in India, whose status is relatively low even at the local village level.

One of the important debates related to the question of the status of women in peasant societies is whether the change from peasant to capitalist farmer or wage laborer (a process often labeled "economic development" or "modernization") improves or degrades the status of women relative to men. Prior to recent questioning by feminist anthropologists, it was generally assumed that economic development would improve women's position in society, absolutely, through a rise in the general standard of living and, relative to men, through the adoption of liberal, democratic ideals. Laurel Bossen, in an examination of several peasant societies, found no case in which this assumption was unambiguously true. Further, the job segregation and wage differentials that contribute to the feminization of poverty* in the United States are also found in developing societies with more devastating consequences, given their lower standard of living and higher unemployment levels.

References. Laurel Bossen, "Women in Modernizing Societies," *American Ethnologist* 2 (1975): 587–601; Michelle Rosaldo, "A Theoretical Overview," in M. Rosaldo and L. Lamphere (eds.), *Women, Culture, and Society* (Stanford, 1974): 17–42; Eric Wolf, *Peasants* (Englewood Cliffs, N.J., 1966).

LYNN WALTER

PEDAGOGY, FEMINIST, emerged as women reclaimed their right to an education as a set of strategies to support them in gaining knowledge without mimicking men's ways of knowing (Rich). Within the context of feminist pedagogy, knowledge is grounded in the context of women's lives and experiences, enabling them better to think and become agents of their own lives.

Feminist pedagogy grows out of a political context. Society sees roles and identities as fixed, as stable, with members of society positioned in social groups based on social characteristics such as gender. Gender is one of the most fundamental social categories. Sociologists term gender a "master status" because it shapes so many of the roles a person plays. No one escapes positioning within gender. An awareness of the power and effects of that positioning leads feminist pedagogy, with its perception that the world is not fixed but, rather, composed of multiple experiences and realities, to becoming a reawakening for female students.

Classical studies in education, learning, and pedagogy, such as those completed by Jean Piaget and Lawrence Kohlberg worked from a perspective of the male as the norm, where the way males learn represents the way "everyone" learns. However, feminist research on gender and learning suggests that because of different experiences women and men do not come to learn the same way.

While Kohlberg's studies suggest that students follow a linear path to knowledge where the knower eventually becomes a rational thinker with individual, universal ethics, Carol Gilligan's work suggests that the context of women's lives is a web, not linear. Women have developed a culture based on the ethics of care, not of separation; women are not separated from others in making decisions. Since women have developed a culture and a language different from men's, schools and other learning environments dominated by masculine rules and language are unsafe for women learners (see Chodorow). Feminist pedagogy works from an awareness of the history of young girls and women in school, recognizing that, traditionally, both materials and methods within the classroom setting have been chosen with the male student in mind.

Pedagogy consists of several components: curriculum, objectives, materials, instructional strategies, projects and assignments, and evaluation. While acknowledging that students bring multiple life experiences and worldviews to the learning situation, thus allying itself with multicultural pedagogy (e.g., see Banks and Banks), feminist pedagogy calls specifically for the inclusion of women's experiences in, and for a feminist analysis of each component of, the teaching-learning process. For example, a feminist curriculum is more inclusive than the traditional curriculum and draws on women's experiences and concerns (see Heilbrun). Feminist objectives include developing students' voice and agency, helping students locate themselves as authors of their own lives and acting in their own interests (see Freire). Feminist materials include accounts of women's lives and achievements, as well as a wider variety of teaching media (e.g., dance, art, "hands-on" learning tools, games, and simulations) in addition to more traditional maps, demonstrations, and models. Feminist instructional strategies extend to active or experiential learning (where students learn through "doing" rather than through "hearing"), to cooperative or collaborative learning (where students learn through activities that depend on sharing materials and ideas to construct and connect a range of concepts or other information in order to develop and test student-generated understandings, rather than repeating teacher-provided models), and to a greater emphasis on reflective and recursive learning (where students review and analyze the paths they took to reach their findings or conclusions).

All these strategies involve bringing the learner to the center of the learning activity rather than positing the learner as the recipient of knowledge generated by authoritative others. Feminist projects and assignments grow out of the strategies just listed. Students work collaboratively in exploratory projects, students help set the goals of the projects, students reflect on their process of discovery and learning, and students identify the linkages among the components of the project and among a specific project and other assignments or activities. Additionally, feminist assignments build in opportunities for students to set learning goals and then to self-assess their work. Feminist evaluation draws strongly on self- and peer-assessment and emphasizes an evaluation of process as well as of final product.

Feminist pedagogy, then, supports the development of voice and authority in the classroom. Women students need to take themselves seriously and to know their own history, to read inclusive literature, and to understand their own biology in order to be empowered persons. Feminist pedagogy establishes connections to the lives of female students, who, like a web, work in collaborative groups. Women students need conferencing and much dialogue to help them identify their own sources of authority and to validate their own learning. Response groups composed of peers help students come to recognize and value the strengths of their minds and the validity of their understandings. Female students should choose topics without fear of censorship if the topics do not fit male interests.

Within an environment shaped by feminist pedagogy, students learn to read and to write beyond stereotypical gender identities and to interact with each other and with the larger world as authoritative learners rather than as vessels filled with knowledge validated by external others. These students, authors of their own lives, are also empowered to disrupt dominant masculinist story lines by exposing the restrictions of society's prescriptive roles.

References: J. A. Banks and C.A.M. Banks (eds.) *Multicultural Education: Issues and Perspectives* (Boston, 1989); M. Belenky, B. Clinchy, N. Goldberger, and J. Tarule, *Women's Ways of Knowing: The Development of Self, Voice, and Mind* (New York, 1986); K. A. Bruffee, *Collaborative Learning: Higher Education, Interdependence, and the Authority of Knowledge* (Baltimore, 1993); Nancy Chodorow, *The Reproduction of Mothering: Psychoanalysis and the Sociology of Gender* (Berkeley, Calif., 1978); P. Freire, *Pedagogy of the Oppressed* (New York, 1989); Carol Gilligan, *In a Different Voice: Psychological Theory and Women's Development* (Cambridge, 1982); C. Heilbrun, *Writing a Woman's Life* (New York, 1988); D. W. Johnson, R. T. Johnson, and K. A. Smith, *Cooperative Learning* (Washington, D.C., 1991); P. M. King and K. S. Kitchener, *Developing Reflective Judgement* (San Francisco, 1994); Lawrence Kohlberg, Essays on *Moral Development*, vol. 2, *The Psychology of Moral Development: The Nature and Validity of Moral Stages* (New York, 1984); M. B. Baxter Magolda, *Knowing and Reasoning in College: Gender-Related Patterns in Students' Intellectual Development* (San Francisco, 1992); C. Meyers and T. B. Jones, *Promoting Active Learning* (San Francisco, 1993); Jean Piaget, *The Language and Thought of the Child* (New York, 1955); Adrienne Rich, "Claiming an Education," *On Lies, Secrets, and Silence: Selected Prose 1966–1978* (New York, 1979).

CHERYL B. SCARBORO

PERFORMANCE ART. A description, rather than a definition, of women's performance art is the intersection of a variety of media such as music, dance, theater, video, and film with a focus on the body and the politics of it beginning roughly with the coming of the second wave of feminism in the 1960s. A performance artist can choose to "display" her work either publicly, privately, or both, in any setting, such as a nightclub, a university, a museum, or on the street, utilize the notion of spontaneity when "composing" a text, construct a written text, and choose to rehearse or not rehearse the "piece." The "work of art" can use the idea of "real time," "theatrical time," or a combination of the two with concern for— or no concern for—the parameters/comfort of closure. The work can include autobiographical aspects but does not rely on autobiography exclusively for its subject matter. These are just a few of the reasons a concise definition of women's performance art is impossible. Another primary explanation for the ephemeral, eclectic nature of women's performance art is the desire of women performance artists to challenge and move beyond patriarchal notions such as classifying ideas to create a new language and system of meaning. In other words, women performance artists want to defy all forms of restrictive practices such as classification to reclaim the power inherent to the notion of giving things and ideas names. To give something a name, be it a tangible object such as a chair or an intangible notion such as love, shows the ability to possess extraordinary control of language and cultural norms.

The origins of women's performance art are as disparate as a description of the phenomenon. Very often the origins are traced to John Cage and Merce Cunningham in the 1950s because of the conceptual nature of their work. This "statement of origin" is convenient rather than correct. While many performance artists were first visual artists who turned to perform-ance in frustration, defiance, and the need for a more inclusive, elastic method of representation for their creativity, the art world cannot claim sole "ownership" for the origins of women's performance art. For instance, if the elements of religious ritual, such as the shaman, are included in a description of women's performance art, the origins can be traced to any part of the globe that used these elements in public and/or private cere-monies. Sue Ellen Case suggests that the salons of the eighteenth century were an exercise in "personal theater." The "happenings" of the 1960s, with their spontaneous acts and engagement of the audience, also fit a description of the origins of women's performance art. The most perplexing facet of the origins of women's performance art is that it is constantly being renegotiated as sex workers, lesbians, and gays write their experiences and history. Therefore, a description of the term and a discussion of the origins are hardly a tidy process. In fact, the origins of the form are historical, ahistorical, individual, common, universal, and unique as a fingerprint. If, indeed, a central metaphor for the description and origins of women's per-formance art is necessary, then the feminist credo gleaned from Kate Mil-lett's *Sexual Politics* that "the personal is the political and vice-versa," with all the connotations and denotations of the phrase attached, with the con-cept of gender included or excluded, is appropriate.

A few of the artists who are looked to as important in the development of women's performance art are Carolee Schneeman, Vali Export, and Judy Chicago. Schneeman's work *Eye Body* (1963) used nudity and was held in a private space, her loft in New York. The use of nudity is essential in her work to redirect the way in which the audience perceives a performer, specifically, a female performer, and, consequently, to move the audience toward a redefinition of the woman as the subject of a text who can make meaning as opposed to the woman as the object in a text who cannot exercise her ability to create meaning since her purpose is to be looked at and nothing more. Schneeman was one of the first female performance artists to attempt to redirect how women could use nudity to their advan-tage and reclaim the power of their bodies. She describes her use of nudity in *Eye Body* as a "shamanistic ritual" (68). Schneeman also had "live snakes" slither over her during one portion of the piece. When she per-formed the piece, she did not recognize the allusion to a "famous statue of a Cretan goddess." Schneeman now credits this performance as one of many reasons to use nudity in her art. Some of Schneeman's other works are *Meat Joy* (1964), which she describes as "a celebration of the flesh as well as an assault on repressive culture," *Body Collage* (1968), *Up to and including Her Limits* (1973–1976), and *Interior Scroll* (1975–1977). Each of these works was as much an act of rage as it was a carnival. *Interior Scroll* was a performance directed at male critics who found her film work unacceptable. In this piece, again using her nude body as the "vessel" for the message, she unrolled a "script" from her vagina and read phrases from the critics who had attacked her (68–74). Schneeman's focus on exposing forbidden societal norms imposed by patriarchal culture that regulate how a woman uses her body, such as having nudity be taboo, was also reflected in the work of Vali Export.

Export's work in analyzing how a nude woman can redirect the male gaze includes *Touch Cinema* (1968). In this piece she wore a box over her upper torso, cut the front out of the box, and placed a piece of cloth to serve as a "curtain" and then invited the audience to participate in the experience by reaching underneath the "curtain" and touching her breasts. Export did this piece in a theater and on the street. In *Erosion* (1970) she rolled on broken glass while nude, to the horror of her audience. She did not draw blood and took precautions with the broken glass to ensure she would not. Her purpose was to make the audience question their reasons for looking at a nude woman ("Angry Women," 186–193).

Judy Chicago became an important contributor to women's performance art early in the 1970s, when she formed the collective Womanhouse (Case). Her notion of how collaboration is an integral part of a woman's existence was already evident in her installation piece, *The Dinner Party* (1978), and her subsequent work, *The Birth Project* (1980). She organized these pieces by bringing together women artists from several different media and from different socioeconomic groups. Each piece is a symphony of media. For example, *The Dinner Party* brings together china painting, embroidery, and sculpture in a monumental installation that focuses on women's history regardless of whether or not the woman symbolized by the place setting actually lived or is a figure of myth. Every plate in the place settings for the "party" depicts Chicago's version of the particular woman's vagina (Case, 56). *The Birth Project* focuses its commentary on the birthing process, a process unique to women's experience, and again, Chicago organized the piece by collaborating with many women artists. This piece uses textiles as the primary medium, then enhances the textiles by paint or embroidery (Chicago). Chicago accomplishes the delicate balance between her vision and the vision of the artists she collaborates with through patience and dedication. Without the collective working together to meet the tone of the subject matter, both *The Dinner Party* and *The Birth Project* would have been time-prohibitive because of their size. Also, they would have failed philosophically, since patriarchy privileges the idea of a "sole artist" instead of a group working together and achieving consensus to create a work of art. Chicago's vital contributions are reflected in the theory and the praxis of performance art to this day.

Linda Montano seeks to eliminate the distinction between "art" and "everyday living" by making the notion of endurance intrinsic to her work. Among the many pieces she has performed to illustrate this idea are *Handcuff* (1973), where she and Tom Marioni, a conceptual artist, were handcuffed together for three days. She defines the piece as "a study in movement and mutual signaling." Montano continued to push the limits between "art" and "life" throughout the 1970s and for a year (1983–1984) she and Tehching Hsiseh lived tied together. She sees this piece as "an attempt to universalize" the idea of two people living together without engaging in sex and, therefore, to look at them as humans, not a man and a woman (Schneeman, 56).

Close to the same time as Montano's endurance pieces, Lori Anderson brought performance art to mainstream culture with her recording *0 Superman* (1980) and her live performance of the piece. Anderson looks to examine "the ways in which communication between people is affected by technological interference and social neglect" (Champagne, 45). She relies on innovations in technology to aid her in her art. Nowhere is the feminist credo of "the personal is the political" more apparent than in the work of Holly Hughes and Karen Finley, who were part of the National Endowment for the Arts funding scandal of 1990. Out of the 18 artists who applied for funding in the "solo performance" category, Hughes and Finley were outright denied funding (Champagne, xiv). Among the many controversial topics each attempts to address in her work are nudity, the taboo of incest, issues of sexual preference, and abortion. Hughes' *World without End* (1989) incorporates themes from childhood trauma and adult disillusionment in monologue form. Like Hughes, Finley also uses monologue style in her art, but, unlike Hughes, Finley offers analysis of a work that interests her, such as Betty Friedan's *The Feminine Mystique* for her work *The Constant State of Desire* (1986) (Schneeman, 3, 71).

When Annie Sprinkle and Veronica Vera, two former sex workers, became part of women's performance art, Sprinkle, in particular, moved beyond simply using nudity to illustrate a point to inviting the audience to inspect her cervix during the performance of *Post-Porn Modernist*, a piece cowritten with Vera. Sprinkle and Vera both believe that women and men are alienated from their bodies and work toward offering their audiences a way to view sexuality openly, free of shame and guilt and as a facet of existence that is as essential as breathing (Schneeman, 23–39).

Clearly, women's performance art includes much more than painting, sculpture, dance, or music and the possible intersection of several media. It is a place for commenting on contemporary culture by viewing a woman's body as a site of exploration, research, and power that provides profound revelations and insights into our state of being.

References. Sue Ellen Case; *Feminism and Theatre* (New York, 1988), ch. 3; Lenora Champagne (ed.), *Out from Under* (New York, 1990); Judy Chicago, *The Birth Project* (New York, 1980); Karen Finley, *Shock Treatment* (San Francisco, 1991); Terry Galloway, *Out All Night and Lost My Shoes* (Tallahassee, Fla., 1993); Kate Millett, *Sexual Politics* (1970); Moria Roth, *The Amazing Decade: Women in Performance Art 1970–1980* (Los Angeles, 1983); Carolee Schneeman, "Angry Women," *Re/Search* 13 (1991); *Women and Performance* 4, 2, issue 8 (New York, 1989).

SUSAN L. TAYLOR

PHILIPPINES. Women participate at every level of the nation's public life. However, women's liberation is a twentieth-century phenomenon. In 1889, when Spain applied its Civil Code to the islands, Filipino women were legally subordinated to men. A married woman could not dispose of her property or engage in business without her husband's consent. In the public sector, women could work only as teachers.

Public education for boys and girls expanded rapidly after Spain ceded the Philippines to the United States in 1899. The University of the Philippines, founded in 1908, admitted women students and employed women faculty and administrators from the beginning. By 1975 the nation's literacy rate was 89.72 percent, one of the highest in Asia, with little difference between the sexes in all levels of school enrollment, except in graduate schools, where 64 percent of the students were women in 1990.

The demand for political equality was reflected in a female suffrage bill introduced to the Philippine assembly in 1907 and was realized in 1933, when women gained the right to vote and hold public office. One year earlier, married women had gained the right to dispose of their personal property without their husbands' consent. Both reforms were included in the Constitution of 1935. The Constitutions of 1935 and 1953 contained provisions protecting women, in this respect classifying them in the same category as minors. The Constitution of 1973, however, stressed equality of treatment between the sexes, which was reinforced in the 1987 Constitution. The 1973 document said that the state shall "afford protection to labor, promote full employment and equality in opportunity regardless of sex, race or creed." It also stipulated equal rights and duties to both parents in matters relating to their children, allowed women to retain their citizenship upon marriage to foreign nationals, and gave mothers the same rights in the transfer of their nationality to their children as fathers. Up to the mid-1990s, divorce was prohibited, and publicly funded family planning was not available, despite an annual population growth rate of 2.5 percent. The Labor Code of 1973 included equal opportunities for employment and promotion and prohibited discrimination based on sex. It prohibited stipulations against marriage as a condition of employment and discharge of women employees on account of pregnancy and confinement. It also enjoined employers to provide maternity benefits.

Since 1937 women have won elective office at all levels and in increasing numbers. In 1973 the first woman was appointed to the Supreme Court. In 1986 Mrs. Corazon C. Aquino was elected president, defeating longtime incumbent Ferdinand Marcos, in a movement called the People's Revolution. She did not seek reelection at the end of her term in 1992.

Women, who accounted for 31.4 percent of the total labor force in 1977, entered the workplace in numbers larger than their proportional numbers in the 1980s (the labor force increased by 5 percent each year during that decade, whereas the working-age population grew by 2.7 percent annually). Although women were found in all fields and professions, they predominated in domestic service (91 percent), professional and technical areas (59 percent), and sales (58 percent). However, they lagged behind men at top-level positions, accounting for about 15 percent in both the private sector and in government in 1990. Women outnumbered men two to one in the rural-to-urban migration in the 1980s. This is explained by the types of work available to women in cities and the underemployment in the countryside. Many women continued to work without compensation in caring for their families.

References. Ronald E. Dolan (ed.), *Philippines: A Country Study*, 4th ed. (Washington, D.C., 1993); Alzona Entrancion, *The Filipino Woman, 1565–1933* (Manila, 1933); Maria Paz Mendoza-Garzon, *The Development and Progress of the Filipino Woman* (Manila, 1951); Virginia A. Miralao, *Male and Female Status and Changing Role of Women* (Quezon City, Philippines, 1985); Isabel Rohas-Aleta et al., *A Profile of Filipino Women: Their Status and Role* (Manila, 1977); Jose V. Roman and Emerlinda R. Roman (eds.), *Corazon C. Aquino, Early Assessments of Her Presidential Leadership and Administration and Her Place in History* (Quezon City, Philippines, 1993).

JIU-HWA LO UPSHUR

PHYSICAL ATTRACTIVENESS is the degree to which a person's appearance conforms to prevailing standards of beauty and therefore is perceived as pleasing to the eye. It derives from an interaction between the expectations of the beholder and the physical characteristics of the beheld. The relative level of one's physical attractiveness generally remains fairly stable over the life span.

Like gender and race, physical attractiveness is an easily observable trait that serves as an information cue. It strongly influences how someone is perceived by others and consequently becomes a source of stereotyping. Although beauty standards are in constant flux, a high level of agreement in ratings of physical attractiveness prevails within a given culture at a given time. Measures of attractiveness based on consensus are quite reliable. Even preschool children can accurately judge the appearance of their playmates and have already begun to stereotype others according to their looks.

There is a strong tendency for people to believe that what is beautiful is also desirable in other ways. Highly attractive people of both sexes are assumed to be happier, kinder, more socially competent, and more successful than less attractive people. They also receive preferential treatment from friends, parents, teachers, and employers in a wide variety of situations. Beauty bias or "looksism" is real and is applied differently to members of each sex.

Considerable evidence indicates that attractiveness is emphasized and valued more highly in females than in males. Parents tend to rate newborn daughters as pretty and cute, while infant sons are seen as strong and active. The cuter the baby, the more likely it is to be judged a girl. Males consistently place greater emphasis on good looks when choosing dates and mates than do females. Female faces are recognized and remembered more readily than male faces. People have better-defined concepts of ideal attractiveness for women than for men, and ratings of attractiveness correlate more highly with ratings of femininity than with those of masculinity. As women grow older, they are judged not only to be less attractive but also less feminine. In contrast, men are seen as less attractive but not less masculine as they age.

Appearance also influences psychological adjustment. When clinicians rated the characteristics of mentally healthy adults, they indicated that a healthy female would be more concerned with her appearance than a healthy male would be. While self-conscious preoccupation with physical attractiveness promotes insecurity and excessive narcissism, such pathology is often overlooked in women because it remains a culturally sanctioned requirement for "healthy" adjustment to the feminine role.

Belief in one's own attractiveness can be as hard to achieve as physical beauty itself. Body image is as much a function of subjective self-perception as of objective attractiveness. In fact, self-ratings of appearance do not correlate highly with evaluations made by others. Women tend to distort body image in the negative direction, just as depressed people of both sexes do. In contrast, men tend to distort body image in a more positive direction, just as nondepressed people do.

Women are less satisfied with their appearance in general and are much more concerned than men about being overweight. Many women have a distorted mental image of a particular body part, such as hips or thighs, and then generalize this distortion to their whole appearance. Adolescent girls express increasing concern about their appearance with every passing year and feel relatively less attractive in comparison to their peers than do boys.

The relationship between physical attractiveness and self-concept is especially salient for people whose appearance is, in some way, unusual or incongruent with the current ideal. Low self-esteem can result from an underlying body loathing, or it can lead to it. Whereas men derive self-esteem from a variety of sources, including achievement, economic status, and fitness, women's sense of personal esteem is more highly correlated with self-ratings of attractiveness.

Good looks can be a liability as well as an asset. Pretty women may be more vulnerable to sexual exploitation and to harassment on the street or on the job. They complain of not being taken seriously at work. As compared to men, attractive women feel more threatened by the loss of good looks with age, and they make greater cosmetic efforts to preserve a youthful appearance.

In the occupational sphere, good-looking people are more readily hired and promoted for positions that are deemed traditionally appropriate for a candidate of that sex. However, attractiveness can also be a professional hindrance. Exceptionally beautiful women are disadvantaged when aspiring to top management jobs because their beauty is seen as incompatible with the traits of leadership and authority that such jobs require. For females, a conflict persists between cultivating beauty and cultivating brains, between pursuing attractiveness and pursuing achievement. Adolescent girls still report that they hide their accomplishments in order to enhance their social acceptance.

Body beautification is a universal social gesture. Rituals of adornment are used by both males and females to display wealth, to signal social conformity, and to accentuate greater contrast between the sexes. Cosmetics, hairstyles, and fashion all create gender differences that are culturally contrived rather than naturally acquired. In many societies males and females decorate differently but equally. However, for the past two centuries in Western culture, body adornment and cosmetic rituals have been highly associated with feminine vanity. Females are referred to as "the fair sex" (as well as the weaker sex) and are encouraged to use physical attractiveness as an important source of social power. Consequently, appearance has become a major arena of competition between women and a key factor in their economic and social survival.

Feminists have been concerned with a variety of issues related to physical attractiveness, including health, mobility, and sexual and commercial exploitation. Fashion reformers a century ago advised women to remove corsets, put on bloomers, and ride bikes to achieve a healthy glow. A New Wave of the women's liberation movement was ushered in when demonstrators picketed the 1968 Miss America contest, protesting the exploitation of women as beauty objects. Feminists of the 1970s were sometimes stereotyped as "homely libbers" or "bra burners," much as the suffragettes a century earlier had been described as "unsexed women devoid of physical attractiveness."

References. S. Brownmiller, *Femininity* (New York, 1984); R. Freedman, *Beauty Bound* (Lexington, Mass. 1986); R. Freedman, *Bodylove* (New York, 1989); L. Jackson, *Physical Appearance and Gender* (Albany, N.Y., 1992); N. Wolf, *The Beauty Myth* (New York, 1991).

RITA JACKAWAY FREEDMAN

PHYSICIANS. See HEALTH CARE PROVIDERS

PICTURE BRIDES were women brought into the United States from Japan, Okinawa, and Korea to correct the sexual imbalance in Hawaii's sugar and pineapple plantations and California's farm communities. The years 1885, 1900, and 1903 marked the first arrivals in Hawaii of immigrant laborers from Japan, Okinawa, and Korea, respectively, who were almost exclusively male. Few women came until the turn of the century. The immigration of women was prevented by labor recruiters' profit motives, restrictive immigration laws, the temporary sojourner situation of male laborers, and cultural traditions of female seclusion and family obligation.

When large numbers of male workers began to realize that their original intention of returning home with savings would not be possible, they arranged picture marriages. Picture brides were matched with prospective grooms through photographs in accordance with the custom of arranged marriage that was prevalent in Japan, Okinawa, and Korea at the turn of the century. A mutual family friend or a relative of the prospective groom serving as a go-between would send the man's photograph to the bride's family. If the bride's family was interested in the marriage offer, it would send a photograph of the bride to the go-between, who then negotiated for the two parties. The Japanese and Okinawan brides usually came from the same home villages as the grooms, while Korean brides came from southern provinces and Korean grooms from northern provinces. Between 1907 and 1924, about 45,000 Japanese and 1,000 Korean picture brides came to Hawaii and California to marry their picture grooms, most of whom were plantation and farm laborers. Their immigration continued until 1924, when the Asian Exclusion Act was passed.

References. Alice Yun Chai, "Korean Women in Hawaii," in Hilah F. Thomas and Rosemary Skinner Keller (eds.), *Women in New Worlds* (Nashville, Tenn., 1981), 328–344; Alice Yun Chai, "Picture Brides: Feminist Analysis of Life Histories of Hawaii's Early Immigrant Women from Japan, Okinawa, and Korea," in Donna Gabaccia (ed.), *Seeking Common Ground* (Westport, Conn., 1992), 123–138.

ALICE YUN CHAI

PIETY/SPIRITUALITY (MEDIEVAL CHRISTIAN) arose naturally in a society in which devotions of the liturgical year and canonical hours of monastic life were major elements of the perception of time. Medieval women participated in vigils, processions, pilgrimages, and devotional prayers, both public and private. However, since women's group events were monitored and controlled by men, we know little of the authentic intentions of women in religious orders. Even less is known of the traditions of piety that accompanied the cycles of the agricultural year, fertility, and motherhood, but the hostility of the Inquisitors toward women and the witch burnings of the early modern period suggest that they existed. (See WITCHCRAFT, CRAZE.)

Many works of medieval literature describe visions and revelations of individual Christian women. These were occasionally written by men, for not all women visionaries were literate. Most of the women seem to have had some understanding of liturgical Latin but rather usually experienced their intense moments of devotion and heard God, the saints, or angels speak in the vernacular. In fact, medieval women contributed greatly to the expansion of literature in European vernaculars and to the tone of Christian devotional writings into the modern age.

Some medieval women mystics, such as Hildegard of Bingen, Julian of Norwich, and Catherine of Siena, were famous and influential. However, permission to live a life of intense spirituality was not limited to the privileged; some women, like Angela of Foligno and Margery Kempe, were determined to be heard at any cost. But the social conditions under which each woman lived, including her class and wealth, made a difference in how easily she could acknowledge and reveal her devotional experiences. Often the authority granted to a woman in the secular sphere was validated by, or a result of, her visionary power. Hildegard, Catherine of Siena, and Joan of Arc were all taken seriously because they were visionaries. (See also ASCETICISM, Ascetics, Recluses, and Mystics [Early and Medieval Christian].)

The spirituality of medieval Christian women did not develop on any sort of evolutionary scheme; Anglo-Saxon women enjoyed far more respect and power than Frenchwomen of the Gothic period. Feminist historians have questioned the concept of "the Renaissance" for women and have shown that women's fortunes followed a complicated pattern in relation to the growth of individualism and the exaltation of reason that symbolize the development of European culture. The tradition of medieval women's piety shows the wisdom of thinking differently about the periodization of Western history, for if one includes baroque Catholic piety and Protestant pietism, it continued for many centuries.

The relationship between medieval women's piety and contemporary feminist spirituality is also very complicated. Many visionary women of the Middle Ages were apologists for their own oppression, hotly defending the hierarchy of the Church and the Inquisition. Nonetheless, all pleaded eloquently for the ultimate truth of their revelations, and even such a conservative as Hildegard of Bingen was aware of the relationship between her body and her visions. In this, medieval women shared a spirituality of immanence and personal experience with modern feminists.

It is striking, though, that the object of much women's devotion was Christ, portrayed as a beautiful, suffering lover. The Virgin Mary was revered as a model of motherhood, and virgin martyrs were remembered as exemplary figures, but the primary imitation was of Christ. In this way, medieval women's spirituality is particularly interesting to women who wish to remain within institutional Christianity.

References. Clarissa Atkinson, *Mystic and Pilgrim: The Book and the World of Margery Kempe* (Ithaca, N.Y., 1983); Caroline Bynum, *Jesus as Mother: Studies in the Spirituality of the High Middle Ages* (Berkeley, Calif., 1982); Barbara Newman, *Sister of Wisdom: Saint Hildegard's Theology of the Feminine* (Berkeley, Calif., 1987); Elizabeth Alvilda Petroff, *Medieval Women's Visionary Literature* (New York, 1986).

E. ANN MATTER

PLAYWRIGHTS, U.S. (TWENTIETH-CENTURY). While women dramatists in the United States have a history as old as the republic, women as playwrights have come to prominence in the twentieth century. Career women playwrights who have made a success of the commercial stage are relatively few in number and are a small proportion of the century's women dramatists. The principal support for production of women's drama has been in regional and little theaters. Magazine publication, while generally rare for plays, has fostered a number of playwrights, and prize competitions offered early validation for women as dramatists. Less commercial forums allowed for, and encouraged, experimentation with nontraditional subjects and techniques.

Throughout most of the century, women playwrights who have achieved commercial success have written in established genres—the social comedy, the farce, the problem play. Clare Kummer, for example, found success in the commercial theater with farces like *Good Gracious Annabelle* (1916). Experimental techniques and form have found their place in regional theaters where playwrights have often been involved in production and selection of plays. Regional companies noted in theater history, especially the Provincetown Players, have been especially important for women's drama.

Women playwrights have often focused on historical situations, recapturing our collective and individual past, including celebration of both famous and typical women as sources of courage and fortitude and as reminders of the oppression of women. Historical focus has been most prominent at critical junctures of social history: in the suffrage movement; in works by minority women during the 1920s, including historical plays for children; in feminist drama of the 1970s and 1980s. Social problems have focused on the constraints impacting individual women's lives.

Early twentieth-century women's plays used domestic settings, employing easily staged, confined interior sets as emblematic of women's usual environment and stage for action. Even in plays that directly challenged the appropriateness and comfort of the domestic sphere, traditional settings (the table, the kitchen, the living room) and scenarios (receiving guests) served to question the reality and facade of women entrenched in domestic life.

Alice Gerstenberg's short plays—especially the often-anthologized *Overtones* (1913), an early feminist play—used innovative techniques of internal monologues and imagined characters to establish a woman-centered world rejecting traditional, sentimental valuations of marriage and domestic life.

Innovative subjects, problem plays, and experimental techniques evolved through regional and little theaters, which developed along with the little magazines. Edna St. Vincent Millay, while principally known as a poet, was instrumental in founding the Theatre Guild and extended both subject matter and technique with a number of verse plays. She also directed her successful, antiwar play *Aria da Capo* (1919).

Women's drama centered on social and political issues was also fostered by social organizations' and magazines' encouragement of minority voices. The National Association for the Advancement of Colored People (NAACP) produced Angelina Weld Grimke's *Rachel* in 1916. Georgia Douglas Johnson developed as a significant black playwright with works like *A Sunday Morning in the South* (1925), on the effects of lynching on a southern family, and her *Opportunity* prizewinner, *Plumes* (1927), a metaphoric play on burial customs.

Of all the early twentieth-century women, Rachel Crothers was the most consistently successful, serious, career playwright. Not only a writer but also a director, set designer, and actress, Crothers established a genre of problem plays on women's issues and helped to develop a popular and critical audience for plays by women. *A Man's World* (1909) and *Mary the Third* (1923) were among her plays that focused audiences' attention on modern women's issues of equity and choice.

Zona Gale, Susan Glaspell, and, later, Lillian Hellman continued the tradition of *A Man's World* with serious problem plays focused on women's situation, building an increasingly forceful portrait of society's destructive pressures. Zona Gale won the Pulitzer Prize in drama in 1921 for an adaptation of her own novel, *Miss Lulu Bett*. Dramatizing the constricted role of the dependent spinster who becomes a servant to her family, *Miss Lulu Bett* indicts the family's relations with the dependent woman, as well as the traditional wife's forgetting of sisterhood.

Susan Glaspell was a founder of Provincetown Players and, like Crothers, a director and actress as well as a writer. Glaspell's plays, most notably *Trifles* (1916), *Women's Honor* (1918), and *Bernice* (1919), directly confronted contemporary women's issues, often using innovative techniques to reinforce her dramatic points. Glaspell's *Alison's House* won the Pulitzer Prize in drama in 1931.

Not all early women's plays provided positive women's images or critiques of the golden cage of domestic life. Clare Boothe's *The Women* (1936) is exceptional in its vitriolic portrayal of women characters, but Boothe's capacity to identify the types of cages women willingly enter and the types of terror they inflict on other women parallels other women's drama. The sense of awakening benighted sisters and of showing the destructiveness of male identification pervades the drama of the era.

Lillian Hellman's *The Children's Hour* (1934) raised new subject matter and controversy with its lesbian theme and was the first of her three decades of finely crafted, well-made problem plays focused on evil in individuals and society. *The Little Foxes* (1939) and *Another Part of the Forest* (1946), two parts of a planned trilogy on the southern Hubbard family, and Hellman's anti-Nazi *Watch on the Rhine* (1941) remain among the best American plays of their kinds.

In comedy, Mary Chase's *Harvey*, the 1945 Pulitzer Prize-winner that had a major Broadway revival in 1970, established her capacity for sensationally popular fantasy. Chase followed *Harvey* with two additional Broadway hits in 1952: *Mrs. McThing* and *Bernadine*.

The 1950s marked a new era in Britain and the United States of exceptional young women playwrights. Carson McCullers' dramatization of her novel *The Member of the Wedding* (1950) won the New York Drama Critics' Circle Award. Filmed in 1953, *Member* inaugurated a series of women's plays that dominated their seasons and went on to become major films of enduring popularity and significance. Lorraine Hansberry became the first black woman to have a play produced on Broadway. *A Raisin in the Sun* brought the black experience and black actors to prominence with mainstream, national audiences and won the Drama Critics' Circle Award as the best play of the 1958–1959 season.

In the 1960s, the numbers of women playwrights began to grow, and by the 1970s and 1980s, women had made substantial gains in commercial theater, though women's theaters and feminist theaters supported the largest volume of new playwrights and productions. Women's plays of the 1960s, like Megan Terry's *Calm Down Mother*, self-consciously and angrily recorded images and roles of women, overtly attacking stereotypes. Alice Childress' plays presented more complex visions of black life and history. *Wedding Band* portrayed the difficulties of a genteel, poor, black/white couple; *Wine in the Wilderness*, set in the racial conflict of the 1960s, showed a black woman confronting the stereotypes of the artist who treats her as a symbol rather than a person. The number of exceptional plays, innovative subjects, and techniques mushroomed in the 1970s and 1980s, as women dramatists explored the conflicts between expectations and women's realities. Marsha Norman's *Getting Out* presented the same woman in two characters, her mature self and her rebellious teenage past. Wendy Wasserstein's *Uncommon Women and Others* carried her story to national audiences. Emily Mann's *Still Life* brought home the effects of the Vietnam War, and Mann was the first woman to direct her own play on Broadway. Norman's *'Night Mother* continued the story of generational differences. Beth Henley, winner of the Pulitzer Prize and New York Drama Critics' Circle Award, had major plays with *Crimes of the Heart* and *The Miss Firecracker Contest*.

The number and diversity of women dramatists in the 1970s and 1980s provide a dramatic antidote to the decades of sparse representation. Playwrights like Mary Irene Fornes attract critical acclaim and productions in previously male preserves. Institutional support has also come to encourage women dramatists. The Women's Project's Directors Forum of the American Place Theatre encourages supportive, noncommercial production and has worked to discourage the isolation of the woman dramatist by establishing active collaboration and instituting concepts of company and repertory. Among Women's Project plays are Lavonne Muller's *Little Victories*, which created a kind of pas de deux with Joan of Arc and Susan B. Anthony, and *Killings on the Last Line*, a working-class, assembly-line drama; and Kathleen Collins' *In the Midnight Hour* and *The Brothers*.

The 1970s and 1980s have also seen a phenomenal development of feminist drama and theaters that include and extend traditional definitions of drama. Much feminist theater has highlighted consciousness-raising *technique: overt use of sex-role reversal, realistic portrayal of women's oppression, and historical characters in and out of historic context as role models of feminism.

Children's drama also came to prominence in the twentieth century, and women playwrights have been especially involved in the creation of significant, new plays for children, including historical treatments by black women writers of the 1920s, Charlotte Chorpenning's dramatizations of traditional stories in the 1940s and 1950s, and contemporary works giving serious treatment to individual and social pressures.

References. Helen Kirch Chinoy and Linda Walsh Jenkins (eds.), *Women in American Theatre* (New York, 1981); Dinah Luise Leavitt, *Feminist Theatre Groups* (Jefferson, N.C., 1980); Karen Malpéde (ed.), *Women in Theatre, Compassion and Hope* (New York, 1983; repr., 1985).

CAROL KLIMICK CYGANOWSKI

"POETESS" entered the English language in 1530, according to the *Oxford English Dictionary*. Its form indicates its debt to the French, via Middle English: *poet* + the feminizing -*ess*; the word means "a female poet." Ironically, "poetess" derives from the Latin *poeta*, which means "poet" and which incorporates grammatical gender—feminine; *poeta* itself derives from the grammatically masculine Greek term *poētēs*, "poet." A related

English word, "poetress," was perhaps more common up to the nineteenth century. Of course, the "generic" term "poet," variants of which have always been current, indicates that men's poetry, the standard, requires no sexist distinction. However, from the sixteenth to the nineteenth centuries, when "poetess" was most used, the majority of publicly successful poets were men, and the sex-specific feminine term allowed for a dubious distinction often perceived as one of quality rather than kind. "Poetess" carries an inherent sexist slur, for it connotes that sex lies at the center of art and that sex is as important as genre in defining a writer.

Unfortunately, during the currency of "poetess," femaleness was equated with various diminutive perceptions of femininity: domesticity, emotionalism, weakness, virginal purity, and so on, and these qualities were transferred onto, or demanded in the "poetess'" work. Twentieth-century consciousness-raising has provoked several changes in the preferred term for a female poet—from "poetess" to "lady poet," to "woman poet," to, simply, "poet." Further, the range of subject matter (and style/language) has broadened; many contemporary female poets might better be called "women's poets," because they have intentionally explored territories particularly interesting to, or concerning, women themselves—territories hitherto often considered inappropriate or socially unacceptable. A fine example of this alteration may be studied in the lifework of Adrienne Rich, who began her career as an academic, mainstream poet often writing from a (false) male perspective and who had thereby achieved literary Establishment acceptance and acclaim. Rich has, like many women, transformed her worldview and poetic perspective over the past several decades; she now identifies herself as a lesbian, a feminist, and an activist, and her poetry has been strengthened by its resultant honesty. Similar in principle are the careers of such poets as Judy Grahn and Susan Griffin, whose published works have sprung from a feminist milieu and have demonstrated a peculiarly women's perspective openly and from the outset, but their acknowledgment by the literary Establishment has been hindered, perhaps purely because of this failure to disguise either their female identities or concerns, for the literary power structure remains largely in male hands. But "poetess" has been, happily, an early casualty of the war against linguistic sexism; concurrently, the numbers of poets who are women have increased, and women rarely hide behind male pseudonyms or initials to gain acceptance, as once was necessary to avoid the typecasting of being a "poetess."

References. Angela Carter, "The Language of Sisterhood" and Alicia Ostriker, "Body Language: Imagery of the Body in Women's Poetry," in Leonard Michaels and Christopher Ricks (eds.), *The State of the Language* (Berkeley, Calif., 1980), Elaine Showalter (ed.), *The New Feminist Criticism* (New York, 1985).

PENELOPE J. ENGELBRECHT

POETS, BRITISH (ROMANTIC). Hundreds of Englishwomen wrote and published poetry between 1770 and 1837 during the literary movement known as British Romanticism. To some degree, their work exhibits the same general philosophical concerns and poetic characteristics as male Romantic poets like Blake, Wordsworth, Coleridge, Byron, Shelley, and Keats. These philosophical concerns include a belief in the healing power of nature, a regard for the simple life of common people, and a faith in the possibility of human transcendency through divine inspiration or the poetic imagination. Typical genres include ballads, metrical tales, romances, songs, sonnets, odes, elegies, satires, and tragic verse dramas. Romantic poems are often set in exotic, medieval, or fantastic locales; they modulate from intellectual to emotional, from gothic to sentimental in tone and plot.

Women poets were among the leaders in Romantic aesthetic innovation. Charlotte Smith (1749–1806) along with Anna Seward (1747–1809) revitalized the sonnet for Romantic purposes; Coleridge used Smith's sonnets as models for his own. Coleridge and Wordsworth's famous *Lyrical Ballads* (1798), containing Wordsworth's treatise on natural language and common people, appeared two years after a similar treatise by dramatist and poet Joanna Baillie (1762–1851).

Yet women poets of this era also differed significantly from the tradition defined by Romantic male writers. Women poets were more interested in expressing unity and community with the rest of the world, including humans, animals, and even plants, rather than portraying the isolated self confronting sublimity. To the women, the natural subject of a poem is a sentient being with whom the poet empathizes, rather than a stimulus to the senses and imagination of an alienated consciousness, as so often with the men. Women's recurrent metaphor is the family, and the concerns and subjects of their poetry are often quotidian. "Sensibility," a sympathetic and emotional response to experience, dominates their tone. As a result, their poetic language is often effusive, flowing, repetitious—the language of affect.

Aspiring women poets were at a disadvantage as the Romantic era began. Most had not received the kind of classical education that prepared male poets for their careers; though the women could and did write in the vernacular, as Wordsworth recommended, they lacked the advantage of a long and careful study of poetics. In addition, it was still considered somewhat unladylike to be in print, and it was hard for a woman to maintain a comfortable self-concept (or to make a living) as a professional writer. Contemporary literary critics judged women's poetry differently from men's, restricting women to "feminine" style and subject matter and condescending to them as "lady poets" in reviews of their work. Despite the odds, however, many women were successful as poets, and their successes were recognized by their contemporaries.

Anna Letitia Barbauld (1743–1825) is sometimes considered the first Romantic woman poet; her *Poems* of 1773 heralded a new generation of women poets. Many, like Barbauld, came from dissenting backgrounds and held both radical and feminist sympathies. Drawing upon the eighteenth-century Enlightenment philosophies pursued by the intellectual "Bluestock-ing" women and following Mary Wollstonecraft's *Thoughts on the Education of Daughters* (1786) and *Vindication of the Rights of Woman** (1792), these poets sought to demonstrate women's rationality. In the 1790s, on the heels of the French Revolution, a radical, feminist tone is exemplified in pieces like the "Epistle to William Wilberforce" by Barbauld, deploring the slave trade; *The Emigrants* by Charlotte Smith, depicting the sufferings of the poor and dispossessed; and poems by Helen Maria Williams (1762–1827), directly celebrating revolutionary France. The more conservative Hannah More (1745–1833) criticized the leaders of the French Revolution, but she published hundreds of broadsides (known as *Cheap Repository Tracts*) to edify and encourage the English poor while criticizing the irresponsibility of the rich. More discovered working-class poet Ann Yearsley (1752–1806) and assisted her with her first publication.

The *Lyrical Tales* of Mary Darby Robinson (1758–1800) helped estab-lish the sympathy for marginalized and victimized people that characterized women's writing throughout the nineteenth century. Nicknamed "Perdita" by the press, Robinson was a Shakespearean actress and an abandoned mistress of the Prince of Wales. Hounded by scandal and disabled by ar-thritis, she published in 1799 a prose treatise in the Wollstonecraft tradition titled *Thoughts on the Condition of Women, and on the Injustice of Mental Subordination.* When reaction to the Reign of Terror and fear of French invasion reached England, and Mary Wollstonecraft's name became anath-ema, the radical sympathies of these poets were discouraged; their polemics lost the attention and support of many English readers. Their hard-won rationalism and their commitment to political discourse came to be super-seded by sentimental and domestic verse.

The early Romantic women poets were very supportive of one another, often corresponding, writing reviews, dedicating poems to each other, and generally welcoming other women into the privileged, if stressful, role of "poet" in the Romantic era. Yet by the end of the period, their initial radical vision had become domesticated into the Victorian idea of the fem-inine "poetess." Among the best-known and most admired writers of the second generation were Felicia Dorothea Hemans (1793–1835) and Letitia Elizabeth Landon (1802–1838). Hemans was admired as a domestic and patriotic poet, quintessentially feminine in style and subject; in *Records of Woman* she sympathetically portrayed women's lives across barriers of space and time, nationality and class. *Songs of the Affections* contains her most popular poems. As for Landon, one critic dubbed her "the female Byron" for the melancholy tone and heightened emotionalism of her po-etry. Overpraise led her to write profusely and abjure revision; yet she remains interesting for her poetry of disillusionment with romantic love, her ill use by the male literary establishment, and her unexplained death by poison in Cape Coast, Africa, where she had traveled with her husband, a sea captain named Maclean.

There were many other popular poets of the Romantic period whose work remains interesting today. Mary Tighe (1772–1810) is chiefly remembered for her lengthy poem *Psyche, or the Legend of Love*, which was said to have influenced Keats' "Ode to Psyche." Amelia Alderson Opie (1769–1853) is admired for her "Elegy to the Memory of the Late Duke of Bedford." The sisters Jane and Ann Taylor (1783–1824 and 1782–1866) wrote memorable verses for children, including "Twinkle, Twinkle, Little Star." Similarly, Mary Howitt (1799–1888) wrote the nursery poem "The Spider and the Fly," as well as numerous popular lyrics and ballads. A group of Scottish nationals, including Anne Lindsay Bernard (1750–1825), Carolina Oliphant (Lady Nairne) (1766–1845), and Janet Hamilton (1795–1873), produced melodic and convincing Scottish ballads in the manner of Robert Burns. Similarly, Sydney Owenson, Lady Morgan (1776–1859) wrote ballads and songs in the Irish tradition. Many popular ballads, both humorous and sentimental, by Lady Caroline Norton (1808–1877) and her sister Helen Sheridan, Lady Dufferin (1807–1867) were set to music; poems like these were performed in British drawing rooms for half a century.

Several women writers had family connections with prominent literary men of the era. Caroline Bowles (1786–1854), who in her metrical autobiography "The Birthday" lamented the restrictions placed upon women and girls in the nineteenth century, later married British poet laureate Robert Southey. Sara Coleridge (1802–1852) published *Phantasmion*, a prose tale with interpolated poetry in the manner of her famous father. Also of renewed interest, though overshadowed by her brother William's achievements, is Dorothy Wordsworth (1771–1855), whose poems were not published in her lifetime.

Many popular women poets published in the "annuals," yearly illustrated collections of contemporary poetry and prose by diverse writers. Often these volumes were edited by aristocrats such as the countess of Blessington (1787–1855) or Caroline Norton, who generally contributed a few pieces of their own and procured one or two poems by established writers like Wordsworth or Sir Walter Scott. Two other popular women poets who contributed regularly to publications like the *Keepsake, Forget Me Not*, and *Friendship's Offering* were Maria Jane Jewsbury (1800–1833) and Mary Russell Mitford (1787–1855); Mitford also authored five volumes of familiar essays on rustic themes collectively titled *Our Village*.

Viewed in the framework of women's writing throughout the centuries, the English women poets of the Romantic period will be seen to participate in many female literary traditions. For example, a recurrent theme is social or political protest, including poetry criticizing the slave trade; lamenting the exploitation, poverty, and displacement of workers caused by the Industrial Revolution; or supporting the struggles for freedom in Greece. Woman's particular lot in life—with its burden of chastity, marriage, motherhood, and sorrow—is a frequent topic, with special attention to the double standard of love and sexuality. The women poets repeatedly express a

love or yearning for freedom, a frustration with restriction and imprisonment, and an empathy with rebellion, all characteristic of the Romantic
political stance. Yet at the same time they express a strong disapproval of
Romantic self-exile and social alienation and seek to resolve these postures
with Christianity. During the decades before and after the turn of the nineteenth century, the many women poets of the Romantic period helped re-
define the role of poet in ways that made it appropriate and accessible to
women writers for many decades to come.

References. Meena Alexander, *Women in Romanticism* (London, 1989); Isobel
Armstrong, "The Gush of the Feminine: How Can We Read Women's Poetry of
the Romantic Period?" in Paula R. Feldman and Theresa M. Kelley (eds.), *Romantic
Women Writers: Voices and Countervoices* (Hanover, N.H., 1995); Stuart Curran,
"Women Readers, Women Writers," in *The Cambridge Companion to British Ro-
manticism* (Cambridge, 1993), and "Romantic Poetry: The I Altered," in Anne K.
Mellor (ed.), *Romanticism and Feminism* (Bloomington, Ind., 1988); Kathleen
Hickok, *Representations of Women: Nineteenth-Century British Women's Poetry*
(Westport, Conn., 1984); Anne K. Mellor, *Romanticism and Gender* (New York,
1993); Marlon B. Ross, *The Contours of Masculine Desire: Romanticism and the
Rise of Women's Poetry* (Oxford, 1989).

KATHLEEN HICKOK

POETS, BRITISH (TWENTIETH-CENTURY). Work by women poets of
British origin in the twentieth century may usefully be scrutinized in terms
of several discrete—if imprecise—periods of activity. The century begins
with a divided moment in which the majority of British women poets arrayed themselves with a less experimental tradition, while a small minority,
sometimes expatriate, experimented with abstract and discontinuous forms
or explored new concepts of the self and consciousness.

The second third of the century was a period of consolidation for women
poets. T. S. Eliot's influence was widely felt, and some of the aspects of
modernism, like free verse, a fragmented narrative line, and use of an as-
sociative symbolic method to suggest the flow of consciousness, were included in the array of techniques used by British poets, women and men
alike. For the most part, however, the relatively few women who were able
to command the attention of critics sought to continue traditional British
poetic modes and forms, experimenting relatively little with continental
forms like surrealism or American revisions of syntax and sense.

In the years immediately after World War II, the number and visibility
of women poets began to swell appreciably, with some women appearing
among the membership of British coteries like "the Movement" or "the
Group." Emphasis usually was on the very precise and nuanced rendering
of limited, often personal subjects, usually within traditional verse forms,
often with an understated irony and almost always with careful avoidance
of rhetorical excess.

A major efflorescence of women's poetry began in the late 1960s, with substantial experiment in new forms, regular examination of highly charged political and emotional material, and exploration of feminist subjects or formerly suppressed elements of women's experience. Participating in this surge of vital poetic production were the women of a new, feminist generation born after World War II, as well as many women born in the 1920s or 1930s, whose careers had been delayed (a pattern that can be noted in a significant number of women poets) or marked by a less visible volume or two. Anthologies designed to showcase the strength of new women's voices played an important role in gaining significant recognition for powerful new women poets, whether they were adopted by the critical Establishment or not. The efflorescence of poetry was accompanied by decisive new critics who used both feminist and Marxist theory to demonstrate the ways in which literary expression is gender-inflected or reflects class positions. As a consequence, the early anthologies were followed by selections and reprints of the work of women poets from the first half of the century, who appeared, in the light of feminist theory and the explosion of women's poetic energies in the last half of the century, to exhibit unrecognized strengths and to be overlooked harbingers of a woman's vision. The effect of these developments has been to make a surprising range of women's voices from throughout the century virtually contemporaneous (an appropriate effect for a literature that often rejects linear orders) and to make visible the strength and extensiveness of female poetic traditions in the twentieth century.

British women associated with the modernist experiment in the first part of the century included Mina Loy (1882–1966), Edith Sitwell (1887–1964), Nancy Cunard (1896–1965), and Iris Tree (1897–1968). By far the most important British woman modernist poet was Edith Sitwell. Her most experimental work fell chiefly in the decade immediately following World War I, while she was editing the important avant-grade annual *Wheels* (1916–1921) and publishing *Twentieth-Century Harlequinade and Other Poems* (with Osbert Sitwell, 1916), *Clowns' Houses* (1918), *The Wooden Pegasus* (1920), *Facade* (1922), *Bucolic Comedies* (1923), the ambitious long poem cycle *The Sleeping Beauty* (1924), *Troy Park* (1925), *Elegy on Dead Fashion* (1926), and *Rustic Elegies* (1927). She saw her poems as "abstract patterns," and the result was a poetry that sometimes suppressed semantic sense or invoked deliberate non sequitur. Sitwell's work notably demonstrates the modernist tension between order and disorder, between the drive for coherence and the celebration of the noncoherent. Her later work fell back from syntactic or narrative disorder; now Sitwell sought to recast traditional myth in terms of a female vision that rejected the violence and destruction of World War II. See *Collected Poems* (1965).

Growing attention is now being devoted to Mina Loy's and Nancy Cunard's contributions to the formation of modernism. Loy's early poetry was published in *Lunar Baedecker* (1923); she was revived in 1958 (*Lunar Bae-*

decker and Time Tables: Selected Poems), and her unpublished poems appeared in 1982 (*The Last Lunar Baedecker: The Poems of Mina Loy*). (Loy became a naturalized American citizen in 1946.) Cunard's contribution as printer and proprietor of the Hours Press is best known, but her early poetry, which drew criticism for obscurity and for expressions of revolt, was also part of the modernist movement. Her collections include *Outlaws* (1921), *Sublunary* (1923), *Parallax* (1925), and *Poems* (1930).

Among the early figures whose work was regarded as more traditional are Alice Meynell (1847–1922), Katharine Tynan (1861–1931), Charlotte Mew (1869–1928), Margaret Sackville (1881–1963), Anna Wickham (1884–1947), Frances Cornford (1886–1960), Elizabeth Daryush (1887–1977), Rose MacCaulay (1889–1956), Dorothy Wellesley (1889–1956), Vita Sackville-West (1892–1962), Vera Brittain (1892–1970), Sylvia Townsend Warner (1893–1978), Ruth Pitter (b. 1897), and Frances Bellerby (1899–1975). Contemporary feminist critics are rediscovering the quieter originality of some of the ostensibly less experimental figures like Mew (*The Farmer's Bride*, 1915; *The Rambling Sailor*, 1929; *Collected Poems*, 1953), Wickham (*Selected Poems*, 1971; *The Writings of Anna Wickham: Free Woman and Poet*, 1984), Daryush (collections from 1911 to 1971; major work from the 1930s; *Selected Poems*, 1972; *Collected Poems*, 1976), Bellerby, and Warner (*The Espalier*, 1925; seven other volumes of poetry, including the posthumous *Twelve Poems*, 1980; *Collected Poems*, 1982; *Selected Poems*, 1985). Newly attentive readers recognize these writers' decentered and self-reflex visions, unrhymed or rhythmically disrupted forms, and nontraditional views of female roles or sexuality as important expressions of women's experience.

Among the poets whose birth dates place their production in the second third of the century (and sometimes later) are Stevie Smith (1902–1971), Sheila Wingfield (b. 1906), E. J. Scovell (b. 1907), Kathleen Raine (b. 1908), Helen Adam (b. 1909, now resident in the United States), Phoebe Hesketh (b. 1909), Kathleen Nott, Anne Ridler (b. 1912), Laurie Lee (b. 1914), Jean Overton Fuller (b. 1915), Betty Parvin (b. 1916), and Muriel Spark (b. 1918). The difficulty of securing publication during the war, the lack of critical encouragement for women poets, and the different patterns for women's lives delayed the careers of all but a few of these women until well after World War II, when their work appeared nearly simultaneously with that of the cohort of women born in the 1920s—Denise Levertov (b. 1923, a U.S. citizen since 1955), Shirley Toulson (b. 1924), Patricia Beer (b. 1924), Elizabeth Jennings (b. 1926), Molly Holden (1927–1981), Gerda Mayer (b. 1927), Anne Beresford (b. 1929), and Freda Downie (b. 1929). In the years before the war Raine experimented briefly with techniques popularized by the surrealist movement; Lee experimented with the neo-Romanticism that was more broadly practiced in England; and Ridler explored the possibilities of religious verse drama. Jennings, chiefly in postwar years, made important use of the confessional mode and used expressionist methods to represent the experience of madness. Most continued to use rhyme and traditional meters a significant part of the time, although in the hands of a poet like Stevie Smith a traditional ballad or nursery refrain could be used with disquieting results. Among these poets, Raine, Jennings, and Levertov are in the vanguard of those with long-established reputations; Smith, Fanthorpe, and Beer have come to prominence with more recent, current generations.

The first cohort of women to enjoy from the beginning of their careers the stimulation of the greatly expanded presence of women writing poetry and assertive critical inquiry into the theory and content of women's writings was born in the 1930s: Elaine Feinstein (b. 1930), Ruth Fainlight (b. 1931), Jenny Joseph (b. 1932), Anne Stevenson (born in 1933 of American parents but now resident in England), Fleur Adcock (b. 1934), Anne Cluysenaar (b. 1936), Sally Roberts (b. 1935), Gillian Clark (b. 1937), and Frances Horowitz (1938–1983). Of these, Adcock, Fainlight, Feinstein, Joseph, and Stevenson comprise a "senior establishment" of women who forthrightly seek to express a gender-inflected (though not necessarily feminist) vision. Cluysenaar, trained in linguistics, has experimented with genre and themes in ways that reflect an acute feminist theoretical awareness (e.g., *Double Helix*, 1982, a joint mother–daughter text that explores the continuities of women's lives through a mixture of poetry and documents— letters, notes, and photographs).

The contemporary generation is a cacophony of powerful voices, many lifted in assertion of feminist themes, lesbian awareness, and the demonstration of poetry as both politically engaged and performative. Among the strong figures in this cohort are Judith Kazanztis (b. 1940), Michelene Wandor (b. 1940), Jeni Couzyn (b. 1942), Nicki Jackowska (b. 1942), Wendy Mulford, Sally Purcell (b. 1944), Carol Rumens (b. 1944), Eavan Boland (b. 1944), Wendy Cope (b. 1945), Valerie Sinason (b. 1946), Penelope Shuttle (b. 1947), Liz Lochhead (b. 1947), Denise Riley (b. 1948), Michéle Roberts (b. 1949), and Alison Brackenbury (b. 1953). There is no single thread. The range includes the complex and powerful title poem in Brackenbury's 1984 collection, "Breaking Ground," a long narrative poem that explores the problems of expressing or even establishing both identity and historical "truth"; Jackowska's feminist recuperation of myth in a brief poem like "Un-Fairytale" (from *Letters to Superman*, 1984); Michéle Roberts' riposte on Jacques Lacan: "Women's entry into culture is experienced as lack" (*Selected Poems 1975–1985*); and Carol Rumens' achingly political "Outside Oswiecim" from *Direct Dialing* (1985) or her philosophically sophisticated reflection of a mystical experience in "In the Cloud of Unknowing."

Three important anthologies in this period sought retrospectively to establish the existence of a rich and varied tradition in women's poetry (both

British and American): *The World Split Open: Four Centuries of Women Poets in England and America, 1552–1950* (Louise Bernikow [ed.], 1974, repr. 1979), *Salt and Bitter and Good* (Cora Kaplan [ed.]), and *Bread and Roses: An Anthology of Nineteenth and Twentieth-Century Poetry by Women Writers* (Diana Scott [ed.], 1982). *One Foot on the Mountain: An Anthology of British Feminist Poetry 1969–1979* (Lilian Mohin [ed.], 1979) first gave wide recognition to the feminist poetry movement, and other volumes have highlighted various feminist or political subgroups or writing collectives, for example, *Cutlasses and Earrings: Feminist Poetry*, edited by Michelene Wandor and Michéle Roberts (1977); *A Dangerous Knowing: Four Black Women Poets*, by Barbara Burford, Gabriela Pearse, Grace Nichols, and Jackie Kay (n.d. [1984?]); *Beautiful Barbarians: Lesbian Feminist Poetry*, edited by Lilian Mohin (1986); *Angels of Fire: An Anthology of Radical Poetry in the 80s*, edited by Sylvia Paskin, Jay Ramsay, and Jeremy Sliver (1986); and *The New British Poetry*, edited by Gillian Allnutt, Fred D'Aguiar, Ken Edwards, and Eric Mottram (1988).

Nearly simultaneously, women's poetry was more broadly recognized by commercial publishers in such volumes as *Making for the Open: The Chatto Book of Post-Feminist Poetry 1964–1984* (Carol Rumens [ed.], 1985), *The Bloodaxe Book of Contemporary Women Poets: Eleven British Writers* (Jeni Couzyn [ed.], 1985), and *The Faber Book of 20th Century Women's Poetry* (Fleur Adcock [ed.], 1987). By this time most of the poets of the postwar generations have produced a number of volumes, and many—like Adcock, Stevenson, Rumens, Fanthorpe, Roberts, and Lochhead—are available in collections of selected or collected poems.

CYRENA N. PONDROM

POETS, BRITISH (VICTORIAN). Although many Victorian women wrote and published poetry, only Christina Rossetti and Elizabeth Barrett Browning have entered the received canon of British poetry. Novelists Emily and Charlotte Brontë and George Eliot have also received recognition as poets. Of the three, Emily Brontë is the most powerful and varied poet.

Women poets had an ambivalent relationship to poetic tradition. Like male poets, they were struggling with the weight of Romantic tradition, but their struggles were more acute. As Mrs. Adby, a writer for the annuals, wrote, "Never may Woman's lays their service lend/Vice to encourage, soften, or defend. . . . No, may we ever on His grace reflect/To whom we owe our cherished intellect."

As Sandra Gilbert and Susan Gubar have argued, this inclination to moralize the "cherished intellect" reveals the Victorian woman poet's sense that to be a "woman poet" or a woman intellectual was in itself psychically risky, if not financially impossible. Women of all classes were generally not well educated. Among those writing verse a classical education or even a systematic education in literature was unusual. A notable exception was

Elizabeth Barrett Browning, an accomplished classicist who also studied Hebrew and modern European languages. Lack of education, lack of a tradition of women's writing poetry, and the general misogyny of the critical Establishment were impediments to any woman wishing to reach an audience beyond that of the newspapers and albums.

Despite these difficulties, Victorian women wrote about classical subjects in dramatic lyric and dramatic monologue. The classical subjects women chose, however, were often not those central to received tradition. In 1840 Caroline Norton meditated on "The Picture of Sappho," and in 1889 Michael Field (joint pseudonym of Katherine Harris Bradley and Edith Emma Cooper) published "Long Ago: Based on Fragments of Sappho." A different kind of reinterpretation of classical and poetic tradition came in dramatic monologues spoken by women, as poets emphasized previously neglected perspectives on history. Mary Russell Mitford celebrated the heroism of Antigone and emphasized her opposition to tyranny and slavery. More interesting are Mrs. Augusta Davies Webster's dramatic monologue "Circe" and Amy Levy's "Xantippe: A Fragment." Levy's poem took the part of Socrates' wife, deliberately making sympathetic a woman who had been for centuries the object of antifeminist diatribe. Other dramatic poems took the points of view of contemporary subjects. Barrett Browning's "The Runaway Slave at Pilgrim's Point" invites compassion for the slave who has murdered the child she was forced to bear after being raped by her master. More common were less politically charged dramatic monologues, represented by Caroline Bowles Southey's "The Dying Mother to Her Infant." Though treating a potentially sentimental subject, Bowles makes real the threat of death in childbirth, and the emotional strength of the poem comes from the dying mother's fears for her infant daughter's own probable future in marriage. A still more striking treatment of this common Victorian subject is Christina Rossetti's "The Last Look," in which the lament for the dead child concludes austerely: "If I remember her, no need/Of formal tokens set;/Of hollow token-lies indeed/No need, if I forget."

Perhaps the most ambitious and successful attempt at transforming literary tradition and at taking up contemporary subject matter was Elizabeth Barrett Browning's combination of novel and epic in *Aurora Leigh*. Barrett Browning deliberately defended the possibility of epic and the responsibility of the Victorian poet to "represent the age." She implied that the modern long poem could be epic and at the same time contemporary and womanly.

Although *Aurora Leigh* was enormously popular with readers, running to five editions in five years, and was praised by poets as different as Walter Savage Landor, D. G. Rossetti, and Algernon Charles Swinburne, it was less well received by the critics, who generally found the plot melodramatic, the treatment of rape and prostitution unladylike, and its epic ambitions disconcerting. The *Saturday Review* labeled it an interesting study for those who would explain "feminine misadventures in art." Nonetheless, *Aurora*

Leigh is, along with William Wordsworth's *The Prelude*, the major nineteenth-century treatment of what Wordsworth called "the growth of a poet's mind."

Usually not claiming epic scope, Victorian women wrote historical narratives or narrative romances on subjects ranging from Charles I to Margaret of Anjou; equally popular were lyric poems on a variety of topics— the beauties of nature, death (especially deaths of infants or mothers), the domestic affections, social injustice, religious experience, and moral sentiments. Much Victorian poetry and fiction, by women and men, treated these subjects in ways that seem to modern readers sentimental and that no doubt reinforced what one anthologizer of poetry by women called the "beautiful conservatism which so gracefully distinguishes women" and which curbs the "levelling tendencies of the opposite sex." Nonetheless, poetry about death of parents, about infant or maternal death, and about orphans not only elaborated the ideology of maternal virtue but spoke to the real situation of Victorian women, who typically were responsible for the care of children, for their sisters in childbirth, and for their aged or dying parents. Such poets as Mary Elizabeth Coleridge, Caroline Norton, Emily Pfeiffer, and Caroline Bowles Southey, moreover, were sometimes openly critical of the sentimental treatment of domestic affections.

A great many Victorian women poets confronted more or less honestly the considerable social problems of their day. Among these women were the many who participated in the Chartist movement, especially between 1838 and 1843. However, poetry by Chartist women and by Victorian working-class women generally remains to be studied.

Many middle-class women also wrote about social injustice, especially poverty and slavery. Mary Anne Browne's "The Embroideress at Midnight" details the sacrifice and suffering of a poor young woman who embroiders finery for the rich to support her invalid mother, and even Laetitia Elizabeth Landon (L.E.L.), who usually dwelt on morbid and sentimental subjects, recorded the effects of industrialization in "The Changed Home." "The Children" by Mary Howitt is an interesting contrast to Elizabeth Barrett Browning's "The Cry of the Children" on the inhumane treatment of children in the mines and to Browning's anti–Corn Law poem "The Cry of the Human." After cataloging the children's suffering, Howitt ends with a divine voice proclaiming, "The Children's prayer is heard!" Browning was less interested than Howitt in heavenly compensation for earthly suffering and more scornful of the callousness of the powerful. "The Cry of the Human" concludes with this stark image: "The poor die mute—with starving gaze/On corn-ships in the offing." Slavery was also opposed, notably by Eliza Cook in her poem on George Washington, by Maria Jane Jewsbury, by Elizabeth Barrett Browning, and by "the blind poetess of Ulster," Frances Brown.

At least as common as domestic themes and social commentary were poems on religious subjects. Many women wrote hymns, some, such as Sara Flowers Adams' "Nearer, My God to Thee," still popular today. By consensus, the greatest writer of religious poetry was Christina Rossetti. Rossetti's religious life as a devout Anglican was essential to much of her greatest poetry. The keynote of her religious experience was resignation, though she could be celebratory, too. For clarity of diction and perfect control of poetic design, her work has no equal in Victorian poetry, except perhaps in the later poetry of Hardy. In poems such as "Up-Hill," "A Better Resurrection," and "The Heart Knoweth Its Own Bitterness" Rossetti uses the traditional imagery of the English Bible and of Anglican belief and liturgy to create a poetry of passionate resignation and of longing for union with God.

Rossetti wrote on other subjects as well. Like Barrett Browning, whose *Sonnets from the Portuguese* is still popular, Rossetti wrote sonnets, including one extraordinary sequence, "Monna Innominata." In addition to religious and devotional verse, sonnets, and poems on secular subjects, Rossetti, like many other Victorian women, wrote children's poetry.

Victorian women poets worked in a variety of forms: narrative, dramatic monologue and dramatic lyric, expressive lyric, hymn, and epic, and they took up the common themes of Victorian culture, particularly those associated with womanhood and the domestic affections. As they worked within the often restrictive conventions of their culture and within financial and educational limitations, many women, not just those few we now most commonly read, wrote with an artistic integrity grounded in personal and social honesty.

References. Sandra Gilbert and Susan Gubar, *The Madwoman in The Attic* (New Haven, Conn., 1979); Kathleen Hickok, *Representations of Women: Nineteenth-Century British Women's Poetry* (Westport, Conn., 1984).

MARY ELLIS GIBSON

POETS, U.S. (BEGINNINGS TO WORLD WAR II) includes more than 200 women from Anne Bradstreet to H. D. (Hilda Doolittle). This topic should be considered together with entries for AFRICAN AMERICAN POETS; CHICANA WRITERS; NATIVE AMERICAN WRITERS.

Anne Bradstreet, America's first major poet, was the only woman to publish a substantial body of verse in the seventeenth century. Bradstreet was born in England, received a good education, and came to Massachusetts in 1630. She wrote many kinds of poems, quaternions, elegies, dialogues, love poems, religious meditations, even an unusual poem about mothering her eight children. "Contemplations"—a long work celebrating God and nature—is generally considered her best. Bradstreet celebrated women. Though seemingly content with her lot, she occasionally reveals a darker side, as where she remarks caustically: "I am obnoxious to each carping tongue/Who says my hand a needle better fits." Women poets were not always greeted affectionately in the colonies.

In the eighteenth century the number of women poets increased exponentially. American women had their volumes published and found opportunities to print their works in the burgeoning number of colonial newspapers. A list of the more prolific among these women, provided by Pattie Cowell, includes 11 poets. Jane Turrell, Phillis Wheatley, and Mercy Warren are probably best known, Turrell because she preceded the others, Wheatley because she was black and had been a slave, and Warren because of her political connections to the revolution. As a group these women sometimes followed Bradstreet's poetic lead, but they extended the range of women's forms to include political satire and verse drama. Many of them knew each other and corresponded about literary matters. However, the strongest influences on these women's poems were male. References to Milton, to Pope, and to classical writers abound.

By 1873 a revised edition of Rufus Griswold's famous *Female Poets of America* included 116 women, and this number excludes some important figures like the black poet Frances Harper and Emily Dickinson. The growing association of the spirit of poetry with women, the marked increase in the number of literate female readers, and the advent of widely distributed women's magazines like *Godey's Lady's Book* all contributed to creating a society in which women could not only publish but also support whole families on the proceeds of their pen.

Maria Brooks, highly respected in England and America for her verse play *Zophiel: Or, The Bride of Seven*, is the first in a series of distinguished women poets. By midcentury conventional women poets like Lydia Sigourney, Sarah Helen Whitman, Anne Lynch, and the Carey sisters were joined by women less conventional and more outspoken on a whole range of issues, like Margaret Fuller, Elizabeth Oakes-Smith, Lucy Larcom, and Frances Osgood. Though few women were critical of men in their poems, many bemoaned the limited sphere of women's lives and the unequal distribution of sorrows and joys. The lyre came to represent not only poetry but the female sensibility: sensitive, thrilling, and melancholy. Yet these "nightingale poets" could occasionally write pungent poetry, as Lucy Larcom does in her dramatic monologues and Frances Osgood does in her love lyrics. In general, the single biggest female influence on these women was the British poet Felicia Hemans.

Emily Dickinson (1830–1886) published only 10 poems during her lifetime but is now generally regarded as one of the greatest poets America has yet produced. Living her entire life in Amherst, Massachusetts, some 20 years of it as a recluse, she nevertheless produced over 1,700 poems, most of them short, enigmatic, verbally playful considerations of nature, God, the inner life, love, and death. Dickinson was a premodernist. Critics continue to dispute about the meaning of her lyrics, which sometimes seem deliberately obscure. Her peculiar style combines abstractions with startlingly specific references to the phenomenal world, as when she describes a chill as "zero at the bone." Her life and her poetry have furnished much material for feminist critics who find in her wit, irreverence, and originality an inner strength that defied the narrowness of her circumstances.

The second half of the nineteenth century saw the work of women poets incorporated into the national literature. Emma Lazarus' "New Colossus" was inscribed on the Statue of Liberty, Katherine Lee Bates wrote "America the Beautiful," and Julia Ward Howe wrote "The Battle Hymn of the Republic." A martial ideal combined with religious fervor also informed the poetry of Louise Imogen Guiney. Guiney, together with Lizette Reese, Anna Branch, and the notorious Ella Wheeler Wilcox, author of *Poems of Passion* (1883), are the women poets usually used to represent the 1890s.

A new era in American women's poetry was ushered in by Amy Lowell (1874–1925). Wealthy, cultured, and ambitious, Lowell, like Gertrude Stein, went to Europe and was converted to modernism. Unlike Stein, who was also an important poetic innovator, Lowell came back to America and worked actively to spread the ideals of "imagism." She published many books of poetry, was very popular in her time, and helped to support the reputations of other women poets like Dickinson, H. D., and Elinor Wylie. Her most famous poem is "Patterns."

In the last years of her life, Lowell saw the poetry scene changing and beginning to be dominated by female lyric love poets. Sara Teasdale and Edna Millay were known especially for their clear, resonant expressions of sentiment. Millay, however, was the more shocking. She wrote openly of sexual love, participated actively in political causes, and defied Victorian conventions. She produced a large body of work, still in print today, but the last decade of her life was blighted by World War II, ill health, and difficulties with her writing.

Together with Lowell, Stein, Adelaide Crapsey, and Mina Loy, Marianne Moore experimented with poetic conventions. Though personally reserved, she earned herself the role of grande dame of the avant-garde. Her highly intellectual poems unite philosophical commentary with quotations from a wide range of reading materials (both literary and scientific) and vivid visual descriptions. Of poetry itself, she wrote: "I, too, dislike it." Many of her poems about animals, like "To a Snail," are justly famous.

The time between the two world wars also produced a number of leftist women poets like Genevieve Taggard, Lola Ridge, Muriel Rukeyser, Margaret Walker, and Babette Deutsch. Often concerned with the plight of the poor and disfranchised, these women never received the critical attention or the acclaim given the love poets and the experimentalists. Yet their work is still admired by women who find in them models of the attempt to combine political engagement with the literary life.

Both Elinor Wylie and Louise Bogan were praised during their lives for the intelligence, musical quality, and lyric sophistication of their poems. Though both women were more strongly influenced by models from the past than by contemporary experiments, they modulated the female lyric voice into a tone memorable for its strength and intensity. They followed Dickinson in preferring condensation over exuberance, reticence over sentimentality, and form over free verse.

Though hardly known 10 years ago, the work of H. D. (Hilda Doolittle) has come increasingly to occupy a central place in considerations of modern female poets. H. D. (1886–1961) wrote poetry for 50 years, and her career goes well beyond World War II. Born in Pennsylvania, she left America in her 20s, never to make it a permanent residence again. H. D. was deeply involved with male modernists like Ezra Pound and D. H. Lawrence, but she was never long an apprentice. Her association with a wealthy and talented English heiress, Winnifred Ellerman, allowed her to move freely throughout Europe. Her early work was highly condensed, imagistic, and influenced by Greek precedents. However, she moved beyond these early forms to write verse epics in her later years. H. D.'s work is informed by her involvement with film, with psychoanalysis, and with hermetic traditions. In some ways, she belongs to all the categories mentioned before. She was a love poet, an experimentalist, an intellectual, bohemian and yet conservative, and her insistence on revising received traditions and giving women mythic embodiment has made her work an important resource for contemporary feminists.

References. Louise Bernikow, *The World Split Open* (New York, 1974); Pattie, Cowell, *Women Poets in Pre-Revolutionary America* (Troy, N.Y., 1981); Alicia Ostriker, *Stealing the Language: The Emergence of Women's Poetry in America* (Boston, 1986); Cheryl Walker, *The Nightingale's Burden: Women Poets and American Culture before 1900* (Bloomington, Ind., 1983); Emily Stipes Watts, *The Poetry of American Women 1632–1945* (Austin, Tex., 1977).

CHERYL WALKER

POETS, U.S. (CONTEMPORARY). Women are responsible for much of the experimentation that has invigorated American poetry in the last 30 years. Moreover, the development since the mid-1960s of a feminist audience for women's poetry has, by reinforcing the connection between poetic communication and urgent social concerns, helped sustain and broaden the current audience for poetry by both men and women.

Contemporary poetry by American women varies widely in poetic form and language, in subject matter and themes, and in approaches to women's experience. Some poets, such as Marilyn Hacker or Maxine Kumin, appropriate the regular poetic forms of lyric tradition. Others, like Denise Levertov or Adrienne Rich, search for more "open" free verse forms and a new "common" language. While many women favor short lyrics or lyric sequences, increasing numbers are attempting ambitious long poems. Some limit their political concerns to feminist issues. Others, such as Carolyn Forché, Gwendolyn Brooks, the late Audre Lorde, Gloria Anzaldua, Lucille Clifton, Joy Harjo, June Jordan—particularly those who have experienced oppression based on class and/or race as well as gender—speak on behalf of other groups or engage a wider range of political issues. Many, including May Swenson, the late May Sarton, Jorie Graham, Mary Oliver, Rita Dove, Carolyn Kizer, and Tess Gallagher, generally leave feminism and politics in the background. A few, Louise Glück or the late Elizabeth Bishop, for instance, have resisted being classed and anthologized as women poets, while others, such as Judy Grahn, Irena Kelpfisz, or Rich, now speak as explicitly lesbian feminists, often addressing a specifically female or lesbian audience. Probably the majority of women poets today are eager to speak as and for women while addressing an audience that is both male and female, heterosexual and homosexual. Because women inevitably write from their own social contexts and points of view, which are significantly shaped by gender, because they are inevitably conscious of being outsiders in a predominantly male literary tradition shaped by patriarchal patterns of thought and language, and because they are conscious of their affinities with other women writers, one can generalize about contemporary women's poetry. Nonetheless, one must do so cautiously, for it would be inaccurate to speak of a single women's poetry movement.

Contemporary poetry has tended to be more personal than the modernist poetry of the first half of the century. The "confessional" movement that began in the late 1950s (associated with such male poets as Robert Lowell and John Berryman) helped women such as Sylvia Plath and Anne Sexton feel free to expose very private anguish in poetry. The individual suffering and fury they were exploring was intimately bound to social expectations of women in the 1950s and early 1960s. While their suicidal energy no longer predominates, much women's poetry has remained intensely personal. Thus, although feminist critics debate whether language is capable of representing women's experience (either because of its inherent nature as sign system or because of its roots in patriarchal culture), many poets have devoted themselves to presenting women's experience as directly and forthrightly as possible. Often invoking personal conversation or passionate outpouring, they involve the reader closely in intimate details of their sexual and emotional lives. Since women traditionally have been the object in poems, not the speaking subjects, this candid self-expression is also a means of artistic self-creation and self-definition.

In the mid-1960s, involvement in the antiwar movement stimulated writers such as Levertov and, more influentially, Rich to insist on the continuity between their private struggles and public events. Since then, women poets have tended to treat their private experience as indivisible from larger political experience. The political dimension of their writing has grown more visible, and the personal details in their poems have assumed increasingly obvious political significance. In taking as their subjects women's experiences previously regarded as trivial—crafts such as weaving or embroidery, domestic tasks, child rearing, and bonds among women—they foreground the traditionally unrecognized dignity and significance of ordinary women's lives.

Many women poets today place their work within a female literary tradition. Among twentieth-century poets, they look to the daring innovations of Marianne Moore, Gertrude Stein, and H. D. or to the political force of Muriel Rukeyser. Inspirational models from earlier centuries include Anne Bradstreet, Emily Dickinson, the Brontë sisters, Elizabeth Barrett Browning, Dorothy Wordsworth. Because more women in the past published novels than poems, recent poets also draw upon the achievements of women novelists, who often excelled as recorders of social and domestic details. The poets are equally conscious of the innumerable women diarists and letter writers whose creations may assist in the discovery of distinctively female voices and language. The burgeoning of women's history has fostered interest not only in previously neglected women writers and literary genres but also in women's historical achievements. Thus, a common type of contemporary women's poem imaginatively re-creates the voices of earlier historical women. Matrifocal cultures, matriarchal rites, and myths about supernatural females have provided imagery as well as subject matter for contemporary women poets. Many, including Sexton, Mona Van Duyn, Olga Broumas, Diane DiPrima, and Alicia Ostriker, have revised patriarchal fairy tales to represent more fully and sympathetically the witches, evil stepmothers, old maids, dangerous sirens, and trapped maidens portrayed there. Revisionary mythmaking has become a major strategy for challenging gender stereotypes.

To the extent that they choose to stand outside the male tradition, women poets seek alternative forms, alternative approaches to poetic language, alternative subjects, and alternative treatments of poetic themes. Some who approach poetry as a tool for political change and empowerment, such as Marge Piercy and Grahn, aim for an accessibility that contrasts with the often elitist obscurity dominant in modernist poetry. Recent women's tones have often been harsh, angry, defiant, their forms loose and talky. The title of Rich's 1984 selected poems, *The Fact of a Doorframe*, suggests the widespread impulse not only to root poetry in the commonplace but to keep it true to the tangible details of domestic life. Women's bodies and the experiences of female sexuality, pregnancy, parturition, menstruation, and menopause have become important topics as well as sources of imagery. At the same time, some poets, such as Alice Fulton, are tapping the resources of current scientific concepts and language to avoid reinscribing inherited constructions of gender. Others regard political change as dependent on more radically disrupting authoritative conventions of literary form and language. Thus, avant-garde poets such as Leslie Scalapino, Susan Howe, Bernadette Mayer, Rachel Blau DuPlessis, Carla Harryman, Beverly Dahlen, Erika Hunt, Kathleen Fraser, Joan Retallack, Lyn Hejinian, and Rae Armantrout deliberately rupture and fragment the forms of conventional lyric, rejecting a single controlling and personal voice, refusing the traditional coherence of narrative, epiphanic moment, or linear movement. In so doing, they attempt to subvert the dominant systems of meaning and value in which woman has been defined and to invent a linguistic space within which a genuinely different female aesthetic may emerge.

References. Rachel Blau DuPlessis, *The Pink Guitar: Writing as Feminist Practice* (New York, 1990); Suzanne Juhasz, *Naked and Fiery Forms: Modern American Poetry by Women, a New Tradition* (New York, 1976); Lynn Keller, *Forms of Expansion: Recent Long Poems by Women* (Chicago, 1997); Diane Wood Middlebrook and Marilyn Yalom (eds.), *Coming to Light: American Women Poets of the 20th Century* (Ann Arbor, Mich., 1985); Jan Montefiore, *Feminism and Poetry: Language, Experience, Identity in Women's Writing* (New York, 1987); Alicia Suskin Ostriker, *Stealing the Language: The Emergence of Women's Poetry in America* (Boston, 1986).

LYNN KELLER

POLAND, REPUBLIC OF. In modern-day Poland women formed the basis of resistance against communism and were active members of the Solidarity movement, fulfilling many important functions. However, none of their services to the movement were recognized after the bloodless revolution and victory over the communist regime in 1989; and women bear the consequences of change in Poland.

Demography. At the end of 1990 Poland had a population of 38.2 million, of whom 21.2 million were women. For every 105 women there were 100 men. After age 41 the proportion of women increased markedly because of a very high mortality rate among men aged 35–45. There were 145 women for every 100 men over the age of 60, and the imbalance was even higher in the uppermost age group.

Significant demographic differences exist between urban and rural areas and among provinces, depending on the economic basis of the province. Migration to towns caused a gradual decrease in the number of women living in rural areas; in cities women outnumbered men by an average of 108 to 100.

There had been significant and constant decrease in the birthrate. In 1990 the rate was 4.6 per thousand, the lowest since 1948. This low rate is attributable to such factors as a decrease in the number of live births, emigration, bad health, and the difficulties of everyday life. Because of the low birthrate, women are now asked to stay home and take care of the family. The powerful Polish Catholic Church is applying pressure on women. The liberal legislation on abortion in existence in communist Poland was changed and was very restricted under President Lech Walesa. The government of President Kwasniewski revised the legislation and made it more liberal and considerate of women's needs.

Employment and Education. Polish women are a vital force in the labor market. Over 70 percent of women aged 18 to 60 are in the labor force; the majority of workingwomen are aged 35–44.

Women constitute 48.3 percent of the working population, but, in urban areas, they predominate. Women's share in state production industries is high. They constitute 58 percent of workers in communications and 37 percent in industry. In manufacturing they account for 37.4 percent of workers, with the highest percentage in the textile and electric industries. They make up 84.2 percent of the labor force in finance and insurance and 80.2 percent in health and social services (doctors, paramedics, pharmacists, dentists, nurses, social workers).

The teaching profession is dominated by women, in particular on the lower level. Thus, 98.7 percent of teachers in nursery schools and kindergartens are women; 81.4 percent in elementary schools; and 48.6 percent, in vocational schools. In addition, they constitute 66.4 percent of the teaching staff of academic lycea and are similarly well represented in the faculties of universities and institutes, although the majority are to be found in the lower ranks. Although women constitute 35.1 percent of the teaching staff (all ranks), only 13.0 percent of all professors are women. They make up 19.3 percent of the rank docent, 33.3 percent of adjuncts, 37.0 percent of research assistants, 41.3 percent of lecturers, and 49.3 percent of other staff.

Women are taking advantage of the opportunities to acquire an education. In 1990 they constituted 46.7 percent of all graduates of vocational schools, including branches devoted to training in technology, agriculture, forestry, economics, education, health, and fine arts. Women also constituted 53.8 percent of graduates of universities and institutes in law, medicine, liberal arts, and sciences.

Women earn generally 30 percent less than men, with minor variances in wages depending on the area of employment. At the end of 1990, the government established a uniform/equal basis for work evaluation that was applied to all state employees, regardless of their sex.

The general retirement age for women is 60; for men 65.

In communist Poland, as in all communist states, there was officially no unemployment. The collapse of communism and with it the transition to a market economy brought about unemployment. Thus, in 1990, 8.3 percent of the labor force was unemployed. Women accounted for 51 percent of the unemployed.

Social Services. In order to be able to fulfill the role of mother, housewife, and worker, women are eligible for a number of services. They are entitled to maternity leave of from 16 to 28 weeks (the longer period is for multiple births), as well as to special allowances upon the birth of a child. Yet, women are burdened with the "double shift." In addition, certain stereotypes still prevail both in the family and at work.

Politics. The Polish Constitution, written in 1952 and amended many times since, states in article 67, paragraph 2, that all citizens are "equal regardless of sex," and article 78, paragraph 1, confirms the equal rights of women and men in all fields of state, political, economic, social, and cultural activities.

Women have, according to the legal system, the right to participate in political and social life. In practice, however, women's participation in decision making is low. At the end of December 1990, women accounted for 12.7 percent of state administrative staff at the rank of councillor or above and only 5.2 percent of ministerial posts.

There are no women among the 49 local governors, and when the new government was formed at the beginning of 1991, the percentage of women employed in government administration decreased.

In the first fully democratically elected Parliament, of the 100 seats in the Senate women won seven, and in the Sejm they accounted for 13 percent of deputies. But of the six posts of deputy speaker in Parliament (three for each house), three are held by women.

In view of the changes that took place in Polish political life in the period from 1989 to 1990, data on the political affiliation of women are lacking, and their participation in political parties is difficult to estimate. Women are quite active in the two sociodemocratic parties that emerged from the former Communist Party, but their participation in peasant parties is small. Their participation is most significant in the Civic Movement—Democratic Action (ROAD), which has a special women's section. In addition, there are women's organizations such as the League of Polish Women, the Organization of Circles of Rural Housewives, and the National Committee of Women in Cooperatives.

Women in Polish Culture. Polish women have made a significant contribution to the cultural life of Poland and beyond. It must suffice to mention the names of a few of the prominent writers and poets, scientists, and politically active women since the late nineteenth century. Among the most famous writers and poets, mention should be made of Eliza Orzeszkove (1842–1910); Zofia Nalkowska (1888–1910); Maria Dabrowska (1889–1965); Maria Konopnicka (1842–1910); Gabriela Zapolska (1857–1921), also an actress and playwright; Maria Kuncewicz (b. 1911); and Hanna Malewska (b. 1911).

The name of the distinguished physicist Marie Curie-Sklodowska (1867–1934) is well known in the history of science. Other women who left their mark in the fields of education, theater, and revolutionary activity were Helen Modjeska (1840–1909), a famous actress; Jadwiga Szczawinska

(1863–1910), the founder of the Flying University in Russian-occupied Poland; and Ola Szczerbinska (1882–1963), a revolutionary and comrade in arms of Jozef Pilsudski.

Women prominent in Polish cultural life in the 1990s included writers Manuela Gretkowska, Maria Bojarska, Maria Nurowska, and Anna Oniczimowska and, in film and the fine arts, Agnieszka Holland, Barbara Sass, Alicja Helman, Krystyna Muszumańska-Nazar, and Ewa Michnik.

Women prominent in politics, economic life, and women's organizations in the 1990s include Hanna Suechocka, prime minister from 1992 to 1994; Hannah Gronkiewicz-Waltz, director of the State Bank; Danuta Wanicz, chair, Office of the President; Barbara Labuda, representative of Women's Organizations in the Sejm.

References. Barbara Wolfe Jancar, *Women under Communism* (Baltimore, 1978); Bogdan Mieczkowski, *Social Services for Women in Eastern Europe* (Charleston, Ill., 1982); *Poland: Glowny Urzad Statystyczny, Rocznik Statystyczny*, vol. 46 (Warsaw, 1987); Glowny Urzad Statystyczny, *Kobieta w Polsce* (Warsaw, 1975); United Nations, *The Impact of Economic and Political Reform on the Status of Women in Eastern Europe* (New York, 1992); Krystyna Wrochno, *Woman in Poland* (Warsaw, 1969).

TOVA YEDLIN

POLICY NETWORKS, WOMEN'S, is a term used by activists and women's studies scholars to describe feminist strategies within government. The concept of a policy network refers to a constellation of expert or interested groups and individuals, public and private, forming around a policy area. These may include interest groups; the media; experts in government, academe, private sector think tanks, and professional associations; top-level elected and appointed government officials; and public bureaucracies. The workings of a policy system are characterized by continuous interchanges among members at every stage of the policy process from agenda building to implementation. From the perspective of the interest group, membership in such a policy system offers "insider" status. Ready access to elected officials and sympathetic bureaucrats can provide information on new programs and regulations, policy shifts, and effective strategies.

Early Women's Policy Networks. For women, coalition building and networking are a part of the movement canon. Since the 1820s, women working through voluntary associations have traditionally led the major urban reform movements. The National American Woman Suffrage Association was a part of a suffrage policy network, composed of, among others, political parties, labor and church groups, the Red Cross, the National Association of Colored Women, the General Federation of Women's Clubs, the Woman's Christian Temperance Union, and a number of female executives in the war service bureaucracies in Washington, D.C. From 1920 to 1932 a postsuffrage coalition of 10–21 woman's rights groups, the Women's Joint Congressional Committee (WJCC), coordinated lobbying efforts. Members included the American Association of University Women (AAUW), the League of Women Voters (LWV), the National Consumers League, the National Federation of Business and Professional Women's Clubs (BPW), and the National Women's Trade Union League. The WJCC served as a clearinghouse; if three (later five) groups were interested in an issue, a subcommittee was formed. Their social feminist agenda supported education, health care, peace, and protective labor legislation. Their major achievements were the passage of the Sheppard-Towner Maternity Act of 1921 and the Cable Act of 1922, which guaranteed American citizenship for native-born women married to foreign nationals. Although considered the strongest lobby in Washington upon its formation, the WJCC remained effective only through the early 1930s, when an active and visible national feminist movement went into abeyance.

National Women's Policy Network. With the emergence of a new feminist movement in the late 1960s, these new woman's rights groups would ordinarily have operated at a disadvantage in that older groups had developed political allies and achieved an established place in the Washington community. But a half-dozen or so traditional women's organizations such as LWV and BPW were willing to teach feminists the ropes and share their experience and congressional contacts. On the national level today, the women's policy network is composed of feminist organizations such as the National Organization for Women (NOW) and the National Women's Political Caucus (NWPC), traditional women's organizations such as LWV, AAUW, and BPW, the media, female lawyers, women's policy think tanks, educational associations and institutions, other professional women, and, increasingly, other progressive social-movement organizations representing labor unions and public interest, civil rights, and gay rights groups. During the early 1970s, in particular, key roles were played by congresswomen, who sponsored and served as floor managers of woman's rights legislation. Congressional staff members often assist in lobbying campaigns. Women administrators serve as watchdogs in the implementation process and provide feedback. Today, the Congressional Caucus for Women's Issues plays a pivotal role in gathering and disseminating information to woman's rights groups.

Initially, the national women's policy network was maintained on a loosely structured, issue-by-issue basis, without a formal organization. Cooperative relationships were facilitated by the movement media, personal friendships, multiple group memberships, and attendance at rallies, meetings, and conferences. The campaign for the proposed Equal Rights Amendment (ERA) and planning for the International Women's Year (IWY) fueled these interactions. By 1985, almost 90 groups were representing women in Washington, and around 80 percent of these organizations reported participation in coalitions with other women's groups, particularly around one specific issue such as education, poverty, health, abortion, and women in the military. Women's groups also have formed coalitions to place women in presidential administrations and on the federal bench.

In 1985 a number of national women's organizations formed the Council of Presidents, which in each successive year has adopted a set of policy priorities for the coming legislative session. From 17 member groups and one priority issue in 1986, the council has grown to include the leaders of over 90 national, nonprofit women's organizations representing over 6 million women; it annually issues an ambitious multi-issue platform, termed the Women's Agenda. Much like the WJCC, the groups work on issues of their choice but never work against an agenda item. The council holds bimonthly meetings in Washington and, during election years, sponsors the Women's Vote project to raise money for voter education, media outreach about the women's vote, and voter registration. Its current agenda includes the ERA, civil rights, family issues, health care, reproduction rights, employment, violence, and economic equity in pensions, insurance, and Social Security.

State Women's Policy Networks. Parallel women's coalitions on the state level began to emerge in the mid-1970s to work either for ERA ratification or against rescission. Since the demise of the ERA, women have created more permanent and diversified coalitions of organizations to address many women's issues in state government. The National Women's Conference Committee (NWCC) was formed to implement the 25-point National Plan of Action adopted by delegates at the federally sponsored National Women's Conference in Houston in 1977. The NWCC is the only remaining federally constituted citizen body since the Presidential Advisory Commission on Women was eliminated in 1981. It assists networks in 26 states, acts as a network among networks, participates in international conferences on women sponsored by the United Nations, and holds an annual meeting for state networks.

These group coalitions were facilitated by preexisting insider networks in the form of state commissions on the status of women and the rapidly increasing numbers of female elected officials. Spurred by the creation of the national President's Commission on the Status of Women in 1961, every state eventually formed its own commission to gather data on the status of women and document areas of legal discrimination. Although, over the course of 35 years, several of the commissions have been abolished or reorganized or have become inactive, there were 36 active commissions in 1990 and 6 more that were classified as "inactive." Women's groups also recruit women candidates and support them. Increasingly, female state legislators are joining women's groups. In a survey conducted by the Center for the American Woman and Politics at Rutgers University in 1988, 49 percent of women state legislators reported holding membership in two or more women's groups. These legislator-members were found to more strongly support, be more active on, and place a higher priority on feminist and liberal issues.

Local Women's Policy Networks. Local women's groups, too, are well situated to become a part of an emerging policy network. Local feminist groups are pervasive. In 1995 NOW had 511 local chapters, and the NWPC had over 300 local caucuses. Further, because of an association with the home and family, in local politics women have traditionally faced fewer cultural barriers and role conflicts. Local issues are "people" issues, where women are felt to have special expertise. Certain women's issues are most appropriately handled at the local level or lend themselves to participation by those familiar with local conditions. Women's organizations have also gained direct representation in government through local commissions on the status of women. By 1990 there were 204 active local commissions. What are found on the local level are issue-specific women's policy networks formed around women's health, day care, domestic violence, reproduction, sexual assault, and displaced homemakers and made manifest in alternative women's services delivered at the local level. Much of women's group activity is undertaken in cooperation with governmental bureaucracies and elected officials and is oriented toward working within the system to create and expand urban services for women. Although state and national single-issue policy networks are part of these local policy networks, the key actors are drawn from local advocacy groups, women-run alternative services, and urban bureaucracies and elected officials responsible for delivering, funding, and regulating each policy.

The new reality of interest group politics is that only a few organizations focus on several issues; even NOW merely engages in "position-taking" on most women's issues and is active on only a few. The single-issue focus of the policy network mirrors the current model of effective group mobilization in terms of specialization, interorganizational networks, and interdependencies with the bureaucracy and legislators. What currently represents the political interests of feminists is a very sophisticated "insider" network for "outsider" issues, one that frames its goals in liberal, individualistic terms and works to be more inclusive by focusing on racism, classism, and homophobia as well as the core concept of sexism.

References. J. K. Boles, "Local Feminist Policy Networks in the Contemporary American Interest Group System," *Policy Sciences* 27 (1994): 161–178; K. L. Schlozman, "Representing Women in Washington: Sisterhood and Pressure Politics," in L. A. Tilly and P. Gurin (eds.), *Women, Politics, and Change* (New York, 1990), 339–382; R. Spalter-Roth and R. Schreiber, "Outsider Issues and Insider Tactics: Strategic Tensions in the Women's Policy Network during the 1980s," in M. M. Ferree and P. Y. Martin (eds.), *Feminist Organizations* (Philadelphia, 1995), 105–127.

JANET K. BOLES

POLISH WRITERS. Poland's national culture, strongly influenced by Western Europe (classical, Latin, Catholic), blossomed between the fifteenth and the seventeenth centuries. In the late eighteenth century, however, political and economic weakness led to Poland's partitions and political demise. Consequently, for a century and a half, art and literature alone preserved Polish national identity by covertly reworking patriotic motifs. Thus evolved the canon of Polish "national literature," a body of mostly romantic, visionary, messianic poetry, verse drama, and fiction considered as both an expression of Polish national consciousness and a force shaping that consciousness. Regained independence (1918) freed artists from preoccupation with nationhood, until World War II again stifled expression and reimposed concern with national survival. Notable postwar literature indirectly critiqued the official socialist ideology of the Eastern bloc. The dissolution of Soviet alliances (1989) has given Polish writers the second opportunity in two centuries to work in a society free from the dominance of any one official ideology, whether that of a foreign aggressor, a national cause, or the socialist state.

Already the earliest notable Polish women writers combined interest in shared human experience with social concern, local (rather than national) loyalties, and personal modes. Anna Stanisławska (c. 1651–c. 1700) resurrected vernacular lyrics (on love, women, family, social concerns, and memoirs) while foreign, neo-classical modes dominated Polish letters. Elżbieta Drużbacka (c. 1695–1765) followed suit with love and nature lyrics, social satires, and adventure novels. Konstancja Benisławska's (1747–1806) metaphysical religious verse showed no social interests, but Anna Mostowska's (1762–c. 1833) gothic historical fiction had social-didactic goals. Maria Wirtemberska (1768–1845), Poland's best sentimental novelist (*Malwina, or The Intimations of the Heart* [1816]), also promoted women's education, while Klementyna Tańska Hoffmanowa's (1798–1845) activism and fiction (*A Good Mother's Legacy* [1819]) promoted women's public service and civic education.

During the partitions, personal modes, local loyalties, and class and gender politics were not legitimate concerns in a national literature, whose goal was to nourish the national consciousness. Women writers, however, continued to discuss social issues and local concerns. In tune with the pragmatic, socially conscious, realist, prose-oriented trends of positivism, they focused on women's social position, child exploitation and abuse, or ethnic issues. Narcyza Żmichowska's (1819–1876) group of intellectual women, "the Enthusiasts," worked to reform women's education and upbringing. Her verse and fiction, romantic and realist-positivist, advocated gender and social justice alongside national causes. Renowned positivist-naturalist novelist Eliza Orzeszkowa (1841–1910) denounced anachronistic models of femininity (*Marta* [1873]), tackled anti-Semitism and assimilation (*Meir*

Ezofovitch [1878; Eng., 1898]), and indicted rural destitution and superstition (*The Dziurdzia Family* [1885]). She celebrated work- and land-loving rural Poland in her epic masterpiece *On the Niemen River* (1888) and wrote bold essays on patriotism, cosmopolitanism, minorities, and women. Maria Konopnicka's (1842–1910) short stories also championed the dispossessed: the elderly, peasant children, poor Jews. Though criticized for her social radicalism and anticlericalism (as in her verse epic on peasant emigration, *Mr. Balcer in Brazil* [1910]), her editorship of the protofeminist weekly *Dawn* (1984–1986), and her unconventional life, Konopnicka remained popular for decades. Gabriela Zapolska (1857–1921) exposed bourgeois hypocrisy, classism, and sexism in popular novels combining a bold social agenda, naturalist directness, and often melodramatic effect.

Even modernism and the patriotic-celebratory mood of regained independence did not thwart the impulse to critique the official ideologies of gender, class, and conservative national politics. Zofia Nałkowska's (1884–1954) psychological-documentary novels examined radical politics and mainstream ethics (*Prince* [1907]) and social divisions and corruption (*Teresa Hennert's Affair* [1924]) and denounced romantic love, nationalism, and militarism (*Count Emil* [1920]) and classism and sexism (*The Borderline* [1936]). Nałkowska excelled in terse, paradocumentary sketches and character studies (*Medallions* [1946]). In an experimental, lyrical-naturalist idiom, proletarian-born Pola Gojawiczyńska (1896–1963) explored the struggles of working-class women with religious-patriotic idealism and economic, political, and biological realities (*The Girls of Nowolipki* [1935]). Similar populist, naturalist, paradocumentary tendencies abounded in Maria Dąbrowska's (1889–1965) peasant stories (*People from Over There* [1925]; *A Village Wedding* [Eng. 1957]), essays, memoirs, and *Nights and Days* (1932–1934), her masterpiece saga of an impoverished gentry family struggling with economic, political, and ideological forces beyond their control.

Even while exploring individual psyches, women writers often critiqued mainstream concepts of gender and nation. After challenging conventional views of mothering (*A Man's Face* [1928]), Maria Kuncewiczowa (1899–1989) showed strong-willed, artistic femininity and obliquely critiqued nationalism in *The Stranger* (1936; Eng., 1945). She wrote her later psychological fiction abroad (*The Olive Grove* [1961; Eng., 1963]; *Tristan 1946* [1967; Eng., 1974]) before resettling in Poland. Ewa Szelburg-Zarembina's (1899–1986) multivolume, two-generation, coming-of-age novel *River of Lies* (1935–1968) examined women's friendships, loneliness, love, and social pressures in an expressionist idiom. Also noteworthy is Zofia Kossak-Szczucka's (1890–1968) historical fiction on Catholic themes; Aniela Gruszecka's (1884–1976) fiction on trendy artistic milieus; and the idiosyncratic, polyglot writings of Stanisława Przybyszewska (1901–1935), daughter of painter Aniela Pająk and author-philosopher Stanisław Przybyszewski.

Women dramatists also discussed the disfranchised and the workings of ideology. Zapolska's (1857–1921) masterpieces denounced Philistine classism and sexism and tackled minority issues (*Mrs Dulska's Morals* [1907]; *Malka Szwarcenkopf* [1927]). Nałkowska exposed society's masks and self-delusions and questioned the possibility of "truth" (*House of Women* [1930]) Kuncewicz explored the ideologies shaping women's identities, such as that of romantic love (*Maidenly Love* [1932]). Maria Morozowicz-Szczepkowska's (1885–?) *Monika's Case* (1933), filmed in the United States in the 1930s, advocated women's sexual emancipation along with professional and economic independence. Maria Pawlikowska-Jasnorzewska (1894–1945) ridiculed anachronistic gender roles and conventional mores (*Chauffeur Archibald* [1924]). Dąbrowska's historical dramas offered traditional interpretations of Polish history, while Stanisława Przybyszewska's *Danton's Case* (1929), filmed in France (1983), was a fact-based, yet personal, vision of the French Revolution.

Though the canon of nineteenth-century national poetry includes no women, around the turn of the century the most popular poet was Maria Konopnicka, author of folk art–inspired lyrics about the struggles of ordinary people. Though otherwise diverse, women poets remained interested in personal, social, and contemporary issues. The richness of women's experience (also erotic) was first celebrated in Kazimiera Zawistowska's (1870–1902) verse studies of famous and notorious historical and mythical women. Maryla Wolska's (1873–1930) post-Romantic lyrics, rich in Slav mythology and folk art motifs, after 1918 became contemporary in subject matter and direct in expression. Pawlikowska-Jasnorzewska's alluring aphoristic-imagistic verse reflected on body and art, Eros and love, time and death, and the bittersweet joys of the everyday. Inspired by the Parisian avant-garde, Bronisława Ostrowska (1881–1928) critiqued the despiritualized modern world yet celebrated the everyday and the balance between body, spirit, and nature. Kazimiera Iłłakowiczówna (1892–1983) wrote religious verse and free-form, symbolic lyrics on nature, patriotism, and love beyond the individual.

After the hiatus of World War II, writers often evaded issues of class and gender, made obligatory by the official socialist-realist aesthetics. Women's activism dwindled, since official women's organizations and feminism were compromised by their connection to the Soviet regime. Social and gender issues were thus discussed obliquely or in personal terms, as in the psychological novels of Stanisława Fleszarowa-Muskat (1919–1990). A rich diversity of fictional voices has emerged, however. In America Danuta Mostwin (b. 1921) writes psychological-sociological fiction about immigrants, whose everyday existence expresses and makes history. Investigative reporter Hanna Krall's (b. 1937) novels, all fact-inspired, discuss the Holocaust, human dignity in final situations, and the Jewish experience in Poland. Maria Nurowska (b. 1944) explores feminine consciousness catalyzed by ethnicity, history, and politics. In a postmodern, mock sci-fi idiom, Paris- and New York–based Ewa Kuryluk (b. 1946) reflects on this civilization's concepts of love and death, art and life, emotion and intellect, eroticism and physiology (*Century 21* [Eng., 1992; Pl., 1995]). Iza Filipiak, Natasza Goerke, Olga Tokarczuk, and Manuela Gretkowska, all born in the 1960s, write (female) subjectivity, Polishness, history, and politics in individualistic yet universal ways, shaped by their foreign experiences, by Poland's separation from the Soviet bloc (in 1989), and by the resulting collapse of the official discourse.

Women are central in contemporary poetry. Anna Świrszczyńska's (1909–1984) verse evokes war and women's physiology, psychology, and eroticism with simple, striking imagery. Julia Hartwig (b. 1921) writes urbane, reflective verse concerned with universal themes. Wisława Szymborska (b. 1923), awarded the Nobel Prize in literature (1996), always tries new themes and techniques and is often playful yet serious and brilliantly imaginative. Szymborska writes increasingly lyrical, linguistically sophisticated poems combining skepticism with love of humanity, humor and irony with seriousness, elaborate paradox with the celebration of the ordinary (*People on a Bridge* [Eng., 1990]; *View with a Grain of Sand* [Eng., 1995]). Her craftsmanship yields chiseled, sparing verse open to diverse readings. Urszula Kozioł's (b. 1931) intellectual, introspective, lyrical-yet-pithy verse combines classicism with experimentation. Halina Poświatowska's (1935–1967) poems explore women's physicality (in love and illness) and celebrate life, mixing faith and doubt, pain and irony, wit and seriousness. New York–based Anna Frajlich (b. 1942) writes succinct lyrics, emotional yet not sentimental, on exile and uprootedness (Jewish and Polish), aging, childhood, and a ravaged Poland. Ewa Lipska's (b. 1945) reflective, oracular verse uses history to comprehend the present. Her lyrics are sung by Poland's premier performers, as are those of Agnieszka Osiecka (1936–1997), author of over 2,000 witty, ironic, poetic songs. Three poets who reimagine received cultural icons from a feminist perspective are Mira Kuś (b. 1948), whose sarcastic, linguistic verse grapples with the philosophical underpinnings of life and the sexism of Polish culture; Krystyna Lars (b. 1950), whose surreal prose-poetry paints ironic portraits of Poland's holiest historical and mythical figures; and Katarzyna Boruń (b. 1956), who wittily turns the icons of Western pop culture into a ready-found manipulable code for a feminist agenda.

Many prominent women writers have written for children. Maria Konopnicka originated true children's literature in her unstilted, not overly didactic children's poetry. Among the authors mentioned earlier, Hoffmanowa, Kossak-Szczucka, Dąbrowska, Gruszecka, Hartwig, Świrszczyńska, and Iłłakowiczówna wrote extensively for children.

References. Helena Goscilo (trans. and ed.), *Russian and Polish Women's Fiction* (Knoxville, Tenn., 1985); Regina Grol, *Ambers Aglow; Recent Polish Women Poets* (Austin, Tex., 1997); Katharina M. Wilson, *An Encyclopedia of Continental Women Writers* (New York and London, 1991).

URSZULA TEMPSKA

POLITICAL PARTICIPATION. Europe. Voting and Office Holding reflect diverse political and cultural traditions. Women were enfranchised at widely different times. The Scandinavian nations first gave women the vote, beginning with Finland in 1906. Immediately after World War I nine Northern and Central European countries followed suit: Great Britain, Ireland, Luxembourg, the Netherlands, Germany, Austria, and the three Baltic Republics. Woman suffrage was also included in the constitutions of various Soviet Republics. The interwar period saw the full or partial extension of woman suffrage south and east, to Poland, Czechoslovakia, Hungary, Greece, Spain, and Turkey. Then, after World War II women won the vote in the remaining European nations, the last holdout being the principality of Liechtenstein, succumbing in 1984. Thus, while women in Scandinavia have been voting for several generations, women in some other countries have had only limited experience with the franchise. Swiss women were enfranchised for national elections only in 1971; Spanish and Portuguese women have just begun to vote again with the reinstatement of democratic elections in the 1970s.

These different histories of enfranchisement affect the turnout rates of women. In the early-enfranchising nations of Northern and Central Europe women and men today vote at nearly identical rates. In contrast, in late-enfranchising countries women may still lag behind men unless voting is mandatory or quasi-mandatory, as in Italy or Greece. For example, in Switzerland, sex differences in turnout have been (and still may be) quite large; the 1975 Barnes and Kaase survey found an 18 percent difference, with 50 percent of women and 68 percent of men claiming to have voted in the general election. However, these remaining differences in voting rates should narrow, as they did in early-enfranchising nations. Wherever differences have disappeared, women constitute the majority of the electorates because of their predominance in the adult population.

In every Western European country where data are available, women in the early postwar period were more likely to vote for the parties of the Right. This "gender gap" was greatest, more than 10 percent, in Italy and France during the 1950s and in Spain for the 1979 election, the second since restoration of democracy. In these three countries, women particularly favored the Catholic parties of the Right, while men especially supported the Communist and Socialist Parties. The presence of a politically powerful

Catholic Church combined with women's greater religious practice accentuates this gender gap. Women tend to favor Protestant religious parties as well. For example, Norwegian women vote slightly more for the traditional Christian People's Party, and Swedish women for the small Christian Democrats.

Secularization and other factors are currently eliminating this gender gap in voting, however. In fact, a new type of gender gap may be emerging; in certain recent elections in Norway, Denmark, Sweden, and France women slightly favored the socialist parties.

Sex differences still persist in other types of political participation, although they are diminishing. Everywhere women profess less interest in politics and are less exposed to political information via the mass media and interpersonal communications. A 1987 survey of 12 European Union countries showed that attitudes toward women's political activity can still be quite restrictive. When asked if politics should be left to men, roughly two-fifths of West Germans, Luxembourgers, Portuguese, and Spaniards agreed. Denmark turned out to be the most egalitarian, with only 5 percent agreeing with the statement. Besides culture, women's homemaking and child rearing roles constrain their political activity; sex differences tend to be smallest in those types of participation that are most compatible with traditional female roles such as ad hoc and local community activities.

Political parties, essential gateways to political office in Europe, rarely represent women equally to men. In only a few known instances do women make up half or more of the membership: in Great Britain's Conservative Party, Norway's, Denmark's, and Sweden's small religious parties, and a few other conservative or moderate Scandinavian parties. The parties of the Left usually have lower percentages of female members because they recruit more through unions, where women are scarcer. However, these parties' greater commitment to equality often leads to special efforts to increase women's representation, such as quotas for party offices and nominations to parliamentary seats. Nevertheless, the ratio of male to female party members can be quite large, for example, 3 to 1 (or more) in the French and Italian socialist and (former) communist parties and both major parties of Germany. Representation in political office also varies enormously across Europe. Inter-Parliamentary Union data from the mid-1990s show Scandinavia (except for Iceland), Germany, and the Netherlands with the largest proportions of women in national legislatures. There a striking one-third to two-fifths of legislators are female. Other high-ranking countries, with women constituting one out of every four or five legislators, are Great Britain, Spain, Iceland, Austria, Luxembourg, and Switzerland. Because of ideological commitment to equality the communist regimes of Eastern Europe and the former Soviet republics had high proportions of female legislators. However, these proportions dropped sharply with the inception of democratic elections.

In the remaining Western European nations, women's representation in the single or lower house ranges between 6 and 16 percent. Women fare better in countries where voters choose between party lists of candidates, for parties are less reluctant to nominate women when several candidates run as a group. In contrast, single-member districts and plurality election systems lessen women's representation. Great Britain and France, among the few European countries with the plurality electoral system, also had some of the lowest proportions of women in Parliament.

The law of increasing disproportion operates in Europe, as elsewhere. That is, the proportion of women shrinks as the power of the position increases. Thus, women are usually least common in cabinets and government ministries and on the sometimes quite influential consultative committees representing powerful economic interests. Likewise, in the formerly communist Eastern European countries, women were scarcest in the powerful governing organs of the Communist Party, the Central Committee, and the Politburo. Moreover, higher proportions of women usually occur at the local, compared to the national, levels of government. Europe's parliamentary system facilitates women's access to the highest offices. The proportion of women in the cabinets ranges from a low of 6 percent (Italy) to a high of 45 percent (Norway). So far six countries have had a female prime minister: Great Britain, Norway, France, Poland, Lithuania, and Turkey.

References. Samuel Barnes and Max Kaase, "Political Action—An Eight-Nation Study," survey available from the Inter-University Consortium for Political and Social Research, University of Michigan, 1975; Carol A. Christy, "Trends in Sex Differences in Political Participation: A Comparative Perspective," in Marianne Githens, Pippa Norris, and Joni Lovenduski (eds.), *Different Roles, Different Voices: Women and Politics in the United States and Europe* (New York, 1994), 27–37; Commission of the European Communities, *Men and Women of Europe in 1987* (Supplement No. 26, Women of Europe) (Brussels, 1987); Lauri Karvonen and Per Selle (eds.), *Women in Nordic Politics: Closing the Gap* (Brookfield, Vt., 1995); Joni Lovenduski, and Pippa Norris (eds.), *Gender and Party Politics* (London, Thousand Oaks, Calif., and New Delhi, 1993); Marilyn Rueschemeyer (ed.), *Women in the Politics of Postcommunist Eastern Europe* (Armonk, N.Y., and London, 1994); Wilma Rule and Joseph F. Zimmerman (eds.), *Electoral Systems in Comparative Perspective: Their Impact on Women and Minorities* (Westport, Conn., and London, 1994).

CAROL A. CHRISTY

POLITICAL PARTICIPATION. United States. Political participation by women has a history as long as America's. Abigail Adams admonished her husband, John, and the founders of the new nation to "remember the ladies." But even before the American Revolution, colonial women were politically active in behalf of literacy, general education, and religious tolerance.

The first political action organized by women was the Seneca Falls, New York, conference in 1848, called by Elizabeth Cady Stanton and Lucretia Mott. There, over 100 women and some men signed a Declaration of Sentiments, including the resolution "that it is the duty of the women of this country to secure to themselves their sacred right to the elected franchise." From that moment until the Nineteenth Amendment was ratified in August 1920, three generations of women used every political means available in order to secure what is now regarded as a fundamental right. Thus, the protest and demonstration tactics of present-day feminists can be seen as part of a long heritage of political activism by women.

Kansas became an early scene of controversy over woman suffrage and is the first state in which a constitutional amendment granting suffrage to women was introduced. In 1867, two suffrage amendments emerged from the state legislature, one enfranchising black men and the other enfranchising women. The state received nationwide attention, and the fight was fierce. Susan B. Anthony made her famous trek across the state, spending many nights camped out under the stars. Other noted feminists, such as Stanton, Lucy Stone and her husband, Dr. Henry Blackwell, and the Reverend Olympia Brown, the first woman ordained as a minister of the Universalist Church, blazed campaign trails with her. Their efforts were not enough. The woman suffrage amendment failed in popular referendum, by a vote of 9,070 for to 19,857 against.

But by the 1880s, Kansas, like other western territories, enfranchised women for local elections, and women quickly used that power to virtually seize control of many town governments. Wyoming became the first state to enter the union with woman suffrage in 1890. Next came Colorado in 1893, and Utah and Idaho followed in 1896. Some attribute the West's relatively quick move to grant women political rights to the necessity for cooperation between men and women as they pioneered together, although others emphasize that women's "traditional" concerns about public schooling and community affairs were motives for gaining the vote.

Nationally, though, the progress of this early women's movement was not so steady. The movement seemed to slow and falter in the late nineteenth century. New desire for reforms in labor, public health, and social conditions, however, galvanized the movement once more, as reformers thought that a "woman's vote" would help to bring about social change. From about 1908 the struggle intensified, and 12 years later women were enfranchised. All women were first eligible to vote in 1920, and by 1924 their turnout ranged from around 20 percent in the South to a high of 40 percent in Illinois.

For much of this century, women trailed men in their voting turnout rates. Other forms of women's participation, the protesting, petitioning, and marching, in which suffrage activists had engaged, also temporarily disappeared from the scene. Generations of gender-role socialization, teaching women *not* to be politically active, had to be overcome. The World War II years offer an exception: women dominated at the polls in the presidential election of 1944, with so many male voters overseas. But women's war work, as, for example, Red Cross volunteer or Rosie the Riveter, marked an entry of women into public spheres that persisted and grew.

In 1970, on the 50th anniversary of the ratification of the Nineteenth Amendment, a new generation of feminists staged a Women's Strike for Equality. Despite doubts about response, thousands and thousands of women participated, making it one of the first of many mass events of the most recent wave of feminism.* Since then, women have used every political tactic available to them in the quest for equal rights. Women's voting rates also have caught up with, and in some cases passed, men's. By 1980, the gap between men's and women's turnout had completely closed, with 59 percent of each sex voting. Older women and women who have little education, who are blue-collar workers, or who are housewives continue to vote with less frequency than men. This is more than compensated for by well-educated women and women in sales, managerial, and professional occupations, who participate more than do their male counterparts. Since women outnumber men in the population, the identical turnout rates by sex actually means that the majority of voters are women.

Whether this numerical majority would mean a change in the way votes are cast has interested contemporary observers, and evidence suggests that the "gender gap," the phenomenon of men and women preferring different candidates and different public policies, is real. Since 1980, women and men have cast their votes differently. While 61 percent of men voted for Ronald Reagan in 1984, only 57 percent of women did so. More striking are the findings that gender gaps in several states have been great enough to determine election outcomes. Mark White of Texas, for example, believed that he owed his 1982 election to the governorship to women. In 1986, women voters provided the margin of victory for Democratic Senate candidates in Louisiana, North Carolina, Washington, and Colorado. Not all women are alike by any means. But public opinion polling in the 1980s has shown repeatedly that women tend to prefer some policies more than most men do. It may be that the hope of the early activists, that a "woman's vote" would be used for reform and change, will be vindicated.

Women's voting has always been tied to women's participation in other, less traditional kinds of political participation. Women demonstrated, protested, and agitated to *get* the vote, and with each successive wave of feminism, these forms of political participation have gone hand in hand with ever-growing numbers of women at the polls.

References. S. Baxter and M. Lansing, *Women and Politics: The Visible Majority* (Ann Arbor, 1983); E. Flexner, *Century of Struggle* (Cambridge, Mass., 1959); E. Klein, *Gender Politics* (Cambridge, Mass., 1984).

SUE TOLLESON RINEHART

POLITICAL PARTICIPATION. U.S. Political Parties are a source of political influence for women and an increasingly significant outlet for their political ambition.

The two major U.S. political parties seek to win elections to influence the policy-making process. Women's integration into the major parties has occurred across the twentieth century; the parties' contexts have worked to encourage and maintain the extent and direction of women's participation. As the policy-making process is the government's central focus, women's participation in political parties is a significant source of influence for them.

Partisan influence is affected by the nonprogrammatic nature of the major parties. Rather than determine what their candidates' policy stands will be, these parties label candidates Democrat or Republican for voters. The two parties are not strikingly different in ideology; and candidates set their own issue positions.

Partisan participation occurs in a heterogeneous setting. The two major parties are made up of a series of formal organizations; become effectual in several government settings; and are characterized by citizens' strong, moderate, weak, and, for some, nonexistent identification with them.

An early nineteenth-century traveler in the United States, Alexis de Tocqueville, noted that "even the women often go to public meetings and forget household cares while they listen to political speeches. For them clubs to some extent take the place of theaters." Before U.S. women had universal suffrage, they had auxiliaries to the Democratic and Republican Parties. Women also were active in third parties, which operate as pressure valves in the U.S. political system and may lead to changes in the major parties. Third-party activists have included women such as Mary Ellen Lease, who organized and worked in Farmers Alliances and the resulting Populist Party; near the nineteenth century's end the Populist Party set off a realignment of groups underlying the Democratic and Republican Parties. Although the names of the two major parties may stay the same, a realignment changes the two-party system.

Women have run for public office on third-party tickets. In 1872 on the Equal Rights line, Victoria Claflin Woodhull ran for president. In the 1890s women began to be elected to state legislatures on major party lines, and in 1916 on the Republican ticket, Jeannette Rankin (Montana) was elected to the U.S. House. In 1918 she ran unsuccessfully for the U.S. Senate on the National party line, not having received the Republican nomination. In 1940, as a Republican, she won a second term in the House.

In 1920 the Nineteenth Amendment to the U.S. Constitution gave women universal suffrage. Officeholders who led the major parties expected women to vote as a bloc and feared for their own incumbencies. Using quotas, party leaders began integrating women into national, state, and local party committees. These committees administer party business. National American Woman Suffrage Association (NAWSA) president Carrie

Chapman Catt expected women to inform "the whole field of public life with woman spirit" and urged them to join a major political party.

Bypassed by Catt was the National Woman's Party (NWP), a militant offshoot of the NAWSA that advocated a responsible parties system. In this system parties take responsibility for their candidates not only by labeling but also by offering distinctive policy programs and requiring candidates to adopt both label and program. After 1923, the NWP basically offered a "one-plank platform," a constitutional equal rights amendment. Major women's organizations opposed the amendment because it would nullify protective labor legislation, a policy concern of theirs. Neither major party responded to the NWP's sectarian influence; and its "woman for Congress" action did not catch on.

A bloc of women voters did not emerge until 1928 and 1932, because newly enfranchised groups need socialization into the electorate. Republicans ceased to court women so ardently. But women such as Mary (Molly) Willliams Dewson achieved sex-typed posts as Democratic Party regulars and, along with public officials such as Frances Perkins and volunteers like Eleanor Roosevelt, made inroads through the Women's Division of the Democratic National Committee (WDDNC). Entry into the electorate by women, immigrants, and young people and change to Democratic Party labels of black, Jewish, and working-class people contributed substantially to President Franklin Roosevelt's election and led to another major party realignment. Because of the importance in the New Deal's evolution of women activists working through women's clubs, until World War II the WDDNC was so prominent it maintained year-round headquarters with a paid director; among its functions was patronage distribution to key Democratic women.

The presidential nominating conventions first emerged in 1832. Convention delegates operate as a social force in their own right and compose a pool of potential candidates for office. Women convention delegates' history is less known than that of women as party regulars and volunteers. At least since 1912, the major parties have differed proportionately in their integration of women delegates; but women have achieved greater representation as delegates, regardless of party, than as congresspeople or state legislators. Republicans have had fewer women delegates than Democrats, who since 1932 have relied for support on a coalition of disadvantaged social groups. In context the Democratic Party may offer women more political "pleasure" and opportunities than the Republican. In 1972 the Democratic Party's McGovern-Fraser Commission upgraded requirements of proportionate representation among delegations of women, young people, and minorities; Republicans introduced similar changes. Women now constitute 35 to 50 percent of delegations. Like men, these women delegates are socialized to internal party standards and are similarly professional.

Where gender roles* influence women's partisan roles, they influence ambition and type of activism. The context of formal party organization can reinforce or stimulate change in women's ambition and activism. Women and men delegates to the 1972 conventions felt equally ambitious about their party careers, but women showed less ambition than men for public office. Republican women were most likely to shun public office seeking for continued party activism. They did not, however, lack ambition. Differences in the foci of Republican and Democratic women's ambition related to differences in their family-work roles. Among party regulars at Atlanta, Georgia, the ambition levels of Democratic and Republican women stemmed from early learning experiences that varied by party identification; Democratic and Republican men were not so affected. Among white women ambition depended on countersocialization to unconventional gender roles. Black women party regulars' ambition related to politicization in their parental families and also to what they made of their current activities.

A person's party identification is a self-identification likely learned in childhood in the family setting. If there are two parents at home, and the two do not have the same identification, because of her often greater proximity to child rearing the mother may most influence a child's development of an identification. Single-parent homes with children most often are headed by women, increasing opportunity for a mother to influence a child's identification. No distinction by sex is made among children in this transmission. In adulthood, certain situational factors may mitigate or supersede childhood learning. The party identification of women in the paid workforce and of single women especially is least influenced by factors external to them.

Women are said to be "more partisan than men" because women will most likely have a party identification. Women and men with an identification do not tend to differ, though, in desire to see their party prevail in a presidential election; education and an election's circumstances account for any differences. Women and men also do not differ in degree of party loyalty.

Women running on major party tickets in congressional, state legislative, and municipal general elections are as likely as men to win their contests. Democratic women candidates for Congress are more likely than Republican women to win, because Democratic women run in urban districts where most voters are Democrats. Republican women's opportunities to run tend to come in districts not as friendly to their party. Women running on third-party lines lose because third parties lose; more women run on these lines than as Democrats or Republicans. Barriers to women's achievement of public office on a major party line are found in the educational and occupational status of many women; in certain electoral district factors, which also may interact with a candidate's race; and in voters' tendencies to reelect incumbents, who are mostly men.

References. R. Darcy and S. S. Schramm, "When Women Run against Men," *Public Opinion Quarterly* 41 (1977): 1–12; D. L. Fowlkes, J. Perkins, and S. T. Rinehart, "Gender Roles and Party Roles," *American Political Science Review* 73 (1979): 722–780; J. S. Lemons, *The Woman Citizen: Social Feminism in the 1920s* (Urbana, Ill., 1973); V. Sapiro and B. G. Farah, "New Pride and Old Prejudice: Political Ambition and Role Orientations among Female Partisan Elites," *Women and Politics 1* (1980): 13–36.

SARAH SLAVIN

POLITICAL PARTICIPATION. U.S. Women Elected and Appointed Officials have attained several major breakthroughs in the United States following the emergence of the contemporary feminist movement. In 1968 the first black woman, Shirley Chisholm (Democrat, New York), was elected to Congress. In 1974, Ella Grasso (Democrat, Connecticut) became the first woman elected as governor of a state in her own right, rather than in her capacity as wife of a major political figure. In 1978, Nancy Kassebaum became the first woman elected to the U.S. Senate without having first reached Congress by filling the unexpired term of a congressman. In 1981, Sandra Day O'Connor was appointed to the U.S. Supreme Court by President Ronald Reagan and became the first woman justice to serve on that body. In 1984, Arlene Violet (Republican, Rhode Island) became the first woman elected as attorney general of any state, and Geraldine Ferraro (Democrat, New York) became the first woman nominated for vice president by a major political party.

Despite these major breakthroughs and despite substantial increases in the number of women elected and appointed officials in the 1970s and 1980s, the proportion of elective and appointive governmental positions held by women remains low. By the mid-1990s, women held no more than 26 percent of elective positions (except school boards) in the United States at any level of government, and they were about equally as underrepresented in appointive offices.

At the end of the 105th Congress, 1997–1998, women held only 54 of the 435 positions in the U.S. House of Representatives and 9 of the 100 seats in the U.S. Senate. By late 1998, a total of 191 women had served in Congress during its 200-year history. The first was Representative Jeannette Rankin (Republican, Montana), best known because she was the only member of the U.S. House to vote against the entry of the United States into both world wars. Rankin served from 1917 to 1919 and again from 1941 to 1943. The first woman U.S. Senator was Rebecca Latimer Felton (Democrat, Georgia). She was appointed in 1922 to complete the term of a senator who died in office. However, Felton served as a member of the Senate for only one day before giving up her seat to a man who was elected to fill the vacancy. Felton's path into office was not atypical for those women pioneers who served in Congress prior to the contemporary women's movement. In fact, a majority of pre-1970 congresswomen first came to Congress to fill midterm vacancies, often created by the deaths of their husbands. However, the "widow's succession" is no longer a common means for women to gain entry into Congress; most of the women who served in Congress during the 1990s were elected in their own right.

Historically, women have been as absent from high-level, federal appointive offices as they have been from elective congressional offices. The first woman cabinet member was Frances Perkins, who served as secretary of labor from 1933 to 1945 under President Franklin Delano Roosevelt. Only two women in addition to Perkins served in presidential cabinets prior to the administration of President Jimmy Carter. Presidents Bush and Clinton each appointed four women to cabinet-level positions in their administrations, thereby easily surpassing the records of their predecessors. Women also fared better in receiving subcabinet appointments under Presidents Bush and Clinton than under their predecessors. Women were appointed to 19.7 percent of full-time, Senate-confirmed positions in the Bush administration and to 27 percent of all such positions in the first term of the Clinton administration.

Women have made slightly larger gains in most state and local offices than they have at the national level. Progress is perhaps most noticeable at the state legislative level, where the proportion of women among state legislators increased between 1969 and 1987, from 4.0 percent to 23 percent. By 1998 women also held 28.3 percent of appointed positions in governors' cabinets and 26 percent of top statewide elective offices across the 50 states. By the mid-1990s, about 9 percent of all county governing board members and 21 percent of municipal governing boards and mayoral positions were occupied by women. While by 1998 only 15 women had ever served as governors of states, 3 women occupied gubernatorial mansions in that year.

A number of explanations have been put forth to account for women's continued underrepresentation in elective and appointive office. Three sets of factors seem most important.

First, people traditionally have been socialized to believe that men are better suited to politics and that political officeholding is an inappropriate activity for women. These beliefs have limited women's political aspirations and have led men in positions of political power who control access to public office to doubt women's capabilities.

Second, the sexual division of labor* in both the family* and the paid labor force has constrained women's political participation. The fact that women have had primary responsibility for child rearing and household maintenance has meant that most women, particularly those who also work outside the home, have not had the time and flexibility necessary to pursue an activity as demanding as political officeholding. Women who seek elective office often wait to do so until their children are grown; this places them at a disadvantage relative to men of the same age, who often have accumulated political experience while their children were young and are thus better positioned to run for higher-level offices. Women who hold high-level appointive offices in state and federal government are much less likely to be married or to have children than their male counterparts, suggesting that they have had to make a choice between career or family, while men have been able to pursue both.

The sexual division of labor in the paid labor force also affects women's ability to compete for political office on an equal basis with men. Political officeholders have most often come from the fields of law and business where the numbers of women have traditionally been low. Women who seek political office, like women in the population more generally, are concentrated in the fields of nursing, social work, teaching, and clerical work. These female-dominated occupations less often than law or business allow for the leaves of absence and flexible work hours that are necessary for officeholding, less often provide credentials that will be viewed as demonstrating competence for officeholding, and less often serve as inroads into networks that can provide the money necessary for financing political campaigns and the contacts necessary for obtaining political appointments.

The third explanation for women's underrepresentation in public office focuses on basic biases in the way Western democratic political systems operate. These political systems, structured so as to ensure stability, promote the continued tenure of groups and individuals who are in positions of power. Political parties want to win, and party leaders are reluctant to back women's candidacies if they view them as high risk. Women candidates in the United States, more often than not, must challenge incumbents who have huge advantages in terms of visibility and fund-raising. The high costs of campaigning in the United States and the absence of public financing of campaigns for most offices ensure that the have-nots, including most women, will not be able to seek political office. Those who control appointments to high-level executive offices demand loyalty among those they appoint and consequently rely on networks of close friends and associates—networks that are mostly male and very elite—in seeking potential appointees.

Although the barriers to women's election and appointment are considerable, the presence of women in public office has important consequences both for politics and for women's lives. Despite some visible exceptions, most women officeholders do seem to have perspectives and priorities different from those of most men. In the aggregate, women in elective and appointive office are more liberal than their male counterparts on a variety of public policy issues, are more concerned with the effects that various public policy issues will have on women's lives, show higher levels of support for issues like the ERA and abortion* that have been closely associated with the feminist movement, and encourage and assist other women to follow in their footsteps.

References. R. Darcy, S. Welch, and J. Clark, *Women, Elections, and Representation*, 2nd. ed. (Lincoln, Nebr., 1994); S. Thomas and Wilcox (eds.), *Women and Elective Office* (New York, 1998).

SUSAN J. CARROLL

PORNOGRAPHY is one of the largest industries in the United States, larger than the mainstream movie and recording industries. According to *U.S. News and World Report*, hard-core video rentals rose from 75 million in 1985 to 665 million in 1996. About 150 new titles are produced a week and rented and sold in over 25,000 video stores, shown on cable and pay-per-view television, and rented in hotels or motels. Add the phone sex industry, magazines, strip and peep show clubs, and the Internet. Clearly, the question of the effects of pornography is not a trivial issue.

Feminist concerns about pornography emerged in the 1970s with a rally protesting a billboard of a woman in chains with a caption reading, "I'm black and blue from the Rolling Stones and I love it." Women against Violence against Women held a national conference in San Francisco in 1978, staging a "Take Back the Night March." One result was a book of readings on pornography (Lederer) in which feminists viewed pornography as harmful to women. Since then, other factions within feminism have taken different positions on the issue. Some have argued that the protection of freedom of expression is more important to women than the harm of pornography and that banning pornography would not eradicate violence against women. Others have defended pornography on the basis that it liberates women by challenging patriarchal assumptions of female sexuality as monogamous, tied to procreation, and expressed only in committed relations.

The definition of pornography is important in considering its harm. Religious conservatives, considering the sexuality itself as immoral, label an extremely broad range of material as pornographic. In contrast, antipornography feminists reserve the term "pornography" for sexually explicit material that degrades, dehumanizes, or subordinates women or presents women as physically abused in a sexual context. They contend that the subordination of women in pornography, not only the violence against women, has negative effects. Gloria Steinem (Lederer) distinguished pornography from erotica, reinforcing the difference between sexuality expressed in a context of equality and choice and the sexually subordinating.

Social scientists have divided pornography into four categories: (1) nudity without force, coercion, sexual activity, or degradation; (2) sexually explicit material or activity without violence, degradation, submission, domination, or humiliation; (3) sexually explicit material or activity without violence but with degradation, submission, domination, or humiliation; and (4) sexually violent material, including rape and sadomasochistic themes. The first two categories do not appear to have harmful effects. The primary types of pornography investigated are categories 3 and 4, degrading/dehumanizing and violent pornography.

Degrading or dehumanizing, sexually explicit material is most difficult to define. Some researchers consider the indiscriminate sexual availability of women as degrading to women, while antipornography feminists believe that subordination is the key element in degradingness or dehumanization. Those who believe that the dehumanizing focus on genitalia in sexually explicit material is degrading would find most filmed pornography degrades women, regardless of the equality of the sexual participants.

The question of whether pornography harms women requires designation of "harm," as well as specification of the type of pornography. Sexual violence is the harm typically thought of as resulting from pornography. However, harm can also include the development of rape-supportive beliefs and attitudes, the devaluation of women, and the harm to relationships as a result of the expectations and sexual schemas taught by pornography.

Researchers (Donnerstein, Linz, and Penrod) argue that the violence, not the sexuality, is harmful in violent pornography. In contrast, Diana E. H. Russell suggests that pornography can lead to rape through conditioning by pairing of sexually arousing stimuli with violence, reduction of inhibitions, and social modeling. Experimental research has shown that exposure of college men to violent pornography affects their emotions, attitudes, and behavior. Behaviorally, pornography increases aggression typically measured by the willingness to administer shocks to a female confederate in the guise of a learning experiment. An emotional effect of violent pornography is desensitization, which is the blunting or lessening of emotional responses after repeated exposure to some stimulus or event. Desensitization effects of pornography include the perception of victims of violence as less injured and a lowering of empathy toward rape victims. Sexually violent material becomes less anxiety-provoking and depressing with prolonged exposure. Exposure to violent pornography also affects acceptance of interpersonal violence and belief in rape myths, such as the idea that women enjoy rape.

Another effect of exposure to violent pornography among men is an increase in rape fantasies and "rape proclivity" (self-reported likelihood of rape or forced sex if impunity were guaranteed). Although we cannot prove scientifically that pornography causes rape because, of course, the hypothesis cannot be tested in a laboratory study, we can say that pornography causes the types of attitudes rapists hold and creates a social climate that supports violence against women. For example, exposure to violent pornography increases rape myths and belief in rape myths, as a predictor of self-reported sexual aggression.

Various studies have shown that exposure to degrading/dehumanizing material has negative attitudinal and emotional effects, including desensitization and an increase in rape proclivity and, to some extent, behavioral effects on aggression, particularly when the pornography is presented in a visual medium. Dolf Zillmann and Jennings Bryant have shown that men's prolonged exposure to "stag films" desensitizes them to victims of violence and leads to devaluation of their sexual partners, increased sexual callousness, and decreased support of gender equality. James Check and Ted Guloien (in Zillmann and Bryant) found that repeated exposure to sexually violent pornography or nonviolent dehumanizing pornography increased men's proclivity to rape, compared to exposure to erotica. Women have reported that their male partners have tried to get them to engage in behaviors seen in pornography. Charlene Senn (in Russell) found that 24 percent of her female sample had experienced sexual coercion as depicted in pornography.

Pornography works in concert with other factors in predicting sexual violence. Neil Malamuth and his colleagues showed that exposure to pornography magazines, along with hostility toward women and promiscuous-impersonal sex, predicted self-reported sexual aggression among college men. Obviously, we cannot say that pornography turns all the men who view it into rapists. Nor can we say that all men who say they might rape if they could escape punishment will rape. Yet, it is clear that pornography is one piece of the cultural context that supports rape, via a number of attitudinal and emotional effects, and may contribute to violence among men who have the proclivity to rape. Furthermore, many harmful effects of pornography are relatively unexplored, such as the impact of pornography on relationships, on sexual socialization, on satisfaction with one's own and one's partner's body, and with views of women that objectify them as one-dimensional sexual objects.

An important question raised about exposure to pornography is the extent of children's exposure to pornographic materials. Several studies have indicated a large percentage of junior high and high school students who have viewed X-rated films. In a study by Gloria Cowan and Robin Campbell of high school students in southern California, 82.6 percent of the boys and 48.6 percent of the girls had viewed explicit pornography videos. In this study, exposure to pornography was related to belief in rape myths. What are children likely to learn about sex from pornography? Young people are learning that women (and men, too) always want sex, that sex is what people do with their genitals, that sensuality and what is commonly called "foreplay," as well as kissing, caressing, and looking at one's partner, are not an important part of sexuality, and that sex ends with the man's ejaculating on the woman's face, chest, or buttocks. They are learning sexually violent behavior and the rape myths that women want forced sex, that "no" means "yes," and that men cannot control their sexual behavior. They learn that sex is impersonal. A major predictor of college men's sexual violence (in college and 10 years later) is impersonal sex, along with hostile masculinity (Malamuth et al.).

What can be done about pornography? Leaders of the feminist antipornography movement, feminist legal scholar Catherine MacKinnon and writer Andrea Dworkin (in Russell), believe that obscenity law is not appropriate for the regulation of pornography. Obscenity law, grounded in the meaning of pornography as immoral, that is, appealing to lewd and prurient interests, focuses on the sexual standards of the community rather than the subordination of, and violence toward, women. Again, the issue for antipornography feminists is inequality and the effects of pornography on sexual violence. Dworkin and MacKinnon have proposed a legal remedy that gives a victim the right to sue for damages. This does not make pornography a violation of moral standards, nor does it make the production of pornography a crime. It would simply give victims recourse for civil action. This is not censorship. Although versions of this bill were passed in Minneapolis and Indianapolis, the proposed law was declared unconstitutional by federal courts because of the possibility of violation of the First Amendment (*American Booksellers Association v. Hudnut*, 1984, 1985, 1986). Amazingly, the federal court suggested that the very power of pornography to cause harm (as "speech") was sufficient reason for its protection. In Canada, where equality is as important as freedom of speech in its charter, the Canadian Supreme Court, in *Butler v. Her Majesty the Queen* (1992), decreed that obscenity law includes harm to women, so that material that degrades and dehumanizes women is harmful to women as a group and, thus, obscene.

Unfortunately, the question of pornography has become a debate over censorship. The harm of pornography is a scientific question, answerable on its own terms. What should be done about it and whether and how it should be regulated or subject to legal recourse are a political issue. The citizen's right to free speech also entitles individuals to speak out against material they find unacceptable. Private actions, including pickets and boycotts, letter-writing campaigns, and educational efforts, are possible. Enough Is Enough, a national nonprofit organization dedicated to making the Internet safe for children, is educating about the availability of pornography to children on the Internet and offering parents various solutions. At the personal level, people can speak out about material that degrades, objectifies, and dehumanizes women, if only to those with whom it is being viewed. Men who speak out against pornography (e.g., "this is degrading to women") reduce its effect on their peers' laboratory aggression toward a female confederate (Sinclair, Lee, and Johnson). Women and men need not be silent about pornography in fear of being labeled as sexual prudes. If we consider that the latent message of pornography is as much about dehumanization and violence as it is about sex, finding a voice should be easier.

References. Gloria Cowan and Robin Campbell, "Rape Causal Attitudes among Adolescents," *The Journal of Sex Research* 32 (1995): 145–153; Edward Donnerstein, Daniel Linz, and Steven Penrod, *The Question of Pornography: Research Findings and Policy Implications* (New York, 1987); L. Lederer (ed.), *Take Back the Night: Women and Pornography* (New York, 1980); N. M. Malamuth, D. Linz, C. L. Heavey, G. Barnes, and M. Acker, "Using the Confluence Model of Sexual Aggression to Predict Men's Conflict with Women: A 10-Year Follow-Up Study," *Journal of Personality and Social Psychology* 69 (1995): 353–369; N. M. Malamuth, R. Sockloskie, M. Koss, and J. Tanaka, "Characteristics of Aggressors against Women: Testing a Model Using a National Sample of College Students," *Journal of Consulting and Clinical Psychology* 59 (1991): 670–681; Diana E. H. Russell (ed.), *Making Violence Sexy: Feminist Views on Pornography* (New York, 1993); R. C. Sinclair, T. Lee, and T. E. Johnson, "The Effect of Social-Comparison Feedback on Aggressive Responses to Erotic and Aggressive Films," *Journal of Applied Social Psychology* 25 (1995): 818–837; *U.S. News and World Report* (February 20, 1997); Dolf Zillmann and Jennings Bryant (eds.), *Pornography: Research Advances and Policy Considerations* (Hillsdale, N.J., 1989).

GLORIA COWAN

PORTUGAL. To understand the status of women and what has been achieved in obtaining woman's rights since the 1970s, it is necessary to go back to the first steps toward emancipation that occurred at the turn of the century and during the First Republic (1910–1926). Every change in women's status has been the result of a difficult struggle over the years.

By the time of the first Republican Constitution of 1911, women were granted the right to work. By then, one Portuguese woman had already obtained a degree in medicine (1899), and in 1913 another one got a degree in law. From this time on, other changes gradually took place, such as the right to teach in all-male high schools (1926) and the right to vote, though only for women with at least a high school degree (1928). Finally, in 1968 a law was enacted granting women the same political rights as men, except for local elections where only the head of the family (meaning the man) could vote. The first woman in government appeared in 1971 (after the death of Antonio Salazar, ruler of the Second Republic, 1926–1970). In 1972 the publication of a rebellious feminist document, *Novas Cartas Portuguesas*, by Maria Teresa Horta, Maria Isabel Barreno, and Maria Velho da Costa so enraged public opinion that the authors had to answer in court.

On April 25, 1974, revolution restored democracy after 48 years of fascist rule. Since then many social reforms have occurred. At last women are performing active roles in Portuguese society and government (one of them, Maria de Lurdes Pintassilgo, is the founder of the Commission on the Status of Women).

A new Constitution was voted on in 1975 by everyone, men and women, over 18 years of age. In this Constitution justice was at last achieved, with women obtaining recognition at least at some levels. Realizing the limitations on the status of women, the new Constitution has specific articles concerning sexual equality. It states that no one can be discriminated against or privileged on account of that person's sex; husband and wife have the same rights and responsibilities with regard to their children; children born out of wedlock are to be treated the same as other children, and the word "illegitimate" is now forbidden; the same opportunities must be granted to both men and women in work, regardless of sex; and access to, or promotion in, jobs cannot be granted on the basis of sex.

As of November 1977, the Commission on the Status of Women became an official department attached to the prime minister's office. The December 1977 issue of the *Bulletin* of the commission clearly stated that women do not want a status of protection that would be another form of minority treatment but rather desire a status of equality. The purpose of the commission is not to give protection but to grant equality. It also recognized that legal equality, which is what the new civil code establishes, does not mean full equality in practice (Guimarães).

The aims of the commission are given in its objectives: to contribute to the way of thinking of both men and women in order to achieve human dignity; to obtain effective co-responsibility of men and women at all levels of Portuguese social life; to work to get society in general to accept maternity as a social function; to study and do research on women's limitations in social, economic, political, and familial areas in order to pass on information to, and cooperate with, other institutions, both national and international; to grant technical information to the young; and, mainly, to supervise family planning concerns.

The commission's concerns on the status of married women and their rights and duties bolstered a movement that led to the establishment of a new law in 1978. This law provides a more respectable and responsible status for women in social terms: marriage is based on equality—respect, fidelity, cohabitation, cooperation, and assistance are mutual; both marriage partners manage their common property while each one has the right to manage his or her own estate; both have equal authority over their children's physical and intellectual development; a child born out of wedlock cannot be taken by one of the partners into the conjugal home without the consent of the other spouse; and a married woman's child is presumed to be her husband's, but she can deny his paternity under certain conditions.

A law on equal opportunities in work and employment was established in 1979. In 1981 a new law on nationality rights came into existence, guaranteeing a foreign woman the right to choose Portuguese nationality (or not) when marrying a Portuguese man; the same right applies to men marrying Portuguese women. A controversial law allowing the right to abortion under certain specific circumstances was approved in 1984.

These laws represent great advances in women's rights and liberation. If women finally could advance on social and familial grounds they could also progress in the political field, performing high political duties in Parliament and government. In 1979 Maria de Lurdes Pintassilgo became prime minister. Mariana Calhau was the first woman to be appointed as governor of a district (Évora). Rosa Mota first achieved success in international athletics in 1982; she won the Olympic Bronze Medal in 1984 and the Gold in 1988 in the Marathon.

Women's rights during this century were obtained very slowly and with immense difficulties, but the same can be said about the whole of Portuguese society under the negative influence of a dictatorship. Men and women, particularly the intellectuals, fought side by side during 48 years of Fascism. It would be highly unfair not to mention some of the women who, as intellectuals, contributed greatly to the change in Portuguese politics. They were mainly writers but also include researchers, professors, and doctors. The most representative and outstanding among them are Maria Amália Vaz de Carvalho, essayist and historian; Adelaide Cabete, who became a leading Portuguese feminist; Ana de Castro Osório, a novelist and also a leading feminist; Carolina Angelo, a doctor Carolina Michaëlis de Vasconcelos, a philologist appointed as university professor (her appointment produced a major impact on public opinion at that time); Florbela Espanca, one of the best Portuguese poets of all time; and Maria Lamas, a journalist and writer.

These and many other women have contributed very greatly to the abolition of discrimination against women. However, there were also a few men who understood that the position of women needed to be improved. In 1892, under the monarchy, an essayist and aristocrat, D. Antónia da Costa, wrote *A Mulher em Portugal* (Woman in Portugal), manifesting his concern for the poorness of women's education which put an emphasis on training for housework but gave girls no skills for competing with men in social, economic, intellectual and political tasks. Another champion of women's rights was Doctor Afonso Costa, a politician who reached the position of prime minister and who greatly improved women's legal status.

Today women are no longer deprived of their undeniable rights. Their position has been secured by artists such as Vieira da Silva, an internationally acclaimed painter; politicians such as Maria de Lurdes Pintassilgo; and a great number of contemporary women writers responsible for a new vein in Portuguese literature, including, among others, Sophia de Mello Breyner, Agustina Bessa Luís, Olga Gonçalves, Teolinda Gerção, Gabriela Llansol,

Lídia Jorge, Maria Judite de Carvalho, Fernanda Botelho, and Natália Correia.

Reference. Elina Guimarães, *Portuguese Women, Past and Present*, 2d ed., updated (Lisbon, 1987).

DOMINGOS DE OLIVEIRA DIAS

POSTPARTUM DEPRESSION. After giving birth, some women experience feelings that can vary from a day or two of the "baby-blues" to a long period of severe depression. During pregnancy, physiological changes give the mother a sense of well-being. After childbirth, a rapid drop in estrogen and progesterone levels is combined with the reality of incessant demands from a completely dependent infant present 24 hours a day, every day. A first-time mother especially may have difficulty in adapting to the new demands on her life. The severity of postpartum depression has been found to relate to the individual mother's tolerance of stress, the condition of her surroundings, her attitude toward her pregnancy and motherhood, and her relationship with the child's father and others with whom she is closely associated as well as to changes in her hormone levels.

POVERTY still characterizes a large segment of the American population. Between 1959 and 1973, the number of poor fell from 39.5 million to just under 23 million, cutting the poverty rate in half, from 22.4 percent to 11.1 percent. However, between 1973 and 1983, both the numbers in poverty and the poverty rate began to rise; by 1983, these numbers were the highest since 1964, followed over the next decade by a steady poverty level. In 1993, the latest year for which reliable data are available, the number of people in poverty in the United States equaled 15.1 million, for a poverty rate of 14.5 percent.

The composition of the poor has changed as well over the last 35 years. The female share of the overall poverty population was the same in 1983 as in 1966 (the earliest available data). The poor today, though, are more likely to be single females, minor members of female-headed households, elderly females, or members of minority groups.

The growth of female-headed families and their greater representation among the poor have been a particularly noticeable trend over the last 40 years. Between 1959 and 1993, female-headed families in the United States grew from 4.3 million to 12 million, or 18.1 percent of all families. These families are more than four times as likely to be poor as male-headed families. That is, in 1993, 54 percent of all poor families were headed by females, for a total of 8.8 million households, compared to only 2.6 million persons living in female-headed households in 1960.

The increase in female-headed families in poverty has been particularly disastrous for the children in these households. In 1993, 15 million children under the age of 18 lived in households in poverty, including 5 million children aged 5 years or younger. Of all American children, one in four lives in poverty, one in eight has no health insurance, one in four received no prenatal care, and 5 million suffer from hunger. Every 53 minutes, an American child dies from the effects of poverty.

For black and Hispanic families, these trends were even more exaggerated. The number of poor blacks remained nearly constant between 1959 and 1993 (about 10 million). While the 1995 poverty rate for white Americans was 12 percent, that for African Americans was 33 percent, and that for Hispanic Americans was 29 percent. However, the percent of poor blacks living in female-headed households rose from 29.3 to 53.8 percent of all poor blacks in those same years. This means that 75 percent of the black children in poverty lived in female-headed households. A similar pattern holds for Hispanics and other ethnic minorities.

Poor women share many characteristics with poor men. The poor, compared to the nonpoor, have less education, lack market-relevant job skills, and are located in relatively job-poor locations. The greater rates of poverty among women, however, can be traced to three distinctly gender-related causes.

First, women in poverty are more likely than other women to be unmarried and thus to depend on only themselves as income producer. In 1993, female-headed households had only 40 percent of the income of married-couple households ($17,443 versus $43,005 for married-couple families). This disparity increases when female-headed households are compared to married-couple households with wives in the paid labor force ($51,204—almost three times the income for female-headed households). Further, while between 1972 and 1993, married-couple families managed an increase in median family income, the median income for families maintained by women declined almost 5 percent when adjusted for inflation. Thus, 50 percent of all poor American families in 1995 were supported by unmarried females with an average family income 23 percent less than the poverty threshold. Not only do female householders have greatly less purchasing power than do male-headed households, but their relative position has been deteriorating over the last quarter century.

Second, women who head their families often bear most or all of the economic costs of rearing their children. Married women share substantially in the resources obtained by their husbands. The woman's share declines sharply if the husband is absent. For example, in 1975, only 25 percent of the women eligible actually received child support. Roughly one-third of the fathers required by the courts to pay child support never make a payment. Only 5 percent of never-married fathers provide child support.

The number of poor, female-headed households is increased by the growing numbers of unwed mothers. In 1965, about 1 birth in 18 was to an unmarried mother; by 1995 nearly 1 in 3 of all births was to an unmarried woman. Today, one in four American children live in single-parent households. In addition, approximately 60 percent of unwed mothers had incomes under the poverty threshold; three-fourths of the unwed mothers aged 15 to 19 were receiving Aid to Families with Dependent Children (AFDC) in 1993.

Third, sex discrimination* and occupational segregation* in a segmented labor market increase women's representation among the poor. While most women today expect to work or have worked, sex-role socialization* in general and vocational preparation in particular do not prepare women to be primary breadwinners. Further, women are concentrated in what are called secondary sector jobs (marginal, seasonal, sporadic, low-paying positions).

Although many new jobs have been added to the American economy in the last quarter century, these have offered workers little likelihood of moving out of poverty. The vast majority of these new jobs have been in the service sector, which pays much less than primary sector jobs. The wage differential between manufacturing jobs and jobs in retail trade illustrates this point. In 1970, for every dollar earned in manufacturing wages, retail trades workers earned 62¢. By 1995, this differential had increased: for every dollar earned in manufacturing, retail trades workers earned less than 50¢. Women have increased their participation in the labor force, but that increase has gone disproportionately to service jobs so that women's relative share of the national income does not reflect their share of the jobs. Thus, in 1995, 60 percent of all minimum-wage workers were women, and these workers earn wages approximately equal to 70 percent of the poverty threshold.

Even when women enter primary sector jobs, they continue to suffer the effects of sex discrimination. Thus, women aged 25–34 who worked full-time year-round in 1994 earned only 84¢ on the dollar earned by male full-time year-round workers of the same age; for workers aged 55–64, females earn 66¢ for each dollar earned by their male counterparts. Recent changes in women's occupational choices and in litigation and legislation have moderated this disparity somewhat, but the differential remains. Mary Corcoran et al. assert that two-thirds of the wage gap* between white men and white women "cannot be accounted for by sex differences* [between women and men] in skills, work participation, or labor-force attachment." Thus, women income-earners have significantly less money to support themselves and their families than do men income-earners. This disparity continues into retirement: the average Social Security benefit for male retirees in 1994 was $759 per month; for female retirees the benefit averaged $580 per month, a difference of $2,148 per year.

The "culture of poverty" thesis argues that a significant component of the people in poverty constitutes a distinctive subsociety that passes poverty on across the generations. This "permanent underclass," the argument asserts, shares a set of values, norms, attitudes, expectations, and structural arrangements that socialize its members into a pattern that poorly equips them for participation in the larger social and economic structures of American society. Recent data do not support such a thesis. Rather, it appears that there is a continual movement across the poverty threshold, with a sizable number of "floating poor," or individuals and families who remain suspended above the poverty line until illness, rent increases, unemployment, additional children, or family dissolution leads them into the ranks of those officially defined as poor.

Changes in household composition are a better predictor of changes in economic status than variables usually proffered, such as education or achievement orientation. That is, decisions about marriage,* divorce,* or additional children have a strong impact on the resources available to members of a family.* These factors tend to have a greater impact on women than on men.

Marriage or a woman's relationship to a man continues to have the most profound impact on a woman's economic well-being. Entering a marriage typically has an immediate positive effect on a woman's income, while divorce, separation, desertion, and widowhood* tend to have an immediate negative effect. Marriage tends to have the opposite effect for men.

Entering marriage thus tends to promote women to an enhanced economic status, while leaving marriage tends to demote them. Likewise, remarriage leads to greater income gains for women than for men. Since the great majority of divorced women, especially younger women, do remarry, their tenure in poverty is usually temporary. Black women tend to marry or remarry at lower rates than white women, and they tend to stay single longer if they do remarry. Thus, the dip into poverty for black women tends to be of longer duration than that for white women.

Hence, rather than a large cadre of permanently poor, female-headed families characterized by a "culture of poverty" transmitted over the generations, most poor should be seen as transients in poverty. This is illustrated by the tenure of people on welfare rolls. For example, contrary to popular belief, over half of all AFDC families have been on the welfare rolls for under three years; only 7 percent have been recipients for 10 years or more.

While poor adult females share many characteristics with poor adult males, they are distinguished by three specific marks. Poor adult females are more likely to depend on one adult as income producer for the family. Further, female householders bear the economic burdens of child rearing. This is particularly acute for never-married mothers. Finally, females continue to suffer the effects of differential sex-role socialization and of sex discrimination in the occupational structure of our society.

Nevertheless, the majority of female poor do not exist in a transgenerational "culture of poverty." Rather, they should be characterized as transient poor, moving into and out of poverty in response to changes in family composition, in the economy, and in demands on the family budget. Women's marital relationships continue to have a profound impact on women's economic status, so that, for females, the unmarried state increases their likelihood of being poor. Sexual stratification in America continues to exert a primary influence on women's economic status.

References. York W. Bradshaw and Michael Wallace, *Global Inequalities* (Thousand Oaks, Calif., 1996); M. Corcoran, G. J. Duncan, and M. S. Hill, "The Economic Fortunes of Women and Children: Lessons from the Panel Study of Income Dynamics," *Signs* 10 (1984): 232–249; Barbara Reskin and Irene Padavic, *Women and Men at Work* (Thousand Oaks, Calif., 1994); Lillian Rubin, *Families on the Fault Line: America's Working Class Speaks about the Family, the Economy, Race, and Ethnicity* (New York, 1994).

ALLEN SCARBORO

POWER is an important concept for feminist psychology. For example, recent textbooks by Hilary M. Lips and by Rhoda Unger and Mary Crawford employed power as a central organizing construct for feminist psychology. Similarly, Janice Yoder and Arnold Kahn edited a special issue of the *Psychology of Women Quarterly* devoted to the topic of women and power. To date, feminist psychologists have conceptualized power in three different ways: (1) "power over," (2) "power to," and (3) a poststructuralist view of power.

"Power Over." "Power over" refers to dominating, controlling, or attempting to influence the thoughts, feelings, or actions of one or more persons (Yoder and Kahn, "Toward a Feminist Understanding"). Psychological research on "power over" is considerably more extensive than that on the other two conceptualizations of power mentioned and has primarily focused on the interpersonal level, as opposed to organizational or societal levels.

For example, Paula Johnson defined power as the ability to get someone else to do or believe something that person would not otherwise have done or believed. She proposed three dimensions of gender differences in power styles—indirect (e.g., manipulation) versus direct power, personal (e.g., affection, sexuality) versus concrete (e.g., money, knowledge) power, and helplessness versus competence—with the first of each pair presumably being the female style and the second, the male one. According to Johnson, female styles of power are less effective than male ones, and women's use of them sustains their less powerful position in society. Although she advocated that women adopt male power styles, such as direct power, their doing so has interpersonal costs in being seen as more aggressive and unfeminine than women using a sex-congruent power style.

Toni Falbo and Letitia Anne Peplau explored power styles in intimate relationships by asking members of gay, lesbian, and heterosexual couples to indicate how they got their partner to do what they want. They found two independent dimensions to underlie the different strategies respondents reported: direct versus indirect and unilateral versus bilateral. Similar to Johnson's model, the direct-indirect dimension refers to how overt or covert the influence attempt is, with bargaining and discussion being examples of direct strategies of influence and withdrawal and expressing positive affect as examples of indirect ones. The second dimension reflects how much coordination or engagement is required with one's partner, with bilateral strategies, such as arguing, requiring more coordination and engagement than unilateral ones, such as ordering your partner to do something or refusing to speak to her or him. According to Falbo and Peplau, men employ direct and bilateral strategies because they expect compliance from their partners, whereas women employ indirect and unilateral strategies because they expect noncompliance and, therefore, use attempted influence techniques that do not require or presume their partner's cooperation. Likewise, the influence target's sex makes a difference, with male partners in gay and heterosexual relationships eliciting weaker power strategies and more deferential influence attempts than female partners in lesbian and heterosexual relationships (Howard, Blumstein, and Schwartz).

Research in the 1990s suggests two qualifications to previous research and theorizing regarding gender differences in power strategies. First, more recent studies suggest that only a single dimension of goodness-badness or positivity-negativity underlies the different power strategies employed by women and men in either intimate (Frieze and McHugh) or nonintimate, interpersonal relationships (Sagrestano). Second, according to Sagrestano's research, when the participant's gender, target's gender, and the amount of power each partner has are simultaneously taken into account, the amount of power determines the influence strategy women and men select rather than the gender composition of the interpersonal relationship.

"Power To." "Power to" refers to the sense of power or control over one's own self. Feeling powerful and in control of one's own life defines "personal empowerment," a frequent goal of feminist-oriented therapy for women. Jean Baker Miller and other feminist authors dealt extensively with personal empowerment for women. Psychological research on self-efficacy theory suggests that (1) heightening self-efficacy is beneficial for the individual and (2) training programs can enhance a woman's sense of self-efficacy for controlling violent assaults (Ozer and Bandura). Moreover, one's typical power strategies can affect feelings of powerfulness, with strong strategies promoting personal empowerment.

A Poststructuralist View of Gender and Power. Celia Kitzinger questioned the wisdom of psychology's emphasis on personal empowerment, arguing that the autonomous, self-fulfilled (i.e., "empowered") woman is an individualistic myth that encourages viewing power solely as an internal possession located within the self rather than focusing on structural features in society. She suggests as an alternative way of conceptualizing power a poststructuralist view, which focuses on the importance of language and language categories for defining identities and "subjectivities." In this view, power is neither an external force acting upon individuals from outside nor the exclusive possession of any single group (e.g., men). Rather, the meanings and contents of language categories define individuals' sense of selfhood, with the discipline of psychology bearing responsibility for sustaining "gendered" power arrangements by its "technology of subjectivity."

References. Toni Falbo and Letitia Anne Peplau, "Power Strategies in Intimate Relationships," *Journal of Personality and Social Psychology* 38 (1980): 618–628; Irene Hanson Frieze and Maureen McHugh, "Power and Influence Strategies in Violent and Nonviolent Marriages," *Psychology of Women Quarterly* 16 (1992): 449–465; Judith A. Howard, Phillip Blumstein, and Pepper Schwartz, "Sex, Power, and Influence Tactics in Intimate Relationships," *Journal of Personality and Social Psychology* 51 (1986): 102–109; Paula Johnson, "Women and Power: Toward a Theory of Effectiveness," *Journal of Social Issues* 32 (1976): 99–110; Celia Kitzinger "Feminism, Psychology, and the Paradox of Power," *Feminism and Psychology* 1 (1991): 111–129; Hilary M. Lips, *Women, Men and Power* (Mountain View, Calif., 1991); Jean Baker Miller, *Toward a New Psychology of Women* (Boston, 1977); Elizabeth M. Ozer and Albert Bandura, "Mechanisms Governing Empowerment Effects: A Self-Efficacy Analysis," *Journal of Personality and Social Psychology* 58 (1990): 472–486; Lynda Sagrestano, "Power Strategies in Interpersonal Relationships: The Effects of Expertise and Gender," *Psychology of Women Quarterly* 16 (1992): 481–495; Rhoda Unger and Mary Crawford, *Women and Gender: A Feminist Psychology* (Philadelphia, 1991); Janice Yoder and Arnold Kahn, *Psychology of Women Quarterly* 16 (1992): 379–551 (special issue); Janice D. Yoder and Arnold S. Kahn, "Toward a Feminist Understanding of Women and Power," *Psychology of Women Quarterly* 16 (1992): 381–388.

KENNETH L. DION

PRÉCIEUSES are women of seventeenth-century France who flaunted an excessive refinement and affectation of language and manners known as preciosity. Beginning among the aristocracy in Paris, the movement peaked to a fad that swept all France after midcentury, then died in ridicule in the 1660s. Dismissed as a silly pretentiousness of conceited, pedantic women, it has also been identified as a feminist search for identity and self-expression.

The pattern of manners and behavior adopted by the *précieuses* began to form early in the seventeenth century at the first French salon of Catherine d'Angennes, marquise d' Rambouillet, who, repelled by the vulgarity of the French court, set about providing an alternative gathering place. She had a house near the Louvre rebuilt to her own design and there, in the *chambre bleu*, provided a setting and tone that soon attracted the female aristocracy and their satellite gentlemen, including the men of letters of France.

After the social upheaval caused by the Fronde, the last revolt of the aristocracy, 1648–1653, a seven-year period of peace and social stability saw the climax of the phenomenon. Salons multiplied, and members of the bourgeoisie, not just in Paris but all over France, took up the style and mannerisms of *précieuses*.

But in late 1659 and 1660, Molière's one-act *Les Précieuses Ridicules* had Paris laughing at their affectations. Other attacks followed. More importantly, Louis XIV's personal rule, which gathered the aristocracy into a tight social system centered at the court, finished off the *précieuses*.

In reaction to the coarse behavior and speech of the day, the women of the Hôtel de Rambouillet cultivated a deliberate artificiality and stylization of social intercourse. The spirit of refinement in language and literature led to efforts of the women and their satellite literary men to make the language more precise and orderly, a movement taken up and furthered by the newly founded French Academy. The chance to exercise their wits in the shaping and twisting of language led to the exaggerated metaphors, conceits, and circumlocutions for which the *précieuses* were ridiculed. Similar experiments in Spain and England, influenced by the French, led to similar results: Gongorism in Spain and euphuism in England.

The interest of the *précieuses* in literature led not only to the reading and discussion of poetry and novels but to composition as well. The marquise de Sévigné and the comtesse de La Fayette represent the movement at its best. Madeline de Scudéry, the leading spirit of *préciosité* at its zenith, is not up to their literary standards, but her novels, read by all the *précieuses*, are important for their feminist protest.

The *précieuses* phenomenon can be seen as a woman's movement, a search by women, married at or near puberty to strangers chosen for political and economic reasons, to affirm their identity as something other than broodmares. Their protest and their desire to express their own feelings underlie their experiments in startling dress and behavior as well as in the creation of their own language and can also be seen in the proposal of such radical ideas as trial marriage, divorce, birth control, expressing negative attitudes toward marriage, and in the *refus de l'amour*. The artificial atmosphere of the salon emphasized the chivalric and pastoral traditions that idealized women and exaggerated their influence. The ladies, using Arcadian pseudonyms (no lady could be called by her given name in public), discussed many things, but chiefly love. However, it was a love devoid of passion. The possibility of platonic love, an invention of the Renaissance, attracted them. The possibility of enjoying a spiritual relationship with a man, devoid of the dross of materiality, or of enjoying a purely intellectual relationship with a male admirer while keeping for her husband the only part of her he was interested in anyway, her body, was debated endlessly. Hence, despite the preoccupation with love, the *pré-*

cieuses were called the Jansenists (French puritans) of love. It was alleged that love did not arouse their passions but was a kind of religion with them (St. Evremond in his correspondence with Ninon de Lenclos).

Seventeenth-century thought tried to fit everything in the universe, including human nature, within universal laws or types. As females were thought of in terms of sex, all women were classified as either prudes or *galantes* (flirts). As any woman who valued her reputation had to be chaste, the *précieuses* chose to be prudes, or at least to be thought of as such. With the topic of love dominating salon conversation, it had to be made very clear that such talk was not misunderstood; hence, the *précieuses* became celebrated for their prudery. While this was as exaggerated as their circumlocutions and conceits, it does not negate their serious wrestling with, and trying to find answers to, the very real problems of women's sexuality in the seventeenth century.

Reference. Dorothy A. L. Baker, *Precious Women: A Feminist Phenomenon in the Age of Louis XIV* (New York, 1974).

PREGNANCY. See GESTATION

PREMENSTRUAL SYNDROME (also premenstrual Molimina, Premenstrual tension syndrome) is a combination of usually minor, but sometimes serious, psychological and physical symptoms experienced during the week preceding menstruation. These symptoms may include irritability, weight gain, tension, restlessness, depression, swelling, especially of the breasts, headaches, and other discomforts. Observable for most women but not very often incapacitating, these premenstrual problems are popularly called "PMS." In the medical profession, however, the term *"premenstrual syndrome"* is generally reserved for severe physical or psychiatric cases, like unbearable headaches, suicidal tendencies, or acute depression. (See MENSTRUAL CYCLE.)

A number of studies show that the premenstrual syndrome is most intense in women between the ages of 30 and 40; others find that it intensifies after each pregnancy. Some medical researchers say that as few as 20 percent of all women suffer from PMS, whereas others claim that PMS is universal, affecting all women to some degree or another.

The consensus today is that PMS has a physiological origin but that it is accompanied by certain psychological symptoms and that it is not one "disorder" but many. Yet with the overwhelming evidence that the premenstrual syndrome has real physical symptoms, physicians are still not sure how to treat it. Often the theories and experiments of one researcher are not borne out by the work of another.

For nonprofessional treatment of the problems of PMS it is best to watch one's diet, to get plenty of exercise, to restrict salt, to be observant about the effects of tranquilizers or oral contraceptives, and to use a diuretic (although the use of caffeine as a diuretic may possibly exacerbate breast tenderness and hypoglycemic-type symptoms).

Professional treatment varies. According to its leading advocates, the most effective is progesterone therapy, developed by a British doctor, Katharina Dalton. There are no known significant adverse side effects to long-term progesterone use (perhaps mainly because no conclusive studies of long-term progesterone users have yet been published). Antiprostaglandins, along with thyroid treatment and prolactin suppression, are among other medical therapies for PMS relief.

Information for this entry is based on *The Curse: A Cultural History of Menstruation*, by Janice Delaney, Mary Jane Lupton, and Emily Toth (New York, 1976) and on an updated edition (Champaign, Ill., 1987).

MARY JANE LUPTON with JANICE DELANEY

PRISON, MOTHERS IN. At midyear 1985 there were 22,646 women in state and federal prisons nationwide, an increase of about 180 percent since year-end 1974. Roughly 67 percent of the women in prisons had one or more children under age 18; more than 30,000 children were affected by their mothers' incarceration. Studies indicate that one of the greatest concerns of incarcerated mothers is their children. Several studies describe the characteristics of these women, their general feelings about the separation, and the problems confronting agencies in meeting their needs and the needs of their children.

Incarcerated mothers tend to be black more often than white, under 35 years old, usually divorced or never married, and, like most incarcerated women, poorly educated and poorly skilled. With few skills and little education, they have a limited selection of job options. In 1979, those women who had held jobs prior to incarceration usually worked in traditional female positions (i.e., waitress, cook, or secretary) and earned average wages of $2 to $3 per hour, the equivalent of about $6,000 to $9,000 a year.

Most incarcerated mothers have two or three children, and many have children under 13 years old. More than half of them lived with their children prior to arrest, and many had not been separated from their children in the past by incarceration. Although little is known about the quality of the mother–child relationship before the mother's arrest, most inmate-mothers plan to reunite with their children following release; thus, they perceive the separation by incarceration as only temporary.

During the mother's incarceration, relatives, usually the woman's own mother, care for children. If relatives are unavailable or unsuitable to care for children, they may be put up for adoption or, less frequently, placed in foster homes.

Inmate-mothers feel a great deal of conflict, guilt, and shame that their behavior has resulted in the separation. Moreover, many fear that after their release they will be inadequate in disciplining their children. Some mothers fear their children will not know or respect them or may outright reject them because they have been in prison.

Except for very small children, many children apparently understand that their mothers are in prison or, as some women put it, "in jail" or "a place to be punished." Moreover, mothers frequently tell children themselves that they are in prison; often mothers explain at the time of their arrest or prior to imprisonment that they are going away because they did something bad. Inmate-mothers explain their absence realistically because they fear that their children will lose respect for them if they find out the truth from someone else.

Many mothers retain legal custody of children during incarceration; those who voluntarily relinquish custody do so because they feel that caregivers in the community will be better able to obtain services and meet the needs of their children. Although most of the women who gave up custody plan to regain it upon release, they fear their felony conviction will make this process more difficult.

Institutional visitation policies determine the extent of mother–child contact during incarceration. Women's prisons in several states including California, Florida, Georgia, Iowa, Kentucky, Missouri, New Jersey, Texas, Minnesota, Nebraska, New York, Tennessee, and Washington provide parenting programs, extended, daylong visits, or overnight visitation with mothers. The federal women's reformatories at Alderson, West Virginia, and at Pleasanton, California, also provide parenting and extended visitation opportunities. The women's prison at Bedford Hills, New York, has the only nursery in this country where infants born to inmate-mothers after their incarceration may stay with their mothers for up to a year after birth.

However, prisons are security-oriented and foster a sense of dependence, while alternative programs, perhaps in the community, that house inmate-mothers and children together can encourage independence. An important component of this approach is voluntary involvement of inmate-mothers in the development, implementation, and operations of these programs. In order to develop a vested interest in the program and a sense of responsibility, inmate-mothers must participate in determining the selection criteria and process, the nature and directions of the program, rules and disciplinary procedures, and for themselves, whether they want to participate. A less security-oriented environment that encourages independence and personal growth and that provides access to community resources enables inmate-mothers to develop a better sense of responsibility for themselves and for their children and to plan realistically for their transition into the community after their release.

References. P. J. Baunach, *Mothers in Prison* (New Brunswick, N.J., 1985); B. McGowen and K. Blumenthal, *Why Punish the Children?: A Study of Children of*

Women Prisoners (Hackensack, N.J., 1978); A. Stanton, *When Mothers Go to Jail* (Lexington, Mass., 1980).

The views in this article are those of the author and do not reflect the views or policies of the Bureau of Justice Statistics or the U.S. Department of Justice.

PHYLLIS JO BAUNACH

PRISON INMATES. Women currently constitute only 4 percent of the state and federal prison population and 7 percent of the population of local jails. Historically, too, women's numbers have been low relative to those of male prisoners. While these differences may be partly due to "chivalry"—judicial reluctance to commit women (or at least white women) to penal institutions—a better explanation lies with women's much lower crime rates, especially for serious offenses. Socialized to give rather than take, to be nurturant rather than aggressive, women of the past and present have been far less involved than men in crime. Ironically, their low rates of offending and commitment have worked to put women at a disadvantage within jails and prisons.

Through the mid-nineteenth century, women were incarcerated alongside men in predominantly male institutions. Supervised by men, they were subjected to various crimes of sexual exploitation. When scandals ensued, officials tended to blame the women. To minimize contact between male and female inmates, officials gradually isolated the latter into separate cellblocks or small buildings of their own off in a corner of the prison compound. Although isolation improved protection, now women were cut off from whatever services were available. Chaplains, physicians, and teachers found it bothersome to visit the women's quarters and often ignored them entirely. In any case, these officials were male and hence less attuned to the needs of female inmates. Today, their much smaller numbers continue to create similar problems for women who are held in sections of mainly male jails and prisons.

About 1870, officials began to establish separate penal institutions for women, a policy still favored, though it has not been put into practice by jurisdictions whose female populations seem too small to justify the expense of a separate institution. Even when women were given institutions of their own, however, the problem of low numbers continued to pose barriers to equal treatment. The current situation of women held in state institutions provides an example. Most states operate only one prison for women. Whereas the more numerous men's prisons can specialize by security level and type of treatment (drug cases, work camps for those nearing release, a separate institution for the mentally ill, and so on), the state's sole prison for women must attempt to provide the full range of treatment. Usually it fails; states have found it too expensive to deliver, in one small women's prison, the many options available to men. Thus, women have far fewer programs and much more limited access to medical and legal resources. In addition, having but one possible placement, women are more likely to be incarcerated at a considerable distance from family, friends, and community resources.

The numbers problem is not the only source of the inferior conditions of women inmates. Gender, too, has placed them at a disadvantage. Since the prison system began, women have been assigned to stereotyped jobs—cooking, cleaning, and sewing uniforms for male inmates. These jobs have paid less well than those available to men, and they have put women at an employment disadvantage after release. Even today, most women's institutions offer few programs other than cosmetology, typing, and institutional chores. Further, these institutions continue to stress conformity to a narrow definition of the "good woman," pure and passive, as a requirement of early release. Gender has thus combined with low numbers to create the situation in which women experience discrimination on the basis of sex.

For the first time in U.S. history, women inmates recently have begun to challenge discriminatory treatment through the courts. Increasingly, judges are ruling in their favor and requiring jurisdictions to provide equal treatment—not identical, but comparable, care—for incarcerated women and men. Although to date women have won only a handful of these cases, and it is not at all clear how satisfactorily jails and prisons will respond to court orders, this type of litigation has the potential for dramatically improving the lot of female prisoners.

The profile of the woman inmate has not changed greatly since the early nineteenth century. Most female prisoners are young adults, in their 20s. About 50 percent are women of color. Most are poor and poorly educated—currently, 60 percent have not completed high school. Over 40 percent of women incarcerated today were charged with a violent crime, 36 percent with a property crime, 13 percent with substance abuse, and the rest with other types of offenses.

Within institutions, many women join "pseudofamilies," make-believe kinship networks in which an inmate may act as a sibling to some family members, as mother, child, aunt, or uncle to others, and as husband or wife to yet another. As studies since the turn of the century have indicated, black and white women are particularly likely to pair off in couples (this is one reason there is much less racial tension in women's than men's institutions). Sexual activity is less important in the formation and maintenance of pseudofamilies than their ability to provide goods and services, relief from boredom, and substitutes for actual family relationships.

The majority of female inmates have children who, at the time of incarceration, were dependent solely on them. In this respect, too, women differ considerably from male inmates. A man, if living with children at the time of imprisonment, usually leaves them with his partner; women seldom have this option. Finding means to provide for dependent children forms a central anxiety of incarcerated women. Throughout the country, the most successful efforts to help women inmates are being organized around means to relieve this anxiety and maintain ties between the prisoners and their children.

References. Mary Q. Hawks, *Excellent Effect: The Edna Mahan Story* (Laurel Lakes, Md., 1994); Russ Immarigeon and Meda Chesney-Lind, *Women's Prisons: Overcrowded and Overused* (San Francisco, 1992); Nicole Hahn Rafter, *Partial Justice: Women, Prisons, and Social Control* (New Brunswick, N.J., 1990); T. A. Ryan, *State of the Art Analysis of Adult Female Offenders and Institutional Programs* (Washington, D.C., 1984).

NICOLE HAHN RAFTER

PRISON REFORM MOVEMENT, 1870–1930 (U.S.), was a movement to reform the conditions under which women were incarcerated. This effort, which began about 1870, continues to influence women's prisons today. Prison reform was part of the broader social feminist movement that, after the Civil War, carried middle-class women into public life, especially in policy areas involving women, children, and other disadvantaged groups. Enduring about 60 years, the prison reform movement in time challenged nearly every assumption of traditional prison practice. It produced an entirely new model of prison for adults, the women's reformatory, which eventually was adopted by states throughout the country.

The origins of the prison reform movement can be traced to early and mid-nineteenth-century attempts, led by free women in Pennsylvania and New York, to separate female and male prisoners, hire matrons, and provide remedial training. These earlier efforts proved difficult to sustain, mainly because female prisoners and their matrons remained under the control of predominantly male institutions that insisted on male authority and precedence. They did, however, establish the important principle that female prisoners should be held separately and be supervised by other women who might provide role models of "true womanly" behavior. The early endeavors also taught an important lesson—that true reform could not be achieved until women (prisoners and matrons alike) were freed from male control through their removal to autonomous institutions of their own.

The first phase of the prison reform movement, 1870 to 1900, began in the Midwest. Michigan led the way by establishing a prototype of the women's reformatory in the late 1860s. A few years later a Quaker group in Indiana opened the first entirely independent, female-staffed women's prison. Although the Indiana Reformatory Prison held only felons (rather than the misdemeanants on whom the movement later concentrated) and provided few programs, it did create a context in which, for the first time, reformatory principles could be applied without reference to the demands of male prisoners. Owing to the midwestern developments, the idea that women deserved separate, specialized penal treatment under the direction of other women was both legitimated and put into practice.

Shortly after 1870, the thrust of the movement shifted to the Northeast, where, over the remainder of the century, Massachusetts and New York established three more independent prisons for women. Through increasingly bold experimentation, these institutions arrived at what reformers came, by 1900, to regard as the ideal reformatory plan. This plan had three key elements. One was the living unit of the "cottage," the architectural embodiment of the theory that criminal women could be reformed through domestic training in a homelike environment headed by a motherly matron. Second was the theory that reformatories should concentrate their rehabilitative efforts not on felons (the traditional population of state prisons) but rather on misdemeanants and other minor offenders. As a result of this theory, the reformatory movement extended the power of state punishment to a group of female criminals who previously had been sent to local jails, if incarcerated at all, and who had no male counterparts in state prisons. (Most states continued to hold female felons in their mainly male penitentiaries, and there was no movement to establish reformatories for male misdemeanants.) Third, the reformatory plan called for indeterminate sentences that made it possible to hold prisoners, no matter how minor their offenses, for periods of years. Thus, the reformatory plan was based on the acceptance—indeed, an enthusiastic embrace—of differential standards for the imprisonment and rehabilitation of women and men.

Fully articulated by 1900, the reformatory plan was widely and rapidly adopted during the movement's second phase: between 1900 and 1930, 17 women's prisons were founded across the country. As in the earlier phase, the movement was strongest in the Northeast and Midwest. Although none of the institutions fully realized the movement's ideals, they did achieve its basic goal of removing female prisoners from male environments and male control.

Partly because it was so successful in realizing this goal, the reformatory movement lost its energy about 1930. Its end was hastened by the depression: states simply could no longer afford to operate institutions devoted to the moral retraining of petty offenders. The reformatories were not closed, but they changed character. Female felons, traditionally held alongside men in penitentiaries, were now transferred to reformatory grounds or committed directly by the courts; the misdemeanants were squeezed out. After 1930, institutions that had begun as reformatories more closely resembled men's prisons in type of inmate (serious offenders) and treatment.

The accomplishments of the women's prison reform movement were significant for several groups: inmates, who now had a system of independent institutions; the reformers, many of whom entered public life as a result of prison work; and the women who, through administering the reformatories, gained jobs, organizational experience, and in some cases, public prominence. However, these accomplishments had their dark side. Having worked to achieve and maintain segregation of the sexes, reformers and administrators found it difficult to move beyond the narrow world of women's prisons. The movement's concentration on minor offenders meant that many women were incarcerated in state institutions for behaviors (often sexual) for which men were not punished at all or, at worst, received much shorter sentences in local jails. The movement's dedication to rehabilitating women through training in domesticity and sexual propriety limited prisoners' options. Finally, the beliefs about gender differences that lay at the heart of the reform movement have formed a legacy that continues to burden women's prisons—their keepers and the kept—today.

References. Estelle B. Freedman, *Their Sisters' Keepers: Women's Prison Reform in America, 1830–1930* (Ann Arbor, Mich., 1981); Mary Q. Hawks, *Excellent Effect: The Edna Mahan Story* (Laurel Lakes, Md., 1994); Nicole Hahn Rafter, *Partial Justice: Women, Prisons, and Social Control* (New Brunswick, N.J., 1990).

NICOLE HAHN RAFTER

PRO-CHOICE MOVEMENT IN THE UNITED STATES, 1940–1977. In the decades following World War II, the movement for reproductive rights emerged out of the larger demand for women's equality. The so-called second women's movement assumed national prominence in the 1960s, focusing first on issues pertaining to pay equity and equal opportunity in employment between men and women. Increasingly, existing organizations challenged restrictions on abortion, and new organizations were formed to specifically defend a woman's right to choose. By the late twentieth century, issues pertaining to women's reproductive rights and health had assumed a prominent position within national and political debates.

Thousands of women who came of age in the 1960s matured into outspoken pro-choice activists who rebelled against the restrictive family values and gender roles that shaped cultural values in the 1940s and 1950s. During this period, policymakers, popular culture, and the mass media promoted a widely accepted depiction of the American family as the mainstay of social stability and progress. Women married at a younger age than ever before, and birthrates soared for the first time since the early nineteenth century. In what is popularly known as the "baby boom," child rearing was widely embraced as the foremost civic value. Idealized portrayals of marriage emphasized a woman's innate desire to care for, and nurture, a family, while a secure, abundant, suburban life, replete with an array of modern household goods, manifested the ability of a man to support his wife and children (May, 135–137, 162–164).

Although domesticity was portrayed as, and popularly held to be, the feminine ideal, women's participation in the labor force steadily increased throughout the twentieth century and continued to do so following World War II (Kessler-Harris, 251, 347, 380; Ware, 159). As consumerism and quality-of-life spending increased, married women often made financial contributions to support their families (Kessler-Harris, 275). Thus, control of their reproductive lives was a central component of women's ability to remain in the paid labor force. Signs of pregnancy tended to result in dismissal (Rhode, 207–208). Contraception, however, was not legally available to married couples until 1965, while unmarried persons did not have legal access until 1972 (*Griswold v. Connecticut; Eisenstadt v. Baird*). *Griswold v. Connecticut*, 381 U.S. 479 (1965), invalidated a Connecticut statute that prohibited the use of contraceptives, holding that the statute violated the constitutional right of marital privacy; while *Eisenstadt v. Baird*, 405 U.S. 438 (1972), invalidated a Massachusetts statute that prohibited the distribution of contraceptives to unmarried people. The Court held that the constitutional right to privacy extended to reproductive decisions of both married and unmarried people.

In the decades immediately preceding *Roe v. Wade*, an estimated 250,000 to 1 million women each year pursued illegal abortion (May, 153). In most states abortion was illegal regardless of the circumstances, though some states allowed therapeutic abortion if the pregnancy threatened a woman's life or health. With the exception of the last nineteenth century, however, state legislatures tended to be fairly lax in upholding antiabortion legislation. This changed in the 1950s.

The lack of reproductive choices was compounded by increasing enforcement of antiabortion regulation. Beginning in the 1950s, hospitals increasingly created committees to evaluate the reasonableness of a woman's request for therapeutic abortion (Tribe, 36). Hospital committees usually comprised men with the authority to delve into a women's sexual history, to express their personal views on premarital intercourse, or to pass moral judgment on a woman's behavior. These committees increasingly denied a woman's right to choose. Consequently, women's lack of autonomy in making reproductive decisions according to their individual needs and beliefs culminated in the increasing demand for illegal abortion (Reagan, 194; May, 154).

In the 1950s, women frequently consented to "meeting intermediaries, being blindfolded, and driven to a secret unknown place where an unseen person performed the abortion" (Reagan, 97). On one hand, some of the illegal providers were real doctors who provided the services out of sympathy or civil disobedience. On the other hand, many women suffered at the hands of untrained people and poured into the nation's hospitals, suffering from internal injuries created by coat hangers, tubes, and chemicals (Reagan, 222).

While segments of the medical and legal professions advocated policies to liberalize abortion restrictions, the burgeoning women's movement offered other alternatives. Such women began to speak out about their abortion experiences, contending that issues pertaining to reproductive freedom should not be strictly confined to medical or legal perspectives (Reagan, 217). In the late 1960s, two pro-choice organizations developed, one with a broad, equal rights–oriented agenda, the other with a focus on issues pertaining strictly to reproductive rights.

The National Organization of Women (NOW) was founded in 1966 in response to the failure of federal legislation to mitigate gender-based inequalities in pay and employment practices. At first, NOW avoided issues pertaining to reproductive rights, focusing instead on formal legal issues that perpetuated discriminatory attitudes toward women, gradually encompassing the repeal of restrictive abortion laws into its national agenda. The National Association for the Repeal of Abortion Laws (NARAL), now known as the National Abortion and Reproductive Rights Action League, was founded originally in 1969 to organize grassroots support for repealing restrictive abortion laws (Lader; Staggenborg, 16, 18). Both NOW and NARAL emerged as prominent contenders within electoral politics at the national and grassroots levels, promoting agendas that were largely reflective of popular opinion.

According to two national surveys conducted in 1972, 50–57 percent of Americans believed that restrictive antiabortion laws should be reformed to relegate the right to choose abortion as a decision between a woman and her doctor (Rhode, 208). In 1971, a case involving the constitutionality of a Texas antiabortion statute reached the Supreme Court. The now-infamous *Roe v. Wade* 410 U.S. 113 (1973) decision provided the legal support for popular and professional opinion on reproductive freedom.

Antiabortion groups mobilized in the years following *Roe v. Wade* and immediately attacked the women who were most vulnerable. In 1977, they successfully lobbied for the controversial Hyde Amendment, which prohibited Medicaid funding for poor women who sought abortion, except to preserve their lives. Though the constitutional right to choose abortion remained, poor women's access to the procedure was severely restricted. The Supreme Court upheld the Hyde Amendment in *Harris v. McRae* 448 U.S. 297 (1980), ruling that reproductive freedom does not include a constitutional entitlement to financial resources to provide a full range of protected choices (Staggenborg, 81–82).

The Reagan–Bush administration created a conducive climate for antichoice groups to pursue immediate and long-term strategies to end a woman's right to choose. By 1984, the militant wing of opponents to choice increasingly resorted to violent tactics such as bombing family planning clinics and harassment and assault on women who sought abortion and on health care providers (Wilder, 27). This strategy successfully created a climate of fear and terror that reduced the number of willing abortion providers. By 1992, 84 percent of all counties in the United States had no physicians willing to perform the procedure (Tribe, 17).

Antichoice groups worked to circumvent judicial protections of the right to choose by enacting into law restrictions on women's access to abortion services, even though such restrictions were unconstitutional under *Roe v.*

Wade. During his two terms as president in the 1980s, Ronald Reagan bolstered the effectiveness of this strategy by making antichoice appointments to more than half the members of the federal bench and three appointments to the Supreme Court (Wilder, 27–29).

By 1989, the *Webster v. Reproductive Health Services* decision became the first sharp departure from Roe, signaling the Supreme Court's willingness to allow the states greater latitude in restricting access to abortion. Between 1989 and 1992, over 700 antichoice bills were introduced in state legislatures across the country (NARAL, vi).

Three years later, in *Planned Parenthood v. Casey* 505 U.S. 833 (1992), the Supreme Court further enabled state legislatures to enact restrictive abortion-related policies. In this decision, the Court abandoned the "strict scrutiny" standard in favor of a less protective standard that permitted states to impose restrictions as long as they did not "unduly burden" a woman's right to choose. Following *Casey*, legislation to make abortion more difficult for a woman to obtain was introduced in nearly every state.

Since 1994, a refueled antichoice movement has increasingly succeeded at undermining reproductive freedom by reshaping public policy at the state and federal levels. In so doing, antichoice groups have dramatically increased the number of antichoice bills that have restricted women's reproductive choices throughout the nation. These restrictions pose an indirect challenge to the right to choose and in effect are succeeding in rendering *Roe* a hollow promise.

A generation has come of age at a time in which reproductive freedom is constitutionally protected, believing that the right to choose is free and secure. As the nation undergoes a period of rising restrictions on a woman's right to choose, antichoice strategies are more covert. While policymakers do not openly debate legislation to make abortion illegal, current state and federal antichoice policies are denying access to reproductive choice, making it more difficult and dangerous in ways that are reminiscent of conditions prior to *Roe*.

References. Alice Kessler-Harris, *Out to Work: A History of Wage-Earning Women in the United States* (New York, 1982); Lawrence Lader, *A Private Matter: RU486 and the Abortion Crisis* (New York, 1995); Elaine Tyler May, *Homeward Bound* (New York, 1988); NARAL, "Who Decides: A State-by State Review of Abortion and Reproductive Rights" (1997); Leslie J. Reagan, *When Abortion Was a Crime* (Berkeley, Calif., 1997); Deborah L. Rhode, *Justice and Gender: Sex Discrimination and the Law* (Cambridge, Mass., 1989); Suzanne Staggenborg, *The Pro-Choice Movement: Organization and Activism in the Abortion Conflict* (New York, 1991); Laurence H. Tribe, *Abortion* (New York, 1990); Susan Ware, *Modern American Women: A Documentary History* (Chicago, 1989); Marcy J. Wilder, "The Rule of Law, the Rise of Violence and the Role of Morality: Reframing America's Abortion Debate," in Rickie Solinger (ed.), *The Abortion War: A Half-Century of Struggle, 1950–2000* (Forthcoming).

AMY BUTLER

PRO-LIFE MOVEMENT IN THE UNITED STATES. The pro-life movement is a global response to abortion, seeking to protect the lives of human individuals from the moment of conception or fertilization until natural death. In practice, this means to restore legal protection for preborn children, or fetuses, and to maintain laws prohibiting euthanasia and infanticide. Although most of the work concerns opposition to abortion, the movement generally resists the label "antiabortion."

There are several key claims made by the pro-life movement. (1) The life of an individual is precious. This is often put in religious terms: the life of an individual is sacred, because each human person is a child of God. (2) The individual, not society or race or group, matters. Individuals as well as groups have rights. (3) The life of an individual begins in a specific moment; it does not emerge or evolve gradually, gathering value incrementally over time. (4) The beginning moment is objective and discernible, not arbitrary or subject to choice. (5) The beginning moment is conception (or fertilization).

Prior to *Roe v. Wade*, there had been debates about abortion, and some states had already ended legal protection for preborn children. But on January 22, 1973, the Supreme Court struck down the laws of all 50 states and permitted abortion throughout pregnancy by the *Roe v. Wade* and *Doe v. Bolton* decisions.

Pregnancy aid is the largest part of the pro-life movement, with more than 3,000 centers in the United States providing help to women facing unplanned pregnancies. As of 1997, according to the Heartbeat International Directory, there were 3,377 pregnancy service organizations, including pregnancy care centers, medical clinics, maternity homes, and hot lines. The services vary but generally include free pregnancy tests, information about fetal development, counseling and referrals to social service agencies, and support groups. Each center serves hundreds of women and couples annually.

There are three major national organizations or coalitions promoting such services: Heartbeat International, Birthright, and CareNet (formerly Christian Action Council). But many of the centers are independent, since the work is local and does not require a national structure. Some pregnancy centers have become medical facilities, with physicians or physician's assistants in attendance.

The crisis pregnancy centers (or CPCs) are generally staffed by volunteers. Centers may have a paid director, although the oldest network, Birthright, has made a point of avoiding any paid staff at all so that all donations go directly to clients.

Pregnancy centers encourage women to consider adoption. In the United States, there are far more adoptive parents than available children. This is true for children of any background and includes children with disabilities. According to the National Council for Adoption in Washington, there were more than 1 million prospective adoptive parents in 1996, but only 50,000 children were adopted domestically, and 11,000 children were adopted from outside the United States.

Difficulties in the foster care system cause confusion about the availability of children for adoption. Although a White House report on adoption in 1997 found 450,000 to 500,000 children in foster care (temporary placement of a child in a family), most of these children are not available for adoption, as the parents have not relinquished their rights over their children.

In 1984, Project Rachel was started in Milwaukee to help women who had come to regret having had abortions. Many pregnancy centers added this service, starting their own support groups or referring clients to Project Rachel. CareNet developed its own program, called Women in Ramah.

Researchers, including Rev. Michael Mannion and Vincent Rue, Ph.D., collected data on the psychological complications of abortion, but their work was not embraced by other psychologists. For example, DSM-III (*Diagnostic and Statistical Manual of Mental Disorders*, 3d ed.) listed abortion under posttraumatic stress, as a potential stressor; but the next edition, DSM-IV, omitted it. The National Office of Post-Abortion Reconciliation and Healing, started in 1990, does not advertise but receives over 300 calls for help per month. Project Rachel offices in over 100 locations receive over 10,000 calls annually, thus demonstrating the existence of the disorder and the need for postabortion support.

Changing the law (reversing the 1973 decisions) through legislative lobbying and political action has been the most visible part of the movement. The key legislative goal of the pro-life movement is an amendment to the Constitution, declaring that a preborn child—a fetus or even an embryo—has a right to life from the moment of conception or fertilization and is entitled to equal protection under the Fourteenth Amendment. The exact language of the proposed amendment has been debated hotly.

The goal of amending the Constitution shaped the pro-life movement until the early 1980s. The 1980 election of a pro-life president (Ronald Reagan) and 12 pro-life senators seemed to make an amendment possible. But the legislative session in 1981 did not produce any such victory. There was a proposal to end legal abortion by a bill, which would have led to a crisis as Congress and the Supreme Court battled to determine who was the final arbiter of the Constitution. The bill was narrowly defeated.

A second strategy was to bypass Washington and take the matter directly to the states, convening a new Constitutional Convention for the purpose of writing an amendment. This, too, failed, although many state legislatures passed calls for a convention.

A third strategy was to return to the courts, but with a new makeup in the Supreme Court. Pro-lifers turned to the White House for help, asking for pro-life appointees. President Reagan and his successor, George Bush, appointed five Supreme Court justices, a number that would have been enough to reverse *Roe v. Wade*. However, the five new justices did not vote solidly for reversal, and that strategy also failed.

Although they failed in their central legislative goal, pro-lifers were able to attach restrictions on federal funding of abortion. The Hyde Amendment, a funding ban, was attached to appropriations bills each year beginning in 1980. The Hyde Amendment was challenged in federal court. Americans United for Life defended it successfully before the Supreme Court. Many states, including New York and California, provide state funding for abortions, undercutting the federal restrictions.

When their legislators in Washington and in state capitals failed to pass effective pro-life laws, the movement worked to elect people who would do the job. Pro-lifers were able to mobilize from 5 percent to 15 percent of the voters in many elections, enough to swing contested elections.

Education is the third branch of the pro-life movement. Educational groups include the National Right to Life Committee, American Life League and Human Life International, Family Research Council, Feminists for Life, and the Secretariat for Pro-Life Activities of the National Conference of Catholic Bishops.

Pro-life education always includes a description of fetal development and a description of what an abortion does. The principal model for pro-life education was the *Handbook on Abortion* (New York), written by Jack Willke, M.D., and his wife Barbara Willke, R.N.

The descriptions of fetal development emphasize specific points that have emotional resonance. The Willkes point out that the human heart begins to beat on the 18th day after conception, generally before the woman knows she is pregnant. The handbook contains a photo of the feet of a preborn child about 10 weeks after fertilization. The descriptions and pictures of abortion have always caused controversy, with pro-lifers responding that the photos are accurate depictions of what happens and that no woman should decide to have an abortion without a clear understanding of what she is about to do. No other photos of violence are censored in America today.

For over 20 years, pro-lifers were generally ignored when they claimed that the 1973 abortion decisions permitted abortion up to birth. Under *Roe v. Wade*, pregnancy is divided into three trimesters. In the second trimester regulations that are designed to protect the mother are permitted, but regulations designed to protect the preborn child are not. In the third trimester, abortion can be banned unless the mother's life or health is threatened by the pregnancy. The companion decision, *Doe v. Bolton*, decided the same day, defines "health" broadly to include physical, emotional, financial, and social well-being. Since every pregnancy presents some financial or social challenge, this loophole permits abortion in all cases.

In 1996–1997, pro-lifers made an effort to ban an abortion technique used late in pregnancy that they called "partial birth abortion." This type of abortion is considered by many to be infanticide, since the child is killed during the birth process. The ban passed the House and Senate but was vetoed by President Clinton. One positive outcome of this long debate is that the major news media have stopped writing that abortion was permitted only in the first trimester.

Nonviolent direct action, the activist part of the pro-life movement, has included picketing in conjunction with educational and political efforts, "sidewalk counseling," and "rescues."

The term "sidewalk counseling" was coined by Catholics United for Life, a community of hippies from California who converted to Catholicism and launched their own form of activism in the late 1970s. The same kind of counseling and support that pregnancy centers have developed is offered on the sidewalk at the doors of abortion clinics.

Sidewalk counseling has a measurable success rate; in 1989, Karen Black began approaching women outside an abortion clinic in Atlanta that specialized in late abortions; she had more than 1,000 confirmed saves in two years. Msgr. Phillip Reilly, a priest in New York, reported similar success in the 1990s.

The rescue movement started in the 1970s, built largely on the work of Lucy O'Keefe at Harvard University and Jeanne Miller at Yale University, with other members of the Pro-Life Nonviolent Action Group. They distributed the writings of Mahatma Gandhi and Rev. Martin Luther King, Jr., along with practical suggestions for action at abortion clinics. Pro-lifers intervened at clinics by blocking doorways or access to abortion equipment. These "rescues" led to more arrests than any other social justice movement in American history, including over 60,000 arrests between 1988 and 1993. Activists in 25 states participated in rescues.

Rescues declined during the 1980 election campaign but picked up again in 1984, especially in Missouri, Maryland, and Pennsylvania. One rescuer, Joan Andrews, was sentenced to five years in jail for a nonviolent offense in Florida. She spent 18 months in solitary confinement for refusing to cooperate with mandatory strip searches. Her courage eventually gained the attention of prominent ministers, who brought the story to millions via radio and television.

In 1986, Randall Terry persuaded tens of thousands of people to risk arrest in order to protect children and women from abortion. Those arrested included five bishops, numerous ministers, rabbis, several chiefs of police departments, physicians, and a college president. Thousands risked arrest in scores of cities, including New York, Atlanta, Philadelphia, Washington, Wichita, Los Angeles, and Pittsburgh. Numbers declined after 1994, when Congress passed the Freedom of Access to Clinic Entrances Bill, providing stiff criminal and civil penalties for blocking the doors of abortion clinics, but smaller rescues continued.

References. Elizabeth Liagin, *Excessive Force: Power, Politics and Population Control* (Washington, 1995); Rachel MacNair, Mare Krane Derr, and Linda Naranjo-Huebl (eds.), *Profile Feminism Yesterday and Today* (New York, 1995); Fredericka Mathewes-Green, *Real Choices: Listening to Women, Looking for Alternatives to Abortion* (Ben Lomond, Calif., 1997); Bernard N. Nathanson, *Aborting America* (Toronto, 1979); David C. Reardon, *Aborted Women Silent No More* (Chicago, 1987); Jack and Barbara Willke, *Love Them Both* (Cincinnati, 1997). Web sites with pertinent information include <http://www.all.org> and <http://www.africa2000.org>.

JOHN CAVANAUGH-O'KEEFE

PROGRESSIVE MOVEMENT was a surge of reform that swept the United States between the 1890s and 1917. An amalgam of interest groups, Progressivism embraced diverse causes and goals. Trustbusters, who condemned the excesses of monopoly, were Progressives, as were muckraking journalists who exposed corporate abuses and government corruption; municipal reformers who advocated efficient city management through nonpartisan commissions; and settlement workers who strove to improve urban neighborhoods. Some Progressives urged an expansion of democracy through electoral reform. Others promoted economic reforms such as Progressive taxation or railroad regulation. Still others advocated stronger methods of social control, including Prohibition, immigration restriction, and social purity.

Arising in cities and state capitals, Progressivism was promoted by urban, middle-class Americans who shared common aims. Decrying greed, corruption, and poverty, they demanded an end to special privilege and social disorder. Seeking not to end capitalism but to improve it, they tried to impose a more rational, "scientific" order on economic and political life. Overall, Progressives sought to stabilize a society transformed by urbanization, immigration, and rapid industrial growth. By 1910, Progressivism was a national movement.

Middle-class women were a vital part of the Progressive groundswell. Some contributed through journalism, as did Ida Tarbell, whose exposé of the Standard Oil Trust (1902) exemplified muckraking. Many women joined interest groups that endorsed Progressive goals, both restrictive and humanitarian. Through women's clubs, temperance locals, social settlements, suffrage societies, and other associations, women committed their energy to urban improvement and social justice By so doing, they supported and expanded the Progressive agenda. The rise of Progressivism, in turn, legitimated their activism.

A burst of organization, under way by the 1890s, laid the groundwork for women's involvement in Progressive reform. The National Federation of Women's Clubs (founded 1892) turned its attention to urban affairs. By 1910, 2 million club members supported libraries, hospitals, settlements, city services, and protection for women and children in factories. Club women also campaigned for the Pure Food and Drug Law (1906), a major Progressive measure. The huge Women's Christian Temperance Union (founded 1873), which worked for prohibition, also supported such causes as pacifism, labor reform, social purity, and city welfare work.

At the turn of the century women created new organizations to improve urban life and unite social classes. The National Congress of Mothers (founded 1897) sponsored playgrounds and kindergartens, and battled urban problems. The National Consumer's League* (founded 1899) sought to protect women employees in stores and factories and to ensure the safety of products for the home. The National Women's Trade Union League (NWTUL; founded 1903) linked factory employees and reformers in a common cause. First supporting women's unions and strikes, the WTUL later promoted worker education and protective legislation such as minimum wage laws and maximum hour laws. Women also joined the Progressive education movement, the women's peace movement, and urban crusades against prostitution. Women scholars supported Progressive reform by investigating labor conditions, working-class life, and related subjects. Social worker Mary White Ovington, a founder of the National Association for the Advancement of Colored People (NAACP), examined the status of New York blacks in *Half a Man* (1911). Penologist Katherine Bement Davis, who ran New York's Bedford Hills Reformatory and served as New York City commissioner of corrections, studied inmate populations.

The settlement movement, which offered an ideal Progressive solution to urban problems, provided middle-class women with a path to reform and to politics, local, state, and national. By 1910, 400 settlement houses had been established in city ghettos. Running clubs and social services for immigrants, settlements became urban social science laboratories. Settlement residents investigated local conditions, wrote legislative proposals, and supported many Progressive reforms such as juvenile courts, compulsory education laws, housing laws, sanitary measures, factory inspection, child labor regulation, and state protection of women workers. Some settlement leaders, such as those at Hull-House, assumed major roles in public life and Progressive causes. Florence Kelley became a state factory inspector in Illinois, a consumer advocate, and a lobbyist. Child welfare expert Julia Lathrop became the first head of the federal Children's Bureau. Physician Alice Hamilton conducted investigations of lead poisoning in industry. When the Progressive Party first convened in 1912, Hull-House founder Jane Addams made a seconding speech for presidential nominee Theodore Roosevelt. The new party endorsed woman suffrage.

The woman suffrage crusade, finally, profited from the rise of Progressivism. Indeed, the goals of the two movements often coincided. Suffragists capitalized on Progressive support for electoral reform. They viewed their cause as part of the larger Progressive movement to expand democracy, eliminate injustice, and clean up corruption in politics. Progressives, in turn, hoped that women voters would double the educated electorate and help enact reform legislation. The suffrage movement peaked in 1910–1920, with a final surge of support after 1915, when Carrie Chapman Catt took the helm. A woman suffrage amendment was approved by Congress in 1919 and ratified by the states in 1920.

After World War I, the Progressive movement declined, but many women's associations continued to pursue Progressive goals. During the 1920s, women supported protective legislation, worker education, social welfare measures, and pacifism. Among the legacies of women's activism in Progressive reform were two federal agencies, the Children's Bureau (1912) and the Women's Bureau (1919), and two federal amendments, providing for Prohibition (1919) and woman suffrage (1920). Some veterans of Progressive reform, such as social workers Frances Perkins and Mary W. Dewson, became national leaders during the New Deal. (See NEW DEAL.) (See also SETTLEMENT HOUSE MOVEMENT; SOCIAL PURITY MOVEMENT; WOMAN SUFFRAGE MOVEMENT.)

References. Allen F. Davis, *Spearheads for Reform: The Social Settlements and the Progressive Movement, 1890–1914* (New York, 1967); Noralee Frankel and Nancy S. Dye (eds.), *Gender, Class, Race, and Reform in the Progressive Era* (Lexington, Ky., 1992); Seth Koven and Sonya Michel (eds.), *Mothers of a New World: Maternalist Politics and the Origins of Welfare States* (New York, 1993); Molly Ladd-Taylor, *Mother-Work: Women, Child Welfare and the State, 1890–1930* (Urbana, Ill., 1994); Robyn Muncy, *Creating a Female Dominion in American Reform, 1890–1935* (New York, 1991); William L. O'Neill, *A History of Feminism in America*, 2d ed. (New Brunswick, N.J., 1989); Kathryn Kish Sklar, *Florence Kelley and the Nation's Work: The Rise of Women's Political Culture, 1830–1900* (New Haven, Conn., 1995); Ulla Wikander, Alice Kessler-Harris, and Jane Lewis (eds.), *Protecting Women: Labor Legislation in Europe, the United States, and Australia, 1890–1920* (Urbana, Ill., 1995).

NANCY WOLOCH

PROSTITUTION is a form of nonmarital sexual activity characterized by financial reward and absence of long-term fidelity between the parties. This definition includes neither promiscuity without material gain nor concubinage,* in which a couple lives together as husband or wife or, in some legal systems, in an inferior form of marriage in which the man does not convey his rank or quality to the woman, although many discussions of prostitution include one or both of these.

Early History. Whatever its origins, prostitution was well established by the time of the Babylonian empire. Its most famous epic, *Gilgamesh*, features a prostitute sent to entrap and weaken an innocent hero. In fact, the only occupations for women mentioned in the Babylonian law codes (c. 2000 B.C.) are priestess, tavern worker, and prostitute.

These prostitutes of the Tigris-Euphrates Valley were ranked in a hierarchy similar to that found in many parts of the world. First were the temple prostitutes, mistresses of the gods who sometimes took the form of priests or rulers; whether they should be defined as prostitutes is questionable, since their sexual intercourse was a sacred enactment of the annual rebirth of vegetation, not a commercial enterprise. Second were courtesans, entertainers as well as sexual partners. Third were women who worked in taverns or houses of prostitution, and last were slaves of individuals or temples, whose earnings belonged to their owners.

The Old Testament mentions prostitution frequently. Moses forbade fathers to prostitute their daughters, but the law allowed a father to sell his daughter as a concubine. Daughters of priests were forbidden to become harlots, nor could priests marry harlots, but these strictures did not apply to other Israelites. This separation between prostitution and the priesthood may have been a reaction to the sacred prostitution practiced among Israel's neighbors, in which the prostitute herself was regarded as a priestess or sacred person.

The prostitute played a particularly prominent role in the life and literature of classical Greece, where proper women did not participate in public or social life. Prostitution was so accepted that many states levied a tax on it; tradition ascribed the Athenian tax to the legislator Solon, who reputedly filled the brothels with female slaves and used the tax revenue to build a temple to Aphrodite, goddess of love. Brothel prostitutes were lowest in status and price, below streetwalkers and women who worked in inns. Musicians, singers, dancers, acrobats, and other entertainers often added to their income by prostitution. Most respected of the prostitutes were the hetaerae, whose superior education, training, and charm enabled them to win the affections of the most prominent and powerful men of their time. Claiming the patronage of Aphrodite, hetaerae used their skills in dress, makeup, sexual techniques, male psychology, and conversation to amass fortunes and influence the powerful, often establishing long-lasting relationships and winning respect, although not respectability. When Pericles divorced his wife and lived openly with Aspasia, the poets and politicians who had celebrated her wit, wisdom, and beauty when she was his mistress turned on her when she tried to assume a more conventional status; she was insulted openly in the streets and was brought to court on a charge of treasonable impiety.

Roman prostitutes never achieved the influence or status of Greek hetaerae, perhaps because Roman matrons played a larger part in social, commercial, and political affairs than did their Greek counterparts. Since a wife could supply intellectual and social companionship, relationships with prostitutes were purely sexual, which undoubtedly contributed to their low status. No woman of the knight class was allowed to register as a prostitute; prostitutes were not allowed to approach the temple of Juno (patroness of married women) lest they pollute it, and they were often required to dress in styles that distinguished them from proper matrons. Prostitution was tolerated as an evil necessitated by the importance of chastity for respectable women and the fact that many men could not afford to marry at all or until late in life; soldiers, for example, were not allowed to marry during their 20 years of military service. Continence for such men was seen as desirable, but probably biologically impossible. These attitudes permitted prostitution to exist but did not lead to the celebration of the courtesan found among the Greeks.

Although most Romans considered sex a biological necessity, at least for males, Neoplatonist and neo-Pythagorean philosophers considered celibacy an attainable ideal for both sexes. This attitude was adopted and elaborated upon by the early Christians, who combined hostility toward sex with compassion for the prostitute, an attitude encouraged by the tradition of Mary Magdalene, the converted prostitute who was the first witness to the reappearance of Jesus. Although the church fathers imposed a stricter sexual morality than that found in the Old Testament and treated women as sources of temptation to men, they saw the prostitute as a woman who had been led astray and could be saved: Mary the Harlot, Mary the Egyptian, Afra, Pelagia, Thais, and Theodota were all redeemed prostitutes who achieved sainthood.

Islam. Islam regards sex as a gift from Allah, to be thoroughly enjoyed within marriage, but women were seen as the source of male sexual pleasure, not as partners or companions. This attitude produced a special class of high-priced courtesans as well as a larger number of less-skilled prostitutes. Unique to Islam is the *mut'a*, a form of temporary marriage contract lasting from a fraction of a day to several years. The man supports the woman only for the duration of the contract, and any offspring of the union are considered legitimate.

India and China. Hindu women were portrayed as highly sexual beings in need of protection by early marriage. With secluded, uneducated wives, men might seek the company of courtesans well versed in dancing, music, and literature. Their presence was expected during formal visits and required when the king performed certain state ceremonies. Young girls could be donated to temples, where they learned singing and dancing and earned money for the temple through prostitution; there were also secular prostitutes who were allowed to own property.

In China, commercial brothels, located in a special quarter of the city and taxed by the state, reputedly date from the seventh century B.C., and prostitutes who could amuse with songs, dances, and conversation were an indispensable feature of upper-class entertainment. Courtesans skilled in poetry and the arts might become independent and wealthy. Lower-class prostitutes were owned by their brothel keepers and lived under strict supervision, having no choice of customers. Since Taoism and Tantric Buddhism taught that regular intercourse was essential to male well-being, there was a lively market for prostitutes of all classes.

The Middle Ages. The legal basis of medieval prostitution is found in the emperor Justinian's codification of Roman law (c. A.D. 500), which followed earlier practice: toleration of prostitution while trying to curb its worst abuses. The forced prostitution of daughters and slaves was forbidden, and the distinction between prostitution and concubinage was legalized, the latter classified as an informal type of marriage characterized by "marital affection." In the thirteenth century Thomas Aquinas summed up much of medieval thinking when he compared prostitution to a sewer in a palace. If the sewer were removed, the palace would be filled with pollution. Similarly, if prostitution were abolished, the world would be filled with rape and other sexual crimes.

The later Middle Ages brought systematic attempts to segregate prostitutes by confinement to specified sections of cities and by distinctive dress. In Paris, prostitutes lived in the quarter known as the Clapier, which gave the name *clap* to the venereal disease gonorrhea.* Contemporary observers, however, repeatedly noted that prostitutes could be found in all parts of the city, openly soliciting customers. The end of the Middle Ages and beginning of the Renaissance saw the reemergence of the courtesan, the woman whose virtues attracted love as well as lust. Codifiers of courtly love made it clear that such virtues were to be found only in upper-class women; ordinary prostitutes were not worthy of the courtesies and attentions merited by the courtesan.

The Reformation and the Pox. "Renaissance morality" collided with the Protestant Reformation. Both Martin Luther and John Calvin rejected the toleration of prostitution as a means of avoiding greater sins. They preached premarital virginity and marital fidelity for both sexes; Calvin went further, teaching that the primary function of marriage was social, that the wife was the lifelong associate of the husband.

In the sixteenth century, religious hostility toward prostitution was joined by a powerful ally—a particularly virulent outbreak of syphilis. In 1536 the Imperial Diet of the Holy Roman Empire prohibited all extramarital relations, including prostitution. A series of edicts closing brothels and enacting harsh punishments for both prostitutes and customers followed. By the end of the century, however, the fear of the disease and the energy of the reformers both declined. Prostitution resurfaced and, in the seventeenth and eighteenth centuries, blossomed with the elaborate brothels that characterized the London and Paris of that time. Then, at the end of the century, mass mobilization of men for the Napoleonic Wars spread gonorrhea and renewed concern about prostitution throughout Europe. The authorities tried to confine prostitutes to certain areas, register them, and enforce regular medical inspection, often with compulsory hospitalization for those found to have the disease. Given the medical expertise of the time, it proved impossible in most cases to trace the source of contagion, only the most obvious cases could be detected, and the lack of aseptic techniques probably meant that the inspections themselves spread the infection. Nevertheless, variants of this system were to be found all over Europe. England, however, repealed similar regulations in 1886, after a campaign waged largely by women demonstrated not only that the measures virtually legalized prostitution but also that they were ineffective, discriminated against poor and working-class women, and allowed police officers to blackmail and intimidate both prostitutes and innocent women. Prostitution was again practiced openly and without regulation, although Victorian morality of the later nineteenth century dictated greater discretion, at least among the upper classes.

American attitudes toward prostitution tended to reflect those of Europe, modified by the fact that migration and the settlement of the frontier often brought about a dramatic imbalance of men over women. Although many American cities considered regulatory systems, most just tried to confine prostitution to "red-light" districts, allegedly named for the lights trainmen left outside the brothels they were visiting. A 1917 survey, however, found that relatively few cities had been able to maintain such "tolerated" districts.

Twentieth Century. Women who solicit customers on the street often work for pimps, men who collect much of their earnings in return for protection. Others who profit from the earnings of prostitutes are managers or madams who run establishments employing prostitutes or who manage "call girl" services in which prostitutes visit customers in their homes, offices, or hotel rooms. "Escorts" are a modern variation; a customer contracts for female companionship for the evening and then negotiates with the woman herself for sexual services.

In Britain, prostitution itself has been decriminalized, although solicitation on the streets is illegal. Some European countries license prostitutes and restrict them to certain areas of the city, while others have decriminalized prostitution entirely. Communist countries claimed to have eradicated prostitution, but visitors to the formerly communist lands of Central and Eastern Europe questioned these claims, while contemporary reports from China and Cuba reinforce this skepticism. In some Third World countries, on the other hand, entrepreneurs have made commercial sex into a tourist attraction, attracting male visitors with arrangements for golf during the day and visits to prostitutes at night. In the United States, prostitution remains illegal in 49 out of the 50 states, although enforcement is often erratic.

Feminism and Prostitution. Feminist attitudes toward prostitution reflect a basic division in feminist thought about heterosexual activity. One side of that division considers prostitution to be an institution of male supremacy that exploits economically vulnerable and emotionally damaged women for male pleasure; from this vantage point, prostitutes are either unwitting victims of the patriarchy or conscious participants in the degradation of women. The other side sees feminism as supporting a sexual liberation that would remove the moral onus from women's sexual activity; from this point of view, women should be allowed to choose prostitution in the same way as they are allowed to choose any other way of making a living. Because it often seems to deny the legitimacy of their work, prostitutes as a group have been wary of the women's movement, although they maintain that they exemplify feminist values such as sexual self-determination and financial autonomy.

Prostitutes' Rights. In a number of countries, prostitutes have banded together to campaign against harassment and exploitation and to demand recognition and protection. In the United States, the most visible manifestation of this movement is COYOTE (Call Off Your Old Tired Ethics), based in San Francisco, which has worked for the decriminalization of prostitution; tired of trying to influence legislators, COYOTE has turned to working for the election of its own members to lawmaking bodies.

The decline of the double standard, the recognition of women as sexual beings, fear of AIDS, and increased economic opportunities for women have led to the decline, although not the disappearance, of prostitutes, who are still sought by men who want sex with no other obligations, men with unusual sexual proclivities, those who find prostitution sexually exciting, and those who believe that they are unable to attract other women. The sexual liberation and increased earning power of women are producing a group of male prostitutes to service women with the same needs, although their number is small.

References. Vern Bullough and Bonnie Bullough, *Prostitution: An Illustrated Social History* (New York, 1978); Barbara Hobson, *Uneasy Virtue: The Politics of Prostitution and the American Reform Tradition* (Chicago, 1990); Gail Pheterson, *A Vindication of the Rights of Whores: The International Movement for Prostitutes' Rights* (Seattle, 1989); C. Overall, "What's Wrong with Prostitution? Evaluating Sex Work," *Signs: Journal of Women in Culture and Society* 17 (1992): 705–724; Judith Walkowitz, *Prostitution and Victorian Society: Women, Class and the State* (Cambridge, 1980).

DOROTHY H. BRACEY

PROTECTIVE LEGISLATION is a term used to designate labor laws enacted to give exceptional or preferential status to selected categories of workers, notably, women and children. Originating in England in the first decades of the nineteenth century, laws were passed initially to limit the working day of young children and apprentices to 12 hours. By the 1830s the increasing employment of children and women in English factories gave rise to demands for more extensive action by the state for "protection."

Descriptions of physical hardships in factories, textile mills, and coal mines led to official investigations by parliamentary committees. As a result of an industrial survey undertaken by a British Royal Commission, the famous Sadler Report of 1832 documented the "degradation" of factory workers, and, despite the opposition of laissez-faire liberals who opposed all governmental intervention in economic activities, a landmark bill of 1833 forbade employment of children under 9 and limited the working day of those under 13 to eight hours. The Factory Acts of 1842 and 1844 extended the legislation to women, outlawing their labor in mines, prescribing a maximum 12-hour day, and prohibiting night work (between 8:30 P.M. and 5:30 A.M.). Critics of conservative right- and left-wing views agreed that the effects of the factory system were often deleterious for all workers but assumed that their potential to corrupt the health and, especially, the morals of women was worse; furthermore, they assumed that women were by "nature" less able than men to protect themselves. Continental countries followed the British lead. In the 1830s the prestigious Academy of Moral and Political Sciences in Paris commissioned the famous study by Dr. Louis Villermé that exposed the terrible working conditions of women and children and focused on the resulting "demoralization" of the working classes and consequent "degeneration" of the French nation. Villermé also linked the employment of women in factories with prostitution,* which he labeled the "fifth quarter" of the workingwoman's day. Aristocratic Catholic political leaders, socialists, and even some liberal economists called for "English legislation." However, legislation specifically addressing the condition of workingwomen* was adopted only in 1874, when their employment underground was prohibited, leading to a decline in women's share of employment in mining and metallurgy from 9 to 2 percent. Laws comparable to the British legislation of the 1840s waited until the 1880s and early 1890s in Germany and France, respectively, and until the early twentieth century in the United States. In many cases, effective enforcement lagged long behind.

Political leaders, journalists, and social reformers of many persuasions, often opposed on other issues, united in the interest of "safeguarding the reproductive forces" of their nations by limiting women's access to factory labor and thus their potential for exploitation under unhealthy or unsafe working conditions. Working-class men often supported restrictions on female labor as a means of limiting competition for jobs, especially in artisanal industries threatened by the reorganization of work processes and the introduction of machinery that reduced the demand for skilled craftsworkers. By conflating the problems of female industrial labor (outside the home) with other aspects of the woman question, many reformers as well as workers came to accept the passage of protective legislation as a solution to broader, more fundamental issues related to women's changing social roles. Thus, it served to deflate pressures for reform of gender inequalities and, indeed, inaugurated a new form of institutional inequality, for protective legislation, by restricting female factory work, increased the pressures on women, especially those who were married, mothers of young children, older, or in poor health, to work longer hours for lower pay in industrial homework.* Specific injunctions, such as limits on lifting heavy objects or working at night, came to be used as justifications for denying women access to job opportunities; and the general assumption that women were weaker and in greater need of protection than men workers continued to contribute to the denial of equal access to employment even after protection laws were extended to both sexes. Protective legislation also helped channel women into newer white-collar and low-paid service jobs. It also served to create dissension between groups of women reformers, separating "social feminists" (usually educated middle-class women concerned with social reform and supportive of exceptional legislation to "protect" working-class women) against "equal rights feminists" (usually educated middle-class women concerned primarily with reducing gender inequalities). Working-class women themselves sometimes opposed protective legislation out of concern for maximizing their earnings; night work often carried premium wages, and longer hours increased total pay. Professional women viewed protective legislation as further discrimination* against women that "add[ed] another inferiority to all those from which they suffer[ed] already." Conflict over protective legislation has been credited with accelerating the decline of feminist activity in the second quarter of the twentieth century. For the perspective of an American social worker, see Mary Anderson. For an opposing point of view of a French feminist, see the excerpt by Maria Pognon.

References. Mary Anderson, *Woman at Work* (Minneapolis, 1951), esp. ch. 19, "The So-Called Equal Rights Amendment," 159–172; E. F. Baker, *Protective Labor Legislation* (New York, 1925), esp. ch. 7, "The Controversy," 429–456; M. J. Boxer, "Protective Legislation and Home Industry: The Marginalization of Women Workers in Late-Nineteenth, Twentieth-Century France," *Journal of Social History* 20 (1986): 45–65; A. Kessler-Harris, *Out of Work: A History of Wage-Earning Women in the United States* (New York, 1982), esp. ch. 7, "Protective Labor Legislation," 180–214; Seth Koven and Sonya Michel (eds.), *Mothers of a New World: Maternalist Politics and the Origins of Welfare States* (New York, 1993); Susan Lehrer, *Origins of Protective Labor Legislation for Women, 1905–1925* (Albany, N.Y., 1987); Maria Pognon, in *La Fronde* (December 20, 1899), trans. K. M. Offen, in S. G. Bell and K. M. Offen (eds.), *Women, the Family, and Freedom*, vol. 2: *1880–1950* (Stanford, Calif., 1983), 211–213; Mary Lynn Stewart, *Women, Work, and the French State: Labour Protection and Social Patriarchy, 1879–1919* (Montreal, 1989).

MARILYN J. BOXER

PSYCHOANALYTIC CONCEPTIONS OF WOMEN represent a family of theories that are derived from, and related to, the works of Sigmund

Freud (1856–1939). The psychoanalytic approach originated in Freud's scheme of the dynamics, structure, and development of the human psyche. Behavior is motivated by sexual energy (the *libido*) that is directed toward areas sensitive to pleasurable stimulation. With development, these zones of pleasure (erogenous zones) change their locus in a series of successive developmental stages known as the oral, anal, phallic, latency, and genital stages. Structurally, the human psyche is divided into the id (present at birth), the ego, and the superego (emerging during later psychosexual stages). Freud also proposed that one's level of awareness could be either preconscious (accessible to awareness with small effort), conscious, or unconscious (memories and ideas that cannot voluntarily be brought to awareness).

Freud's original ideas on sexual development appeared in *Three Essays on the Theory of Sexuality* (1905). In this work the evolution of male and female sexuality is presented as parallel processes. For males, this means that the original love and attachment for mother during the first two stages of life develop into a "love triangle" during the phallic stage. Now, as the genitals become the primary area of libidinal gratification, the child's attachment to the mother takes on sexual overtones, while at the same time the little boy's father is viewed as a dangerous (i.e., bigger and more powerful) rival. The child's anxiety over this state of affairs is exacerbated by the "realization" that women are castrated and that he, too, might be so punished if his father learns of his desires for his mother. As a result of such fears, claimed Freud, the Oedipus complex is "smashed to bits" when the male child gives up his libidinal attitudes toward his mother and seeks out his father as a source of identification. One important consequence of the Oedipus complex is the development of a superego that leads to a strong sense of justice and morality in men.

While acknowledging that female development was somewhat of a mystery, Freud originally supposed that the preceding oedipal drama was similar for the female. However, in later papers on the subject (e.g., *Some Psychical Consequences of the Anatomical Distinction between the Sexes* [1925] and *Female Sexuality* [1931]), Freud clearly proposed a different and more complicated evolution of female sexuality. According to Freud, preoedipal girls, like preoedipal boys, are strongly attached to their mothers. During the phallic stage, females find the major locus of libidinal gratification to be the clitoris (an "inferior" form of the penis), and their masturbation therefore takes on an active (i.e., masculine) character. The Oedipus complex for the female involves a change in the direction of sexual attachment from the mother to the father and an abandonment of the clitoris for the vagina as the major autoerotic zone. The substitution of the vagina for the clitoris is considered to be essential for the establishment of a feminine (i.e., passive) attitude. Perhaps the major impetus for these significant changes in female sexuality during the phallic period is the girls' observation that they, as well as their mothers, do not have a penis. Freud believed that the female must learn to accept the "fact of castration." But the desire for male genitalia leads to "envy for the penis" and great anger and hostility toward the mother for not having one. The little girl's incestuous feelings toward her father are provoked by the desire to obtain a penis through sexual relations with him. Such penis envy also leads to the rejection of the "inferior" clitoris. Indeed, the Oedipus complex is truly resolved only when the female symbolically obtains a penis through the birth of a child, preferably a male. Thus, the female personality is born out of envy, a sense of inferiority, a change from active to passive modes of sexual expression, and the despair of castration. Women, according to Freud, were narcissistic as a compensation for their sexual deficiencies, as well as vain, frigid, and underdeveloped with respect to their sense of morality.

A number of students of psychoanalytic theory have refined or reformulated Freud's original conception of female psychosexual development. Representative of those who have remained most faithful to Freud's assumption that biology directs psychology is Helene Deutsch (1884–1982), whose work on female sexuality appears in the *Psychology of Women* (1944). Deutsch emphasized that a full understanding of female sexuality must include a consideration of postoedipal events, particularly menstruation, pregnancy, birth, and lactation. The core elements of the female personality, narcissism, passivity, and masochism,* stem primarily from the female anatomy and reproductive functions that direct her toward a passive mode of receptivity and waiting and attract her to pain and suffering (masochism). Failure to switch to the passive, feminine mode of sexuality could lead to a conflict-laden "masculinity complex." A significant extension of Freud's theory involved Deutsch's consideration of the importance of the anticipation and experience of motherhood. Deutsch also recognized that the preoedipal girl had a most significant and complex relationship with her mother that must be acknowledged in its own right.

Erik Erikson (b. 1902) is also a psychoanalyst who has remained close to Freudian theory. However, he does acknowledge the role of culture and historical context in human development and therefore presents female development in a more sympathetic light. The core of Erikson's theory is the negotiation of eight turning points (nuclear conflicts) throughout the course of development. The task before the individual is to seek a positive resolution to each of the successive developmental tasks. Erikson did not specifically address the question of female development until relatively late in his career. The catalyst for his theory of female development was observations of the play constructions of 10-, 11-, and 12-year-old boys and girls. Boys tended to build erect towers and buildings with elaborate cones and cylinders and busy street scenes of animals and cars. Girls constructed enclosed spaces that housed peaceful scenes and static figures. From such spatial representations, Erikson saw parallels to male and female genitalia and ways in which they influenced the experiences of biological and social roles. According to Erikson, the essence of a woman's identity development involves her "inner space," which matches the biological ground plan of womb and vagina and its reproductive potential. Identity is centered on the anticipation and realization of motherhood, not the lack of the male organ as proposed by Freud. Problems for women ensue when their potential for fulfillment of this inner space is not met. In addition, women's psychological interpretation of the inner space leads to a unique constellation of personality characteristics such as warmth, tenderness, nurturance, and compassion.

Representative of psychoanalytic theorists who have significantly departed from Freudian orthodoxy in the accounts of feminine development are Karen Horney (1885–1952) and Clara Thompson (1893–1985). A number of points made by Horney also appear in contemporary criticisms of Freudian theory. For example, Horney emphasizes that psychoanalytic theory presents feminine development from a masculine vantage point. In her revision, Freud's ideas of penis envy, the masculinity complex, female inferiority, and masochism are considered not to be characteristics particular only to women. Horney also refuted the contention that such traits are primarily of biological origin or are significant to female personality development. Rather, such behaviors appear to be culturally related, particularly in cultures where women are denied opportunities to be creative and independent. Horney also objected to the idea that penis envy played a central role in female psychosexuality, pointing out that men can also manifest envy of the anatomical and reproductive functions of the female. The notion that males may experience "womb envy" or manifest a "femininity complex" was developed further in cross-cultural investigations of male puberty rites and male mimicry of birth (couvade*) by Bruno Bettelheim.

Clara Thompson also believed that cultural factors, in terms of whether they impede or promote the need for growth and competence, were more significant to human development than were biological factors. Thus, women's personalities were not a result of their so-called biological inferiority but rather due to the ascription of an inferior status to women in a patriarchal society. Thompson reasoned, for example, that what women envied and desired was not the penis but the position of power and privilege attained by those who had one. Thompson did not deny that many women exhibited feelings of inferiority, a poorly developed superego, rigidity, or, in some cases, masculine behaviors. However, such behaviors were a cultural creation, not of biological origin. While Freud claimed that such traits stemmed from a psychological interpretation of one's biological structures (i.e., "anatomy is destiny"), Clara Thompson pointed to the inferior status of women in society, their dependency* on men, and the goals of marriage* and motherhood as the only pathways of achievement possible.

A number of critiques of the psychoanalytic approach to female development refer to its biological and phallocentric emphases. Freud certainly cast women as psychologically subordinate to men and did not offer any hope for their ability to change and develop. Much of this is probably due to the zeitgeist within which Freud lived and worked. In contemporary psychoanalytic versions of female development, the fusion of the psychoanalytic fundamentals with the acknowledgment of cultural factors has led to a more forgiving and/or positive view of the psychology of the female.

Reference. J. Strouse (ed.), *Women and Analysis: Dialogues on Psychoanalytic Views of Femininity* (New York, 1974).

ILLENE NOPPE

PSYCHOANALYTIC THEORY (CONTEMPORARY) is personality development theories derived from, and related to, the works of Sigmund Freud (1856–1939). Freud's instinct or drive theory is a conflict theory: mental life develops from the conflict of asocial impulses (id) with socially enlightened defenses against them (ego). All motivational, developmental, and structural phenomena can be explained in terms of drive derivatives and defenses against drive derivatives. All relations with others are directly or indirectly linked to their use in, and relevance to, drive gratification. Thus, the individual seeks others because they may result in tension reduction.

Psychoanalytic theory can no longer be equated with classical Freudian theory. There are two major revisions of classical theory: (1) ego psychology, represented by the works of Heinz Hartmann (1894–1970) and Margaret Mahler (1897–1985); and (2) object relations theory, represented by the works of W.R.D. Fairbairn (1889–1965) and D. W. Winnicott (1896–1971). Within traditional psychoanalytic theory, Freud's notion that all behavior and all psychic functions are derived from, and secondary to, instincts was first seriously questioned with respect to ego functions. While attempting to preserve the basic id-ego structural model and the basic assumptions of traditional theory, ego psychologists reworked its structural components. They focused on the development of adaptive (rather than defensive) ego abilities.

Object relations theorists emphasize human connections, a focus that was largely undeveloped in classic Freudian theory. Their work calls into question the relationship between object relations and the underlying conceptual foundations of drive. Within this broad theoretical framework, two major strategies have been used for dealing with relations with others. One involves abandoning the drive model completely. Theorists such as Fairbairn deal with object relations by replacing drive theory with a different conceptual framework in which relations with others determine mental life and replace drive discharge as the force motivating human behavior. Thus, people seek objects (persons) as an end rather than as a means to achieve tension reduction. In the other approach, loyalty to classical drive theory is maintained. The classical model is adapted to recognize the importance of object relations and of self. One adaptation involves utilizing the concept of diagnosis. Otto Kernberg (b. 1928), for example, holds that classical theory is appropriate for neurosis, while a model focused on object relations is required for more severe disorders such as borderlines, narcissistic personality disorders, and developmental arrests. Within a second adaptation, sequence is considered in order to encompass relational processes and issues. Winnicott, for example, maintains allegiance to the drive model by keeping instinctual and relational issues temporarily separate, with relational issues at an earlier developmental time. Thus, these theorists start with relational assumptions and move to the traditional version of the Oedipus complex. A third revision of classical theory is self psychology, represented by the works of Heinz Kohut (1913–1981). Self psychology stresses the strivings of people to become and remain cohesive and to fulfill a creative/productive potential. This approach questions the centrality of drive theory.

Contemporary psychoanalytic theorizing on female psychology has been influenced by theoretical psychoanalytic formulations that emphasize object relations and the concept of self rather than instinct as well as cultural changes, findings from research on infant observation and academic psychology, and feminist criticism of Freudian theory. While some formulation of women's development is based on the drive model, most contemporary reappraisals are based on object relations theory.

Freud's theory on female sexuality, derived from his theory about male sexuality, emphasized organs, bodily sensations, reactions to the discovery of anatomical differences between the sexes that lead to penis envy, feelings of inferiority, and the Oedipus complex. Girls blame mother for their castration; turn to father; relinquish masturbation; and become passive, masochistic, and narcissistic. Within this theory, girls' desire to be mother is seen as a conversion of penis envy and desire to be masculine. The girl's task in the oedipal period is to become heterosexual, which, according to Freud, involves a change of object, a change from activity to passivity, and the shift of primary organ of sex gratification from clitoris to vagina.

Representative of reformulations based on drive theory is the work of Irene Fast (b. 1928), who indicates that masculinity and femininity* are parallel constructs. Young children are not attuned to sex differences* or aware of the limitations in belonging to a particular sex. Thus, while Freud pointed to girls' lack and envy, Fast points to the envy of both sexes. Fast draws implication for the oedipal process resulting from boys' and girls' overinclusive perspective.

Much of contemporary psychoanalytic theorizing on female psychology is based on object relations theory. An important work is that of Nancy Chodorow (b. 1944), a sociologist who uses object relations theory to account for gender-related aspects of personality development. Chodorow considers psychodynamic processes within their social and political context. She considers and accounts for the psychological dissimilarities between men and women by pointing to differential effects of the mother's gender on males and females during preoedipal years. Men have a more impersonal and autonomous orientation. Women have an interpersonal orientation in which their attachments to others is central in their lives. These differences result from infants having their first social relationship with women. Boys must develop a masculine role without the continuous presence of a father. As mothers experience their sons as different, mothers treat sons as separate persons. The identity of boys, therefore, is more diffuse. Since girls are parented by a person of the same gender, they experience themselves as more continuous with, and related to, the external world. Mothers experience their daughters as extensions of themselves and unconsciously communicate this sense of connection and identification. Girls, in turn, have more difficulty separating and individuating from their mothers than boys do. The oedipal conflict has been reformulated based on the revised preoedipal relationship. While the boy's oedipal attachment to his mother is perceived as an extension of his preoedipal attachment, the girl's oedipal attachment to her father is seen as an attempt to free herself from mother and experience a sense of self. Engagement with father is important as it fosters separation and individuation.

Contemporary views on female development stress the preoedipal mother: the differential impact of mother on the gender of boys and girls; the role of learning in gender role identity; and the centrality of separation-individuation. Presently, masculinity and femininity are seen as parallel constructs. It is no longer believed, as did Freud, that all children are originally masculine or that girls' desire to be mothers develops other than as a conversion of penis envy and the desire to be masculine. The earliest gender differentiation is believed to be the result of sex assignment, and the behavior of infant males and females differs before sexual distinctions are known, contrary to Freud's belief. Further, gender identity or the knowledge that one biologically belongs to one or the other gender is firmly and irreversibly established by age 3 for both sexes, rather than as a consequence of the oedipal conflict. Contemporary thinking is that penis envy, while a phase-specific developmental phenomenon, undergoes reworking in subsequent stages and is not an inevitable outcome of the anatomical differences between the sexes, as Freud held.

Reference. J. L. Alpert (ed.), *Psychoanalysis and Women: Contemporary Reappraisals* (Hillsdale, N.J., 1994).

JUDITH L. ALPERT

PSYCHOSEXUAL STAGES OF DEVELOPMENT are a five-stage model of the normal development of personality proposed by Sigmund Freud.

Freud posited that the major determinants of personality in later life were the result of an invariant sequence of stages occurring, for the most part, very early in life. He believed that the newborn is a sexually charged entity seeking sexual gratification through a predictable sequence concentrating on specific parts of the body termed "erogenous zones." Movement within and between stages is important for satisfactory and healthy adult sexual functioning. There were, however, numerous pitfalls and conflicts to be resolved at each stage. Successful transition through stages allowed enjoying, but not becoming obsessed with, the expression of personal sexual energy. His five stages are:

Oral stage (approximately the first year of life). Innate sexual energy is focused on oral behaviors. Pleasure is derived from one's lips and oral cavity associated with the taking of sustenance and exploring the environment through oral means. Later in this stage, oral activity also involves biting, a form of aggression. Weaning presents a crisis for the child, who must forsake the breast or bottle, even though it provides intense sexual pleasure.

Anal stage (approximately the second year and part of the third). Sexual energy is concentrated on the abilities to "hold on" and to "let go" associated with toilet training. The ability to control one's eliminative functions is seen by Freud as a source of pleasure. As in the oral stage, there is a conflict between satisfying parental demands and the release of sexual tension.

Phallic stage (approximately the third through the fifth years). During this period children become aware of the sexual pleasure associated with the touching of their genitals. Conflict with parental concerns over masturbation is important in this stage. Freud believed this the most critical stage because of the Oedipus complex.

Males experience the Oedipus complex-aggressive, competitive feelings against their fathers coupled with desires to sexually possess their mothers exclusively. The boy resents father, his rival for mother, but hides his hostility because he fears paternal retaliation in the form of castration. The normal resolution of this crisis is sex-role identification with father, in particular, and males, in general. What is motherly or feminine is renounced.

Females are assumed to go through a similar, but separate, process called the feminine oedipal complex (Jung coined the term "Electra complex"). Generally, Freud expended little theoretical specificity on women until late in his career. Girls, like boys, start out loving mother and resenting father because he is a rival for mother's attention. In this stage, however, the girl discovers that she has no penis and feels incomplete and inferior to males, particularly blaming mother for her shortcoming. "Penis envy" is the outcome, and the girl is seen as growing into womanhood still unconsciously stricken by this lack of an organ. She eventually expresses her desire for her father as she identifies with her mother and the feminine role. Only with marriage and especially with the birth of her first male child does this crisis of her incompleteness become resolved.

Latency period (from approximately 6 to 12 years of age). Sexuality "goes underground" in this period, only to reawaken with puberty. Females continue to feel inferior based on their nonresolution of penis envy.

Genital stage (from late teens until senility). In this final stage of psychosexual development, immature, but pleasurable, infantile sexuality is integrated with mature healthy functioning in a unified hierarchical organization. Personal sexual pleasure is finally channeled outward as sexual expression and love for another person merge. Women without a male child may be aggressive and hostile to men in an unsuccessful attempt to compensate for their anatomical deficiency.

Freud believed one could become fixated (stuck) in a stage if there is either too much or too little gratification at that stage or regress (revert to an earlier stage) when faced with sustained frustration—outcomes by definition abnormal. Crucial to Freudian thought is the premise that the foundations of personality are laid down by the age of 5, and little can be done to change afterward, outside of in-depth psychoanalysis or intense life experience.

Freudian theory holds that these conflicts are powerful and threatening to the individual and hence are driven into the unconscious. Freud believed that "anatomy is destiny," and the demeaning nature of his theory toward women has been the focus of much feminist interest both in and out of the psychiatric profession. Vestiges of these notions still pervade the male-dominated domain of Freudian psychoanalysis.

References. C. S. Hall and G. Lindzey, *Theories of Personality*, 3d ed. (New York, 1978); J. Strachey (ed.), *Freud: The Standard Edition of the Complete Psychological Works* (London, 1953).

STEVE L. ELLYSON

PUBERTAL DEVELOPMENT encompasses several interrelated processes that result in girls' becoming young women both in form and function. The change from child to adult holds significance and meaning for young adolescent girls, with their responses to their development affecting their feelings about themselves. In addition, these same changes in appearance signal to others that girls are becoming adults; the responses of others to pubertal development also help shape girls' feelings about themselves.

Most adolescents take four to five years to go through the primary processes of puberty. Although age norms have been established by J. M. Tanner and others, Tanner notes that sizable variation exists among individuals in the age of onset and the rate of progression through pubertal development. During the course of puberty, girls experience growth and development in different physical systems.

Alterations occur in the central nervous system that coordinate the development and ultimate functioning of the reproductive endocrine system (glands that secrete internally). The reproductive endocrine system is organized during prenatal development but becomes dormant either by or shortly after birth. In middle childhood, frequency and amplitude of hormone releases increase, stimulating the development of other pubertal processes. Levels of hormones continue to increase until they are sufficient to stimulate negative feedback loops. These feedback loops produce the cyclic secretions of hormones that result in the menstrual cycle.

Secondary sexual characteristics (breast development, pubic hair growth) develop in connection with maturation of the reproductive organs. Initial increases in gonadal hormones result in the first signs of breast development (budding) around 10 years of age. (Initial changes of puberty begin about two years later for boys. See References for a detailed description of boys' and girls' development.) Breast budding is followed shortly by initial growth of pubic hair. Menarche occurs fairly late in the pubertal process, at around 12.5 years of age. Variation in timing of menarche or onset of secondary sexual characteristics has been associated with exercise, nutrition, and dieting. In addition, the National Heart, Lung and Blood Institute Growth and Health Study Research Group reported that African American girls begin puberty earlier than their white peers. Twice as many 9- and 10-year-old African American girls had begun breast development than had same-age white girls. These girls were also taller and heavier and had higher percentages of body fat. At this time, it is unknown why this race difference occurs, but the greater health risks among African American women (e.g., higher blood pressure and obesity) may stem from the same cause as the earlier onset of puberty.

Growth during puberty is the most rapid after fetal and neonatal development. Growth spurts in both height and weight occur along with changes in the distribution of fat and muscle mass. Adolescent girls add 10–14 inches to their prepubertal height, acceleration beginning a few months before the first changes in breast development and peaking in midpuberty. Most girls attain final adult stature by age 18; however, growth in bone mass continues into young adulthood. The growth spurt in weight, with increases in both fat and muscle mass, lags growth in height slightly during puberty. Peak growth in muscle mass occurs at midpuberty, and peak increases in fat occur in the later phases of puberty. Fat deposition differs by gender, resulting in more curvaceous figures for girls.

Changes in the respiratory and circulatory systems, although less often examined, also occur as part of pubertal development. Specifically, the heart and lungs experience a growth spurt that results in an increase in the size of these organs in proportion to the rest of the body. An overall increase in strength and endurance occurs for both girls and boys.

Given that puberty has such global effects on physiology and physical structure, it is not surprising that it also has emotional effects on adolescents themselves. As might be expected with such pervasive changes, emotional response to puberty is mixed. An extensive cross-cultural literature exists on the personal and cultural significance of menarche. Menarche has been associated with increased maturity, peer prestige, higher self-esteem, and increased feelings of self-consciousness. Negative feelings about menarche are most often associated with being unprepared for this event or experiencing menarche earlier than one's peers. A more limited literature exists on the experience of breast development, but some parallels are found. That is, more advanced breast development seemed to promote positive feelings about oneself in peer relations and self-esteem, but in the social context, this aspect of development often elicited teasing from peers and even family members (Brooks-Gunn, Newman et al.).

In the later stages of puberty, after weight spurt and menarche, girls often experience a decline in body image. Increases in body fat have been linked to increased dieting and unhealthy eating practices in white adolescents. Links between weight changes at puberty and adjustment have only begun to be examined for African American girls or girls from different ethnic backgrounds. Interestingly, initial findings suggest that African American girls in the early stages of puberty also increase their dieting and drive for thinness in response to weight gains and criticism from others about their weight, but they are not necessarily dissatisfied with their appearance (Striegel-Moore et al.).

It is clear across studies that the significance of puberty to adolescent girls is shaped by their family, peer, and school environments. The responses of others to a girl's development are often the best indicator of how she feels about her development. In particular, whether a girl goes through puberty earlier, at about the same time, or later than her peers is often an important determinant of how she feels about the experience and whether her pubertal experiences set her on a course for less healthy adjustment. Girls who mature earlier than their peers seem to be at particular risk for poorer body image, the development of eating problems, and, in some cases, more severe mental health disorders (Graber et al., 1997). It is likely that earlier development poses unique challenges for girls because they are less likely to be prepared for not only the physical changes of puberty but also for the social response to it. Girls who already are experiencing behavioral or emotional difficulties in childhood seem to be particularly at risk for longer-term behavioral problems if they also begin puberty earlier than peers. The timing of puberty accentuates the childhood difficulties (Caspi and Moffitt).

It is important to note that the hormonal changes of puberty may stimulate behavioral change either by directly affecting moods and behavior or through an interaction of hormonal stimulation and social forces that combine to affect behavior. For example, it has been suggested that hormonal changes at puberty may result in a feeling of general arousal, and the extent to which the arousal is interpreted as negative, positive, or neutral is dependent on the adolescent's predispositions and prior experiences with physiologically arousing conditions (Brooks-Gunn, Graber, and Paikoff).

In addition, hormonal changes do not just stimulate behavioral or emotional change in the individual; the hormonal system is itself responsive to the environmental conditions that the individual is experiencing. Hence, the social context may exert influences on the hormonal changes themselves. As indicated, behaviors such as exercise and dieting can act on the developing physiological system to delay puberty. In addition, we and others have found evidence that interpersonal stress (e.g., family conflict and lowered family warmth) also influences the timing of girls' development (Graber, Brooks-Gunn, and Warren).

Clearly, puberty is a set of dynamic processes in development that not only affect, but are affected by, the psychological and social processes existing in connection with it. These changes make the early adolescent period particularly challenging and exciting for girls themselves and those who interact with them.

References. J. Brooks-Gunn, J. A. Graber, and R. L. Paikoff, "Studying Links between Hormones and Negative Affect: Models and Measures," *Journal of Research on Adolescence* 4, 4 (1994): 469–486; J. Brooks-Gunn, D. Newman, D. C. Holdeness, and M. P. Warren, "The Experience of Breast Development and Girls: Stories about the Purchase of a Bra," *Journal of Youth and Adolescence* 23, 5 (1994): 539–565; J. Brooks-Gunn and A. C. Petersen (eds.), *Girls at Puberty: Biological and Psychosocial Perspectives* (New York, 1983); J. Brooks-Gunn, A. C. Petersen, and D. Eichorn, "The Study of Maturational Timing Effects in Adolescence," *Journal of Youth and Adolescence* 14 (1985): 149–161; J. Brooks-Gunn, and E. O. Reiter, "The Role of Pubertal Processes in the Early Adolescent Transition," in S. Feldman and G. Elliott (eds.), *At the Threshold: The Developing Adolescent* (Cambridge, 1990), 16–53; C. M. Buchanan, J. S. Eccles, and J. B. Becker, "Are Adolescents the Victims of Raging Hormones: Evidence for Activational Effects of Hormones on Moods and Behavior at Adolescence," *Psychological Bulletin* 111 (1992): 62–107; A. Caspi and T. E. Moffitt, "Individual Differences Are Accentuated during Periods of Social Change: The Sample Case of Girls at Puberty," *Journal of Personality and Social Psychology* 61 (1991): 157–168; J. A. Graber and J. Brooks-Gunn, "Biological and Maturational Factors in Development," in V. B. Van Hasselt and M. Hersen (eds.), *Handbook of Adolescent Psychopathology: A Guide to Diagnosis and Treatment* (New York, 1995), 69–101; J. A. Graber, J. Brooks-Gunn, and M. P. Warren, "The Antecedents of Menarcheal Age: Heredity, Family Environment, and Stressful Life Events," *Child Development* 66 (1995): 346–359; J. A. Graber, P. M. Lewinsohn, J. R. Seeley, and J. Brooks-Gunn, "Is Psychopathology Associated with the Timing of Pubertal Development?" *Journal of the American Academy of Child and Adolescent Psychiatry* 36 (1997): 1768–1776; R. M. Lerner and T. T. Foch (eds.), *Biological-Psychosocial Interactions in Early Adolescence* (Hillsdale, N.J., 1987); National Heart, Lung and Blood Institute [NHLBI], Growth and Health Study Research Group, "Obesity and Cardiovascular Disease Risk Factors in Black and White Girls: The NHLBI Growth and Health

Study," *American Journal of Public Health* 82 (1992): 1613–1620; R. H. Striegel-Moore, G. B. Schreiber, K. M. Pike, D. E. Wilfley and J. Rodin, "Drive for Thinness in Black and White Preadolescent Girls," *International Journal of Eating Disorders* 18 (1995): 59–69; J. M. Tanner, *Growth at Adolescence* (Springfield, Ill., 1962).

JULIA A. GRABER and JEANNE BROOKS-GUNN

PUBLIC OFFICE, IMPACT OF WOMEN IN. The 1992 election, popularly referred to as the Year of the Woman, brought with it the message that women, particularly at the highest levels of politics, were severely underrepresented. Before the election, women made up only 6 percent of Congress. Afterward, women made up 10 percent of members.

Today, many feel that great strides have been made. If the problem of women's underrepresentation and, therefore, their opportunity for impact has not been solved, much has been done to remedy past inequities.

In some respects, that is true. In many others, such interpretations misperceive the extent to which women in political office, in both the elective and appointive arenas at the local, state, and national levels, are still underrepresented compared to their proportions in the population.

For example, in 1996 (prior to the November election), women still made up 10 percent of Congress, including 8 in the U.S. Senate and 47 in the House of Representatives. Of these, only 14 were women of color, 10 African Americans, 3 Hispanics, and 1 Asian American.

On the state level, women made up 21 percent of state legislatures and held 26 percent of statewide offices. However, there was only one woman governor, Christine Todd Whitman of New Jersey. Women of color were 6 percent of those women holding statewide elective office and 14.3 percent of women holding state legislative seats.

To bring some historical perspective to this discussion, very few women have served in elective and appointive office over our history. Although there were always exceptional women who took on the challenge of shattering barriers to public sphere participation, the fact that even today we talk about "firsts" is illustrative of the progress yet to be made.

The first woman elected to the Congress was Jeanette Rankin of Montana, who began her service in 1917. Rebecca Latimer Felton of Georgia, appointed in 1922, was the first woman senator. Ten years later, the first woman was elected to the Senate, Hattie W. Caraway of Arkansas. In 1968 Shirley Chisholm of New York became the first African American woman elected to the U.S. House of Representatives; Carol Moseley-Braun, elected in 1992, was the first African American woman in the U.S. Senate.

On the state level, the first women legislators came from Colorado and began their service in 1895: Clara Cressingham, Carrie Clyde Holly, and Frances S. Klock. Nellie T. Ross from Wyoming was the first woman governor. She served from 1925 to 1927. To date, only 15 women have ever served as governor. The largest number to serve simultaneously was four in 1994.

A famous first was Geraldine Ferraro, who, in 1984, was the first woman to run for the vice presidency on a major party ticket. She ran with Democrat Walter Mondale.

In the appointive realm, in 1933, Frances Perkins became the first woman appointed to a presidential cabinet position. She served as the labor secretary in Franklin D. Roosevelt's administration. In 1965, Lorna Lockwood of Arizona became the first woman chief justice of a state supreme court. In 1981 Sandra Day O'Connor became the first woman on the U.S. Supreme Court.

The question of the impact of women in politics or the difference women make in office is often raised. It is useful to ask why scholars, journalists, commentators, activists, and citizens are interested in women's impact as a group rather than whether specific individuals are competent, active, contributing, successful, or making a difference. After all, we rarely ask whether men make a difference in politics.

Several answers to this question are available. Whenever a group that has typically been outside the public sphere takes its place beside those traditionally present, interest in its progress is high. Because women were barred from politics until relatively recently (the right to vote was won only in 1920), their progress as a group is a natural focus of attention.

Another reason that women's group impact, rather than individual impact, is of interest is that women are assumed by many, either as a result of life experience and social construction or of innate difference, to view the political world differently than men do. This is presumed to translate into distinctive interests and distinctive behaviors of women and sometimes to a quite uniform set of interests and behaviors.

A final reason that women's collective impact in politics has been of interest concerns the desire by some in society to see women take a different political approach than has been the norm. Some see women as having the potential to clean up politics and to take it to a higher level.

Scholarly research over the past 25 years attests that the impact of women's increased representation among elected and appointed officials has been significant. One way its impact is demonstrated is that women politicians of both parties tend, more often than their male peers, to be supportive of issues relevant to women such as increased child care availability, funding for domestic violence shelters, funding for medical research on women's health care issues, and child support enforcement.

Several sets of findings about women in legislative office are illustrative of women's impact throughout the political arena. Women representatives are more likely than men to consider representing the interests of women to be very important and to take pride in accomplishments that further the status of women. Most tellingly, women legislators also tend, more often than men, to make priorities of issues of women, children, and family and to successfully usher those priorities through the legislative process. It is important to note that women in politics do not limit themselves only to certain kinds of issues; they are involved and are successful in the full range of items in the political arena. What is clear, however, is that women are more active and involved than men on issues that flow from their differential life experience.

A recent example of the ways in which women make a difference in the political arena comes from the former Congressional Caucus for Women's Issues. An October 13, 1994, news release reported that, with 66 successful measures, the 103d Congress broke all records of passage of legislation of importance to women. Caucus cochair Pat Schroeder of Colorado noted, "In 1992, the voters said they wanted change. . . . The list of accomplishments we are releasing today represents a healthy return on the voters' investment, one that should finally put to rest the question, 'What difference does having more women in Congress make?' " (Congressional Caucus for Women's Issues).

Recent studies also indicate that women officeholders may bring a new dimension to the political decision-making process itself. Female politicians have been found to be more likely than their male counterparts to conceptualize public policy problems broadly and, as a result, seek different types of solutions. One example concerns crime. Whereas male officeholders tend to view the problem as one of individual flouting of legal mandates, female officeholders are more likely to search for societal antecedents of criminal activity. Hence, women's legislation is more likely than men's to address the roots of the problem rather than its most recent symptoms.

Another way to think about impact concerns the effort devoted to further diversification and inclusiveness. Women in politics, more than their male counterparts, believe in, and are active in, increasing the proportion of women in office by participation in recruiting, training, and supporting them.

Finally, the impact of women in politics may also be affected by their proportions in office. Theories of critical mass suggest that when a large enough group of newcomers enters, or a unified group is present in, the organization, their attitudes and behaviors will permeate the mainstream. Recent research suggests this is happening in the political arena.

When we talk about impact and what difference it makes that women are in the political arena, the best answer is that when representation is expanded, so is the range of opinions about what is appropriately political, the range of issues that are introduced into the agenda, and the range of solutions considered. Do women have an impact? The answer is an unqualified yes.

References. Congressional Caucus for Women's Issues, *News Release: Record Accomplishments for Women in Congress* (October 13, 1994); Debra L. Dodson (ed.), *Gender and Policymaking: Studies of Women in Office* (New Brunswick, N.J., 1991); Debra L. Dodson and Susan J. Carroll, *Reshaping the Agenda: Women in State Legislatures* (New Brunswick, N.J., 1991); Lyn Kathlene, "Alternative Views of Crime: Legislative Policymaking in Gendered Terms," *The Journal of Politics* 57 (August 1995): 696–723; Nancy E. McGlen and Karen O'Connor, *Women, Politics, and American Society* (Englewood Cliffs, N.J., 1998); Sue Thomas, *How Women Legislate* (New York, 1994).

SUE THOMAS

PUBLIC SPHERE is the sphere of activity outside the home. Relationships with nonfamily members and business other than that related directly to the consumption needs of the family* are carried out in the public sphere. Employment outside the home, political activity, and economic activity beyond consumer buying of retail purchases for the home are part of the public sphere that, in patriarchal societies, has generally been monopolized by men. Especially during the nineteenth-century "Cult of True Womanhood"* the public sphere and domestic sphere* were looked upon as, ideally, mutually exclusive domains, the public sphere under man's control; the domestic sphere, under woman's.

PURDAH is a term for specific gender relations based on the subordination of women, including rigid behavioral prescriptions and proscriptions, seclusion and prohibition against fulfilling visible social roles, limited physical mobility, and hierarchical deference patterns.

The customs and traditions associated with purdah have a long history and are integral to Islamic cultures of the Middle East and to Hindu and Muslim cultures in South Asia. Interpretations of purdah by outsiders, whether colonial administrators, social reformers, or female observers, have generally depicted the tradition of purdah as epitomizing the suppression and subordination of women in non-Western cultures.

Academic analyses of purdah have shifted in focus from a delineation of characteristics and symbolic meanings generic in particular ethnographic settings to delineations of purdah in relation to more encompassing societal issues affecting women, such as class, Islamic fundamentalism, and patriarchal modernization.

Much of the literature dealing with purdah in South Asia has focused on differences in purdah observance among Hindu and Muslim women. Basic distinctions are made regarding the function of women's seclusion. Among Muslims, for example, it is argued that women are restricted in their physical movements and enjoined to cover themselves when venturing in areas outside their homes in order to protect themselves from outsiders, particularly non-kin males. Patterns of hierarchal deference and avoidance among Hindus are internally directed at orchestrating intrafamilial relations to ensure harmony and minimize conflict and strife.

Sylvia Vatuk criticizes the preceding interpretations as being too narrowly focused on particular sets of behaviors and derived functions and instead suggests considering purdah as part of the general modesty codes structuring women's lives in South Asia. Veiling and seclusion, she argues, are only special manifestations of a whole array of behaviors constituting gender relations. The gender relations of purdah, in other words, combine reciprocal, yet asymmetrical, duties and obligations between men and women, including patterns of avoidance, proper etiquette, and gender-specific forms of exhibiting "shame" and "shyness." (Men in both Hindu and Muslim communities are to announce their presence before entering the women's part of the household and are not to spend time in the women's portion of the house except for eating or sexual activity; young boys are considered to show appropriate "shyness" when they learn to spend most of their time outside the women's domain.)

South Asian societies have two major cultural concerns with respect to women's place in the social order. One is women's sexual vulnerability, which includes ideas about female sexuality and women's inability to control their sexual impulses, hence, the need for external constraint. Sheltering women from the threat of sexual advances is necessary for their sake and for the honor of the families. Sheltering activity is not only found in Muslim societies but is afforded women cross-culturally in a variety of ways, that is, through standards of dress and restricted expressions of emotion and chaperonage in addition to face veiling and/or physical seclusion. The second major concern is with women as a disruptive influence on group unity and group cohesion. Avoidance relationships or structured patterns of deference also include relationships among women. These, too, are not unique to Hindu society but are found in other South Asian societies as well.

A broadened approach to women's subordination would facilitate the understanding of intra- as well as intercountry differences in the status and condition of women and could promote comparative studies of female behavioral codes. Not all women who are Muslim observe seclusion or veiling strictures, even within the same country, and restrictions on women's behavior vary widely among different Muslim countries. Moreover, an approach that would attempt to link the particular condition of Muslim women to the general condition of women in India would facilitate the understanding of similarities without ignoring the differences. The importance of enhancing commonalities lies in the potential it holds for increased political alliances and support for the mutual concerns of all women, such as violence against wives, dowries, and divorce. (See DOWRY, In India.)

References. Shelley Feldman and Florence E. McCarthy, "Purdah and Changing Patterns of Social Control among Rural Women in Bangladesh," *Journal of Marriage and the Family* 45 (November 1983): 949–959; Hanna Pananek and Gail

Minault (eds.), *Separate Worlds: Studies of Purdah in South Asia* (Delhi, 1982); Sylvia Vatuk, "Purdah Revisited: A Comparison of Hindu and Muslim Interpretations of the Cultural Meaning of Purdah in South Asia," in H. Papanek and G. Minault (eds.), *Separate Worlds: Studies of Purdah in South Asia* (Delhi, 1982).

FLORENCE E. McCARTHY

ISBN 0-313-31072-6

90000>

EAN

9 780313 310720

HARDCOVER BAR CODE